Suharto's Cold War

OXFORD STUDIES IN INTERNATIONAL HISTORY
James J. Sheehan, series advisor

THE WILSONIAN MOMENT
Self-Determination and the International Origins of Anticolonial Nationalism
Erez Manela

IN WAR'S WAKE
Europe's Displaced Persons in the Postwar Order
Gerard Daniel Cohen

GROUNDS OF JUDGMENT
Extraterritoriality and Imperial Power in Nineteenth-Century China and Japan
Pär Kristoffer Cassel

THE ACADIAN DIASPORA
An Eighteenth-Century History
Christopher Hodson

GORDIAN KNOT
Apartheid and the Unmaking of the Liberal World Order
Ryan Irwin

THE GLOBAL OFFENSIVE
The United States, the Palestine Liberation Organization, and the Making of the Post–Cold War Order
Paul Thomas Chamberlin

MECCA OF REVOLUTION
Algeria, Decolonization, and the Third World Order
Jeffrey James Byrne

SHARING THE BURDEN
The Armenian Question, Humanitarian Intervention, and Anglo-American Visions of Global Order
Charlie Laderman

THE WAR LORDS AND THE DARDANELLES
How Grain and Globalization Led to Gallipoli
Nicholas A. Lambert

FEAR OF THE FAMILY
Guest Workers and Family Migration in the Federal Republic of Germany
Lauren Stokes

POLITICS OF UNCERTAINTY
The United States, the Baltic Question, and the Collapse of the Soviet Union
Una Bergmane

SUHARTO'S COLD WAR
Indonesia, Southeast Asia, and the World
Mattias Fibiger

Suharto's Cold War

Indonesia, Southeast Asia, and the World

MATTIAS FIBIGER

OXFORD
UNIVERSITY PRESS

Oxford University Press is a department of the University of Oxford. It furthers
the University's objective of excellence in research, scholarship, and education
by publishing worldwide. Oxford is a registered trade mark of Oxford University
Press in the UK and certain other countries.

Published in the United States of America by Oxford University Press
198 Madison Avenue, New York, NY 10016, United States of America.

CIP data is on file at the Library of Congress

ISBN 978–0–19–766722–4

DOI: 10.1093/oso/9780197667224.001.0001

Printed by Integrated Books International, United States of America

Portions of the manuscript are adapted from: Mattias Fibiger, "A Diplomatic Counterrevolution: Indonesian
Diplomacy and the Invasion of East Timor," *Modern Asian Studies* 55, no. 2 (March 2021): 587–628.
Copyright © The Author(s) 2020. Published by Cambridge University Press. Reprinted with permission.

Mattias Fibiger, "The Nixon Doctrine and the Making of Authoritarianism in Island Southeast Asia,"
Diplomatic History 45, no. 5 (November 2021): 954–982. © The Author(s) 2021.
Published by Oxford University Press on behalf of the Society for Historians of American Foreign Relations.
All rights reserved.

For Maggie

CONTENTS

ACKNOWLEDGMENTS

I owe an enormous debt of gratitude to the people and institutions who made the publication of this book possible.

Thanks must be given first to an extraordinary group of mentors. I began this book as a dissertation at Cornell University. Fredrik Logevall was a sterling doctoral advisor who set a model for incisive thinking and elegant writing. His guidance, support, and good humor was nothing short of invaluable. Chen Jian introduced me to the craft of international history and pushed me to situate my arguments in a global context. Eric Tagliacozzo encouraged me to think across the borders of postcolonial Southeast Asia and about the *longue durée*. And Tom Pepinsky embodied an unusual combination of rigor and generosity in introducing me to the field of comparative politics. I hope to live up to the stellar scholarly examples they set.

I was inspired to pursue an academic career by my professors at the University of California, Santa Barbara. Tsuyoshi Hasegawa first ignited my intellectual interests and helped me find purpose in academic work. Salim Yaqub taught me how to think like a historian, how to conduct research in an archive, and how to navigate university life. Laura Kalman showed me the power of history to captivate. I owe them more than they can ever know.

An exemplary array of language teachers helped me acquire the faculties necessary to write this book. At Cornell, Jolanda Pandin and Maria Theresa Savella guided me through the early stages of learning Indonesian and Tagalog with unfailing grace. *Maraming salamat po* and *terima kasih banyak*. At Universitas Negeri Malang, Peni Anggari (*mendiang*), Az' Arie Bachtiar, Basori, Elva Maharani, and Agnes Aisyah Suprihatin taught me how to operate in *bahasa jalanan* rather than *bahasa diplomasi*. I am grateful to them all.

I transformed a rather unwieldy dissertation into a more cohesive book after joining the Business, Government, and International Economy Unit at Harvard Business School. HBS provided the time and resources necessary to reconceptualize and rewrite the entire manuscript. The trial by fire in global political economy that all new faculty members in the BGIE Unit endure also led me to rethink many of my key arguments and made the book immeasurably stronger. I thank all my colleagues for creating such a rich intellectual atmosphere. In addition, Jeremy Friedman, David Moss, Sophus Reinert, Meg Rithmire, and Dick Vietor read parts or all of the manuscript and offered insightful critiques and suggestions. The support staff in the BGIE Unit, especially Sarah Antommaria, provided invaluable logistical assistance.

A wider network of scholars helped shape the ideas in the book. I thank the members of my graduate cohort at Cornell, Kaitlin Pontzer, Ai Baba, Nicholas Bujalski, Shiau-Yun Chen, Kyle Harvey, Jason Kelly, Matthew Minarchek, Margaret Moline, Joshua Savala, and Osama Siddiqui. Also at Cornell, Fritz Bartel, Sean Fear, Christopher Tang, Brian Cuddy, Hoang Vu, Nathaniel Rojas, and Taomo Zhou shared ideas on international history. In Cambridge, I have benefited from conversations with and advice from William Kirby, Erez Manela, Jay Rosengard, Lou Wells, Arne Westad, and many attendees at various talks and seminars. I also thank Mark Atwood Lawrence, Jana Lipman, Wen-Qing Ngoei, Lien-Hang Nguyen, Bradley Simpson, and audience members at myriad conferences and workshops for offering commentary on various chapter drafts that improved the book.

For financial support that enabled me to conduct archival research, I thank the Social Science Research Council, the Judith Reppy Institute for Peace and Conflict Studies, and the Division of Research and Faculty Development at Harvard Business School. A Critical Language Scholarship from the United States Department of State facilitated language study. Universitas Indonesia and Universiti Malaya offered affiliations that allowed me to obtain research visas.

Thanks are due to myriad archivists at the national archives of Australia, Indonesia, Malaysia, the United Kingdom, and the United States; the presidential libraries of Gerald Ford, Richard Nixon, and Ronald Reagan; the Carlos Romulo Library; the World Bank and the International Monetary Fund; the Rockefeller Archive Center, the Minnesota State Historical Society, and the Hoover Institution; and the special collections reading rooms at Columbia University, Cornell University, Harvard University, the University of the Philippines at Diliman, and the University of California, Berkeley. Nadia Esham, Margaret Kenna, and Fitria Sis Nariswari provided outstanding research assistance tracking down documents after my departure from various archives. Isabelle Lewis made beautiful maps.

It was a distinct pleasure to work with Susan Ferber and Oxford University Press. Susan's keen eye for everything from indelicate phrasing to incomplete thinking rescued me from mistakes both large and small. For her editorial judgment and consummate professionalism, she has my enduring gratitude.

I also thank the reviewers for OUP whose trenchant commentary bettered the manuscript.

My foremost debts are to my loved ones. My parents always taught me to pursue what I love, and that lesson led me to the position of thanking them here. I owe them everything. My siblings Kate, Dan, Piers, and Tor are an endless source of inspiration and laughter. I have treasured every moment with them and with my wider family: Greg Stephan, Gail Plecash, Kyle Melvin, Anna Melvin, Sophie Melvin, Emmett Melvin, Lauren Hurst, Neve Fibiger, Kai Fibiger, Lauren Capozzi, Jordan Tetreau, Easton Tetreau, Krista Capozzi, Scott Moline, Jayne Moline, Dan Moline, and Anna Staudacher.

And then there is Maggie. She came into my life when this book was no more than an idea. Over the course of its path from inception to publication, she read every word and discussed every idea. But the book's journey paled in comparison to our own. We built a home, a life, and as this book came into being we learned we would be building a family as well. Words cannot capture the love and energy she devoted to our journey together. Through it all she tolerated my absence when I was traveling to far-flung archives and my presence when I was sulking about writer's block. She has my gratitude, my admiration, and my love—always. This book is dedicated to her.

NOTE ON SPELLING, NAMES, AND TRANSLATION

The orthographic system governing the Indonesian language underwent significant changes during the years covered in the narrative ahead. In 1947, the Dutch-influenced *oe* was simplified into the Indonesian *u* (*goeroe* into *guru*) and the glottal stop indicated by ' was denoted with *k* (*ra'jat* into *rakjat*). In 1972, the Suharto regime implemented a "perfection" of Indonesian spelling that shifted *tj* into *c* (*tjatatan* into *catatan*), *dj* into *j* (*Djakarta* into *Jakarta*), *j* into *y* (*rakjat* into *rakyat*), *nj* into *ny* (*banjak* into *banyak*), *sj* into *sy* (*masjarakat* into *masyarakat*), and *ch* into *kh* (*achir* into *akhir*). In quotations and citations, I have preserved the spelling of words as they were written in the documents in question.

Indonesians were free to maintain or alter the spelling of their names as they saw fit. Thus the man born Soemitro Djojohadikoesoemo became Sumitro Djojohadikusumo in 1947 but not Sumitro Joyohadikusumo in 1972. In the text, I have adopted the newest orthography for most names for the sake of simplicity. Most notably, I use Suharto even though the man preferred Soeharto. I have made exceptions for names that are almost exclusively rendered in the old orthography, such as William Soeryadjaya and the aforementioned Sumitro Djojohadikusumo. Most Indonesians do not have a family name, and many have only one name. I therefore use the name by which they were most commonly known rather than the final part of their name. For example, while I refer to Ali Murtopo as Murtopo, I refer to Alamsjah Ratu Perwiranegara as Alamsjah. In quotations and citations, I have preserved the spelling of names as they were rendered in the documents in question. Occasionally this includes a practice whereby the initial Su- prefix common in Javanese names is dropped and an honorific Bapak/Pak, Bang/Bung, or Ibu/Bu is added. For instance, Suharto was often referred to as Pak Harto.

Indonesian newspapers changed their names in accordance with new regulations surrounding spelling, meaning the military newspaper *Angkatan*

Bersendjata became *Angkatan Bersenjata.* In quotations, citations, and the text, I have preserved the spelling of newspapers as they were rendered at the time. Many Indonesian place names have changed as well. For example, the city of Ujung Pandang was renamed Makassar. I have adopted the most recent name for all place names. I refer to the western half of the island of New Guinea (variously known in Indonesia as West Irian, Irian Jaya, and Papua) as West Papua to differentiate it from Papua New Guinea on the eastern half of the island. In quotations and citations, I have preserved the names of places as they were rendered in the documents in question.

Unless otherwise noted, all translations are my own.

ABBREVIATIONS

ABRI	Armed Forces of the Republic of Indonesia
Apodeti	Timorese Popular Democratic Association
ASA	Association of Southeast Asia
ASDT	Timorese Social Democratic Association
ASEAN	Association of Southeast Asian Nations
Askrindo	PT Asuransi Kredit Indonesia
Aspri	Personal Assistants
Bakin	State Intelligence Coordinating Body
Bappenas	National Development Planning Agency
BE	Export Bonus
Berdikari	Standing on One's Own Feet (Self-Sufficiency/Autarky)
BKK	Campus Coordinating Body
BKPM	Investment Coordinating Board
BPI	Central Intelligence Board
BSDU	Barrio Self-Defense Unit
Bulog	National Logistics Board
Caduad	Army General Reserve
CPP	Communist Party of the Philippines
CSIS	Center for Strategic and International Studies (Jakarta)
DAP	Democratic Action Party
Dekon	Economic Declaration
DNU	Department of National Unity
DPR	People's Representative Council ("Parliament")
DPR-GR	People's Representative Council–Mutual Cooperation
FBSI	All-Indonesia Labor Federation
Fosko	Forum for Study and Communication
Fretilin	Revolutionary Front for an Independent East Timor

G-30-S/PKI	September Thirtieth Movement/Communist Party of Indonesia
GAM	Free Aceh Movement
GBHN	Broad Outlines of State Policy
Gerakan	Malaysian People's Movement Party
Golkar/ Sekber Golkar	Functional Groups/Joint Secretariat of Functional Groups
Golput	White Group
GPII	Indonesian Islamic Youth Movement
Hankam	Ministry of Defense and Security
Hankamrata	Total People's Defense and Security
ICCS	International Commission of Control and Supervision
ICHDF	Integrated Civilian Home Defense Forces
IGGI	Inter-Governmental Group on Indonesia
IMF	International Monetary Fund
IPC	Investment Promotion Council
IPKI	League of Upholders of Indonesian Freedom
ITB	Bandung Institute of Technology
Kadin	Chamber of Commerce and Industry
KAGI	Indonesian Teacher Action Front
KAK	Anti-Corruption Committee
KAMI	Indonesian Student Action Front
KAP-Gestapu	Action Command to Crush the September Thirtieth Movement
KAPPI	Indonesian High School Student Action Front
KASI	Indonesian Scholar Action Front
KAWI	Indonesian Women Action Front
KBL	New Society Movement
Kesban	Security and Development
KIK	Small Investment Credit
KIN	State Intelligence Command
Kista	Special Course
KMKP	Permanent Working Capital Credit
KNIL	Royal Netherlands Indies Army
KNPI	National Indonesian Youth Committee
Kogam	Crush Malaysia Command
Kopassandha	Secret Warfare Command
Kopkamtib	Operational Command for the Restoration of Security and Order
Kostrad	Army Strategic Reserve Command
Koti	Supreme Operations Command

Lemhannas	National Resilience Institute
LNG	Liquefied Natural Gas
MAF	Malaysian Armed Forces
Mahmillub	Extraordinary Military Tribunal
Malari	January Fifteenth Catastrophe
Manipol	Political Manifesto
MAP	Military Assistance Program
MCA	Malaysian Chinese Association
MFA	Armed Forces Movement
MIC	Malaysian Indian Congress
MM	Students Accuse
MNLF	Moro National Liberation Front
MPR	People's Consultative Assembly ("Assembly")
MPRS	Provisional People's Consultative Assembly
MUI	Indonesian Ulama Council
Nasakom	Nationalism-Religion-Communism
NCC	National Consultative Council
NEDA	National Economic and Development Authority
Nekolim	Neocolonialism, Colonialism, and Imperialism
NIEO	New International Economic Order
NKK	Normalization of Campus Life
NOC	National Operations Council
NPA	New People's Army
NSC	National Security Council
NU	Nahdlatul Ulama
OIC	Organization of the Islamic Conference
OPEC	Organization of Petroleum-Exporting Countries
Opsus	Special Operations
P4	Directive for the Realization and Implementation of Pancasila
PAP	People's Action Party
Parmusi	Muslim Party of Indonesia
PAS	Pan-Malaysian Islamic Party
PDI	Indonesian Democratic Party
Permesta	Charter of Universal Struggle
Peta	Homeland Defense Force
PIBA	Pacific Indonesia Business Association
PKI	Communist Party of Indonesia
PKP	Partido Komunista ng Pilipinas
PNI	Indonesian Nationalist Party
Polkam	Council on Political Stabilization and National Security

PPP	United Development Party
PRRI	Revolutionary Government of the Republic of Indonesia
PSI	Socialist Party of Indonesia
Repelita	Five-Year Development Plan
RPKAD	Army Paracommando Regiment
SEAARC	Southeast Asian Association for Regional Cooperation
SEATO	Southeast Asia Treaty Organization
Spri	Personal Staff
SRI	Stanford Research Institute
SSKAD/Seskoad	Army Staff and Command School
Supersemar	Order of March Eleventh
Trikora	Three Commands of the People
Tritura	Three Demands of the People
UDT	Timorese Democratic Union
UMNO	United Malays National Organization
Wanhankamnas	National Defense and Security Council

Suharto's Cold War

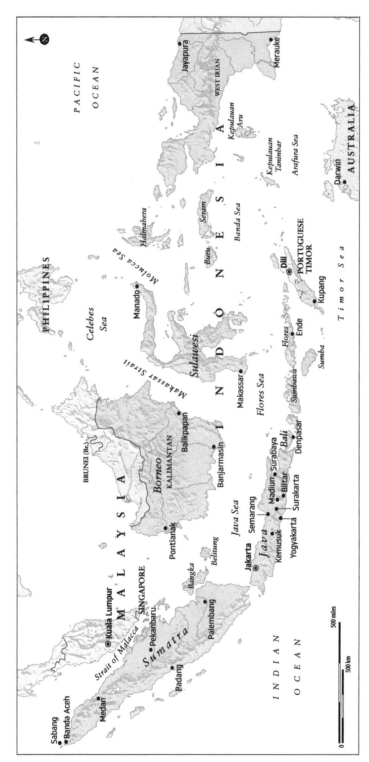

Indonesia in 1970

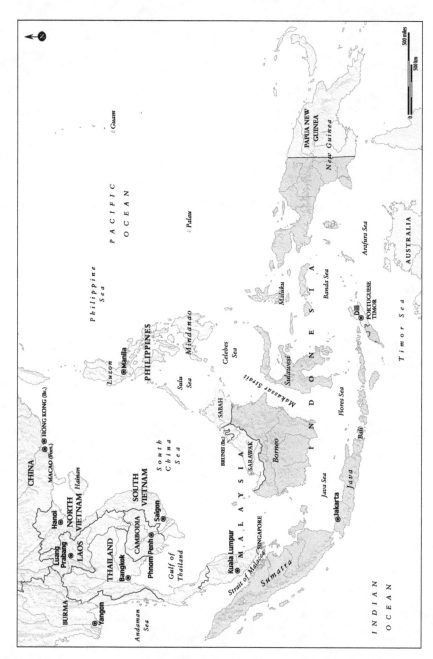

Southeast Asia in 1970

Introduction

An atmosphere of crisis enveloped Jakarta over the course of 1965. Indonesian society seemed to be coming apart at the seams, and denizens of the capital sensed an impending climax. But General Suharto was preoccupied by other matters on the morning of October 1. He had spent the evening at the hospital caring for his three-year-old son, who had suffered serious burns in a kitchen accident a few days earlier.[1] It was after midnight by the time Suharto went home to care for his infant daughter. At half past four, he was awoken by a knock on the door by a cameraman for the national television station. The man was returning from an overnight film shoot and said he had heard gunfire at several locations across the capital. Distracted and exhausted, Suharto "didn't give much thought" to the news. Half an hour later, a neighbor knocked at the door and announced that he too had heard gunshots. Suharto felt a pang of anxiety. Two more visitors arrived in rapid succession. One reported that a handful of senior army officers had been kidnapped. Another revealed that troops had taken up positions near the presidential palace, situated on the north side of Merdeka Square in central Jakarta. Suharto donned his uniform and climbed into a vehicle. Alone, he drove toward his office at the headquarters of the Army Strategic Reserve Command (Kostrad), located on the east side of Merdeka Square about half a mile from the palace. As he approached the Kostrad building, he looked across the square and saw the mysterious troops for himself. The long-awaited climax had arrived.[2]

But the nature of the events unfolding around Suharto remained unclear. Who were the troops occupying the square? What had happened to the leaders of the army? And where was President Sukarno? Shortly after Suharto arrived at Kostrad, the national radio station broadcast a ten-minute statement by Lieutenant Colonel Untung, a commander in the president's palace guard. Untung explained that he led a group called the September Thirtieth Movement that had arrested several army leaders. He accused the movement's captives of belonging to a "Council of Generals" that was allegedly working with the

Suharto's Cold War. Mattias Fibiger, Oxford University Press. © Oxford University Press 2023.
DOI: 10.1093/oso/9780197667224.003.0001

Central Intelligence Agency (CIA) to overthrow Sukarno. Untung reassured his listeners that the president and other key political figures were under the September Thirtieth Movement's "protection." He announced that the move-ment would take immediate action against "agents and sympathizers of the Council of Generals" across Indonesia. An "Indonesian Revolution Council" would be established and wield broad executive authority. Untung's statement stressed that the September Thirtieth Movement was "solely a movement within the Army directed against the Council of Generals."[3] But Suharto remembered Untung as a "disciple" of Alimin, a former chief the Communist Party of Indonesia (PKI). The party had twice before staged revolutionary uprisings, first in 1926 and again in 1948, and the kidnappings and formation of a revolutionary council pointed unmistakably in the direction of a coup. Suharto concluded that the September Thirtieth Movement represented nothing less than an attempt by the PKI to "seize the power of the state by force."[4]

Whether the events of October 1, 1965, did amount to a coup attempt re-mains unknown. Precisely what transpired that morning, who exactly was be-hind the plot, and what the plotters intended cannot be definitively answered over a half-century later.

This much is clear: in the early morning hours, teams of soldiers climbed into jeeps at Halim Perdanakusuma Air Force Base on the southern outskirts of Jakarta and rumbled toward the homes of seven of Indonesia's most senior generals in the city center. They attempted to kidnap the generals, but their plan quickly went awry. Three of the movement's seven targets were killed and another escaped. The conspirators then brought captives and corpses alike to an uninhabited rubber grove called Lubang Buaya near Halim. They shot the living and interred all the bodies in a derelict well, which they covered with branches and leaves.

As these murders were carried out, troops loyal to the September Thirtieth Movement occupied Merdeka Square, the symbolic seat of political power in cen-tral Jakarta. In the center of the square sat the half-finished National Monument, a tall obelisk symbolizing the country's independence struggle, its construction halted amid an ongoing economic crisis. Along the square's borders lay the key installations of the Indonesian state: not only the presidential palace and the Kostrad building but also the headquarters of the army, the ministry of defense, the telecommunications building, and the national radio station. Curiously, the troops occupying the square numbered only about 1,000—a tiny fraction of the total number of Indonesian soldiers in Jakarta that morning. The radio station soon began issuing bizarre broadcasts stating that Sukarno's existing cabinet would be "decommissioned" and all ranks above lieutenant colonel would be abolished.[5]

Back at Halim, Untung and his military co-conspirators remained in hiding in a small house. Also on the grounds of the base, in another house less than a mile away, were the PKI leader Dipa Nusantara Aidit and several close aides from the party's shadowy Special Bureau. They were soon joined by none other than Sukarno, who had spent the night at the home of one of his wives and was not in fact under the September Thirtieth Movement's protection. After he heard Untung's initial radio broadcast, the president traveled to Halim, where his plane was on permanent standby in case he needed to make a quick escape from the city. Upon arriving at the base, Sukarno met with one of Untung's subordinates. The president ordered a halt to all violent actions, appointed a loyalist as "caretaker" of the army, and summoned a crowd of deputies to Halim, including the commanders of the navy, police, and palace guard. The nationalist hero seemed unfazed by the cascade of events. "This kind of thing will happen in a revolution," he mused.[6]

The drama of October 1 seeded a litany of historical mysteries. Why would the architects of the September Thirtieth Movement neglect to target Suharto, who was in Jakarta and in command of a considerable number of Kostrad troops? Why would the plotters' radio broadcasts describe the movement as an effort to protect Sukarno and then announce the dissolution of the president's cabinet and the formation of an alternative government in which Sukarno was apparently uninvolved? Why would the movement's ostensible leaders remain hidden in two separate houses at Halim—isolated from each other, from their troops, and from the public? Why would the leaders of the PKI move to upend a political system that had proved so hospitable to the expansion of communist influence? Whoever masterminded the plot and whatever their ultimate purpose, the September Thirtieth Movement was either so poorly conceived or so shoddily implemented as to be almost incomprehensible in hindsight.[7]

Suharto responded decisively to the chaos. As he later recounted to an American journalist, "I realized the Army was in danger and I decided to assume leadership."[8] He called the officers in command of the troops occupying Merdeka Square to Kostrad headquarters. He told the mutineers that their actions amounted to a revolt and ordered them to surrender. One of the battalions occupying the area laid down their arms in the early afternoon. The other battalion fled to Halim. Troops loyal to Suharto recaptured the critical infrastructure surrounding the square by early evening. Once the radio station was secured, Suharto took to the airwaves to denounce the September Thirtieth Movement and inform the Indonesian public that "the general situation is again under control and security measures are being actively carried out."[9] Suharto then turned his attention to the air force base. He refused to allow any army officials, including the man Sukarno appointed caretaker of the army, to answer the president's summons. Instead, Suharto sent a courier to Halim to order the president to leave the area—a remarkable feat of insubordination that portended a political struggle.[10] Late that evening, crack Army Paracommando

Regiment (RPKAD) troops amassed around the base. By then, Sukarno had fled to his Bogor palace, located about thirty-five miles south, and the leaders of the September Thirtieth Movement had fanned out across Java. The movement collapsed before most Indonesians even knew it existed.

Suharto used the September Thirtieth Movement as a pretext to destroy the PKI and usurp state power. Over the subsequent six months, he orchestrated a politicide that literally drenched Indonesia's soil in blood and clogged its rivers with corpses—among the most violent episodes of the second half of the twentieth century. A recurring pattern occurred across the archipelago: a pause after October 1, the arrival of army units who ignited anticommunist bloodshed, a carnival of violence as civilian paramilitaries associated with religious organizations and political parties took to killing, and a return to peace after the army reimposed order. Communists and their fellow-travelers constituted the overwhelming majority of the victims, but others were killed on account of ethnic animosities, clan loyalties, and personal rivalries. When all was said and done, at least half a million Indonesians were dead and perhaps a million more were imprisoned.[11]

I

Existing scholarship on the September Thirtieth Movement and the Indonesian mass killings has implied that this brief but tumultuous period marked an abrupt about-face, both in Indonesia and in the wider world. Over the final years of Sukarno's rule, the PKI grew to become the world's largest non-ruling communist party and Indonesia gravitated toward the communist bloc. A Western official captured the prevailing sentiment in January 1965 when he lamented that "before long Indonesia may be for all practical purposes a Communist dictatorship."[12] In the wake of the rupture of October 1, Suharto annihilated Indonesia's political Left, which remained moribund for generations to come. Atop the bones of hundreds of thousands of Indonesians he erected the New Order, a counterrevolutionary dictatorship that reigned for more than three decades. Suharto also fastened Indonesia—which contemporary American policymakers were fond of referring to as the "greatest prize" in Southeast Asia in light of its geographic, demographic, and economic significance—to the capitalist bloc.[13] In so doing, he decisively altered the strategic balance in Asia and the trajectory of the global Cold War.

The wager of this book is that that the gruesome violence of 1965–1966 marked not an *end* but a *beginning*—the opening salvo of Suharto's Cold War. Suharto was determined to purge Indonesia of communist influence and ensure that communism could never again take root in the archipelago's lush political soil. Possessed of an almost paranoid conviction that communism could sprout from social dislocation, economic deprivation, or foreign subversion, he conceived of his mission as far more expansive than presiding over a massacre of suspected leftists. He sought to establish political stability, stimulate economic development, and promote regional security—not simply to salt the earth but rather to cultivate an entirely new ecosystem toxic to leftism. But Suharto confronted a nation riven by political polarization and mired in economic chaos. To extract the resources necessary to implement his ambitious agenda out of the domestic population would have required him to sacrifice that agenda at the altar of compromise with rival military branches, political parties, religious organizations, and student and youth groups who belonged to a broad anticommunist coalition but held divergent visions of Indonesia's future. Faced with this seemingly intractable dilemma, Suharto turned to the outside world. He mobilized international resources made available through the global Cold War to wage his own domestic and regional Cold Wars, first erecting a developmental authoritarian regime in Indonesia and then propagating authoritarian reaction elsewhere in Southeast Asia. In short, Suharto's devastating campaign of destruction was followed by a much more contingent, contested effort of construction.

What follows in these pages is a narrative of Suharto's Cold War that unfolds across three levels of analysis: the national, the regional, and the global. At each level of analysis different arguments come to the fore. Weaving these arguments together is a single thematic thread: anticommunist Cold War.

Suharto is something of a paradox. He was the most corrupt dictator in modern history and a mass murderer responsible for the deaths of hundreds of thousands of people.[14] But he was also the "father of development" who lifted tens of millions of Indonesians out of abject poverty. As one longtime observer of Indonesia has remarked, evoking an enduring trope about repressive but developmental dictatorships, the New Order was "at once one of the worst and one of the best governments of the twentieth-century world."[15] Scholars wrestled with this apparent contradiction as they attempted to define the nature of the New Order. Many saw in the Suharto regime's subjugation of society a recrudescence of the old—what Ruth McVey and Benedict Anderson depicted, respectively, as the apotheosis of the late colonial *Beamtenstaat* or the self-aggrandizing colonial "state-qua-state."[16] Others saw in the Suharto regime something altogether more modern, describing the New Order as a bureaucratic polity, a neopatrimonial regime, or a bureaucratic authoritarian regime.[17] Yet these interpretive debates disguised broad agreement over the autonomy and capacity of the Indonesian state under Suharto. This book explains how such a state came into being. It describes the elaboration of the Suharto regime as a contingent historical process—one of, by, and for the Cold War, in which anticommunism was simultaneously ends and means. It charts how Suharto inherited the deteriorating political, economic, and ideological infrastructure of the Old Order and built his New Order in response to unexpected crises and opportunities both at home and abroad.

And the outside world was pivotal in the rise of the New Order. Suharto himself is often depicted, sometimes in crude Orientalizing terms, as a provincial Javanese uninterested in the world beyond the Indonesian archipelago.[18] While he may have been inclined toward traditional Javanese culture, Suharto was also a consummately international figure known to keep an upside-down globe on the desk in his home office. Analyses of the regime he built often exhibit a similar nationalist myopia. Political scientist Dan Slater's *Ordering Power* argues that authoritarian governments in Indonesia and elsewhere in Southeast Asia cohered when national elites surrendered their resources to the state, banding together to form "protection pacts" against urban, class-based contentious politics that they perceived as endemic and unmanageable under more pluralistic institutional arrangements.[19] Suharto did dramatically expand the revenue base of the Indonesian state, but his fiscal appetites consistently exceeded his extractive capabilities. Moreover, he worried about saddling the Indonesian population with the financial burdens of his anticommunist ambitions. Suharto therefore worked to tap a deep reservoir of resources made available through the global Cold War: foreign aid and investment. Foreign aid alone accounted for more than 20 percent of total Indonesian government revenues during most of Suharto's reign, reaching almost 30 percent during the critical juncture in which he established his New Order. Moreover, the lion's share of all capital formation in Indonesia's investment-starved economy originated abroad in the crucial years of regime consolidation.[20] This book devotes special attention to the New Order's efforts to court global capital, arguing that "protection pacts" were international—dependent upon the cooperation of foreign financiers of authoritarian rule in addition to the collective action of domestic elites.

Scholars of political economy have long recognized the importance of international capital to the Suharto regime. Early observers cast the New Order as a paradigmatic comprador regime defined by its intermediary role in the purportedly "neocolonial" relationship between Indonesia and extractivist Western purveyors of aid and investment.[21] But the comprador thesis proved incapable of explaining the Suharto regime's turn toward economic nationalism in the 1970s. Subsequent scholarship put forth alternative perspectives on the relationship between the Suharto regime and global capitalism. Richard Robison characterized the New Order as the guardian of a constellation of capitalist forces within Indonesian society, ruling "with their general acquiescence and in their general interests." In his account, the Suharto regime nurtured a domestic capitalist class and then gradually displaced foreign capital before finally regularizing "the process of accumulation within a legal and predictable framework."[22] Jeffrey Winters disputed the existence of an indigenous capitalist class, which he insisted was no mere than a mere "capitalist crust." Instead, he argued that the New Order was, like all governments, responsive to a basic "investment imperative." For most of Suharto's time in power, the Indonesian state met the investment imperative with foreign capital and embraced market-based mechanisms for the allocation of resources in accordance with the preferences of international investors. During the oil boom of the 1970s and early 1980s, however, Indonesian policymakers met the investment imperative with petroleum revenues and embraced discretion-based mechanisms of distribution in accordance with the preferences of state officials.[23] These highly structuralist accounts portrayed the Suharto regime as a mechanistic reflection of capitalist power relations. What differentiated them was ultimately the New Order's *telos*—a pendular pattern for Winters and a Weberian modernization for Robison.

This book presents a different account of the international political economy of the New Order. It argues that the Cold War served as the nexus between the Suharto regime and international capital. Suharto considered the army the sole institution in Indonesia capable of safeguarding the archipelago from what he regarded as the persistent and pervasive threat of communism. An array of international actors in the United States, Western Europe, and Japan shared Suharto's determination to forestall a communist resurgence in Indonesia and furnished him with the resources necesary to sustain his bid to transform the archipelago. Suharto harnessed international capital to subjugate poles of countervailing power with Indonesia that he saw as impediments to his agenda. Put differently, Suharto enlisted international capital to build his authoritarian state from the outside-in, shrinking the internal constituencies upon which state power depended and obviating the domestic bargaining that characterized inside-out state-building in Europe.[24] Authoritarianism in Indonesia was thus an international construct. Centering the Cold War in the Suharto regime's engagement with international capital reveals the New Order as a dynamic agent capable of driving historical change. Put differently, Suharto's project was not one of mere management of a capitalist order—it was one of defense and ultimately of counterattack in what Indonesians perceived as a struggle of apocalyptic proportions. It required a consistent effort to orient state and society against a shifting matrix of threat and opportunity. And because the Cold War operated at the regional and global levels in addition to the national level, it necessitated a field of vision that spanned beyond Indonesia itself.

The two decades following Suharto's ascent were as turbulent for Southeast Asia as they were for Indonesia. The most dramatic changes unfolded in Indochina, where communist movements triumphed over their anticommunist opponents before fracturing the façade of socialist unity by waging wars against one another. But the tumult in Indochina disguised the consolidation of a broader "arc of containment" in the rest of Southeast Asia.[25] The Association of Southeast Asian Nations (ASEAN) gradually knit together the region's anticommunist states, vanquishing a reputation for endemic conflict that led an observer to dub Southeast Asia the "Balkans of the Orient" as recently as 1962.[26] Economic integration went hand-in-hand with political interconnection. Intra-ASEAN exchange expanded from 6.3 percent of the total trade of the organization's member states in 1967 to 14.9 percent in 1979 amid the earliest rumblings of what would eventually be called the "East Asian Miracle."[27] Finally, democratic governments faltered and authoritarian regimes gained footholds across the region. Shifting from the national to the regional level of analysis, this book excavates an Indonesian crusade to promote anticommunism in Southeast Asia by forging an autonomous architecture of regional security and by remaking the region in its own developmental authoritarian image—a crusade long overshadowed by the dense historiographic canopy arising from the militarized jungles of Indochina. If the Suharto regime was a product of the international system, so too was it an agent of change within the international system.

The New Order employed the traditional tools of statecraft to promote counterrevolution across Southeast Asia. For instance, Suharto provided President Ferdinand Marcos with diplomatic aid to roll back the internationalization of a secessionist struggle in the Philippines and gave Prime Minister Lon Nol material aid to combat a burgeoning Khmer Rouge insurgency in Cambodia. Indonesia's efforts to internationalize counterrevolution in Southeast Asia mirrored other forms of Third World anticommunist internationalism long overlooked in the historiography of the Cold War.[28] These internationalisms reveal that counterrevolution did not simply radiate outward from Washington but was instead adopted, adapted, and propagated by elites in the Third World who were embedded in their own particular histories and political struggles. Suharto's counterrevolutionary offensive in Southeast Asia flowed from the Indonesian army's long-standing domestic conflict with the PKI, since anticommunist army officers interpreted the PKI's activities in Indonesia as one manifestation of a broader revolutionary thrust emanating from the People's Republic of China. And like other forms of Third World anticommunist internationalism, Suharto's counterrevolutionary drive confirms that middle powers exercised considerable agency in the unfolding of various "regional Cold Wars."[29] In Southeast Asia, Suharto's counterrevolutionary offensive helped ensure the region remained attached to the anticommunist bloc even as communist forces in Vietnam, Cambodia, and Laos dealt the United States its most profound defeat of the Cold War era. The region's arc of containment was built from within.

Suharto's regional Cold War also encompassed novel approaches to international relations. Through diplomatic meetings, military exchanges, and public speeches, Suharto urged other Southeast Asian leaders to reorganize their states and societies in accordance with the New Order's doctrine of *ketahanan nasional*, or national resilience. A totalizing doctrine of securitization, the idea of national resilience subjected the realms of ideology, politics, economics, society, and culture to the imperatives of national security.[30] It abstracted from Indonesian experiences to prescribe an authoritarian government, a developmental bureaucracy, a system of total people's defense, and an official state ideology. Suharto's proselytization of the national resilience doctrine reverberated across the region. When national leaders in Malaysia, the Philippines, Cambodia, and Thailand faced political shocks, they self-consciously drew upon the Indonesian model to construct and consolidate newly authoritarian regimes. They pioneered novel institutional and ideological formations with few if any domestic precedents that, taken together, constituted a remarkable process of authoritarian convergence. Indonesian influence was not solely responsible for the turn toward authoritarian governance in Southeast Asia, nor did it extinguish all national particularities, but it contributed to a reconstitution of the foundations of political order in the region.

The result was a counterrevolutionary wave. Scholars have long recognized that revolution cannot be understood within a framework of methodological nationalism.[31] By contrast, scholarship on counterrevolution remains surprisingly parochial.[32] Odd Arne Westad's magisterial work on the global Cold War suggests that the turn toward authoritarianism in the Third World was propelled by common structural conditions—the failure of development schemes, the deepening of rural discontent, and the emergence of a new generation of postcolonial elites.[33] When scholars acknowledge the international dimensions of counterrevolution, these linkages tend to be vertical in nature, emblematized by American sponsorship of regime change in Iran and Guatemala in the 1950s and promulgation of military modernization in Bolivia and Indonesia in the 1960s.[34] This book argues that Indonesian efforts to internationalize counterrevolution contributed to a synchronous turn toward authoritarianism in Southeast Asia in the 1960s and 1970s in a process featuring horizontal logics of both contagion and emulation. Jeffrey James Byrne has chronicled the manifold ways in which Ahmed Ben Bella's Algeria became a beacon for national liberation movements across the Global South—from Angola to Vietnam to Palestine. If Algiers served as a "Mecca of revolution," a site to which pilgrims from national liberation movements across the Global South traveled to deepen their engagement with revolutionary theologies, then Jakarta became a Mecca of counterrevolution that inspired and abetted a wave of authoritarian retrenchment across Southeast Asia.[35]

The Southeast Asia that emerges in the pages that follow was a dynamic field of exchange in which international influences were polyvalent and reciprocal.

Elements of the Suharto regime looked beyond the Indonesian archipelago as they charted the course of the New Order—particularly toward Japan as a paragon of social cohesion and economic development, but also toward South Korea and Taiwan as more recent vintages of developmental states par excellence.[36] Other Southeast Asian regimes also held themselves up as models for anticommunist development.[37] What made Indonesian influence so powerful was its institutionalization through ASEAN. Like the Suharto regime itself, ASEAN is a subject of scholarly contention, particularly within the field of international relations.[38] Skeptics, often hailing from the realist tradition, cast the organization as little more than an ineffectual "talk shop."[39] Boosters, usually emerging from the constructivist tradition, depict ASEAN as giving rise to norms of noninterference and cooperation that sustained a "security community."[40] The narrative ahead argues that ASEAN emerged from the New Order's anticommunist project and served as a key channel for the diffusion of the Suharto regime's counterrevolutionary vision. As the United States and United Kingdom pulled back from Southeast Asia, Indonesian officials worked to bind the region's noncommunist states together in a united front against the People's Republic of China. Facing resistance to the idea of fashioning ASEAN into a formal military pact, the Suharto regime used ASEAN to promulgate its authoritarian state-building doctrine of national resilience, which culminated in ASEAN's endorsement of the idea of "regional resilience" as the Vietnam War came to an end.

The transformations unfolding in Southeast Asia reflected broader upheavals in the world's geopolitical and geoeconomic landscape. With the advent of détente and triangular diplomacy between the United States, the Soviet Union, and China, the Cold War was institutionalized and embedded within the structure of the international system.[41] But forces of decay also began to erode the foundations of the high Cold War order. The economic recovery of Western Europe and Japan from the ravages of the Second World War combined with the renascent forces of globalization to strain the institutional arrangements that upheld the postwar settlement.[42] Meanwhile an age of fracture produced a splintering effect that called an end to ideological uniformity within developed societies and to bipolarity between them.[43] The twin forces of ossification and decay within the international order—the former made manifest in superpower condominium and the latter in the rise of the human rights movement, the collapse of the international monetary system, and the emergence of North-South conflict—threatened Suharto's ability to mobilize Cold War resources. He consequently navigated the treacherous eddies of Indonesian and Southeast Asian politics with an eye toward the horizon of a protean global order.

Existing accounts of the Cold War emphasize the diffusion of ideologies to explain why, although the superpowers and much of the developed world experienced the conflict as what John Lewis Gaddis calls "long peace," for the states of the Global South the Cold War resembled what Odd Arne Westad labels a "semipermanent civil war."[44] From Afghanistan to Zimbabwe, Cold War ideologies inflected domestic struggles over modernity, independence, development, and identity and often instigated violence.[45] This book pays heed to the transnational circulation of Cold War ideologies, not only pandemic strains like communism and modernization theory but also more localized variants like *ketahanan nasional*. But it emphasizes the deployment of capital—both public and private—to explain the trajectory of the Cold War in the Global South. Suharto and the Indonesian army's bid to violently remake Indonesia depended upon an ability to tap reservoirs of foreign capital. After ascending to power, Suharto mobilized foreign aid and investment to bankroll coercive institutions, finance economic development programs, and facilitate corrupt accumulation. Absent international capital, he would have found little alternative but to moderate his Cold War ambitions in Indonesia and Southeast Asia. The trajectory of regimes like Suharto's reveals that it was Cold War capital that enabled national leaders in the Global South to wage war against their own people and their neighbors.

If international capital fueled violence, so too did it construct states. Historian David Engerman's exploration of the economic Cold War in India concludes that international aid "weakened Indian political institutions and ultimately constrained the nation's exercise of sovereignty."[46] The Cold War fueled an entirely different economic trajectory in Indonesia. International capital enabled Suharto to construct a highly capacious, autonomous, developmental state with the ability to "see" Indonesia's society and economy and orient them in a more or less coherent fashion toward an imagined future.[47] The Indonesian state had withered under Sukarno, with the civil service shrinking from 855,000 employees in 1953 to only 608,000 in 1963, whereupon the state ceased publishing statistics entirely and Indonesia careened into crisis.[48] Foreign aid and investment helped Suharto to rebuild the state. The civil service expanded to number 1.6 million employees by 1974 and became better-educated as well.[49] The enlarged state apparatus orchestrated a remarkable effort at development, publishing a series of five-year plans that guided the economy and implementing an array of initiatives designed to deliver the benefits of prosperity to ever-greater numbers of Indonesian citizens—all the while enabling Suharto to maintain an iron hold on political power.

Summing up a new generation of scholarship, Robert McMahon suggests that historians "have forged a rare scholarly consensus"—"that the Cold War constituted a truly global contest, in which the Third World served as a critical theater."[50] The rivalry between the United States and Soviet Union, as well as the clash between capitalism and communism that animated it, suffused the globe, polarizing and militarizing societies across the world and orienting the international outlooks of almost every state on the map. But to speak of a singular, global Cold War risks implying an ahistorical uniformity to the international relations of the latter half of the twentieth century. The Cold War was not only an international order, a grammar of geopolitics, but also an agglomeration of distinct yet interrelated political projects, each with its own themes, geographies, and temporalities. Some of these political projects were propelled by the global Cold War, such as the conflicts over the disposition of Germany and the Korean peninsula. Others, including the Arab-Israeli conflict and the rivalry between India and Pakistan, were braided into the global Cold War by the efforts of local elites to secure international support for their own idiosyncratic agendas. Still others were linked to the global Cold War through the perceptions of policymakers in Washington, Moscow, and Beijing.[51] Disaggregating the Cold War into its constituent parts reveals that Third World elites exercised considerable agency, often pulling the Cold War into the periphery to channel it toward their own particular purposes rather than having it unwittingly pushed upon them by the superpowers. It also reveals that these Cold War projects could, and often did, contradict each other.[52] Sometimes these contradictions were matters of geographic or temporal scope, but at other moments they amounted to fundamental disagreements over the meaning of Cold War itself. For instance, Suharto's Cold War was avowedly anti-Chinese, which explains why Indonesia continued to work to isolate China at the very moment that the United States sought to integrate the People's Republic into the international system.

The narrative ahead telescopes between the national, regional, and global levels of analysis while emphasizing the connections and contradictions between them. For example, Suharto's determination to insulate Indonesia from communist influence propelled his efforts to internationalize counterrevolution and fashion an anticommunist regional order in Southeast Asia. His regional activism in turn won him goodwill in Washington, where policymakers fixated on the Vietnam War lavished Suharto with aid that fueled the consolidation of the New Order in Indonesia. Suharto's domestic and regional Cold Wars thus depended in no small measure on the existence of the global Cold War. And yet other developments internal to the global Cold War or other regional Cold Wars, including the political transformations ushered in by the human rights revolution and the economic dislocations engendered by the oil shocks, occasionally threatened the continuity of Suharto's Cold War projects. National, regional, and global—all were irretrievably intertwined.

II

This book begins with a chapter that traces the coming of the Cold War to Indonesia in the decades before the September Thirtieth Movement. It argues that Suharto's project of Cold War emerged from his experience in the Indonesian army, an institution that absorbed the fascist values of the Japanese empire and nurtured a skepticism of civilian authority and a hostility toward communism. It also makes the case that Indonesian politics assumed the logic of Cold War as Sukarno collapsed a kaleidoscope of contestation into a single anticommunist-communist axis of conflict under the rubric of Guided Democracy. The Indonesian army then worked to link its Cold War project to the global Cold War by cultivating ties with counterrevolutionary powers like the United States. As a whole, the first chapter shows that the Cold War emerged largely endogenously in postcolonial Indonesia and that Indonesian actors subsequently grafted their political projects onto the global Cold War.

The next two chapters chart Suharto's chaotic efforts to dislodge the Sukarno regime, establish the New Order, and revitalize the economy in the three years following the September Thirtieth Movement. Chapter 2 examines Suharto's efforts to forge an anti-Sukarno political coalition while overseeing a campaign of eradication against the PKI. It argues that he generally eschewed positive international assistance in order to preserve his nationalist legitimacy but embraced negative international assistance—including promises to starve the Sukarno regime of international aid and thereby deepen an ongoing political and economic crisis. Chapter 3 explores Suharto's push to attract international aid and investment after he secured a political foothold in early 1966. It makes the case that Suharto's relatively limited access to international capital forced him to compromise with his unruly domestic coalition and moderate his Cold War ambitions, allowing a limited role for political parties and civil society organizations that favored a democratic order. Together, the two chapters reveal the unsettled nature of the period between 1965 and 1968 and demonstrate that Suharto's ability to mobilize international capital dictated the rhythms of his drive to power and the nature of the regime he built.

The subsequent two chapters trace Suharto's projection of his Cold War outward into Southeast Asia. Chapter 4 analyzes the New Order's drive to reintegrate Indonesia into networks of regional diplomacy and cohere the anticommunist states of Southeast Asia into an anti-Chinese axis through ASEAN. It argues that the national resilience doctrine helped the Suharto regime envision an autonomous architecture of regional security that transcended domestic and regional objections to a formal military pact. Chapter 5 delves into Suharto's effort to promote counterrevolution in Southeast Asia by promulgating the national resilience doctrine. It contends that other Southeast Asian leaders facing political crises embraced the Indonesian model to build new authoritarian regimes. Combined, the two chapters reveal the internationalist ambitions embedded within Suharto's Cold War project and the centrality of concerns about China in the evolution of regional geopolitics.

The following two chapters return to the domestic realm. Chapter 6 tracks how Suharto's increasingly successful efforts to attract Cold War capital enabled him to narrow his domestic coalition and abandon some of the consensual, inside-out state-building policies he pursued in the early years of the New Order. In rapid succession, Suharto clamped down on the remnants of the Indonesian communist movement, restive students and youth, and rival branches of the armed forces. Chapter 7 explores how elements of Suharto's domestic coalition resisted the narrowing of the New Order while the human rights movement, the collapse of the Bretton Woods order, the end of the Vietnam War, and the rise of triangular diplomacy collectively threatened Suharto's access to international capital. Domestic and international trends combined to produce a moment of maximum danger for Suharto's anticommunist project. Side by side, these two chapters argue that Suharto's turn toward outside-in state-building rendered his regime increasingly fragile.

The final two chapters chart the last gasps of Suharto's Cold War. Chapter 8 explores how Suharto mobilized windfall petrodollar revenues following the 1973 oil crisis to surmount the challenges facing the New Order, embarking upon a wide-ranging program of repression and cooptation at home while resisting the erosion of the Cold War abroad. It argues that Suharto's Cold War reached full bloom as the New Order was rendered increasingly auton-omous of both its domestic and international constituents. Chapter 9 traces how Suharto responded to the rising threat of political Islam in the late 1970s by adopting new approaches to governance. It claims that Suharto called an end to his Cold War project and Indonesia entered a post–Cold War world that was no longer defined by the competition between capitalism and communism.

Undergirding the narrative ahead are the available records of a number of crucial bureaucracies of the New Order held at the National Archives of the Republic of Indonesia: the Cabinet Secretariat; the Coordinating Ministry of Economy, Finance, and Industry; the Office of the Vice President (under both Sultan Hamengkubuwono IX and Adam Malik); and the Office of the State Secretariat for Special Affairs. These sources offer valuable windows into the New Order, whose inner workings have long been obscured by restrictions on access to archival records that endured decades after the collapse of the New Order and the advent of a flawed yet inspiring Indonesian democracy. The archives of the Foreign Ministry, the Armed Forces, the National Development Planning Agency, and the Office of the President remain inaccessible to researchers. Where the official archival record leaves the trajectory of events sketchy, Indonesian periodicals, memoirs, and government publications step into the breach. Meanwhile, sources from the region—Malaysia, Singapore, and the Philippines—and beyond—the United States, the United Kingdom, and Australia—situate Indonesia in its international context.

These sources necessarily shape the contours of the narrative.[53] Events in government offices and on university campuses in Jakarta emerge more clearly than developments in outlying provincial capitals, to say nothing of the rural villages where more than 80 percent of the Indonesian population lived in the 1960s and 1970s. The words and deeds of policymakers in Washington, Tokyo, and Paris reverberate more fully than those in Moscow and Beijing. More often than not, these voids in the archival record present no irresoluble dilemmas, since events in Jakarta and Western capitals proved most fateful for the course of Suharto's Cold War. But some grainy details, such as the twists and turns of Indonesian engagement with other Global South states, necessarily fall out of focus. Much work on the international dimensions of Indonesia's experience during the Cold War remains to be done.

Of the silences in the archival record that impose limits on the arc of the narrative, one in particular merits further comment. An outpouring of enormously valuable recent work by scholars, artists, and activists has revealed a great deal about the causes and consequences of the mass killings that swept Indonesia in 1965 and 1966. The conclusion of the most cutting-edge scholarship is simple and inescapable: the Indonesian army under Suharto bore primary responsibility for the horrific violence. This book does not contest that conclusion. Yet the narrative herein only rarely strays beyond Jakarta to analyze what one path-breaking study has branded the ground-level "mechanics of mass murder."[54] The partial elision of the violence of 1965–1966 in the narrative ahead reflects a gap in the archival record that is itself the product of a deliberate and ongoing campaign of silencing undertaken by the New Order, its Western sponsors, and its contemporary inheritors—a campaign that makes it challenging to draw precise connections between decisions in the capital and deaths in riverbeds and rice paddies elsewhere in Indonesia. But it also reflects a sense of historiographic unease with the air of inevitability that the newest scholarship on the mass killings occasionally imparts to the subsequent consolidation of the New Order. It is a grotesque but crucial truth that the mass killings represented a phase of Suharto's Cold War that encountered comparably little sustained, organized, contemporaneous resistance, either within Indonesia or in the outside world.[55] And even after the mass killings subsided, a considerable number of obstacles stood in the way of the consolidation of the New Order in Indonesia and the transformative regional and global reverberations it portended.

Suharto responded to the September Thirtieth Movement by embarking upon an anticommunist Cold War. Although the core component of Suharto's Cold War was a campaign of eradication waged against the PKI, his ambitions

spanned far beyond the mass murder of hundreds of thousands of his fellow citizens. He sought nothing less than to use the existing global order to remake
Indonesia and Southeast Asia. His was a project in which many, both in Indonesia
and around the world, were implicated. But on the evening of October 1, 1965,
it remained unthinkable how transformative a project Suharto's Cold War would
become—for Indonesia, Southeast Asia, and the world.

1

The Path to Power

Suharto was an unlikely Cold Warrior. Until October 1, 1965, he was known as a capable officer with few ideological predilections beyond a devotion to his soldiers. His career had traced modern Indonesia's encounter with the world: the rise of anticolonial nationalism, the waning of empire, the interregnum of the Second World War, the struggle to secure independence. And on the morning of October 1, he was catapulted to the center of an epic struggle over postcolonial Indonesia's path toward modernity.

Suharto's world-historic role owed first and foremost to his profession. He was neither a revolutionary nationalist in the mold of Vietnam's Ho Chi Minh nor a patrician conservative in the mold of Singapore's Lee Kuan Yew. He was a soldier through and through. And it was the Indonesian army that delivered him to his position as paragon of counterrevolution. Forged by the Japanese army during the occupation, the Indonesian army imbibed many of its fascist progenitor's ideals—nationalism, militarism, hierarchy, and order. It carried those values forward into the Indonesian revolution following Japan's defeat. Four years of revolutionary struggle fortified the army's conservative outlook with a mistrust toward civilian authority and an animus toward communism. The army nursed those antagonisms during the tempestuous years of parliamentary democracy that followed the achievement of independence in 1949, as ceaseless partisan infighting paralyzed the mechanisms of government, regional rebellions threatened the territorial integrity of the state, and a renascent communist party grew to command unprecedented popular loyalty. The army then banded together with President Sukarno to end democratic rule in Indonesia and initiate a period of martial law in 1957. Already possessed of a deeply conservative sociopolitical orientation, the army acquired a conservative economic orientation when it assumed control of key firms across the archipelago. But the revolutionary challenge persisted. Under Sukarno's protection, the Indonesian communist movement wielded ever greater influence. The Cold War slowly came to define Indonesian life.

Suharto's Cold War. Mattias Fibiger, Oxford University Press. © Oxford University Press 2023.
DOI: 10.1093/oso/9780197667224.003.0002

The emergence of a rivalry between the Indonesian army and the PKI was to a large extent a domestic phenomenon. But in the context of a world cleaving amid the global Cold War, the conflict between the army and the PKI inevitably assumed international dimensions. The army worked to cultivate ties with the United States, the world's preeminent counterrevolutionary power, and the PKI nurtured ties with the People's Republic of China, the world's most strident revolutionary power. The internationalization of the domestic struggle only stoked the flames of conflict. By the time the September Thirtieth Movement upended Indonesia's unstable political equilibrium, both the army and the PKI were convinced that the other was on the cusp of a daring move to seize power and deliver Indonesia into the camp of its international sponsor.

I

Suharto was born into an "age in motion." At the turn of the twentieth century, the Dutch rulers of what was then known as the Netherlands East Indies embarked upon an "Ethical Policy." Uplift replaced exploitation as the principal rationale of colonial rule—in rhetoric if not entirely in reality. The colonial state implemented developmental programs focusing on education, health, irrigation, and infrastructure, which nurtured a rapidly expanding if overwhelmingly poor population. But a small sliver of the people of the Indies gained access to the appendages of modernity that enabled them to think, communicate, and act in novel ways—giving rise to a swirl of revolutionary sentiment avant la lettre and an inchoate nationalist movement that could not yet speak its name.[1]

Suharto was not among these privileged few. His native village of Kemusuk lay in the fertile rice plains of Central Java, six miles west of the court city of Yogyakarta. There Suharto entered the world in June 1921. Kemusuk did not go untouched by the transformations unfolding elsewhere on Java, but what tumult Suharto experienced in his youth emanated from family quarrels rather than ideological awakenings. Suharto's mother experienced what was then described as a nervous breakdown (and would in later times likely be diagnosed as postpartum depression) shortly after giving birth and quickly divorced her husband. Suharto's father, a minor village official, subsequently entrusted the six-week-old child to the care of a relative. Thus began a peripatetic childhood. Suharto would live with no fewer than seven families by the time he came of age. His father frequently sent him to the house of one relative or another—partaking of the traditional Javanese practice of *ngenger*—and his soon-remarried mother occasionally dragged him back to Kemusuk. Amid this difficult upbringing, Suharto acquired an education through the network of village schools established under the guise of the Ethical Policy and through tutelage in the principles of Javanese mysticism. His was a modest education compared to that of children of elite Indonesian families, who usually enrolled in the parallel Dutch-medium school system that led to a university education and a desirable career.

The young Suharto soon became a soldier. He had hoped to continue his education, but his family's means were depleted amid the Great Depression. At eighteen years of age, with only ten years of schooling under his belt, his father told him he had no alternative but to find a job. He eventually found employment as a clerical assistant at a local bank—a position he held for only a year and for which he expressed little enthusiasm. The following year, he applied to join the Royal Netherlands Indies Army (KNIL), the Dutch force responsible for the conquest and pacification of the archipelago. Decades later, Suharto claimed that he joined the colonial army out of a desire to "make myself useful in the struggle for our country's independence." That assertion revealed an enduring tendency toward mendacity: Suharto remained unmoved by the churn of anticolonial nationalism, which by then had split into distinct communist, Islamist, and nationalist *aliran* (streams). More likely, his motives for enlisting with the KNIL lay in a desire for stable employment and, possibly, a thirst for adventure in a life that presented few other opportunities.[2]

As with so much in Suharto's life, the personal became political. The Dutch surrendered to Nazi Germany in May 1940, only two weeks before Suharto joined the KNIL. The young soldier quickly climbed the ranks of the manpower-hungry colonial army, reaching sergeant by the time the Japanese conquered Java in May 1942—an unusually high position for a man of his modest origins. But Suharto displayed no particular attachment to the Dutch. He abandoned his KNIL uniform in the face of the Japanese invasion and soon thereafter joined the police force under a new imperial master. Although some Indonesians were galvanized by the idea of "Asia for the Asians" that undergirded Japan's Greater East Asia Co-Prosperity Sphere, Suharto was once again driven by want for employment rather than loftier ideals.[3] After nearly a year as a police officer, he signed up for the Homeland Defense Force (Peta), which the Japanese established in October 1943 to mobilize the Indonesian population against a brewing Western counteroffensive in the Pacific.

Peta became the fountainhead of the Indonesian army. Young soldiers imbibed the ideals of Japanese militarism, with its emphasis on discipline and *semangat* (spirit).[4] Japanese training also enlivened traditional Javanese military values among Peta trainees, including the images of the *ksatria* and *jago*—the elite warrior and populist champion, respectively, both imbued with an irrepressible personal dynamism capable of channeling popular energies in times of crisis.[5] These ideological ballasts, with their elevation of martial ardor over material potency, reflected the impoverished conditions of 1940s Java. They also shaped the future Indonesian army's embrace of a "territorial" strategy of "Total

People's Defense and Security" (Hankamrata), whereby units led by charismatic officers would integrate themselves into particular locales and mobilize the population to defeat an occupying force.[6] The result was that Peta officers and soldiers came to regard themselves as both emerging from and guarding over the people.

For his part, Suharto garnered a reputation for quiet competence among his Japanese superiors and Indonesian comrades alike. He ascended the Peta ranks at an impressive clip, weathering grueling training exercises and degrading punishments meted out by Japanese officers. But discontent within Peta mounted as the Japanese military was beaten back across the Pacific and as socioeconomic conditions on Java deteriorated. A detachment of Peta soldiers enraged by the abuse inflicted by the Japanese upon the local population (and upon themselves) revolted in the Blitar region of East Java in February 1945.[7] "My experiences in Peta convinced me that the behavior of most Japanese officers was unacceptable to us," Suharto recalled in his memoirs. "My desire to fight back against those who hurt us grew."[8] If he conveyed his desires truthfully, he never acted on them. Such was his reputation for reliability among the Japanese that he was tasked with rebuilding the very Peta battalion that rebelled in Blitar. He was serving in that capacity when American planes dropped atomic bombs over Hiroshima and Nagasaki in August 1945 and the Second World War came to an end.

II

Across Asia, the months following August 1945 were defined by exhilaration and immiseration.[9] In Japanese-occupied Jakarta, nationalist leaders Sukarno and Mohammad Hatta proclaimed the independence of the Republic of Indonesia on August 17, 1945. But little united Indonesian nationalists beyond a desire for independence. Would the postcolonial Indonesian state be secular or Islamic? Individualistic or collectivistic? Unitary or federal? Sukarno had long served as an instrument of synthesis, seeking to bind the fissiparous archipelago together through formulas like his 1926 call for unity between the forces of "Nationalism, Islamism, and Marxism."[10] He assumed that role once more in the waning months of the war by articulating a national ideology of Pancasila, meaning five principles: nationalism, internationalism, democracy, social justice, and belief in God.[11] Whether this vague vision could surmount widespread contestation over the contours of state and society remained to be seen.

As these momentous events unfolded, Suharto was busy training Peta replacements in a remote area of East Java. After conducting training exercises on the morning of August 19, he was told by a Japanese officer that Peta would be disbanded. Suddenly demobilized, Suharto made his way back to Yogyakarta, a city that was a cauldron of nationalist ferment. Sukarno sensed an opportunity to capitalize on the "Rooseveltian moment" opened by the proclamation of the Atlantic Charter and was determined to lead Indonesia into the postcolonial era via the path of *diplomasi* (diplomacy) rather than *perjuangan* (struggle).[12] The Republic's foreign minister went so far as to tell one of the first Americans who arrived in Java following the Japanese surrender that "What is best for Java is almost surely what your country has done for the Philippines—an assurance of a future independence, with a date set, and a program for arriving at that independence."[13] But in Yogyakarta as elsewhere in the archipelago, *pemuda* (young people) intoxicated by the euphoria of revolution began seizing arms from the Japanese and hoisting the red-and-white Indonesian flag above public buildings.[14] Suharto joined with several of his former Peta comrades to form a *lasykar* (militia) and launched a series of raids to capture weapons from Japanese encampments around Yogyakarta.[15]

The nascent Republican government attempted to establish a measure of control over the countless armed groups sprouting up across the archipelago by establishing the organization that would become the Indonesian army and appointing ex-KNIL officers as its leaders. Most *lasykar* led by former Peta commanders integrated themselves into the new army. But an array of operationally independent *lasykar* under the command of local powerbrokers seethed against the central government's cautious, diplomatic strategy. These irregular forces began waging war against both Japanese units that attempted to restore law and order and Allied troops that landed on Java beginning in late September 1945.[16] One such Allied detachment (with Dutch colonial officials in tow) arrived in the coastal city of Semarang in October and began moving inland. Suharto's unit participated in combat that pushed the Allied advance from the inland area of Magelang back to Semarang. His performance won him promotion to the rank of lieutenant colonel and command of his Yogyakarta-based regiment.[17]

The brewing rivalry between civilian and military poles of authority deepened amid the early days of Indonesia's war for independence. A group of army commanders from Java and Sumatra held a conference in November 1945 and elected the twenty-nine-year-old former Peta officer Sudirman as commander-in-chief and the Yogyakarta Sultan Hamengkubuwono IX as minister of defense. At almost the exact same moment, Sukarno's presidential cabinet collapsed as a result of opposition to his corporatist, Japanese-inspired political program and the aristocratic, collaborationist composition of his cabinet. In its place emerged a parliamentary cabinet led by Prime Minister Sutan Sjahrir. A democratic socialist, Sjahrir had belonged to an underground opposition movement during the occupation. He was known for his hostility toward Japanese fascism and his affinity for European thought.[18] Among Sjahrir's first moves was to appoint his own minister of defense, Amir Sjarifuddin. The leftist Sjarifuddin quickly embarked upon an effort to assert civilian control over an army that he regarded as hopelessly tainted by Japanese militarism. Although he accepted Sudirman's election as commander-in-chief, Sjarifuddin sought to indoctrinate the members of the armed forces by introducing a political commissar system modeled on that of the Soviet Red Army. He also began cultivating the remaining independent *lasykar*, which competed with the army for weapons and popular support, as a counterweight to Sudirman's force. By the time the Republic moved its capital from Jakarta to Yogyakarta to escape the expanding Allied presence in January 1946, the stage was set for confrontation between a Japanese-influenced army devoted to *perjuangan* and a Western-influenced government wedded to *diplomasi*.[19]

Suharto found himself at the center of this brewing civil-military rivalry when a group of disaffected army officers kidnapped Sjahrir in June 1946. Sukarno responded by assuming extraordinary powers and declaring martial law. Fearful that internecine strife would provide grist for the mill of Dutch propaganda about Indonesians' purported inability to govern themselves, Sukarno issued a radio broadcast denouncing what he called an "attempted coup d'état" and demanding Sjahrir's immediate release. The president sent a written order to Suharto instructing him to arrest the mastermind behind the kidnapping. After he learned that General Sudirman had distanced himself from the affair, Suharto cast his lot with the government and complied with the order. Sjahrir was released to continue his diplomatic offensive.[20]

Sjahrir's *diplomasi* eventually delivered the Linggadjati Agreement of November 1946. Under the terms of the agreement, the Dutch recognized de facto Republican authority in Java and Sumatra, and both Dutch and Republican officials pledged to work toward the creation of a federal United States of Indonesia within a vague Netherlands-Indonesian Union. The agreement reflected the emerging Cold War. The United States was determined to promote the reintegration of the Indonesian archipelago into the global economy and to prevent the Soviet Union from establishing a foothold in the decolonizing world. American officials were also aware of developments in nearby Indochina, where a French effort to subjugate the newly proclaimed Democratic Republic of Vietnam hardened the revolutionary regime's communist character and plunged the wider peninsula into what would become known as the First Indochina War. Washington therefore moved beyond its prevailing hands-off approach and pressed The Hague to adopt a more conciliatory posture in negotiations with the Indonesian Republic.[21]

A tenuous sense of stability took hold in Java following Linggadjati. Sudirman worked to incorporate the *lasykar* into a reorganized Indonesian army in accordance with a decree issued by Sukarno in May 1947. But deteriorating economic circumstances impeded Sudirman's efforts to stanch the centrifugal tendencies within the army. Republican coffers grew increasingly bare, and army and *lasykar* units continued to finance themselves. Like other officers across the archipelago, Suharto began working with smugglers (of materiel, food, and opium) to sustain his soldiers during the lean months of early 1947.[22]

The calm did not last long. In July, the unpopularity of Sjahrir's diplomatic concessions led to the dissolution of his cabinet. As a new government led by Sjarifuddin ascended to power, the Dutch launched a euphemistic "police action" against the Republic, seizing control of most of Java and key areas of Sumatra. Suharto served with Republican forces on the front lines of Central Java and helped prevent the Dutch from destroying the fledgling Republic entirely. But the key lesson he drew from the police action and its aftermath concerned the possibilities opened by the emerging geopolitical configuration of the global Cold War. In his memoirs, he recalled that "the outside world's reaction to Dutch aggression was overwhelming."[23] Islamic societies the world over rallied behind their coreligionists in Indonesia. Australian stevedores refused to load Dutch ships bound for the archipelago in what they called a "black armada" campaign. Indian and Australian diplomats raised the Indonesian cause at the United Nations Security Council, where the Republic also garnered support from the Soviet Union and Poland. Most consequentially, US policymakers anxious to avoid alienating the decolonizing world urged the Dutch to halt their offensive and threatened to exclude the dollar-starved Netherlands from the Marshall Plan unless it agreed to negotiate with the Republic.[24]

The Hague eventually relented in the face of overwhelming international pressure. Negotiations between Dutch and Indonesian officials resumed in late 1947 and resulted in the Renville Agreement of January 1948, which established a ceasefire along the so-called Van Mook Line connecting the farthest-advanced Dutch positions. The Republic's territory was left significantly diminished and choked by a tightening Dutch blockade—a humiliating outcome for a government that put its faith in *diplomasi*. As Republican soldiers retreated from West Java, Islamists under Sekarmaji Marjan Kartosuwiryo formed Darul Islam to fight the Dutch and eventually establish an Islamic state.[25] Within the shrunken Republic, meanwhile, opposition to the Renville Agreement quickly led to the collapse of Sjarifuddin's cabinet. A government led by Mohammad Hatta took its place. The new prime minister faced a groundswell of internal problems: huge numbers of refugees fled from Dutch-occupied territory into Republican areas, which led to a surfeit of manpower and a scarcity of materiel visible in an elevenfold increase in rice prices in the year following August 1947.[26] Hatta knew Republican forces had generally fared poorly in combat against the Dutch, so he pledged fealty to Renville despite Dutch violations of its terms. With an increasingly immiserated population straining against a cautious leadership, the Republic's Central Javanese stronghold became a hotbed of political contention.

One manifestation of that ferment was an uprising by the PKI in the Republican-controlled city of Madiun in September 1948. Established in May 1920—the first communist party in all of Asia—the PKI quickly succumbed to irrelevance after launching an ill-fated uprising in 1926. The party revived itself following the Second World War and supported Sjahrir's and Sjarifuddin's left-wing governments. But as Soviet policy toward the decolonizing world took on an increasingly militant cast in the wake of ideologist Andrei Zhdanov's proclamation of his two-camp doctrine in September 1947, and as ever more leftist Indonesians despaired of the path of *diplomasi* and urged a turn to *perjuangan*, the PKI assumed a more avowedly oppositionist posture in domestic politics. The party directed a wave of strikes and prepared for an insurrection. As these plans gathered momentum, the erstwhile PKI leader Musso unexpectedly arrived in Republican territory after more than a decade of exile in the Soviet Union. He came bearing what he called the "Gottwald Plan," named after the Czechoslovakian communist who seized power in a February 1948 coup d'état. Musso was quickly anointed leader of the PKI. But the hurtle of events preempted his bid to seize power. Hatta had implemented a program of "rationalization" designed to reduce the size of the military (then numbering about 350,000 soldiers) and deepen its hold on the remaining *lasykar* (then estimated at 470,000 irregulars on Java alone). At the core of Hatta's rationalization plan lay a proposal by Colonel Abdul Haris Nasution for a guerrilla warfare–oriented military divided between fully armed mobile strike forces and sparsely equipped territorial defense forces.[27] After conflict broke out between Nasution's West Java-based Siliwangi division and defiant left-wing forces slated for demobilization in the opposition stronghold of Surakarta, *lasykar* in the nearby city of Madiun staged a revolt against the central government. Musso and the PKI ascertained they had been presented with a fait accompli and had no choice but to support the uprising.[28]

Suharto was soon pulled into the chaos. Determined to avoid a split within the armed forces, General Sudirman instructed Suharto to travel to Surakarta and warn another officer against joining the Left's struggle against military rationalization. That officer invited Suharto to travel to Madiun to see the situation for himself. Upon arriving at the epicenter of the uprising, the two men encountered Musso. "Wouldn't it be better if we abandoned the hostilities between us and united against the Dutch?" Suharto recalled asking the PKI leader.[29] But Musso was evidently unmoved by Suharto's appeal. Sukarno had delivered a radio address denouncing the rebellion and calling on the population to "make a choice between following Musso and his Communist Party, who will obstruct the attainment of an independent Indonesia, or following Soekarno Hatta, who, with the Almighty's help, will lead our Republic of Indonesia to become an independent Indonesia which is not subjected to any other country whatsoever." Musso replied with a radio message of his own urging the Indonesian population to "wrest the powers of the state into their own hands."[30] No mass uprising materialized. The Siliwangi division entered Madiun in late September and crushed the rebellion, killing both Musso and Sjarifuddin and arresting some 35,000 people (mostly *lasykar* irregulars sympathetic to the PKI) in the process. Like many other members of the armed forces, Suharto came away convinced that the PKI was treacherously anti-national. The Madiun rebellion established a pattern of hostility between the army and the left that would endure for decades.

No sooner had the Madiun uprising had been dispatched than the Dutch launched a second "police action" against the embattled Republic. In December 1948, Dutch forces stormed across the Van Mook Line and quickly overran the Republic's remaining territory in Java and much of its writ in Sumatra as well. Their first target was the Republican capital of Yogyakarta. In the face of the Dutch offensive, Sukarno, Hatta, and a coterie of other civilian leaders abandoned their plans to retreat to the countryside to lead a guerrilla struggle. Instead, they went willingly into Dutch captivity—reasoning that their capture would stoke international support for the revolutionary cause and reduce the likelihood that the Dutch would assassinate the Republic's leadership. But the army remained inclined toward *perjuangan* rather than *diplomasi*. Suharto and his men evacuated Yogyakarta and began staging attacks on the capital to demonstrate the Republic's survival and frustrate Dutch ambitions. In one particularly daring maneuver, Suharto commanded forces that attacked Yogyakarta in March 1949 and allegedly held the city for six hours—an event ripe with symbolism whose significance would later be exaggerated and mythologized.[31] Suharto and other military officers also came to assume unprecedented authority over matters of public administration and mass mobilization as they worked to sustain the Republic against the Dutch onslaught.[32] By the time Indonesia achieved its independence, many army leaders had come to resent their civilian counterparts as either feckless or contemptible. They had also concluded that the army was the sole force in Indonesia that had proven itself both willing and able to act in the national interest.[33]

For all the daring of the Indonesian military's *perjuangan*, it was the civilian government's ceaseless efforts at *diplomasi* that prevailed. By March 1949, the Truman administration formalized a dramatic shift in US policy toward Indonesia and the rest of Southeast Asia. NSC-51 held that French and Dutch efforts at recolonization were "anti-historical in direction" and "the greatest factor contributing to the expansion of communism in SEA [Southeast Asia]."[34] Several calculations lay behind this reorientation. Within Indonesia, the Republic's suppression of the PKI uprising at Madiun had demonstrated its anticommunist bona fides. American policymakers were determined not to vanquish the Hatta government's hopes for international deliverance lest they precipitate its collapse and the emergence of a left-wing alternative. In Asia writ large, 1948 witnessed the eruption of communist rebellions in Malaya, Burma, and the Philippines as well as advances by Mao Zedong's Chinese Communist Party against Chiang Kai-shek's Kuomintang. American policymakers were anxious not to push nationalist movements across decolonizing Asia into the Soviet orbit. And at the global level, the Dutch police actions and subsequent mopping-up operations violated a series of United Nations decrees. American policymakers were unwilling to sacrifice the architecture of the postwar global order at the altar of Dutch imperialism. Washington therefore abandoned its hitherto indulgent posture toward the Dutch and threatened to halt Marshall Plan aid to the Netherlands unless it negotiated an expeditious path toward Indonesian independence.[35]

Indonesian and Dutch negotiators finally came to an accord in December 1949. The Dutch extracted an array of painful concessions from their former colonial subjects. The independent Indonesian state would assume a federal rather than unitary structure—meaning the Republic would exist alongside fifteen Dutch-created puppet states with equal juridical status. The federalized Indonesian state would also enter into a Commonwealth-like union with the Netherlands. So too would independent Indonesia guarantee Dutch investments in the archipelago and, more controversially, assume responsibility for the lion's share of the debts accumulated by the Dutch colonial state, including for expenses accrued during the war against the Republic. Finally, the Dutch would retain sovereignty over West Papua until future negotiations could determine the territory's ultimate dispensation. With these conditions satisfied, Indonesia secured its independence on December 27, 1949.

III

The Indonesian revolution delivered an independent state. But the revolution also posed a number of questions about relations between center and periphery, the role of the military, and Indonesia's orientation within a cleaving global order. Indonesians' efforts to answer those questions soon gave rise to a yawning polarization along cross-cutting political, economic, religious, ethnic, and geographic axes.

The political structure of the Indonesian state became the subject of immediate contestation. The federal system smacked of the divide-and-rule tactics employed by the Dutch. The states of Central and West Java voted to dissolve themselves and merge with the Republic in January 1950. The same month, a

Dutch military captain staged a coup in Bandung in order to preserve the West Javanese state of Pasundan and the federal system more broadly. Siliwangi troops quickly crushed the coup attempt and the Republic absorbed Pasundan as well. Over the ensuing eight months, pro-Republican sentiment mounted across the archipelago, and most federal states liquidated themselves to merge with the Republic. The last bastion of opposition to unitarism was in East Indonesia— the oldest, largest, and most autonomous of the puppet states created by the Dutch. Rogue military elements in East Indonesia orchestrated a coup against a newly installed regional commander in April 1950. Sukarno denounced the rebels as traitors and ordered the military to conquer East Indonesia. An expeditionary force that included Suharto's brigade arrived in Makassar toward the end of the month and rapidly re-established order.[36] Only three days after the arrival of Republican troops, the government of East Indonesia announced it was prepared to merge into a unitary Indonesian state. The federal system was liquidated on August 17, 1950.

Independent Indonesia became a parliamentary democracy with its capital in Jakarta. No elections would be held until 1955, so seats in parliament were allocated to parties based on estimates of their popular support. Masyumi, representing Islamists, obtained 21.1 percent of seats, while the Indonesian Nationalist Party (PNI), representing nationalists, obtained 15.5 percent of seats. The early cabinets were led by prime ministers from one of these two parties. Still tainted by the Madiun uprising, the PKI obtained only 5.6 percent of seats to represent the communist *aliran* of the anticolonial movement. Post-revolutionary leaders assumed control over an archipelago in dire economic straits, with per capita output in 1950 reaching only 71 percent of its 1941 peak.[37] Post-independence cabinets consequently prioritized political consolidation and economic reconstruction—not, to the chagrin of Sukarno and other revolutionary nationalists, the reclamation of West Papua. But the compromises inherent in such a pragmatic approach inflamed popular opinion and fueled partisan maneuvering that felled seven cabinets in seven years, a rate of turnover that precluded the formulation and implementation of farsighted policy. After the cabinet of Prime Minister Sukiman Wirjosandjojo signed an aid agreement with the United States that pledged Indonesia to contribute to the "defensive strength of the free world," for instance, the prime minister was quickly forced to resign for transgressing Indonesia's nonaligned, *bebas aktif* (free and active) foreign policy doctrine.[38]

The army fractured amid political instability. The legendary General Sudirman died in January 1950. Hatta and Hamengkubuwono then installed a coterie of former KNIL men like Nasution in senior positions in the armed forces—reasoning that their Dutch education rendered them more amenable to the principle of civilian supremacy than Japanese-influenced ex-Peta officers like

Suharto. The army worked hand in hand with the civilian governments to bind the nation together by suppressing holdout federal states in the Outer Islands and combatting the continuing Darul Islam rebellion in West Java. The civilian governments also supported Nasution's efforts to create a more disciplined and professional military, particularly his rationalization scheme that aimed to cut the army's size to 150,000 soldiers by 1953. But the demobilization of hundreds of thousands of revolutionaries inspired trenchant opposition from former Peta commanders and *lasykar* leaders whose units were most likely to be made redundant. These men made common cause with Sukarno and other populist critics of the technocratic cabinets by denouncing the army's leadership as "Westernized" and insufficiently devoted to the revolution. Under their influence, parliament soon passed a motion providing for the establishment of an official commission to report on "the possibility of improvements in the leadership and organization" of the military.[39] The prospect of civilian interference in military matters enraged segments of the officer corps. On October 17, 1952, a cabal of officers at army headquarters organized a rally of 30,000 civilians in Jakarta and dispatched tanks to train their cannons on the presidential palace. Representatives of the cabal went to the palace to meet Sukarno and demanded the immediate dissolution of parliament and the expeditious organization of elections. The president refused. He then counterpunched by instigating mutinies by ex-Peta dissidents against regional commanders loyal to army headquarters. Nasution was suspended and his allies were removed from their posts. Central control of the army attenuated to such an extent that it once again resembled a network of loosely interconnected but largely autonomous and self-sufficient fiefdoms.[40]

In these years Suharto remained stationed in Central Java. He presided over the demobilization of five of his nine battalions—a task made easier by the revolt of one battalion comprising former Islamist *lasykar* irregulars that defected to join the Darul Islam rebellion. But he kept himself aloof from politics, recording in his autobiography of the October 17 contretemps, "I did not understand what that incident was about at all."[41] As direction and funding from Jakarta dried up in the wake of the episode, which coincided with the end of the Korean War economic boom that inflated the prices of Indonesian exports, Suharto was forced to devote himself ever more fully to financing his regiment.[42] The same was true of regional commanders in the Outer Islands, who erected massive smuggling enterprises that starved the state of vitally important tariff revenues.

Indonesia grew increasingly polarized throughout the 1950s. The PNI became antagonistic toward political Islam and hewed toward radical nationalist positions on matters of foreign and economic policy, which strained the Masyumi-PNI coalitions that undergirded two of the first three post-independence cabinets.[43] As the PNI moved away from Masyumi, it gravitated toward the PKI. The communists had adopted a united front policy under Aidit's leadership and sought to build an alliance of workers, peasants, and national bourgeoisie. Between 1954 and 1955, PKI membership grew tenfold to more than 1 million, the overwhelming majority of whom resided on Java.[44] Meanwhile Nahdlatul Ulama (NU), which represented rural, traditionalist Muslim communities concentrated in East and Central Java, split from Masyumi. The rump Masyumi was left to cater primarily to urban, modernist Muslim communities located in West Java and the Outer Islands.[45] As this political realignment transpired, the government maintained an overvalued exchange rate for the rupiah that served as an implicit subsidy for the import-dependent island of Java and an implicit tax on the export-oriented Outer Islands. Resentment against the Javanese-dominated central governments reached a fever pitch with the eruption of Islamist revolts in Aceh, South Sulawesi, and South Kalimantan that eventually linked themselves to the simmering Darul Islam rebellion in West Java.

The elections that were finally held in October 1955 laid bare the depth of Indonesia's polarization: with more than 90 percent of eligible voters casting ballots, the PNI won 22.3 percent of the vote, Masyumi 20.9 percent, NU 18.4 percent, and the PKI 16.4 percent. No other party won more than 3 percent. More than 85 percent of all ballots marked for the PNI, NU, and PKI came from Java, home to just 66.2 percent of the country's population, whereas only 51.3 percent of ballots tallied for Masyumi came from Java.[46]

As was the case elsewhere in the Third World, polarization drew in the Cold War. PNI Prime Minister Ali Sastroamidjojo organized the landmark Asian-African Conference in Bandung in April 1955 in a bid to bolster his party's popularity before the forthcoming elections.[47] When the conference convened, Sukarno delivered a soaring address denouncing the persistence of colonialism in "its modern dress" and proclaiming it was necessary to give "content and meaning to our independence"—"not material content and meaning only, but also ethical and moral content."[48] Although his audience was decidedly global, his words reflected a deepening frustration with the decline of revolutionary élan amid the crucible of parliamentary politics and with the figurehead presidential role assigned to him under the parliamentary system. Soon thereafter he began delivering speeches excoriating "fifty-percent-plus-one" democracy as ill-suited to Indonesian society.[49]

To disrupt Indonesia's sclerotic parliamentary system, Sukarno turned to the outside world. The president embarked on two grand tours in 1956: first to the United States, Canada, and Western Europe, then to Yugoslavia, Czechoslovakia, the Soviet Union, Mongolia, and China. He predicted that, when he returned from his overseas voyages, "I will be able to say for certain what would be the best course for us to follow in our task of nation building."[50] Sukarno thus devoted considerable attention to the political and economic systems of the countries he visited. He was astonished by the prosperity he witnessed in the United

States but concluded that it did not represent a viable model for Indonesia given the developmental gap that existed between the two countries. His visit to the Soviet Union was far more productive, and he came away with an agreement for $100 million in concessional aid.[51] "Years ago," he recalled in his autobiography, "I asked the USA for a loan. Not a gift. I felt like a hungry relation whimpering at the door of a rich uncle. . . . Finally I asked Khrushchev for the one hundred million. It was bitter cold, yet he came out of the Kremlin into the street to embrace me. . . . There were no long, cold negotiations. Nor did they dictate my future behavior before giving me my crust of bread."[52] Even so, the president was disillusioned by the prevalence of social problems in the Soviet Union, especially the maltreatment of Muslims. The Soviets could offer the president material aid but apparently not ideological inspiration. It was in China that he found a model. Sukarno concluded that Mao had perfectly combined strong leadership and mass mobilization for the achievement of revolutionary goals.[53]

Upon his return to Indonesia, Sukarno delivered a fiery speech to youth leaders. "If we want to build as people have in other countries I have seen, for example, in the Chinese People's Republic," he remarked, "we must transform the party system completely." He called political parties a "disease" that led the people to "forever work against one another!" "Bury the parties," went the refrain of his speech.[54] Two days later, he revealed that he had devised a *konsepsi* (conception) for resolving Indonesia's political problems that he called Guided Democracy. Sukarno's efforts to impose his vision on Indonesia would define the next stage of the archipelago's history.

IV

A drawn-out crisis within the army eventually morphed into a mortal threat to the Indonesian state and provided Sukarno with an opportunity to implement his *konsepsi*. Army officers stationed at headquarters and in regional commands had grown increasingly discontented with dwindling budgetary outlays and escalating civilian interference in personnel matters in the years following the October 17 affair. In February 1955, some 270 officers gathered in Yogyakarta to sign a Charter of Unity and issue a resolution demanding "clarification of the limits of political influence on the army."[55] A renewed showdown between civilian and military claimants to political power awaited.

The trigger came with the resignation of the army's chief of staff in May. The cabinet attempted to install a pliant and relatively junior figure in his stead, continuing the time-tested strategy of divide-and-rule that preserved civilian supremacy over the army over the preceding three years. But the acting chief of staff refused to surrender authority to his anointed successor. He announced he could not allow the army, the "backbone of national potential," to succumb to political interference.[56] Opposition parties rallied behind the army and soon precipitated the collapse of the Ali Sastroamidjojo cabinet, whose support in parliament had already waned due to its indulgent attitude toward the PKI. A Masyumi-led government then immediately moved to reach a settlement with the army. Officers purged following the October 17 affair were allowed back into the fold. Foremost among them was Nasution, who returned as army chief of staff. Nasution quickly renewed his long-standing effort to subject the unwieldy army to central control—notably by transferring regional commanders to new posts in a bid to sever the bonds of loyalty and patronage that enabled them to act as local warlords. In so doing he stoked lingering tensions within the army. Recalcitrant regional commanders staged an unsuccessful coup attempt in Jakarta before capitalizing on popular unrest and usurping power across Sumatra in late 1956 and early 1957. Around the same time, the regional commander in East Indonesia declared martial law. One of his deputies then produced a "Charter of Universal Struggle" (*Piagam Perjuangan Semesta*, or Permesta) explaining that the region was "not breaking away from the Republic of Indonesia" but was instead "fighting for the betterment of the fate of the Indonesian people and the settlement of remaining issues of the National Revolution."[57] Although commentators remarked on the ethnic, religious, and ideological orientation of the rebellions, the key grievance animating the rebels concerned center-periphery relations and the structure of the military—not the existence of Indonesia as such.[58]

Sukarno finally revealed his *konsepsi* as the Indonesian state veered toward collapse. In a February 1957 speech entitled "Saving the Republic of the Proclamation," he reiterated his denunciation of Western liberal democracy as "not a democracy which is in harmony with our spirit" because of its emphasis on "the idea of opposition." He proposed a new system based instead on the Indonesian village traditions of *gotong royong* (mutual aid), *musyawarah* (deliberation), and *mufakat* (consensus). More concretely, he advocated the reorganization of the cabinet to include representatives of all political parties seated in parliament, including the PKI. He also urged the creation of a National Council composed of representatives of "functional groups" including workers, peasants, intelligentsia, entrepreneurs, religions, regions, the armed forces, and more.[59] Responses to the president's proposal from political parties varied. The PKI endorsed the *konsepsi*, which the Politburo regarded as consonant with its policy of prioritizing national over class struggle. In any case, the party's leaders remained convinced that the PKI depended on Sukarno's protection for its survival in the face of a hostile army. The PNI also signaled its grudging acquiescence, determined as it was to maintain Sukarno's favor. But the other major parties, NU and Masyumi, united against bringing the PKI into the government.

The Indonesian army chose to support Sukarno's *konsepsi* and bury parliamentary democracy. Although officers remained implacably hostile to communism and wary of Sukarno's desire to cultivate the PKI, Nasution had come
to share the president's distaste for political parties and the polarization they
incited among the population. "Partisan excess," he argued in 1955, "has inflicted
serious harm on the country."[60] At Nasution's urging, Sukarno declared martial
law across the archipelago in March 1957. The combination of Sukarno's political offensive and the eruption of regional rebellions dealt a fatal blow to the
ruling cabinet. In its place Sukarno installed a new cabinet led by the nonpar-
tisan, technocratic figure Djuanda Kartawidjaja. But it wielded little influence.
Sukarno and the army had established themselves as the predominant forces in
Indonesian politics.

The president then worked to navigate Indonesia toward his *konsepsi* of
Guided Democracy.[61] His rudder was foreign policy. He began delivering
speeches railing against enduring Dutch economic dominance over Indonesia
and continuing Dutch sovereignty over West Papua. A critical turning point
came with a dual crisis in November 1957. That month, the United Nations
General Assembly failed to pass an Indonesian-sponsored resolution calling
for international intervention in the dispute over West Papua—the third such
failure in four years. Trade unions affiliated with the PKI and PNI then began
seizing Dutch property across Indonesia, including shipping lines, financial
firms, and agricultural estates. The day after the UN vote, a band of Islamist
youth attempted to assassinate Sukarno with grenades as he was leaving a cer-
emony at his son's Jakarta elementary school. The president was unharmed, but
eleven people were killed and dozens more were injured. The army blamed the
attacks on the rebels in Sumatra. A sense of crisis built across Indonesia, one that
Sukarno believed he could manipulate to serve his own purposes.[62]

But the army seized the initiative. Nasution announced that the army
would assume control over the management of Dutch firms seized by trade
unionists. At a stroke, the army became one of the most economically powerful institutions in Indonesia, in command of enterprises that accounted for
a combined 20 percent of the archipelago's economic output.[63] It also moved
to subjugate the regional rebellions. In the initial months following Sukarno's
declaration of martial law, Nasution had engaged in negotiations with the rebels.
After all, their objectives were limited and their tactics fell within a long tradition of adventurous military politicking in Indonesia. Following the dual crisis
of November 1957, however, the rebellions escalated. A coterie of prominent
civilians, including two former Masyumi prime ministers, fled to West Sumatra
and joined the rebels. On February 15, 1958, they proclaimed the existence of
the Revolutionary Government of the Republic of Indonesia (PRRI). Two days
later, the Permesta rebels in Sulawesi announced they would join the PRRI.

The turn toward separatism proved intolerable for Nasution. "We shall take action without any exception against all who support or say they will support the rebels," he announced. "We do this in the interests of our State's survival."[64] The air force began strafing rebel strongholds, the navy began blockading rebel territories, and the army dispatched troops to combat rebel soldiers.

The PRRI-Permesta rebellion became a decidedly international affair, drawing the global Cold War deeper into Indonesian politics. In a misguided effort to arrest Indonesia's leftward drift under Sukarno, the United States covertly supported the rebels with materiel and even mounted bombing runs against Indonesian soldiers. So too did the network of American and British clients in the region including Singapore, Malaya, the Philippines, Taiwan, and South Korea offer aid to the rebels. They did so not merely at the behest of Washington or London but because regnant elites in each country possessed their own strategic concepts that dictated the pursuit of anticommunist internationalism.[65] As the PRRI-Permesta rebels turned to the West, Sukarno turned to the East. In late 1957, he dispatched an arms-buying mission to Yugoslavia, Czechoslovakia, and Poland to accumulate the weaponry necessary to subdue the regional rebellions.[66] Over the next eight years, Indonesia would acquire approximately $1.1 billion worth of aid from the Soviet Union, accounting for more than one-fifth of all Soviet aid to non-socialist developing countries during that period.[67] The Indonesian army retook all major rebel-held cities by June 1958, though guerrilla warfare continued in the countryside for several more years.

The army emerged from the rebellions with unprecedented cohesion and power. Nasution became the most powerful army officer since Sudirman. Regional commanders who had resisted central authority for reasons of ideological conviction, political calculation, or personal expediency were purged. The army also retained broad authority under the state of martial law that persisted until 1963. Nasution commanded a military hierarchy that paralleled the civilian administration down to the village level. Through this shadow bureaucracy the army became deeply enmeshed in matters like collecting taxes and granting licenses, which combined with profits derived from the management of firms seized from the Dutch and ample aid from the Soviets to supply the institution with a diversified revenue stream. The army thus became a deeply conservative force in Indonesian life oriented toward the preservation of social order and the maintenance of economic production.[68] Nasution gave ideological veneer to the army's expanding political and economic remit in 1958 when he explained the army would chart what he called a "Middle Way": "We do not and we will not copy the situation as it exists in several Latin American states where the army acts as a direct political force," he intoned, "nor will we emulate the Western European model where armies are the dead tools (of the government)."[69] The result was that the army moved away from its traditional role as guardian of the Indonesian revolution and toward a new role as partisan actor in the maw of Indonesian politics. The institution's sense of mission was increasingly diluted by the pursuit of naked self-interest.[70]

Sukarno embraced the army's expanded role as key to the realization of Guided Democracy. He responded favorably to Nasution's call to return to the 1945 constitution, which provided for a powerful executive responsible to an assembly (MPR) that convened at least once every five years and whose membership comprised members of parliament (DPR) and representatives of functional groups. The president restored the old constitution by unconstitutional presidential decree in July 1959 and quickly moved to renovate the institutional structures that undergirded Indonesian politics. He appointed a cabinet in which roughly one-third of the available posts went to current or former military officers and none to leading figures in political parties. He also banned Masyumi and the Socialist Party of Indonesia (PSI), whose leaders were implicated in the PRRI-Permesta rebellion. By mid-1960 Sukarno had dissolved the DPR in the face of parliamentary obstinacy over a budget resolution and replaced it with a new *gotong royong* parliament (DPR-GR) comprising 154 representatives of functional groups (including 35 from the military) and 129 representatives of political parties. The members of the DPR-GR also took seats in a temporary assembly (MPRS) alongside 333 representatives of functional groups. All these bodies were appointed rather than elected and would remain so for the remainder of Sukarno's presidency. No formal checks constrained executive authority, meaning Guided Democracy was altogether more guided than democratic.

The ideological underpinnings of Guided Democracy proved far more revolutionary than its institutional scaffolding. Beginning in 1959 Sukarno unveiled a series of slogans like *Manipol* (Political Manifesto) and *Nasakom* (nationalism-religion-communism) that were designed to serve as lodestars for Guided Democracy and quickly assumed the cast of state-enforced orthodoxy. The upshot of these vague formulations was an effort to weave the PKI ever more deeply into the fabric of Indonesian governance. Sukarno regarded the party as the last bastion of the revolutionary fervor he sought to recover under Guided Democracy, and he considered the communist movement's mobilizational capacity vital to counterbalancing the burgeoning power of the army.[71]

And it was the PKI that posed the greatest threat to the army's conservative mission. Alone among major parties, the PKI sought to overturn the existing socioeconomic order. The party's program of land reform, wage increases, and price controls proved resoundingly popular given the deplorable state of the economy, and its exclusion from positions of power under parliamentary democracy meant the party was untainted by the rampant corruption of the period. Elections held across Java between June and August 1957 confirmed the PKI was the most popular on the island, winning 31.6 percent of all ballots cast.

The party grew even more popular with the resumption of Dutch-Indonesian conflict over the ultimate dispensation of West Papua.[72] In early 1960, The Hague announced a ten-year plan that would culminate in the independence of West Papua and prepared to organize elections for a representative council in the territory. Sukarno broke off relations with the Netherlands in August and launched a small-scale military campaign to recover West Papua. The conflict simmered at a low level until late 1961, when Sukarno formed the Supreme Command for the Liberation of West Irian and delivered a speech issuing the *Trikora* (*Tri Komando Rakyat*, or Three Commands of the People): prevent the Netherlands from establishing a puppet state in West Papua, fly the Indonesian red-and-white flag in West Papua, and prepare for the mass mobilization of the population to defend the independence and unity of Indonesia. But nationalist mobilization continued to outpace military action. The PKI orchestrated massive rallies across Indonesia demanding the fulfillment of the foremost promise of the revolution—the assertion of Indonesian sovereignty over the entirety of the former Netherlands East Indies, from Sabang on the northwest tip of Sumatra to Merauke on the southeast coast of West Papua. A US-brokered diplomatic settlement signed in August 1962 ultimately delivered West Papua into Indonesian hands and forestalled military escalation. As one of the foremost proponents of the West Papua campaign, the PKI recovered much of the nationalist legitimacy that it had lost at Madiun in 1948.[73]

The rise of the PKI prompted the Indonesian army to look to the United States—a great power possessed of unparalleled resources, a conservative orientation, and a growing interest in Southeast Asia. The army had first built ties with the United States in the late 1940s and began sending some ten officers per year to American military academies in the early 1950s, reasoning that the United States served as a model for a military that was modern without being Dutch.[74] Among the trainees was Colonel Ahmad Yani, who spent a year at Fort Leavenworth, Kansas, beginning in June 1955 before returning to Indonesia to take up a position as one of Nasution's deputies. Yani then dramatically expanded the number of Indonesian officers sent to the United States for training to about 150 in 1957 and 300 in 1958. The uppermost echelons of the army came to be inhabited overwhelmingly by graduates of US training programs, and the army's domestic curricula soon relied almost entirely on translated US materials.[75]

It is undeniable that the United States wielded significant influence over Indonesian army thinking through the training programs of the 1950s. Even so, it would go too far to conclude that Indonesian officers were blank slates upon which their American trainers etched Cold War ideas. The army's formative moments occurred under the Japanese, not the Americans. And though attendees at US training programs were enlisted in seminars with titles like "The Characteristics of Communism," the recollections of Indonesian officers suggest it was training in operational matters like "intelligence problems, personnel control problems, logistics problems" that made the most powerful impression. Indeed, one Indonesian officer remembered that it was not difficult to discern the gap between the rhetoric of freedom and the reality of discrimination in the United States. "The problem of 'skin color' was still very sensitive," he recalled, and signs on public transport still read "colored people are expected to take a seat at the rear of the bus."[76] The anticommunism of Indonesian army leaders held distinct internal lineages and was not simply diffused outward from the United States. What American training programs offered was means rather than ends.

US support for the PRRI-Permesta rebellions led to a fraying of ties between the Indonesian and American armies. But the Indonesian army turned once again to the United States in the face of a burgeoning PKI. It found a willing partner in the administration of President Dwight Eisenhower, whose Joint Chiefs of Staff concluded in the wake of the defeat of the PRRI-Permesta rebellions that the army was "the only non-Communist force in Indonesia with the capability of obstructing the progress of the PKI toward domination of the country."[77] American military aid to Indonesia tripled to $15 million between 1958 and 1959. The incoming administration of John F. Kennedy doubled down on the budding emphasis on "military modernization" in US foreign policy toward the Third World through a promotion of so-called civic action programs in which militaries combated insurgencies by contributing to social and economic development.[78] Once again, however, the United States did not so much determine the doctrine of the Indonesian army as it did provide the resources necessary to implement and expand preexisting army plans.[79] The notion of civic action dovetailed with long-standing army beliefs about its sociopolitical role emanating from its territorial structure, its emphasis on guerrilla warfare, its Hankamrata strategy, and its ever-expanding political and economic footprint. Emblematic of the Indonesian army's growing civic mission was *Operasi Bhakti*, an army-led development effort to reconstruct West Java following the final defeat of the Darul Islam rebellion in 1962. Through this operation soldiers built or repaired 31,310 mosques, 372 schools, 269 dams, 353 bridges, 32 markets, 917.5 kilometers of road, 720.5 kilometers of drainage culvert, and 152.6 kilometers of embankment, and cultivated massive quantities of crops by mid-1963.[80] In a conversation with a US military attaché, Yani characterized the army's civic action program as designed to bring the army into villages to compete with the PKI for the hearts and minds of the Indonesian citizenry—an objective that predated American efforts to cultivate the army.[81] Nor did the army shy away from coercive methods. Across the archipelago, regional commanders used their martial law authority to periodically round up PKI leaders, ban PKI newspapers, and obstruct PKI activities.[82]

What emerged in Indonesia by 1962 was a triangular configuration of power.[83] At its inception, Guided Democracy represented a bargain between Sukarno and the army to overturn parliamentary rule in Indonesia. But Sukarno knew the leadership of the army held misgivings about his revolutionary ambitions. And the president in any case preferred to rule by cultivating countervailing sources of power and interposing himself as a vehicle of creative reconciliation. He therefore fostered the PKI as a counterweight to the army. The result was to collapse the phantasmagoria of political conflicts in 1950s Indonesia—between Java and the Outer Islands, between secularists and Islamists, between liberals and non-liberals, and among myriad political parties—into a single axis of political contestation: communist versus anticommunist. The Cold War had come to structure Indonesian politics.

V

Suharto was largely uninvolved in the fateful events that brought the Cold War to Indonesia. His attitude toward national politics in the mid-1950s is encapsulated by his remarks in his memoirs on the Bandung Conference and the 1955 elections, calling them "momentous events in and of themselves" but "beyond my areas of responsibility."[84] Nor did Suharto travel to the United States for military training as ties between the Indonesian and American armies broadened in the late 1950s. His horizons remained decidedly limited, rarely reaching beyond Central Java.

Only as he ascended the army ranks did Suharto develop a political consciousness. A key turning point came with his appointment as commander of Central Java's Diponegoro division in September 1956. Devotee of national unity that he was, he rejected any appeasement of the regionalist sentiment ascendant during that period as a "perverse partiality."[85] His most powerful political commitment, however, was an unyielding anticommunism. "In those years I saw the activities and influence of the PKI growing larger by the day," he remembered decades later. The party represented a threat to the traditional social order that he prized, one whose tranquility was already disrupted by the propulsive forces of modernity. Suharto's was thus an indigenous anticommunism that emanated from forces within Indonesian society rather than beyond it. When Sukarno visited Central Java to attend an anniversary celebration for the Diponegoro, Suharto went so far as to warn the president that the PKI was "dangerous." But he was rebuffed. "Suharto," the president responded, "you are a soldier. Political problems are my concern. Leave them to me."[86] Suharto proved unwilling to follow Sukarno's instructions to the letter. As divisional commander, he built ties with local political figures, particularly from the conservative wing of the PNI, who worked to suppress communist activity.[87]

The anticommunist initiatives Suharto implemented as Diponegoro commander flowed from his techniques of military leadership. He had always paid heed to the livelihoods of his soldiers, which he claimed delivered "great benefits in cultivating the morale of soldiers and peace within their families." By the same logic, securing the loyalty of the population toward the existing order depended upon the achievement of a degree of material prosperity. He accordingly assembled a coterie of young officers including Yoga Sugama, Ali Murtopo, and Sudjono Humardani as well as entrepreneurs like Bob Hasan to assist him in a developmental push in Central Java. Together they established an array of so-called foundations whose mission Suharto described as "carrying out various efforts in the economic and financial fields to make it possible to help the farmers, the people in the villages" by "providing agricultural equipment, seeds, and fertilizers."[88] The foundations raised money by taxing local economic activity and soliciting donations from established firms. They then made loans to individual peasants and invested in local firms, particularly those concerned with the marketing and distribution of primary commodities.[89]

Suharto's efforts to stem the popularity of the communist movement in Central Java ultimately delivered him to the epicenter of the struggle between the army and the PKI in Jakarta. The pervasive role of his foundations in Central Java's economy provided a pretext for relieving Suharto of his command over the Diponegoro division in 1959 and sending him to the Army Staff and Command School (SSKAD) in Bandung for a training course. In those years Nasution was engaged in a thoroughgoing anti-corruption campaign both within and beyond the army designed to bolster the institution's legitimacy as a national political force.[90] But it seems plausible that the real reason for Suharto's transfer lay in an effort by his Sukarnoist and perhaps PKI-leaning chief of staff in the Diponegoro to halt his anticommunist activities.[91] Whatever the true reason, Suharto arrived in Bandung in late 1959.

At SSKAD, army thinkers were deeply engaged in work to elaborate the intellectual underpinnings of the institution's expanded role under Guided Democracy. Crucial in that effort was Colonel Suwarto, a former Siliwangi officer and devotee of the modernizing PSI who was then deputy commander of the school. Suwarto graduated from a training program at Fort Leavenworth in 1959 and nurtured ties with American academics, particularly Guy Pauker of the RAND Corporation. Upon his return to Bandung, he set about remaking SSKAD (soon to be rebranded Seskoad) in RAND's image, cultivating expertise on matters of military effectiveness but also on subjects like politics, economics, and ideology. During his time at the school, Suharto contributed to debates on the army's doctrine of territorial warfare and its attendant civic action mission—subjects that to a large extent represented a formalization of the developmental and anticommunist practices he had engaged in as Diponegoro commander.[92]

Suharto was transferred to Jakarta to take up a position as first deputy to Nasution following his time in Bandung. Soon thereafter he was named commander of the Army General Reserve (Caduad), the Indonesian army's first mobile strike force under the control of army headquarters rather than a regional commander. And in early 1962 he was named as commander of the newly created Mandala command responsible for the reclamation of West Papua. He moved his headquarters to Makassar in March and prepared a massive offensive involving land, sea, and air units designed to establish a beachhead on Papua from which Indonesian forces could oust the Dutch presence. Despite his insistence that the offensive would result in a world-historic defeat for the Dutch akin to Japan's defeat of Russia in 1905, Suharto's plan was preempted by the diplomatic settlement brokered by the United States.[93] He returned to Jakarta with a reputation as an accomplished and effective military leader and resumed his position as commander of the army's strike force, now renamed the Army Strategic Reserve Command (Kostrad). Such was his prestige that Suharto began standing in as acting army commander when his boss was overseas.

The Jakarta to which Suharto returned was defined by the escalating competition between the army and the PKI. In June 1962, Sukarno sought to undermine the army's power by installing Nasution in the newly created position of armed forces chief of staff, separating the commander from his base of power in the army. Into the vacant post of army chief of staff Sukarno maneuvered the comparatively junior Yani, who alongside the chiefs of staff of the other military services would report directly to Sukarno.[94] Although Yani was a staunch anticommunist like Nasution, he was a womanizer and bon vivant who lacked his predecessor's puritanical outlook; of Javanese heritage, he could also be expected to adapt himself more readily to the corrupt palace culture of Guided Democracy.[95] The following year, Sukarno dealt the most severe blow to the army's authority when he ended martial law.

Sukarno's effort to curb the influence of the army produced a brief reorientation in Indonesia's economic trajectory. Following the resolution of the dispute over West Papua, the president turned his attention to a mounting economic crisis fueled by a decline in overall production and an increase in the money supply. The most evident manifestation of the crisis was a mounting inflationary spiral. Between June 1961 and June 1962, the price of rice in Jakarta surged by 250 percent and the black market exchange rate of the rupiah collapsed from 200 to 800 per dollar.[96] The president allowed the technocrat Djuanda, then serving as first minister, to prepare a stabilization plan that included fiscal consolidation, currency devaluation, price liberalization, and monetary tightening in exchange for aid and debt relief from the United States, its Western European and Japanese allies, and the International Monetary Fund. Why the president abided this rightward turn in foreign and economic policy remains somewhat unclear—perhaps he sought to curb the army's expansive claims on the state budget, perhaps he sought to divert American resources from the army to the state, or perhaps he simply sought to manipulate the army into supporting unpopular economic policies.[97] Whatever his rationale, the president offered a tepid endorsement of an effort at economic recovery in a March 1963 address that he called the Dekon (*Deklarasi Ekonomi*, or Economic Declaration).[98] Two months later, the government implemented an array of economic policies in line with the US-backed stabilization plan. Exports surged and prices moderated. But firms faced mounting liquidity challenges and the population endured a searing cost-of-living crisis.[99]

The PKI began a massive political offensive to thwart a rightward turn in Indonesia. By December 1962 the party claimed over 2 million members, which made it the largest non-ruling communist party in the world. The party's various front organizations could boast some 12 million additional members. Aidit and a fellow PKI leader had been appointed as special ministers without portfolio in the cabinet in March 1962, but they resented their limited influence under Guided Democracy. The Politburo derided the stabilization plan as the work of "false Manipolists" seeking to subvert the Indonesian revolution and implement the will of "U.S imperialists."[100] Aidit himself traveled to Seskoad and admonished senior officers that the army was an "instrument of state authority" whose sole duty was the implementation of Sukarno's political ideology—a direct rejection of Nasution's Middle Way doctrine.[101] The PKI urged Sukarno to impose a broader "retooling" of the state apparatus, meaning its cleansing of allegedly counterrevolutionary elements.[102] Aidit went so far as to threaten civil war should communist representation in the cabinet not increase.[103]

A renewed foreign policy crisis ultimately reversed Indonesia's brief turn to the West. The crisis revolved around the creation of Malaysia. The United Kingdom had granted independence to Malaya in 1957 but retained possession of its colonies in Singapore, Sabah, Sarawak, and Brunei. Since then, British officials had occasionally suggested merger with Malaya as a viable path to decolonization for their remaining Southeast Asian territories. Malayan prime minister Tunku Abdul Rahman finally offered his assent to the scheme in May 1961.[104] Indonesia offered no formal objections. Foreign Minister Subandrio wrote to the *New York Times* in November 1961 asserting "we do not show any objection toward this Malayan policy of merger."[105] Within Indonesia only the PKI denounced the Malaysia Plan. As early as July 1961, the party excoriated the merger as a neocolonial scheme designed to suppress the aspirations of the peoples of Malaya, Singapore, and Borneo and encircle Indonesia with hostile powers.[106] That position gained more widespread acceptance among Indonesian elites after British forces crushed a December 1962 revolt against the creation of Malaysia in Brunei. Indonesia soon proclaimed a policy of *Konfrontasi* (Confrontation) modeled on the campaign to recover West Papua, mixing limited military offensives, aggressive diplomatic pressure, and pervasive mass mobilization. Even the army proclaimed its support for *Konfrontasi*. Doing so served domestic political purposes: it would burnish the army's nationalist legitimacy and preserve its claims on the state budget as martial law came to an end. But the army's support of *Konfrontasi* also possessed a geopolitical logic. Senior officers believed Indonesia ought to exert hegemonic influence in Southeast Asia, feared former rebel strongholds in Sumatra might gravitate toward Malaysia, and worried Malaysia itself might fall under the control of its ethnic Chinese population and thereby under the thumb of Beijing.[107]

Indonesia's pursuit of *Konfrontasi* oscillated between periods of escalation and conciliation over the first nine months of 1963. But *Konfrontasi* reached a point of no return when Malaysia came into existence in September 1963. Sukarnoist organizations orchestrated a massive rally in Jakarta that culminated with demonstrators barraging the British embassy with stones. Malaysia suspended diplomatic ties with Indonesia the following day. The ruling party's youth wing then marched on the Indonesian embassy in Kuala Lumpur, pilfered the building's emblem, and delivered it to the Tunku. Indonesian demonstrators responded by returning to sack the British embassy, where they ignited fires that left the facility a burned-out shell. British cars, homes, and businesses across the capital, including the expatriate community's beloved cricket club, were attacked that evening by marauding gangs of young people. Sukarno then announced that Indonesia would sever economic ties with Malaysia and assume control over British property across the archipelago.[108] The flow of Western aid to Indonesia slowed to a trickle, and the necessity of economic stabilization gave way to a new imperative: *Ganyang Malaysia* (Crush Malaysia), as the ubiquitous political slogan demanded.[109] Economic deterioration resumed.

Konfrontasi propelled a radicalization of the PKI's outlook as well. Since the emergence of the Sino-Soviet split in the 1950s, the party had maintained a posture of formal neutrality. But Aidit ended that neutrality over the Malaysia dispute. The Chinese supported the anti-Malaysia crusade, while the Soviets urged a return to economic stabilization.[110] In September 1963, upon returning from a nine-week tour that took him to the Soviet Union, Cuba, East Germany, China, and North Korea, Aidit announced that anticolonial revolution rather than peaceful coexistence represented the foremost objective of the international communist movement. Evoking Maoist ideas, he held that "if the world revolution is to be victorious there is no other way than for the world proletariat to give prominence to the revolutions in Asia, Africa and Latin America, that is to say,

the revolutions in the villages of the world." He arrogated for Indonesia a vanguard role in the world revolution, reasoning with a series of mixed metaphors
that the "victory of the Indonesian revolution will signify a mighty breakthrough
in the fortress of imperialism, it will signify a great stride forward in the anti-
imperialist struggle and its rays will shine from afar, even beyond the borders of
Southeast Asia."[111]

Despite the internationalist pretensions of the PKI's new line, the party
remained focused squarely on the domestic arena. Cognizant that an escalation of *Konfrontasi* could lead to a resumption of martial law and redound to
the benefit of the army, the party did not urge any massive military escalation
of Indonesia's conflict with Malaysia. Aidit instead worked to curb the army's
power. He promoted the "*Nasakom*-ization" of the armed forces—a vague initiative that most interpreted as calling for the reintroduction of a political commissar system. He also proposed the creation of a "Fifth Force" of armed workers
and peasants that would threaten the military's monopoly on the instruments
of violence.[112] Most dramatically, the PKI launched a campaign of "unilateral
action" (*aksi sepihak*) in the countryside to forcibly implement land reform laws
that were enacted in 1959 and 1960 but went largely unenforced in the interim.[113]
Peasants affiliated with the party began occupying agricultural land and seizing
agricultural produce, particularly in Central Java, East Java, and Bali. Local elites
affiliated with the PNI and NU mobilized to defend their landholdings against
redistribution. Bloody conflicts soon erupted between militant peasants, on the
one hand, and party militias often aided by local authorities, on the other. The
Cold War permeated Indonesia as never before, polarizing and militarizing the
population even in rural villages.[114]

In August 1964, Sukarno delivered a National Day address proclaiming
that Indonesia was embarking upon a "year of living dangerously." He knew of
what he spoke. By mid-1965 the capital was rife with rumors that a "Council of
Generals" within the army was plotting to overthrow Sukarno. The discovery
of a mysterious document only heightened the prevailing confusion. Typed on
British embassy letterhead above the name of Ambassador Andrew Gilchrist,
the document referred to a joint US-UK operation in concert with "our local
army friends." The army and foreign diplomats insisted the document was a fake.
But Sukarno was sufficiently alarmed to summon senior army commanders to
the palace and claim that he possessed evidence that imperialist forces planned
to assassinate him, Subandrio, and Yani.[115] The president redoubled his efforts to
cultivate the PKI and curb the army. He moved to appoint left-leaning officers
from other services—those who had embraced the PKI's proposals for a Fifth
Force and Nasakomization—to key posts in institutions formed to oversee
Konfrontasi. He presided over a purge of anticommunists within the political
system, notably by instigating the removal of some 150 conservative leaders

within the PNI. Sukarno also appeared to be maneuvering Indonesia toward the communist camp, particularly toward China. He withdrew Indonesia from the United Nations in January 1965 after Malaysia was granted a temporary seat on the Security Council. He also offered tacit support to violent demonstrators who ransacked US diplomatic facilities across Indonesia and announced the Indonesian government would assume control for the management of many American firms in the country.[116] By August, Sukarno had withdrawn Indonesia from the International Monetary Fund and the World Bank as well.

The extent of Indonesia's radicalization became clear when Sukarno delivered his 1965 National Day address. He derided army leaders as corrupt and counterrevolutionary, "swindlers of state wealth" and "force[s] of reaction!" He announced he would soon make a decision on the proposal for the Fifth Force. With his assertion that the armed forces "will form an invincible power if they unite with the people like fish in water," and his admonition that "water can exist without fish, but fish cannot exist without water," Sukarno clearly foreshadowed his approval of the Fifth Force. The president also proclaimed the existence of a "Jakarta-Phnom Penh-Hanoi-Beijing-Pyongyang Axis."[117] The hurtle of events gave the unmistakable impression that Sukarno had abandoned his traditional balancing role. Rather than seek to accommodate and counterpose the major political forces in Indonesian life, the president seemed to have thrown his weight behind the PKI against the army.[118]

The leadership of the army gathered over the course of 1965 to take stock of the rapidly evolving political situation.[119] Some scholars have interpreted these meetings as proof that a "Council of Generals" was indeed preparing to usurp state power and orchestrate a purge of the PKI.[120] In the context of escalating political conflict and deepening economic crisis, however, it would be unusual if the brass did not gather to discuss threats to the army's corporate interests. The best evidence that the army was plotting a coup comes from one of the generals who attended these meetings. The army's chief of intelligence, General Siswondo Parman, told the US ambassador in January 1965 that the army was "developing specific plans for [a] takeover of government [the] moment Sukarno steps off stage"—and possibly earlier if the president endorsed the PKI's Fifth Force proposal.[121] But Parman may have been seeking to forestall a total cutoff in US aid then under consideration in Washington. In any case, there is little concrete proof that the army was preparing for a massacre of the kind that followed the September Thirtieth Movement. An American military attaché recalled being told by General Yani in July 1965 that "We *have the guns*, and we have the kept the guns out of their [the PKI's] hands. So if there's a clash, we'll wipe them out."[122] But Yani may have been musing about a grisly hypothetical rather than confirming the existence of a plan for mass murder. Even after the Madiun uprising of 1948, only about 8,000 people (mostly rebel soldiers) were killed and 35,000 more were arrested.[123] A politicide of the magnitude that occurred in 1965 and 1966, directed almost entirely against the civilian population, thus went beyond what one scholar has dubbed the army's "repertoire of violence."[124] Precious little direct evidence from Indonesian sources indicates the army was preparing to assume unilateral authority and orchestrate a mass slaughter of communists. That does not alter the undeniable fact that the army under Suharto's leadership *did* engage in the unforgivable murder of hundreds of thousands of Indonesian citizens whom it professed to represent. But it would go too far to assert with a high degree of confidence that the army's usurpation of state power and bloody campaign against the PKI was entirely premeditated and awaited only a suitable pretext.

It was the September Thirtieth Movement that unleashed the mounting political pressures in Indonesia. In the wake of the revelation of the so-called Gilchrist Letter, Aidit attempted to ascertain the veracity of the rumors of an impending army coup. To do so he turned to his aide Sjam, then in charge of a clandestine PKI body called the Special Bureau whose purpose was to cultivate communist influence within the military. Sjam affirmed that a coterie of right-wing generals was plotting a coup. Aidit then instructed Sjam to determine whether he could mobilize leftist and Sukarnoist officers to preempt the coup. Sjam apparently developed a plan whereby progressive officers would kidnap the allegedly treasonous generals and expose their perfidy to Sukarno. The architects of the plan likely hoped Sukarno would either dismiss or imprison the generals and usher the PKI into the halls of power. As the plan took shape, Sukarno's health became the subject of widespread speculation. Just two weeks before he was to deliver his National Day address in August 1965, the president collapsed and vomited while he was receiving an official delegation.[125] Because the PKI's political position depended on Sukarno's support, and because Sjam's plan included a role for the president, the prospect of Sukarno's impending demise proved alarming. Despite widespread anxieties among the plotters over the soundness of the plan, Aidit and Sjam pressed ahead with what came to be called the September Thirtieth Movement.[126] On the morning of October 1, 1965, army units acting in coordination with these PKI leaders left Halim Perdakusuma Air Force Base to capture anticommunist generals. The chaos that unfolded that day set off a new era in Indonesian history.

Suharto's path to power traveled through the Indonesian army. From its inception under the Japanese, the army regarded itself as the exemplar of the nation. It quickly found itself at loggerheads with other claimants to popular legitimacy, including a succession of civilian governments and various political parties.

Contestation over the commanding heights of the state was thus inherent to postcolonial Indonesia. Such contestation gradually assumed the shape of a Cold War. Indigenous revolutionaries inspired and aided by the international communist movement sought to overturn the existing order in Indonesia. But theirs was only one of many movements seeking to transform Indonesia in the vibrant and chaotic 1950s. Only as Sukarno sought to impose his vision of Guided Democracy on Indonesia and cultivate the PKI as a counterweight to the army did a political system defined by multiple and overlapping axes of contestation collapse into a Cold War system defined by a single communist-anticommunist axis of conflict. In the face of a burgeoning PKI sponsored by Sukarno, a relatively heterogeneous group of conservative Indonesian elites comprising party leaders, religious chieftains, urban bourgeoisie, rural landlords, and nationalist youth banded together with the army in an anticommunist coalition.[127] And the army itself began building ties with the United States, the world's preeminent counterrevolutionary power, to support its domestic struggle against the Indonesian communist movement. Indonesia's experience is thus emblematic of how diverse and localized strains of conservatism across the Third World could graft themselves onto the global Cold War. Still, it bears emphasizing that the army's outlook blended social conservatism with a modernizing impulse arising in opposition to Sukarno's economic mismanagement, which distinguished it from the military regimes that took power in Latin America and mounted rearguard defenses against socioeconomic change.

The September Thirtieth Movement marked the explosive culmination of the Cold War in Indonesia. The PKI struck first but failed to land a fatal blow against the army. With his superior officers either dead or incapacitated, Suharto found himself thrust to the helm of the army's anticommunist project. He came to his newfound position informed by his experiences over the previous forty-three years. He was determined not only to mount a devastating counterattack against the Indonesian communist movement but also to launch an effort to remake Indonesia so that it would never again fall under the sway of communist influence. And as time went on, Suharto's Cold War in Indonesia would come to exert influence on the course of the global Cold War itself.

2

In the Shadow of Vietnam

The September Thirtieth Movement inaugurated a critical juncture. Indonesia's existing order was all but certain to collapse, but the future remained open. On the morning of October 2, Suharto confronted a country wracked by interlocking political and economic crises. Sukarno clung to the presidency and made it clear he would deploy his still-considerable political talents and personal prestige to rally the population behind his leadership. The military was divided, with the army riven by factional conflict and the leadership of the navy, air force, marines, and police generally loyal to Sukarno. Polarization and mobilization combined with an overarching sense of chaos to stretch Indonesia's political fabric to the point of tearing. Hyperinflation was eroding standards of living, a balance-of-payments crisis left Indonesia unable to finance vital imports or service its massive debt obligations, labor and capital sat idle, and the country's infrastructure was in shambles. Many ordinary Indonesians subsisted on the brink of starvation.[1]

The Indonesian army was about to embark upon an anticommunist politicide to crush the PKI—the opening salvo of Suharto's Cold War. But Suharto was aware that would need to do far more than murder hundreds of thousands of Indonesians to forge a new political and economic order inimical to a recrudescence of communist influence. In addition to destroying the PKI, Suharto intended to dislodge Sukarno from power, establish a military-dominated regime, and ignite economic recovery. In short, he sought nothing less than to remake Indonesia from the top down.

But Suharto possessed neither the resource base nor the popular mandate to pursue his maximalist ambitions. He therefore forged partnerships with allies in civil society—paramilitary bodies, religious organizations, student groups, political parties, and others—to further his exterminationist agenda against Indonesian communists and his political campaign against Sukarno. Although these partisans pined for a new regime in Indonesia, they held no unified vision of the archipelago's future. Many anticipated a return to democratic governance and loathed the prospect of military rule. Suharto also began building

Suharto's Cold War. Mattias Fibiger, Oxford University Press. © Oxford University Press 2023.
DOI: 10.1093/oso/9780197667224.003.0003

international partnerships with Western governments and firms that could finance his Cold War projects. Determined to avoid tarnishing his nationalist credentials, however, Suharto kept these nascent international partnerships both limited and secret. He secured small-scale material aid, promises of non-interference, and assistance in delegitimizing Sukarno. This broad coalition of countervailing power helped Suharto pursue a campaign of annihilation against the PKI and sustain a condition of political and economic crisis that ultimately enabled him to dislodge Sukarno and launch his broader Cold War.

I

Suharto quickly determined that the September Thirtieth Movement represented another of the PKI's periodic efforts to seize state power. Yoga Sugama, one of Suharto's intelligence deputies at Kostrad, remembered remarking to a colleague on the morning of October 1, "This is definitely the work of the PKI. We just need to find proof."[2]

He would find his proof soon enough. On the morning of October 2, the PKI daily *Harian Rakjat* published an editorial attesting to "the correctness of the action taken by the September 30th Movement to preserve the revolution and the People."[3] (Why exactly the newspaper was allowed to publish on October 2, after its offices had been occupied by the army and all other non-army newspapers in Jakarta had been shuttered, remains a tantalizing mystery.) The following afternoon, Suharto received word that his slain colleagues' bodies had been discovered in the well near Halim.[4] He went to Lubang Buaya on the morning of October 4 to supervise the exhumation of his comrades' remains. Waiting until an array of journalists, photographers, and television cameramen had assembled, Suharto ensured the proceedings would be broadcast across Indonesia.[5] After the last corpse was brought to the surface, he delivered a short, angry speech in which he excoriated the PKI and the air force for their alleged involvement in the plot.[6] Suharto reminisced in his memoirs that, upon "witnessing with my own eyes what had been discovered at Lubang Buaya, my primary duty was to crush the PKI, to smash their resistance everywhere."[7] He kept vigil over the bodies that night. The following day, in lieu of the annual Armed Forces Day parade, he organized an elaborate funeral procession ending at the national heroes' cemetery. The entire affair was carefully choreographed to stoke fury against the PKI—emblematized by the contemporaneous publication of a short book accusing the party of orchestrating the September Thirtieth Movement.[8]

The performance succeeded. As one Sri Lankan journalist put it, "Almost immediately the Army's campaign against the PKI and its affiliates became a people's movement. The masses . . . turned on the communists with a fierce heat

Figure 2.1 A stern Suharto, in camouflage attire at front left, attends the funeral for
the generals murdered by the September Thirtieth Movement on October 5, 1965.
Associated Press.

which I have seen only once before in my experience as a reporter," during the
Vimochana Samaram of late 1950s Kerala. Slogans like "*Aidit Gantung*" (Hang
Aidit), "*Bubarkan PKI*" (Ban the PKI), and "*PKI Anti-Tuhan*" (the PKI is anti-
God) soon adorned "every inch of wall space and road space" in Jakarta.[9]

The journalist grasped the eruption of public anger, but he missed the extent to which it was the product of army manipulation. The Indonesian army
under Suharto fabricated stories that communist-affiliated women's groups had
visited horrific tortures upon the generals before murdering them, including
gouging out their eyes and cutting off their genitals.[10] General Sugandhi, the
director of the military newspaper *Angkatan Bersendjata*, coined a portmanteau for the September Thirtieth Movement that scholar Benedict Anderson
remarked "would have pleased Goebbels": Gestapu.[11] Syntactically incorrect in
Indonesian, the neologism was devised to evoke comparisons to the Gestapo
and signal (particularly to Suharto's prospective Western sponsors) that the
army was engaged in a struggle against an evil of world-historic proportions.[12]

Indonesian politics under Guided Democracy had assumed an agitational
quality in which a group's legitimacy was seen as a function of its ability to mobilize the populace. In the wake of October 1, the army consequently presided
over the creation of an array of civilian bodies dedicated to legitimizing its
anticommunist campaign through protests, marches, and rallies. Foremost

among them was the Action Command to Crush the September Thirtieth Movement (KAP-Gestapu).[13] Led by Subchan Zaenuri Echsan, a notable figure within Nahdlatul Ulama, and Harry Tjan Silalahi, a grandee of the Catholic Party, KAP-Gestapu staged a small rally on October 4 and called upon all Indonesians "to assist the Armed Forces in destroying the 'Counter-revolutionary September 30th Movement' down to its roots."[14] A few days later, the group held another, much larger rally that culminated in the ransacking and burning of the PKI's Jakarta headquarters. As this attack occurred, army units and civilian fire brigades watched idly from the side of the road.[15] Other army leaders simply ordered citizens to rise up against the PKI. In Aceh, General Ahmad Yunus Mokoginta issued a simple statement: "It is mandatory for the People to assist in every attempt to completely annihilate the Counter Revolutionary Thirtieth of September Movement along with its Lackeys."[16]

The army also mobilized civilian proxies as it embarked upon an anticommunist politicide. It began first in Aceh, where only days after the September Thirtieth Movement Mokoginta's subordinate General Ishak Djuarsa traveled across the province and held public meetings encouraging the population to eliminate the PKI. Paramilitary and vigilante groups associated with anticommunist political parties and religious organizations met the army's call and began raiding homes and buildings associated with the PKI, rounding up suspected communists, and surrendering them to the authorities. The army transported most of the captives to a concentration camp near a military base before releasing them to death squads established by the same anticommunist civil society groups. The death squads then transported detainees to isolated killing sites on plantations, rice fields, river beds, and beaches. They executed their captives with crude instruments of death, including guns, knives, sickles, machetes, spears, clubs, and wire—sometimes after engaging in wanton acts of torture. The bodies that were not interred in mass graves were dumped in wells or tossed into rivers or the sea.[17]

This pattern recurred across the archipelago. The onset of violence occurred soon after the September Thirtieth Movement in Central and East Java, where regional army command possessed both the capability and intention to mount a campaign of annihilation against the PKI. In North Sumatra, Bali, and East Nusa Tenggara, where the regional army command was politically divided, lacking in troops, or encountered resistance, the killings began only after the local balance of power shifted—often following the arrival of elite troops under Suharto's authority. Meanwhile in West Java, where the regional army command was united against a campaign of mass killing, the army's campaign against the PKI became one of mass imprisonment. Although civilians perpetrated most of the killings, the variation in the timing and intensity of the violence revealed that Suharto and the army bore primary responsibility for the wave of death that swept across Indonesia in 1965 and 1966.[18]

As Suharto and the Indonesian army purged Indonesia of communism, they drew upon international assistance. In the aftermath of the September Thirtieth Movement, Indonesian army leaders established ties with American, British, and Australian officials in the close-knit Western diplomatic community in Jakarta. Their conversations were tepid and indirect at first. On October 10, an envoy close to Suharto approached the American military attaché in Jakarta and elliptically requested assurances that Britain would not take advantage of the army's preoccupation with its anticommunist crusade to escalate *Konfrontasi*—the simmering guerrilla conflict between Indonesia and Britain over the creation of Malaysia. American diplomats coordinated with their British counterparts and formulated a response stating that Washington harbored "no intention of interfering in Indonesian internal affairs" and had "good reason to believe that none of our allies intend any offensive action against Indonesia."[19] When the American attaché delivered the message to the Indonesian envoy on October 14, he received word that "this was just what was needed by way of assurances that we (the army) weren't going to be hit from all angles as we moved to straighten things out here."[20]

Captivated by the prospect of stamping out the world's third-largest communist party, and unmoved by reports of ongoing slaughters, Western governments were determined to do more than offer simple reassurances of noninterference. In the weeks following the September Thirtieth Movement, Western diplomats worked in parallel with the Indonesian army to incite hatred of the PKI.[21] In the words of the US ambassador in Jakarta, Marshall Green, Western powers mobilized their propaganda networks in Indonesia, the region, and the wider world to "spread the story of [the] PKI's guilt, treachery and brutality," noting that "this priority effort is perhaps the most needed immediate assistance we can give [the] army."[22] Australian diplomats urged Radio Australia to depict the Indonesian army "as restoring law and order . . . with the widespread support of wide sectors of the people."[23] Western propaganda also played up the possibility of Chinese involvement in the movement, stirring up latent anti-Chinese sentiment in Indonesia and contributing to a surge of ethnic violence that accompanied the army's bloodletting against the PKI. In fact, the most pressing worry among Western officials was that the army would restrict its assault to "those directly involved in the murder of the Generals" rather than unleash a murderous campaign against the entire communist movement.[24]

It was not long before the army sought more concrete forms of aid. On October 13, the same army envoy who had solicited assurances from Britain over *Konfrontasi* approached the American embassy and requested portable communications equipment for guards protecting senior army officers. Green approved the request and handed over three walkie-talkies the following day.[25] He outlined his rationale in a cable to Washington: the United States should be prepared to assist the army on a "covert or semi-covert basis related to specific, small, ad hoc needs."[26] As the bloody campaign against the PKI gathered momentum in Central Java in November, the army began testing the limits of American support. General Sukendro met with an American diplomat and requested medical supplies, communications equipment, and small arms.[27] Green relayed the request up the chain of command, recommending his superiors approve the provision of communications equipment and medical supplies and investigate whether the United States could supply small arms indirectly so as to avoid public detection.[28] Washington ultimately approved Sukendro's request for medical supplies. An American official met with Sukendro in Bangkok to deliver the news and indicate Washington's "general willingness to consider Army requests for small-scale covert assistance."[29] The general was pleased, but he once again lodged a request for communications equipment and small arms, which his American interlocutor assumed would be used "to arm Moslem nationalist youths in Central Java for use against the PKI"—a campaign that American consular officials described as a "reign of terror."[30] Washington approved the requests.[31]

Sukendro was not the only Suharto associate to approach prospective international benefactors in the weeks following the September Thirtieth Movement. Green reported that "People we haven't heard from in years . . . are coming out of [the] woodwork." In early December, anticommunist politician and diplomat Adam Malik approached the American embassy in Jakarta and requested 50 million rupiah to finance the activities of KAP-Gestapu. Green endorsed the request in a telegram to Washington, noting that the "army-inspired but civilian-staffed action group is still carrying [the] burden of current repressive efforts targeted against [the] PKI, particularly in Central Java."[32] American diplomats in Jakarta also provided the Indonesian army with lists of names of thousands of suspected communists who were subsequently hunted down and either imprisoned or killed.[33] Even as Western officials remained uncertain as to who exactly was behind the September Thirtieth Movement—many analysts doubted the PKI would deliberately disrupt a political system that had proved so hospitable to its growing influence—the prospect of the Indonesian army destroying the world's largest non-ruling communist party proved too attractive to pass up. "More Communists have been killed here in three months than in the whole Vietnam War," Green exulted to his Australian counterpart in mid-December.[34]

II

The army's campaign of extermination against Indonesian communists represented only the opening shot of Suharto's Cold War. As Suharto became convinced that Sukarno was defending the PKI against the army's onslaught and was even seeking to reintegrate the party into the nation's political system, he orchestrated a slow-moving coup d'état that entailed undermining Sukarno, forging a political coalition, and establishing his own institutional authority. Conscious of the need to avoid inflaming nationalist opposition by appearing as a lackey of the United States or other Western powers, Suharto deliberately shunned international ties during this early stage of his deepening Cold War.

At Kostrad on the morning of October 1, Suharto asked Yoga whether Sukarno was involved in the September Thirtieth Movement. Yoga answered affirmatively, though the evidence he offered was hardly airtight. "The suspicion that there was a close connection between Bung Karno and the Revolutionary Council controlled by the PKI was not without reason," Yoga recalled, because "in the last few years there have been some similarities in views between Bung Karno and the PKI."[35] Suharto remained unsure of the precise nature of the relationship between Sukarno and the September Thirtieth Movement. He accordingly adopted a posture of cautious defiance toward the president. When Sukarno summoned an array of Indonesian military leaders to his Bogor palace on the morning of October 2, Suharto sent word that he was too busy to attend immediately. He eventually made his way to the palace in the afternoon, where the president, his deputies, and the chiefs of the other branches of the Indonesian military were waiting. During a tense, five-hour meeting, Suharto refused to accept Sukarno's appointment of a loyalist as caretaker of the army. He finally acceded to the arrangement on the condition that Sukarno grant him overarching authority for the "restoration of security and order."[36]

Sukarno had established a delicate political balance between the army and the PKI during the years of Guided Democracy. He was determined that the September Thirtieth Movement would not upset that equilibrium. On the evening after his contentious meeting with Suharto, the president delivered a speech over radio reassuring the public that he remained in command of the Indonesian state and expressing his intention of "quickly settling the problem of the so-called September 30th Affair."[37] He broadcast another speech the following evening exonerating the air force of complicity in the September Thirtieth Movement and imploring his listeners to "prevent the playing off against one another of the Air Force and the Army."[38] Suharto bristled against the president's efforts to sweep the September Thirtieth Movement under the rug. The movement was launched from an air force base, and Air Force Commander Omar Dani had issued a statement on October 1 that hailed the movement as intended "to secure and safeguard the Revolution and the Great Leader of the Revolution against foreign subversion."[39] "It is impossible that there is no involvement in this affair of elements of the Air Force," Suharto scolded in his speech after supervising the exhumation of the murdered generals on October 4.[40] Suharto was increasingly incensed by the president's posture of nonchalance. Sukarno chose not to attend the funeral for the slain generals on October 5, and he called a cabinet meeting on October 6 that included representatives of both the PKI and the air force. Suharto claimed in his memoirs that the meeting took place in an "environment of hearty laughter," which enraged him given the tragedy that had just befallen his colleagues.[41]

The perpetrators of the September Thirtieth Movement continued to find sanctuary in the uppermost echelons of the Indonesian state. Suharto therefore worked to establish alternative institutions under his control and to either purge existing institutions of communist influence or dismantle them entirely. On October 10, he erected the Operational Command for the Restoration of Security and Order (Kopkamtib). The new body coordinated the army's campaign against the PKI and would eventually become the institutional core of Suharto's New Order regime. The following week, Sukarno recognized that Suharto had established de facto control over the army and appointed him army commander. Suharto was also named chief of staff of Supreme Operations Command (Koti), the cabinet-like body that Sukarno created to coordinate Indonesia's takeover of West Papua from the Dutch and then maintained to wage his campaign of *Konfrontasi* against the creation of Malaysia. Triply empowered, Suharto ordered a purge of communists and communist sympathizers from the organs of state in mid-November.[42] In early December, Suharto announced a reorganization of Koti to include more army representatives as well as specialists on political, economic, and social affairs, signaling the widening scope of his ambitions beyond destroying Indonesia's communist movement.[43] He also ordered the subsumption within Koti of the Central Intelligence Board (BPI), Indonesia's most powerful intelligence agency which had long under the control of the leftist iconoclast and outspoken foreign minister, Subandrio.[44]

Even vested with his new authority, Suharto was anything but secure. Yoga remembered that "the Army was already in the hands of the Kostrad commander" on the morning of October 2 because of "an informal agreement among senior Army officers to support Major General Suharto."[45] But just because the army was generally anticommunist and rallied behind Suharto to turn back the September Thirtieth Movement did not mean he could count on the institution's unstinting support if he moved to fundamentally reshape Indonesian politics. Several generals at army headquarters in Jakarta remained loyal to the president, as did the chiefs of the Siliwangi and Diponegoro divisions and much of the Brawijaya and Diponegoro officer corps. Other generals were reluctant to allow Suharto to adopt a leadership role for which they considered themselves better qualified. "People like Nasution and Kemal Idris only gave him six months in 1966," remembered an Indonesian journalist of influential army personages.[46] Beyond the army, the leaders of the police, the marines, and the air force were pro-Sukarno, as were the broad masses of Indonesian soldiers, sailors, marines, aviators, and police officers, who regarded the president as Indonesia's revolutionary hero and even the embodiment of the nation itself.[47] More perceptive than Yoga was a KAP-Gestapu leader who met with Suharto on October 4. "It was clear he was vulnerable," the man recalled. "His grasp on the Army was tentative. He was very new, and there were only two people he trusted in headquarters. . . . The rest were all either dead or flip-flopping. You couldn't tell whether their loyalty lay with Suharto or with Sukarno."[48]

Because the general staff had been decimated by the September Thirtieth Movement, Suharto could install allies in vacant positions after being appointed army commander on October 16. He brought General Maraden Panggabean, General Basuki Rachmat, General Sugih Arto, General Sumitro, General Hartono Rekso Dharsono, General Hartono Wirjodiprodjo, General Daryatmo, General Alamsjah Ratu Perwiranegara, and General Umar Wirahadikusumah into the fold in the weeks after October 1.[49] The deluge of new appointments meant only one Sukarnoist officer remained in the army general staff by early November, but it did not guarantee Suharto's uncontested authority. Of the new appointments, only Alamsjah had a close, preexisting relationship with Suharto. The rest he could count as reliably anticommunist and in favor of aggressive stances against the PKI and Sukarno, but not necessarily personally loyal. Suharto's most likely rival at army headquarters was Nasution—the architect of the Indonesian army who still cut an imposing figure on the national stage. But Nasution seemed either unable or unwilling to mount a bid for power. He had suffered injuries during a hair-raising escape from the captors sent to his home on the morning of October 1, and he was mourning the death of his young daughter from injuries sustained during the attack. With his position in army headquarters solidifying, Suharto turned to consolidating his control over the army writ large by laying the groundwork for a purge of the institution. Inspection teams within Kopkamtib began crisscrossing Indonesia to gather intelligence on PKI infiltration of the army and other state institutions.[50]

Suharto's allies within the army also began deepening their ties with civil society groups to further their campaign to eradicate the PKI and usurp state power. Among the most obvious potential allies were students and youth, historically a revolutionary vanguard in the country. Indonesia's student population had grown increasingly discontented under Sukarno. The number of students enrolled in university-level education surged from 1,000 in 1950 to 50,000 in 1960, yet graduates found little opportunity for meaningful employment given Indonesia's descent into economic crisis.[51] In late October 1965, General Syarif Thayeb and the leaders of KAP-Gestapu organized a gathering of various anticommunist student groups, which led to the creation of the Indonesian Student Action Front (KAMI). A division of labor emerged between the two groups, with KAP-Gestapu (soon renamed the Pancasila Front) taking charge of high politics and KAMI of mass demonstrations. KAMI leaders remained in close contact with a number of army figures who often spoke at the group's rallies—including General Kemal Idris, Colonel Sarwo Edhie Wibowo, Colonel Ali Murtopo, and Colonel Yoga Sugama.[52] At a November 3 rally at the University of Indonesia, KAMI pledged "to help ABRI [Armed Forces of the Republic of Indonesia] crush the counterrevolutionary G-30-S/PKI [September Thirtieth Movement/PKI] movement and all political parties and mass organizations that directly or indirectly participated in it."[53] KAMI staged raucous protests over the next few months to which the army trucked huge numbers of students. Attendance estimates reached the hundreds of thousands.[54] As KAMI's demonstrations mounted, KAP-Gestapu worked to convince the leaders of Indonesia's political parties to abandon Sukarno and throw their weight behind Suharto. As Jusuf Wanandi, a KAMI and Pancasila Front leader, remembered, "Bit by bit, Suharto was bringing in others he could rely on, but there was no question he needed all the help he could get. That was where we felt we could be useful, as his 'shock troops,' although frankly we were hoping too for some protection from the Army."[55]

The balance of power in Indonesia shifted in the last three months of 1965. Soldiers and civilian militias slaughtered PKI members, arrested communist leaders, and demolished the party's institutional and mobilizational capacity. Suharto gained control over army headquarters in Jakarta, secured an institutional position within Kopkamtib and Koti, and built an alliance with the leaders of Nahdlatul Ulama, the Catholic Party, the army-linked League of Upholders of Indonesian Freedom (IPKI), the banned Socialist Party of Indonesia, and an array of bourgeois groups including students, journalists, intellectuals, and lawyers. Its growing social base allowed the army to mobilize throngs of young people to demonstrate in the streets. But when General Sumitro walked upstairs to meet with Suharto at army headquarters in early 1966, he remembered that "Pak Harto seemed hesitant." He listened intently as Suharto agonized over what to do about Sukarno. The army chief recognized the president remained wildly popular in much of Indonesia, just as he appreciated that the army was divided and the other branches of the military were generally loyal to Sukarno.[56] He needed to undermine Sukarno's popularity. The deepening economic crisis provided an ideal opportunity for Suharto to escalate his Cold War.

III

The crisis was born of mismanagement. Sukarno had presided over a dramatic expansion of government budget deficits from approximately 15 percent of total

revenue in 1955 to more than 175 percent of total revenue in 1965. To finance
its mushrooming obligations, the Indonesian government simply printed more
money. The money supply expanded from 12 billion rupiah to more than 2.5
trillion rupiah over the same time ten-year period.[57] The predictable result was
a hyperinflation that escalated dramatically in late 1964. In Jakarta, the overall
price level of consumer goods rose at an annualized rate of nearly 1,300 percent
in the last quarter of 1965.[58] Farmers began hoarding agricultural produce rather
than exchanging it for cash that would swiftly lose its value. Food riots erupted
in urban areas as consumers found markets bare of basic commodities like rice,
sugar, and eggs.[59] Meanwhile, because Sukarno had focused his energies on the
grandiose task of forging a new international order rather than the relatively
mundane work of routine economic maintenance, the archipelago's infrastructure was in shambles. According to the World Bank, 84 percent of Indonesia's
roads were in bad or very bad condition in 1966, and even those in good condition were built according to 1940s standards and were incapable of bearing
the heavy loads of modern, large-axle trucks. Moreover, Indonesia's harbors and
waterways were filling with silt, and there was a 45 million cubic meter dredging
backlog. State-owned enterprises expropriated from the Dutch in the late 1950s
likewise suffered from persistent mismanagement. Hyperinflation and underin-
vestment combined with a foreign exchange policy that forced exporters to sell
their hard currency for rupiah at below-market rates to sap the competitiveness
of Indonesian exports, which caused export revenues to collapse from $954 mil-
lion in 1957 to $707 million in 1965.[60]

As domestic production cratered and foreign exchange grew scarce, Sukarno
found himself forced to turn to sovereign debt markets to finance vital imports like
rice, factory equipment, and motor vehicles. He racked up towering quantities
of international obligations. But rather than investing these loans in domestic
production capacity, Sukarno channeled them toward prestige projects, consumer goods, military equipment, and cronyist arrangements.[61] Seeing little
hope of repayment and little political return on their economic investments,
Indonesia's creditors eventually grew unwilling to throw good money after bad
and constrained Sukarno's ability to borrow.

The Indonesian nationalist hero then turned to a rhetoric of self-sufficiency.
Alas, for the broad masses of Indonesians, what Sukarno called *berdikari* (*berdiri
diatas kaki sendiri*, or standing on one's feet) might have better been called
starving on one's knees. Lack of access to imported spare parts meant buses
and trains were left idle and power plants dark, which resulted in transportation bottlenecks and production stoppages. Industrial output in 1965 reached
only 20 percent of capacity. As rice imports cratered from more than 1 million
tons in 1964 to fewer than 190,000 tons in 1965, famines broke out in parts
of the archipelago, and per capita caloric intake plunged to one of the lowest

levels in the world.[62] Malaria, largely eliminated in Java by 1964, returned because Indonesia lacked the hard currency to purchase insecticides or parts for spraying equipment.[63] Living standards fell and the country sank deeper into poverty as population growth outstripped economic growth almost every year between 1960 and 1965. Real GDP per capita was lower in 1965 than it was in 1941—and lower than comparable figures for China following the Great Leap Forward and the Democratic Republic of the Congo following Belgium's retreat from empire.[64] One development economist commented at the time that "Indonesia must surely be accounted the number one failure among the major underdeveloped countries."[65]

And a precipice loomed. In mid-December 1965, Indonesia's foreign exchange reserves dropped so low that the government announced it would not be able to pay on letters of credit worth $2 million to Japanese exporters and was effectively in default. Shortly thereafter, it admitted it could not repay American and West German export-import bank loans.[66] With more than $2.3 billion in total foreign debt, and with debt service payments coming due in 1966 a full $100 million more than Indonesia's anticipated export revenues for that year, the country's economy was teetering on the knife-edge of catastrophe.[67]

Economic chaos fueled opposition to Sukarno. Facing mounting financial difficulties amid the hyperinflation of late 1965, Sukarno's government announced hikes in the prices of petroleum (from 4 to 1,250 rupiah per liter) and other state-subsidized commodities. The move came only weeks before the Lebaran holiday—when many Indonesians returned to their home villages to celebrate the end of Ramadan—and enraged urbanites who suddenly found bus fares and train tickets prohibitively expensive. On January 10, 1966, KAMI staged a rally of several thousand students at the University of Indonesia. The headline speaker was RPKAD commander Sarwo Edhie, recently returned to the capital after presiding over the slaughter of tens of thousands of suspected leftists in Central Java. The students at the rally proclaimed the *Tritura* (*Tri Tuntutan Rakyat,* or Three Demands of the People): disband the PKI, purge the cabinet of communist sympathizers, and reduce prices. Over the next five days, waves of protest pummeled the capital, cresting with a massive rally in front of the Bogor palace on January 15, as Sukarno was preparing to hold a cabinet meeting. Throngs of young people endured the soaking rain to taunt the arriving ministers and demand that Sukarno accede to the *Tritura*. Members of the presidential guard nervously fingered the triggers of their guns and fired warning shots above the heads of students who tried to climb the fence surrounding the palace.

Sukarno was unmoved. He delivered a characteristically bombastic speech in which he likened himself to Martin Luther and declared himself responsible to the nation, almighty God, and the prophet Muhammad. The president called

Table 2.1 **Indonesia's foreign debt as of December 31, 1965 (millions of US dollars)**

Country	Medium/Long Term	Short Term	Total
Western Countries			
United States	172	7	179
West Germany	112	10	122
France	113	2	115
Italy	84	7	91
United Kingdom	40	2	42
Netherlands	12	16	28
Switzerland	0	3	3
Other	6	1	7
Communist Countries			
Soviet Union	980	10	990
Yugoslavia	108	7	115
Poland	98	2	100
Czechoslovakia	58	19	77
East Germany	70	2	72
Hungary	17	2	19
Romania	15	1	16
China	13	0	13
Other	2	0	2
Other			
Japan	168	63	231
Pakistan	0	20	20
India	8	2	10
United Arab Republic	3	1	4
IMF	102	0	102
Total	2,181	177	2,358

Source: "Survey of Recent Developments," *Bulletin of Indonesian Economic Studies* 2, no. 4 (June 1966): 5.

on his supporters to assemble into a Sukarno Front to defend his regime against counterrevolutionary students.[68] He also told Suharto to "handle" the crowds outside the palace. The army commander did as he was told: he simply walked outside into the rain, climbed atop a fence post, and addressed the crowd with a megaphone. "Go home," he appealed, "we've already won."[69]

But the general knew he had not won just yet. Only by igniting an economic recovery could Suharto ensure huge numbers Indonesians did not once again embrace communism. No expert on economic affairs, Suharto reached out professors of economics at the University of Indonesia—a group later dubbed the Berkeley Mafia by New Left muckrakers because many had pursued post-graduate study at the University of California's flagship campus.[70] In so doing, he drew upon preexisting ties between the army and the coterie of technocratic economists. As the Indonesian economy careened in the early 1960s, Colonel Suwarto of Seskoad had become convinced that army leaders should be pre-pared to take greater control over the nation's political, economic, and social life. He invited the members of the Berkeley Mafia to lecture to the officers enrolled in Seskoad programs, including Suharto. As one of the scholars who belonged to the Berkeley Mafia remembered, "At first the relationship between the mil-itary and the academics was exploratory, but over time the bond became insti-tutional."[71] That institutionalization deepened in January 1966, when KAMI organized a ten-day seminar on the economy attended by University of Indonesia economists, senior army officers like Nasution, and important civilian allies of Suharto like Hamengkubuwono, Malik, and Subchan. Suharto sent a written message lamenting that, for all the economic sloganeering under Sukarno, the Indonesian people were no more prosperous. He asked the attendees at the sem-inar to deliver concrete policy proposals for overcoming the country's economic crisis.[72]

Often compared to the market fundamentalist "Chicago Boys" who administered "shock therapy" on the Chilean economy under the dictator Augusto Pinochet, the budding technocrats of the Berkeley Mafia in fact favored state intervention in the economy in order to direct the process of economic de-velopment.[73] They were active participants in a swirling transnational discourse on the logics of the developmental state. Widjojo Nitisastro, first among equals within the Berkeley Mafia, dedicated his inaugural address as a faculty member at the University of Indonesia in 1963 to the necessity of state-led development planning.[74] A few days before the KAMI conference, Widjojo told a senior eco-nomics student that "the People's Republic of China and Korea are earlier than us in preparing their economic development, [and] they made long preparations to have long-term development plans. We must also have a long-term plan as a guidance."[75] The members of the Berkeley Mafia took inspiration from a wide array of sources beyond the neoclassical orthodoxy they learned in the United

States, including the developmentalist model pioneered by Japan's Ministry of International Trade and Investment and subsequently emulated by South Korea and Taiwan, the Soviet-influenced planning efforts of Prasanta Chandra Mahalanobis's Indian Statistical Institute, the "middle road" between capitalism and communism adopted by Egyptian policymakers under Gamal Abdel Nasser, and even the planned economy of Mao's People's Republic of China.[76] Moreover, the members of the Berkeley Mafia were dedicated nationalists. One of their erstwhile teachers and enduring interlocutors remembered that they often sought advice from foreign advisors but noted that "the most common experience of the foreign advisor is one of frustration" because his advice is "more frequently than not" ignored.[77]

The Berkeley Mafia's chief complaint against Sukarno was not his *dirigisme* per se but rather his disregard for any economic rationality. Indonesia's revolutionary leader was fond of deriding economics as "textbook thinking," and he went so far as to ban books by renowned economist John Maynard Keynes. Over the course of KAMI's ten-day seminar, the members of the Berkeley Mafia delivered lecture after lecture explaining the backwardness of Sukarno's economic policies. Emblematic was a speech by Mohammad Sadli excoriating Sukarno's anti-inflationary policies as hopeless, his subsidies for fuel and rice as counterproductive, and his foreign policy grandstanding as a drain on national wealth. Sadli explained that Indonesia needed to attract new international credits and channel scarce foreign exchange toward the revitalization of the country's agricultural and industrial sectors if it were to escape the maw of poverty.[78]

Sukarno was in fact seeking international aid to overcome Indonesia's crippling economic and humanitarian crisis and restore his political legitimacy. The president had burned bridges with the West and the international institutions it controlled, famously telling the United States to "go to hell with your aid" in January 1965 and then withdrawing from the United Nations, the International Monetary Fund, and the World Bank. Western governments either ignored or refused his requests for hundreds of millions of dollars of aid in the months following October 1.[79] But Sukarno retained close diplomatic ties with Japan, spending no fewer than 117 days in the country between 1957 and 1964 and taking a Japanese woman, Dewi Sukarno, as one of his wives. In the months after the September Thirtieth Movement, Japanese leaders leaned toward Sukarno in his conflict with Suharto and the army. Only Sukarno had demonstrated an ability to contain Indonesia's centrifugal tendencies and maintain the stability of what was, for Japan, a vital source of raw materials, a large potential export market, and a critical choke point through which most of the country's oil imports passed. In late December 1965, Japan agreed to furnish Sukarno with $6 million in credit to finance textile imports before the Lebaran holiday (for which new clothing was a common gift).[80] But amid anticommunist bloodletting and economic chaos, Japanese policymakers concluded Sukarno would not be able to recover his political authority. The Japanese government began hedging its bets, announcing it would no longer insure exports to Indonesia, which effectively halted trade between the two countries. The flow of aid from Japan dried up by February 1966.[81] That left Sukarno almost totally isolated on the international stage. Only communist China remained willing to extend aid to Indonesia, offering 10,000 tons of rice to overcome food shortages on January 30.[82]

Suharto was content to allow Indonesia's economic crisis to fester and sap Sukarno's political legitimacy. His allies even sought to exacerbate the crisis. University of Indonesia economist and Berkeley Mafia godfather Sumitro Djojohadikusumo, then living in exile in Bangkok, went so far so to press the Japanese government to refrain from aiding Sukarno.[83] Army officials also attempted to starve Sukarno's government of foreign exchange by demanding multinationals like Caltex and Goodyear deposit the Indonesian share of natural resource revenues into army-owned accounts rather than the central bank.[84]

Some army representatives delivered appeals for Western support. Facing a food shortage that was especially acute among soldiers and civil servants, an undersecretary in the Ministry of Foreign Affairs, Alfian Yoesoef Helmi, approached Western diplomats and asked for assistance in obtaining 300,000 tons of rice from Thailand and Burma, alleging he was acting on behalf of the army.[85] The request perplexed Western officials. Helmi was the brother-in-law of longtime Suharto confidante Alamsjah, but other high-placed figures like Nasution and Malik had specifically asked Western governments *not* to provide any aid to Indonesia lest it ease the pressure on Sukarno or allow him to paint the army as a lackey of the West.[86] After some consultations among themselves, Western officials denied Helmi's request. Only a month later, General Achmad Tirtosudiro implored American officials to provide him with a letter of credit to purchase 200,000 tons of rice from Thailand. His effort met a similar fate.[87] Some reports have suggested that Ali Murtopo and other Suharto confidants traveled to anticommunist dictatorships like Thailand, South Korea, and Taiwan to raise funds on Suharto's behalf, but the available archival record offers no definitive proof of these missions.[88] Beyond modest quantities of materiel for use in its campaign against the PKI, the army generally eschewed international assistance in the critical months following the September Thirtieth Movement.

Despite his calculated rejection of immediate foreign aid, Suharto did not ignore the outside world. He worked to pave the way for a resumption of large-scale aid by assuring Western governments that an army-dominated Indonesia would prove more amenable to their interests than Sukarno's leftist regime. Central to this effort was his maneuvering in Indonesia's oil industry. Shortly before the September Thirtieth Movement plunged Indonesia into crisis,

Sukarno had ordered his deputies to expedite negotiations over the purchase of foreign oil assets in Indonesia and to oversee a transfer in the management of American oil companies to Indonesian hands by the end of 1965—a prospect that American oil executives believed amounted to de facto nationalization.[89] After US officials warned army leaders that the move could trigger the Hickenlooper Amendment, which forbade the provision of aid to any country that expropriated American property, Suharto acted to halt any momentum toward nationalization. On December 6, 1965, he interrupted a meeting organized by Sukarno's underlings to discuss the takeover of Stanvac and Caltex and announced that the army would not allow any moves against foreign oil companies.[90] Although Suharto's intervention won the army considerable goodwill, its allies told Western governments to continue holding off on delivering aid to Indonesia. "Wait," Malik told the American ambassador, "I will let you know when we want your help."[91]

The backdrop to those negotiations was a Jakarta on the brink of civil war. As hyperinflation spiraled unchecked and students returned from the Lebaran holiday for the new semester, KAMI and the Sukarno Front engaged in pitched battles on the streets of the capital, attacking each other with fists, sticks, and stones.[92] "We don't want Monuments, we need Industry!" and "We are tired of Speeches," came the chants from anti-Sukarno protestors.[93] As chaos mounted, Sukarno attempted to reassert his authority. In quick succession in mid-February, the president drained Koti of its political and economic authority and renamed it the Crush Malaysia Command (Kogam), reiterated his call for the Sukarno Front to defend his leadership against counterrevolutionary forces, demanded the release of hundreds of thousands of communist prisoners, removed Nasution and several prominent anticommunists from the cabinet, and reinstalled loyalists in important military posts.[94]

Sukarno's maneuvers incensed Suharto's civilian allies. On the day the new cabinet was scheduled to be installed, student protestors amassed in Jakarta. They drained the air from the tires of cars across the city, bringing traffic in the capital to a standstill. Rowdy demonstrations reached the presidential palace, where arriving ministers walked on foot and weaved between immobilized vehicles. This time Sukarno's guards fired directly at the protestors, killing a university student named Arief Rachman Hakim. Hakim's death galvanized more protests. Fifty thousand people attended his funeral in Jakarta, marching through the city and demanding that Sukarno accede to the *Tritura*.[95] Sukarno responded by banning KAMI. Anticommunist youth simply formed an alphabet soup of new action fronts for high school students (KAPPI), women (KAWI), scholars (KASI), teachers (KAGI), and more. Other KAMI figures formed the Arief Rachman Hakim Militia, moving their base of operations into Kostrad headquarters and receiving training and weapons from RPKAD troops. Increasingly

Figure 2.2 RPKAD forces joined by KAMI activists on the streets of Jakarta on March 14, 1966 to celebrate the *Supersemar*. Algemeen Nederlands Persbureau/Redux.

militant students began ransacking government offices, including the Foreign Ministry, Education Ministry, and State Secretariat, as well as Chinese consular, trade, and media facilities.[96] Pro-Sukarno students staged demonstrations of their own. Thousands chanted in front of the American embassy, burning twenty-two vehicles and tossing Molotov cocktails through the building's windows.[97] Violence spread to Surabaya, Makassar, and other provincial capitals in February and March 1966.

The army-managed chaos threatened to devolve into outright anarchy. On March 4, Suharto appealed to Sukarno to allow him to arrest cabinet ministers suspected of involvement in the September Thirtieth Movement. The mood within the ranks of the army was so vengeful, he warned, that soldiers would join students on the streets of Jakarta if figures like Subandrio continued to walk free. The president refused the request outright. Instead, Sukarno called a series of meetings with leaders of political parties, mass organizations, military regiments, and the cabinet to demand declarations of loyalty.[98] By then, Suharto had already laid plans to arrest leftist members of the cabinet without Sukarno's authorization.[99] Shortly after he called a cabinet meeting to order on the morning of March 11, Sukarno was informed that unidentified troops had surrounded the presidential palace. (The soldiers were RPKAD troops who had stripped off their insignias and telltale red berets.) Doubtless aware of Suharto's conspicuous absence from the meeting, Sukarno and his closest confidants, Subandrio and Chaerul Saleh, rushed to the Bogor palace by helicopter.

Three generals present at the suspended cabinet meeting, General Basuki Rachmat, General Mohammad Yusuf, and General Amirmachmud, then traveled to Suharto's home and requested permission to follow Sukarno to Bogor. They asked Suharto whether he had any message for Sukarno. "Convey my greetings and respect to Bung Karno," came his reply. "Report that I am sick. If I am given command and his confidence, I will overcome the current situation."[100] Upon arriving in Bogor, the three generals pressured Sukarno to sign a letter endowing Suharto with the authority to restore order and promised the president his family would be unharmed. After some hesitation, Sukarno signed what became known as the *Supersemar* (*Surat Perintah Sebelas Maret*, or Order of March Eleventh). The letter gave Suharto authority to "take all measures deemed necessary to ensure security and calm as well as the stability of the running of the Government and the course of the Revolution." "This hands over power," Amirmachmud marveled as he read the letter while driving back to Jakarta.[101]

Supersemar became the founding document of the New Order. Upon receiving the letter from Amirmachmud, Suharto immediately ordered General Sucipto, the head of the Kogam division for sociopolitical affairs, to ban the PKI.[102] Sucipto delegated the task to two assistants, Colonel Sudharmono and Captain Murdiono. After some debate about the legality of their task, since they knew full well Sukarno would oppose the move, the men drew up an order banning the PKI and all its affiliated mass organizations throughout Indonesia.[103] Radio Republic Indonesia announced the ban on the morning of March 12, and RPKAD troops under Sarwo Edhie paraded through the streets of Jakarta, with KAMI activists joining soldiers on top of tanks—characterized by the American ambassador as "carefully and effectively staged" to exhibit the army's political dominance.[104] A week later, the army arrested more than a dozen leftist members of Sukarno's cabinet, including Subandrio, thought by many to be Sukarno's most likely successor. Suharto had achieved a signal victory.

The period between October 1965 and March 1966 marked the onset of Suharto's Cold War. In these momentous months, Suharto and the Indonesian army launched a campaign of extermination against the PKI. But Suharto's Cold War remained mostly disarticulated from the global Cold War. The anticommunist bloodletting in Indonesia flowed primarily from Suharto's rage at the murder of his comrades and the Indonesian army's long-standing antipathy toward the PKI. The politicide likely would have unfolded in much the same way had international actors absented themselves from the scene entirely in the months following the September Thirtieth Movement. Indeed, that is precisely what Suharto and his allies requested of their prospective Western sponsors: disengage from Indonesia while the army cleansed the archipelago of communism. As these grisly events unfolded, Suharto also set the stage for the next phase of his Cold War. He began institutionalizing his authority and cultivating a broad constellation of social forces that could serve as a source of countervailing power against Sukarno. Already at this early stage a key feature of Suharto's Cold War was coming into view—its improvisational, even capricious quality, responding to the swirl of crises and opportunities by forging ad hoc partnerships to further the agenda of anticommunism.

But Suharto knew that achieving his longer-term domestic objectives would require international assistance. He lacked the means to remake Indonesian politics and rejuvenate the Indonesian economy, and he knew a mandate to destroy the PKI was anything but a mandate to implement his broader anticommunist vision. He therefore began laying the groundwork for a partnership with Western governments and firms that could fuel his Cold War agenda at the opportune moment. He would begin drawing upon that partnership in earnest in the wake of the *Supersemar.*

3

A New Order

The *Supersemar* marked a moment of both victory and uncertainty for Suharto. Sukarno remained Indonesia's president and commanded the loyalty of the leaders of the navy, marines, air force, and police—at least one of whom offered to send his troops into battle against pro-Suharto regiments on the streets of Jakarta. Civilian-led religious organizations and political parties, having participated in the slaughter of hundreds of thousands of communists, were determined to secure positions of influence in the emerging New Order. Youth protest lulled during a moment of exhilaration following March 12 but would soon re-emerge. Most pressing of all, banning the PKI and the purging the cabinet did nothing to address the third pillar of the *Tritura*—lowering prices. Indonesia remained mired in political and economic crisis.

Suharto turned to the outside world to consolidate his initial Cold War victory. He appealed for debt relief, aid, and investment from countries such as the United States, Japan, the United Kingdom, West Germany, and the Netherlands; from international institutions like the International Monetary Fund, the World Bank, and the Paris Club; and from multinational firms interested in Indonesia's petroleum, logging, and mining sectors. To attract Cold War capital, Suharto and his allies warned that failure to support Indonesia's political and economic reorientation would lay fertile soil for the resurgence of communist influence.

International capital flowed into Indonesia beginning in 1966, but not in sufficient quantities or with sufficient regularity to allow Suharto to rapidly consolidate power. He therefore cooperated with rival military branches, political parties, Muslim organizations, and student groups that he considered threats to his authority and impediments to his agenda. He even coexisted with Sukarno rather than ousting him from the presidency. Only when international aid and investment began arriving in significant amounts and with longer time horizons in 1967 and 1968 did Suharto accelerate his drive toward power. Suharto's ability to draw upon resources made available through the global Cold War thus

Suharto's Cold War. Mattias Fibiger, Oxford University Press. © Oxford University Press 2023.
DOI: 10.1093/oso/9780197667224.003.0004

determined the scope, pace, and intensity of his domestic Cold War as well as the nature of the regime he built.

I

The arrests of high-ranking members of the cabinet left a vacuum in Indonesia's political leadership. On March 28, Sukarno, under pressure from Suharto, formed a new cabinet in which Suharto, Hamengkubuwono, and Adam Malik effectively ruled as a triumvirate.[1] The three men took charge of a country sinking deeper into economic crisis. The annualized rate of inflation crept upward to above 1,500 percent. Indonesia's Central Javanese breadbasket was experiencing historic flooding, which would cause a rice shortfall estimated at 250,000 tons.[2] The resulting food crisis could easily morph into a political crisis for the New Order.[3] As General Sukendro put it to the Australian ambassador on March 23, "the Army was now clearly responsible for the welfare of the people and the rice situation was critical."[4]

Beginning in late March, Malik and other Suharto allies began canvassing Western governments for emergency infusions of aid. US ambassador Marshall Green, having counseled a "low profile" approach following the September Thirtieth Movement, recommended that the United States "be prepared to move rapidly in helping meet" the needs of the Indonesian government after Suharto "banned the PKI, arrested his [Sukarno's] top lieutenants and appointed [an] interim government clearly controlled by responsible moderates."[5] Washington agreed to a "one-shot emergency shipment" of 50,000 tons of rice and another shipment of 75,000 bales of cotton whose combined value reached almost $20 million, though US officials made clear that "this is not repeat not [the] beginning of an aid program."[6] Tokyo indicated it would supply 10,000 tons of rice as well as some yarn and medicine worth a combined total of $5 million. Canberra, London, and Bonn offered smaller contributions of emergency aid.[7] Indonesia received a total of $60 million in emergency aid over the first half of 1966, enough to finance the country's import needs through August.[8]

Emergency aid could sustain Indonesia through a crisis, but it could not rebuild the country's economy. Conservative estimates suggested Indonesia's economic recovery would require hundreds of millions, even billions of dollars in aid and investment. But Sukarno's expropriation of foreign property had alienated Indonesia from most sources of international investment. And the 1960s was a decade of stagnation in flows of official development aid, which meant a massive aid increase appeared unlikely. When Indonesian officials raised the possibility of debt relief and long-term aid with international creditors, they were given a laundry list of preconditions. Among the issues raised in early talks were the status of American oil companies, restitution for Dutch and British firms whose property had been nationalized by Sukarno, Indonesian re-entry into the United Nations and other international institutions, the end of *Konfrontasi*, the dismantling of Sukarno's "Beijing-Pyongyang-Hanoi-Phnom Penh-Jakarta Axis," and the elaboration of a plan to overcome Indonesia's economic turmoil. In short, Western creditors demanded nothing less than the wholesale reorientation of Indonesia's domestic and international policies.

Suharto and his allies needed no convincing, for they shared the same goals. In early April, Malik and Hamengkubuwono launched a propaganda offensive designed to prove they intended to set Indonesia on a new trajectory. Malik delivered a series of speeches that outlined the foreign policy of the New Order. He proclaimed that "the demands of the people which spring straight from their suffering hearts will become a compass for our foreign policy and diplomacy." The principle that "foreign policy should be dictated towards the prosperity of the people" led Malik to announce that Indonesia would seek a peaceful resolution of *Konfrontasi*, re-enter the United Nations, and cultivate better relations with Western countries—a staggering volte-face for one of the most strident states of the Global South.[9] Meanwhile, Hamengkubuwono gave speeches that articulated the New Order's economic policies. Challenging Sukarno's insistence that Indonesia's economy remained stable, the sultan offered a sober accounting of Indonesia's yawning fiscal deficit, declining export revenues, and mounting sovereign debt burden. He pledged the New Order would tame inflation by implementing an austerity program and offering greater leeway to market forces. Hamengkubuwono also explained that the government would channel precious foreign exchange to enterprises that could most productively generate hard currency earnings in order to surmount a balance-of-payments crisis. Finally, he stated that Indonesian negotiators would consult with international creditors regarding "a just settlement enabling our country to fulfill its commitments without making our present economic difficulties at home more complex."[10]

Malik and Hamengkubuwono looked first to Japan. They dispatched financial experts led by Second Deputy Foreign Minister Umarjadi to Tokyo in May 1966 to lay the groundwork for a visit by the sultan himself the following month. Umarjadi's team described Hamengkubuwono's economic stabilization and rehabilitation program and presented debt rescheduling proposals. The Japanese were unimpressed. They lamented to Australian diplomats that the "Indonesians explained their economic policy and reconstruction plans only in broad and rather abstract terms" and offered nothing more than the scantiest data on the state of the Indonesian economy. Hamengkubuwono's follow-up visit in June went more smoothly. The sultan focused on political stabilization rather than economic recovery, assuring his hosts that "there was no chance of Sukarno making a comeback."[11] He left Tokyo with an agreement for $30 million in economic aid, less than the $50 million he requested but more than the $16 million Japan's Ministry of Finance was prepared to offer. According to Australian diplomats, Japanese prime minister Sato Eisaku hoped the offer would "break the ice and facilitate steps by other countries to extend aid."[12]

Sato's hopes proved excessively optimistic. From Tokyo, the Umarjadi mission continued on to Western Europe, where the Indonesian delegation planned to visit the Netherlands, West Germany, the United Kingdom, France, and Italy to negotiate aid and debt relief.[13] Only Bonn agreed to furnish additional aid. Australian diplomats in London reported that Umarjadi had learned that "no-one was prepared to sign blank cheques for Indonesia" and that Western officials regarded the economic plans he presented as "wholly unrealistic."[14] French diplomats told their Australian counterparts that they "want to see the Indonesians showing some signs of getting a grip on their economy before expressing any willingness to help."[15] A British diplomat griped that Umarjadi seemed unwilling to contemplate steep cuts in expenditures on the military and civil service lest Suharto alienate critical domestic constituencies. Western diplomats urged Indonesia to invite an IMF delegation to Jakarta to help draw up a more robust economic stabilization program.[16] While the Umarjadi mission negotiated with Western creditors, Malik prepared to travel to the Soviet Union and other Eastern Bloc countries in July. But shortly before his departure, he received word that the Soviets would be unwilling to receive him until at least August.[17] Indonesian hopes for the rapid initiation of an aid program were quickly extinguished.

Suharto himself appealed for aid using anticommunist language he anticipated would resonate with American officials. On May 26, he met Ambassador Green for the first time. "Unless something could be done to alleviate [the] suffering of [the] people," Suharto stressed, the "door would be open for [the] resurgence of communism." He requested aid for an ambitious—and expensive—transmigration scheme that would transport people from Java to Indonesia's Outer Islands in order to build agricultural and forestry industries and address demographic pressures. Green's response was noncommittal, noting that a resumption of large-scale aid could only take place "against [a] background of improving relationships and improved handling of Indo[nesian] economic problems."[18] Malik and Hamengkubuwono followed up in July with a request for $495 million in aid that was all but laughed off by American officials.[19]

It had become clear that Western governments would refuse to consider meaningful relief until they saw significant changes in Indonesian policies. "So it boils down to this," an editorial in the Foreign Ministry–controlled, English-language *Indonesian Herald* put it in July 1966: "As long as Indonesia does not really terminate its Confrontation towards Malaysia, no aid or loan substantial enough for the reconstruction of the Indonesian economy will be forthcoming. This is painful truth which our leaders have to accept whether they like it or not."[20] An official at the central bank lamented the Catch-22. Until the country presented a viable economic plan, it would have no idea how much foreign exchange would be available to it. But without an idea of how much foreign exchange would be available, Indonesia could not produce a meaningful economic plan.[21]

II

The triumvirate's failure to win large-scale economic aid in the first months following Suharto's seizure of power in March 1966 shaped the coalitional logic of the New Order. Suharto was forced to engage in consensual rather than coercive modes of governance and delay the establishment of an army-led regime. Studies of the New Order often suggest that Suharto's caution was innate to his personality—or even inherent to his cultural outlook, in line with the Javanese proverb *alon-alon asal kelakon*, which translates roughly to "slowly but surely." In fact, Suharto's moderation stemmed more from his inability to mobilize sufficient resources from either domestic or international sources to implement his maximalist agenda. General Nasution remembered that the country was "on the threshold of civil war" between forces loyal to Sukarno and Suharto in the aftermath of the *Supersemar*.[22] Without massive amounts of international aid to shore up a faltering Indonesian state, Suharto could ill afford to mount an aggressive challenge to his political opponents.

Polarization struck Suharto's anticommunist coalition in the months following the *Supersemar*. On one side were the New Order radicals. Led by General Kemal Idris, Colonel Sarwo Edhie Wibowo, and General Hartono Rekso Dharsono, the radicals were generally secular in orientation and distrustful of political parties. They demanded the abolition of all existing parties and the creation of a new political format based on functional rather than ideological lines.[23] Moreover, their self-conception as "modernizers" led them to value technocratic expertise over democratic legitimacy.[24] Sarwo Edhie in particular decried the "leaders of the Armed Forces, even the Army, who adhere to 'life and death' discipline" in their respect for civilian authority. American observers speculated he might stage a coup that dislodged both Sukarno and Suharto.[25] On the other side were the New Order moderates, including Nasution and key figures from Nahdlatul Ulama, the Indonesian Nationalist Party, and a number of smaller Christian parties who anticipated a resurrection of political party influence after the wilderness years of Guided Democracy. Nasution made known his belief that "military dictatorship was impossible in Indonesia" and insisted the armed forces "never had any intention to suppress political parties."[26] Most student activists sympathized with the radicals. But some more religious and constitutionalist factions within the anticommunist student movement rallied behind the moderates. In other words, although the radicals and moderates were united against the PKI, they clashed over the nature of the New Order—particularly the balance of power between the army and political parties.

Suharto shared the radicals' skepticism of political parties. He viewed them as vehicles of conflict that stirred up parochial, primordial rivalries among the Indonesian population and thereby impeded economic development. But parties retained large social bases across the archipelago, especially on Java, and their opposition could destabilize the nascent New Order. Suharto's limited resource base led him to adopt a strategy of coercive inclusion rather than outright exclusion toward Indonesia's political parties. His underlings policed the boundaries of political discourse and intervened in party affairs to ensure they chose pliant and uninspiring leaders who would pose no threat to the army's power.

The most conspicuous threat came from Sukarno's PNI, which remained popular in Central and East Java. Factional conflict between Sukarnoists and anticommunists had cleaved the party well before the momentous events of October 1, 1965. As the army began turning its attention from anticommunist bloodletting to political consolidation in the spring of 1966, it directed the PNI to hold a "Unity Congress." Suharto opened the proceedings by demanding that the party undertake self-criticism. He warned the attendees that the PNI would "be put to death by the people themselves" if it opposed the New Order—an ominous threat given the violence still sweeping the archipelago.[27] Suharto's army allies then ensured party leadership fell into the hands of the anticommunist faction under Osa Maliki Wangsadinata.[28] Some of the party's regional wings, in Central and East Java and in some Outer Island provinces, continued to shelter PKI refugees and publicly support Sukarno. But the PNI's national umbrella rallied squarely behind the New Order.[29]

The next-largest party in the archipelago, NU, experienced similar turbulence in the period leading up to October 1, 1965. Party leaders in Jakarta accommodated themselves to Sukarno's dictatorial rule while party elites at the local level bristled against the president's alliance with an increasingly assertive PKI. After Suharto seized power in March 1966, NU leaders began cooperating with the New Order in order to maintain control over the Ministry of Religion—the fiefdom through which the party traditionally dispensed patronage to its supporters. The party's accommodationist leadership, headed by Idham Chalid, faced challenges from charismatic insurgents like Subchan, the swashbuckling Pancasila Front activist who decried Suharto's efforts to consolidate military rule as akin to replacing "a lion with a crocodile."[30] But Idham and his allies remained firmly in control of NU's political apparatus.

Suharto sealed his tentative alliance with political parties in June 1966, when the national assembly met for the first time since April 1965. In the months before the meeting, the army purged roughly 150 members of the assembly suspected of holding leftist sympathies, including chairman and Sukarno confidant Chaerul Saleh. Suharto maneuvered Nasution into the vacant chair, which neutralized the general as a potential threat and secured the loyalty of moderates within the New Order coalition. Under Nasution's leadership, the assembly added a veneer of legality to Suharto's seizure of power by endorsing the *Supersemar*, affirming the ban on the PKI, prohibiting the dissemination of communist ideas, revoking Sukarno's title of president-for-life, and ordering Suharto to form a new cabinet. These moves enraged Sukarno. The president delivered an obstinate and evasive speech called the *Nawaksara* in which he defied expectations that he would offer an account of his relationship to September Thirtieth Movement. Instead, he demanded that "the entire People, including members of the MPRS, always follow, implement, and finalize everything that I give through my leadership."[31] The dissatisfied assembly then voted to require the president to complete a report of responsibility regarding the September Thirtieth Movement and the deteriorating state of the country. While the assembly did not remove Sukarno from office entirely, it commissioned Suharto to form a new cabinet and ruled that elections involving political parties would be held no later than July 1968. Suharto formed a new Ampera (*Amanat Penderitaan Rakyat*, or Message of the People's Suffering) Cabinet following the assembly session and announced the presidium would include himself, Malik, Hamengkubuwono, the NU figure Idham Chalid, and the former PNI leader Sanusi Harjadinata.

Suharto's nonconfrontational policy also characterized his efforts to secure control over the army and other branches of the Indonesian military. Opposition to the New Order was fiercest in the strongholds of Sukarno's authority in Central and East Java, home to the Diponegoro and Brawijaya divisions of the army as well as the headquarters of the navy and the marines. Troops from these outfits regularly attacked local KAMI demonstrations while shouting slogans like "long live Sukarno!"[32] Internecine conflict within the military reflected not only divergent attitudes toward Sukarno but also the divergent interests of different branches. Because the air force, navy, and marines relied overwhelmingly on Soviet-supplied equipment, they opposed Suharto's reorientation of Indonesian foreign policy toward the West; and because they emphasized the projection of power outside Indonesia's borders, they opposed Suharto's reorientation of the military toward internal security and economic development.

The forces under Suharto's command likely could have subjugated the Sukarnoists in the army. But a full-frontal assault risked igniting violent factional conflict that could quickly spiral out of control. Suharto instead replaced the leaders of Java's Siliwangi, Diponegoro, and Brawijaya commands with political allies. Emblematic of his approach were orders given to General Sumitro, who took over the Brawijaya division, to prevent outright clashes between different branches of the armed forces in East Java.[33] Other high-ranking army leaders whose loyalties Suharto doubted were replaced over the course of 1966. By early 1967, Suharto appointees inhabited all three of the army's interregional commands and all seventeen of its regional commands.[34] From there the purge of Sukarnoists descended down the army hierarchy. Some 2,600 soldiers from the Diponegoro division, the locus of support for the September Thirtieth Movement within the army, were eventually dishonorably discharged or otherwise punished.[35]

Purging the other branches of the military of communists and Sukarnoists required even greater finesse. The army was most aggressive toward the air force, whose involvement in the September Thirtieth Movement was incontrovertible. In March 1966, Sri Mulyono Herlambang resigned as commander of the air force and was replaced by Rusmin Nuryadin.[36] By the middle of April, more than 300 air force officers had been arrested, including Herlambang and his predecessor Omar Dani.[37] Toward the police, navy, and marines, the army acted less directly. Police commander Sutjipto Judodihardjo, a staunch Sukarnoist listed as a member of Untung's Indonesian Revolution Council, attempted to stay ahead of army purges and dismissed hundreds of officers suspected of involvement in the September Thirtieth Movement.[38] But there were approximately 125,000 members of the police, of which the few hundred who were purged represented only a tiny fraction. Sutjipto finally sealed his fate in early 1967 when he said he would "declare war" on the New Order if Sukarno was brought to trial.[39] Admiral Mulyadi of the navy and General Hartono of the marines refused to accede to army pressure to purge Sukarnoists and communists. Especially in East Java, sailors and marines continued to clash with action fronts and occasionally even skirmished with detachments of army soldiers. Determined not to outpace the limits of his power and incite civil war, Suharto bided his time rather than mobilize the army against the navy and marines.

Suharto further consolidated his authority by building new institutions. In August 1966, he formalized his Personal Staff (Spri), led by the military entrepreneur General Alamsjah Ratu Perwiranegara and rounded out by General Sunarso, Colonel Sudjono Humardani, Colonel Slamet Danusudirjo, Colonel Abdul Kadir, General Suryo Wirjohadiputro, Colonel Yoga Sugama, and Colonel Ali Murtopo.[40] Suharto would come to rely on Spri as a kind of kitchen cabinet even as civilian critics harangued the body as an unaccountable locus of corruption. Suharto also abolished Subandrio's Central Intelligence Board and tasked Yoga with building a new State Intelligence Command (KIN), later renamed the State Intelligence Coordinating Body (Bakin).[41]

As Suharto imposed his stamp on military personnel, he also worked to shape military doctrine. Back in April 1965, some 230 officers had gathered at Seskoad to formulate the army's defense doctrine. There Sukarno defended his vision of the Indonesian revolution as not only a war for national independence but also a broader struggle to "tear down colonialism, neocolonialism, and capitalism" across the world. Sukarnoist army officers ensured the doctrine that emerged over the following week bore the imprint of Sukarno's ideas. The resulting codex was called the *Tri Ubaya Çakti*, or Three Sacred Vows. Pledging fealty to Sukarno and his teachings, the army embraced its duty to what the Indonesian leader called the "New Emerging Forces" of nationalism in Asia, Africa, and Latin America against the "Old Established Forces" of neocolonialism, colonialism, and imperialism (Nekolim). General Ahmad Yani proclaimed that the army would embrace a strategy that was "offensive-revolutionary in spirit" and "galvanize the people of Southeast Asia to become one great power to crush all the forces of NEKOLIM in this region." Moreover, the *Tri Ubaya Çakti* held up solidarity between "Indonesia, the Democratic Republic of Vietnam, the People's Republic of China, and the Democratic [People's] Republic of Korea" as vital to the struggle of the New Emerging Forces in Asia.[42] "What I cannot forget about the first seminar," remembered Sumitro, "was how vocal and bold the PKI exponents within the ranks of the army were."[43]

In August 1966, Suharto organized a Second Army Seminar at Seskoad to subject the *Tri Ubaya Çakti* to a "total correction" and purge army doctrine of Sukarnoist influence.[44] It was here that the army for the first time systematized the philosophical foundations of the New Order. Seskoad chief General Suwarto divided the seminar participants into three syndicates: military, political, and economic. The military syndicate assumed responsibility for reformulating the army's defense doctrine. It all but eliminated the army's duty to support the global anticolonial struggle. The revised *Tri Ubaya Çakti* disavowed "any foreign interference in the internal affairs of various countries"—an implicit renunciation of the "offensive-revolutionary" doctrine it superseded. It went on to explain that "communist infiltration and subversion, especially originating from the People's Republic of China and Chinese population centers in Southeast Asia," represented the key threat facing Indonesia. Where its precursor emphasized the "spiritual-material" dyad in the elaboration of army doctrine, the revised *Tri Ubaya Çakti* held that "at the current stage of the Revolution, material prosperity will be given special emphasis." The doctrine that emerged from the 1966 seminar also marked a shift in the army's domestic role. As a result of overlapping crises including "communist subversion and infiltration" and "economic chaos," the revised codex asserted, the army was forced, "in addition to its duty in the field of defense, to become a stabilizing and dynamizing element in the political and economic life of the nation." The army thus arrogated for itself a position not only as a "military force" but also as a "social-political force."[45] The revised *Tri Ubaya Çakti* signaled a step beyond Nasution's "Middle Way" framework and legitimized the army's assumption of a decisive political role.[46] It foreshadowed the formal adoption of the concept of *dwifungsi*, or dual function, which Nasution had first articulated in 1960 but would not be enshrined into law until 1969.[47]

Only three months after formulating the revised *Tri Ubaya Çakti*, the army's new doctrine was extended to the air force, navy, and police as the *Çatur Dharma Eka Karma*, or Four Missions, One Deed. The new "national defense and se-curity doctrine" used less stridently anticommunist language than did the *Tri Ubaya Çakti*, but it deepened the military's focus on maintaining political sta-bility and igniting economic growth, outlining specific ideological, political, economic, and sociocultural roles for the armed forces.[48] The army's effort to stamp its doctrine on the other military services also represented a break with the past and Sukarno's efforts to maintain his authority by pitting one service against another. "For the first time in its history," Suharto enthused upon the document's publication, "ABRI has a national defense and security doctrine."[49]

The most visible manifestation of Suharto's inability to press his agenda due to his limited resource base was what Indonesians referred to as "dualism"—a ri-valry between two countervailing poles of political power: Sukarno and Suharto. Though Suharto had won extraconstitutional authority through the *Supersemar*, and though he worked to expand his institutional and ideological authority over the military, political parties, and civil society groups, he remained unable to mount an open takeover of the Indonesian state.

III

Resource constraints had left Suharto with little choice but to moderate his Cold War. But he did not moderate his ambitions. Even as he worked to coopt, sub-vert, and contain potential rivals, he charted a new course in Indonesian political, economic, and diplomatic life in order to win the international aid and invest-ment necessary to pursue his transformative ambitions. He moved quickly to end *Konfrontasi*, reorient Indonesian foreign policy more broadly, and flesh out the New Order's program of economic stabilization. The dramatic moves illus-trated Suharto's efforts to harness the global Cold War to serve his domestic and regional Cold Wars and their objectives of promoting development, unifying Southeast Asia, and containing China.

Army leaders had initially rallied behind *Konfrontasi*. Despite their misgivings about the wisdom of the campaign, they shared Sukarno's skepticism of British intentions in Southeast Asia in light of the fact that London had supported the

PRRI-Permesta regional rebellions in Indonesia in 1958. Moreover, they believed a limited conflict could expand the army's claims on the state budget and burnish its nationalist credentials. But most army leaders soured on the campaign by 1965. *Konfrontasi* redounded to the benefit of the PKI by rendering Indonesia an international pariah with few allies beyond the People's Republic of China. It also generated public support for the creation of a so-called Fifth Force of armed peasants that could defend Indonesia against Malaysian subversion—and would threaten the military's monopoly on modern instruments of violence. In mid-1965, months before the September Thirtieth Movement upended Indonesian politics, General Yani met with Suharto and two of his Kostrad deputies, Ali Murtopo and Colonel Benny Murdani, to discuss bringing *Konfrontasi* to a close. Murtopo mused that "We have to try to end it. Why should we kill each other and have to face the Chinese after that?" The meeting gave rise to Special Operations (Opsus), a secretive military command within Kostrad that would assume responsibility for much domestic and international intrigue under the New Order. Shortly thereafter, Murtopo met with Ghazali Shafie, the permanent secretary of Wisma Putra, the Malaysian foreign ministry, in a bid to end hostilities between the two states.[50] The talks led Malaysia to release some Indonesians captives as a gesture of goodwill. But with Sukarno still in charge, Indonesia and Malaysia could not move toward a broader resolution of *Konfrontasi*.[51]

The momentum toward Indonesian-Malaysian rapprochement waned in the period following the September Thirtieth Movement. So too did *Konfrontasi* itself, as the Indonesian army slowed the pace of military operations on Borneo in order to focus on its campaign of eradication against the PKI.[52] Only after the *Supersemar* endowed him with political authority did Suharto move toward a negotiated settlement with Kuala Lumpur. In May 1966, Murtopo produced a secret Opsus memorandum recommending that Indonesia make peace with Malaysia in order to obtain foreign aid from the West and unite Southeast Asia against what he described as the overarching threat posed by China.[53] A group of military intelligence figures including Murtopo, Murdani, and Yoga drew upon their network of overseas contacts to open lines of communication with Malaysia's deputy prime minister, Tun Abdul Razak. Meanwhile Adam Malik, newly installed as foreign minister, made a series of conciliatory public gestures hinting at Indonesia's desire to wind down *Konfrontasi*. In a speech at a student rally on May 20, he linked the end of *Konfrontasi* to the New Order's overriding goal of economic recovery. "We must have peace," Malik proclaimed, "otherwise prices cannot be kept down."[54] Although Sukarno inveighed against rapprochement and even forbade Malik from leaving the country, Malik traveled to Bangkok to meet Razak at the end of May. The two men negotiated an end to hostilities between Indonesia and Malaysia and a renewal of diplomatic relations. Of the populations of Sabah and Sarawak on the island of Borneo, whose inclusion in Malaysia incensed Sukarno and ignited *Konfrontasi* in the first place, Malik and Razak agreed they would be given an opportunity to "reaffirm" their desire to join the federation by taking part in general elections in 1967—little more than a face-saving formula, since there would be no option to dissent.[55] As if to demonstrate Indonesia's newfound focus on development rather than conflict, a large billboard on Jakarta's largest thoroughfare that once depicted Indonesia crushing Malaysia was papered over with advertisements for spark plugs and cooking utensils.[56]

As Indonesia pursued rapprochement with Malaysia, it also opened diplomatic ties with Singapore. During *Konfrontasi*, Indonesian saboteurs worked to destabilize Singapore and even carried out acts of violence, most infamously the March 1965 bombing of MacDonald House that killed three people and wounded dozens more.[57] In April 1966, Malik announced that Indonesia would recognize Singapore. Diplomatic relations between the sprawling archipelago and the tiny city-state opened in June. Two months later, Malik admitted frankly that "Indonesia needed Singapore's technical and entrepreneurial skills."[58] After trade ties between the two countries opened, Singapore extended credit worth more approximately $32.5 million to Indonesia.[59]

Suharto also worked to formulate an economic program that could attract Western creditors and donors disaffected by the perfunctory plan Umarjadi presented. In May 1966, action fronts of university students and scholars joined with the budding technocrats in the Berkeley Mafia to organize a public seminar at the University of Indonesia called "The Awakening of the Spirit of '66—Exploring a New Path." Although sessions explored ideology, politics, diplomacy, society, and culture, the most important focused on economics. Widjojo Nitisastro began the proceedings by commenting approvingly on the change in government. Economists' complaints about mismanagement had previously been greeted by closed doors, he remarked, but critics of economic irrationality faced no need to "break down doors that were already open."[60] The seminar concluded that the new government needed to balance Indonesia's state budget and its international trade ledger as well as rebuild infrastructure, increase food production, and expand tax collection. Its conclusions became the basis for a national assembly decree on economic, financial, and development policies issued at the momentous June 1966 session. The decree endorsed an economic recovery program focused first on controlling inflation, then on restoring production, and finally on igniting economic development. Still less a thoroughgoing development plan than a sketch of first principles, the decree reflected the Berkeley Mafia's preference for state-planned but market-oriented economic development.[61]

While the assembly was meeting, an IMF team arrived in Jakarta to negotiate Indonesia's return to the IMF and the World Bank and begin consultations on the New Order's economic stabilization and rehabilitation program. The Indonesians presented the economic development program that Umarjadi had hawked to Western creditors, which the IMF delegation described as a "draft ... still at [an] early stage." The delegation asked tough questions about the surfeit of government employees, excessive military spending, continuing subsidization of state-owned enterprises, and Indonesia's seemingly rosy projections for a rebound in export revenues.[62] These discussions marked the beginning of a close relationship between the IMF and technocrats in the Indonesian government that burnished the international legitimacy of the New Order.

The New Order coalition's effort to create a more detailed economic development program continued at the Second Army Seminar held at Seskoad in August 1966. There Suwarto established an economic syndicate comprising members of the Berkeley Mafia as well as roughly twenty civilians and seventy army officers tasked with considering Indonesia's economic plight. General Hartono Wirjodiprodjo explained the syndicate's overarching objective as stemming the tide of hyperinflation, which he warned could "give rise to tensions in the sociopolitical and socioeconomic realms" and destabilize the New Order. But he also tasked the syndicate with expanding access to food and clothing, rebuilding vital infrastructure like ports, and incentivizing export activities.[63] The syndicate recommended an austerity program that included significant cuts to subsidies for public utilities and the privatization of inefficient state-owned enterprises. But rather than demobilize segments of the Indonesian military, which was far larger than necessary to meet the country's defensive needs and exhausted 45 percent of all government revenues, the syndicate recommended the army expand its civic mission and allocate men and equipment toward economically productive activities.[64] Mohammad Sadli remembered that the seminar was important because it "presented to the Army leadership—the crucial element in the New Order—a 'cookbook' of 'recipes' for dealing with Indonesia's serious economic problems."[65] It also revealed that the technocrats in the Berkeley Mafia were willing to accommodate themselves to the army's particularistic interests. Suharto was so impressed by the economists that he recruited all five members of the Berkeley Mafia into a Team of Experts on the Economy and Finance with responsibility for drafting a more formal economic stabilization and rehabilitation program.[66]

The Berkeley Mafia then worked hand in hand with IMF experts to create a comprehensive economic program. An internal report from the Coordinating Ministry of Economics, Finance, and Industry explained that the collaborative effort at once enabled Indonesian policymakers to draw upon international expertise and also provided the New Order with international credibility, noting the "IMF is important because it is very influential in the operations of Congress," which could exercise a veto over US aid to Indonesia.[67] After weeks of work and negotiations with army leaders, the economic recovery program was unveiled on October 3, 1966. It envisioned nothing less than the wholesale restructuring of the Indonesian economy. It provided for a balanced budget, which the government would achieve through a mix of spending cuts and expanded tax collection. Subsidies for key commodities like water, rice, fertilizer, gasoline, electricity, and public transportation would continue undisturbed, though IMF representatives in Jakarta reported that the technocrats "still support higher key [commodity] prices" and would send proposals to curtail subsidies to the presidium at a later date.[68] The stabilization program also mandated massive hikes in interest rates from 14 to 29 percent per year to between 6 and 9 percent per month to curb the growth of bank credit, which was a key source of inflationary pressure. Finally, it aimed to bring Indonesia's balance of payments into harmony by simplifying the complex and inefficient system of multiple exchange rates, reducing the effective rate of taxation on exports, and devaluing the rupiah. Suharto also made it clear he had directed his economic stabilization team to prepare a foreign investment law that would exempt foreign investors from a variety of taxes and all but guarantee their property against expropriation.[69]

IV

As Suharto and his allies reoriented Indonesia's diplomatic and economic posture, creditor countries began discussing forming a consortium to oversee the rescheduling of Indonesia's debts.[70] They saw little alternative. As US secretary of state Dean Rusk put it, the collapse in Indonesia's balance of payments meant "success enjoyed by either private or governmental negotiators of creditor nations in arranging payment will mean that Indonesians will have to rob Peter to pay Paul."[71] Creditor governments drew upon two distinct institutional mechanisms in aiding Indonesia: the club, through which creditor countries oversaw debt rescheduling and restructuring arrangements with countries whose sovereign debt burdens had become unsustainable, and the consortium, through which donor countries coordinated the provision of economic aid to developing countries.[72] These models were helpful, but they provided only so much guidance. As an Australian diplomat remarked of previous clubs and consortia, "none of these operations has been as large and complex as the Indonesian case."[73] The towering size of Indonesia's debts in relation to its export revenues, the need to make service payments on short-term loans Sukarno had contracted at sky-high interest rates, the puzzle of how to coordinate between communist and noncommunist creditors, and the question of which government would take responsibility for organizing the proceedings—all these issues made the prospect of a multilateral arrangement an exceedingly complicated proposition.

Japanese officials first proposed that a "Tokyo Club" of Indonesia's creditors meet to discuss debt rescheduling in advance of Hamengkubuwono's visit to the country in mid-1966. But the sultan let the Japanese know he preferred to wait until after his bilateral talks with Indonesia's creditors over the summer—hopeful, perhaps, that he could play Western governments against one another and secure more favorable terms for aid and debt relief.[74] That gambit failed. Representatives of ten Western governments met in July and determined that "a multilateral approach was necessary to solve the difficult problems which Indonesia is now facing."[75] Confronting an escalating balance-of-payments crisis, Indonesian officials agreed to meet Western creditors in Tokyo in September.

Suharto dispatched the Indonesian delegation to Tokyo with a letter reaffirming his commitment to complete Indonesia's "political transformation" and implement the economic program drawn up with the help of the IMF. In return, he asked for a moratorium on debt repayment and additional aid worth $350 million for 1967.[76] Tun Thin, the head of the IMF's Asia desk who had led the mission to Jakarta a few months earlier, endorsed Suharto's proposal. But a division emerged among Indonesia's creditors over how to respond. European states were interested primarily in recouping their investments in Indonesia and advocated at most a temporary pause in debt repayment. The French delegate refused to consider any additional aid, noting in blatantly racist terms that "the Indonesian people had a natural tendency toward indolence" and asserting that any indulgence of that tendency would blunt the momentum behind necessary reforms. The United States, Japan, and Australia, on the other hand, proved keen to revitalize the Indonesian economy in order to sustain the consolidation of the New Order. The Americans hailed the rise of Suharto as a "political miracle" and promoted a more accommodative debt rescheduling arrangement and the provision of additional aid. Negotiations stretched well past midnight on the day the conference was scheduled to conclude. When the meeting finally adjourned, creditor countries had agreed in principle to reschedule debts due over the next fifteen months. But they left a final settlement regarding the rescheduling of Indonesian debt for a subsequent meeting, to be held in December, after the IMF would have more time to evaluate the Indonesian economy. Although disagreement among Indonesia's creditors prevented them from coming to an accord on new multilateral aid, the joint communiqué issued at the conclusion of the Tokyo meeting also noted that individual countries represented at the conference would extend emergency aid to Indonesia on a bilateral basis.[77]

Malik and Hamengkubuwono had already begun canvassing for emergency assistance. Hamengkubuwono's itinerary took him to The Hague, London, Paris, Bonn, Rome, Tokyo, New Delhi, and Washington.[78] Malik was scheduled to visit the Soviet Union and other Eastern Bloc creditors after his canceled August trip, but the Soviets again announced that they were not yet prepared to welcome an Indonesian mission.[79] Instead, the foreign minister traveled to Bangkok, Belgrade, Algiers, Cairo, New Delhi, New York, and Washington. The teams led by Hamengkubuwono and Malik were authorized to speak about Indonesia's new foreign and economic policies in pursuit of additional aid, but their briefs instructed them to "avoid going into too much detail and avoid taking too much time."[80] To the Americans they were instructed to focus on anticommunism. One report from the Indonesian embassy in Washington stated frankly that Americans were willing to "pay for national security" and explained that "Indonesia's victory over communists in 1948 and 1965 *without* American aid in any form, direct or indirect, helped the 'national security' of the United States."[81] In talks at the State Department, Hamengkubuwono spoke about his plans to revitalize the Indonesian economy.[82] Meanwhile Malik met with President Lyndon B. Johnson, Vice President Hubert Humphrey, and officials at the State Department and suggested that the New Order required considerable international aid to head off a "resurgence of Communism."[83] The junkets proved successful. Indonesia won additional economic aid from the United States worth $40 million, the Netherlands worth $18 million, and India worth $13 million. By late October, Suharto's emissaries had secured no less than $174 million in aid.[84]

Malik also made progress in winning a resumption of military aid. Washington agreed to resume a formal Military Assistance Program (MAP) for Indonesia. American officials noted that "there is no direct military requirement for an Indonesian MAP," so the amount of aid given would be small, but they considered a program worthwhile because it would "allow us to influence and strengthen the hands of those who will be running this country for the next several years."[85]

Finally in October, Eastern Bloc countries made clear they were willing to receive an Indonesian technical mission led by Malik to discuss debt rescheduling.[86] In Moscow, Belgrade, Warsaw, and Prague, Malik laid the groundwork for an agreement rescheduling $785 million of Indonesia's $1.2 billion in Eastern bloc debt, including a three-year moratorium and a repayment schedule that spanned thirteen years.[87] An Indonesian delegation led by General Suprayogi remained in Eastern Europe through early December and negotiated the suspension of large aid projects contracted under Sukarno as well as an agreement to provide spare parts for military equipment on a cash basis.[88] Coming only weeks before the follow-up to the Tokyo meeting to be held in Paris in December 1966, Malik's agreement with Indonesia's communist creditors removed a principal roadblock: Indonesia's Western creditors would not agree to reschedule Indonesian debt repayment, let alone begin the process of issuing new aid, if the credits they provided would be used to repay debts to communist countries. It also gave Indonesian negotiators leverage. Quipped one Indonesian diplomat to an Australian counterpart in November 1966, "We hope you will encourage the Americans to be more generous with us than the Russians."[89]

Before Hamengkubuwono and Malik departed Indonesia, they asked the IMF to dispatch another delegation to Jakarta to create a specific debt rescheduling proposal and work on additional economic stabilization measures.[90] Through October and November, IMF economists worked with Indonesian technocrats to wring some coherence out of the country's maze of economic statistics and prepare balance-of-payments projections and debt-servicing estimates, which they completed in early December. Experts from the IMF and economists at the US embassy (who maintained open lines of communication with American firms) also helped Indonesian technocrats draft a foreign investment law that parliament enacted on January 1, 1967.[91] The law broke with Sukarno's policy of self-sufficiency and noted that "the principle of relying on our own capability may not be allowed to arouse a reluctance to exploit the potential capital, technology, and skill available from abroad." It offered foreign investors a five-year reprieve from corporate taxes, an exemption from import duties and an accelerated depreciation schedule for fixed capital equipment, the right to repatriate profits unimpeded by government restrictions, and guarantees against expropriation and nationalization without compensation.[92] The law marked not only an attempt to woo foreign investors with generous provisions—an unlikely prospect in the immediate future given the economic crisis still enveloping Indonesia—but also an effort to reassure Western creditors that Suharto had definitively broken with Sukarno's economic policies.

When the Paris conference convened on December 19, 1966, Indonesian diplomats requested a lengthy moratorium on all debt servicing, with repayment taking place over ten years beginning in 1973. Other than the Netherlands, European governments facing financial challenges of their own scoffed at such a generous proposal. They instead suggested rescheduling as little as 85 percent of Indonesian debt and requiring repayment over five years beginning as early as 1968. American and Australian negotiators countered that such harsh terms risked destabilizing the New Order, reasoning that Suharto had just pushed through a raft of harsh austerity measures and needed something to show for them lest he be sapped of his domestic legitimacy. Ultimately, the creditors reached a compromise. They agreed to reschedule Indonesia's $357 million in debt coming due in 1966 and 1967, which would be repaid in steadily rising increments between 1971 and 1978.[93] The delegates also spent a great deal of time discussing whether Indonesia should be required to make other commitments such as promises to raise additional revenue and avoid contracting new debt. The Indonesians maneuvered to retain as much freedom of action as possible, while the Europeans proved anxious to lash Suharto to the mast of austerity. Once again, the Americans brokered a compromise that committed Indonesia to "take advantage of the advice and assistance of the IMF" but did not dictate precise conditions.[94] "Without the effective efforts of the US delegation," the Dutch minister of finance later remarked, "there would have been no agreement."[95]

The Paris meeting eased Indonesia's debt burden. But economic planners in Jakarta still anticipated massive budgetary and foreign exchange shortfalls in 1967. As the Paris conference drew to a close, Dutch officials offered to host a separate meeting at which Indonesia's creditors could discuss the extension of additional aid to finance the country's economic stabilization and rehabilitation program.[96] The first meeting of what came to be called the Inter-Governmental Group on Indonesia (IGGI) convened in late February 1967. Suharto sent a written appeal for aid, noting that Indonesia had reshaped the archipelago's regulatory framework through the new law on foreign investment and had also tamed inflationary pressures.[97] The IMF concluded that "these measures reveal a high order of courage and determination in reversing the policies of past years" and endorsed Jakarta's request for $200 million in aid over the course of 1967. The IMF also defended Suharto's proposal to disburse aid through Indonesia's export bonus (BE) scheme—a market for foreign exchange—which limited donor countries' ability to impose rigid ties on aid and allowed the Indonesian state to channel scarce hard currency toward particular sectors.[98] After what the chief of the Indonesian delegation called a "fierce debate," only France and Italy demurred.[99] Convinced by the IMF's endorsement of the New Order's economic program, the IGGI collectively agreed to provide the $200 million Indonesia requested. Although the participants had made it clear that pledges were not expected upon meeting's conclusion, the United States unilaterally announced that it would provide one-third of the aid. A journalist explained that American officials felt that Suharto "needed something concrete in the way of aid to answer the growing number of critics in Indonesia of his austerity program."[100] Under considerable American pressure, Japan also announced that it would furnish an additional one-third of the aid.

The whirlwind negotiations between Indonesia and its Western creditors from roughly June 1966 until February 1967 eased the financial burden on Suharto. It assured him of international support and enabled him to make difficult domestic decisions. In February 1967, for instance, he reduced fuel subsidies, causing an eightfold increase in the price of gasoline, kerosene, and diesel and a twentyfold increase in the price of some public utilities. These changes spurred renewed inflation in consumer prices, violated a key plank of the *Tritura*, and incensed the action fronts. He also increased taxes, but mainly by expanding duties on exports and imports rather than direct taxes on the Indonesian population. This decision reflected the crushing poverty of the majority of Indonesians and Suharto's sense that the Indonesian populace was unwilling to surrender additional resources to the state. The fiscal space Suharto gained also allowed him to consider moving more aggressively against Sukarno. As one IMF observer put it during the Paris conference, "General Suharto reportedly has given the signal to the impatient 'new order' supporters to launch an intensive and 'final' campaign to sweep the President from office."[101]

V

As Suharto's allies secured initial commitments for debt relief and emergency aid, political conflict and economic chaos threatened to plunge Indonesia into disorder. On August 17, 1966, Sukarno delivered a National Day address entitled "Never Forget History" (*Jangan Sekali-kali Melupakan Sejarah*, which Nasution cleverly fashioned into a portmanteau with communist connotations: *Jas Merah*, meaning Red Jacket). The president castigated the assembly for usurping his presidential authority via its legitimization of the *Supersemar*. His speech enraged New Order radicals. Action front demonstrations erupted with new-found vigor. Buoyed by his newfound access to international capital, Suharto banned protests in September, but students ignored his order much as they had ignored Sukarno's earlier ban on demonstrations. On October 1, the first anniversary of the murder of army leaders, students gathered in front of the presidential palace. They chanted slogans accusing Sukarno of masterminding the September Thirtieth Movement and demanding the president be tried by Extraordinary Military Tribunal (Mahmillub). The protest continued for three days. On the third day, after the students ignored orders to disperse, soldiers attacked them with rifle butts and bayonets, injuring sixty-two and killing one. Watching the carnage unfold from the balcony of the nearby army general staff building, Suharto prevented General Maraden Panggabean from stopping the soldiers. He "did not want to be controlled or dictated to by his partners" in civil society, Panggabean remembered.[102] At KAMI's anniversary celebrations held at the end of the month, Suharto warned students that "in the New Order KAMI should avoid physical clashes and confrontations."[103]

Suharto pressed his campaign against Sukarno even as he sought to curb what he regarded as the excesses of his civilian allies. The Mahmillub put Subandrio on trial for treason in October 1966 and tried Omar Dani on the same charge in December. The army used the Mahmillub trials to publicize damaging information about Sukarno, including his womanizing and his mismanagement of public finances. The most damning stories concerned Sukarno's behavior on the morning of October 1, 1965, and his communication with PKI leader Aidit following the September Thirtieth Movement's botched attack on army leaders. Malik joined the fray upon returning from his world tour in November and publicly implored Sukarno to step down. He suggested Sukarno might join his wife

Dewi in Japan and presented Egypt and Yugoslavia as alternative sites of exile. But the president responded that he had no desire to be "given the Nkrumah treatment," referring to the Ghanaian president who was overthrown by a military coup in early 1966 and lived the rest of his days in Guinea.[104] With Sukarno unresponsive to Malik's gentle suggestions, the army began a more aggressive campaign. On December 21, the commanders of all four branches of the military jointly pledged to "take strong action" against all who deviated from Pancasila or the constitution or who refused to implement the decisions of the summer 1966 assembly session—a reference to Sukarno's failure to follow up on the body's demand that he complete a report of responsibility.[105] The New Order radical Dharsono predicted that "1967 will be a decisive year; only victory for the New Order can bring stabilization in all fields."[106]

Sukarno found himself boxed in by the army and the action fronts. In January 1967, he relented and delivered a written supplement to his *Nawaksara* address. The president denied that the assembly had the authority to question him on matters beyond the broad outlines of state policy. He blamed the September Thirtieth Movement on the PKI leadership, the forces of "neocolonialism," and unidentified "bad elements," and he disavowed responsibility for Indonesia's "economic setbacks and moral decline."[107] His belligerent rejection of accountability further inflamed political tensions. KAMI activists marched in the streets deriding Sukarno as a "Peking dog," and the assembly and every Indonesian political party except the PNI deemed the supplement unacceptable.[108]

A key turning point came on February 3, 1967. General Sumitro had been called back to Jakarta to take up the positions of army deputy for operations and Kopkamtib chief of staff. Before he departed East Java, Sumitro formed the Greater Brawijaya Family in order to "consolidate" the New Order's control over the generally Sukarnoist division. He took a group of Brawijaya officers to Jakarta to meet with Sukarno; they "painted a clear picture for Bung Karno so that he would not get the impression that Brawijaya would stand unquestionably behind him."[109] A few days later, on February 7, Sukarno wrote to Suharto with an offer to surrender day-to-day control of the government while retaining broad authority to determine the direction of the Indonesian revolution. Suharto rejected the offer because it did nothing to end the "dualism" in national leadership.[110] Meanwhile parliament, recently fortified by 108 new members appointed directly by Suharto, called for a special session of the assembly to remove Sukarno from office entirely. What followed was an intense series of negotiations between Suharto, Sukarno, and key military and political leaders— the details of which remain shrouded in mystery even decades later. Sukarno ultimately preempted the assembly and invited Suharto and the leaders of the navy, air force, and police to the presidential palace to witness him signing an order surrendering power to Suharto.[111] The president announced the transfer of power to what one participant remembered was a "speechless, silent" cabinet on February 22.[112] Slowly and then suddenly, the Sukarno era came to an end.

The special session of the assembly proceeded on March 7 in an environment of extraordinary tension. Some 80,000 troops were in Jakarta. The army and marines were poised for conflict on the streets of the capital, and the navy armada was floating in the harbor at Tanjung Priok. Elements of the military certainly would have rallied behind Sukarno if he had attempted to retain power by force of arms. Indonesia seemed to be teetering once again on the brink of civil war.[113] Aware that he could not yet monopolize power, Suharto chose to chart a middle path. He spoke to the assembly and said Sukarno would relinquish executive power but would not be prosecuted.[114] Days of contentious debate followed. When the session ended, the assembly withdrew its mandate from Sukarno and banned him from political activities until the election scheduled for 1968. Indonesia's founding father was shortly thereafter divested of his many titles and placed under "political quarantine"—essentially house arrest—while his health rapidly deteriorated. Suharto was named acting president.[115] He addressed the assembly and told the delegates that "the trust and honor you have placed in us is in fact trust and honor in all of ABRI."[116] He knew of what he spoke: Indonesia was now ruled by a military government whose raison d'être was anticommunism.

But Suharto did not possess total authority. The leaders of the navy, air force, and police had united against Sukarno, but their loyalty to Suharto was anything but guaranteed. The bosses of established political parties continued to vie for influence, to which they believed they were entitled for their role in destroying the PKI, while the New Order radicals in the army demanded all existing political parties be disbanded. Although student protest lulled for a time after Suharto was declared acting president, the action fronts continued to menace Indonesia's hard-won stability.[117] Without the unifying enemy of Sukarno, the New Order coalition threatened to dissolve. The question of what Indonesia's political system would look like post-Sukarno remained largely unresolved.

Conflict over the contours of the Indonesian political system resumed as soon as Suharto was declared acting president. Army leaders had fleshed out their political program at the Second Army Seminar in August 1966, where Suwarto established a political syndicate led by General Daryatmo. Influenced by the work of American modernization theorists who emphasized the importance of political order as a prerequisite to economic development, the syndicate advocated a wholesale dismantling of Indonesia's party system and a deep program of de-Sukarnoization. It proposed replacing Indonesia's proportional representation system with a single-member district system and remodeling the legislature to limit elected representatives to only 50 percent of the seats in parliament—institutional changes that would pose a fundamental threat to the power of Indonesia's established political parties.[118] Suharto's allies in parliament introduced bills to this effect in early 1967.

The PNI and NU remained in thrall to the army's burgeoning power and mounted little opposition. In March 1967, Koti described NU as likely to "continue to practice a politics of looking for opportunities for advantage" and "easily persuaded to compromise."[119] Opsus had begun channeling funds to the PNI-owned Bank Umum Nasional, which was in danger of collapse amid the ongoing economic calamity, in order to render the party dependent upon state financial support.[120] PNI leader Osa returned the favor, telling the press in July that he believed it was important that the public "give the new Ampera Cabinet an opportunity to work."[121]

More threatening than PNI and NU was what remained of Masyumi, the modernist Muslim party banned by Sukarno for involvement in the regional rebellions of the late 1950s. Beginning in 1966, former Masyumi leaders petitioned the army to allow them to reconstitute their party.[122] Suharto refused. He wrote to a Masyumi leader who had served as vice prime minister in the early 1950s and asserted the New Order would not tolerate any groups that had rebelled against the legitimate government.[123] But it quickly became clear that the modernist Muslim community would not abide perpetual political marginalization. Former president Mohammad Hatta proposed the creation of a new political party that would include modernist Muslims as well as displaced socialists. Other modernist figures joined with New Order radicals in the army to establish Komando Jihad, an umbrella group for modernist Islamic youth organizations engaged in the anti-Sukarno struggle.[124] Djarnawi Hadikusuma, the leader of Muhammadiyah, a mass organization of modernist Muslims whose members often voted for Masyumi in the 1950s, sent a missive to Suharto noting that modernists had "stood behind you in destroying the adventures of the Gestapu/ PKI/anti-God group" and requesting permission to create a new political vehicle to represent modernist Muslims.[125] Suharto knew he lacked the capacity to suppress escalating modernist mobilization. In July 1967, he addressed the leadership of Muhammadiyah and explained that the government would allow the creation of a new "partisan vessel that can unite and accommodate all existing Islamic forces and organizations that have not been incorporated into a party."[126] Contentious negotiations ensued between army officials and modernist leaders over which Masyumi figures would be permitted to join the new party and whether they would be allowed to assume leadership roles. Eventually, the Muslim Party of Indonesia (Parmusi) was established under Djarnawi's leadership in February 1968.[127]

Even Indonesia's neutered parties resisted the proposals emanating from the Second Army Seminar. Replacing the proportional representation system with a single-member district system would revoke the power of party leaders to determine which candidates assumed seats in parliament. It would also open pathways to power for candidates who claimed popularity at the local level but possessed no meaningful connections with party leaders. After Suharto held a series of meetings with party leaders between March and June 1967, he was forced to disavow the political syndicate's recommendations. He explained at a press conference in July that he was not "anti-party."[128] Ultimately, the government and the parties agreed to a compromise that allowed the government to appoint 100 of the 460 members of parliament, with the remainder being chosen through a proportional representation system.[129] Yet Suharto also worked to ensure that renewed political contestation would not threaten his hold on power. At the same press conference in which he distanced himself from the New Order radicals' proposals for a renovation of the party system, he announced that it was unlikely that elections could be held by the July 1968 statutory deadline.[130]

The nature of the political system Suharto aimed to establish was one he dubbed Pancasila Democracy. He emphasized that Pancasila Democracy differed from liberal democracy in that it "reflects and represents all interests of the Indonesian people" and "puts the people's interest first and not group or private interests." Free and fair elections, an independent press, and programmatic political parties had no place in this system. Suharto insisted that elections must "guarantee the success of the New Order's struggle," the press must "reflect the orthodoxy of the New Order," and Pancasila must serve as the "ideology of each political party and all other organizations."[131] Scholars often suggest that Pancasila Democracy reflected Suharto's ideological predilections—particularly his sense that liberal democracy's individualistic underpinnings were alien to Indonesia's sociocultural fabric.[132] But the question remains: why democracy at all? Certainly, the Indonesian population was accustomed to rhetorical invocations of democracy, as were many of the New Order's creditors and donors. The answer also lies in the contingent rhythms of Indonesia's engagement with the outside world in the two years following the September Thirtieth Movement. In the context of persistent economic challenges, centrifugal tendencies within the New Order coalition, and still-limited access to international capital, the army lacked the capacity and legitimacy to mount a bid for a regime entirely autonomous of Indonesia's existing political parties. The system of Pancasila Democracy was the result of Suharto's need to square modest means and maximum ends.

VI

As Suharto worked to establish what in Indonesian discourse was called a "political format," he continued to seek international aid and investment to abet his consolidation of power. His economic recovery program was beginning to succeed as monthly inflation subsided to 1 percent in April 1967—even before the wet season rice harvest that usually brought declines in food prices. But a combination of fiscal austerity and monetary tightening strangled economic activity and brought further political difficulties. Military figures mounted a challenge to the market-oriented policies favored by the Berkeley Mafia at a cabinet meeting in May 1967, and the Siliwangi division passed a resolution lamenting the effects of the New Order's economic policies on "social and political stability."[133] Only by driving forward economic development could Suharto maintain the unity of the increasingly fractious New Order coalition.

After the passage of the Foreign Investment Law, New Order officials began canvassing for international investment. In this effort they found an ally in the American ambassador, who according to the Indonesian government spent a period of leave in the United States "providing information about the situation and opportunities in Indonesia."[134] The earliest interest came from American, British, West German, and Australian firms, though most preferred to wait until their governments had negotiated investment guarantees with the Indonesian government.[135]

The first bona fide international investor in Indonesia was Freeport Sulphur. In June 1966, the American firm submitted a request to the Indonesian government to mine copper ore deposits at the Ertsberg mine in the Carstenz mountain range in West Papua. A Freeport employee surveyed the area in the early 1960s, but the technological difficulties of mining copper in such a remote, rugged location and the political instability of the wider archipelago led Freeport to shelve the project. Negotiations between Freeport and Indonesian officials resumed in the wake of Suharto's takeover. In March 1967, the two parties inked an agreement drafted entirely by Freeport.[136] The agreement obligated Freeport to invest approximately $76.5 million in the mine and granted the firm a three-year tax holiday. In exchange, Freeport would pay the Indonesian government either 35 percent of net profits or 5 percent of net sales, rising to 41.75 percent of net profits or 10 percent of net sales after ten years—generous provisions that contradicted key planks of the Foreign Investment Law.[137] Indonesian authorities justified the exemptions by citing the uncertainty of Jakarta's sovereignty over West Papua. One economic policymaker added that "a quick agreement with Freeport will add to the reputation of the Government in its efficiency of implementing foreign direct investment projects."[138] The gamble succeeded. The Ertsberg turned out to be the largest copper mine in the world, and Freeport proposed an additional investment of $150 million in 1968.[139] The Suharto regime soon attracted interest in other mining projects in Sulawesi, Sumatra, Kalimantan, and beyond.[140]

Indonesian officials also began courting firms in other industries. In April 1967, the oil magnate Julius Tahija led a delegation to Sydney to attend a Pacific Industrial Conference sponsored by the Stanford Research Institute (SRI).

Tahija delivered a presentation on the Foreign Investment Law that garnered an enthusiastic reception, and the SRI agreed to sponsor a meeting of the Pacific Indonesia Business Association (PIBA) in August. The meeting attracted more than 170 executives from fourteen different countries and led to the creation of an Investment Promotion Council (IPC) within PIBA. The IPC began acting as an intermediary between international firms and Mohammad Sadli's Technical Team for Foreign Investment, which supervised foreign investment into Indonesia. The council presented a report concluding that "the internal situation in Indonesia is not yet ideal for capital investment," although it detected among foreign investors a "conviction and confidence toward the good intention and determination of the Government which will be able to provide the necessary condition required for economic development." Among the regulatory changes the IPC recommended were revisions to the corporation law, alterations to labor regulations, and an overhaul of the tax system.[141] IPC members also embarked upon what Tahija colorfully dubbed "investment safaris" to court multinational firms considering investing in Indonesia.[142]

It was not only technocratic figures who sought out private international capital. In April 1967, an Opsus delegation led by Colonel Suhardiman traveled across Asia, Europe, and the Middle East to "search for credit and natural resource markets." Their vehicle was PTPP Berdikari, a military trading company established the year before to take over assets expropriated from Sukarno cronies.[143] Over the course of their journey, Suhardiman and his colleagues received credits worth at least $40 million.[144] Later that year, a group of Taiwanese investors arrived in Indonesia as guests of PTPP Berdikari and promised credits worth $20 million, but the deal fell through as a result of the Taiwanese government's insistence that Indonesia withdraw its support from the People's Republic of China at the United Nations.[145] PTPP Berdikari eventually fell within the ambit of the National Logistics Board (Bulog), established in 1967 to stabilize the prices of basic commodities like rice and sugar. Under the command of General Achmad Tirtosudiro, Bulog became a critical reservoir of what an IMF representative called "extra budgetary" funding in the New Order.[146] On one occasion, Bulog borrowed from the central bank at a low rate of interest and then deposited the funds in accounts at private banks that accrued higher rates of interest. When several of these banks collapsed and undermined Bulog's carry trade, the institution was left without the capital necessary to finance some of its rice purchases. The Berdikari-Bulog scandal garnered unfavorable public attention and underlined how Suharto and the army used foreign investment to both drive economic recovery and consolidate their authority.[147]

The most important military-controlled institution that generated foreign exchange was the state oil company. When the September Thirtieth Movement struck, control over Indonesia's oil industry was divided between three state enterprises: Permigan, Pertamin, and Permina, each of which had negotiated profit-sharing agreements with major international oil firms. General Ibnu Sutowo of Permina cannibalized Permigan and Pertamin's production and overseas marketing rights over the course of 1966 and subsequently absorbed Permigan entirely. Ibnu then negotiated production-sharing agreements with smaller, independent oil companies for offshore production in the Java Sea—a novelty in the global oil market. Sharing production rather than profit meant the military-controlled Indonesian oil companies rather than the technocrat-dominated Ministry of Finance would lay first claim to most of the country's oil revenue.[148] An American diplomat soon dubbed Ibnu "Mr. Oil in Indonesia."[149]

Nasution, the Berkeley Mafia technocrats, Minister of Mines Slamet Bratanata, and Pertamin chief Saleh Siregar soon mounted bureaucratic challenges to Ibnu's steadily expanding control over Indonesia's oil industry. They regarded his freewheeling financial practices as a threat to Indonesia's fragile credibility among international donors, creditors, and investors. They also preferred to rely on international firms rather than domestic industry—an early manifestation of an emerging conflict between technocrats amenable to free trade and economic nationalists like Ibnu, who remembered thinking that "management must be in our hands."[150] The Permina chief fended off his rivals by mid-1967, largely because Suharto viewed Ibnu as an asset in his political struggle. Ibnu became a vital source of off-budget financing for the Suharto regime. As he put it to a *Wall Street Journal* reporter in early 1967, "I wouldn't say that I have financed the Army; you could say rather that I have simply helped it a bit. It has become a habit for Army officers and Ministers to come to me for assistance. What can I do? I have the funds they need for their roads. The central financial authorities don't give them the money they need, so I must."[151]

The excitement with which foreign investors regarded the new Indonesia became clear in late 1967. A year earlier, *Time-Life* publisher James Linen traveled to Bali at Hamengkubuwono's invitation. Upon his return, he suggested to American officials that "*Time-Life* might play a useful role in encouraging American private investment in Indonesia." The publisher explained that "he had in mind a grouping of major American companies which could help to develop American interest in Indonesian economic development."[152] Conversations between representatives of the American and Indonesian governments and *Time-Life* progressed over the following months, and Linen's idea for a gathering of American firms was broadened to include representatives of European, Australian, and Japanese business interests.[153] The result was an Indonesian Investment Conference held in Geneva in November 1967 to which Sadli remembered that "Linen invited all his friends and cronies."[154] Hamengkubuwono, Malik, Sadli, and more than fifteen other Indonesian officials traveled to Geneva to hobnob with senior executives from banks like Lehman Brothers and Chase Manhattan, petroleum conglomerates like Shell and Standard Oil, and logging and mining firms like Weyerhauser and Freeport. These luminaries of capital listened to Indonesians describe the archipelago's wealth of human and natural resources and participated in roundtables on topics like manufacturing, finance, extractive industries, and taxation. At every instance, the Indonesians emphasized their determination to preserve political stability and economic openness—if necessary by suppressing opposition to their agenda of development. They also appealed to business leaders' sense of responsibility for the stewardship of the international capitalist system. "It is inconceivable to me," Chase president David Rockefeller summed up, "that the impression they have made on such a group as this will not result in a very warm response in terms of investment."[155]

The investment conference evolved into an annual roundtable between Indonesian officials and Business International, a publishing and advisory firm headquartered in New York that catered to multinational enterprises. The first of these roundtables was held in Jakarta in September 1968.[156] Japanese investors also grew particularly interested in Indonesia. The Keidanren (Federation of Economic Organizations, which represented more than 700 large enterprises) established an Indonesia Committee in October 1967 and secured meetings with Sadli and other members of the Technical Team for Foreign Investment shortly thereafter.[157] Burgeoning investor interest in Indonesia was evident in bookings at Hotel Indonesia, the standard accommodation for foreign businesspeople visiting Jakarta, where reservations increasingly had to be made one or two months in advance. By mid-1968, thirty-four foreign investment projects worth approximately $150 million had won government approval.[158] To continue courting international investors, the Suharto regime established Foreign Investment Service bureaus at Indonesian embassies and consulates in The Hague, Geneva, Paris, London, New York, Washington, San Francisco, and Tokyo.

Table 3.1 **Capital flows to Indonesia, 1966–1969 (millions of US dollars)**

	1966	1967	1968	1969
Aid	96*	273	298	325
Debt Repayment		−54	−75	−40
Net Private Capital	50	100	33	55
Net Capital Flows	146	319	256	340

* The $96 million aid figure in 1966 represents aid less debt repayment.

Source: Lawrence J. White, "Problems and Prospects of the Indonesian Foreign Exchange System," *Indonesia* no. 14 (October 1972): 131.

But progress in attracting foreign investment remained slow. One investor remarked that dealing with Indonesia's still-plodding bureaucracy was akin to "wading through syrup."[159] Given the time lag between the proposal, approval, and realization of foreign investment projects, international aid remained Suharto's most important source of international capital—and the key resource that would enable Suharto to deepen his Cold War. After the February 1967 meeting of the IGGI in Amsterdam, Suharto and other leading figures within the New Order continued to canvass for international aid.

VII

The two-track Paris Club and IGGI system proved extraordinarily cumbersome for Indonesian diplomats. Because the Paris Club rescheduled only one-third of Indonesia's total debt to Western countries, it was certain that Indonesia would need to renegotiate additional debt rescheduling agreements beginning in 1969. The IGGI was even more onerous. After creditor countries reached an accord on delivering $200 million in aid to Indonesia in 1967, New Order officials engaged in bilateral negotiations with no fewer than thirteen individual governments to iron out the terms of particular aid commitments. Because each country offered loans or grants under different political, economic, and legal constraints, these negotiations served as a study in managing complexity. One missive to Hamengkubuwono went so far as to advise the sultan that, in light of the logistical challenges facing Indonesian negotiators, "we should not make Indonesia's economic stabilization/rehabilitation plan dependent on offers of assistance or fresh credits."[160] In Japan, for instance, legal restrictions precluded the government from offering loans at the low rate promised by the IGGI, so the government of Prime Minister Eisaku Sato had to offer a portion of its aid in grant form in order to bring down the total effective rate of interest. Moreover, parliamentary challenges and bureaucratic conflicts between the Foreign Ministry and the Ministry of International Trade and Industry also meant the Sato government struggled to meet its commitment to furnish one-third of IGGI aid.[161]

The results of such a byzantine system became clear shortly before the IGGI met in June 1967 to review aid commitments to Indonesia. Only $126 million of the promised $200 million had been delivered. Delays in the delivery of aid interrupted economic planners' efforts to craft budgets and make financial projections, which resulted in difficult choices between taking inflation-generating advances from the central bank or sacrificing imports of fertilizer and spare parts vital for economic rehabilitation.[162] Indonesian officials hurried to organize a preliminary meeting with representatives of creditor countries and expressed "great anxiety with the pace at which agreements on new assistance have been concluded so far."[163] "It was obvious," remembered Widjojo, that such an arrangement "could not become the basis of a viable long-term settlement of Indonesia's debt crisis."[164]

The June 1967 IGGI meeting succeeded in bridging the gap between collective aspirations and individual commitments of aid to Indonesia. But no sooner did the meeting adjourn than Indonesian officials prepared to begin the whole process anew.[165] In July, the Indonesian ambassador in Washington, Suwito Kusomowidagdo, met with American policymakers to request additional aid for 1968. He was told that the Vietnam War was generating extraordinary budgetary pressures that would make it difficult for the United States to meet its aid commitments in forms other than PL-480 food aid.[166] Indonesian diplomats held similar meetings with their counterparts in the Netherlands, Italy, Belgium, Switzerland, West Germany, and Japan.[167] Representatives of the New Order also began broadening their focus beyond bureaucrats to the populations of aid-granting countries. "Our diplomacy is now aimed at the American people," said Suwito of his embassy's efforts to attract investors, tourists, and ordinary people to Indonesia.[168] In Europe, a key concern was an upsurge of anti-Indonesia activism. The army reported that PKI elements continued to engage in "guerrilla politics" outside of Indonesia and foment antipathy toward the New Order among students and youth, especially in the Indonesian diaspora. It recommended a "Special Operation" to "completely destroy G30S/PKI political guerrillas abroad, especially in Europe" and "defend international faith in Indonesia."[169]

Not all aid-seeking ventures proved as onerous as Indonesia's negotiations with its Western creditors. As New Order officials turned their sights from economic stabilization to economic development, they worked to build relationships with the World Bank, which Indonesia rejoined in April 1967. The following month, Indonesia invited the institution to send a mission to Jakarta to "study our economic performance and prospects" and help draft the government budget for 1968. World Bank economists spent five weeks in Indonesia evaluating specific development projects and producing a 130-page report on Suharto's economic stabilization program. They concluded that Indonesia would require between $500 and $750 million per year in foreign assistance between 1969 and 1973—up to four times the sum the IGGI pledged for 1967.[170] Meanwhile, private development enterprises began dispatching teams to Indonesia. The most important were the Harvard Development Advisory Service and a Dutch team under the leadership of Jan Tinbergen.[171] Although their presence was small at first, these teams would work closely with Indonesian technocrats and their counterparts in the IMF and the World Bank in drafting economic development plans.

But the United States remained the most important donor given its coordinating role within the IGGI. Suharto and his allies raised the communist bogey to loosen the purse strings on American aid. Ambassador Green recalled that Indonesian frustrations over delays in aid disbursement meant that "I found myself denied access to Suharto for several months" beginning in early 1967. The military men who blocked Green from the palace told him that no meeting could be arranged unless he would be "the bearer of good news." Only in July did Green finally secure an audience with Suharto.[172] The acting president "expressed doubt as to whether we [the United States] attached sufficiently high priority to Indonesia." He lamented that "I have regarded [the] US as potentially our greatest friend, but if I cannot be sure of your assistance then I will have to make another plan."[173] A week later, Sudjono Humardani and Ali Murtopo traveled to the United States and appealed directly to Vice President Humphrey, National Security Advisor Walt Rostow, and key leaders in Congress.[174] President Johnson regarded Indonesia as a "showcase" and wanted to increase aid to the New Order. But the Vietnam War continued to exhaust vast sums of the foreign aid budget and inspire congressional attempts to curb overseas spending.[175] In September, Suharto warned Green that, if the United States did not exceed its commitment to meet one-third of Indonesia's aid needs through the IGGI, the "New Order would be in serious trouble."[176] Green traveled to Washington and urged the cabinet to find a way to meet Indonesia's aid requests. "This is Indonesia's critical hour of need," he said, and "our sacrifices in Vietnam avail little if we do not take strong and swift steps to foster the growth and strength which the new Indonesia can achieve."[177]

Green's diagnosis hit the mark: the New Order confronted a critical juncture. Inflation had been brought under control, but at considerable social cost. Unemployment persisted at distressingly high levels. Wages for soldiers and bureaucrats were, in real terms, lower than ever; smuggling and corruption remained widespread. Industry continued to operate at below 50 percent of capacity. The country's infrastructure was still in what one observer called "appalling condition." Foreign exchange shortages depressed fertilizer imports, which drove food production down and prices up.[178] Moreover, just as the New Order appeared to break the back of inflation, a rice crisis threatened the country's hard-won stability. A long drought at the beginning of the wet season generated expectations for a meager off-season rice crop and led to speculation-driven increases in food prices in September 1967.[179] Because commodity exporters, manufacturers, and the government paid many employees in kind, increasing rice prices drove wage costs up across the archipelago and strained the state budget. Combined with sagging world prices for rubber, a key Indonesian export, prospects for the country's economic takeoff appeared dramatically worse in the last quarter of 1967 than they had only a few months earlier.[180] And economic difficulties brought concomitant political tensions. Action fronts began protesting food shortages and decrying the

Table 3.2 **Rice prices in Jakarta**

Date	Price of 1 Kilogram of Rice in Jakarta Retail Markets (Rupiah)
May 31, 1967	17.50
September 30, 1967	30
October 31, 1967	35
November 31, 1967	46.25
December 31, 1967	47.50
January 31, 1968	86.25

Source: J. Panglaykim, D. H. Penny, and Dahlan Thalib, "Survey of Recent Developments," *Bulletin of Indonesian Economic Studies* 4, no. 9 (February 1968): 26.

corruption they saw enveloping the emerging New Order.[181] "If the price of rice does not go down the Government should go," exclaimed a KAMI leader to approximately 1,000 demonstrators who breached the veranda of the cabinet office in late September.[182]

It was in this milieu that Indonesian officials once again traveled to Europe to attend a meeting of the Paris Club in October and the IGGI the following month. In Paris, Indonesia's creditors agreed to extend the same terms under which they had rescheduled the country's debts falling due in 1967 to debts falling due in 1968—and all but promised to offer the same terms to Indonesian debts coming due in 1969 and 1970.[183] The next month, in Amsterdam, Indonesian officials lodged a request for $325 million in aid for 1968, broken down by $250 million for balance-of-payments support and $75 million for specific infrastructural and development projects, especially surrounding agricultural irrigation and fertilizer production.[184] The IMF tepidly endorsed these requests as "not unreasonable," and American negotiators expressed their willingness to continue meeting their commitment to furnish one-third of Indonesia's aid requirements. But Japanese diplomats doubted their government could meet its one-third share of this enlarged commitment, and several European representatives announced their governments did not plan to increase aid to Indonesia. Donor countries ultimately agreed to "take note" of the $325 million request "in connection with decisions they would make as to their responses to the Government of Indonesia's request for assistance."[185] This nonbinding formulation reflected the increasing contention among and within donor countries over the trajectory of international aid to Indonesia. Even so, the consensus surrounding the figure requested by the Indonesian government represented a vote of confidence in Suharto's stabilization and rehabilitation program.

In between the Paris Club and IGGI meetings, Suharto welcomed Hubert Humphrey to Jakarta—the first vice presidential visit to Indonesia since Richard Nixon traveled to the archipelago in 1953.[186] Humphrey sympathized with the New Order. Earlier in the year, he had lamented "the great timidity of the United States Government on the question of Indonesia and a lack of interest in some circles."[187] Suharto expressed hope that the United States could furnish $150 of the $325 million in aid the IGGI endorsed for 1968. "If progress is not achieved in 1968," he warned, "there could be the most serious consequences." Humphrey told Suharto that ongoing legislative processes prevented him from making a firm aid commitment, but he promised that "a strong effort would be made, both at home and to enlist [the] support of other nations."[188] On his return, Humphrey told a joint meeting of the National Security Council (NSC), the cabinet, and senior lawmakers that the "stakes are very high in Indonesia; as high as those in Japan and India."[189] Johnson was convinced. He wrote a simple memo to his national security advisor: "I want to do everything I can for Indonesia—as quickly as I can. Send me a program."[190]

VIII

Renewed infusions of foreign aid and the first signs of foreign investment in the second half of 1967 enabled Suharto to mount his final drive toward the presidency. A month after the June 1967 IGGI meeting that generated additional commitments for disbursements of foreign aid, Suharto hosted a cabinet meeting and outlined a "consolidation phase" to be completed by the beginning of 1968. In working to establish what Suharto called the *Panca Tertib*, or Five Orders—political, economic, social, legal, and military—the Ampera Cabinet would pursue the stabilization and unification of political authority, the expansion of the bureaucratic-institutional power of the state, the crystallization of the social authority of the New Order, and the "redisciplining" of the country's coercive institutions.[191] Because domestic revenues remained anemic, international capital was vital for Suharto to consolidate his authority.[192] As he explained in a September 1967 cabinet meeting, it was critical to "estimate the amount or source of money from abroad that we can explore and exploit" to further the process of what he called "New Orderization."[193]

The consolidation of authority over the military remained Suharto's foremost concern. Suharto emphasized that the achievement of order in the military sphere would have a "very large influence on the realization of order in other fields." He achieved early success in extending his authority within the army. In early July, the commanders of the three Java-based divisions met in Yogyakarta and agreed to "strengthen the unity of New Order forces" and "take strong actions against any individuals or groups that seek to restore the power of the Old Order and the leadership of Sukarno."[194] On July 20, Suharto met with Kostrad commander Kemal Idris to discuss the "cleansing" of the Indonesian army of Old Order elements, especially the East Java–based Brawijaya division in which Sukarnoist sentiment held considerable sway.[195] Over the following month, Brawijaya commander Mochamad Jasin orchestrated a dramatic purge of the division before calling in a battalion of special forces to mount a show of force against holdout Sukarnoist elements. More broadly, at least seventy-five generals or other senior army leaders were arrested by the end of August.[196]

Suharto also extended his control over the other branches of the Indonesian military. In early September, he announced that the commanders of the army, navy, air force, and police would report to a new minister of defense: himself.[197] The following month, he removed the commanders of individual services from the cabinet.[198] Suharto's ability to subjugate rival branches of the armed forces reflected his control over the foreign-domestic nexus and the steady degradation of the old, Soviet-acquired equipment on which the navy and air force relied. Admiral Mulyadi attempted to circumvent Suharto by traveling to the Soviet Union in late 1967 to request spare parts for vessels in need of repair, but he was told the parts were available exclusively on a cash basis.[199] And as Suharto and the army halted or assumed control over seaborne smuggling—until that point one of the navy's key sources of hard currency—navy leaders found little alternative but to accommodate themselves to Suharto's expanding authority.[200]

As Suharto deepened his hold on Indonesia's political institutions, he elaborated the modus vivendi between the New Order and political parties. Across the second half of 1967, New Order radicals stationed on Sumatra purged local PNI branches of Sukarnoists and even banned the party from operating entirely. In mid-December, PNI leaders met with Suharto and assured him that the party and its associated mass organizations would distance themselves from Sukarno's cult of personality, defend the New Order against the remnants of the PKI, and cultivate a partnership with the armed forces and other branches of the government. Upon receiving these assurances, Suharto instructed regional army commanders to "help and give opportunities to the PNI to undertake the crystallization and consolidation of the New Order within the organization," and he dispatched General Panggabean to Sumatra to negotiate an end to army bans on PNI activities.[201] Army leaders elsewhere also policed the boundaries of political contestation by partisans of NU and Parmusi. In Jakarta, for instance, Amirmachmud banned Komando Jihad and engaged in consultations with local ulama to ensure that devotional addresses steered Muslims away from confrontational forms of politics.[202]

Establishing greater control over the action fronts proved more challenging. Without the common enemy of Sukarno to bind them to the army, some students and youth began protesting the growing militarization and corruption of the New Order.[203] As one April report to the cabinet put it, "both in the capital and in the regions, via gossip and via the press, it is widely said that violations by men in uniform are becoming more prevalent."[204] Suharto continued to court the action fronts in spite of these brewing tensions. He appointed student and youth leaders to parliament and appeared at anniversary celebrations for their organizations.[205] He succeeded in earning the trust of the action fronts. But it quickly became clear that this was a hierarchical form of trust that did not extend to the whole of the New Order.[206] In July and August 1967, KAMI ignored army prohibitions on public protests and staged large demonstrations beseeching Suharto to move forcefully against corruption and purge political parties of PKI sympathizers.[207] A KAMI congress in January 1968 called on the action fronts to rally behind Suharto while urging the acting president to battle inflation, cleanse the corrupt bureaucracy, and reform the structure of parliament. The action fronts continued to regard themselves as a "moral force" and could turn against the New Order if it failed to fulfill their expectations.[208]

As a measure of stability returned to Indonesia's political life, work began on Indonesia's first five-year economic development plan. In July 1967, Suharto appointed Widjojo head of the National Development Planning Agency (Bappenas). The agency became the major institutional body around which Indonesia's other technocrats in the Ministry of Finance, the central bank, and the foreign investment team revolved.[209] One recalled that "it was Widjojo who was the real architect of the economic policies of the New Order. He was the *dalang*, or puppeteer, who directed the play, while we, the other economic technocrats, were the players, the *wayang*."[210] In consultation with economists from the IMF and other bodies, Indonesia's technocrats decided to focus on agricultural development. Agriculture consumed nearly 80 percent of Indonesia's labor and accounted for 70 percent of Indonesia's hard currency earnings. Food shortages were a major source of political ferment in cities. Moreover, Indonesia remained dependent upon rice imports and lacked the capital necessary to pursue a large-scale industrialization drive. The technocrats therefore drew up a plan through which the export of primary commodities like oil and timber would finance the expansion of irrigation networks and the creation of upstream industries like fertilizer production and downstream industries like food processing.[211] Their goals were admittedly modest but nevertheless depended upon foreign capital. In submitting his 1968 budget to parliament, Suharto acknowledged that, because the Indonesian state's ability to extract resources from the population was limited, "without financial assistance from abroad, it is almost impossible for us to revive the economy."[212]

The first three months of 1968 marked the denouement of Suharto's consolidation of power in Indonesia. In January, a renewed rice crisis gripped the capital and other major cities. Having doubled in the last six months of 1967, the price of rice doubled again by the end of January—the result of rumors that the government would soon end disbursements of rice to civil servants and soldiers as part of its austerity program.[213] Action fronts staged three days of "down to the street" protests in Jakarta to demand the government lower the price of this critical staple.[214] Economic challenges did little to arrest Suharto's drive toward the presidency. Throughout January and February, he met with representatives of action fronts, mass organizations, political parties, Islamic groups, and military factions to engage in customary *musyawarah* (consultations) and discuss the future of Indonesian politics.[215] Suharto recalled in his memoirs that he was told repeatedly that "there is no one else" capable of leading Indonesia.[216] But he left nothing to chance. He appointed nearly 200 new members of parliament in early February.[217] The body convened toward the end of the month and passed a resolution calling on the national assembly to undertake a similar "refreshing" of its membership and then convene several months ahead of schedule to appoint Suharto full president, postpone national elections for five years, and endorse the outline of the five-year economic development plan prepared by Widjojo.

The period leading up to the national assembly session revealed Suharto's consolidation of authority. Rosihan Anwar, Indonesia's leading columnist, remarked to a foreign journalist that the mood of hope and exhilaration that accompanied Sukarno's downfall two and a half years earlier had given way to a mood of resignation and frustration.[218] The military clamped down on Jakarta in the days before the assembly convened. Thirty battalions were posted at critical points across the city—at the city's universities and high schools, at all routes in and out of the capital, at the homes of lawmakers, and at vital installations and thoroughfares.[219] Suharto also appointed almost 150 new members to the assembly, ensuring that his allies dominated the proceedings. As Nasution remarked wryly to an aide, "according to the constitution the assembly chooses the president, now the president chooses the assembly."[220] Suharto's forceful tactics did inspire discontent. Leaders of political parties like PNI and NU raised their voices In protest. Action fronts splintered between those who proclaimed the New Orderization of Indonesia's state their foremost objective and those who demanded Suharto hew to constitutional principles. Some action fronts took to the streets to express their displeasure with Suharto and the army's monopolization of power, carrying signs reading "democracy is not arbitrary" and "establish the rule of law."[221] A small group commandeered two fire engines and drove them into a line of soldiers near Hotel Indonesia as foreign businessmen watched from above.[222]

The final showdown between Suharto and his rivals within the New Order coalition took place when the assembly convened in March 1968. In his opening speech, Suharto explained that "differences of opinion among New Order forces must be immediately ended and resolved." He went on to warn his audience that "dark PKI cells continue to work to carry out consolidation and spread subversion among us."[223] Despite his dire warnings about communist intrigue, the key challenge to Suharto's drive for unity came from Nasution, the chairman of the assembly. Dedicated to the provision of the 1945 constitution that the assembly embodied popular sovereignty and determined to create a more inclusive political system, Nasution worked to curb Suharto's emergency powers and impose some legislative constraints on presidential authority.[224]

The weeklong assembly session featured a dizzying array of negotiations on subjects ranging from the role of the assembly to the timing of elections, the place of Islam to the path of economic development, and the extent of regional autonomy to the enumeration of basic rights. No voices were raised in opposition to Suharto's elevation to the presidency or the approval of the five-year development plan. But the assembly deadlocked over two questions: When would elections be held? And how would power be divided between the executive and the legislature? Suharto and his allies advocated a five-year delay in elections during which time Suharto would wield supreme authority. Others favored a three-year delay in elections and proposed imposing limits on Suharto's authority by revoking the *Supersemar*, formalizing Broad Outlines of State Policy (GBHN), and enumerating the basic rights of the citizenry. Under considerable pressure from Suharto's allies, Nasution's camp reached a compromise.

Figure 3.1 Suharto takes the oath of office as president on March 11, 1968, as a religious officer holds a Quran over his head. AFP via Getty Images.

The emergency powers bestowed upon Suharto through the *Supersemar* were restricted to use against communists and those undermining the state, the constitution, and democracy. Elections were postponed for three years rather than the five Suharto preferred. But Suharto was appointed to a full five-year presidential term during which time no legislative guidelines would constrain his authority. He now wielded uncontested power.

Suharto's elevation to the presidency depended on his growing ability to mobilize international capital. Even the timing of the assembly session owed to the imperatives of Indonesia's engagement with the outside world. As renewed economic difficulties faced the New Order in early 1968, Suharto believed a reaffirmation of his authority and an approval of his plans to transform Indonesia were necessary before two key events in April: his first presidential voyage overseas, when he would travel to Japan to court aid and investment, and the fourth meeting of the IGGI, when donor countries would gather in Rotterdam to take stock of Indonesia's request for $325 million in aid for 1968.

None of this was foreordained. The two years following the *Supersemar* witnessed a profound eruption of human energy as Indonesians fashioned a New Order. Many fought for their ideals—for nationalism, for religion, for liberalism, and for justice as they saw it. Others simply fought for an end to Indonesia's slide into chaos and poverty. The churn of protest revealed both the potency and the limits of Suharto's power. He acted as a *dalang*, a puppet-master in traditional Javanese shadow theater, giving direction to the swirl of events from behind the scenes and mobilizing the population against the remnants of the Old Order. But he lacked the institutional capacity and political legitimacy to mount an immediate takeover of the Indonesian state, and he therefore accommodated himself to a rising tide of opposition. In short, this was no mere coup d'état: this was a crisis, a rebellion in which the army was one actor among many. A vast array of different futures suddenly became possible.

What narrowed those possible futures was Indonesia's encounter with the outside world. Suharto mobilized resources made available through the global Cold War to wage his own domestic Cold War. Emergency rice and cotton imports helped stabilize the prices of these basic staples with profound political significance and won the army considerable goodwill. Debt relief agreements enabled Suharto to maintain Indonesia's standing in sovereign credit markets. Renewed infusions of foreign aid then helped Suharto address balance-of-payments challenges and channel resources toward productive investment, both political and otherwise: the rehabilitation of dilapidated infrastructure, the promotion of agriculture and industry, and the distribution of official largesse. As hyperinflation subsided and the green shoots of economic recovery sprouted, Suharto purged the army and began bringing the other branches of the military into line. He coopted political parties and rendered them dependent upon the state, and he began a long effort to tame the enfants terribles of the action fronts. Suharto thus harnessed international capital to win political legitimacy and create a more exclusionary, personalized regime than would otherwise have been possible.

As the first stage of his Cold War came to a close, Suharto began casting his gaze outward. Determined to continue attracting international aid and to preserve the security of his anticommunist stronghold in Indonesia as the Vietnam War reached its crescendo, he began projecting his developmental authoritarian vision outward into Southeast Asia.

4

An Anti-Chinese Axis

"Promise in Indonesia," read the headline in the January 1968 issue of *Foreign Affairs*. In the preeminent American outlet for commentary on international affairs, Indonesian foreign minister Adam Malik bluntly appealed for $110 million in foreign aid from the United States and a "good measure of American equity investment." His arguments were by then familiar to Western observers of Indonesia. Although Sukarno and the PKI had been vanquished, Malik explained, the New Order "has to score substantial successes in the economic field; it has to 'deliver the goods.'" But there was something new in Malik's pitch for Cold War capital. Not only would US aid and investment stabilize a "vital region of the world" by preventing a resurgence of communism in Indonesia itself, but it would also further the Suharto regime's efforts to promote anticommunist stability in a region menaced by leftist insurgencies. Emphasizing that "the task of the Indonesian Government now is to regain the confidence" of the international community, Malik declared that the New Order would adopt a leading role in "working toward the establishment of regional cooperation in Southeast Asia."[1]

Malik's article laid bare the international ambitions embedded within Suharto's Cold War project. Having destroyed the Indonesian communist movement, established a measure of control over the Indonesian state, and subjugated political parties and civil society groups, Suharto cast his gaze beyond the archipelago. Only by ensuring that Indonesia was not surrounded by hostile communist powers could Suharto remain confident in the security of his anticommunist stronghold. What Indonesia required was, in the words of General Benny Murdani, "stability-in-depth."[2]

Suharto believed the People's Republic of China posed the greatest threat to regional stability. China had provided material support to communist insurgencies across the region, and Suharto suspected Beijing of involvement in the September Thirtieth Movement. Going forward, Suharto feared China would mobilize the tens of millions of overseas Chinese who inhabited Southeast

Suharto's Cold War. Mattias Fibiger, Oxford University Press. © Oxford University Press 2023.
DOI: 10.1093/oso/9780197667224.003.0005

Asia to undermine the region's anticommunist governments—evoking long-standing, racially motivated anxieties about regional security.[3] He also doubted Southeast Asia's noncommunist states possessed the capacity or legitimacy to fend off threats from Chinese-sponsored national liberation movements. Suharto therefore worked to construct an anti-Chinese axis in Southeast Asia. He began in the domestic realm, where he subjected Indonesia's ethnic Chinese population to violence and oppression. He then turned to the wider region. Indonesian diplomats helped create a new regional organization whose fundamental purpose was the containment of Chinese influence: the Association of Southeast Asian Nations (ASEAN).

Suharto's regional Cold War both flowed from and fed into his domestic Cold War. The New Order used ASEAN to promulgate the security doctrine of *ketahanan nasional,* or national resilience, which emerged from the Indonesian army's efforts to address the challenge posed by the PKI. And promoting regional cooperation in Southeast Asia would win the New Order goodwill in Washington, Tokyo, Canberra, and beyond. Particularly as the United States and United Kingdom began withdrawing their forces from the region, Suharto believed Indonesia's bid to revive anticommunist regionalism would facilitate the flows of aid and investment upon which his New Order depended.

I

What Suharto called the "Chinese problem" predated the New Order.[4] Between 2 and 3 million ethnic Chinese called Indonesia home in 1965. Although ethnic Chinese had inhabited the archipelago for centuries, *pribumi* (indigenous) Indonesians sometimes regarded them as compradors or fifth columns. The Dutch had encouraged Chinese immigration during the colonial period and bestowed favorable legal status on overseas Chinese, employing some as tax farmers, retail traders, and other economic intermediaries between the colonial state and the indigenous population. In the postcolonial era, ethnic Chinese continued to wield disproportionate influence in the commercial networks that knit the Indonesian economy together and connected the archipelago's primary commodity producers to the wider global market.[5] Meanwhile, the rise of popular nationalism in China at the turn of the twentieth century and the rivalry between Chinese nationalists and communists galvanized segments of the overseas Chinese community in Indonesia. Skepticism about the loyalty of the archipelago's ethnic Chinese population took hold among Indonesian *pribumi* experiencing a national awakening of their own. Sporadic outbreaks of anti-Chinese violence erupted during Indonesia's national revolution in the 1940s and recurred in the 1950s and 1960s. The army-orchestrated politicide that convulsed the archipelago following the September Thirtieth Movement targeted followers of the PKI rather than ethnic Chinese. But the links many Indonesians drew between identity and ideology led some ethnic Chinese to suffer considerable violence, and the relative prosperity of other ethnic Chinese left them vulnerable to intimidation and extortion.[6]

As early as October 1965, action fronts and Islamic groups began targeting symbols of Chinese power in Indonesia. Enraged by the Chinese embassy's refusal to lower its flags to half-mast on the day of the funeral for officers slain by the September Thirtieth Movement, protestors amassed in front of Chinese consular facilities and demanded Sukarno sever ties with the People's Republic. Suharto and other senior army figures bluntly accused China of masterminding the attempted coup and suggested Beijing continued to plot against the Indonesian government. But even after the *Supersemar* endowed him with far-reaching legal authority in March 1966, Suharto did not sever diplomatic relations with communist China. Indonesia's nonaligned posture and its *bebas aktif* (free and active) foreign policy doctrine held profound domestic political resonance. Perceived transgressions of the *bebas aktif* line had inspired protests and even toppled governments during the country's chaotic experiment with parliamentary democracy in the early 1950s. Suharto thus played a balancing act. He sought to undermine Sukarno by castigating him as a handmaiden of Chinese subversion while also cultivating an image as the guardian of Indonesia's nonaligned posture after Sukarno's alleged deviations.

New Order partisans also targeted Indonesia's ethnic Chinese community. In late October 1965, they burned down Res Publica University in Jakarta, run by the Consultative Body for Indonesian Citizenship—an organization devoted to advancing the interests of ethnic Chinese in the archipelago whose official line had hewed toward communism beginning in the late 1950s. Thus began what one Australian observer called a "reign of terror" against ethnic Chinese people and property across Indonesia.[7] Over the spring of 1966, action fronts occupied Chinese-language schools and pressured the government to ban all foreign-operated educational institutions, which deprived some 200,000 ethnic Chinese children of education for the next eighteen months.[8] Army commanders in North Sumatra began rounding up ethnic Chinese for expulsion from Indonesia. The deportees were sent to squalid refugee camps to await deportation. An American diplomat traveling on the northern coast of Java reported that "several new mounds were noted in two Chinese cemeteries," remarking that "their number and freshness were conspicuous enough to raise the possibility that they might have been the fatal results of a recent anti-Chinese action."[9] Toward the end of the year, local army commanders in West Java, South Sulawesi, and West Kalimantan adopted anti-Chinese policies that resembled those pioneered in Sumatra. Suharto issued a statement disavowing these "racialist actions."[10] But the groundswell of anti-Chinese action continued to mount. In January 1967, East Java commander General Sumitro issued a slate of anti-Chinese policies that he dubbed a "New Year's gift": imposing a head tax of approximately $320 on Chinese nationals, prohibiting ethnic Chinese from engaging in trade outside the provincial capital, closing all Chinese temples and religious sites, and banning speaking or writing in Chinese.[11]

Ethnic Chinese communities mobilized against repression over the early months of 1967. One ethnic Chinese man wrote Suharto a letter comparing the treatment of his coethnics to that of Jews under Hitler and appealing for a halt to the "scapegoating."[12] Ethnic Chinese traders protested against mounting restrictions on their ability to do business. After an ethnic Chinese man was arrested for distributing incendiary pamphlets in April and committed suicide in custody by dousing himself with boiling water, the ethnic Chinese residents of Jakarta began staging more aggressive demonstrations. But the protests only stoked what Nasution called the "exclusivism" of the Indonesian masses.[13] *Pribumi* counterprotests quickly devolved into ferocious communal violence. Marauding bands of indigenous Indonesian youth rampaged through Jakarta's Chinese quarter, smashing shop windows and beating ethnic Chinese, killing at least three. Anti-Chinese rampages occurred across the archipelago.[14]

Suharto found himself caught between his anticommunist and developmental impulses. He garnered nationalist legitimacy by positioning himself as the guardian of *pribumi* interests, and his anticommunist coalition favored the expropriation of Indonesia's ethnic Chinese community. Koti reported in late April 1967 that overseas Chinese engaged in a range of subversive economic activities such as speculation, shadow banking, and smuggling. The body concluded that ethnic Chinese in Indonesia represented a subversive political force and "a vital tool for the implementation of Beijing's strategy in Southeast Asia."[15] An Indonesian technocrat spoke to an Australian diplomat around the same time and "painted a pretty cold-blooded nationalistic picture of a long[-]range intention decided at [the] army seminar in Bandung [in August 1966] to wrest business out of the hands of the alien Chinese and give it to Indonesians."[16] But Indonesia lacked an indigenous capitalist class. Violence against the archipelago's ethnic Chinese community risked generating an exodus of capital and expertise, which would exacerbate the country's foreign exchange shortages, fuel further economic disintegration, and quite possibly alienate the international creditors and investors vital to the country's economic recovery. As *The Economist* surmised, "It would be a bold foreign capitalist ready to take over Indonesia's small-scale and decapitalized industry and commerce from which the enterprising Chinese community is being driven out."[17]

Suharto squared this circle by harnessing ethnic Chinese capital to his Cold War ambitions. He offered *cukong*—ethnic Chinese capitalists—favorable access to licenses, contracts, concessions, and credits and enabled them to build up diversified conglomerates whose reach would eventually extend into every nook and cranny of the Indonesian economy. In return for access and protection, *cukong* channeled a portion of their profits back into the coffers of the New Order. This centralized reservoir of resources enabled Suharto to finance military expenditures and a range of other clientelist obligations while imposing a measure of discipline on unbridled rent-seeking by senior civil servants whose monthly salaries usually covered less than a week of expenses.[18]

The broad masses of ethnic Chinese in Indonesia received no such reprieve. Suharto established a State Committee for Chinese Affairs and charged the body with ensuring that the "Chinese problem does not become a force that harms the aspirations of the Indonesian nation."[19] It formulated an array of policies designed to undermine ethnic Chinese political and economic power and promote assimilation into the Indonesian body politic. In June 1967, Suharto banned entry permits for new Chinese immigrants, shuttered all foreign schools and social organizations, froze Chinese capital across the archipelago, and mandated that all Chinese in Indonesia be referred to by the derogatory term *Cina* rather than the long-standing, gentler *Tionghoa*.[20] Six months later, noting that "Chinese religion, beliefs, and traditional customs in Indonesia which focus on the country of their ancestors ... can give rise to inappropriate psychological, mental, and moral influences on Indonesian citizens," Suharto issued more discriminatory regulations forbidding the public observance of Chinese religious practices or the public celebration of Chinese religious festivals. He also ordered ethnic Chinese to adopt indigenous-sounding Indonesian names.[21] The repression of ordinary ethnic Chinese served Suharto's anticommunist objectives while also keeping *cukong* in line by reminding them of their vulnerability as pariah capitalists.

Sectarian conflict within Indonesia contributed to a deterioration in Sino-Indonesian relations. Action fronts repeatedly laid siege to Chinese consular facilities in the months following the September Thirtieth Movement. But the People's Republic adopted a generally restrained posture toward these attacks, casting them as the work of a "small clique" of right-wing elements. Beijing abandoned its moderate approach following the *Supersemar* and an attack on the Chinese embassy in April 1966 in which a Chinese diplomat was shot while protecting his country's flag.[22] Chinese propaganda began inveighing against the "fascist regime" in Jakarta and denouncing the violence directed against Indonesia's ethnic Chinese population. As the Cultural Revolution churned in China and pulled the Foreign Ministry into its orbit in January 1967, Chinese denunciations of the New Order grew increasingly strident before culminating in a call on the Indonesian people to embark upon a program of Maoist guerrilla warfare against the New Order.[23] Convinced that Beijing's propaganda contributed to the surge of ethnic Chinese activism in early 1967, Suharto declared two leading Chinese diplomats personae non gratae in April.[24] Conscious of the need to maintain Indonesia's nonaligned image while his grip on power remained insecure, however, he did not break diplomatic ties with communist China. Suharto also worked to ensure that outright violence against ethnic Chinese Indonesians ebbed in order to preserve the New Order's international legitimacy. One report to the cabinet suggested that communist sympathizers incited Chinese protests in order to provoke violent reactions by the army, Islamic groups, and action fronts, which would "show the world that Indonesia . . . undertakes fascist actions." The report concluded that "it is hoped that the world's view of Indonesia could thus be changed" and the Suharto regime could be starved of vital aid and investment.[25] If Suharto wanted to use resources made available through the global Cold War to continue waging his domestic Cold War, the suppression of Indonesia's ethnic Chinese population needed to be achieved without excessive violence.

Suharto's anticommunist allies in civil society held no such calculus and continued to mobilize against all things Chinese. Action fronts stormed the Chinese embassy in Jakarta in August 1967 and set two buildings alight. Chinese diplomats defended themselves by firing on the intruders, killing four.[26] The following month, Indonesia suspended trade with the People's Republic as anticommunist generals began establishing commercial relationships with Taiwan—although Malik insisted that this was not a prelude toward diplomatic recognition.[27] On October 1, thousands of club-swinging action front cadres stormed the Chinese embassy for the forty-third time and roughed up diplomats, smashed equipment, burned automobiles, and raised the Indonesian flag over the compound. After five hours, Indonesian troops who had been watching the melee unfold finally took over the embassy, boarded up the building, and lowered the Indonesian flag.[28] The Ampera Cabinet announced later that day, exactly two years after the September Thirtieth Movement thrust Indonesia into an uncertain future, that Jakarta would "freeze" its relations with Beijing.[29]

II

Suharto began extending his Cold War beyond Indonesia even before Sino-Indonesian relations collapsed. The first indications of his regional aims emerged in the diplomacy that brought an end to *Konfrontasi*. When Colonel Ali Murtopo met with Philippine officials in Bangkok in April 1966, he suggested a peaceful resolution of *Konfrontasi* would enable Southeast Asia's noncommunist states to band together against China.[30] The proposal struck a chord with other Southeast Asian leaders. Alarmed at what they saw as Chinese-sponsored aggression in Vietnam and Chinese-supported subversion among the region's overseas Chinese communities, Malaysian and Thai officials had already begun floating the idea of revitalizing either Maphilindo or the Association of Southeast Asia (ASA)—two regional organizations founded in the early 1960s that had quickly sputtered into irrelevance.[31] Philippine diplomats had also expressed interest in a renewed effort at regionalization. Once Ferdinand Marcos ascended to the presidency in 1965, he de-emphasized his predecessor's irredentist claim to the Malaysian state of Sabah and pursued a broader reorientation of Philippine foreign policy toward renewed partnership with the United States and cooperation with other anticommunist states in Southeast Asia.[32] Suharto was determined to further the regionalist project. Arguing "with real conviction," an American interlocuter reported, he asserted in May 1966 that the "sole reason" he sought an end to *Konfrontasi* was to "pave [the] way for closer association with neighboring countries against [the] menace of Communist China."[33] When he hosted Deputy Prime Minister Tun Abdul Razak in Jakarta in August 1966 to re-establish formal diplomatic ties between Indonesia and Malaysia, Suharto announced that Indonesian foreign policy would work toward the creation of a "cooperative and mutually beneficial relationship among the states of Southeast Asia" so that "this region can stand strong in the face of outside influence or intervention, both economic and military, from wherever they may come."[34]

Momentum toward the creation of a new regional organization built in late 1966. In December, General Panggabean told Indonesian army officers at Seskoad that "there is a need to have a joint defense organization among countries in Southeast Asia in view of the fact that the People's Republic of China is now strongly engaged in strengthening its influence in this part of the world," notably by mobilizing the region's overseas Chinese communities. Panggabean went so far as to claim that the Indonesian military should "be able to operate in any neighboring country needing defense assistance"—a suggestion Malik and his aides in the Foreign Ministry quickly disavowed. Aware of the domestic political resonance of the country's *bebas aktif* foreign policy doctrine and regional wariness about Indonesian expansionism, the foreign minister asserted that Indonesia would never join a military pact.[35] As he explained to a Western diplomat, "so long as some of these Asians have bilateral defence arrangements with the Western powers, Indonesia cannot go in with them" because "to do so would be to expose the new regime here to criticism and attack."[36]

Malik then took charge of negotiating Indonesia's reintegration into networks of diplomacy in Southeast Asia. He had already dismissed the idea of revitalizing either Maphilindo or ASA and instead joined with Thai foreign minister Thanat Khoman to draw up a proposal for a new body provisionally called the Southeast Asian Association for Regional Cooperation (SEAARC). The authors of the draft charter, conscious of the challenges that had scuppered earlier efforts at regionalism, limited SEAARC's remit to promoting economic, cultural, and technical cooperation. But they also included language that reflected Indonesia's nonaligned principles. The draft charter asserted that foreign military bases in Southeast Asia were temporary in nature and that collective defense arrangements in the region should not serve the interest of any great power. It also included sops to Indonesian army leaders' determination to establish an autonomous architecture of regional security, proclaiming that "the countries of Southeast Asia share a primary responsibility for ensuring the stability and maintaining the security of the area." Malik's deputies in the Foreign Ministry traveled to Kuala Lumpur, Bangkok, Manila, and Singapore to hold consultations on the draft proposal. They also visited Yangon and Phnom Penh—two other nonaligned capitals in Southeast Asia whose participation in SEAARC would affirm the ecumenical nature of the new regional organization.[37]

Indonesian diplomats encountered considerable skepticism about the value of a new regional body.[38] The most vocal, Malaysian prime minister Tunku Abdul Rahman, remained wary of Indonesian ambitions and continued to prize Malaysia's defensive ties with the United Kingdom. He also resisted mothballing the pro-Western ASA, whose creation he had overseen only six years earlier. The Tunku derided Malik's SEAARC proposal as "pointless" in April 1967, noting that "we already have our regional organization in ASA."[39] Singaporean officials toed the Tunku's line, keen to avoid upsetting Kuala Lumpur and preserve their own security arrangements with London.[40] Misgivings about the Malik-Thanat proposal surfaced in the Philippines as well. Marcos was determined to maintain the archipelago's defensive links with the United States, which encompassed a mutual defense treaty and membership in the American-sponsored Southeast Asia Treaty Organization (SEATO). More broadly, Philippine officials questioned whether Southeast Asian states could maintain regional stability absent international assistance. At a SEATO meeting held in April, Secretary of Foreign Affairs Narciso Ramos explained that the Philippines was "convinced more than ever before of the validity of the SEATO idea" and that the organization remained a vital "defensive shield for our region."[41] The more nonaligned states in Southeast Asia joined their pro-Western neighbors in expressing resistance to the SEAARC proposal. Burmese and Cambodian officials quickly made it known they would not join the prospective organization, seeing it as a Western-sponsored anticommunist initiative thinly shrouded by a nonaligned veil.[42]

Malik, Thanat, and their deputies engaged in shuttle diplomacy to overcome Malaysian, Singaporean, and Philippine concerns. In the spring of 1967, Indonesian and Thai officials met their counterparts in formal conference rooms and at airports during layovers. They agreed to alter the wording of the provision in the SEAARC charter concerning the responsibility of Southeast Asian states for regional stability and security. But Malik insisted he could not drop the provision emphasizing the temporary nature of foreign military bases in Southeast Asia without imperiling the Indonesian army's support for the new body. Deadlock was avoided only because of two extraregional developments. First was the steady drip of news about an impending British retrenchment from positions "east of Suez," including Malaysia and Singapore, and the escalation of protests against the Vietnam War in the United States, which together signaled to anticommunist leaders in Southeast Asia that the Western umbrella they relied upon for protection might be folded up sooner than expected.[43] Second was the transnationalization of Mao Zedong's Cultural Revolution as radical firebrands seized control of the Foreign Ministry in Beijing and consular personnel stationed abroad began encouraging overseas Chinese communities to launch cultural revolutions of their own. Threat perceptions in regional capitals shifted, and Southeast Asian leaders warmed to the SEAARC proposal.

Malik also needed to convince Indonesian army commanders who envisioned a formal military pact that a softer form of regional agglomeration was a worthwhile project. His underlings began emphasizing the links between economic development, political stability, and national security. One of the foreign minister's deputies told a Western diplomat that SEAARC would enable "the countries of the region to help each other in creating cohesive societies which could stand against Chinese-inspired aggression or subversion and maintain national solidarity in the face of large and essentially unreliable minorities."[44] Soedjatmoko, one of Malik's key advisors, elaborated on that theme at a lecture delivered in Australia in July 1967. He argued the key threat facing Southeast Asia was political rather than military, noting that "for all its military strength as a land power, China's ability to project that strength beyond its borders is quite limited." A new regional body, even one limited to the economic and cultural realms, could further "the twin processes of nation-building and modernization" and thereby develop "the indigenous political strength on which stability and security rest."[45]

The foreign ministers of Indonesia, Thailand, the Philippines, and Singapore, as well as the deputy prime minister of Malaysia, gathered in Bangkok in August 1967 to inaugurate a new regional organization. Concluding that SEAARC sounded too much like "shark," the assembled diplomats agreed to change the name of the body to ASEAN.[46] But not all their negotiations were so superficial. Ramos mounted a final effort to delete from the organization's charter the planks surrounding foreign bases and regional security. Malik prevailed on him to drop his objections by arguing that omitting these passages would give fodder to opponents of the New Order in Indonesia and disrupt Suharto's drive toward the presidency. The preamble to the final draft of the ASEAN Declaration asserted that the countries of Southeast Asia "share a primary responsibility for strengthening the economic and social stability of the region" and are "determined to ensure their stability and security from external interference"—a slightly watered-down version of Indonesia's early proposals concerning regional security. The preamble also proclaimed that "all foreign bases are temporary and remain only with the expressed concurrence of the countries concerned."[47] The New Order had given rise to a new organization that Indonesian officials hoped would become the cornerstone of an autonomous architecture of regional security in Southeast Asia.

What emerged from the Bangkok meeting was nevertheless a compromise. ASEAN would facilitate cooperation in the fields of economics, society, culture, technology, science, and administration through an annual meeting of foreign ministers and the creation of a standing committee and various subcommittees to deal with specific issues.[48] Although Malik had succeeded in ensuring the inclusion of articles linked to Indonesia's nonaligned posture in ASEAN's founding document, the *Far Eastern Economic Review* observed that disavowals of security arrangements with great powers were "conspicuously absent" from the ASEAN Declaration.[49] Malik himself remembered that the Bangkok Declaration was "the maximum result that could be achieved . . . in accordance with the situation and condition of the time."[50] Singaporean foreign minister Sinnathamby Rajaratnam was less oblique. "All of our modest hopes have been realized," he quipped of the new regional body.[51] Its obvious institutional limitations notwithstanding, ASEAN became a core instrument of Suharto's Cold War in Southeast Asia.

III

As Malik navigated the treacherous shoals of domestic and regional politics to make landfall at Bangkok, Suharto and other New Order military figures developed a holistic national security doctrine of "national resilience." Drawing upon and universalizing earlier Indonesian experiences and ideas, they theorized that a country's resilience against threats both internal and external arose from a combination of economic prosperity, sociopolitical cohesion, and military strength. The national resilience doctrine at once reflected and reinforced the institutional and ideological formations that sustained the authority of the New Order.

The institution responsible for delineating the national resilience doctrine was the National Defense Institute (Lemhannas). Its origins lay in an October 1962 proposal by Nasution to cohere disparate efforts by Seskoad, the army, and Sukarno to formulate a defense doctrine based on Indonesia's historical experiences and national endowments rather than supposedly universal theories—much as the People's Republic of China and Democratic Republic of Vietnam had schematized defense doctrines rooted in their distinct revolutionary experiences rather than Marxist-Leninist orthodoxy.[52] Lemhannas first formalized the national resilience doctrine in a 1968 primer. It defined national resilience not as "an element of defense" but rather something that encompassed "all fields of national and state life," which enabled Indonesia to "face all threats coming from without or within, that directly or indirectly endanger the survival of the state and the nation."[53]

Ideology represented the pivotal font of national resilience. The pride of place afforded to ideology reflected the challenge of building a nation in a territory like Indonesia's, with its gulfs of geography, ethnicity, language, religion, class, and politics. To unify the archipelago's nearly 70 million inhabitants, Sukarno proclaimed Pancasila as the philosophical foundation of the Indonesian state. The ideology's five ambiguous principles proved sufficiently malleable to bind Indonesia together through the challenges of decolonization. Amid the tumult of the 1950s, Sukarno used Pancasila to stress revolutionary contention. Upon his ascent to power beginning in late 1965, Suharto promulgated a far more stifling interpretation of Pancasila—one that stressed unanimity, harmony, and the subservience of the individual to the state. "The primary source of National Resilience is Pancasila," read the Lemhannas primer, because it led all Indonesians to "prioritize the national interest over individual and group interests."[54] In the New Order's formulation, Pancasila represented a timeless set of values that united the population and rendered it capable of vanquishing internal and external threats.[55]

The Lemhannas primer explained that national resilience emerged from four other domains: political, economic, sociocultural, and military. The primary requirements for political resilience were "strong leadership" that could "arouse the dignity and obedience of the people" and a passive population that would "put the people's interest first and not group or private interests." The decidedly authoritarian, integralist vision of governance embedded within the concept of political resilience emanated from Lemhannas's evaluation of Indonesia's turbulent experience under parliamentary democracy. "The various types of political systems practiced in the past only brought the result of weakening resilience in the political field," the Lemhannas primer explained. Rapid political turnover and ceaseless partisan infighting produced "congestion in the implementation of governance" and "opportunities for the proliferation of infiltration and subversion." Lemhannas concluded that Indonesia required a state highly autonomous of society, one capable of instilling "national discipline" and pursuing farsighted policy. Suharto's stultifying vision of Pancasila Democracy marked the realization of Lemhannas's vision of political resilience.[56]

The cause for which Suharto promoted political stability was economic development. The former, he explained around the time Lemhannas released the national resilience codex, was an "absolute requirement" for the latter.[57] And economic development was itself a key component of national resilience.

"The problem of national prosperity can no longer be separated or detached from the problem of national security," read the Lemhannas primer, "because the two problems have a reciprocal relationship."[58] Unless the material needs of the Indonesian population could be met, the country would be vulnerable to revolutionary contagion. The pursuit of economic resilience underpinned the transformation of the Indonesian economy under the New Order, including the mobilization of international capital and the elaboration of a technocratic development plan.

Lemhannas also explained that the traditions of Indonesian village life instilled in the population an "awareness that, with mutual cooperation, deliberative consensus, and unity, social problems can always be minimized, so that the tranquility of national life can be preserved."[59] The concept of sociocultural resilience reflected the mythologized ideal of an allegedly eternal Indonesian character, one influenced by colonial-era scholars who posited that the nation's *adat* (customs) prized hierarchy, unity, and order.[60] A key proponent of this school of thought was legal scholar Sudiman Kartohadiprodjo, who taught at the Military Law Academy. By proffering a vision of Indonesian society and culture as monolithic, Sudiman cast democracy, individualism, social justice, popular sovereignty, and the very idea of politics as a competition of interests as Western imports that "go against our souls."[61] The national resilience doctrine appropriated such organicist ideals to frame Indonesian social and cultural mores as complementary to the New Order's explicitly antipolitical, developmental vision of Indonesian life.

Military resilience was the final component of national resilience. The idea of military resilience did not refer simply to the ability of the armed forces to repulse external threats but more broadly to the "consciousness that all people possess the right and duty to defend the State and the Nation . . . against threats from wherever they arrive and whatever their shape and manifestation." Suharto and other New Order generals, including the theoreticians at Lemhannas, believed that most threats to the continuity of the Indonesian republic had emerged from within the archipelago. They also concluded that the mobilization of the masses by the armed forces represented the key to overcoming those threats. During the Indonesian revolution, when the ragtag Indonesian military fought Dutch attempts at recolonization, Nasution developed a system of "Total People's Defense and Security" (Hankamrata). This system envisioned a small, underequipped, and poorly trained military overcoming its deficiencies by mobilizing the population against external invaders or internal enemies.[62] A related doctrine of "Territorial Warfare and Territorial Management" emerged as a result of the rebellions that erupted in the 1950s, when the armed forces began stationing its units throughout the archipelago, where they adopted political and economic roles parallel to the local civilian

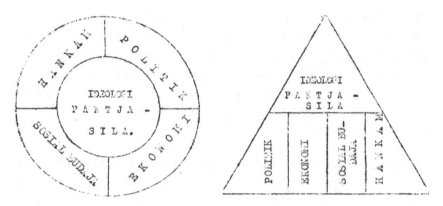

Figure 4.1 The Components of National Resilience. Lemhannas, *Ketahanan Nasional*, 13.

administration.[63] The Lemhannas primer on national resilience suggested that military resilience emerged from the role of the armed forces as "dynamizer and stabilizer," blending the roles of Leninist vanguard party and Maoist guerrilla force.[64] That insight led Indonesian policymakers to announce that all citizens would be required to undergo militia training to ensure they could participate in the defense of the nation in 1969.[65]

The Lemhannas codex made clear that the four components of national re-silience encircling ideological resilience—political, economic, sociocultural, and military—constituted an interlocking whole. A decline in one form of re-silience spelled decline for the others. Absent a unified sociocultural outlook, the Indonesian population would not mobilize for national defense behind the armed forces; without a stable political system undergirded by strong leadership, economic development would falter and render the population vulnerable to subversive ideas.[66] The national resilience doctrine thus located every domain of Indonesian life within the realm of national security.

IV

The national resilience doctrine looked inward. But as Suharto consolidated his authority over Indonesia's state and society, he began extending his Cold War outward into Southeast Asia—for no matter how strong its military, no matter how prosperous and united its citizenry, Indonesia could not hope to remain stable if it were surrounded by hostile communist powers. Suharto and other Indonesian military thinkers came to see the proliferation of Indonesia's national resilience doctrine as integral to the preservation of anticommunist stability in Southeast Asia. As one Indonesian strategist put it, "threats that come from a totalitarian and totalizing system like communism . . . can only be overcome with a system that is total and totalizing as well, namely national resilience."[67]

Southeast Asia's regional order experienced tectonic shifts as the Suharto regime elaborated the national resilience doctrine. General Suwarto, the Seskoad commander whose thought did much to shape the New Order, told an Australian interlocutor in April 1967 that the "historic trend" in Southeast Asia was "one of Western withdrawal," so the region's states needed to develop some capacity to defend themselves.[68] In the official mind of the New Order, the key threat facing Southeast Asia remained China's efforts to foment revolution by manipulating the region's ethnic Chinese population. An academic who interviewed Lemhannas personnel in May 1967 concluded that "the greatest fear expressed by these Generals was of the overseas Chinese communities in Indonesia and South East Asia."[69]

Suharto and other Indonesian army leaders worked to fashion ASEAN into a vehicle of anticommunist internationalism as they grappled with how to contain communism without the involvement of Western powers. As Jusuf Wanandi, a key aide to Murtopo, remembered, "ASEAN had been established in 1967 to withstand the dominoes likely to fall to communism after Vietnam. The socio-economic 'front' of ASEAN was just a cover for the strategic build-up of a force that could withstand communist pressure in the region, because we simply didn't know what was going to happen in the Vietnam War."[70]

The New Order's drive toward regionalism drew upon a matrix of ideas about regional security that predated the September Thirtieth Movement. In 1964, thinkers at Seskoad had begun contemplating the creation of a new confederation of Southeast Asian states. They anticipated a bid for regional agglomeration would enable Indonesia to recover the confidence of the international community, secure international aid and investment, and fuel economic recovery. A follow-up paper in 1966 entitled "Concept for the Establishment of a Confederation of Southeast Asian Countries" argued that such a confederation would present a number of benefits. Indonesia could adopt a leadership role in maintaining regional security and "contain and localize" war away from the archipelago itself. Jakarta could also disseminate the ideals of Pancasila, the "Indonesian army's and armed forces' doctrines," and even the Indonesian language to other states in Southeast Asia.[71] When Indonesian army leaders met at the Second Army Seminar in August 1966 to chart the course of the New Order, they elaborated a new army doctrine that anticipated that "military cooperation between Southeast Asian states" would arise "in the near future."[72] Already at the dawn of the New Order, army leaders harbored plans to remake Southeast Asia in Indonesia's image and institutionalize military cooperation across the region.

New Order leaders sensed an opportunity to implement those plans through ASEAN in the first months of 1968. In rapid succession, the United Kingdom formalized its decision to withdraw military forces from Malaysia and Singapore, the Tet Offensive exposed the enduring vulnerability of American forces in Vietnam, and President Lyndon Johnson foreshadowed an US withdrawal from Indochina by announcing he would halt most of the American bombing of North Vietnam and would not seek re-election. In this context Suharto proposed that ASEAN institutionalize defense and security cooperation.[73] Even Malik suggested during a visit to Singapore in March 1968 that ASEAN should "bring new ideas, including defence," into the group, making headlines by asserting that "the 200 million people represented in ASEAN need not worry about any communist threat" because Indonesia "shall protect them even if the threat comes from Genghis Khan."[74] These trial balloons were quickly punctured by other ASEAN leaders who still harbored anxieties about a revanchist Indonesian nationalism. Malik lamented in a July 1968 memorandum to Suharto that "there is not or is not yet common ground on the functions and goals of ASEAN"— the organization was little more than "an 'extension' or continuation of national programs."[75] The idea of transforming ASEAN into a guardian of regional security remained anathema to other Southeast Asian leaders.

The eruption of intramural strife within ASEAN delivered another setback to the Suharto regime's efforts to forge an autonomous infrastructure of regional order in Southeast Asia. In March 1968, Manila dailies published articles alleging the Philippine military had recruited Muslim men from Mindanao and Sulu to infiltrate the Malaysian state of Sabah, where they would sow chaos and secessionist sentiment as a prelude to Philippine reclamation of the territory. But the recruits mutinied against their commanding officers during training and were subsequently executed. The stories ignited a scandal in the Philippines. Senator Benigno Aquino, Marcos's chief political rival, set out to investigate the killings and delivered a searing address on the senate floor accusing Marcos of seeking to ensure "his continuity in power and achieve territorial gains" through illegitimate means.[76] In Malaysia, the Tunku lodged a formal note of protest and demanded an explanation from Marcos. He also announced that twenty-six Filipinos had been arrested in Malaysian territory in possession of small arms and explosives.[77] What followed were a series of failed negotiations and diplomatic escalations that culminated in the suspension of diplomatic relations between Malaysia and the Philippines in September 1968.[78] The Tunku also joined with the chief minister of Sabah, Tun Mustapha bin Harun, to foment separatist sentiment in the southern Philippines. Malaysian operatives contacted Congressman Rashid Lucman, a lawmaker from Mindanao who had called for Marcos's impeachment in light of the massacre of Muslim recruits. They offered to "train young Muslims from the Philippines, with 10,000 arms, continuous supply of ammunition, and all needed logistical support for 10,000 boys."[79] Lucman agreed and organized a group of ninety Moros to travel to an island off the coast of peninsular Malaysia for military training. Among the attendees was Nur Misuari, who would eventually form the Moro National Liberation Front (MNLF).[80] Malaysian sponsorship thus helped give rise to what would, in time, become a massive separatist insurgency that threatened the territorial integrity of the Philippines: the Bangsamoro rebellion of the 1970s.

The Malaysian-Philippine dispute over Sabah paralyzed the institutional mechanisms of ASEAN. Indonesian officials immediately set to work mediating the conflict. Ali Murtopo carried personal messages from Suharto to the Tunku and Marcos in the summer of 1968.[81] Philippine and Malaysian officials agreed to parley during the inaugural meeting of ASEAN foreign ministers in Jakarta that August. There Indonesian diplomats secured agreement for a "cooling-off period."[82] But that ambiguous formulation failed to avert the suspension of Malaysian-Philippine diplomatic ties the following month. Malik and Thanat then negotiated an agreement for another "cooling-off period" in December. Persistent diplomacy eventually helped heal the rift between Manila and Kuala Lumpur. In March 1969, General Sunarso crisscrossed the region and secured assurances from the Marcos government that Philippine diplomats would not raise their country's claim to Sabah at a preparatory meeting for a gathering of ASEAN foreign ministers later that year. Malaysian and Philippine representatives met face-to-face in May, which led Sunarso to exult that "ASEAN can go on despite the existence of the Sabah issue."[83] When ASEAN leaders convened in Malaysia's Cameron Highlands in December 1969, Razak and Philippine foreign minister Carlos Romulo agreed to re-establish diplomatic ties "in the spirit of goodwill and friendship and because of the great value Malaysia and the Philippines placed on ASEAN."[84]

In the face of enduring regional rivalries and mistrust of Indonesia, Suharto and his military colleagues concluded there was no hope of fashioning ASEAN into a defensive alliance. Instead, they worked to mold the organization into a vehicle for promoting national resilience. The New Order anticipated the promulgation of Indonesia's national resilience doctrine would give rise to an autonomous architecture of regional security in Southeast Asia without the need for a formal military pact. In April 1969, Malik published an article in the Seskoad journal *Karya Wira Jati* arguing that ASEAN could help member states "increase their national resilience, so they can prepare themselves to face the changes to come" as Western powers pulled back from the region.[85] Like other architects of the New Order, Malik saw Indonesia's neighbors in Southeast Asia as suffering an ideological deficit that rendered them vulnerable to communist subversion. This was a lesson not only of Indonesia's historical experience but also of the Vietnam War. As Murtopo later explained, the threats facing the region were "ideological in character even though their manifestations may have been physical and their operation has penetrated into the social, political, economic, and cultural fields." He argued that "because such threats have been motivated by a certain ideological concept or outlook, we must also face them with a definite conception or outlook, for despite their frequently physical manifestations, physical force alone, no matter how strong, would not suffice to deal with them. The Vietnam experience is case in point."[86] Indeed, Suharto himself would routinely criticize American policymakers for giving the South Vietnamese things to fight *with* but nothing to fight *for*.[87] What other Southeast Asian states required was an indigenous system of values that would prevent their populations from being inspired by foreign ideologies like communism or liberalism.

The New Order's efforts to evangelize the national resilience doctrine were designed to preserve, protect, and promote Indonesia's regional interests. But they were also designed to further the New Order's consolidation of power by winning additional military and economic aid from the United States. Shortly after President Richard Nixon's inauguration in 1969, General Sumitro sent a telegram to US National Security Advisor Henry Kissinger emphasizing Indonesia's determination to adopt a leadership role in Southeast Asia. Sumitro's telegram underlined the importance of "building 'national resilience' in SEA [Southeast Asia]," suggesting that "Indonesia can make [a] contribution to [the] maintenance of security in SEA without repeat without [a] formal 'military pact.'" He added that "we must strive to create [a] uniform regional security system thru [the] application of Indonesia's concept of Total People's Defense and Security." With American financial assistance, Sumitro wrote, Indonesia would establish close diplomatic, military, and intelligence ties with other Southeast Asian states and promulgate the national resilience doctrine.[88] Given the Nixon administration's determination to devolve responsibility for the maintenance of regional security to client states in Southeast Asia, Latin America, the Middle East, and Africa through the Nixon Doctrine, Indonesian military leaders believed their adoption of a leadership role in ASEAN would win them goodwill in Washington and ensure they received a larger percentage of a declining foreign aid budget.

Lemhannas took charge of the New Order's efforts to fashion ASEAN into a vehicle for the promotion of national resilience in Southeast Asia.[89] Indonesian officials disseminated the national resilience doctrine through all manner of ASEAN meetings, conferences, and exchanges. In December 1970, for instance, the Indonesian Human Resources Development Foundation sponsored an ASEAN regional workshop on "The Role of Leadership in Development," where attendees from all five ASEAN member states listened to papers on the importance of authoritarian leadership for economic development. Summing up the proceedings, the steering committee wrote that, "although democratic means of leadership are preferred, with respect to certain types of problems, authoritative means of leadership" often proved necessary.[90]

Alternative visions of regional order asserted themselves as the structural changes sweeping Southeast Asia became apparent. In January 1968, the Malaysian parliamentarian Ismail Abdul Rahman called on the United States, Soviet Union, and China to guarantee the neutralization of the region.[91] The proposal languished until Tun Abdul Razak became prime minister in 1970. Razak tapped Ismail as deputy prime minister and instructed him to unify ASEAN around the neutralization scheme at the organization's March 1971 meeting.[92] The idea generated anxieties in several ASEAN capitals. Singapore and the Philippines maintained defensive ties with Washington and London and worried Malaysia's proposal would accelerate Western withdrawal from the region.[93] But nowhere did it incite more skepticism than in Jakarta. Superpower-guaranteed neutralization contradicted the New Order's determination to forge an autonomous regional order that did not depend on the benevolence of great powers—to say nothing of the Indonesian army's persistent distrust of China. Malik argued that a great power guarantee of neutralization was likely to be "as brittle and unstable" as the triangular relationship between Washington, Moscow, and Beijing. He insisted that a stable regional equilibrium could emerge "only through developing among ourselves an area of internal cohesion and stability, based on indigenous socio-political and economic strength."[94]

After eight months of delicate negotiations, ASEAN diplomats endorsed a watered-down statement at a special ministerial meeting held in November 1971. They proclaimed their determination "to exert initially necessary efforts to secure the recognition of, and respect for, South East Asia as a Zone of Peace, Freedom, and Neutrality, free from any form or manner of interference by outside Powers."[95] Malik signed his name to what became known as the ZOPFAN Declaration because it omitted any mention of relying on great powers and because he regarded its decidedly vague ambitions as a first step toward Indonesia's vision of an autonomous architecture of regional order. The national resilience doctrine lay at the core of that vision.

V

A series of geopolitical realignments beginning in 1971 posed enormous challenges to the New Order's approach to Southeast Asia. Nixon announced in July that he would visit China in early 1972. Soon the Suharto regime's principal benefactor and paramount enemy would enlist each other in a tacit alliance against the Soviet Union. Amid the drama of détente, Ali Murtopo and Sudjono Humardani felt insufficient attention was being devoted to strategic matters within the New Order and sponsored the establishment the Center for Strategic and International Studies (CSIS) to serve as a think tank for Indonesian foreign policy.[96] Three months after its September 1971 founding, CSIS issued a report on the major problems facing Southeast Asia, which concluded that Beijing sought to reclaim various territories along its borders, win the loyalty of all overseas Chinese, and assert leadership of the international communist movement. The report lamented that within ASEAN there existed neither consensus over "who really is the common enemy" nor "a determination on behalf of member states to defend the region together." Noting that if "a disturbance that occurs in one country in this region, its vibrations will immediately be felt in other countries," CSIS recommended that Indonesian policymakers should work to strengthen ASEAN as a "diplomatic infrastructure for the sake of defense."[97]

To forge this diplomatic infrastructure and move ASEAN toward a common security posture, Suharto and Malik introduced the concept of regional resilience. At an April 1972 ASEAN ministerial meeting, Malik likened ASEAN to a chain—only as strong as its weakest link. If one member state lacked national resilience and proved vulnerable to communist subversion or infiltration, other member states would have to divert precious resources away from development and toward defense, which would diminish their own national resilience. Conversely, the achievement of national resilience across the region would prevent threats from spilling over beyond the borders of one member state to others and enable each state to focus on development and other domestic imperatives. Malik's proposal earned plaudits from representatives of Malaysia and Thailand. The joint communiqué issued upon the meeting's conclusion stated that ASEAN member states must "develop national resilience which would enable them to face the present changes and challenges of the future with greater confidence."[98] For the first time, the Suharto regime's idea of national resilience entered the official lexicon of ASEAN.

What then was regional resilience? As one general who served as Indonesia's ASEAN secretary explained, "regional resilience can only be increased based on the national resilience of ASEAN member states."[99] But the whole was greater than the sum of its parts. Achieving regional resilience required a broader convergence of institutions, ideologies, and identities within ASEAN in order to facilitate regional cooperation against shared threats. Panggabean argued that the achievement of regional resilience necessitated "common views, a common understanding and approach."[100]

More changes in the balance of power in Southeast Asia rendered other ASEAN member states receptive to Indonesia's vision of regional resilience. In January 1973, American and Vietnamese negotiators signed the Paris Peace Accords that brought an end to US involvement in the Vietnam War. The treaty foreshadowed a massive cut in American military and economic aid to ASEAN states, which declined by 55 percent in 1973.[101] ASEAN foreign ministers met in Kuala Lumpur in February to consider the implications of the American withdrawal. There they offered a first, tepid endorsement of the Indonesian idea of regional resilience, concluding it "could be the foundation on which Southeast Asian countries" establish "the peace and security of the area."[102] Other ASEAN member states also began recognizing the importance of Indonesian leadership for regional stability. As Marcos put it in July 1973, Indonesia must serve as "the base and anchor of Southeast Asia."[103] Suharto embraced the Indonesia's role as regional hegemon and used it to promote the ideas of national and regional resilience. The Broad Outlines of State Policy issued in March 1973 consecrated national resilience as the lodestar of Indonesian foreign policy and instructed officials to "take steps to consolidate the stability of the Southeast Asian area" by "enabling the countries in the region to manage their own futures through the development of national resilience."[104]

But Suharto's strategic calculus differed from that of other ASEAN leaders. Indonesian military officials continued to regard China as the overriding threat facing Southeast Asia and advocated the diplomatic isolation of the People's Republic.[105] Indonesia's appeals to its ASEAN partners to continue the policy of containment fell on deaf ears, especially after China emerged from the Cultural Revolution and assumed Taiwan's seat at the United Nations in 1971. Malaysia, the Philippines, and Thailand all initiated the process of establishing diplomatic ties with the People's Republic in the early 1970s—determined as they were to either neutralize Chinese support for local insurgencies or to focus what they regarded as a more pressing threat from Vietnam.[106] Razak went so far as to push

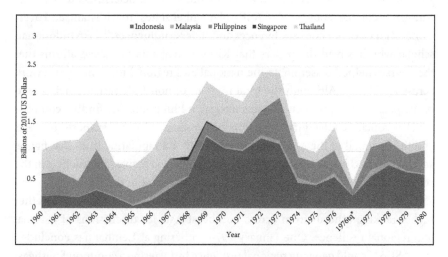

Figure 4.2 US Military and Economic Aid to ASEAN States, 1960–1980. Compiled by author from US Agency for International Development, "U.S. Overseas Loans and Grants: Obligations and Loan Authorizations, 1945–2013."

*The US fiscal year shifted from July 1–June 30 to October 1–September 30 in 1976, necessitating a three-month "transition quarter."

Suharto to resume diplomatic ties with Beijing, noting that China was "different" and "no longer aggressive." The Indonesian strongman subsequently told his Council on Political Stabilization and National Security (Polkam) in September 1974 that it was "only a matter of time" until diplomatic relations with Beijing resumed. He issued a variety of instructions to pave the way for renewed ties.[107] But the New Order's suspicion of Chinese interference in Indonesia and its enduring skepticism about the loyalty of the archipelago's ethnic Chinese community prevented Suharto from bending with the regional wind.[108] In his rigid diplomatic posture he was joined by Singaporean prime minister Lee Kuan Yew. Resolute about the need to forge a common Singaporean identity and sever any bonds that connected the city-state's population (the majority of which claimed Chinese ancestry) to the Chinese mainland, Lee announced that he would be the last ASEAN leader to recognize Beijing.

The Suharto regime mounted a wide-ranging effort to proselytize its resilience-based strategic outlook following the Paris Peace Accords. Believing that national resilience was a concept "universal" in its applicability and that its promulgation would "stabilize ASEAN," Lemhannas organized annual Special Course (Kista) training programs for high-ranking military and civilian officials from the national defense institutes of each ASEAN country beginning in 1973.[109] Three of the first four Kista sessions were held in Jakarta, and the course subsequently rotated between ASEAN capitals. At each meeting Indonesian officials lectured their counterparts on the national resilience doctrine.[110] Emblematic was a talk given at the 1974 Kista seminar in which an Indonesian official insisted that "only national resilience" could enable ASEAN member states "to withstand and overcome all kinds of outside interferences and adverse influences."[111] An Indonesian scholar who has read the papers that Kista participants produced affirms that the courses helped disseminate the national and regional resilience framework across ASEAN.[112] Although the total number of non-Indonesian officials who participated in the program remains unclear, a Philippine fact-finding commission has concluded that fifty-three Filipinos graduated from Kista between 1973 and the downfall of the Marcos regime in 1986. Extrapolating from that figure, several hundred high-ranking ASEAN officials likely received instruction in the principles of national resilience through Kista programs in the 1970s.[113]

CSIS and Lemhannas also organized conferences that brought together higher-ranking officials from across Southeast Asia for discussions of national and regional resilience. One January 1974 gathering at Lemhannas concluded that ASEAN could generate regional resilience by fostering a common Southeast Asian identity, which would induce member states to alter their economic structures to become more complementary, their foreign policies to become more harmonious, and their security postures to become more cooperative.[114] A longtime contributor to New Order thought gave a lecture at Lemhannas later that year calling this process a "collectivisation of interests."[115] Around the same time, CSIS hosted a conference on regional security. There Malaysian minister of home affairs Ghazali Shafie endorsed the ideas of national and regional resilience, confirming the desirability of a "correlated response on the part of ASEAN member states" toward "largely uniform internal security requirements." He elaborated that ASEAN could help member states develop "a national ethos to which dissimilar components of the state can relate"—a national ideology—"as well as socio-economic reconstruction to provide them with tangible evidence of the benefits to be accrued from participation in the national system."[116] These points were echoed by Alejandro Melchor Jr., who served as executive secretary to Marcos and played a critical role in designing the institutions of martial law in the Philippines.[117]

The communist takeovers of Cambodia, South Vietnam, and Laos in 1975 further altered the strategic environment in Southeast Asia. New Order officials were not altogether surprised by the cascade of communist victories. As early as September 1974, Suharto explained to Lee Kuan Yew and Tun Abdul Razak that "sooner or later—maybe in the coming two or three years—all of Vietnam and Cambodia will become 'red.'"[118] Suharto and his allies doubted a Vietnam reunified under communist rule would pursue an expansionist foreign policy. This rather subdued sense of threat reflected a chauvinistic and romantic view of Vietnamese communism among Indonesian officials, who saw the Vietnamese revolution through the prism of their own and assumed it was fundamentally nationalist rather than internationalist. As Murtopo surmised in April 1975, "I do not think it likely that a communist Indochina would pose a direct threat of open invasion to the rest of Southeast Asia." He claimed Hanoi and Phnom Penh "need plenty of time and resources for internal consolidation and national reconstruction" and would adopt a posture "independent from either Moscow or Peking on account of their strong nationalism nurtured by a long history of struggle against foreign domination."[119]

The Suharto regime did nevertheless consider 1975 a moment of vulnerability for Southeast Asia. Indonesian officials feared the communist triumphs in Indochina would inspire communist movements elsewhere in Southeast Asia, and that $5 billion in captured American weaponry would find its way into the hands of communist insurgents across the region.[120] In early April 1975, Suharto told Polkam that communist victories in Cambodia and Vietnam "will have an effect on communist elements in Southeast Asia via ideological solidarity" and will lead indigenous communist movements to "increase their opposition to or resistance against" noncommunist governments. To "face the possibility of danger," Suharto continued, "the national resilience of ASEAN states must be strengthened."[121] Yet China remained the overriding threat fixating the New Order. Much as Beijing increased its aid to Vietnamese communists after the end of the Korean War, Indonesian officials reasoned, so too might the People's Republic accelerate its support for Southeast Asian revolutionary movements after the end of the Vietnam War. One New Order defense official went so far as to remark that the communist takeovers in Indochina could be a "blessing in disguise" if they inspired other Southeast Asian leaders to extend ASEAN co-operation to encompass "the political and security, or as we call it in Indonesia the regional resilience areas" in light of the overriding threat posed by China.[122]

ASEAN foreign ministers gathered informally in Kuala Lumpur in mid-May to take stock of the new regional environment. Malik emphasized that "the danger that might be faced by ASEAN states will not take the form of open ag-gression but of subversion and infiltration."[123] The largest risk he envisioned was that the weapons the United States had supplied to the defunct anticommunist regimes in Phnom Penh and Saigon would find their way to leftist insurgencies beyond Indochina.[124] But other ASEAN states did not necessarily share Indonesia's sanguine attitude toward developments in Indochina. Vietnam's military commanded more soldiers than the militaries of all other ASEAN states combined, and it could call on decades of experience of almost non-stop fighting against extraordinarily powerful adversaries. So alarmed was Lee Kuan Yew after the fall of Saigon that he summoned his family to his bedroom and said he would remain in Singapore "until the bitter end" but assured his loved ones that they "need not feel obliged to stay."[125] The prospect of Vietnamese expansionism prompted a strategic reassessment in several ASEAN capitals. Thailand and the Philippines accelerated their normalization of relations with Beijing. Malaysia had already done so in June 1974, hoping to burnish its non-aligned credentials and reduce Chinese support for an indigenous communist insurgency dominated by ethnic Chinese guerrillas. In the wake of the ASEAN meeting in Kuala Lumpur, Suharto told Polkam that Indonesia still needed to convince other Southeast Asian states to adopt the national resilience doctrine, particularly its ideological core.[126] The following month, he remarked to an American diplomat that "Indonesia [is] encouraging other ASEAN leaders to develop [their] own national philosophy. Without such [a] philosophy, commu-nism can creep in easily."[127]

Disagreements about the source of the peril notwithstanding, a renewed com-munist threat hung like a shadow over Southeast Asia. In that context ASEAN leaders threw themselves headlong into deepening regional cooperation. The Kuala Lumpur meeting was only the first of a flurry of ASEAN meetings in the wake of the communist takeovers of Cambodia and Vietnam. Suharto met with Lee in Bali over two days in early September 1975. The Singaporean lamented that "the governments of Malaysia and Thailand underestimate the communist danger." Suharto and Lee agreed that ASEAN states needed to deepen their cooperation and "strengthen their national resilience to face the communist threat." Because economic resilience was "the weakest link in the chain," they concluded that economic cooperation should be the "primary concern." While they recognized that "military resilience is also needed," they decided to avoid highlighting security issues to "avoid the impression that ASEAN will grow into a kind of military pact." Instead, Suharto and Lee decided to promote security cooperation beyond the confines of ASEAN itself.[128] Suharto reiterated that conclusion during a Polkam meeting in November. He insisted that the New Order should "maintain cooperation in the defense and security field between ASEAN members to improve their defense and security capacity and strengthen their national resilience" and thereby "preserve stability and security in Southeast Asia." But he was resolute that "there should be no impression that we will form a military pact" because he did not want ASEAN to "provoke hostility from other parties."[129]

The accelerating pace of informal gatherings culminated in the first meeting of ASEAN heads of state in Bali in February 1976. There ASEAN leaders signed the Treaty of Amity and Cooperation in Southeast Asia, which pledged member states to mutual cooperation and noninterference; the Declaration of ASEAN Concord, which affirmed national and regional resilience as ASEAN's formal security framework; and the Agreement on the Establishment of the ASEAN Secretariat, which provided for the creation of a central hub for ASEAN in Jakarta.[130] The February 1976 meeting revealed a fundamental shift in the role of ASEAN. Where before it had promoted regional reconciliation after the conflicts of the 1960s, now it preserved regional security after the realignments of the 1970s. Bilateral forms of cooperation began blossoming under the ASEAN canopy. Indonesia had since the late 1960s pursued joint training exercises with other ASEAN militaries as part of its effort to become a hub for regional defense. These military exercises achieved real momentum in the period following the communist takeovers in Indochina.[131] One contemporary Soviet author was not far off the mark when he evaluated the proliferation of bilateral security cooperation as an indication that ASEAN amounted to a "hidden military pact."[132]

The specter of China haunted Southeast Asia as Suharto launched his Cold War in October 1965. The communist giant to the north financed national liberation movements across Southeast Asia, most notably in Vietnam. Furthermore, tens of millions of overseas Chinese dispersed across the region raised the prospect of fifth columns undermining noncommunist states. Containing Chinese influence thus became a key objective of Suharto's Cold War. The New Order worked to sever the bonds of culture, language, religion, and family that Indonesian officials feared linked the archipelago's ethnic Chinese inhabitants to the People's

Republic. Suharto also worked to cohere anticommunist states across Southeast
Asia into an anti-Chinese axis capable of guarding against Chinese aggression
and subversion. The complexities of grafting his Cold War onto the global Cold
War proved challenging, as Suharto was compelled to restrain the suppression of
the ethnic Chinese population in Indonesia in order to maintain the confidence
of international donors and investors whose capital sustained the consolidation
of the New Order.

Persistent divisions within Southeast Asia prevented the Suharto regime
from building ASEAN into a formal military alliance. But Indonesian officials
promulgated the New Order's security doctrines of national and regional resilience through ASEAN and institutionalized bilateral security cooperation
underneath the multilateral ASEAN umbrella. The Suharto regime's efforts to
evangelize the institutions and ideologies that undergirded the authority of the
New Order would ultimately reverberate in profound ways and contribute to a
remaking of political order across much of Southeast Asia.

5

Internationalizing Counterrevolution

Philippine president Ferdinand Marcos declared martial law in September 1972. The following year, he published *Notes on the New Society of the Philippines*. Rife with amateurish political theory, the meandering book offered a personal account of Marcos's decision to dismantle democracy in the Philippines and inaugurate a period of authoritarian rule. Marcos wrote that martial law emanated from what he called the September Twenty-First Movement. By this he meant not any particular event or movement but simply his own recognition on the day in question that the "remaking of society was not just an imperative of national development but of national survival." And the imperative of national survival itself necessitated an effort to build what Marcos dubbed a New Society. The lexicon of Marcos's nascent authoritarian regime—"New Society," "September Twenty-First Movement"—revealed his emulation of Suharto. Indeed, Marcos anticipated his effort to model his regime on Suharto's would garner a favorable reception on the world stage, not least from the United States and other international sponsors of authoritarian rule. "Has there been any outraged cry," he asked early in *Notes*, "over the martial law in Indonesia?"[1]

Suharto did not merely inspire Marcos from afar. In the months leading up to Marcos's declaration of martial law, Indonesian officials offered advice to their Philippine counterparts on matters ranging from military strategy to economic development. Suharto himself visited the Philippines and encouraged Marcos to draw upon Indonesia's experience in order to surmount an ongoing political crisis. Suharto's Cold War in Southeast Asia thus spanned beyond an effort to fashion the Association of Southeast Asian Nations (ASEAN) into a bulwark against communist aggression and subversion. The Indonesian strongman also sought to internationalize counterrevolution across the region. Possessed of boundless confidence in the universal applicability of the Indonesian model, Suharto and other New Order officials evangelized the institutions and ideologies that undergirded their authority in Indonesia by promoting the national resilience

Suharto's Cold War. Mattias Fibiger, Oxford University Press. © Oxford University Press 2023.
DOI: 10.1093/oso/9780197667224.003.0006

doctrine as a solution to instability in Malaysia, the Philippines, Thailand, Singapore, Cambodia, and South Vietnam.

Across the region, the Indonesian example was in the air—a ready solution to unexpected problems. When leaders elsewhere in Southeast Asia faced political shocks, they drew upon the Indonesian model to construct and consolidate authoritarian regimes. They embraced institutional and ideological formations with few if any domestic precedents that, taken together, revealed the breadth of Indonesia's international influence. This process of authoritarian convergence did not erase all national particularities, but it did reshape the foundations of political order in Southeast Asia.

I

Malaysia became a key target of Indonesian diplomacy. As New Order officials negotiated an end to *Konfrontasi*, a number of other borderland security issues demanded joint Indonesian-Malaysian attention. Most pressing were piracy in the Strait of Malacca and insurgency on the island of Borneo. More broadly, Indonesian military leaders regarded Malaysia as a divided society whose ethnically based political system was a powder keg of instability. With that in mind, they worked not only to institutionalize military cooperation with Malaysia but also to convince Malaysian leaders of the need for a new approach to politics aligned with Indonesia's national resilience doctrine. But Malaysia's political and military establishment continued to nurse anxieties about Indonesian expansionism and remained reluctant to cooperate more fully with the New Order. Only after race riots plunged Malaysian society into crisis in May 1969 did the Suharto regime's efforts to promulgate the national resilience doctrine in Malaysia gain traction.

Shared security concerns first brought about collaboration between the Indonesian and Malaysian militaries. In early 1967, General Mokoginta welcomed a Malaysian military delegation to Sumatra and then traveled to Kuala Lumpur to organize intelligence-sharing measures to combat piracy and smuggling in the Strait of Malacca. He also reiterated General Panggabean's suggestion that Indonesia and Malaysia band together to form an indigenous Southeast Asian military alliance to contain the spread of communism in the region.[2] Not long thereafter, Indonesian and Malaysian officials negotiated agreements on border crossing and joint operations against communist guerrillas on Borneo.[3]

Joint operations commenced in April 1967 with Operation Clean Sweep I, led by Indonesian General Mussanif Ryacudu in coordination with Malaysia's Third Infantry Brigade. But the campaign was hindered by ill-trained troops and poor intelligence. Indonesian and Malaysian forces suffered more casualties than the communist guerrillas they hunted. As a result, Suharto replaced Ryacudu with General Witono Sarsono, who had served as deputy assistant for logistics during the army's bloody campaign against the PKI.[4] Indonesian and Malaysian officials also agreed to establish twenty-seven outposts on either side of their shared border on Borneo to surveil local communities and facilitate intelligence gathering in the borderlands.[5] Reinforced by new troops from Java and Sumatra, Witono organized Operation Clean Sweep II in August 1967. He attempted to deprive communist insurgents of local support by evacuating the ethnic Chinese population from the rural areas of northern Borneo. Indonesian soldiers engaged in bloody "sweeping" operations that drove south from the border and included massacres of innocent ethnic Chinese families. They also mobilized the indigenous Dayak population to engage in anti-Chinese bloodletting—reminiscent of the army's use of civilian militias to press its politicide against the PKI. Several thousand people died amid the fighting and some 60,000 refugees fled to cities along the west coast of Borneo, where they were subjected to starvation, disease, and violence.[6] The brutal campaign laid the groundwork for further military cooperation between Indonesia and Malaysia. In December 1967, Malaysia agreed to furnish Indonesian troops in the border region with rations, medical equipment, and aviation fuel worth $20,000 per month.[7]

Joint campaigns in Borneo did little to alleviate Indonesian concerns about Malaysia's vulnerability to communism. When an unprecedented political crisis rocked Malaysia in May 1969, New Order leaders seized the opportunity to proselytize the national resilience doctrine.

The crisis followed a dramatic election. Malaysians went to the polls in May and delivered an unexpected setback to the ruling Alliance government. A consociational regime comprising the United Malays National Organization (UMNO), the Malaysian Chinese Association (MCA), and the Malaysian Indian Congress (MIC), the Alliance presided over a delicate political-economic bargain. The regime distributed power and patronage among its diverse constituencies, largely preserving ethnic Malay political preeminence and ethnic Chinese economic hegemony.[8] But opposition parties denounced the status quo in increasingly strident terms in the late 1960s. The Pan-Malaysian Islamic Party (PAS) seized on the degradation of Malay cultural and educational institutions, as well as pervasive Malay unemployment, to castigate the Alliance for failing to preserve the perquisites for ethnic Malays enshrined in the country's constitution. Many UMNO voters deserted the party for the PAS. Meanwhile, non-Malay opposition parties like the Democratic Action Party (DAP) and the Malaysian People's Movement Party (Gerakan) campaigned for a "Malaysian Malaysia" in which racial categories would carry less political weight. These parties attracted votes from ethnic Chinese and ethnic Indians who felt that special Malay privileges denied the rest of the population access to adequate schooling, fulfilling employment, and meaningful political participation. The results of the May 1969 election results shocked observers: the Alliance received only 48 percent of the popular vote. Gerrymandering and a disunited opposition left it with an enduring parliamentary majority, but the regime had lost the two-thirds majority that allowed it to amend the constitution—and much of its legitimacy as well.

Opposition parties staged raucous post-election celebrations. DAP and Gerakan partisans made clear their intent to bring sweeping political change to Malaysia. Some paraded through the streets while waving brooms to illustrate the point. During these rallies, later reports averred, ethnic Chinese supporters of the opposition hurled racial epithets at ethnic Malay bystanders.[9] Young UMNO partisans then organized marches of their own. The largest march was set for dusk on May 13. As demonstrators gathered at the residence of a prominent UMNO politician, fisticuffs broke out between ethnic Malay marchers and ethnic Chinese onlookers. One American stationed in Kuala Lumpur remembered that "we then had a first class example of that old Malay word *amok*, and its meaning"—evoking the persistence of colonial stereotypes about allegedly languid Malays who could be worked up into a frenzy by real or imagined slights.[10] Groups of Malays broke off from the marchers and stormed through Chinese neighborhoods, slashing and stabbing people they encountered with ceremonial *parang* and *kris* blades. Ethnic Chinese and Indian Malaysians organized local self-defense forces to repel the attackers. Some also targeted ethnic Malay property, including the headquarters of UMNO. The Malaysian army was called in to restore order, but many soldiers joined in on the violence and shot indiscriminately at ethnic Chinese people, homes, and businesses.[11] By the time order was restored nearly three days later, ethnic violence had claimed hundreds of lives, the overwhelming majority of them of Chinese heritage.

The leaders of UMNO responded swiftly. Blaming "communist terrorist" saboteurs for the eruption of racial strife, Prime Minister Tunku Abdul Rahman suspended parliamentary democracy and announced the formation of an all-powerful National Operations Council (NOC) headed by his deputy, Tun Abdul Razak. "There is no doubt now that democracy is dead in this country," said one government official.[12] The NOC arrested opposition leaders, banned political speech, censored the press, and announced a ten-battalion expansion of the army and police. Much like his Indonesian counterpart, the Tunku appealed to the United States for aid in constructing his newly authoritarian regime. The Nixon administration responded favorably to his request for assistance in expanding the intelligence capabilities of a new government bureau in charge of suppressing dissent from what the prime minister described as communists and other "extremists."[13]

The NOC also sought to restore political stability and ethnic harmony by reordering Malaysia's politics along Indonesian lines. Razak tapped Foreign

Minister Ghazali Shafie to head a new Department of National Unity (DNU). In a July 1969 speech broadcast on radio and television, Ghazali explained his task as the "systematic formulation of the National Ideology" that could transcend "the affiliations of race, religion, culture, class and political parties."[14] Razak also announced the creation of a National Consultative Council (NCC)—a forum where representatives of most political parties and various religious, social, and professional groups could "establish positive and practical guidelines for inter-racial co-operation and social integration for the growth of a Malaysian national identity." The Tunku urged the NCC at its first meeting to "think afresh" and create a novel political and economic framework for Malaysian life that would allow for the restoration of parliamentary governance.[15] In a series of secret sessions held over the following months, the NCC debated the establishment of strictures on the public discussion of sensitive political questions, such as the special rights and privileges afforded to ethnic Malays. Meanwhile the DNU devised a new national ideology, which Ghazali called *Rukun Negara* (often rendered as Rukunegara). The ideology was adopted by the NOC and announced to the public on August 31, 1970. Rukunegara enumerated five principles to animate Malaysian life: belief in God, loyalty to king and country, upholding the constitution, the rule of law, and good behavior and morality. Razak then worked to implant Rukunegara in all aspects of Malaysian life, making its recitation compulsory in schools and featuring it prominently in national speeches.[16]

The DNU and NCC sketched an economic development plan as they formulated Rukunegara. A DNU paper from March 1970 proposed a "New Economic Policy" that would redress the income and wealth disparities between ethnic Malays and the rest of the population, which it identified as a key source of the discontent that engulfed Malaysia in May 1969. A subcommittee report on the New Economic Policy issued in August 1970 recommended an array of policies designed to improve the welfare of ethnic Malays. Over the following year, the NCC drafted the Second Malaysia Plan, with a "two-pronged objective" of "eradicating poverty, irrespective of race, and restructuring Malaysian society to reduce and eventually eliminate the identification of race with economic function." The plan called for a massive mobilization of both domestic and foreign capital to fuel agricultural investment and rural development in the agrarian Malay heartland; it also aimed to increase ethnic Malay ownership in the urban manufacturing and commercial sector from 2 to 30 percent within twenty years. By harnessing international capital to drive state-directed development, the Second Malaysia Plan aimed to stabilize national politics under a newly authoritarian regime.[17]

Domestic imperatives propelled the work of the DNU and NCC. But these institutions embraced an overarching conception of governance as the management of discrete political groups for the promotion of economic development under a unifying ideology—a functionalist vision brought into focus by the Indonesian example. In March 1970, Suharto traveled to Malaysia at Razak's invitation, where the two men planned to discuss the communist threat in Borneo and economic cooperation within ASEAN.[18] Suharto quickly steered the conversation toward the national resilience doctrine. According to his official chroniclers, Suharto insisted that "the concept of national resilience is the only answer to the challenges faced by Southeast Asia" and told Razak that ideology represented the cornerstone of national resilience.[19]

Rukunegara failed to impress Indonesian officials. General Abdul Thalib, the Indonesian ambassador in Kuala Lumpur, sent a letter to Suharto in December 1970 in anticipation of Razak's upcoming visit to Jakarta. "At a glance, Rukunegara is a kind of Pancasila," wrote Thalib, noting that "this was indeed the purpose of the Malaysian leaders." But the ambassador regarded the two as fundamentally different. Malaysia's new national ideology, he argued, represented a "set of guidelines for the achievement of national goals" that were "shallow and short-term" and could not answer the question of "what next?" Pancasila, on the other hand, constituted an "eternal wellspring that animates all national thinking including national goals."[20] The New Order's skepticism about the political utility of Rukunegara did not, however, prevent Indonesian officials from finding other ways to cultivate national resilience in Malaysia.

Thalib recommended that Suharto evangelize Indonesia's Hankamrata system during Razak's forthcoming visit to Jakarta. "It is clear that at some point in the future," he wrote, "Malaysia *must* adopt and (voluntarily) implement a portion of the aforementioned strategy for the sake of Malaysia's own security interests and those of the Republic of Indonesia." He noted that Razak and other Malaysian leaders had already "to a certain extent" realized the necessity of adopting a Hankamrata system, and he predicted that they would do so "sooner or later" even without Indonesian encouragement. But he warned that Malaysian thinking remained hamstrung by "traditional habits and ties"—namely the country's reliance on the United Kingdom in matters of national security. By the time Malaysian leaders recognized the Hankamrata imperative, Thalib cautioned Suharto, "it may be too late" to stave off an imminent crisis: Malaysia's ethnically based political system was already "extremely vulnerable," and the early 1970s would be "years of crisis" in Southeast Asia as the British military withdrew from positions east of Suez and the American military presence in Vietnam dwindled. Thalib concluded his letter by reiterating the need to "persuade Malaysia that the Hankamrata Doctrine is the most appropriate doctrine for a developing country."[21] Shortly before Razak's arrival in Jakarta, Thalib requested permission for a seventy-member delegation from Lemhannas to visit Kuala Lumpur to "study and understand the problems in countries neighboring Indonesia and exchange ideas about the problems faced together by Southeast Asian countries."[22]

Any surviving records of discussions between Suharto and Razak, and between the Lemhannas delegation and Malaysian officials, remain inaccessible to historians, but the available evidence suggests Indonesia promoted the national resilience doctrine to Malaysian officials through a multitude of channels. Malaysian military officers were guaranteed seats in Indonesian military intelligence and command schools where they imbibed the national resilience doctrine.[23] The Indonesian military newspaper *Angkatan Bersendjata* published a series of articles in May 1969 narrating the efforts of one Indonesian officer stationed in Kuala Lumpur to explain to his Malaysian counterparts the philosophy and mechanics behind *dwifungsi*, the doctrine that arrogated a social-political role for the Indonesian armed forces in addition to its defense-security role.[24] In light of the multilayered cooperation between the Indonesian and Malaysian militaries, Razak "thanked ABRI . . . for the training given to the Malaysian Royal Army" during a visit to Jakarta in December 1970.[25]

The New Order's efforts to promote Hankamrata contributed to the Malaysian government's adoption of a Security and Development (Kesban) program. Though not formally adopted by the National Security Council until 1980 as "the sum total of all efforts undertaken by the MAF [Malaysian Armed Forces] and other government agencies to strengthen and protect society from subversion, lawlessness, and insurgency," the ideas and programs behind Kesban emerged a decade earlier. Razak argued that the "primary task of the Armed Forces is to fight the communists. But at the same time, they must also help implement the Government's development plan—this is part of the fight against the communists. Defence and development go hand-in-hand."[26] In short, Razak tasked the military with promoting economic development in order to preserve social cohesion and inoculate the population against radicalism. The Malaysian military's increasing responsibility for domestic security was exemplified by *Operasi Setia*, launched to combat the resurgence of communist insurgency in the northwestern state of Perak in 1971. Malaysian security forces worked to isolate guerrillas from the population by fencing off villages, imposing a twenty-four-hour curfew, exerting control over the food supply, registering households and tenants, demolishing illegal squatter homes, and providing residents with increased access to government services.[27]

The Kesban doctrine held distinctly Malaysian precursors dating to the era of the Emergency. Among them were the Briggs Plan, which forcibly resettled 10 percent of the population in "New Villages" to starve communist insurgents of support, and Field Marshal Sir Gerald Templer's "hearts and minds" campaign, which aimed to win the loyalty of the population through the promotion of political and economic development.[28] But the Kesban doctrine also encompassed some programs that possessed no domestic Malaysian precursors. For instance, in 1975 Razak introduced the Neighborhood Watch (*Rukun Tetangga*) program, which obligated all able-bodied males between the ages of eighteen and fifty-five to receive military training and patrol their neighborhoods to guard against communist threats. "The idea," Razak explained, "is to make everyone responsible for their own security and that of their neighbours by taking turns guarding their areas."[29] The military mobilization of the masses in the name of national security closely resembled Indonesia's Hankamrata system.

The Suharto regime's promotion of the national resilience doctrine in Malaysia did not transform Malaysia into a facsimile of Indonesia. Razak possessed a civilian background, as did future Malaysian leaders. And the Malaysian military remained strictly apolitical and never developed a doctrine akin to *dwifungsi*. The regime's fundamental character remained stable. Even so, the Suharto regime's efforts to internationalize counterrevolution did shape the nature of the programs launched by the Razak regime and its successors. From Rukunegara to Kesban, Indonesian influence became increasingly visible throughout Malaysia in the 1970s.

II

The New Order also worked to promulgate the national resilience doctrine in the Philippines. Indonesian policymakers regarded the Philippine archipelago as remarkably vulnerable to insurgency and excessively reliant on American protection. For years, senior New Order figures courted Philippine officials and encouraged them to draw upon the Indonesian example to fashion a more durable political and economic order. After President Ferdinand Marcos declared martial law in September 1972, he looked to Indonesia as a lodestar while he built his counterrevolutionary dictatorship.

Links between the Suharto regime and the Marcos administration emerged slowly. General Alamsjah visited the Philippines toward the end of 1967 to cultivate ties between the New Order and the Marcos administration. He was granted a diplomatic honor denoting meritorious services to the Philippines and established a close working relationship with Marcos's executive secretary, Rafael Salas.[30] Alamsjah also invited Marcos to visit Indonesia and meet Suharto for the first time. In January 1968, the two leaders discussed the Vietnam War, ASEAN, and economic development, agreeing that the key threat facing Southeast Asia was not external aggression but internal subversion. Marcos enthused at a press conference on the last day of his visit that, "under the leadership of President Suharto, Indonesia is making progress and will become the greatest nation in Southeast Asia."[31] He also remarked on the Chinese threat to Southeast Asia and floated the possibility of creating "arrangements for collective security on the basis of ASEAN principles and purposes."[32] Marcos continued to echo Suharto's views on regional security in the months ahead. He warned the Overseas Press Club in Manila in late February that there was a looming "security gap" in Southeast Asia and predicted "those of us in Asia could very well be left fending for ourselves under the shadow of the Chinese colossus" after the United States and United Kingdom withdrew from the region.[33]

Indonesian and Philippine negotiators held bilateral talks on political, economic, and sociocultural issues as the relationship between Suharto and Marcos grew closer.[34] The accelerating pace of diplomacy reflected the extraordinary changes sweeping Southeast Asia, notably President Richard Nixon's announcement that Southeast Asian states would be required to bear more of the burdens of anticommunist defense. "Events are beginning to show the diminishing value of reliance on one's 'friends,'" Carlos Romulo remarked upon becoming Philippine foreign minister in January 1969.[35] Yet the search for a new foreign policy orientation amid a reconfiguration of regional geopolitics did not alone drive the Philippines toward accepting Indonesia's national resilience framework. Much as in Malaysia, it was a domestic crisis that led Marcos to adapt the Indonesian example in a bid to remake the Philippines.

Marcos delivered his annual state of the nation address on January 26, 1970, months after becoming the first Philippine president to win re-election. The hectoring speech sounded the theme of "national discipline" while tens of thousands of young demonstrators protested outside the Philippine Congress on Manila's Padre Burgos Avenue. Chants of "*Rebolusyon!*" "*Marcos puppet!*" and "*Makibaka, huwag matakot!* [Struggle, don't be afraid!]" echoed from the crowd. The protestors belonged to a diverse array of movements, from moderate opposition groups to communist front organizations. Speakers at the demonstration railed against Marcos's manipulation of the country's democratic institutions and against dwindling goods and rising prices in the country's markets.[36] So too were the young demonstrators aggrieved by barriers on youth political participation: Philippine law prohibited citizens under the age of twenty-one, at least 70 percent of the population, from casting ballots in national elections.[37] The protest grew riotous and trapped Marcos and his listeners inside the halls of Congress. When the police escorted the president and his family to the front door and hustled them to a waiting limousine, demonstrators tossed stones and bottles at the first family and pelted the president in the back with what different witnesses described as a papier-mâché crocodile or a cardboard coffin—the former apparently intended to symbolize Marcos's greed and the latter his "dead promises."[38] The authorities responded with a show of force that an opposition senator later excoriated as a police riot. "Go on, demonstrate!" shouted one officer as he bludgeoned a pair of fallen students with his rattan nightstick.[39]

Four nights later, tens of thousands of young people gathered in front of the presidential complex at Malacañang Palace to protest against police violence.

A group of agitators commandeered a fire engine and smashed it through the metal gates surrounding the palace. Hundreds of angry students stormed the compound and lobbed Molotov cocktails into parked automobiles. "This is no longer a riot," said one police officer. "This is an insurrection."[40] Marcos called in the military to restore order. Secretary of Justice Juan Ponce Enrile remembered that the authorities turned the area surrounding the palace into a "war zone," killing four protestors and injuring hundreds more.[41]

Thus began the First Quarter Storm—a series of protests that convulsed Manila and outlying provincial capitals between January and March 1970 and politicized huge numbers of urban Filipino youth. The demonstrations followed years of student protest against the Vietnam War and coincided with a rise in violent crime and the growing visibility of narcotics, gambling, and prostitution rackets that seemed to erode the foundation of public order. Perhaps most alarmingly for the Marcos government, the First Quarter Storm occurred alongside a resurgence of the Philippine communist movement. In early 1969, Jose Maria Sison and a dozen comrades rechristened the Communist Party of the Philippines (CPP), a Maoist splinter from the largely defunct, Soviet-aligned Partido Komunista ng Pilipinas (PKP). A few months later, Sison joined with a young rebel named Bernabe Buscayno (better known by his nom de guerre Kumander Dante) to establish a CPP military wing called the New People's Army (NPA).[42] The CPP and NPA worked to carry out agrarian revolution and establish rural base areas from which the communist movement could encircle and overwhelm the cities.[43] Writing under the pseudonym Amado Guerrero, Sison argued in 1970 that the Marcos government's repressive behavior would alienate moderate Filipinos and contribute to the development of a broad anti-Marcos front: "By resorting to more counterrevolutionary violence, the Marcos puppet regime is enraging the people and hastening the collapse of the semicolonial and semifeudal system."[44] The urban and rural strains of revolution commingled and invigorated the anti-Marcos revolution. That much was evident in the popularization of a new word in Manila's radical lexicon: *mamundok*, which literally means "to go to the mountains" but came to connote joining the NPA's guerrilla war.[45]

Marcos flirted with a shift toward authoritarian rule amid the swell of protest and disorder. He had Enrile prepare orders for the declaration of martial law, but Marcos found himself lacking a suitable pretext to issue the order.[46] "I secretly hoped the demonstrators would attack the palace [again] so that we could employ the total solution," the president recorded in his diary. "But it would be bloody."[47]

The next two years witnessed their fair share of bloodshed. In August 1971, unknown assailants tossed grenades onto a stage at Manila's Plaza Miranda, where opposition Liberal Party candidates were campaigning for upcoming legislative elections. Nine people died and more than 100 were injured. Marcos responded to the attack by suspending the writ of habeas corpus and proclaiming "I am asserting the power of government over disorder, over rebellion, over subversion."[48] Marcos then orchestrated additional attacks that intensified popular fears of a breakdown in law and order and served as pretexts for further repressive measures. During the summer of 1972, special operations crews detonated bombs around Manila, which Marcos blamed on communist saboteurs.[49] The campaign of false-flag attacks culminated in September, when soldiers staged an ambush on Enrile's limousine, peppering it with bullets as the defense minister rode safely in an escort car.[50] On September 21, Marcos organized a meeting with the American ambassador to explain that he would declare martial law in order to "reform our society and eliminate the communist threat." He exulted in his diary that night that the American "agreed that there seemed to be no other solution."[51] On September 23, Marcos issued Proclamation 1081 declaring martial law. "We will eliminate the threat of a violent overthrow of our Republic," the president intoned during his first address to the nation after issuing the declaration, "but at the same time, we must now reform the social, political and economic institutions in our country," warning the population that, "if you offend the New Society, you shall be punished."[52] In short order, Marcos imprisoned opposition politicians, shuttered unfriendly media outlets, disbanded the legislature and political parties, tortured and disappeared dissidents, and pilfered vast sums from public coffers.

Marcos deliberately modeled his authoritarian regime on the New Order. Over the previous seven years, he had closely watched Suharto's consolidation of power. Enrile remembered Suharto as one of "the two Asian leaders whom President Marcos respected and highly regarded."[53] As recently as February 1972, Suharto visited the Philippines and spoke of the necessity of strong leadership and stability for nation-building, emphasizing the lessons of Indonesia's experience. "In facing earlier challenges we have found an answer, which we have dug up from our own experiences, which is our conception of national resilience," Suharto explained. "We must strengthen our national ideology which is rooted in our personality, we must reinforce political stability by developing a democratic life that recognizes responsibilities, we must implement economic development which is just in assuming the burden and enjoying the results of development, we must preserve a sense of shared destiny and social harmony, and we must have adequate security and defense forces that become the responsibility of the entire nation with military forces as its vanguard."[54] Not without reason did the print organ of the Communist Party of the Philippines, *Ang Bayan*, suggest that a primary purpose of the visit was "to teach each other how to suppress the people and preserve a brutal and corrupt regime subservient to U.S. imperialism."[55]

Over the following months, Philippine military and intelligence officials repeatedly solicited advice from their Indonesian counterparts.[56] Only three weeks before declaring martial law, Marcos received General Panggabean and bestowed upon him the same honor he had given to Alamsjah five years earlier. The Filipino president expressed "hope that the close understanding now existing between the Philippines and Indonesia shall continue to be further strengthened by frequent exchange of visits" and affirmed that the two countries "are joined by geographical propinquity, common ideology, common origin and common destiny."[57] Indonesian military delegations visited the Philippines often over the next several years and consistently pressed the Marcos regime to adopt Indonesia's national resilience framework.[58]

Marcos was convinced that the Philippines needed an ideology akin to Pancasila to promote a spirit of public interest and weld together the Philippine archipelago's disparate clans, classes, ethnolinguistic groups, and religious communities. "The new covenant—the political bond—must take the form of a national ideology," he wrote in *Notes on the New Society*. It was the old ideology, Marcos explained, which "viewed politics as essentially a competition for public power and privilege among individuals, political parties, and pressure groups, and only secondarily as a means of promoting the general welfare and the public interest" that accounted for the desultory state of Philippine political and economic life and "led to the martial necessity."[59] Complaints about the venality of Philippine politicians were nothing new. But Marcos's belief in the ability of the state to use an official ideology to promote cooperation and development all but certainly reflected Indonesian inspiration and the Suharto regime's ceaseless efforts to promote the national resilience doctrine.

Over the following years, Marcos established the infrastructure through which a new national ideology might be promulgated—including a pliant national media that could serve as a government mouthpiece, a primary and secondary education system that could indoctrinate pupils, and a single national political party that could serve as an umbrella group for political disputes. But he never articulated an ideology in anything but the vaguest terms. Marcos's rhetoric brimmed with phrases like "national discipline," "revolution from the center," "new society," and "the new Filipinism," which revealed aspirations rather than any shared beliefs upon which Philippine unity, stability, and prosperity could be built. As late as 1982 he still characterized the national Philippine ideology as "emergent."[60]

The Filipino dictator also emulated Suharto's efforts to promote economic development. New Order officials championed Indonesia's economic policies in bilateral and multilateral meetings within ASEAN as well as in more technical fora, including the Japanese-sponsored Southeast Asian Ministerial Conference on Economic Development and the Asia Society–run Southeast

Asia Development Advisory Group.[61] After declaring martial law, Marcos established the National Economic and Development Authority (NEDA).[62] Led by US-trained technocrats, the institution drafted plans for expanding tax collection and liberalizing trade and investment that would have been unthinkable under the democratic governments that preceded martial law. "Economic reforms suddenly became possible under martial law," wrote one Philippine technocrat.[63] Marcos also entrusted cronies with monopolies and other rent-generating arrangements and funneled the proceeds toward patronage and outright corruption.[64] Although the absence of archival documentation from the Marcos regime prevents drawing definitive conclusions, it stands to reason that Suharto's success in promoting technocratically planned, internationally sponsored growth in Indonesia inspired Marcos's nearly identical efforts in the Philippines.

To safeguard the political and economic programs of the martial-law state, Marcos bolstered the role of the armed forces. He insisted in 1972 that "our martial law is unique in that it is based on the supremacy of the civilian authority over the military."[65] In fact, Marcos quickly used the military to subjugate all strongholds of civilian authority save his own, and military officials adopted civilian functions in vastly greater numbers. "The people's regard for our soldiers has justified my faith in you," Marcos told a military audience at Camp Aguinaldo in December 1972, "and this is the reason I have given you greater responsibilities, indeed a major role in nation-building."[66] The Philippine military thus adopted a tacit doctrine of *dwifungsi*.[67]

Military involvement in politics predated martial law and accelerated after Marcos first ascended to the presidency in late 1965. Marcos's first four-year plan proclaimed that the military, "with its manpower, material, and economic resources plus its organizational cohesiveness and discipline possesses a tremendous potential to participate in economic development which should be exploited to the maximum."[68] Before the issuance of Proclamation 1081, the military had acted as a tool of civilian authority animated by a professional, apolitical ethos and only occasionally involved in domestic programs. By contrast, under martial law it became a coequal partner of the civilian administration deeply enmeshed in political competition, the exercise of patronage, and the preservation of domestic security.[69] The military's budget quadrupled in the four years following Marcos's declaration of martial law. Manpower rose from approximately 60,000—where it had hovered since 1950—to more than 140,000, far exceeding military expansion in other Southeast Asian countries.[70] The enlarged military constructed roads, bridges, and schools; assumed responsibility for managing public utilities, media outlets, and certain industries; and exercised influence over systems of education, justice, and diplomacy. The military's expanded civic mission was formalized in 1981 through *Oplan*

Katatagan (Operational Plan Stability), which held that the causes of rebellion lay "in the political, social and economic environment of [the] country."[71]

So too did Marcos preside over a militarization of society by the armed forces, adopting a counterinsurgency program that resembled Suharto's Hankamrata doctrine. The prevalence of civilian militias was a long-standing fact of life in the Philippines' decentralized political system. Landed oligarchs fielded militias that they used to enforce their personal authority and occasionally to help the central government suppress rebellions. In 1970, Marcos worked to circumvent the armed power of rival elites by launching the Barrio Self-Defense Unit (BSDU) program, under which representatives of the military trained, armed, and supervised local men in barrios throughout the Philippine archipelago. His secretary of defense explained the official rationale behind the program: "Arming the people themselves against the dissidents was the best and most effective way to dislodge the Huks [communist rebels] in Central and Southern Luzon."[72] The BSDU program represented a precursor to Marcos's efforts under martial law to sever the bonds of loyalty and patronage that enabled landed elites to act as local warlords. Around 1973, Marcos rebranded the BSDU as the Integrated Civilian Home Defense Forces (ICHDF), which grew to include some 25,000 paramilitaries who became known for wanton human rights abuses.[73] Because the ICHDF paid farmers and laborers for paramilitary service through national rather than local coffers, Marcos was able to assert a measure of central control over the local militias throughout the archipelago.

The Philippine military thus significantly widened its remit under martial law—assuming unprecedented political authority, embarking upon a civic action mission, and militarizing the citizenry. The military presented a means through which Marcos could address purely domestic imperatives by suppressing a burgeoning insurgency and centralizing a fragmented political system. But Marcos's horizons spanned beyond the Philippines. Indonesia became a model for the preservation of national security. Both were poor, archipelagic, and fractionalized states confronting unrest and rebellion. The United States supported Marcos's "effort to transform the Philippine army into an effective Civic Action force," suggesting that Marcos was influenced by transnational discourses of military modernization emanating from Washington.[74] Marcos also identified Japan, South Korea, and Taiwan as models for his efforts to promote economic development in the Philippines.[75] These international influences shaped how the Marcos regime responded to the domestic challenges it faced.

Finally, Marcos emulated Suharto's reorganization of the party system. Having witnessed the effectiveness with which party formations in Indonesia, Singapore, and Malaysia reinforced the authority of regnant elites, he worked to institutionalize his domination of Philippine politics by establishing a new political organization halfway between party and machine that he called the New Society Movement (KBL). KBL attracted support from local government officials and agents of the national bureaucracy, from urban capitalists and landed elites, and from Marcos's partners in the military. Like his efforts to emulate Pancasila, Marcos's efforts to emulate Golkar disappointed. KBL did not hold its second meeting until two years after its inaugural conference. Little more than a formal shell—a vehicle of vote-getting cast over the vast informal networks of patronage, corruption, and bossism—KBL never became a locus of political power. Marcos's authoritarian regime remained personalist in style and reliant on military rather than civilian institutions. A leading figure in the Jakarta-based Center for Strategic and International Studies lamented in the mid-1980s that "the Philippines may rely more on its armed forces in the future for the simple reason that they have become the principal remaining factor for the maintenance of internal stability."[76]

The Suharto regime's efforts to promote national resilience did not alone transform Philippine politics, but authoritarian cooperation and emulation mattered. Marcos adopted many of the innovations that Suharto had pioneered in Indonesia, including the elaboration of a national ideology that delegitimized political contestation and the expansion of the military's role into almost all realms of Philippine life. Indonesia's efforts to internationalize counterrevolution shaped even if they did not determine the nature of the authoritarian regime Marcos built.

III

Singapore became another focus of the Suharto regime's efforts to promote the national resilience doctrine. Indonesian officials were of two minds on the city-state. On the one hand, they worried Singapore's ethnic Chinese majority would become a seedbed for subversive campaigns elsewhere in Southeast Asia; on the other hand, they believed Singapore's demographic composition and economic prosperity could be harnessed to the New Order's advantage. Seskoad chief Suwarto suggested the New Order had much to learn from Singapore about inculcating a sense of national loyalty among Southeast Asia's ethnic Chinese population. In April 1967, he dispatched two officers to Singapore to study the question of ethnic Chinese loyalty to postcolonial Southeast Asian states in coordination with Goh Keng Swee, the prime minister's right-hand man and Singapore's minister of defense.[77] New Order leaders also anticipated the British withdrawal from Southeast Asia would present opportunities to enlist Singapore in Indonesia's effort to forge an autonomous architecture of regional security— points made by General Panggabean in a 1965 paper that Indonesian officials told Australian diplomats two years later "was still the basic policy document."[78] But Singapore remained aloof from Indonesia and dubious of the national resilience framework.

Prime Minister Lee Kuan Yew and his colleagues in the ruling People's Action Party (PAP) regarded Singapore as an ethnic Chinese island in a sea of ethnic Malays. And the prospect of Indonesian and Malaysian expansionism led Lee to look elsewhere for allies and archetypes. As Lee remarked in July 1966, "The strangest thing about countries is: your best friends are never your immediate neighbour!"[79] The transition from Sukarno to Suharto did little to alleviate his anxieties about Indonesia. "You can change governments but there are basic compulsions of a people grouped together as to the things they want to do," Lee remarked the same year.[80] With these considerations in mind, Singaporean diplomats entered the negotiations that led to the formation of ASEAN somewhat reluctantly—and only after British officials told Lee that they would withdraw their forces from Singapore within a decade. When financial strains led London to accelerate its timetable for withdrawal from Southeast Asia in 1968, Lee traveled to the United Kingdom in a futile attempt to reverse the decision. He told Labour prime minister Harold Wilson that he "did not fear attack from Malaysia but from Indonesia."[81] The Indonesian ambassador in London cabled Jakarta that Lee's overwrought performance in television interviews in which he urged the British public not to abandon Singapore made it appear "like he was drunk."[82] Even then Lee cultivated ties with other Commonwealth countries and more distant partners rather than cast Singapore's lot with Southeast Asia. He worked to establish a consultative defense arrangement with Australia and New Zealand and redoubled his efforts to cultivate security ties with Israel and Taiwan, other small countries facing potentially hostile neighbors. He told participants at an ASEAN ministerial meeting in 1969 that the organization should restrict its focus to economic cooperation and suggested those "preoccupied with ideological and security problems could perhaps profitably set up other organizations for this purpose."[83]

A dispute that erupted in 1968 threatened the fragile ties between Indonesia and Singapore as well as the broader ASEAN project. Three years earlier, during *Konfrontasi*, two Indonesian marines disguised as civilians had slipped into Singapore and carried out a bombing at MacDonald House. The marines were captured and sentenced to death by hanging. After Suharto edged Sukarno from power, he sent an aide to Singapore to deliver a letter (which was simultaneously published in Indonesian newspapers) requesting the sentence be commuted.[84] But his appeal fell on deaf ears. The execution of the marines in October 1968 left Suharto "angry and disappointed," according to General Sumitro, who then "observed a consistent worsening of relations between the two countries as the days passed."[85] Action front activists stormed the Singaporean embassy in

Jakarta, and Suharto called a cabinet meeting to discuss potential retaliation.[86] Foreign Minister Adam Malik succeeded in convincing Suharto that adopting a confrontational posture would impede Indonesia's economic development and harm its international reputation. Yet relations between Indonesia and Singapore became frosty. When the new Singaporean ambassador to Indonesia arrived in Jakarta in July 1970, he proposed a meeting between Suharto and Lee and received a quintessentially Javanese rebuff: Suharto said Lee "could come any time," though he lamented his schedule made timing difficult.[87]

The Indonesian and Singaporean heads of state crossed paths for the first time at the Non-Aligned Summit in Lusaka in October 1970. The two leaders discussed the conflict in Indochina and agreed that a premature American withdrawal from Southeast Asia would engender instability. "We found we shared some common views about developments and dangers in the region," Lee remembered.[88] The communist threat facilitated diplomatic rapprochement. The Singaporean ambassador in Jakarta called on Ali Murtopo in early 1971 to once again propose a formal meeting between Lee and Suharto. Murtopo explained that the hanging of the Indonesian marines had humiliated Suharto. But he insisted that Indonesia favored a strong, independent Singapore, not least because it would demonstrate to overseas Chinese communities across Southeast Asia that they could thrive without paying fealty to either Beijing or Taipei. Murtopo ended the meeting by suggesting Suharto would invite Lee to Jakarta for talks shortly after Indonesia's July 1971 elections. The polls came and went, and no invitation arrived.

Months elapsed before General Sumitro took up the reins of Indonesian-Singaporean relations. He arranged a tête-à-tête with Lee in April 1972. Sumitro explained that Suharto continued to nurse grievances over the execution of the marines, especially since Indonesia was working to end *Konfrontasi* and promote regional reconciliation when the sentences were passed down. The Singaporean prime minister protested that his was a country of laws. Turning the tables, he asked Sumitro whether he could be sure "the new man governing in Indonesia now will not return to the style and characteristics of the previous man in power?" Sumitro assured Lee that Suharto was a soldier rather than a politician and that his only aim was the improvement of the welfare of the Indonesian population.[89] Both men left the meeting reassured of the other's goodwill. Meanwhile, Bakin chief Sutopo Juwono and Singaporean Security and Intelligence Division head S. R. Nathan began nurturing a close relationship. Lee remembered that these conversations helped convince New Order officials that "we shared their views on the big issues."[90]

Changes in the balance of threat in Southeast Asia finally healed the rift between Indonesia and Singapore. As the Vietnam War reached its denouement and China emerged from the Cultural Revolution, Singapore tempered its skepticism toward ASEAN and began promoting regionalism. "The importance of ASEAN has been enhanced rather than diminished by recent international developments," Foreign Minister Rajaratnam explained at the April 1972 meeting of ASEAN ministers.[91] Suharto embraced the shift in Singaporean policy. He invited Goh Keng Swee to Jakarta and "stressed the importance of closer cooperation between leaders of South-East Asian countries."[92]

Lee Kuan Yew traveled to Indonesia to meet with Suharto in May 1973. At the recommendation of his ambassador, he agreed to lay flowers on the graves of the executed Indonesian marines during his visit as a gesture of goodwill. Beyond the realm of diplomatic symbolism, Lee remembered that the "bull point" in his discussions with Suharto was the containment of Chinese influence in Southeast Asia.[93] According to a joint communiqué issued after the meeting, Suharto "explained to the Prime Minister of Singapore the Indonesian efforts to develop its own as well as regional resilience," emphasizing in particular "the concept of national resilience, particularly in order to maintain national unity and cohesion, political stability, economic progress, and national security." Lee's response indicated he was "sympathetic to, and expressed his support for, the Indonesian efforts." But he explained that Singapore possessed its own "effort of nation building," which diverged from the Indonesian model and would "contribute to stability and harmony in Southeast Asia."[94]

The institutions and ideologies that undergirded authoritarianism in Singapore resembled their Indonesian counterparts. But they possessed distinct genealogies. For all his bluster about his disdain for ideology and his supposedly "pragmatic" outlook, Lee did promote what he called an "ideology of survival."[95] After Singapore's rancorous divorce from Malaysia in 1965, which Lee said rendered the city-state a "heart without a body," the PAP saw Singapore as vulnerable to destabilization. The simple imperative of survival then justified heavy-handed state intervention in almost all spheres of Singaporean life, especially the preservation of political stability, the protection of social harmony, and the promotion of economic development.[96] If Pancasila delegitimized political contention in Indonesia, the ideology of survival did the same in Singapore, though unlike Rukunegara and the New Filipinism it owed little to Indonesian inspiration.

Lee also built a powerful military and expanded ties between the military and the citizenry. But his model was Israel rather than Indonesia. In October 1965, Goh secured an agreement with Israel to dispatch a military mission to Singapore. Israeli trainers disguised as Mexicans subsequently helped transform Singapore's military from a small force of regular soldiers supplemented by volunteer reservists into a mass force sustained by conscription and mandatory reservist service.[97] Unlike most other militaries in Southeast Asia, whose political and economic clout increased in the 1960s and 1970s, Singapore's armed forces steadily shed their internal security role and focused instead on developing an offensive conventional warfare capability.[98] Indeed, Lee lamented the growing political and economic roles of militaries across the developing world in a June 1969 speech.[99] Additionally, even after Lee reoriented Singapore's foreign policy toward ASEAN, he chafed against the organization's efforts to oust the superpowers from the region. While touring the United States in 1973, he insisted that any regional equilibrium "must allow the four major world powers (the United States, Japan, Russia, and China) equal access and fair competition for political and economic interests."[100] Singapore's unique condition—ethnically distinct, territorially meager, and globally oriented—thus combined with Lee's enduring skepticism toward Indonesia to constrain the New Order's efforts to promote the national resilience doctrine in Singapore.

IV

Mainland Southeast Asia appeared more vulnerable to revolutionary contagion than Indonesia and its neighbors, so it was a natural target for the Suharto regime's efforts to internationalize counterrevolution. The New Order's most sustained effort to reinforce an authoritarian regime on the mainland took place in Cambodia. In addition to proselytizing the national resilience doctrine, Indonesian officials worked to confer both diplomatic legitimacy and military wherewithal upon the embattled Lon Nol regime.

In a desperate effort to maintain Cambodia's sovereignty in the early 1960s, Prince Norodom Sihanouk aligned Cambodia with North Vietnam and China, allowing Cambodian territory to serve as a sanctuary and transit point for men and materiel making their way into South Vietnam. He also struggled to manage Cambodia's increasingly polarized domestic political system. Elections held in September 1966 ushered in a conservative national assembly and a new prime minister in General Lon Nol, the commander of Cambodia's army. Sihanouk's increasingly erratic, ineffectual management of Cambodian political and economic life resembled the latter-day governance of Sukarno, whom Sihanouk called his "older brother."[101] As Cold War conflict threatened to swallow Cambodia, Lon Nol and his deputy Sirik Matak staged a coup in early 1970. Both the coup and the nature of the regime that arose in its wake reflected Indonesian influence.

The Suharto regime's involvement in Cambodia reflected two contradictory imperatives: on the one hand, Suharto's determination to maintain Indonesia's nonaligned image as he consolidated his domestic authority; and on the other hand, his effort to promote counterrevolution across Southeast Asia to reinforce regional stability. He decided to make Cambodia one of the two countries he visited on his first trip abroad as president, arriving in Phnom Penh in April 1968.

Although Sihanouk hewed toward the communist bloc and Suharto tilted toward the capitalist world, the two leaders embraced each other as leading lights in the Non-Aligned Movement. Sihanouk also awarded medals to a retinue of Suharto's traveling companions, including Adam Malik, Sudjono Humardani, and Frans Seda.[102] But beneath the façade of diplomatic propriety, New Order officials worked clandestinely to support Lon Nol. As early as 1966, according to a Sihanouk confidant, Suharto's ascent to power in Indonesia had "emboldened" the Cambodian right, which then chose "the initially reticent General Lon Nol to be the instrument of a similar operation in Cambodia."[103] In his memoirs, Sihanouk accused Suharto of dispatching "psychological warfare specialists from Indonesia who had engineered the slander campaign against the late President Soekarno" to Cambodia to help the country's right wing whip up "a campaign against the monarchy."[104]

Evaluating the extent of Indonesian interference in Cambodia during the period leading up to Lon Nol's March 1970 coup remains challenging. *Newsweek* magazine alleged that a small contingent of Cambodian army officers traveled to Indonesia in late 1969 to study how the army had dislodged Sukarno.[105] The Indonesian ambassador to Cambodia told one scholar that General Dharsono, then stationed in Bangkok, made frequent trips to Phnom Penh to cultivate ties with Lon Nol.[106] In early 1970, General Djuarsa informed Nasution that he was helping to lead a project on Cambodia dubbed "Military Area Command 17"—an ominous notion given there were only sixteen such commands in Indonesia at the time. He continued by noting that American-equipped Indonesian soldiers might be dispatched to the country.[107] The efflorescence of ties between the New Order and forces loyal to Lon Nol suggest that the Suharto regime played a significant role in precipitating counterrevolution in Cambodia.

If Indonesian inspiration and assistance midwifed the anti-Sihanouk coup, so too did the Suharto regime sustain counterrevolution in Cambodia. Within weeks of Sihanouk's ouster, the Nixon administration hatched a scheme to reinforce the nascent Lon Nol regime by asking Suharto to furnish the new Cambodian government with AK-47 rifles and ammunition.[108] The administration formalized the plan at an April 1970 meeting of the National Security Council.[109] Suharto was eager to assist a fellow anticommunist leader. But he was reluctant to deprive the already underequipped Indonesian military of valuable weapons for what seemed like an uphill battle against communism in Cambodia. He agreed to the Nixon administration's plan on the condition that the United States replace the old, Soviet-made AK-47s Indonesia shipped to Cambodia with new, American-made M-16s. An Opsus team traveled to Cambodia in mid-April to lay the groundwork for Indonesian military assistance.[110] Around the same time, the State Secretariat under General Sudharmono tasked the Legal and Analysis Bureau with preparing a memorandum on how the New Order could square aid to Cambodia with Indonesia's *bebas aktif* foreign policy. The bureau reported back that providing aid to Cambodia—while technically justifiable as an effort to combat Vietnamese imperialism, preserve Cambodian independence, and protect Indonesian interests—"should be a special case, an exception imposed by circumstance." It envisioned an aid package anywhere between a minimal program of small arms and training and a maximal program that included heavy equipment like trucks, tanks, helicopters, and planes.[111]

Foreign Minister Malik discovered the arms-for-Cambodia scheme in mid-April. Convinced that providing military aid to Lon Nol would undermine Indonesia's nonaligned reputation, he worked with sympathetic American diplomats to derail the scheme. He told the US ambassador in Jakarta on April 19 that American policymakers should "drag our feet on responding to Suharto on [the] proposal that U.S. replenish Indonesian arms supply to Cambodia."[112] He also opposed the idea publicly. He told the Indonesian press that the New Order could offer Cambodia only prayers, not weapons, because "we don't have any" arms to offer. He also noted that funneling American armaments to Lon Nol would violate congressional restrictions and "Nixon could fall."[113] But Malik's opposition to the arms scheme did not imply he opposed Lon Nol's government or Indonesian efforts to promote anticommunist stability in the region. Two weeks after Lon Nol seized power, Malik told the press that "what is happening in Cambodia at present is a change of government and that Indonesia recognizes the government currently in power in that country."[114] Instead, Malik convinced Suharto that Indonesia should promote a diplomatic solution to the Cambodian crisis and prove to the region and the wider world that Asian problems should be solved by Asians themselves.[115] He began laying the groundwork for a conference whose objectives were the restoration of Cambodia's neutrality, the withdrawal of all foreign troops from Cambodian territory, and the reconstitution of an international commission to monitor the implementation of the agreement.[116]

Malik sent invitations to twenty-one countries for a conference in Jakarta. The foreign minister then implored, cajoled, and browbeat his counterparts to attend. To his chagrin, no communist or neutral governments accepted the invitation. Malik grew so worried that the composition of the impending conference would tarnish Indonesia's nonaligned reputation that he called a meeting of Arab ambassadors in Jakarta to disavow them of the notion that Indonesia had abandoned its *bebas aktif* foreign policy or become an American stooge.[117] He was at least partially vindicated when Nixon announced on April 30 that American and South Vietnamese forces were invading Cambodia, which followed a year of withering bombing campaigns unleashed by American B-52s.[118] In the two weeks before the Jakarta conference opened, the attendees failed to agree on a draft communiqué that encompassed their wildly different outlooks toward the Cambodian question. No fewer than seven different drafts circulated in the Indonesian capital on the eve of the conference. During his opening address, Suharto all but admitted that the conference was unlikely to bring about a resolution of the Cambodian imbroglio, explaining that he was "realistic" about what the delegates could achieve and did not anticipate they would solve the problem "all at once."[119] A journalist was blunter, noting that the American invasion imbued the proceedings with an "air of futility."[120] After two days of speeches and negotiations, the assembled delegates released a modest communiqué that did little more than reiterate the goals of the conference and promise to raise the Cambodian issue at the United Nations.[121] In the end, the Jakarta conference did little to bolster international confidence in Indonesia's leadership, revealed the hollowness of the New Order's supposed nonalignment, and cast in stark relief the challenges of constructing an autonomous architecture of regional security in Southeast Asia.

As the desultory results of Malik's diplomatic offensive became clear, Suharto returned to the idea of arming Lon Nol. The Jakarta conference concluded only days before he traveled to the United States. During his weeklong trip, Suharto engaged in numerous discussions with American officials focusing on the conflict in Indochina and Indonesia's desire for additional military and economic aid. If Suharto elliptically scolded Nixon for the Cambodian incursion in public and called for "the withdrawal of all foreign forces from Cambodian territory," he abandoned his nonaligned pretensions in private conversations and praised the invasion of Cambodia. He also told Nixon that Indonesia would "consider military aid to Cambodia but first we would have to be assured of replacements in view of our limited capabilities."[122] Kissinger was furious that he had never been apprised of the New Order's proposal that the United States replenish any Indonesian military equipment sent to Cambodia. He told the chairman of the Joint Chiefs of Staff that it was "unbelievable" that "they told our Ambassador three weeks ago that they wanted to do something and I have never heard about it or seen anything."[123] Nixon gave the order to implement the scheme.[124] Kissinger met twice with Suharto's military emissary, General Sumitro, in early July. Over the course of those meetings, the two men finalized an arrangement whereby Indonesia would furnish Cambodia with 25,000 AK-47 rifles and the United States would in turn provide Indonesia with 30,000 M-16s.[125]

Indonesia continued to supply Cambodia with military aid in subsequent years. In January 1971, the Cambodian foreign minister traveled to Jakarta to thank Indonesia for the aid it had given the Lon Nol regime thus far and to ask for additional assistance. Suharto told the emissary that Indonesia was "willing to provide such assistance in accordance with its capabilities."[126] Military cooperation between Indonesia and Cambodia was already being institutionalized. Colonel Seno Hartono traveled to Phnom Penh in September 1970 and remained in the country for nine months, visiting dozens of bases and battlefields. The Cambodian military had suffered years of neglect and numbered only 30,000 soldiers—a problem Lon Nol was in the midst of rectifying through a sixfold increase in the manpower of the armed forces. But Seno concluded that the Cambodian military was failing due to lack of training rather than shortage of manpower. He recommended that the New Order put sixty Cambodian soldiers through airborne and commando training courses. The handpicked recruits arrived in Indonesia in September 1971 and graduated in June 1972. They were then shipped to South Vietnam for additional training in reconnaissance before finally returning to Cambodia to fight against the Khmer Rouge.[127] Lon Non, the younger brother of Lon Nol who served as Cambodia's minister of interior, traveled to Jakarta in October 1972 and urged the Suharto regime to continue supporting Cambodia until the last North Vietnamese and Viet Cong soldiers left Cambodian territory.[128]

Suharto's aid and inspiration also shaped Lon Nol's regime. A reporter stationed in Phnom Penh recalled in his memoirs that Lon Nol "brought in a crew of advisors from Indonesia" and "was taking notes from them on the conduct of internal security." In the aftermath of the coup, Cambodian soldiers loyal to Lon Nol massacred hundreds of Vietnamese civilians around Phnom Penh alleging they were communists. The prime minister then gave Vietnamese forces forty-eight hours to leave the country and, when his ultimatum was ignored, mobilized tens of thousands of new recruits to wage hopeless war against better-trained, better-equipped Vietnamese guerrillas.[129] In December 1970, a Suharto ally named Imron Rosjadi traveled to Phnom Penh and met with Lon Nol, who "was especially interested in Rosjadi's comments on territorial warfare as perfected by the Indonesians."[130] The dictator then embraced the New Order's strategy of militarizing society. "Young and old, civil and military, all have risen to defend their country from danger," Lon Nol enthused in 1972.[131] "The military are everywhere," reported a correspondent for *Le Monde* that March.[132] Apparently on Indonesian advice, Lon Nol also announced over Radio Phnom Penh shortly after seizing power that "the gravity of the situation" meant Cambodia must "accept all unconditional foreign aid, wherever it may come from."[133] But little international aid materialized beyond American military assistance. And a web of corruption enveloped the country as officers lined their pockets with money sent from the United States to finance salaries for Cambodian soldiers.[134]

Much as was the case elsewhere in Southeast Asia, Cambodia's emulation of Indonesia was most visible in the realm of ideology. Lon Nol unveiled a new national ideology of neo-Khmerism in a rambling pamphlet published in 1970. Based on three pillars of national renaissance, republican democracy, and popular welfare, neo-Khmerism articulated an ethnonationalist conception of

Cambodian identity. While the contents of the ideology betray little Indonesian inspiration, Lon Nol used neo-Khmerism in much the same way that Suharto used Pancasila: to delegitimize political contestation in the name of economic development. As Lon Nol wrote in his tract, "historical experiences teach us that we must fight the enemy not only on the military battlefield, but also on the ideological battlefield."[135] Given the density of connections between the military regimes in Jakarta and Phnom Penh, Lon Nol's efforts to establish a novel ideology for Cambodia likely owed much to the Indonesian example.

Suharto and Lon Nol's desperate efforts to build national resilience in Cambodia were in vain. They could not prevent the small country from being swallowed up by the expanding Vietnam War. Even so, Suharto continued to furnish Lon Nol with aid until the bitter end. As Khmer Rouge forces encircled Phnom Penh in preparation for a final assault, Suharto instructed his representative in the Cambodian capital to urge Lon Nol to wage a campaign modeled on Indonesia's experience.[136] When the Cambodian dictator finally decided to flee the country in early April, he traveled to Indonesia to obtain an American visa and spent a week vacationing at cottages in Bali owned by the Indonesian oil giant Pertamina. There Suharto visited Lon Nol and promised he would do everything in his power to effect a peaceful resolution of the Cambodian conflict.[137]

V

The New Order also built bridges with the other anticommunist states on the Southeast Asian mainland: Thailand and South Vietnam. But the Suharto regime's determination to maintain a nonaligned posture prevented Jakarta from opening formal diplomatic relations with Saigon. And political turmoil in Bangkok limited opportunities for New Order officials to convince Thai officialdom of the wisdom of the national resilience doctrine.

Although Malik joined with Thai foreign minister Thanat Khoman to engineer the creation of ASEAN, relations between Indonesia and Thailand remained somewhat cool. Thai officials resented what they perceived as a sense of chauvinism among their Indonesian counterparts and regarded Bangkok rather than Jakarta as the hinge around which the region should turn. For their part, military officials within the New Order dismissed their Thai counterparts as hamstrung by their reliance on the United States and by their extravagant corruption—a striking charge given the deeply entrenched corruption within the Indonesian armed forces. "They don't care if Thailand becomes dependent on the United States, they just don't care who does what," said one Indonesian general of the government in Bangkok.[138] Suharto dispatched General Dharsono to serve as ambassador to Thailand and instructed him to "strengthen the struggle of the New Order abroad."[139] He visited the country himself in March 1970.[140] But the onset of a period of endemic political instability in Thailand then undermined the Suharto regime's efforts to evangelize the national resilience doctrine in Bangkok. Escalating social unrest culminated in student demonstrations that brought down the ruling military junta in October 1973. Under subsequent civilian governments, Thailand shifted toward neutralism. Thai officials negotiated the withdrawal of American forces stationed in Thailand and cultivated ties with both China and the Soviet Union.[141]

Thailand's diplomatic maneuvers were of a piece with its traditional bamboo-bending-with-the-wind foreign policy posture. But they contravened the Suharto regime's efforts to erect an autonomous architecture of regional security in Southeast Asia and undermined Indonesia's bid to promote counterrevolution across the region. Despite the New Order's misgivings about the wisdom of Thailand's posture, Bangkok's realignment was not altogether unexpected in Jakarta. Ali Murtopo wrote in 1973 that Thailand's leaders suffered from a "psychological dependency" on foreign powers that is "deeply rooted in the structure of their existence" and "could only be reduced gradually."[142]

Ultimately, a combination of economic decline and political insecurity fueled a conservative backlash in Thailand that returned the military to power in October 1976.[143] Already in the wake of the collapse of anticommunist governments in Cambodia and South Vietnam in April 1975, New Order diplomats had advised Thai officials that "they should improve civilian-military cooperation and should develop their own ideology based on king, Buddhism and economic/social development."[144] Suharto sensed a renewed opportunity to promulgate the national resilience doctrine in the wake of the October 1976 coup. The Thai king tapped Thanin Kraivichien, a hard-line anticommunist who embraced a political role for the military, to serve as prime minister in the aftermath of the coup.[145] Mere weeks after he was installed in office, Thanin traveled to Jakarta for talks with Suharto.[146] During this visit, Suharto explained that both Indonesia and Thailand were in the midst of nation-building and were thus "vulnerable to disturbances." He urged Thanin to embrace the national resilience framework to surmount the threats facing Thailand.[147] When Thanin's successor, General Kriangsak Chamanan, traveled to Indonesia in February 1978, Suharto once again urged his Thai counterpart to "increase national resilience for the sake of regional resilience."[148]

Thailand was no stranger to international emulation. Field Marshal Sarit Thanarat remodeled the country's military along American lines in the 1950s and pursued a similar "modernization" of the country's political and economic institutions after seizing absolute power toward the end of that decade.[149] He also sacralized the nation-religion-king triad as the ideological foundation of Thai national identity, mobilizing the monarchy and the Buddhist *sangha* (clergy) to serve his developmental, unifying, and anticommunist ambitions.

It was after the rupture of October 1976 that the institutions and ideologies of authoritarian rule in Thailand tilted decisively toward the Indonesian example. In the wake of the violence that accompanied the military's return to power, Thailand's National Security Council concluded that the existing nation-religion-king triad no longer inspired the population. The council anticipated that the Thai public, left "confused, anxious, and without a common standpoint," would be vulnerable to appeals from a left-wing opposition possessed of a "rigid and stimulating ideology, which will hegemonize the thinking of the people." What Thailand required to confront emerging threats to national security was a new "national ideology" capable of reconciling a deeply polarized country. The council canvassed the demands of what in the Indonesian context would be termed functional groups—farmers, workers, capitalists, civil servants, and students—to determine what different segments of the population required of a national ideology. The conservative intellectual Kramol Thongthammachart then took charge of an effort to elaborate that ideology. As examples guiding his work he cited the national ideologies of Indonesia, Burma, Malaysia, and China, revealing the rich transnational currents shaping techniques of authoritarian governance across the region. Kramol ultimately proposed a new ideology that was, like Pancasila, a five-point schema. The nation-religion-king triad constituted its first article, while the remaining four articles outlined paths for politics, economics, administration, and society and culture. The new ideology represented an effort to reverse what Benedict Anderson called the "secular demystification" of Thai politics. The king was framed as the embodiment of the nation who internalized the interests of all Thai people, obviating democratic institutions and delegitimizing political contestation. An array of new government bodies sprouted up to promulgate the new king-focused ideology, including the National Culture Commission and the National Identity Board. Transgressions of the Thai state's effort to re-mystify the monarchy were punished severely, as prison terms for violations of lèse-majesté laws were increased from three to fifteen years.[150]

The Thai military also pioneered an array of programs designed to mobilize the citizenry in ways that resembled Indonesia's Hankamrata system. To combat a simmering insurgency in northeast Thailand along the border with Laos, leaders in the Border Patrol Police pioneered a program called Village Scouts in 1971. They trained villagers in Boy Scout principles to prepare them to contribute to economic development and prevent them from embracing communist ideology. These local pilot projects attracted attention from King Bhumibol Adulyadej and the Thai military, which then presided over the expansion of the program in other borderland regions and ultimately the entire country.

After the military returned to political dominance in 1976, the Village Scouts program underwent massive expansion. One and a half million Thai villagers completed the weeklong training session in its first five years of existence, and another million did so over the following eighteen months.[151] The Thai military also pioneered an array of other programs expanding its role in the country's political, economic, social, and cultural life, including the National Defense Volunteer, Volunteer Development and Self-Defense Villages, and Military Reservist for National Security programs, through which some 50,000 villagers were trained as paramilitaries and informants. Although these programs had domestic precursors, including the military's limited civic action mission under Sarit, one scholar of the Thai military concludes that they "did not come from the concept of civic action that the Thai Army had learned from the U.S. in the early 1960s" and that other international influences were crucial in their elaboration and implementation.[152] It stands to reason that the New Order's national resilience doctrine was one among many strands of thought underpinning the growing political role of the Thai military and its Hankamrata-esque mobilization of the citizenry.

Indonesia's ties with South Vietnam were even more tenuous than its ties with Thailand. Too cozy a relationship with the anticommunist government in Saigon, almost universally regarded as an American puppet regime, risked contravening Indonesia's carefully managed nonaligned image. Moreover, Indonesian officials regarded North Vietnam's revolutionary struggle as akin to their own: a valiant effort to throw off the yoke of foreign domination and secure national independence.[153]

Formal diplomatic relations between Indonesia and Vietnam traced their origin to the period following the Bandung Conference in 1955. Adopting a policy of equidistance consistent with its nonaligned posture, Indonesia established consulates in both Saigon and Hanoi that year. But as Sukarno veered toward the communist bloc, he closed the Indonesian consulate in Saigon, permitted the National Liberation Front to establish a representative office in Jakarta, and upgraded diplomatic ties between Indonesia and North Vietnam to the ambassadorial level. After Suharto's ascent to the presidency in Indonesia, a debate emerged over the future of Indonesia's relationship with the two Vietnams. Malik and the Foreign Ministry favored maintaining diplomatic ties with North Vietnam in order to preserve Indonesia's nonaligned image; he also floated the idea of Jakarta acting as an intermediary to facilitate negotiations between the Washington and Hanoi. Some military officials within the New Order instead favored cultivating ties with South Vietnam, which they believed represented an opportunity to generate goodwill from Indonesia's pivotal benefactor, the United States, and to ensure its primary enemy, China, remained focused on the war in Indochina rather than probing elsewhere in Southeast Asia.[154]

Relations between Indonesia and North Vietnam did not succumb to the same xenophobic and anticommunist swell that produced a freeze in Sino-Indonesian relations. In a May 1966 speech in which he first articulated the international outlook of the New Order, Malik proclaimed that Indonesia "continues to stand firmly in support of the Vietnamese people in opposition to United States military intervention" and urged "the United States to withdraw its military forces from Vietnam and hand over the solution of the Vietnam issue to the Vietnamese people themselves"—a striking statement from a foreign minister whose overriding objective was winning American economic aid.[155] Notwithstanding Malik's efforts to preserve ties with Hanoi, the North Vietnamese unsurprisingly adopted a posture of aloofness toward a regime that had recently presided over a politicide of suspected communists and fellow-travelers. The foreign minister received permission to dispatch a new ambassador to Hanoi in May 1967 after the previous left-leaning ambassador defected to China following the September Thirtieth Movement. Nugroho took up the post in August and reminisced upon the conclusion of his three-year tenure that relations between Indonesia and North Vietnam were "cold but not inimical."[156] The increasingly evident strain between the two states reflected the preponderant influence of the army in Indonesian foreign policy. Malik routinely insisted that "our struggle against communism is strictly of a local character and, therefore, does not necessarily mean that we have to involve ourselves in the global anti communist campaign, e.g. the Vietnam War."[157] But the army thought otherwise. Emblematic was an October 1967 editorial in the military newspaper *Angkatan Bersendjata* that questioned Indonesia's "policy of playing ostrich by encouraging Hanoi" and argued that the Suharto regime needed to "drive the communist danger as far away as possible from our borders."[158]

The army began building ties with South Vietnam as Suharto consolidated power in Indonesia. The first contacts between the nascent New Order and South Vietnamese officials occurred in early 1966 but remained secret. Ali Murtopo led an Opsus delegation to Saigon in December 1966. In conversations with Murtopo, Prime Minister Nguyen Cao Ky raised the possibility of opening a South Vietnamese embassy in Jakarta. Suharto rejected the idea for fear of providing Sukarno and his allies with a political cudgel. But he ordered Murtopo to continue sending his underlings to the embattled anticommunist republic over the next six months.[159] Indonesian delegations from Opsus, Bakin, and Koti repeatedly visited Saigon sub rosa over the course of 1967 and established a web of informal ties with the regime in Saigon.[160] The New Order also limited Indonesian engagement with the National Liberation Front of South Vietnam, whose office in Jakarta an observer described as "dormant" by late 1967.[161]

It was only in 1968 that the Suharto regime's policy toward Vietnam shed its ambivalence. An American politician who traveled to Jakarta in January noticed a new "hawkishness" in Indonesian views. Suharto told him that the Vietnam War was the product of Chinese aggression, which was "extremely hard to combat and essentially required the development of indigenous ideologies."[162] The Indonesian strongman was also heartened by reports that President Nguyen Van Thieu had resisted American pressure to participate in negotiations, which according to an intelligence officer convinced Suharto that "Thieu's government could stand on its own feet and was no longer an American puppet."[163] General Sumitro visited Saigon later that year and recalled that, his admiration for Vietnamese revolutionaries notwithstanding, he "wanted to delay or at least to hinder the rapid advancement of North Vietnam" by rectifying what he described as the South Vietnamese regime's "erroneous political concept."[164] Relieved of the need to protect his domestic flank after his ascent to the uncontested presidency and guided by the national resilience doctrine, Suharto embarked upon an effort to save the anticommunist regime in Saigon.

Ties between Indonesia and South Vietnam blossomed in the late 1960s. After a senior South Vietnamese official traveled to Jakarta in late 1969 to meet with Malik and Murtopo, Indonesia and South Vietnam agreed to establish in each other's capitals trade offices whose representatives would possess the authority to speak as ambassadors.[165] South Vietnamese diplomats in Jakarta cultivated ties with highly placed Indonesian military and political figures, including General Supardjo, who headed the Asia desk in the Ministry of Foreign Affairs, and Subchan and Imron Rosjadi, who chaired the foreign affairs committees in parliament and the assembly.[166] Suharto himself finally met South Vietnamese foreign minister Tran Van Lam in May 1970. In these exchanges, senior New Order officials routinely urged their South Vietnamese counterparts to elaborate a national ideology capable of binding together their population and to promote political stability and economic development—pillars of the national resilience doctrine.[167]

The Suharto regime also worked to reinforce the Thieu regime through diplomatic channels. Although the New Order maintained a public posture of opposition toward American involvement in Vietnam consonant with its nonaligned principles, Indonesian officials privately urged the Nixon administration to remain in Indochina as long as it took to preserve the Thieu regime and the region's other anticommunist governments—even if that entailed an American presence lasting more than ten years.[168] As negotiations between the United States and North Vietnam unfolded in Paris, Malik volunteered Indonesia to participate in the International Commission of Control and Supervision (ICCS) that would monitor the implementation of the peace agreement. New Order officials anticipated participation in the ICCS would bolster Indonesia's leadership role in Southeast Asia and present an opportunity to reinforce the Thieu regime.[169] Most of the men Indonesia dispatched to Vietnam were veterans of the anticommunist politicide of 1965 and 1966.[170] Ultimately, however, whatever advice Indonesian participants in the ICCS offered to their South Vietnamese interlocutors failed to remedy the fundamental weakness of the Thieu regime or alter the course of the war. In late March 1975, General Kharis Suhud predicted an imminent South Vietnamese collapse and recommended the withdrawal of the Indonesian ICCS contingent.[171] The last Indonesians left Saigon on April 27, 1975.[172]

Because the New Order kept its dealings with the Thieu regime secret, there are few records of the substance of Indonesian–South Vietnamese cooperation. And because historians have paid little attention to the Thieu regime, little is known of how Indonesian influence shaped South Vietnamese governance. But the Thieu regime was decidedly international in its orientation, working to expand its diplomatic footprint in Southeast Asia and around the world and also drawing inspiration from the likes of South Korea and Taiwan.[173] Whatever the extent of its influence, then, Indonesia's role in South Vietnam was yet another manifestation of its devotion to anticommunist internationalism in Southeast Asia, which focused on remaking the region in its own image through the doctrine of national resilience.

The Suharto regime faced considerable obstacles in its efforts to internationalize counterrevolution by promoting the national resilience doctrine in Southeast Asia. The notion of unity between the military and the population at the heart of the Hankamrata system emerged from Indonesia's particular revolutionary experience—using guerrilla tactics to repel a foreign force bent on recolonization. It did not obviously translate to Malaysia or the Philippines, where decolonization occurred more peacefully and the principal threats to national stability in the postcolonial era emerged from domestic insurgencies. The idea of military leadership in the political and economic realms reflected the leading role of the army in the Indonesian revolution and the institutional decay that plagued Sukarno's Guided Democracy regime. It held little appeal for Malaysian, Philippine, or Singaporean elites who emerged from outside the armed forces and prized military subservience to civilian institutions. These impediments notwithstanding, Suharto's Cold War in Southeast Asia contributed to a broad authoritarian convergence in the 1960s and 1970s. Across the region, national elites drew upon Indonesian resources, both material and ideational, to overcome political challenges and build authoritarian regimes.

As Suharto expanded his Cold War into Southeast Asia, he acquired the means to deepen his Cold War in Indonesia. The New Order's increasingly prominent role as a guarantor of anticommunist stability in Southeast Asia won Indonesia goodwill in the United States, Japan, Australia, and other aid-granting countries. Increasingly flush with international aid at the dawn of the 1970s, Suharto tightened his grip over Indonesia's stage and society, implementing plans to promote political stability and ignite economic development.

6

Capital and Consolidation

The day after Indonesia's national assembly elected him president in March 1968, Suharto departed Indonesia for a state visit to Japan. He stayed in Tokyo for a week—three days longer than his original itinerary—working to secure $100 million in aid. He met with Prime Minister Eisaku Sato, Emperor Hirohito, officials in the Foreign Ministry and Ministry of Finance, members of the Diet, and leaders of the Keidanren federation of businesses. But he left empty-handed. As a sign of his displeasure, he refused to sign a joint communiqué with Sato upon his departure.

The visit was the brainchild of General Alamsjah, the head of Spri, Suharto's kitchen cabinet. Alamsjah and Sudjono Humardani, who managed economic and financial matters within Spri, assumed responsibility for Indonesian relations with Japan in 1966. They traveled to Tokyo two months before Suharto for preliminary talks with Sato's government over Japan's reluctance to furnish one-third of the $325 million in aid that Indonesia requested from the IGGI that year—a stance that imperiled the agreement between the United States and Japan to deliver two-thirds of total IGGI aid and thus Suharto's ability to mobilize international capital more broadly.[1] Japanese officials informed Alamsjah and Sudjono that legal restrictions prohibited Japan from lending to Indonesia at the low rate of interest the IGGI promised. Moreover, balance-of-payments challenges and reports of misuse of the previous year's credits had inspired opposition parties in the Diet to lodge objections to Sato's proposed foreign aid budget for 1968.[2] Yet upon their return to Jakarta, Alamsjah and Sudjono assured Suharto that a presidential visit to Tokyo would break the logjam in negotiations. The Japanese sent signals to Foreign Minister Adam Malik that they were not prepared to grant the aid Indonesia sought, but Suharto ignored these warnings in the face of optimistic assessments from his confidants in Spri. One source in Ali Murtopo's Opsus command told an interlocutor that the Japan imbroglio was "the worst of Alamsjah's many blunders."[3]

Suharto's Cold War. Mattias Fibiger, Oxford University Press. © Oxford University Press 2023. DOI: 10.1093/oso/9780197667224.003.0007

International capital remained integral to the coalitional logic of the New Order. As Suharto extended his control over the armed forces, neutered political parties and civil society groups, launched a five-year economic development plan, and orchestrated national elections, he continued to rely on international aid and investment. Despite the desultory results of his first overseas voyage as president, he soon won dramatically expanded amounts of international aid by manipulating Western concerns about a post–Vietnam War political equilibrium in Southeast Asia. As the floodgates of international aid opened in late 1968 and early 1969, Suharto abandoned some of the consensual, inside-out state-building policies he had pursued in the early years of the New Order.

I

The economy remained Suharto's foremost concern. Drought struck Java in 1967 and led to a sixfold increase in Jakarta rice prices in the six months preceding March 1968. Because the government provided a rice ration to soldiers and civil servants, the state budget came under increasing strain. At the same time, the central bank continued to extend credit to the government to finance subsidies for consumer goods. Both the fiscal deficit and the money supply threatened to exceed the limits Indonesia agreed to in a stand-by agreement with the IMF.[4] Inflation surged. And external challenges reinforced domestic instability. The IGGI's tepid posture toward Indonesia's request for $325 million in aid stoked rumors that the flow of international aid to Indonesia would soon abate. The devaluation of the pound sterling in November 1967 then prompted a burst of speculative activity on the foreign exchange market. The rupiah cratered in value from 140 to 285 per dollar, fueling inflationary pressures and undermining budgetary planning as imported goods grew more expensive.[5] Suharto faced a contradiction between his twin goals of political and economic stabilization. Curtailing subsidies for rice and other consumer staples would lead to further cost-of-living challenges, violate a key pillar of the *Tritura*, and enrage the civil society groups that helped propel him to the presidency. But continuing to use fiscal and monetary artistry to finance consumption in excess of production would inevitably generate further inflation and alienate the international donors whose largesse propped up the New Order.

Indonesian officials explained this dilemma at an April 1968 meeting of the IGGI held in Rotterdam. The ostensible purpose of the meeting was to ensure that individual donor commitments combined to reach Indonesia's request for $325 million in total aid. The IMF, World Bank, and Asian Development Bank circulated reports on the state of the Indonesian economy in advance of the meeting. Summarizing these documents, the IMF's deputy director for Asia noted that, despite the challenges that cropped up at the turn of the year, "the measures taken by the Indonesian authorities during 1966 and 1967 may be said to have had a considerable degree of success." He implored IGGI member states to "commit an adequate amount of aid to Indonesia . . . as quickly as possible."[6] Some IGGI donors expressed skepticism about the New Order's commitment to its stabilization plan in light of the emergence of popular protest. The Indonesian delegates scolded the skeptics. They noted that disbursements of aid had waned during the challenging months of early 1968, leaving the New Order with "no choice but to face the crisis practically alone." Indonesian officials warned the IGGI that "there is a limit to what the people are prepared to endure."[7] Their protests fell on deaf ears. Although the United States affirmed its willingness to provide one-third of Indonesia's $325 million aid request if other donors committed to providing the remaining two-thirds, Japan and other IGGI members continued to demur, citing political and legal hurdles.[8] Upon the conclusion of the proceedings the Indonesian delegation lamented that "hope deferred is not a marketable commodity."[9]

Suharto confronted serious challenges in reining in fiscal and monetary excess. The state subsidized commodities like gasoline and kerosene, the prices of which remained fixed even as the overall price level doubled between 1967 and 1968. By the time the Rotterdam meeting of the IGGI adjourned, a liter of gasoline was cheaper than a cup of coffee.[10] These subsidies drained the government's coffers and encouraged the inefficient use of fuel that could otherwise be exported for scarce foreign exchange. "It is a matter for regret that no adjustment has yet been made to the prices of petroleum products," the IMF mission chief told the IGGI in April.[11] But key Indonesian military officials believed fuel price hikes would endanger the New Order. "Ali Murtopo was panicky," Suharto remembered. "He even cried in front of me. . . . 'If you make a decision like this,' he said, 'the people will revolt and the government could fall.' "[12]

Squeezed between the demands of his domestic and international constituencies, Suharto plotted a middle-of-the-road approach. He agreed to liberalize fuel prices but, during a meeting with the American ambassador, insisted that "full [liberalization] measures could not be instituted at this time in [the] face [of] current political realities." Instead, he envisioned a more gradual " 'two-bite' program."[13] Suharto appeared on television on the evening of April 24 and announced that the government would quadruple the price of gasoline and double the price of kerosene effective immediately. These price hikes then radiated through the economy, generating increases in the prices of goods and services that depended on fuel inputs. The action fronts erupted in fury. They staged demonstrations demanding the resignation of the finance minister, one of which turned violent and ended with one student dead and several more injured.[14] Public fury prompted Suharto to retreat from his plans for additional price liberalization. He told two technocrats that "further petroleum price increases would not be politically possible this calendar year."[15] But he pressed forward with an increase in utility prices and an imposition of import tariffs on textiles, which led to more price hikes for politically sensitive consumer goods but reduced strain on the government's budget and preserved Indonesia's reserves of hard currency.[16]

Suharto worked to shore up his international flank in the wake of the Rotterdam meeting. Indonesian officials canvassed the globe and pleaded for quick disbursements of aid. Bappenas chair Widjojo Nitisastro and fellow technocrat Emil Salim traveled to the United States in May 1968. They told Vice President Hubert Humphrey that the results of the most recent IGGI meeting were "very disappointing" and warned that "Indonesia cannot survive a second crisis."[17] By then US policy toward Indonesia was in the midst of a realignment. American policymakers had become increasingly confident that Suharto could establish a durable regime capable of driving political and economic change in Indonesia and Southeast Asia more broadly. Moreover, the US embassy in Jakarta believed that "the present year will be crucial to the success of these efforts, for during 1968 trends will be set in motion which determine the course of this important nation for many years to come."[18] Widjojo and Salim succeeded in extracting an emergency infusion of $46 million in aid, which for the Johnson administration meant exceeding the one-third formula that was popular with a Congress increasingly hostile to foreign aid and useful as a cudgel among other members of the IGGI facing economic difficulties of their own.[19]

Other Indonesian officials secured commitments for additional food relief from a number of European IGGI members and made progress in coaxing Japan to commit to providing one-third of Indonesia's aid needs.[20] By year's end Indonesia would obtain some $350 million in international aid—a full $25 million above the amount deemed necessary by the IGGI in November 1967. Renewed infusions of international aid tempered inflationary pressures in Indonesia. International capital also enabled Suharto to adopt a more exclusionary and coercive posture toward his domestic coalition. He betrayed an air of confidence when he warned a nationwide gathering of university student leaders that, although he embraced the "vanguard" role of youth in Indonesia, he expected students to allow themselves to be "directed," lest their activism become "harmful."[21]

Reinforced by the resumption of international aid, Suharto embarked on an effort at institutionalization. He unveiled his cabinet on June 10, 1968—aptly dubbed the First Development Cabinet. Although soldiers retained control over portfolios with implications for national security, they were outnumbered in the cabinet three-to-one by civilians.[22] Notable among those elevated to ministerial posts were Sumitro Djojohadikusumo, to oversee trade, and Ali Wardhana, to direct finance. Beneath the cabinet level, Widjojo retained his chairmanship of Bappenas, the most powerful economic policymaking body.[23] Suharto also disbanded Spri—a frequent target of student protest and press criticism. In its place he formed a new body called Personal Assistants (Aspri), to which he appointed the most influential members of Spri, including Sudjono Humardani and Ali Murtopo. Suharto presented his newly remodeled policymaking network with five main goals: achieving political stability, restoring order and security, holding national elections, continuing the "cleansing" of the state apparatus, and implementing a five-year economic development plan.[24]

The economic ministers in the First Development Cabinet continued to court new sources of international capital. In July 1968, the government unveiled a domestic investment law designed to encourage ethnic Chinese entrepreneurs to repatriate capital to Indonesia after they had channeled untold sums to Taiwan, Hong Kong, and Singapore following the September Thirtieth Movement. The new law offered domestic investors the same incentives and protections extended to foreign investors one year earlier, including various tax holidays and guarantees against expropriation and nationalization. Said one money changer, "the big push was to pull the 'hot money' back into the country."[25] Foreign aid also remained paramount. Widjojo published an article in the *Financial Times* in October 1968 noting that "the basic objective of Indonesia's current economic policy is to secure a breathing space of a few years during which the economy can recover from the damage inflicted on it during the Sukarno era. It is essential that during this period Indonesia should receive sufficient assistance from abroad and that it should be spared the burden of excessive foreign debt servicing."[26]

Indonesian technocrats found an eager partner in the new president of the World Bank, Robert McNamara. Recently ousted from the Pentagon after he became disenchanted with the Vietnam War, McNamara brought himself up to speed on the World Bank's operations by opening an atlas and noting the institution's total lending to various developing countries. He noticed that Indonesia, which he had dubbed "the greatest prize of all" in Southeast Asia back in 1964, was the most populous country other than China that received no World Bank assistance.[27] World Bank officials quietly informed Suharto that McNamara had decided "to count Indonesia as being amongst his principal concerns and priorities."[28] He decided to visit the archipelago on his first overseas trip in his new position.[29] In June 1968, he arrived in Jakarta for four days of meetings with Suharto, other political leaders, economic planners, and international observers. Sumitro told McNamara that "the people were becoming very impatient" and suggested that "Indonesia might need to accept hard loans, or even supplier credits, since the debt was a lesser problem than popular revolt."[30] During breaks in the talks, McNamara bonded with other Indonesian technocrats over their fondness for the Berkeley economist Malcolm Davisson, who taught both the World Bank chief and many of his Indonesian interlocutors when they attended the university.[31] McNamara came away impressed. "No other country I have ever visited, particularly in Southeast Asia," he enthused "has a sounder approach to its economic problems, backed by so many resources, as Indonesia. And in no other country are the top men responsible for the nation's economy so well qualified as in Indonesia."[32]

McNamara ordered the establishment of a World Bank resident mission in Jakarta headed by Bernard Bell. The first of its kind in the Bank's history, the mission was staffed by what McNamara called "the top 2–3 per cent of the Bank's personnel" and intended to provide managerial and technical expertise to Indonesia's economic policymakers.[33] Given that Bell had already made known his belief that "the present level of aid to Indonesia is inadequate," Indonesian technocrats hoped that the mission would also bolster Indonesia's efforts to secure additional IGGI aid.[34] When McNamara sat down with IGGI ambassadors and Indonesian policymakers during his visit to Jakarta, Sumitro and Ali Wardhana told the group that further delays in aid disbursement would endanger Indonesia's economic progress.[35]

Indonesian technocrats enlisted a broad cast of consultants from the World Bank, the IMF, and the Harvard Development Advisory Service to elaborate the Suharto regime's first five-year development plan (Repelita). As one foreign economist involved in its formulation remarked, the plan "was premature in terms of the available data and the necessary preparatory work, but it was timely in signalling the shift of emphasis from stabilization to rehabilitation and development."[36] The plan thus represented a bid for additional aid with longer time horizons as much as a realistic guide for economic development. It focused first and foremost on the expansion of agricultural production through the rehabilitation of irrigation and anti-erosion systems; the promotion of fertilizers, pesticides, and high-yield seeds; the reconstruction of transportation networks connecting producing, consuming, and exporting areas; and the upgrading of electrification and communication systems.[37] Such lofty ambitions came with a sizable price tag. Repelita envisioned a 1.42 trillion rupiah spending program, of which 59 percent would be financed by foreign aid and another 14 percent by foreign investment. Measured in hard currency, the plan hinged on massive infusions of approximately $550 million in foreign aid and $130 million in foreign investment per year.[38] Those projections became a source of some controversy in Indonesia. Sarbini Sumawinata, a colleague of many technocrats at the University of Indonesia, rescuscitated the rhetoric of self-sufficiency popular under Sukarno and argued that "funds for financing the plan must be sourced domestically," which would remind the Indonesian public that "development requires sacrifice."[39]

Table 6.1 **Sources of funding for Repelita I**

	Billions of 1968 Rupiah	*Percent of Total*
Aid Counterpart	393	27.7
Project Aid	440	30.9
Foreign Investment	200	14.1
Total Foreign Sources	1033	72.7
Budget Surplus	226	15.9
Bank Credits	95	6.7
Domestic Investment	66	4.6
Total Domestic Sources	387	27.2
Total	1420	100

Source: Compiled by author from Government of Indonesia, *Rentjana Pembangunan Lima Tahun 1969/70–1973/74* (Jakarta: Departemen Penerangan, 1969).

II

As Suharto and Indonesian economic policymakers prepared Repelita, they worked to negotiate further debt rescheduling agreements. Absent such postponements in the repayment of Sukarno-era debts, the Suharto regime would require an additional $160 million in annual capital inflows to finance the five-year plan.[40] The World Bank mission in Jakarta believed the year-by-year rescheduling ritual consecrated annually in Paris served only to "postpone the problem into the 1970s," when Indonesia would be required to remit more than $200 million per annum in debt service payments—more than 40 percent of its projected export revenues in some years.[41] Indonesian technocrats had long expressed similar frustrations. The chief of the central bank remembered that "Indonesia's negotiators began to see themselves as the financial equivalent of Sisyphus," because upon the conclusion of a debt rescheduling agreement they were immediately presented with even larger debt burdens that required rescheduling.[42] The most recent iteration of that ritual occurred in October 1968, when the Paris Club agreed to reschedule Indonesia's debts falling due in 1969 on the same terms that debts falling due in 1967 and 1968 had been rescheduled: repayment over eight years following a three-year grace period.[43]

Most stakeholders came to agree on the necessity of a wholesale settlement of Indonesia's debt burden. The Paris Club enlisted Dr. Hermann Abs, the chairman of Deutsche Bank who had negotiated the rescheduling and partial cancellation of Germany's World War II debt, to study Indonesia's balance of payments and formulate a sustainable solution.[44] The German banker would present his proposals no later than mid-1969.

A week after the Paris Club meeting, the IGGI met in the coastal district of Scheveningen in the Netherlands. There Indonesian officials lodged a request for $500 million in aid for 1969: $365 million in economic aid and $135 million in food aid. Both the IMF and the World Bank endorsed the request in light of the considerable progress the New Order had made in stabilizing the Indonesian economy, especially in bridling galloping inflation and preparing a development plan. The United States made known its willingness to provide one-third of the economic aid Indonesia required in addition to a "fair share" of food aid—a formal deviation from the formula whereby the United States provided one-third of all IGGI aid, since "fair share" was interpreted to mean at least half.[45] But the Japanese delegate said it was "difficult to recognize the need for an even larger amount" of aid in 1969 and asserted that "the Government of Japan could not accept a formula" that would require Japan to pledge one-third of IGGI aid. A number of delegations suggested they wanted to wind up the IGGI altogether and revert to bilateral discussions with Indonesia on economic aid. Steadfast diplomacy by the United States preserved the IGGI as a going concern and led the assembled governments to endorse Indonesia's request for $500 million in aid.[46]

By the end of April 1969, Hermann Abs had sketched the outlines for a plan to manage Indonesia's sovereign debt burden. The principal on all existing Indonesian debts (to both non-communist and communist creditors) would be consolidated and repaid in equal installments over a period of thirty years, while the past and future interest due on those debts would be cancelled. The proposal would lower Indonesia's total debt burden from $2.2 billion to $1.7 billion and entail annual debt service payments of $57 million. Economists at the IMF and World Bank feared the proposal would impose undue burdens on Indonesia's balance of payments during the critical juncture of the first five-year plan, when $57 million would constitute a relatively larger proportion of gross domestic product and total export earnings.[47] US officials also worried that, because communist countries were not providing additional aid, the plan risked being characterized as a transfer of American aid to the Soviet bloc at a moment when the foreign aid program faced unprecedented congressional skepticism.[48] Abs lobbied Paris Club governments to embrace his proposal. At one point in mid-1968, he told the Japanese minister of finance that Indonesia's already-rescheduled debts "must be rescheduled again" and, if Japanese law didn't permit as much, "the law would simply have to be changed."[49] After several months of consultations with creditor countries about the draft proposal, Abs completed the final, largely unchanged version of his plan in late July 1969.[50]

The Soviet Union rejected the Abs proposal outright, proclaiming that "a workers country could not be philanthropic and reduce interest to zero."[51]

But the Abs plan became the basis for negotiations between Indonesia and its Western creditors.[52] Before the Paris Club met to discuss the Abs plan in December, American diplomats worked diligently to ensure it won broad international support.[53] Meanwhile New Order envoys sought a modification of the payment schedule to ease Indonesia's debt service burden during the first years of the plan.[54] It quickly became clear that Indonesia's Western creditors would not agree to the Abs plan as written. The disagreements within the Paris Club revolved around two matters. First was the retroactive imposition of a zero interest rate and lengthy repayment period, which some Western governments feared would set an overgenerous precedent for other indebted sovereigns. Second was the question of whether Indonesia's already-rescheduled debts would be rescheduled again—something proponents of the Abs plan believed necessary to give the New Order leverage in negotiations with the Eastern bloc but opponents considered a bridge too far. American officials warned other creditors that failure to reschedule Indonesian debts under the generous terms Abs proposed would bring "strategical and general consequences" and predicted that "the contagion of setback and economic dislocation could quickly spread to neighboring countries."[55] The American appeal to geopolitics failed. The most the Paris Club would endorse was a standstill on Indonesian debts falling due in 1970 to provide breathing room for negotiations to continue.[56]

Over the first months of 1970, the New Order and its Western creditors came to an agreement on a slightly modified version of the Abs plan.[57] Indonesia gave ground on the no-interest provision of the original Abs proposal and agreed to pay the accumulated $445 million in interest on Sukarno-era debts over fifteen years beginning in 1985. Creditor countries in turn conceded Indonesia the option of deferring at 4 percent interest up to 50 percent of the payments due on the principal during the first eight years of the new repayment schedule to the last eight years—a version of what in the world of international credit was known as a "bisque clause."[58] Malik then worked to win Soviet assent to the plan. He traveled to Moscow in March 1970 and again in August and eventually secured agreement to repay the Soviet Union on the same terms as the Indonesia's Western creditors. Agreements with other Eastern bloc countries followed not long thereafter.[59]

As Indonesian diplomats prepared for final negotiations over the Abs plan, they also readied themselves to lodge a request for $600 million in aid at the December 1969 meeting of the IGGI. Malik traveled to Washington in November and told President Richard Nixon that "he hoped the US would continue and possibly increase its present level of aid, which was crucial in maintaining Indonesia's stability and accomplishing its five-year plan."[60] His anxieties about the willingness of the international community to continue

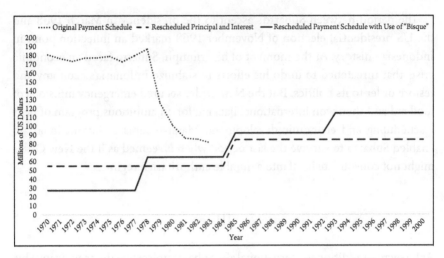

Figure 6.1 Indonesian Debt Repayment before and after the Abs Plan. H. W. Arndt, "Survey of Recent Developments," *Bulletin of Indonesian Economic Studies* 6, no. 2 (July 1970): 16.

furnishing Indonesia with aid appeared to be misplaced. The World Bank and the IMF both endorsed the Indonesian aid request and delegates of creditor countries accepted it without controversy. American officials remarked on the "great degree of unanimity" at the meeting, at which even traditionally skeptical creditor country delegations "joined with other donors in [a] positive view of overall Indonesian performance."[61] The Indonesian delegation proved correct when they labeled the year one of "transition."[62] Subsequent gatherings of the IGGI were shorn of much of the drama and uncertainty that pervaded the body's early meetings. The relationship between the Suharto regime and international capital achieved an unprecedented degree of regularization.

But storm clouds lurked on the horizon. Indonesia's ambassador to the United States, Soedjatmoko, wrote Suharto to note that the December 1969 meeting of the IGGI contained several "warning signals." The World Bank had only reluctantly deleted from its report to the IGGI several negative passages concerning corruption in the state oil company Pertamina and the rice procurement agency Bulog. And the Dutch delegation had predicted that general elections in April 1971 would likely bring to power a government in The Hague hostile to aiding the "military regime" in Jakarta. Soedjatmoko argued that anti–New Order sentiment was also ascendant in United States, West Germany, and the United Kingdom and would soon endanger the Suharto regime's ability to mobilize international capital. "Only concrete actions in Indonesia will be able to change this negative outlook," the ambassador warned, such as clamping down on graft and organizing democratic elections.[63]

The period between Suharto's ascent to the presidency in March 1968 and the US presidential election of November 1968 marked an inflection point in Indonesian history. At the moment of his triumph, Suharto faced an economic crisis that threatened to undo his efforts to stabilize Indonesia's economy and restore order to its politics. But the New Order secured emergency infusions of food aid and then won international backing for an ambitious program of debt rescheduling and economic development. Massive sums of international aid enabled Suharto to survive the last period when it seemed as if the New Order might not consolidate itself into a durable authoritarian regime.

III

As he secured additional international aid, Suharto unleashed the army against his political rivals, forcibly incorporated West Papua into the Indonesian state, and clamped down on the student movement and the press. Indonesians recognized that the alliance between the New Order and international capital was ena-bling Suharto to build his authoritarian state from the outside-in. Opposition mounted against his increasingly exclusionary approach to governance.

The slaughter of half-a-million suspected communists and fellow-travelers in 1965 and 1966 and the imprisonment of hundreds of thousands more decimated the PKI. Surviving party leaders nonetheless made periodic attempts to resus-citate the Indonesian communist movement. Most embraced Maoist ideas that prized the mobilization of the peasantry for agrarian revolution.[64] Politburo member Sudisman organized a new central committee in 1966 but was arrested by the army in December. The party's Central Java and East Java chiefs then knit together a network of covert PKI cells over the course of 1967. The rural South Blitar district of East Java eventually emerged as the focal point for this renewed effort to revive the party.

East Java was a deeply polarized province. Islamic militias associated with Nahdlatul Ulama had taken advantage of the chaos following the September Thirtieth Movement to target the PNI (whose regional branch leaned to the left) in addition to the PKI. General Sumitro was appointed commander of the army's East Java–based Brawijaya division in June 1966 and tasked with ensuring that violence did not widen beyond the campaign against the PKI. "My mindset at the time was simple: maintain balance," he recalled, affirming that "religious forces should not become too strong" and "the PNI should not be to-tally destroyed."[65] As international aid reinforced his domestic position, Suharto expanded his political objectives in East Java. He appointed General Mochamad Jasin as Sumitro's successor in April 1967. Jasin surmised that his appoint-ment showed Suharto wanted a "hard-liner" (*orang keras*).[66] He orchestrated a purge of Sukarnoists in the Brawijaya division as well as provincial and local governments and banned the PNI from operating in the province.[67] Jasin's purge led many Sukarnoist members of the armed forces to defect and join the renascent PKI in South Blitar. They trained and armed local peasants and refugees from army repression elsewhere in Java. The PKI soon began staging ambushes on army convoys and terrorizing landlords and religious elites complicit in the anticommunist bloodletting of 1965–1966.[68]

The escalating violence in East Java quickly attracted attention in Jakarta. Five thousand soldiers from the Brawijaya division arrived in Blitar in June 1968 and established direct military control over civilian life in the region as part of *Operasi Trisula*. The troops conscripted locals and forced them to take part in a "fence-of-legs" campaign in which they linked civilians in a human chain and marched them through the countryside to flush out PKI remnants taking refuge there. Villagers thought to harbor leftist sympathies were made to take part in the execution of suspected communists, sometimes using nothing more than rocks and sharpened sticks. By the time *Trisula* concluded in September, more than 2,000 people had been killed and thousands more detained.[69] The PKI would never again represent even a minor irritant to the Suharto regime. The party became little more than an imagined threat—a "latent danger," in the political lexicon of the New Order—that justified the preservation of authoritarian rule.[70]

Suharto's increasingly assertive posture also emerged in his approach to West Papua. In May 1968, he told a group of students and youth at the presidential palace that he considered "the development of West Irian as a national project."[71] Indonesia had assumed responsibility for the administration of the territory from the Netherlands following the 1962 New York Agreement. But the accord required Indonesia to orchestrate no later than 1969 an "act of free choice" through which the inhabitants of West Papua would be allowed to decide between integration with Indonesia and outright independence. Indonesian administration of West Papua fell far short of the noble terms set out in New York Agreement. One of the few foreigners able to travel to the territory noted that the Indonesian army "was left to its own heavy-handed devices," perpetrating "numerous beatings, shootings and gaolings in order to ensure a passive population." Meanwhile "development projects either languished or in many instances were totally abandoned. Imported foods disappeared and many urban Papuans used to artificially high wages and full employment under the Dutch were forced to return to subsistence gardening in order to get enough food to eat."[72] The brutality of the Indonesian occupation and the recognition that Jakarta would not permit a genuine act of self-determination to take place gave rise to a West Papuan opposition movement that narrated itself in increasingly nationalistic terms.[73]

For reasons both personal and political, Suharto was determined to cement Indonesian control over West Papua. He had led the military campaign to seize the territory in 1962 and believed its fate was intertwined with his own.[74] The overwhelming majority of Suharto's political allies regarded securing uncontested sovereignty over the entirety of the former Dutch East Indies as an unfulfilled promise of the national revolution.[75] West Papua was also home to the Ertsberg copper mine—the first project that had attracted foreign investment under the New Order and therefore a barometer of Indonesia's attitude toward international capital. As an American dispatch put it in January 1968, Freeport expressed concern about "the 'ascertainment' of popular wishes as to Indonesian rule which is scheduled for 1969."[76] To permit the emergence of an independent West Papua would thus threaten Suharto's personal legitimacy, his domestic popularity, and his international credibility. But Suharto was unwilling to forego entirely the act of free choice promised by the New York Agreement lest the New Order sacrifice its reputation for legalism both at home and abroad—which Indonesian officials routinely contrasted with Sukarno's proclivities for erratic governance and his disregard for legal constraints in order to attract international capital.[77]

Rather than disavow the act of free choice as an insult to Indonesian sovereignty, Suharto enlisted Opsus to ensure the referendum delivered the desired result.[78] As Malik told the American ambassador in February 1968, Indonesian officials anticipated that they could dispense "favors" to indigenous power brokers to secure their support for integration.[79] Lest inducements prove insufficient, Suharto also transferred General Sarwo Edhie, the New Order radical who had played a key role in the anticommunist violence of 1965–1966, from Sumatra to West Papua in mid-1968.[80] Reinforced by several thousand new troops, Sarwo told the local population that, although the act of free choice would be implemented in 1969, "Irian is unconditionally part of Indonesia." He warned West Papuans to "cease opposing [the] GOI [Government of Indonesia] or face strong countermeasures."[81] Unwilling to leave anything to chance, New Order officials also manipulated the mechanics of the act of free choice itself. Arguing that Papuans were too primitive for a one-man, one-vote system, Indonesian leaders disavowed the idea of a traditional plebiscite. Instead, they hand-selected 1,025 West Papuans out of a population of approximately 800,000 to vote publicly on the question of integration versus independence. Although American diplomats estimated that 85 to 90 percent of the population "are in sympathy with the Free Papua cause," the 1,025 voters expressed a unanimous desire to join Indonesia.[82] Credible reports of intimidation abounded. Not without reason have scholars dubbed the affair an "act of no choice."[83]

West Papua became a province of Indonesia in September 1969. Even after the so-called act of free choice concluded, the Suharto regime worked to mobilize international capital to consolidate its authority over the poor, restive province. One general told a high-ranking American diplomat in Jakarta that the New Order would require "additional foreign assistance . . . to continue developing West Irian" after integration.[84] Pertamina quickly solicited bids for 55,000 square kilometers of oil concessions in and around the province.[85] Suharto himself traveled to the provincial capital of Jayapura to welcome West Papua to Indonesia in September 1969 and proclaimed that the overarching task of national development required Indonesians to "dig up all the natural resources and all the funds that we have."[86]

Further evidence of Suharto's increasingly coercive approach to governance emerged in his effort to muzzle the Indonesian media. Sukarno's Guided Democracy regime had entailed a guided press.[87] A labyrinth of regulations and licensing requirements together with periodic bans on publications that failed to accept the media's government-prescribed role as an "instrument of national struggle" delivered a quiescent fourth estate.[88] But Suharto's rise to power ushered in a period of remarkable intellectual ferment. Notwithstanding the shuttering of some forty-six publications accused of acting as organs of the PKI, the media subjected the nascent New Order regime to considerable scrutiny and aired contentious debates over Indonesia's future.[89] So vibrant was the period that one cabinet minister compared it to the Prague Spring.[90]

Suharto soon came to regard the cacophonous press as a threat to the New Order's twin goals of political stabilization and economic development. In November 1969, the Jakarta daily *Indonesia Raya* published a searing indictment of General Ibnu Sutowo's management of Pertamina's finances. It followed the Pertamina articles with exposés of waste and corruption in Bulog.[91] The resulting discontent gave rise to a new organization of Indonesian youth called Students Accuse (MM) that defined its role as a moral force whose aim was "not to overthrow the government" but instead to provide "critical support for the government."[92] Youth groups like MM staged large protests against corruption that spread from Jakarta to Bandung to Yogyakarta and to Medan—the first major expressions of popular discontent within the New Order.[93]

Reports of corruption did far more than alienate segments of Suharto's domestic coalition. They also threatened to stanch the flow of international aid that sustained the New Order. Mochtar Lubis, the editor of *Indonesia Raya*, published an editorial suggesting that Ibnu's freewheeling financial practices ought to make international donors reluctant to continue funding Indonesia's economic development.[94] Malik, who was visiting Washington to secure international acquiescence to West Papua's integration into Indonesia, sent a cable to Suharto relaying a conversation with an American diplomat who told him that some IGGI donors would refuse to authorize the aid Indonesia sought in light of the Pertamina scandal.[95] Facing both domestic and international criticism,

Suharto appointed a special Commission of Four to investigate corruption. The commission's inflammatory report was promptly leaked by the newspaper *Sinar Harapan* in July 1970.[96] Another new youth organization, the Anti-Corruption Committee (KAK), staged silent protests centered on Hotel Indonesia, the symbolic seat of international capital's presence in the archipelago.[97]

Suharto was determined to prevent revelations of additional scandals that could imperil the flow of aid and investment. He was also increasingly willing to alienate the student and youth groups whose activism had propelled him to the presidency. He banned KAK in August and began clamping down on the press.[98] *Sinar Harapan* came in for particular punishment. The paper's editor was hauled in front of the body that regulated the press and told that he might be held to account under the state secrets law. "Since when did corruption become a state secret?" he acerbically responded. *Sinar Harapan* was permitted to continue publishing. But after the paper leaked details of the government's budget proposal eighteen months later, the Suharto regime revoked the its permit to print and threatened to shutter it entirely unless the editor was removed.[99]

Suharto did not completely dismantle the free press. He was cognizant of the disaffection such a move could inspire among the New Order's international sponsors, whose publics and legislatures had begun to express opposition to aiding authoritarian regimes.[100] Antiwar lawmakers in the United States excoriated not only the war in Indochina but also the provision of aid to Taiwan, South Korea, Greece, and other countries ruled by authoritarian governments, reasoning that such aid abetted human rights violations and could lead the United States into another Vietnam.[101] Meanwhile the human rights organization Amnesty International had begun publishing accounts of the travails of Indonesian political prisoners.[102] The institution's central council determined in early 1970 that Amnesty would "give the highest priority to Indonesia."[103] As the human rights revolution—a project that emerged within the global Cold War—roiled the world, Suharto found his ability to continue waging his domestic Cold War limited.

IV

The most pressing challenge for Suharto was consolidating his control over the armed forces. Resistance to the New Order remained prevalent in the navy and the marines after March 1968, and some forty sailors were arrested during the army's *Trisula* operations against the PKI in South Blitar.[104] In July 1968, the outspokenly leftist navy newspaper *El Bahar* aired accusations that the Suharto regime was inviting foreign powers to establish military bases in Indonesia—a charge certain to spark a nationalist outcry.[105] An Opsus deputy told an

American diplomat the same month that "the Navy and Marine Corps together now harbor the strongest concentration of leftist and Sukarnoist influence in the Indonesian Armed Forces, and the Suharto government would like to begin tackling this problem as it already has done to some extent in the Air Force and Police."[106]

Suharto mobilized international capital to secure his control over these recalcitrant branches of the military. The munitions and materiel upon which the navy and marines relied came largely from the Soviet Union, and the supply of spare parts dried up as Indonesian links with the West deepened during Suharto's ascent to power. Audits conducted in mid-1969 revealed that only 20 percent of the air force's planes and 40 percent of the navy's vessels were operational.[107] If Suharto could attract military aid for the navy and marines, he could ensure their loyalty to the New Order. But the Johnson administration had until 1968 limited US military aid to Indonesia to what the American embassy in Jakarta called a "small but important" civic action program focused on public works beneficial to the civilian population.[108] And Ambassador Soedjatmoko warned Suharto in June 1968, "regarding military aid, there is no possibility that this assistance will be enlarged."[109]

Indonesia's prospects for attracting American military aid brightened considerably with the election of Richard Nixon in November 1968. Suharto had begun cultivating Nixon well before the election. He met with the future president in Jakarta in April 1967 during one of the American's globe-spanning trips. Having just seized executive power from Sukarno through the *Supersemar*, Suharto emphasized to Nixon the "need for spare parts for [the] military" and suggested "communism could come back . . . because its ideological roots are so deep."[110] Bakin reported the following month that Nixon believed South American countries needed "De Gaulle–style democracy with a strong leader at the top." Although he was "concerned about the survival of representative democracy," the future president was equally mindful of "the rate of economic development." Moreover, he "wants South America's major countries—Brazil and Argentina— to take over the police role which the US has traditionally undertaken in the area."[111] The parallels with Indonesia were not difficult to discern. Like Brazil and Argentina, Indonesia was an authoritarian state draped with only the barest trappings of democracy. It too was ruled by a military strongman whose legitimacy rested upon a narrative of economic development. And it too occupied a region from which American leaders wanted to disengage after lengthy periods of direct military intervention—but in which they worried about the possibility of instability.

That Nixon could be induced to expand American military aid to Indonesia became obvious in his October 1967 *Foreign Affairs* article entitled "Asia after Viet-Nam." Like McNamara before him, Nixon called Indonesia "by far the greatest prize in the Southeast Asian area." He celebrated the regionalist and developmentalist impulses arising across the region, of which the Suharto regime was emblematic, and he suggested the United States ought to help "the nations of non-communist Asia become so strong—economically, politically and militarily—that they no longer furnish tempting targets for Chinese aggression."[112] There emerged a remarkable (although not total) complementarity in grand strategic outlooks between the incoming Nixon administration and the Suharto regime.

Suharto wasted little time lobbying the new Nixon administration for heightened levels of military aid. In a March 1969 conversation with Marshall Green, the outgoing American ambassador in Jakarta newly promoted to the top job at the State Department's Asia desk, Suharto explained he wanted to "explore [the] means by which the Indonesian armed forces can be brought to an acceptable state of readiness." He argued that only a revitalized Indonesian military could fend off the threats posed by the PKI, Vietnam, and China. Suharto also hinted that a re-equipped Indonesian military could be dispatched to combat communist threats elsewhere in Southeast Asia, such as Malaysia.[113] These were talking points designed to appeal directly to Nixon's determination to devolve responsibility for the maintenance of international stability to regional clients. Nixon perused Green's report of the conversation with interest, making several marginal notations as he read. He ordered his chief foreign policy aide, Henry Kissinger, to invite Suharto to the United States "as soon as possible."[114]

Not all Indonesian policymakers favored the expansion of military aid that Suharto requested. Two days after he met with Suharto, Green sat down with Malik. The Indonesian foreign minister remarked that American military aid in Asia "should be limited in scope so as to avoid disproportionately large military establishments. He added wryly: "What [the Indonesian] military needs more than weapons and tools is greater political sophistication."[115] Aware that an increase in military aid would render action fronts, political parties, and religious organizations less vital to the coalitional logic of the New Order, the civilian and wily bureaucratic operator Malik hoped to forestall the provision of additional military aid to Indonesia and thereby prevent the armed forces from accumulating uncontested political power. He also sought to preserve Indonesia's nonaligned image, which a massive US military aid program would belie.

Nixon traveled across Southeast Asia in late July 1969 as part of his effort to chart a new course for American foreign policy. During a stopover on the Pacific island of Guam, he announced what would become known as the Nixon Doctrine: the United States would furnish its Asian allies and friends with the military and economic aid—but no longer the manpower—necessary to subdue threats that arose within their national borders.[116]

The articulation of the Nixon Doctrine confirmed the Suharto regime's plans to win additional aid by casting the New Order as a bulwark against communism both at home and abroad. Briefing books from Indonesia's Ministry of Foreign Affairs emphasized that Nixon harbored a "hard-line" anticommunism, a desire to manage foreign policy from the White House, a favorable outlook toward developmental dictatorships, and an obsession with credibility as American forces withdrew from Vietnam. They informed Suharto that the United States still regarded Indonesia with a combination of "hope and anxiety" and encouraged him to play on both emotions as he lobbied for heightened levels of aid. Repelita, for instance, required "very large quantities of American assistance." Its success would make Indonesia "more resistant to the communist threat," while its failure would mean "an Indonesia that is continuously economically weak that can easily become a communist target." The books also noted that Suharto should explain that, with "sufficient arms aid and military equipment," the Indonesian military could combat communist threats across Asia, whether caused by Chinese or Soviet meddling or by the end of the Vietnam War. Nixon himself, the briefing books remarked, harbored a "special interest in forms of regional cooperation" that would allow "Asian countries to defend themselves (and defend American interests)." The books therefore suggested that Suharto emphasize Indonesia's leading role within ASEAN as "the most concrete proof of Indonesia's cooperative efforts with other Southeast Asian countries."[117]

Air Force One touched down in Jakarta on July 27. In conversations with Nixon, Suharto said Indonesia would need some $3 billion in economic aid and $1 billion in debt relief over the coming five years to finance Repelita. He also urged Nixon to support an additional $200 million in aid for a power complex, a steel foundry, a fertilizer plant, and a cement factory that would lay the groundwork for the second five-year plan and serve as "monumental projects that would enhance U.S.-Indonesian relations over the long haul." Beyond economic aid, Suharto asked Nixon to furnish the Indonesian military with additional weapons, equipment, and training.[118] General Sumitro and a coterie of other senior military leaders met with Kissinger at the same time. The generals echoed Suharto's request for military aid and began the process of setting up a communications backchannel that bypassed civilian officials in the US State Department and Indonesian Foreign Ministry that they (correctly) believed opposed reinforcing the Indonesian armed forces.[119]

Upon his return to the United States, Nixon told Kissinger that he regarded "our discussions with Indonesian Generals on military assistance" as "personal Presidential commitments." He wanted American officials to "follow through without fail."[120] He overrode a consensus within the foreign policy bureaucracy held over from the Johnson administration that the Suharto regime faced "no serious external or internal threats" and an increase in military aid risked leading the New Order to ignore the vital tasks of fostering "a popular base for the regime" and "institutional channels for the expression of discontent."[121] On August 11, Kissinger sent Sumitro a telegram noting that Nixon looked "with great favor on your proposal" and requesting more information about the scope of Indonesia's military needs.[122]

Conversations between Indonesian and American leaders during Nixon's visit to Jakarta dramatically inflated Suharto's expectations regarding the future of US military aid. Confident that a flood of munitions and materiel would enable him to win the loyalty of the navy and marines, he embarked upon a more aggressive purge of suspected leftists and Sukarnoists in those branches of the armed forces. In October 1969, he reorganized the Indonesian military to eliminate each service's operational independence and bring them all under the central control of the Ministry of Defense and Security (Hankam).[123] He then kicked the reigning chiefs of the navy and marines upstairs to ambassadorships—appropriately enough in Moscow and Pyongyang—and installed loyalists at the command of those services.[124] Admiral Sudomo, who became head of the navy, worked to more tightly integrate the marines into the navy's command structure. He quickly announced that his first priority was "cleansing the navy of the remains of the September Thirtieth Movement" and embarked upon a purge of the institution.[125] So thorough was Sudomo's purge that some regime insiders began joking that the navy was likely to have more ships than officers to command them.[126] As Sudomo's purge radiated down the ranks of the navy and marines, Suharto sought to ensure the flow of equipment to those services. He also installed Marshal Suwoto Sukendar as chief of the air force and ordered the new commander to "continue" purging the service of leftist elements.[127]

Indonesian officials pressed the Nixon administration to follow through on what they regarded as commitments for a massive military aid program. In October 1969, Sumitro approached the American embassy in Jakarta and requested the United States "study the possibility of equipping the Indonesian armed forces over the next 5–7 years."[128] But the Nixon administration delivered far less than the Indonesians hoped. After a contorted and contentious bureaucratic process, Washington agreed in March 1970 to triple American military assistance to Indonesia to $15 million per year.[129]

Suharto traveled to the United States in May 1970 in a bid to secure additional military aid.[130] Shortly before departing Jakarta, he received a report from Yoga Sugama, then serving as chief of the intelligence division within Hankam. Yoga wrote approvingly that the "Nixon administration has outlined a non-discriminatory policy toward other countries, whatever their form (dictatorship or democracy) and whichever group rules (military or civilian)." But he warned that "within the American people there is a tendency not to sympathize with governments led by the military." He alleged that several New Left

Figure 6.2 A political cartoon illustrates the sorry state of Indonesia's naval capabilities. *Indonesia Raya*, April 14, 1969.

"anti-Indonesia" groups as well as unfriendly media outlets like the *New York Times* and NBC News were seeking to undermine US support for the New Order. Moreover, Yoga explained that Congress sought to "make cuts to the budget not directly related to the people's welfare (defense and foreign aid)." To navigate these challenging political waters, Yoga advised Suharto to emphasize both American credibility and the communist threat: the Nixon Doctrine faced a "test case" brought about by the accelerating withdrawal of American forces from Vietnam, and the United States needed to "give the countries of Southeast Asia a reasonable ability to defend themselves against the communist threat."[131]

Suharto followed the script when he arrived in the Oval Office. He raised the communist bogey to argue for expanded military and economic aid, predicting that "issues such as the revival of Communism" would "become more critical" if his five-year development plan failed. He added that, during his first few years in office, "I have put top attention on economic strength, but now Indonesia must give attention to military strength as well. Assistance is especially needed for the navy and air force." Suharto concluded by noting that an expanded military would be vital in enabling Indonesia to play a stabilizing role in Southeast Asia as the United States withdrew from Vietnam—a realization of the Nixon Doctrine's vision of a devolution of geopolitical authority to guarantors of regional stability. The president was impressed, promising once again that he would "give Indonesia's requests very sympathetic consideration."[132]

General Alamsjah followed up with Kissinger the next day. For nearly a decade, the general explained, all Indonesian military equipment came from the Soviet Union. The current state of Soviet-Indonesian relations was so poor that obtaining spare parts for this equipment had become impossible, leaving "a Navy without gunboats" and "pilots without aircraft." Alamsjah suggested that a massive American program to re-equip the Indonesian military was necessary to preserve stability in Southeast Asia because "Indonesia was being depended upon" by other countries in the region. Yet he hinted at a second rationale behind Suharto's requests when he insisted that military aid should be delivered before Indonesia's elections scheduled for July 1971.[133] Once again officials in the American foreign policy bureaucracy began worrying about the "possibility of exaggerated expectations" regarding military assistance.[134]

Those worries proved well placed. Sumitro traveled to the United States in July 1970 for meetings with Kissinger on the specifics of Suharto's request for additional military aid. Reiterating the New Order's determination to play a stabilizing role in Southeast Asia, Sumitro presented Kissinger with a shopping list that a National Security Council staffer described as "a complete force modernization plan"—it included such extravagant items as B-52 bombers and intermediate-range ballistic missiles—whose "price tag would run to billions of dollars."[135] Kissinger finally punctured the New Order's inflated hopes for a massive infusion of military aid at a follow-up meeting the next week. He lamented that the Nixon administration faced congressional and budgetary constraints on its military assistance program and would not be able meet the Suharto regime's expansive aid requests. But he insisted that Nixon "was in favor of helping" and agreed to dispatch a specialist from the NSC to oversee a study of Indonesia's military requirements.[136] Finally in August 1970, General Panggabean sent a note to the American ambassador outlining Indonesia's priorities for military aid: communications and electronic equipment for the army and transportation and patrol vehicles for the air force and navy.[137] Not without reason, American bureaucrats understood the requests as "directly related to Indon[esian] armed forces (ABRI) top priority mission—to prepare for and support national elections in mid 1971 and to maintain internal security before, during and after national elections."[138]

Suharto and his underlings characterized Indonesia's appeals for military aid as a realization of the Nixon Doctrine. They claimed a reinforced Indonesian military would adopt a vanguard role in promulgating its doctrines of national resilience and Hankamrata in Southeast Asia. They went so far as to promise the Indonesian military would project power outward into the region to suppress so-called wars of national liberation that threatened other non-communist governments. But Suharto's overarching objectives were domestic. An expanded military aid package from the United States would allow Suharto to consolidate his authority within the military and allow the military to consolidate its authority within Indonesia. Much of the military aid that Indonesia received from the United States over subsequent years went to the air force and the navy, which solidified support for the New Order within those recalcitrant services. And the aid that went to the military helped Suharto orchestrate a national election and secure popular mandate for his rule.

V

Having mobilized international capital to launch the five-year plan, broaden and deepen the authority of the state, and consolidate his control within the military, Suharto turned to the delicate task of legitimizing his rule through a popular mandate. During his drive toward the presidency, Suharto's limited ability to mobilize international capital left him with little alternative but to set aside his distaste for political parties and permit them a role in the New Order. Instead, agencies like Opsus intervened in the internal affairs of parties to ensure they adopted programs amenable to Suharto's Cold War agenda. Suharto also agreed to hold elections no later than July 1971. By the time inflows of international aid expanded in the late 1960s and allowed Suharto to consolidate his authority, political changes in aid-granting countries meant he had to maintain the trappings of democracy that he had permitted during the period immediately following the September Thirtieth Movement.

Suharto therefore required a vehicle of electoral legitimation. But the form that vehicle would take and the channels of competition it would navigate remained uncertain. The late 1960s became a period of experimentation within the New Order and negotiation between the Suharto regime and its domestic and international constituencies. In early 1969, the New Order radicals General Dharsono, commander of the Siliwangi division, and General Kemal Idris, commander of Kostrad, implemented a forcible reorganization of the party system in West Java, merging the region's parties into a "dwigrup" structure comprising a government-development group and an opposition-correction group oriented toward the same goal: formulating and implementing the government's economic program.[139] Such coercive measures inspired strident complaints from party leaders like NU's Yusuf Hasyim, who wrote directly to Suharto demanding the government roll back the changes. General Amirmachmud, newly installed as interior minister, responded on Suharto's behalf and ordered the undoing of the New Order radicals' reorganization of West Java's party system. He asserted that the population's desire to fashion a new political system "must be channeled through democratic and constitutional avenues that are national in scope" rather than arise through a chaotic process of regional experimentation.[140] Dharsono was relieved of command and sent to serve in an ambassadorial post in Bangkok, while Kemal Idris was reassigned to become interregional commander for East

Indonesia—positions from which the radicals would wield far less influence over the course of national politics.

Events in West Java appeared to confirm that parties would serve as the conduits of political competition in the New Order. But Suharto could not claim the uncontested loyalty of any existing party. Some of his supporters approached him in early 1969 and urged him to establish his own party. He refused out of concern that doing so would cost him the support of the anti-party segments of the army. Instead, Suharto ordered Murtopo and Opsus to resuscitate the Joint Secretariat of Functional Groups (Sekber Golkar) and fashion it into a political machine through which he could secure electoral legitimation. Established by the military in 1964 as a counterweight to the mobilizational power of the PKI, Golkar was a corporatist umbrella organization for various civilian bodies, including groups of farmers, workers, teachers, and students. Even after undergoing anticommunist purges in the wake of the September Thirtieth Movement, however, Golkar remained riven by factionalism and controlled by officers with Sukarnoist leanings. Moreover, what little reputation the institution's leaders possessed outside Jakarta came from corruption and womanizing. Murtopo's efforts to mold Golkar to serve Suharto's political objectives consequently proceeded slowly. As late as November 1969, the *Far Eastern Economic Review*'s well-connected Jakarta correspondent reported that Suharto "has not yet established a party base from which to make his bid for a second term."[141] Even Golkar chief General Sokowati briefed Suharto and suggested that holding elections might "destabilize politics and disturb development" and was thus "totally unconstitutional and not beneficial to the common interest."[142]

By that point Ali Murtopo's Opsus group had penned a series of internal memoranda urging a further postponement of the elections. They reasoned the party system had not yet been reorganized and it was not yet clear that holding the election would "bring victory to the New Order" and "guarantee political and economic stabilization."[143] Word of the possibility of an additional delay in the holding of elections percolated through Jakarta. These rumors elicited widespread condemnation from the leaders of major political parties and strongly worded editorials in many newspapers.[144] Furious, Suharto called Murtopo and his aides to a meeting. "If the people hang me, you all will clap your hands and laugh at me," he scolded. He reiterated his determination to fashion Golkar into a political vehicle and affirmed that the elections would be held on time.[145]

The Suharto regime then accelerated its efforts to mold Golkar into a vehicle of electoral legitimation. Golkar had mushroomed from sixty-four member organizations in 1965 to more than 200 by early 1969, which strained the body's coherence and left it vulnerable to eruptions of factional strife. The Indonesian army engineered a reorganization of Golkar in late 1969 that subsumed the hundreds of member organizations into one of seven umbrella groups, all but one of which was led by a military officer.[146] These institutional changes rendered Golkar far more responsive to the institutional whims of the Suharto regime—and far more able to siphon capital from the reservoirs of the state and its appendages, notably Pertamina. Golkar approached the elections with a vague program emphasizing service to the New Order's causes of stability and development as well as opposition to the ideologically oriented politics of the Sukarno era.[147] It could thus anticipate winning the support of the self-consciously modernizing segments of the New Order coalition. But it could not hope to inspire converts from existing political parties deeply rooted in Indonesian political life. An internal report suggested Golkar's key challenge was winning over "the bulk of the mass": Indonesians it characterized as "emotional, impulsive, and suggestible."[148] Rather than emphasize ideological appeals, Golkar instead relied on patronage. Opsus financed a new newspaper, *Suara Karya*, that toed the Golkar line and doubled its initial circulation to more than 50,000 copies within a year—making it one of the five most read papers in Indonesia. Golkar also brought Muslim voters into the fold by funneling official largesse toward *hajj* voyages and the maintenance of Islamic boarding schools.[149]

Amirmachmud played an especially consequential role in building Golkar. The Interior Ministry exercised responsibility for overseeing Indonesia's elections, and Amirmachmud was determined that his institution would serve as "a pioneer in the struggle for the New Order." In December 1969, he issued an order endowing Golkar with the authority to appoint functional group representatives in regional legislatures and prohibiting those representatives from belonging to political parties. Two months later, he issued another regulation forbidding civil servants and members of the armed forces from joining political parties—effectively making Golkar, framed as a functional rather than political organization, the only electoral organization to which Indonesians on the state payroll could belong. Amirmachmud went further still by forcing the professional association of some 800,000 Interior Ministry employees and their wives to declare "monoloyalty" to Golkar and "work to bring victory to the New Order" in the upcoming elections. Rumors circulated that local government officials across the archipelago were assigned quotas for the number of Golkar votes they needed to tally in their jurisdictions.[150] Such heavy-handed moves enraged the leaders of political parties and earned Amirmachmud the nickname "Bulldozer."[151]

Opsus operatives also continued to intervene in the internal affairs of political parties to ensure they remained prostrate. After Suharto's hand-picked leader of the PNI, Osa Maliki Wangsadinata, died in September 1969, Opsus ensured that a PNI conference held in April 1970 elevated Suharto's longtime associate Hadisubeno to the position of party chairman rather than the popular acting chairman who had criticized the political dominance of the military.

As party delegates traveled to the site of the conference from Jakarta, they were told by Opsus agents that "if so-and-so is not elected general chairman, the PNI will have difficulties in surviving."[152] Murtopo and his allies engaged in similar skullduggery toward Parmusi. When the party held its inaugural congress in November 1968 and elected as chairman the former Masyumi leader Mohammed Roem, the government refused to recognize the new leadership and announced it would deal only with the party's current leader, Djarnawi Hadikusuma. But when Djarnawi grew increasingly solicitous of Masyumi influence over the course of 1969 and 1970, Opsus engineered a split within Parmusi. In October 1970, a Murtopo ally inside the party accused Djarnawi of hostility toward the military and declared himself party leader. Suharto then stepped in to mediate between the dueling factions and appointed as Parmusi chairman Mohammad Syafa'at Mintaredja, a reliable member of his cabinet.[153]

By the time the campaign got underway, both the PNI and Parmusi were left in the hands of pliant politicos determined not to mount a serious challenge to the authority of the military should they win majorities in the 1971 elections. Amirmachud and other military leaders then carefully screened prospective candidates, purging 768 candidates from party lists, with PNI and Parmusi accounting for almost half of the deletions. The military also prohibited more than 2 million suspected communist sympathizers from casting ballots.[154]

With the scales definitively tilted toward Golkar, the campaign kicked off in late April 1971. Nine parties and Golkar vied for votes. But few expressed anything but the most tepid opposition to Suharto. The most strident partisan rhetoric came from the NU firebrand Subchan, elected as second-in-command of the party's *Tanfidziyah* (executive political committee) in 1967 and re-elected in 1971 over the objections of the older, more accommodationist elites who dominated the party's central institutions. Subchan peppered his campaign speeches with caustic attacks against Suharto, Murtopo, and Golkar.[155] Attendees at NU rallies brandished posters with audacious slogans like "The people want to be free" and "The Republic of Indonesia is the possession of all the people, not the possession of one group."[156] Opposition also emerged from a group of disaffected students and intellectuals in Jakarta, who formed Golput (Golongan Putih, or White Group, a play on Golkar) and urged voters to spoil their ballots in protest.

Although soldiers were prohibited from voting, the armed forces rallied behind Golkar. The military censored criticism of the Suharto regime and banned Golput.[157] It also worked to ensure Golkar triumphed at the polls. Some military functionaries traveled around villages and told residents, "If you choose another party it could be misinterpreted as being anti-military and maybe even pro-PKI"—an obvious threat of violence only five years removed from the savagery of 1965–66.[158] Credible reports of military abuses abounded, including the kidnapping, beating, and torture of opposition figures. To complaints that the military placed undue pressure on voters to support Golkar, Amirmachmud responded that "intimidation from New Order elements which is not anti-elections can be educative and persuasive."[159]

Golkar won a commanding victory when voters went to the polls in July. Of 58 million eligible voters, some 54.5 million cast ballots. Golkar tallied 62.8 percent of the vote. Parmusi and the PNI, both regarded as tools of the New Order, secured only 5.4 and 6.9 percent of the vote, respectively—declines of more than 15 percent from the 1955 elections that marked the high point of liberal democracy in Indonesia. Only NU managed to maintain a semblance of popular support and raked an impressive electoral haul of 18.7 percent, likely because its role as a genuine opposition party did nothing to alienate (and perhaps even inspired) its rural Javanese constituents. In the end, Golkar controlled 236 of the 360 elected seats in parliament. After taking advantage of its right to appoint the remaining 100 members, the Suharto regime held a 73 percent majority in parliament. This all but guaranteed the national assembly—of which parliament constituted about half the membership—would re-elect Suharto as president when it convened in 1973.

Golkar's victory in the 1971 elections both reflected and reinforced the New Order's ability to mobilize international capital. Massive quantities of aid and investment had helped jumpstart the economy and fund development projects across the archipelago, which inspired genuine loyalty and admiration among large swathes of the Indonesian population. But they also enabled Suharto to channel capital toward the military and the civil service, which then used more underhanded methods of securing Golkar's triumph at the polls. The vote was also important in enabling Suharto to continue attracting aid and investment as publics across the Western world expressed increasing concern over democracy and human rights in Indonesia. The American ambassador warned Suharto that "Congress and others in the United States" would likely be upset by "bad publicity of army arm-twisting or other rough tactics."[160] As the US State Department's Bureau of Intelligence and Research put it, Suharto's victory would allow the New Order to portray "itself to aid-donor countries as a government enjoying popular support and at least nominally committed to democratic norms."[161]

———

A phase shift in the New Order's ability to mobilize international capital occurred in the wake of Suharto's installation as uncontested president in March 1968. IGGI aid grew from $167 million in 1967 to $361 million in 1968 to $547 million in 1969. Just as important as the quantity of international capital was its quality—its regularity, longevity, and predictability. The IGGI was transformed from an ad hoc body undergirded largely by American power to a durable international organization sustained by multiple committed stakeholders. The Paris Club presided over a comprehensive settlement of Jakarta's Sukarno-era debts, more than doubling overall maturity profile of Indonesia's obligations and backloading rather than frontloading its largest debt service payments. The Suharto regime also expanded its partnerships with an array of other international bodies, including the IMF, the World Bank, the Asian Development Bank, and several private development consultancies. The result was to endow the New Order with greater certainty in its capacity to secure international capital and to afford policymakers in Jakarta with longer time horizons.

Suharto tapped these reservoirs of international capital to wage his Cold War. He launched a five-year economic development plan that depended on international aid and investment for more than 70 percent of its total expenditures, and he extended his authority over recalcitrant branches of the armed forces by furnishing the navy and air force with military equipment from the United States. The New Order rested on increasingly narrow domestic foundations. Even so, the legacies of the compromises in the critical period of regime formation and growing concerns about democracy and human rights in Western capitals began to threaten Suharto's ability to channel international capital toward his particular purposes. As countervailing forces within Indonesia witnessed the narrowing of legitimate channels of political contestation around them, they would mount increasingly aggressive protests against the Suharto regime—bids for a vision of Indonesia that international aid and investment were rendering evanescent.

The Travails of Development

Suharto emerged from Indonesia's July 1971 elections triumphant. His Golkar electoral machine controlled 336 of the 460 seats in parliament. Student groups, religious organizations, and political parties all appeared united behind the army and its program of modernization and development. So too did the international community. Western governments and international financial institutions funneled ever-larger sums of aid to the Suharto regime through the IGGI. The New Order was at the apex of its legitimacy both at home and abroad.

But Suharto did not intend to aggregate the interests and ideals of a capacious domestic coalition. To the contrary, he intended to marshal international resources to create a highly autonomous state capable of reshaping Indonesian society in accordance with his anticommunist ambitions. Rather than the state embodying its citizens, its citizens would embody the state. Suharto revealed the nature of political authority in the New Order shortly after the elections when he announced a reshuffling of his cabinet to include twelve PhDs, four military officers, and only three representatives of political parties.[1] Elements of the New Order coalition recognized the increasingly exclusionary nature of the Suharto regime and mobilized to reorient the trajectory of Indonesian life. Suharto responded by cracking down against all manner of opposition—igniting a dialectic of repression and resistance.

A key lesson of the period since October 1, 1965, was that Suharto could rely on international resources to surmount domestic challenges. But Suharto soon confronted unprecedented threats to his ability to channel to the global Cold War to wage his own domestic and regional Cold Wars. Those threats emerged from processes endogenous to the global Cold War, including the rise of the human rights revolution, the end of the Vietnam War, and the collapse of the Bretton Woods system, all of which impeded Suharto's ability to mobilize international aid and investment. But they also emerged from the erosion of the Cold War itself. The advent of détente and triangular diplomacy meant the world was no longer divided along ideological lines. For Suharto, the geopolitical

Suharto's Cold War. Mattias Fibiger, Oxford University Press. © Oxford University Press 2023.
DOI: 10.1093/oso/9780197667224.003.0008

reconfigurations of the 1970s risked undermining the salience of Cold War imperatives in international politics. What emerged was a chaotic interregnum in which Suharto engaged in a series of desperate maneuvers to sustain his access to international capital and confront renascent domestic challenges.

I

International capital fueled the revival of the Indonesian economy and the consolidation of the Suharto regime. Between 1968 and 1973, the gross domestic product expanded at an average clip of 7.9 percent per year and inflation slowed to single digits. Recovery from a decade of economic chaos won the New Order the goodwill of vast numbers of Indonesians and furthered Suharto's efforts to cement his authority. "The Indonesian economy has turned a corner," remarked one keen observer of the archipelago in July 1969. But that observer also noted that "stability, internally and externally, is still heavily dependent on foreign aid."[2]

The all-important agricultural sector confirmed the extent to which economic growth and political stability continued to rely on international capital. Most of Indonesia's irrigation systems were constructed under the Dutch, and almost no maintenance had been undertaken since the Second World War. Of 4.3 million hectares of irrigated land in Indonesia, 1.9 million required rehabilitation in 1968. The inaccessibility of water meant rice yields fell between 1960 and 1967, generating persistent food shortages and fueling inflation in the wider economy.[3] The government did not possess sufficient hard currency to purchase the equipment necessary to repair Indonesia's irrigation systems. World Bank chief Robert McNamara remembered that he promised the Suharto regime that "our first efforts would be to help them grow more rice."[4] The Bank provided a $5 million loan to purchase the equipment required to rehabilitate irrigation systems on 198,000 hectares of paddy, which it anticipated would increase rice production by 39,000 tons and save Indonesia $6.6 million in foreign exchange by obviating some rice imports. The project ultimately expanded to cost $54 million.[5] An alphabet soup of other international development agencies conducted agricultural surveys, educated farmers about fertilizer usage, and more.[6] Together with the adoption of Green Revolution rice varietals, international aid helped Indonesia dramatically expand its rice production. Between 1968 and 1973, annual rice production surged from 11.6 million tons to 14.5 million tons, and yields per hectare increased nearly 20 percent.[7] Because rice remained central to Indonesia's political imaginary, the production increases redounded to the benefit of the New Order.

International aid also contributed to a revitalization of Indonesia's physical infrastructure. Suharto's first five-year development plan (Repelita) channeled vast sums of international capital toward electrification, transportation, and tel-ecommunication projects. The World Bank also allocated $101 million toward electric power and $91 million toward transportation and communication be-tween 1968 and 1974. Indonesia's electricity-generating capacity consequently surged from 448 megawatts in 1965 to approximately 2,250 megawatts in 1975.[8] Statistics reveal a massive increase in infrastructural capacity between 1970 and 1975: the length of roads expanded at some 4.4 percent per year, the tonnage of inter-island cargo shipping at 8 percent, the weight of domestic air cargo at 44 percent, and domestic telephone calls at 17.6 percent.[9] As the streets of downtown Jakarta began to clog with traffic in 1972, the governor banned *becak* pedicabs to make way for automobiles.[10] Expanding connectivity enabled both the creation of economies of scale and the projection of state power.

International assistance also helped the New Order formulate and imple-ment policies designed to promote economic growth. In April 1970, Suharto announced a raft of policies elaborated with the help of the IMF that harmonized Indonesia's dual exchange rates at a single, devalued rate and slashed an array of taxes and regulations on exports.[11] Exports of major commodities including timber, rubber, copra, palm oil, coffee, tin, and nickel expanded considerably, bringing Indonesia's non-oil export earnings from $569 million in 1968 to $1.9 billion in 1973.[12] This rapid expansion in commodity earnings occurred even while overall prices for these commodities stagnated.[13] Technocrats from institutions like the IMF also contributed to the New Order's adoption of var-ious import-substitution policies.[14] For instance, the Suharto regime announced revisions to the automobile tariff structure in 1969 that offered lower rates to semi-knocked down and completely knocked down kits than completely built-up units, which incentivized local assembly.[15] Domestic automobile production subsequently rose from 1,442 units in 1969 to 36,959 units in 1973—or from 7.5 percent to 86.3 percent of automobile imports.[16] Similar protectionist policies nurtured a boom in domestic textile production.[17] More broadly, manufacturing output grew at an average annual rate of 13 percent between 1969 and 1973, outpacing growth in overall economic output. And in both the commodity and industrial sectors, licenses, concessions, and credits flowed overwhelmingly to military-linked firms run by ethnic Chinese *cukong*. These firms then churned a portion of their profits into so-called foundations controlled by powerful mil-itary figures, allowing the Suharto regime to tap a deep reservoir of capital to finance all manner of "off-budget" expenditures.[18]

The New Order continued to court foreign investment even while it ringfenced key industries from foreign competition. A delegation of senior Indonesian policymakers and business leaders flew to the United States in late 1969 to drum up interest in Indonesia among American capitalists. They visited Honolulu, Seattle, Chicago, Minneapolis, Washington, and New York.[19] These "investment

safaris" notwithstanding, foreign investment arrived in smaller quantities and
at more dispersed intervals than foreign aid. Less than 10 percent of the approximately $600 million worth of foreign investment projects approved by
Mohammad Sadli's Technical Team for Foreign Investment had been realized
by 1970. Sadli was forced to cancel an appearance at the American Management
Association that year to avoid an embarrassing reception. He cabled Jakarta
that the problem was not "lack of interest among American investors." Instead,
he concluded that the New Order needed "to remove bureaucratic and other
implementational obstacles which still harass incoming investors" and present
capital controllers with a "list of concrete investment opportunities with feasibility studies."[20]

Throughout the period between 1968 and 1973, foreign aid outpaced foreign investment by a ratio of roughly four-to-one. Sadli's foreign investment
team approved $2.8 billion in investment in Indonesia between 1968 and
1973, but only $1.1 billion was realized.[21] The challenges of attracting foreign
investment were exemplified by the construction of the Asahan hydroelectric
power-generating and aluminum-smelting complex. Shortly after the passage of
the Foreign Investment Law in 1967, an executive in the Japanese engineering
firm Nippon Koei approached General Sudjono Humardani about harnessing
the power of the Asahan River to generate electricity and fuel industrial development in North Sumatra.[22] Nippon Koei presented a preliminary report to
Sudjono in July 1969 and signed contracts to undertake more detailed feasibility
studies in July 1970.[23] The firm completed these studies the following year and
estimated the project would cost approximately $500 million. Sudjono traveled
to Japan in April 1971 to meet Prime Minister Eisaku Sato and returned ex-
ultant, with one magazine proclaiming that Japan had agreed to finance the project as "a monument of friendship of the type of the Aswan Dam built by Russia
in Egypt."[24] But when Indonesia solicited tenders in January 1972, a consortium
of five Japanese and two American firms failed to submit a bid.[25] Negotiations
then stretched on for more than eighteen months, confronting a seemingly endless array of bureaucratic obstacles before the American firms finally withdrew
from the venture.[26]

The economic expansion that took place under the New Order was remarkable. As foreign aid helped rebuild Indonesia's infrastructure, the agricultural,
industrial, and commodity sectors experienced breakneck growth. Nor did economic expansion come at the expense of equality. Between 1965 and 1975,
inequality in per capita consumption income declined by a small margin.
Destitution remained widespread—ranging from about 15 percent in rural areas
beyond Java to about 26 percent in urban areas in Java.[27] But the Suharto regime had clearly reversed the deterioration in standards of living that occurred
under the Sukarno regime. Economic growth endowed the New Order with

considerable legitimacy among the Indonesian population, even if it did not erase perceptions of inequality, since growth was concentrated in particular sectoral, geographic, and even ethnic enclaves. Nor did Indonesia join the ranks of the so-called tigers—Taiwan, South Korea, Singapore, and Hong Kong—in achieving growth through the export of industrial goods. Indeed, precisely because international donors exhibited forbearance surrounding the Suharto regime's import-substitution policies, which protected fledgling but inefficient domestic firms from international competition, the commodity sector remained the Suharto regime's most important source of foreign exchange.

II

As the Indonesian economy expanded, the Suharto regime collected more revenues. Between 1968 and 1973, government revenues increased sixfold while GDP grew threefold, meaning receipts grew from 10 to 15 percent of GDP. But the New Order's ability to tax did not grow at the same clip as its ability to spend. The tax base in 1969 was only 250,000 people of a population of approximately 115 million—a "ridiculously low number," according to the *Far Eastern Economic Review*.[28] The New Order's ability to secure international aid tempered the imperative to expand domestic revenues and obviated the political compromises that such efforts would entail. The portion of government revenues accounted for by non-oil taxes decreased from 62 percent in 1968 to 41 percent in 1973, while the portion accounted for by oil and foreign aid grew from 37 percent to 57 percent.

Oil represented Indonesia's most promising asset. Indonesia's continental shelf housed vast oil reserves with low sulfur content—approximately 0.2 percent compared to the 2–4 percent common in Middle Eastern crude. Indonesian oil was thus less polluting and more attractive to developed markets like Japan and the United States, where environmentalist sentiment was on the rise.[29] But at the moment of Suharto's ascent to the uncontested presidency in March 1968, the Indonesian oil sector remained fragmented between Permina, led by General Ibnu Sutowo, and Pertamin, led by General Marah Yunus. Under Yunus, Pertamin mounted a renewed effort to level the playing field with Permina by working to recover the international marketing rights over which Ibnu had established a monopoly in 1966.[30] To repulse Yunus's challenge, Ibnu enlisted the support of international oil firms and the Japanese government, both of which were enraged by Pertamin's efforts to secure a higher price for Indonesian oil.[31] The precise trajectory of events remain unclear, but Ibnu ultimately prevailed upon Suharto that competition within the Indonesian oil industry had become counterproductive. In August 1968, Suharto ordered the merger of Permina and

Pertamin into a new megafirm called Pertamina, which Ibnu would lead.[32] The Pertamina chief wielded unrivaled influence within the Indonesian oil industry for the next seven years.

Ibnu shifted the state oil company's focus away from a strategy of vertical integration in which the firm pursued exploration, production, refining, transport, and marketing and instead embraced a simpler profit engine: signing production-sharing agreements with international oil firms, including for the first time majors like Mobil and Caltex. Crude oil production rose from 219 million barrels in 1968 to 490 million barrels in 1973, and oil proceeds expanded from 22 percent to 36 percent of government revenues.[33] By 1973, Indonesia was the tenth largest producer of oil in the noncommunist world. Freed of the need to invest in every link of the petroleum supply chain, Ibnu established subsidiaries in a vast array of different industries, including insurance, aviation, shipping, housing, agriculture, healthcare, tourism, and corporate services—emulating the *keiretsu* constellation of firms that played a key role in Japan's postwar economic growth and revealing the transnational circulation of development models across Asia.[34] Much like other firms granted quasi-monopolistic arrangements under the New Order, Pertamina also recycled portions of its profits back into the New Order. The oil giant became the military's most important source of nonbudgetary funds. Suharto also assigned Pertamina with responsibility for massive white elephant projects like the completion of the Krakatau Steel project in West Java, estimated to cost hundreds of millions if not billions of dollars. In addition, Ibnu helped finance the construction of the *Bina Graha* presidential office complex and a number of other edifices of state power.[35]

Ibnu's freewheeling financial practices drew considerable criticism. The Commission of Four lambasted Pertamina as a "state within a state" in a 1970 report on corruption.[36] But Ibnu was unrepentant. "Pertamina is more than just an oil company," he told an audience in Geneva in 1973. "We are a development company for Indonesia."[37] "We were struggling for our independence," the Pertamina chief remembered, "to free ourselves as quickly as possible from dependence on the outside world for our needs, like fertilizer, cement, steel, and the like."[38] Ibnu's lavish lifestyle also became a source of discontent. When he was not jet-setting abroad, he was often spotted cruising through Jakarta in one of his fleet of Rolls Royce sedans. The extravagant wedding festivities he put on for his daughter inspired widespread condemnation. Ibnu was equally ill-disposed toward criticism on this front. "It is simply not psychologically possible for men who wear threadbare clothing and who ride in old cars or *becaks* to negotiate satisfactorily with men who earn $50,000 a year and fly by company jet aircraft," he remarked of his need to keep up appearances for the sake of business.[39]

Unlike major petrostates like Saudi Arabia, Indonesia funded its oil-related spending through leverage rather than retained earnings. After securing

$10 million in New York for the first time in 1968, Pertamina continued to raise capital on international credit markets to finance its developmental and clientelist obligations. Ibnu contracted with Edmund "Pat" Brown, former governor of California, to obtain international financing for Pertamina and represent the New Order as a lobbyist.[40] Brown drew upon his personal connection with Robert McNamara to reinforce the World Bank's nascent relationship with Indonesia, and he proved helpful in placing what one broker called "well-secured Indonesian paper" in burgeoning Eurodollar markets.[41] Japanese banks, increasingly prominent in Southeast Asia in the 1970s, also became major sources of credit for Pertamina.[42] In many cases these private creditors inked loan agreements with Pertamina without requiring a full appraisal of the company's finances. Ibnu's efforts to tap private credit markets began to rival Suharto's efforts to secure sovereign aid, with Pertamina accruing no less than $350 million in loans in 1972 and $870 million in 1973.[43] And much as the global Cold War enabled the Suharto regime's ability to secure international aid, so too did it enable Pertamina's ability to mobilize private capital.[44] Given the importance of Pertamina to the New Order and the importance of Indonesia to Southeast Asia, the *New York Times* explained, private creditors "were confident that the governments of Indonesia and of their own countries would never permit a default to take place."[45]

Pertamina's mushrooming obligations, as well as its focus on grandiose development schemes rather than rural infrastructure and labor-intensive industry, produced considerable anxiety among Indonesian technocrats and their allies in the IMF, the US Treasury, and elsewhere.[46] After the Commission of Four report excoriated Ibnu, parliament passed a law creating a board of commissioners to oversee Pertamina's affairs and ensure proper remission of oil proceeds to the government. Despite the board's de jure mandate, it exercised little de facto authority. Only when the IMF and the members of the IGGI pressured Suharto to rein in Ibnu beginning in 1972 did the president agree to impose meaningful constraints on Pertamina's borrowing.[47] In October 1972, Suharto required all state enterprises to obtain the finance minister's permission to assume international debt obligations.[48] But the directive went unenforced, which prompted Indonesia to lose its access to IMF funding facilities and delayed the approval of an American loan worth $50 million.[49] In May 1973, the Ministry of Finance at last issued regulations establishing limits on Pertamina's ability to borrow at maturities of between one and fifteen years—reasoning that Pertamina was unlikely to secure long-term credits and that short-term flexibility was necessary for working capital financing.[50] But the quadrupling of world oil prices that followed the eruption of war in the Middle East in October 1973 allowed Ibnu to elude these restrictions by modifying the term structure of Pertamina's balance sheet. Foreign banks eagerly extended massive quantities of short-term loans to Pertamina, which Ibnu rolled over at ever-greater interest rates.[51] By the mid-1970s, Ibnu's borrowing spree had made the Indonesian state oil company the largest corporate borrower in the developing world.[52]

Economic growth and international aid also fueled military expansion. Indonesian military expenditures grew from roughly $300 million in 1968 to $535 million in 1973. By the early 1970s, Jakarta's military spending rivaled that of Hanoi and Saigon. According to the annual budgets prepared by the Indonesian government, the military's share of routine government spending (which the New Order kept distinct from so-called "development" spending) hovered around 25 percent in the early 1970s.[53] But the New Order's publicly available budgets understated total military expenditures. Off-the-books sources of financing, including revenues diverted from Pertamina and other military-owned or military-linked businesses, remained extraordinarily important. A March 1970 editorial from the armed forces newspaper *Angkatan Bersendjata* confirmed that the official budget covered only half of the Indonesian military's needs.[54] Measured by its overall spending as a percentage of routine government expenditures, then, the Indonesian military likely commanded a greater share of resources than every other military in the world in the early 1970s, except that of the Soviet Union and South Yemen.[55] And Suharto would mobilize the state's expanding coercive apparatus against Indonesians who opposed the New Order in spite of its record of economic achievement.

III

The Suharto regime confronted a series of unexpected domestic challenges in the period following the July 1971 elections. Student and youth organizations disillusioned by corruption began demonstrating against Suharto and the New Order. A coterie of military leaders became convinced that the Suharto regime's suppression of dissent threatened the legitimacy of the armed forces and worked to alter Indonesia's political trajectory. And political parties mobilized against their inability to further their agendas. Although dissent emerged from different groups, it possessed common wellsprings. Countervailing forces within Indonesia saw Suharto marshaling international capital to shrink the domestic constituencies upon which his power depended and narrow legitimate channels of political contestation. These disaffected elements of Indonesian society mounted increasingly aggressive protests against the exclusionary nature of the New Order.

Golkar's victory in the 1971 elections led General Sumitro to reason that the communist threat facing Indonesia had been addressed and "political stability had been established." He advised Suharto to disband Kopkamtib, Aspri, and Opsus and return to a "standard institutional structure." He even suggested that Suharto cultivate a civilian, Widjojo Nitisastro, to take his place as president. Sumitro and other military leaders including Bakin chief General Sutopo Juwono, Hankam Chief of Staff General Hasnan Habib, Army Deputy Chief of Staff General Sayidiman Suryohadiprojo, and Ambassador to South Korea General Sarwo Edhie Wibowo came to resent what they saw as "feudalism" taking root within the New Order. They believed that the blatant corruption of so-called political and financial generals like Ali Murtopo and Sudjono Humardani undermined efforts to achieve law and order, imperiled the professional discipline of the armed forces, and threatened the military's sociopolitical role. "We must have the courage to say 'I do not agree.' . . . We must have the courage to say 'that is wrong, this is right,' " Sumitro recalled telling his staff.[56] Opposition to Suharto's mechanisms of rule thus mounted within the New Order itself.

Student and youth groups also staged protests against corruption. Unlike previous outbursts of youth unrest, these protests began targeting the New Order itself, revealing an erosion of hierarchical trust in the Suharto regime. Suharto's wife Siti Hartinah (commonly known as Ibu Tien) became a key source of public discontent. Inspired by a visit to Disneyland and the construction of monuments to cultural diversity in Thailand and the Philippines, Ibu Tien had had dreamed up a theme park that would include life-size dioramas of traditional homes from each of Indonesia's twenty-six provinces. She established the Our Hope Foundation to finance what became known as the Beautiful Indonesia-in-Miniature Park (colloquially Taman Mini) and indelicately suggested Indonesian business leaders donate to the foundation should they wish to retain Suharto's favor. Plans for the park called for the clearing of 100 hectares of land in eastern Jakarta. The combination of Ibu Tien's ham-fisted fundraising tactics, the forcible eviction of poor residents from the proposed site, and the extravagant cost of the project for a nation still mired in poverty led many young Indonesians to take to the streets in December 1971.[57] The demonstrations offered definitive proof that the student and youth movement, so crucial in the emergence of the New Order, had grown alienated by the exclusionary and opaque nature of the Suharto regime.[58]

The protests against Taman Mini inspired a massive reaction. Suharto wielded the coercive institutions of the Indonesian state against his political opposition. The regime mobilized violent counterdemonstrators who attacked protestors with fists, machetes, and pistols. Officials also instructed the media against covering the protests.[59] "Watch your tongues," a gathering of editors of Jakarta newspaper editors were warned.[60] In an extraordinary impromptu speech suffused with vitriol, Suharto suggested protestors sought to "discredit the government" and "expel ABRI from the executive branch." He declared that he would "pummel" those who challenged his constitutional authority and threatened to dust off the *Supersemar* to legitimize a crackdown.[61] Sumitro issued an order outlawing "extra-parliamentary" activity and dissolving the key organizations behind the protests, which he attributed to the increasingly porous boundary between the foreign and the domestic. Lamenting that young Indonesians had looked to the West for inspiration, he proclaimed that "the lives of our teen-youths must be saved." The government tightened regulations prohibiting the entrance of "hippies" into Indonesia and rounded up long-haired young men for haircuts and lectures on national identity at army barracks—eliding a more culturally salient referent for long-haired youth: the *pemuda* who galvanized the Indonesian revolution in the heady days of late 1945.[62]

A rice crisis that erupted in mid-1972 threatened to fuel the ascendant opposition. An unusually long spell of exceptionally dry weather after the monsoon generated anxieties about production shortfalls and food shortages. The rice procurement agency Bulog had failed to accumulate sufficient stocks to counteract a shortage, purchasing only 150,000 tons of its 400,000-ton target.[63] Moreover, the same El Niño that caused drought conditions in Indonesia also brought harsh weather across the region, to which increasingly common Green Revolution rice varietals were particularly vulnerable. World food production dropped for the first time in twenty years, and global rice prices surged 33 percent.[64] In Indonesia rumors of scarcity prompted hoarding. Domestic rice prices doubled between June and December 1972. With the average Indonesian family still spending 60 percent of its income on food—and half of that on rice—such massive increases produced considerable anxiety. Students demonstrated against rising prices in Jakarta, blaming official corruption and hoarding by ethnic Chinese rice merchants.[65]

Suharto worried that political parties might capitalize on the eruption of discontent within the New Order coalition and destabilize his anticommunist regime. As early as 1970 Ali Murtopo produced a tract that characterized liberal democracy as a "disease that made it possible for Communism to return."[66] Murtopo's deputy Jusuf Wanandi told an American diplomat shortly before Indonesia's July 1971 elections that the Suharto regime would trim the number of electoral vehicles to four after the polls, preserving only Golkar, PNI, NU, and Parmusi.[67] Suharto agreed that the number of parties needed to be reduced, reminiscing in his memoirs that, "If the road is already there, the one and only, why must we have so many cars, as many as nine? Why must we have speeding and collisions?"[68] Even four parties proved challenging to manage, evident in NU's unexpectedly vigorous oppositionist posture.

Suharto delivered a coup de grâce against political parties in January 1973 amid protests over corruption and food prices. The Indonesian state forcibly agglomerated Indonesia's existing parties into two new parties under the leadership of pliant figureheads: the United Development Party (PPP) for Muslim parties and the Indonesian Democratic Party (PDI) for nationalist and Christian parties.[69] Sumitro declared in a public speech that "the government will not hesitate to take decisive actions against parties that do not agree to fusion."[70] By then, Murtopo had theorized that the Indonesian population should form a "floating mass" freed from the supposed burdens of politics so they could devote themselves entirely to economic development.[71] Although it was not written into law until several years later, the floating mass doctrine was immediately enforced across the archipelago. Parties were prohibited from maintaining offices at the village and subdistrict levels, fraying their ties with the population and impeding their ability to channel popular discontent. This restriction nominally applied to Golkar as well, but the organization's ties with the civil service and military meant the rule was honored in the breach.[72]

The imposition of additional restrictions on partisan activity generated a sense of disillusionment among many political parties. For instance, when the national assembly re-elected Suharto as president in March 1973, some 150 delegates were absent from the proceedings. With the results entirely foreordained, many lawmakers apparently didn't wish to brave the pouring rain to attend such a dull affair.[73] Even so, the Suharto regime enlisted international aid to ensure it was ready for any outbreak of opposition. In response to an Indonesian request in advance of the session, the United States ordered, procured, and installed a mobile communications network for Jakarta's police in just 100 days—a process that one official remarked would normally take three years or more.[74]

Having mounted the most vigorous opposition to Suharto's Golkar machine in the 1971 elections, Islamic parties mobilized against the narrowing of political horizons under the New Order. They focused on repulsing challenges to what they perceived as Islamic interests. The first challenge related to the Broad Outlines of State Policy (GBHN), a document prepared by the assembly to guide the president during his five-year term. The draft GBHN tabled by the government in 1973 included references not only to state-sanctioned scriptural religions but also to Javanese mysticism (*kepercayaan*). If mysticism were recognized as coequal to religion, many nominally Muslim Javanese would likely alter their formal religious identification, diminishing the political power of Islam. The PPP's protests against the inclusion of references to mysticism in the GBHN proved unsuccessful. But the party did prevent the Suharto regime from formally elevating *kepercayaan* to the status of a state-sanctioned religion. The second challenge related to civil law. The government introduced a draft bill bringing marriage, divorce, and other family matters like adoption under the jurisdiction of secular courts rather than religious authorities. Muslim groups objected to more than twenty provisions in the bill that allegedly violated Islamic law, including one that would have permitted marriage between people of different faiths.[75] Hundreds of protestors pushed their way into parliament and interrupted a debate on the bill in September 1973. The following month, PPP lawmakers staged a walkout.[76] Suharto relented. He ordered Sumitro and Sutopo Juwono to work with Islamic leaders to revise the bill to prohibit interreligious marriages by Muslims, permit polygamy under certain conditions, and address other complaints from religious organizations.[77]

Student and youth groups bristled against the narrowing space for opposition as well. Befitting their reputation as a moral and political vanguard in Indonesia, they held seminars on a range of sensitive subjects like corruption and inequality. After a period of calm following the Suharto regime's violent reaction to the protests against Taman Mini, students again began leaving their campuses and staging "down to the street" protests against inflation, corruption, and the New Order's dependence upon foreign capital.[78] The Suharto regime responded to the swell of protest by working to extend its control over the student and youth movement through the same corporatist methods that neutralized Indonesia's political parties. In July 1973, Suharto established the National Indonesian Youth Committee (KNPI) as an umbrella organization under which all student and youth groups would be subsumed.[79] Led by the former action front leader turned Murtopo ally and Golkar lawmaker David Napitupulu, KNPI was generally seen by students and youth as a contravention of their rights to free association. Political party leaders lambasted the organization as a bid to "monopolize" students and youth on Golkar's behalf.[80]

Opposition mounted in spite of the Suharto regime's efforts at corporatist control. Popular unrest increasingly assumed a sectarian cast. Javanese and Outer Islanders clashed in Yogyakarta in April 1973 after a dispute over pedicab fare devolved into communal violence. Four months later, anti-Chinese riots erupted in Bandung after three ethnic Chinese beat a Javanese man who hit their Volkswagen with his horse-drawn carriage. The ensuing violence resulted in at least one death (and possibly as many as fifteen), more than fifty injuries, the destruction of 1,500 Chinese homes and businesses, and the burning of hundreds of vehicles—all told, more than 1 billion rupiah in property damage.[81] Student activists characterized the outbreak of communal violence as a consequence of the Suharto regime's neutralization of political parties and youth organizations, which meant most Indonesians lacked what the students called a "satisfactory outlet" for the expression of discontent.[82]

Suharto's reaction to the resurgence of unrest reflected the New Order's bargain with international capital. A regime that depended on the support of a broad domestic coalition might have turned toward a more inclusive approach to politics to defuse popular discontent. But Suharto's key coalition partners were foreign rather than domestic. On August 7, he told his Council on Economic Stabilization that the eruption of communal strife could "influence the outside world's view of Indonesia," which meant that "repressive measures are needed."

The ethnic Chinese community became a particular target of his animus. He lamented that because "there are still many Indonesians of Chinese descent who cannot adapt their lives to the lives of the people around them, it is necessary to make efforts to bring about an awareness among those Indonesians of Chinese descent to conform, so that they do not only 'assert their rights,' but also fulfill their obligations as good and responsible citizens."[83]

Repression bred resistance. Students enamored of the *dependencia* literature emanating from Latin America began applying this analysis to Indonesia and excoriating the New Order as a comprador regime.[84] Reviving the rallying cry against Sukarno, student protestors articulated a new *Tritura* (Three Demands of the People): disband Aspri, lower prices, and eradicate corruption.[85] The University of Indonesia Student Council published a petition on October 24, 1973, demanding the Suharto regime review its development strategy, reinforce the institutional channels through which the public expressed its opinions, and free Indonesians from corruption, inflation, abuse, and uncertainty.[86] A rising oppositionist tide swept beyond university campuses to other venues. In November 1973, Mochtar Lubis moderated a discussion at the Jakarta Cultural Center focused on the question of whether foreign investment was good or bad for Indonesia.[87] That same month, poet and dramatist Willibrordus Surendra Rendra staged a play called *Mastodon and the Condors*. Set in an unnamed Latin American country, the drama followed the rise of a revolutionary student movement in opposition to a developmental dictatorship. One protagonist, a student leader, raged against the regime's tendency to "ally itself with foreign *cukong*" at the expense of the domestic population. "O, my homeland," he lamented, "how fertile your valleys, yet how miserable the lives of your people."[88] Another young artist, novelist Ashadi Siregar, began publishing a series of "campus stories" in *Kompas* that depicted the stultifying effects of an increasingly authoritarian environment through the lives of university students navigating political, economic, cultural, and generational change.[89]

Perhaps most alarming from Suharto's perspective, senior New Order officials appeared to be making common cause with students. General Sumitro was traveling to university campuses across Java promising a "new leadership pattern ... based on two-way communication" rather than the top-down style that characterized the Suharto regime.[90] He even met with Rendra, praising his work and proclaiming he had no objection to staging *Mastodon*.[91] Informed observers understood Sumitro's campus barnstorming as an indication of a cleavage at the upper echelons of the New Order. On one side stood "pragmatic" generals like Ali Murtopo, Sudjono Humardani, and Ibnu Sutowo concerned above all with furthering economic development. With that objective in mind, they embraced pervasive rent-seeking, promoted economic nationalism, and advocated closer relations with Japan. On the other side stood "principled" generals like Sumitro determined to ensure the military was not tarnished by corruption. To that end, they advocated civilian government, urged economic liberalization, and promoted the maintenance of ties with the United States.[92]

As protests against his regime escalated, Suharto worked to resuscitate the notion of a communist threat. In February 1973, Kopkamtib issued a directive instructing all government bureaucracies to ensure their employees read the military newspapers *Angkatan Bersenjata, Suara Karya,* and *Berita Yudha*—renowned for their tendency to present alarmist accounts of the communist threat to Indonesia.[93] In November 1973, Suharto complained to his cabinet that "both in society and in certain government circles there is a presumption that the problem of the G-30-S/PKI is finished and that the government is using the G-30-S/PKI as a reason (scapegoat) to cover up government deficiencies and failures in various fields." He asserted that the PKI remained a "latent danger," which he explained by resorting to an "iceberg" theory: although "the former PKI no longer functions as an organization," vast numbers of communists lurked below the surface and inhabited an "organization without form." He instructed the cabinet to ensure the domestic population remained "responsive" to the communist threat and "did not take action that could lead to the growth of tension, upheaval, and conflict in society, which is fertile soil for G-30-S/PKI infiltration." But he also reminded them to avoid giving the impression to the international community that Indonesia "was not safe" for aid and investment.[94]

A top-secret document produced by Sutopo Juwono's Bakin in December 1973 cast the regime's renewed anxieties about political contestation in stark relief. Entitled "Basic Text on Subversion and How to Tackle It," it emphasized that "the threat to Indonesia in the near and immediate future is not going to take the form of an invasion but will take the form of subversion and infiltration." The report identified subversion as "any activity that aims to amend or replace the national philosophy of Pancasila, whether done legally, through democratic-parliamentary means, or illegally." It outlined an array of "preventive and repressive" measures to combat subversion, not limited to "investigating, arresting, combatting, and eradicating" subversive elements but also utilizing "educational institutions, the mass media, i.e. the press, radio, television, film, *wayang kulit* [shadow puppet] shows," and other forms of mass communication to "raise Pancasila consciousness . . . so it becomes engrained in the lives of the people."[95]

IV

International challenges rose in tandem with domestic dissent. As Indonesian officials prepared to lodge a request for $640 million in aid at the December 1970 meeting of the IGGI, Soedjatmoko told American officials that he anticipated relations between Indonesia and the United States, still the key player in the IGGI, would "deteriorate in the future because of the 'New Left.'"[96] His anxieties proved prescient. The IGGI endorsed Indonesia's aid request. But over the following three years, international developments threatened to stanch the flow of aid from Western governments to the New Order. Human rights advocates began pressing international donors and creditors to curb the disbursement of aid to the Suharto regime. The demise of the Bretton Woods system and mounting stagflation in developed economies diminished the reservoir of funds available for foreign aid. And the tortuous end of the Vietnam War augured a decline in US military and economic aid to Southeast Asia.

Human rights advocates seized upon the Suharto regime's maintenance of a massive complex of gulags following the September Thirtieth Movement to demand the curtailment of international aid to Indonesia. At first, Suharto attempted to mollify the nascent human rights movement through dialogue and engagement. "We had to make the media our friends in order to counter negative reports," recalled Sumitro of his efforts to cultivate goodwill in the United States, the United Kingdom, West Germany, and the Netherlands.[97]

The New Order allowed Australian jurist Julius Stone and Amnesty International staffer Stephanie Grant to travel to Jakarta to investigate the detention of political dissidents in late 1969. Amnesty reported that the delegation was "extremely well received and was able to have full discussions with Cabinet Ministers and senior officials."[98] Shortly after the delegation departed, the New Order announced the release of 26,000 political prisoners.[99] The following year, Suharto traveled to West Germany and the Netherlands in part to counteract growing impressions that he was, in the words of his official chroniclers, a "military dictator."[100] He faced tough questions from politicians, journalists, and protestors about the status of political prisoners in Indonesia.[101] During Suharto's journey, an Amnesty representative approached State Secretary Sudharmono and inquired whether another delegation could travel to Indonesia.[102] Indonesian officials granted visas to the delegation and sought to impress upon its members that the continued imprisonment of suspected communists was vital not only for national security but also for the safety of those imprisoned—nonsensically claiming that a vehemently anticommunist Indonesian population would exact vengeance upon released prisoners. In February 1971, Amnesty sent a private memorandum to Suharto based on the observations of its two delegations. While "appreciating the extremely difficult and dangerous situation" that Suharto faced in 1965 and 1966, Amnesty said the "continued detention of vast numbers of persons who are uncharged and untried" contravened international law and was "highly damaging to the image of Indonesia in the outside world."[103]

Amnesty saw little change in the number or conditions of Indonesian political prisoners. The organization therefore changed tack from a strategy of private engagement to one of public agitation. In August 1971, Amnesty published the private letter it had sent to Suharto expressing concern over the plight of political prisoners, hoping to draw "attention to the continuing detention of at least 70,000 political prisoners."[104] The letter quickly attracted attention from policymakers. Senator J. William Fulbright, the dovish chair of the Senate Foreign Relations Committee, asked the State Department for a comment on the Amnesty report shortly before the IGGI convened to discuss Indonesia's aid request for 1972.[105]

The New Order ultimately despaired of convincing Amnesty representatives that the indefinite detention of suspected leftists was necessary. Suharto abandoned his conciliatory approach in favor of a more adversarial posture. In May 1972, the military newspaper *Angkatan Bersendjata* denounced Amnesty as a "front organization of the New Left" that "defends political detainees, especially the communists who are imprisoned in various countries outside the communist bloc ... but 'remains silent in a thousand languages' about political detainees in communist lands."[106] One civilian minister who normally served as a reliable intermediary between Amnesty International and the Suharto regime stopped replying to Amnesty's letters after he was formally censured at a cabinet meeting for "corresponding with communists."[107] The regime began denying visas to members of Amnesty delegations and prevented foreign journalists and advocates from visiting Indonesian prisons.[108] Kopkamtib worked to stifle discussion of the political prisoner issue in Indonesia, canceling a seminar on the topic out of concern that "the discussion of political prisoners could be exploited by international organizations that want to discredit the Indonesian government, like Amnesty International, the Cornell group, and the Wertheim group"—the latter two items referring to Western academic networks ill-disposed toward the Suharto regime.[109]

As the Suharto regime came under increasing scrutiny from human rights organizations, changes in the structure of the global economy posed further challenges to the New Order's ability to mobilize international capital. The fixed exchange rate system established at Bretton Woods in 1944 came under strain beginning in the 1960s—the result of growing productivity in Western Europe and Japan and rising inflation in the United States, as well as the nascent power of global finance to elude controls on the movement of capital across national borders and thereby exploit yawning macroeconomic imbalances. The Nixon administration began pressing for a revaluation of foreign currencies relative to the dollar to address the deterioration in the US balance of payments. Facing a mounting drain on American gold reserves and resistance to revaluation in Europe and Japan, Nixon announced a sudden suspension of dollar convertibility in August 1971 as well as a 10 percent cut in foreign aid. Negotiations between finance ministers from North America, Europe, and Japan then produced an agreement signed at the Smithsonian in December 1971 to devalue the dollar against gold from \$35 to \$38 per ounce and revalue other currencies against the dollar. But the dollar remained fundamentally overvalued.

CSIS reported in January 1972 that the Smithsonian Agreement was unlikely to solve the "fundamental" problems of the international monetary order. Moreover, it predicted the turmoil in the international monetary system would threaten Indonesia's continued economic development. As the Nixon administration worked to address a resurgent deterioration in the US balance of payments, CSIS suggested, it might make further cuts to the country's foreign aid program. And as European central banks adopted contractionary policies to counteract the inflationary effects of capital inflows, demand for the raw materials produced by developing countries like Indonesia might fall. In short, the demise of the Bretton Woods order threatened a reduction in all three of Indonesia's primary sources of hard currency: aid, investment, and exports.[110]

The ongoing Vietnam War also fueled political changes that further threatened the flow of US aid to the New Order. Disillusioned by the war, a number of influential senators, especially left-leaning members of the Foreign Relations Committee, began wielding the power of the purse to demand a stronger hand in the shaping of American foreign policy. These doves mounted steadily rising opposition to funneling aid to authoritarian regimes like the New Order—some because they feared the United States could be dragged into another Vietnam, others because they lamented the human rights abuses perpetrated by American allies.[111] The numbers reveal an astonishing shift: in the decade before 1968, Senate roll-call votes on defense bills numbered one every two years, but in the three years after 1968 more than twenty such votes occurred every single year.[112] Emblematic of the shift in congressional attitudes was an October 1971 speech given by Senator Frank Church, a longtime proponent of a robust foreign aid program. "While experience has shown that our aid programs have little if any relevance either to the deterrence of communism or the encouragement of democracy," the Idaho Democrat opined, "they have been effective in certain instances in keeping unpopular regimes in power."[113] Shortly thereafter, the Senate voted to kill foreign aid entirely. The program was revived only after considerable legislative surgery that separated economic and military aid into two separate bills and imposed substantial limits on each.[114]

The turmoil over the monetary order, foreign aid, and human rights converged as New Order officials were preparing for the December 1971 meeting of the IGGI, where they planned to submit a request for \$670 million in aid for 1972. The Indonesian ambassador to the United States received reassurances that "there would be a continuing aid program," though he was also warned that it would likely be "at somewhat reduced levels."[115] Nixon's treasury secretary, John Connally, traveled across Asia in November 1971 to press Japan to agree to revalue the yen and reassure American partners like South Vietnam, Thailand, the Philippines, and Indonesia that US aid programs would be restored. When Connally met with Suharto in Jakarta, he explained that Nixon's cuts to the foreign aid program represented an effort at "doing something about the U.S. balance of payments situation." He suggested similar motives, rather than human rights concerns, lay behind Congress's mounting skepticism toward foreign aid, noting that the sudden demise of foreign aid legislation reflected "the conviction of the American people that the U.S. had too long been bearing all the burdens of foreign assistance and common defense" while other countries were "taking advantage of the U.S." He concluded the meeting by optimistically telling Suharto that there was "no certainty it would affect the Indonesian program at all."[116] Upon returning to Washington, Connally summarized his meetings with anticommunist leaders in Southeast Asia for Nixon as "quite reassuring to all of them. And I think it particularly was to Suharto."[117]

Whatever hopes Suharto carried out of his conversation with Connally were dashed shortly thereafter. The American ambassador in Indonesia informed New Order officials that the United States might reduce its aid to Indonesia and abandon the formula whereby it provided one-third of the non-food aid and a "fair share" of the food aid endorsed by the IGGI.[118] The rationale, according to the secretaries of state, agriculture, and the treasury, was that "the U.S., due to congressional action, is in a poor position to carry as heavy an aid burden as before." Moreover, international financial institutions like the World Bank planned to increase their pledges, and other donors planned to maintain or increase their aid commitments as measured in their own, newly revalued currencies, which meant the dollar value of their aid to Indonesia would increase.[119] Alarmed at the symbolic implications of an American aid drawdown, Suharto wrote a letter to Nixon arguing that such a move would "greatly influence in a negative sense the attitude of other donor countries" and would also "add to the arguments used by certain groups in our society, skeptical of United States policies, to doubt even more the present Indonesian government's domestic and foreign policies."[120] Sumitro followed Suharto's letter with two messages to Kissinger sent through the backchannel the men had established two years earlier.[121] These missives struck their targets. Nixon overrode his underlings and ordered the United States to once again pledge to meet one-third of Indonesia's non-food aid requirements.[122]

When the IGGI convened in Amsterdam in late December 1971, the IMF and the World Bank endorsed Indonesia's request for $670 million in assistance for 1972. The New Order continued to secure ever-larger amounts of foreign aid in spite of an increasingly challenging international environment. But threats to the Suharto regime's ability to mobilize international capital mounted and rendered the future uncertain.

V

The human rights revolution, the international monetary crisis, and the end of the Vietnam War were developments internal to the global Cold War. But it was the institutionalization of the global Cold War itself that posed the most serious obstacle to the Suharto regime's ability to maintain the flows of international aid to Indonesia. As détente and triangular diplomacy reshaped the international order and altered the valence of Cold War imperatives in global politics, Indonesian officials began to look elsewhere for sources of foreign support, including regional networks and energy markets.

Indonesian policymakers were stunned by Nixon's July 1971 announcement that he would travel to the People's Republic of China in early 1972. "We are confronted with unexpected events and those we previously regarded as impossible," remarked one army newspaper.[123] Adam Malik's Foreign Ministry had launched a campaign to restore diplomatic ties between Indonesia and China as early as 1969. Malik predicted economic development would inevitably give the People's Republic a stake in the preservation of the international order and believed Indonesia should avoid overreliance on the United States as it pulled back from Southeast Asia.[124] But the military put a quick stop to Malik's outreach efforts and held firm to a policy of isolating mainland China—a policy that senior New Order officials believed reinforced their efforts to secure American aid.[125] Nixon's about-face on China thus put the Suharto regime in an awkward position. In October 1971, the military directed Indonesia's representatives at the United Nations to vote in favor of a US-sponsored resolution to preserve Taipei's membership in the body and then abstain from an Albanian-sponsored resolution to admit Beijing. A respected Indonesian journalist reported that the New Order's posture reflected fear of the "repercussions toward the flow of aid to Indonesia through the IGGI in which America and Japan play an important role."[126]

The Suharto regime's willingness to toe the American line on China elicited widespread condemnation in Jakarta. The action front newspaper *Harian Kami* claimed the New Order had shed its nonaligned pretentions and Indonesia had become little more than a "client state."[127] In its determination to preserve the flow of international aid, the regime had imperiled its domestic legitimacy.

The New Order continued to regard China as the key threat facing Indonesia even as triangular diplomacy integrated the People's Republic into the international order. A secret CSIS report prepared in January 1972 suggested Beijing's foreign policy remained fundamentally expansionist: dedicated toward reclaiming territories across the South China Sea (including territory claimed by Indonesia) and keen to mobilize overseas Chinese communities across

Southeast Asia to further China's efforts at domestic development and international subversion. The report also predicted that Southeast Asia would become the primary field of Sino-Soviet competition following an American withdrawal from Vietnam.[128] Suharto came to fear that an imperative of the global Cold War—preserving US hegemony by playing the Soviet Union and China against each other—contradicted the imperatives of his Cold Wars in Indonesia and Southeast Asia—preserving the stability of the New Order and containing the spread of Chinese influence in the region. Suharto met with the American ambassador in Indonesia in January 1972 to express alarm at the prospect of communist (particularly Chinese) expansionism in Southeast Asia.[129] Reports of Indonesian anxieties reached the White House and led Nixon to pen a letter to Suharto. The American president informed his Indonesian counterpart that he had ordered a near-doubling of US military aid to Indonesia to $25 million per year. He reassured Suharto that he would "have your country's interests very much in mind as I go to Peking and then to Moscow in the coming months."[130]

Indonesian officials soon concluded that the advent of a more multipolar order represented an opportunity rather than a crisis. In March 1972, the National Defense and Security Council (Wanhankamnas) prepared a report on superpower relations in the era of détente. The report echoed CSIS's conclusion that both Beijing and Moscow would seek to extend their influence in Southeast Asia. In that context, the United States would likely adopt an "off-shore strategy" of relying on regional allies to either "balance or fill the vacuum" that would emerge as American forces withdrew from Vietnam. Because "an Indonesia under the influence of Moscow or Beijing" would threaten the overall American strategic posture in Asia, the report concluded, Washington would continue to furnish the Suharto regime with military and economic aid and would encourage other developed countries like Japan to do the same. In other words, Indonesia's "bargaining position toward the United States is quite strong."[131] This was a statement of unusual boldness for a regime as dependent upon international aid as Suharto's.

Why did Indonesia not embark upon a triangular diplomacy of its own by deepening its ties with Moscow? The Wanhankamnas report on superpower relations characterized the Soviet Union as a power in decline. Reformist and revisionist movements had risen up against Soviet authority across Eastern Europe, delivering "shocks that endanger the integrity" of the Warsaw Pact. Moscow thus faced a dilemma "between the imperative of maintaining hegemony in Eastern Europe and the imperative of giving channels for the aspirations growing in socialist countries." The Soviet empire's command economy had also revealed its inability to keep pace with technological progress in the West, and it would soon require massive infusions of foreign capital to meet the demands of its clients. Wanhankamnas suggested that the Soviet Union's "primary strategic objective" was the containment of China. It would likely "put ideological interests aside" and seek to build diplomatic relationships with Southeast Asian states rather than foment insurgencies across the region.[132] That much had become clear as early as 1969, when Soviet general secretary Leonid Brezhnev had proposed a collective security arrangement for Asia.[133]

Soviet economic difficulties meant Moscow represented an unlikely source of the international capital upon which the Suharto regime depended. But Suharto's unwillingness to deepen ties with the Soviet Union was as much a product of his deeply engrained Cold War mentality as it was a product of pragmatic calculation. A top-secret May 1972 report from Kopkamtib characterized Soviet cultural and economic diplomacy in Indonesia—including seemingly innocuous programs like offering Russian language courses, screening films about Soviet life, and hosting industrial exhibitions—as a manifestation of an ideological "offensive," one "inseparable from subversive interests" and a "threat that, if left unchecked, will at some point escalate to become a national danger."[134] Suharto would wait until November 1973 to tell his cabinet that the signing of trade agreements with socialist countries was a "good political step," though he hastened to add that "the ability of our security apparatus to prevent subversion and infiltration must be taken into account in the implementation" of the agreements.[135]

Triangular diplomacy went some way toward institutionalizing the Cold War and undermining the salience of Cold War imperatives in the superpowers' engagement with the Third World. In that context, geopolitics grew more fluid and regional diplomacy took on added importance. Suharto recognized these trends and worked to broaden Indonesia's ties in the Asia-Pacific. He traveled to Australia and New Zealand in February 1972 and secured Canberra's agreement to donate to the Indonesian air force sixteen F-86 fighter jets and the training and spare parts necessary to keep them operational. The planes helped Suharto deepen his hold on the air force.[136] But even these victories revealed challenges ahead. The Antipodes did not go untouched by the global human rights revolution, and small but vocal protests greeted Suharto on trips to both countries.[137] Suharto found himself confronted by the press with uncomfortable questions about Indonesia's political prisoners.[138] He blamed the disturbances on communists.[139] A few months later, Suharto traveled to Japan for discussions on an oil-for-loans agreement outside the purview of the IGGI. At least one Japanese official suspected Suharto's motives for the agreement lay in the fact that "his position was less secure than generally believed and that he needed the loan to 'placate' elements in the Indonesian power structure."[140] According to reports of the trip given to American diplomats, Suharto also delivered an alarmist assessment of the communist threat facing Southeast Asia and proposed a "Tokyo-Djakarta-Canberra-Wellington understanding in dealing with Asian matters."[141]

High-ranking military officials in the New Order tended to ignore the developing world beyond Southeast Asia. But as détente reshaped the international order and globalization remade the world economy, other elements within the New Order worked to strengthen Indonesia's ties with the Global South. Adam Malik's Foreign Ministry cultivated the Non-Aligned Movement, which played key roles in legitimizing the *bebas aktif* foreign policy that remained a third rail of Indonesian politics. Suharto himself attended the September 1970 meeting of the Non-Aligned Movement in Lusaka, which a briefing book stated would represent "reaffirmation of Indonesia's free and active foreign policy principles and the refinement of their implementation by the New Order government."[142] Disillusioned by his experience in Lusaka—one report to Bakin characterized the conversations at the conference as entirely "inconsequential"—he subsequently divorced himself from networks of Global South diplomacy.[143] But Malik remained an active participant in the Non-Aligned Movement and worked to blunt the organization's radical predilections. He walked out of an August 1972 ministerial meeting in Guyana to protest the admission of the Provisional Revolutionary Government of South Vietnam.[144] The following year, at a summit in Algiers, he rejected calls to support national liberation movements and insisted that "we must never let the concept of the struggle for freedom become an excuse for instigating a civil war within an already independent and sovereign state, or even worse, an excuse for the intervention of a foreign power."[145] Given its role as a voice of moderation, the New Order's participation in Global South fora at once sustained its domestic legitimacy and furthered its efforts to attract international aid.

Most consequential of all were the activities of Ibnu Sutowo and other leading figures of the Indonesian oil industry. By early 1973, the New Order had become confident that a looming global energy crisis would present opportunities to expand the fiscal capacity of the Indonesian state. One wild-eyed estimate suggested Indonesia could secure $22 billion in windfall oil revenues—enough to free Indonesia of all of its debts and finance the entirety of its development needs—because rich countries "will be forced to accept the conditions demanded by Indonesia."[146] The New Order also hoped to tap the windfall profits accruing to larger oil-producing states. In April 1973, the Indonesian ambassador in Saudi Arabia reported that Riyadh was willing to invest its mushrooming oil riches in "the development of Islam, the struggle against Israel, and anticommunism." He recommended that the New Order send a mission to the kingdom to appeal for investment in Indonesia.[147] Finally, the emergence of a market for liquefied natural gas (LNG) presented additional opportunities for the Suharto regime to secure international capital. Pertamina signed letters of intent with foreign buyers for LNG beginning in late 1972, including with electric utilities in Japan and California.[148] Director of Oil and Gas Wijarso explained that Indonesia would seek to export as much oil and gas as possible and utilize coal or imported Middle Eastern crude (whose price was cheaper than Indonesia's "sweet" variety) to meet its domestic energy needs.[149]

Indonesian officialdom's efforts to secure other sources of fiscal capacity did not erase the regime's anxieties about declining aid. Beginning in 1971, a quartet of young members of the US House of Representatives eked out positions of influence in subcommittees within the Foreign Affairs Committee and curtailed the power of the committee's leadership, which had exhibited a tendency to defer to the White House. These lawmakers hired young, idealistic staffers and held public hearings on a number of controversial issues, including US military aid to the junta in Greece.[150] The increasingly assertive legislative branch slashed nearly $300 million from the Nixon administration's military aid budget in the spring of 1972.[151] Sensing the danger to the New Order, the Indonesian ambassador quickly scheduled meetings with a number of American lawmakers to emphasize Indonesia's need for "hardware" to "carry out its responsibilities for regional security." He strained credulity when he insisted that, although the Suharto regime accepted the Nixon Doctrine, the United States possessed "not a low profile but 'no profile at all'" in Indonesia.[152] Not long thereafter, idealistic supporters of Senator George McGovern crafted a Democratic Party platform that advocated an overall "curtailment of military aid" and immediate cutoffs in US aid to authoritarian governments not only in Indochina but also in Greece

Figure 7.1 Protestors amass outside the Amstelhotel in December 1973 to demand the IGGI halt aid to the Suharto regime. BNA Photographic/Alamy.

and Portugal.[153] Although McGovern's radicalism alienated voters and led to a landslide victory for Nixon, the Republican Party did not fare so well in the legislature. "EEK! The Senate," wrote one aide in a memorandum to Kissinger, noting that the president's party "will be much diminished on crunch national security votes."[154]

Similar developments occurred beyond the United States. Suharto traveled across Europe in November 1972—stopping in France, Austria, Switzerland, Belgium, Italy, and the Vatican—to drum up aid commitments in advance of the following month's meeting of the IGGI. Adam Malik described the trip as an effort to "encourage France and other European nations to bring balance to [the] Asian situation through participation in economic development" after the United States and United Kingdom withdrew from the region.[155] With that goal in mind, the mission met with moderate success. France agreed to increase its aid to Indonesia by 20 percent, and Austria and Switzerland agreed to join the IGGI.[156] When the body convened in December, it endorsed the New Order's request for $760 million in aid for 1973 and also promised to provide an additional 250,000 tons of rice to help Indonesia surmount its food crisis.[157]

But warning signs flashed throughout Suharto's journey and the IGGI meeting. Especially in France, leftist groups staged demonstrations denouncing Suharto's role in the mass murder that accompanied his rise to power and the continuing detention of tens of thousands of political prisoners.[158] And diplomats from donor countries expressed worries to the Indonesian delegation about the enduring corruption within the New Order.[159] Meanwhile, Australia's December 1972 elections brought an end to twenty-three years of uninterrupted conservative rule. The new prime minister, Gough Whitlam, linked himself to the burgeoning human rights movement and promised to upend the Cold War and Commonwealth orientation of Australian foreign policy in favor of a deeper engagement with Southeast Asia.[160] How he would reconcile those ambitions with regard to Indonesia—Australia's closest neighbor but a notorious dictatorship—remained an open question for the Suharto regime at the dawn of 1973.

VI

Nineteen-seventy-three was a year of crisis for the Suharto regime. The end of US involvement in the Vietnam War, the flowering of the international human rights movement, and the advent of a floating exchange rate system combined to threaten the flow of international aid that sustained the New Order. Student protest also escalated in Indonesia and elsewhere in Southeast Asia, raising the threat of a destabilizing regional contagion.

The United States and the Democratic Republic of (North) Vietnam signed the Paris Peace Accords that brought an end to American involvement in the Vietnam War in January. Senior New Order officials doubted a Vietnam reunified under communist rule would pose a threat to Indonesia. "We could already see that Vietnam would become a communist nation," Sumitro recalled, "but we were certain that a communist Vietnam would not endanger its environment."[161] What they feared was not a Vietnamese offensive into Southeast Asia. Instead, they feared that the end of the war would lead US aid to dry up while insurgents and subversives across the region tapped a newly available reservoir of weaponry. Suharto met with Spiro Agnew during the US vice president's tour through Southeast Asia in early 1973 and made what the American embassy reported was a "strong pitch" for "additional economic and military assistance."[162] Upon his return to Washington, Agnew told Nixon that Suharto "was apprehensive about the future of Indochina and anxious to be reassured concerning our continued presence and support."[163] American policymakers made efforts to buoy Indonesian officials, but the Indonesian embassy in Washington reported that Congress's hostility toward foreign aid remained an impediment to the New Order's efforts to secure international capital.[164]

Suharto worked to court the Whitlam government in Australia as well. In a briefing paper prepared before Whitlam visited Jakarta in February 1973, the Coordinating Ministry of Economics, Finance, and Industry reported that, as a result of "events in Southeast Asia with the end of the Vietnam War" as well as the "intrinsic politics of the Labour Government," Australia was likely to "increase its military and economic aid to Indonesia."[165] During his visit, Whitlam agreed to expand economic aid to Indonesia, which totaled approximately $15 million per year between 1970 and 1972, to $26.2 million for 1973.[166] Toward the end of the year, Suharto also hosted New Zealand prime minister Norman Kirk. The two leaders issued a statement affirming their intent to deepen international cooperation in the Asia-Pacific region.[167]

As the Suharto regime grappled with an evolving regional equilibrium, international monetary developments once again threatened to destabilize the Indonesian economy. The recalibrated exchange rates agreed to at the Smithsonian in December 1971 came under strain beginning in January 1973. By mid-March, American policymakers loosed the dollar from gold and the world groped uncertainly toward a new era of floating exchange rates. Indonesian monetary policymakers were determined to preserve the international credibility conferred by a fixed exchange rate and an open capital account. Bank Indonesia therefore maintained a peg of 415 rupiah per (weakening) US dollar, which required lowering interest rates to discourage capital inflows and facilitated a dramatic expansion of the money supply. The currency peg transmitted increases in the prices of internationally traded goods into Indonesia. The result was a spike in inflationary pressures, with retail prices in Jakarta rising at an annualized rate of more than 40 percent over the last three quarters of 1973, only months after Indonesia surmounted the rice crisis of late 1972. Given the ongoing discontent surrounding price increases across Indonesia, the inflationary consequences of the regime change in international finance stoked further domestic protest.[168]

So too did the turmoil in the monetary system pose challenges to the New Order's efforts to court international investment. One foreign journalist reported in mid-1973 that many potential investors, frustrated by seemingly endless bureaucratic obstacles, anticipated directing their capital elsewhere. A doctor who catered to the community of foreign investors remarked that "the number of nervous breakdowns, ulcers and cases of alcoholism within the foreign community is higher than anywhere I've seen."[169] Suharto worked to mollify these concerns by creating the Investment Coordinating Board (BKPM) under Barli Halim to serve as a one-stop destination for investors seeking information, permits, and licenses.[170] At the same time, however, Suharto sought to counteract a growing sense that the New Order was a comprador regime beholden to the whims of international capital. After Barli delivered a report suggesting that changes in the international monetary system would lead foreign firms to gain a larger share in joint ventures with Indonesian companies, Suharto insisted that, as a matter of principle, the Indonesian share should increase and that additional foreign funds should take the form of debt rather than equity.[171] Bridging these two objectives proved challenging. In September 1973, Suharto and Vice President Hamengkubuwono hosted a mission from Japan's Mitsui Group, which since 1968 had invested some $46 million in Indonesia in industries including cement, textiles, tires, and forestry. New Order officials courted additional investments from Mitsui but demanded the conglomerate offer a majority position to local counterparts in upstream industries and urged it to channel capital toward the agricultural sector.[172] Representatives of the Suharto regime also encouraged Mitsui to ensure its agents in the archipelago tempered what many Indonesians regarded as a supercilious mien.[173]

The human rights movement gathered steam across the world and posed further challenges to the Suharto regime's ability to secure international aid. In 1973, Amnesty International's Dutch section published *Indonesia Special*, a glossy thirty-two-page magazine focusing on political imprisonment in Suharto's Indonesia.[174] Amnesty also began lobbying members of the IGGI to use aid as a weapon to force the Suharto regime to address the plight of Indonesia's political prisoners.[175] A memorandum from the group's secretary general suggested "the possibility of making some further publicity about the Indonesian political prisoner situation at the time of the IGGI meeting" because "the Indonesian authorities are increasingly concerned about public opinion in those countries on which they depend for aid."[176] Around the same time, Carmel

Budiardjo, a former political prisoner freed as a result of Amnesty's activism, established TAPOL, the British Campaign for the Release of Indonesian Political Prisoners.[177] The organization's first publication appeared in August 1973. It encouraged activists to rally popular opinion against the Suharto regime in "those countries whose governments aid Indonesia over the flagrant violation of human rights in that country."[178] TAPOL quickly won the support of influential lawmakers. British members of parliament Eric Lubbock and Peter Archer visited the Indonesian embassy in London in August 1973 to "express the deep concern felt by themselves and many members of Parliament in both Houses over the plight of Indonesia's *tapols*," using the Indonesian portmanteau for political prisoners.[179]

In the United States, meanwhile, Congress amended Section 32 of the Foreign Assistance Act to proclaim the "sense of Congress that the President should deny any economic or military assistance to the government of any foreign country which practices the internment or imprisonment of that country's citizens for political purposes." Although such language was not legally binding, it reflected a burgeoning threat to the ability of authoritarian regimes like the New Order to win American aid. The unfolding Watergate scandal only heightened the legislature's willingness to challenge the Nixon administration's foreign policy priorities, including funneling military and economic aid to key Nixon Doctrine clients like Indonesia.

Portentous political change also occurred in the Netherlands, another of Indonesia's most important purveyors of international aid. A center-left cabinet led by Prime Minister Joop den Uyl of the Labor Party came to power in May 1973. Den Uyl appointed as minister for development cooperation Jan Pronk, a lawmaker in his early thirties with New Left predilections. In July 1973, the US ambassador in Jakarta warned Indonesia's attorney general that, although "Indonesia's prisoner problem has not been a factor in IGGI deliberations," it could yet "be used against Indonesia abroad in various forums."[180] So anxious were IGGI diplomats about the possibility of domestic political pressure affecting the flow of aid to Indonesia that they gathered for a lunch in August to discuss the matter.[181] Indonesians themselves began to worry. Frans Seda, who moved from a ministerial post to a roving ambassadorship in Europe, reported that Pronk was an "intelligent and very dogmatic" devotee of the New Left who disagreed with the concentration of Dutch development aid on Indonesia. He predicted that Pronk would serve as a "catalyst for a latent view that will gradually influence public opinion in Europe" and could endanger Indonesia's ability to obtain international aid in the near future.[182]

Regional developments reinforced the sense of ascendant threat. In October 1973, student protestors brought down the military government in Thailand, which some New Order officials worried would endow the Indonesian student movement with a renascent sense of momentum.[183] The director of research at the Ministry of Foreign Affairs told an American diplomat that "many Indonesian students and even young military officers . . . harbor similar grievances against the Indonesian military leadership for its corruption and irresponsibility."[184] Protests in Jakarta did indeed grow more frequent. Prohibitions on demonstrations, arrests of some opposition leaders, and divisions within the student movement meant these protests generally attracted fewer than forty people.[185] But leaders of the University of Indonesia Student Council succeeded in wringing a measure of coherence out of the fractious student movement. By the end of 1973, opposition marches attracted upward of 1,500 protestors, including not only students but also workers, farmers, and pedicab drivers.[186] American diplomats sensed what the ambassador described as "a feeling that the discontent among youth is both deeper and more dangerous than perhaps I or other, more senior officers, yet believe."[187] Youth dissatisfaction also increasingly found an outlet in the pages of moderate opposition newspapers like *Indonesia Raya*, *Abadi*, and *Harian Kami*.[188]

Student protest ultimately coalesced around the issue of Japan. Tokyo represented one of the Suharto regime's key sources of international capital, and its representatives possessed close ties with reputedly corrupt figures in Aspri. In early December 1973, Sudjono Humardani convened the first of what became many Japanese-Indonesian conferences at the CSIS building in Jakarta. He called the conference to order by remarking that Indonesia had no alternative but to mobilize foreign aid and investment, and he praised Japan for its role in promoting the archipelago's economic development. He went on to explain that, in Indonesia, "development is not regarded by the people solely in terms of economics" but rather as part of a larger "process of nation building," a belief that animated the "open discussions regarding foreign investments, including that of Japan, in the context of [a] development strategy of Indonesia still seeking for an equilibrium."[189] If one purpose of the conference was to convince the public that Sudjono was not sacrificing Indonesia's national interests at the altar of foreign capital, it backfired considerably. Two senior CSIS officials remembered that the conference further inflamed anti-Japanese sentiment.[190] Students burned effigies of Ali Murtopo, Sudjono Humardani, and representations of "ugly Japanese."[191] As it happened, Japanese prime minister Kakuei Tanaka was scheduled to arrive in Jakarta in mid-January. Students resolved to stage massive demonstrations during his visit. "The situation was heating up in Jakarta in more ways than one," Sumitro recalled. "The situation weather itself seemed hotter than usual. The situation in general was such that it felt as if we were on a roasting spit over a fire."[192]

Indonesia was on the verge of a crisis. Since Golkar's triumph in the 1971 elections, Suharto had mobilized vast sums of international capital to sustain his Cold War projects of political consolidation and economic development. Indonesia experienced a period of stability and prosperity unprecedented in a quarter-century of independence. But opposition was mounting against the alliance between the Suharto regime and international capital. Civil society groups in Indonesia saw possibilities for evolutionary change evaporating before their eyes and mounted more frequent and more intense protests against the New Order. In the United States, the United Kingdom, the Netherlands, Australia, and beyond, human rights groups lobbied their governments to curb the provision of aid to authoritarian regimes like the New Order. These dynamics became self-reinforcing. As the Suharto regime cracked down on dissent within Indonesia, it provided ammunition to human rights activists abroad to vilify the New Order; and as human rights movements held up Indonesian dissidents as heroes, they provided a rationale for the Suharto regime to suppress demonstrators as foreign agents. All the while, the collapse of the Bretton Woods system, the end of the Vietnam War, and the advent of détente and triangular diplomacy corroded the means and motives behind flows of international capital to Indonesia.

As Suharto confronted threats on numerous fronts, war erupted in the Middle East. Already in September 1973, Indonesian officials detected a change in the willingness of moderate petrostates like Saudi Arabia to unleash the "oil weapon."[193] After Egyptian and Syrian forces launched a coordinated strike on the Israeli-occupied Sinai Peninsula and Golan Heights in October and the United States began a massive airlift of arms and materiel to reinforce Israel, Arab oil exporters announced price hikes, production cuts, and an embargo against the United States and other countries that supported Israel. The price of Arab crude rocketed to more than $11, quadrupling in a matter of weeks.[194] Indonesia would soon reap massive petrodollar windfalls that diminished the importance of foreign aid to the New Order's fisc and sustained Suharto's Cold War.

The Age of Oil

Monsoon rain soaked Jakarta as 1973 turned to 1974, but the streets of the capital teemed with protest. Young demonstrators railed against the corruption that sapped public wealth, against the authoritarianism that stifled civic demands, against the inflation that eroded popular livelihoods, against the conspicuous consumption that exposed persistent inequality, and against the foreign domination that shaped the Indonesian economy. Major protests also erupted in Yogyakarta, Bandung, Surabaya, Makassar, and Medan.[1]

Simmering popular discontent finally boiled over during Japanese prime minister Kakuei Tanaka's visit to Jakarta in mid-January 1974. On the evening of January 14, students and youth breached the perimeter of the capital's newly opened international airport and unfurled anti-Japanese banners as Tanaka's plane came to a halt on the runway.[2] The following day, university students organized a "long march" from the campus of the University of Indonesia to the campus of Trisakti University. As the march progressed, bands of teenagers broke off from the procession and began deflating tires, lowering flags, and smashing windows. Eventually, demonstrators converged on the National Monument in Merdeka Square. When the student marchers arrived in the city center, they encountered a cordon sanitaire of soldiers and armored vehicles that denied them access to the square. Raucous protest then devolved into chaos as angry demonstrators scattered across the city. They set fire to hundreds of vehicles, ransacked a Coca-Cola factory, and burned the showroom of PT Astra—a Toyota partner owned by the ethnic Chinese Suharto crony William Soeryadjaya. Joined by tens of thousands of unemployed urban poor, young agitators engaged in widespread looting. Security forces at first attempted to disperse the demonstrators and rioters through moral suasion but quickly resorted to deadly force. By the time order was restored late on January 16, 144 buildings were damaged or destroyed, 807 cars and 187 motorbikes smashed or burned, and 160 kilograms of gold stolen from jewelry stores.[3] Eleven people were killed

Suharto's Cold War. Mattias Fibiger, Oxford University Press. © Oxford University Press 2023.
DOI: 10.1093/oso/9780197667224.003.0009

Figure 8.1 A child watches as demonstrators set fire to vehicles in the Senen district of Jakarta during the protests of January 15, 1974. *Tempo.*

and almost 200 injured. Suharto was forced to use a helicopter to ferry Tanaka back to the airport on the seventeenth rather than drive him through the city's debris-strewn streets.[4]

Malari (*Malapetaka Lima Belas Januari*, or January Fifteenth Catastrophe) was a moment of maximum danger for the New Order. As inflation galloped and food grew scarce in parts of the archipelago, students and youth appeared once again to represent a vanguard of revolutionary change in Indonesian history—the sharp wedge of a broad political coalition that included disaffected middle classes and immiserated urban poor. Moreover, the Suharto regime itself appeared to be fracturing between two poles of authority: the Sumitro group in Hankam and the Ali Murtopo group in Aspri. One regime insider remembered that the combination of widening elite polarization and escalating popular mobilization "could easily have opened the way to instability and even civil war."[5] Beyond the archipelago, the end of US involvement in the Vietnam War diminished the geopolitical salience of Southeast Asia in Washington and Moscow. Meanwhile, mounting economic challenges and the churning human rights revolution rendered other donors reluctant to channel aid to the New Order. International investors, already disaffected by the bureaucratic morass they encountered in Indonesia, grew alarmed at the prospect of further instability. Suharto's ability to sustain the financial inflows that undergirded his Cold War projects appeared in doubt.

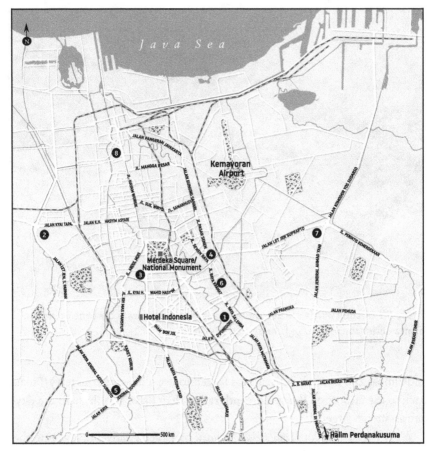

Significant Events of the Malari Incident in Jakarta, January 15, 1974

1 Students gathered at the University of Indonesia and began a long march through the capital. Many carried signs with slogans like "Get Out Japan!" and chanted "We are not traitors!"

2 The long march culminated at Trisakti University. There students held an assembly and burned Japanese prime minister Kakuei Tanaka in effigy.

3 General Sumitro encountered demonstrators at the southwest corner of Merdeka Square. He urged them to march away from the presidential palace on the north side of the square.

4 The Senen shopping complex was burned to the ground. Student leaders denied involvement in the arson. Many came to suspect General Ali Murtopo's shadowy intelligence network had engineered the chaos to discredit General Sumitro.

5 The headquarters of PT Toyota Astra was ransacked and burned. The firm had become an emblem of Japan's growing presence in Indonesia.

6 A Pertamina building was ransacked and its contents burned on the street. The state oil company had become synonymous with official corruption.

7 A Coca-Cola factory was burned. The product had come to symbolize the displacement of local artisans by international brands.

8 Widespread looting erupted in the Glodok/Chinatown neighborhood. Some wealthy ethnic Chinese Indonesians ran businesses with close links to the Suharto regime and became targets of the indigenous population's rage.

Figure 8.2 The *Malari* incident across Jakarta.

As Indonesia descended into political turmoil, faraway developments rescued choice from circumstance. *Malari* occurred just weeks after the Organization of Petroleum Exporting Countries (OPEC) announced the doubling of oil prices for the second time in only two months. Indonesia reaped petrodollar windfalls that, while minuscule in per capita terms, reshaped the political economy of the New Order. Oil revenues spiked to about 50 percent of total government receipts while foreign aid declined to about 15 percent, rendering the New Order more autonomous of its domestic and international constituencies alike. Suharto channeled Indonesia's newfound resource rents back into his Cold War. He worked to restore political stability through coercive repression and corporatist cooptation. Freed of his need to placate international capital, he also unveiled a developmental, protectionist, and redistributionist economic program and launched an invasion of the tiny Portuguese colony of East Timor. His Cold War projects of political stabilization, economic development, and regional securitization reached their crescendo.

I

Restoring political stability became Suharto's overriding objective in the wake of *Malari*. "Once again ABRI soldiers are called by history to save the people, the nation, and the state," he told a group of military officials on January 17.[6] Security forces detained almost 800 people during and after the riots, including student leaders like Hariman Siregar as well as other opposition figures including human rights lawyer Adnan Buyung Nasution, editor Rachman Tolleng, economist Sarbini Sumawinata, and even former ambassador to the United States Soedjatmoko. The New Order then clamped down on activism by students and journalists. Gatherings of more than five people were prohibited and a curfew was imposed. Schools and universities were ordered to close for a week. The newly appointed minister of education issued a decree requiring student councils to obtain permission for all on-campus activities. Several action fronts of high school students were banned. Twelve critical media outlets were shuttered, only two of which were allowed to reopen. Reporters from the closed papers were blacklisted from employment in the industry. The spectrum of opinion accessible through the press narrowed considerably, and criticism of the government vanished entirely from the pages of newspapers.[7]

In early February, Suharto established the Council on Political Stabilization and National Security (Polkam) to coordinate the New Order's response to *Malari* and centralize control over the Indonesian state's coercive institutions.[8] At the council's first meeting on February 12, he instructed Indonesia's military and intelligence officials to "continue the implementation of comprehensive preventive and repressive measures in all fields to overcome the effects of the incident."[9] Suharto accelerated the ban on the publication of Chinese-language newspapers and ordered increased surveillance of the Chinese population in Indonesia.[10] He also adopted a stricter posture against crime. "Lawbreaking activities with a political background, especially those aimed at obstructing or undermining development," he told Polkam in May 1974, "should not be considered as mere criminal acts so that the punishment imposed becomes lenient, because it will encourage criminal acts orchestrated by underground political movements." Although he admitted it was difficult to force judges to dispense harsh penalties, he stressed the need for magistrates to "secure the path of development."[11]

Repression alone was unlikely to achieve Suharto's goal of cultivating an anticommunist population. Corporatism consequently became a key strategy for preventing a recurrence of civil unrest. Suharto explained to Polkam in early March that the formation of the National Indonesian Youth Committee (KNPI) six months earlier was "intended to cultivate Indonesian youth so that they cannot easily be divided and are not fragmented by the narrowness of group politics and ideology." He ordered Polkam to "revisit" the decision to establish KNPI as a federation rather than a unitary body.[12] A few months later, he directed Polkam to ensure the inaugural KNPI congress scheduled for October 1974 ran smoothly, disbursing 50 million rupiah to finance the event.[13] Suharto himself opened the congress and told the attendees that KNPI was a "vessel to develop a new orientation for Indonesian youth" and to cultivate "their role in national development."[14] Cognizant of KNPI's corporatist purpose, the leaders of five major student groups issued a joint statement expressing concern about the dangers of an overly "structural" approach to civic life and calling on military leaders to recognize the importance of pluralism in Indonesian society.[15]

Suharto was unmoved. After the congress, he instructed Polkam to continue "the cultivation of KNPI so that it can support national stability." More specifically, he sought to use KNPI to mobilize Indonesian youth behind the cause of economic development rather than political change. "With the youth's understanding of the problems and efforts of development," Suharto explained, "a recurrence of events like the 'January 15 Incident' can be prevented" and "the youth can be saved from having its potential manipulated by other forces."[16] Suharto hosted the newly elected leaders of KNPI at the Merdeka Palace in late November and told them the efforts of Indonesian youth should be "channeled to agricultural extension, credit, processing, marketing, and distribution . . . because the farmers in the villages need a helping hand from the youth to increase production."[17] He remained gripped by a fear of student and youth unrest. "Do not hesitate in giving the right direction to the activities" of student groups, he told Polkam the same month. "Although it seems small, if left to drag on this experience can have substantial consequences in the future."[18] Independent student and youth organizations continued to exist, albeit under considerable government surveillance. However, by May 1976 Suharto ordered that KNPI should "become the one and only vessel for the cultivation of the youth generation."[19]

The Suharto regime also sought to corporatize Indonesian labor. After a series of unsuccessful attempts at cohering Indonesia's political party-based labor movement through Golkar, the New Order established the All-Indonesia Labor Federation (FBSI) in February 1973.[20] General Ali Murtopo worked through Bakin to host a series of meetings of Indonesian labor leaders that resulted in a declaration of unity proclaiming that the "essence of the struggle of Indonesian workers . . . is not only to protect the social and economic interest of workers, but also to enhance its participation in that process of development." Only after *Malari* upended Indonesian politics did Suharto forcibly assimilate all independent trade unions across the archipelago into FBSI. With the institutional mechanisms already in place, Murtopo then turned to the ideological underpinnings of corporatism. He presided over a December 1974 conference of government officials, FBSI representatives, business leaders, and intellectuals that gave birth to the idea of "Pancasila Labor Relations."[21] Under such a system, tripartite cooperation among unions, firms, and government would surmount the antagonistic relationship between capital and labor prescribed by Marxist doctrines of class conflict. Murtopo elaborated on his concept in a 1975 volume entitled *Workers and Peasants in Development* in which he suggested that relations between capital and labor must be "synchronized, harmonized, and attuned." He linked the Indonesian model to a nascent culturalist discourse of so-called Asian values by suggesting that "If we want to get to the bottom of our industrial relations philosophy, it is to the sources of our National Culture . . . that we must look."[22] The FBSI grew extraordinarily rapidly. By January 1976, it encompassed more than 2,500 branches located in each region of Indonesia and all major sectors of the economy except mining.[23]

Similar corporatist organizations coopted farmers and fisherman over the same period. And it was Cold War calculation that animated the New Order's renewed corporatist thrust. "The background to all these actions," recalled the general secretary of Golkar, "was to destroy the PKI because the backbone of the PKI were laborers, farmers, fishermen and youth."[24]

Suharto also worked to reinforce the New Order's control over political parties in the wake of *Malari*. At a Polkam meeting on March 12, he ordered his underlings to "consolidate" the fusion of political parties. He explained that it was in the government's interest to promote the continued "viability" of the reorganized parties and ensure they "do not need to ask for help in improper ways." The New Order began paying Golkar, PDI, and PPP monthly subsidies of 2.5 million rupiah as well as lump sums of 30 million rupiah to hold congresses at which they would ratify agglomeration.[25] The following month, he ordered Polkam to prohibit PDI from publishing an official newspaper in order to "safeguard political stability."[26] Isolated from their constituents and increasingly dependent on the state for financial support, the PDI and PPP were rendered docile players in the New Order's choreographed political system.

The Suharto regime formalized restrictions on party activity in 1975. In January, the government submitted a bill on political parties to parliament. The bill would give de jure legitimacy to a number of long-standing de facto changes to Indonesian politics: the "simplification" of the party system, prohibitions on party operations below the district level (areas of up to 500,000 people further divided into subdistricts and villages), and restrictions on party recruitment of civil servants. It would also grant the president the right to "freeze" the leadership of political parties. Most controversially, it would require political parties to accept Pancasila as their "sole foundation," which posed a particular threat to the Islamic PPP. Party leaders expressed strident opposition to the bill and deadlocked negotiations over the first six months of 1975. Suharto intervened in June and called Golkar, PDI, and PPP leaders to the Merdeka Palace, where he told them in no uncertain terms that he expected movement on the bill.[27] The bill became law in August, though only after Suharto backed down on the "sole foundation" plank.[28]

The virulence of resistance to the sole foundation plank foreshadowed a divergence between the PDI and PPP. A combination of hostile parties and factions, the PDI suffered endemic internecine conflict. Mohammed Isnaeni and Sunawar Sukowati, both of PNI backgrounds, vied for influence within the enlarged PDI—the former earnestly working to make the merger work and the latter attempting to secure the dominance of former PNI elements. Sukowati won a series of bureaucratic victories over the course of 1974 and seemed poised to be named general chairman of PDI. But Suharto told Polkam that the other parties within PDI felt slighted and ordered the leadership of the PDI to be "redeliberated, with instructions not to allow fusion to become raw again."[29] Isnaeni and Sukowati eventually stepped down from the PDI board, and leadership of the party fell to Sanusi Harjadinata and Usep Ranawijaya.[30] On the eve of the party's first congress in April 1976, former navy chief and Suharto confidant Sudomo met repeatedly with various factions of the PDI to ensure the party elected Sanusi and Usep.[31] Sudomo's relentless efforts to cohere the PDI led some wits to dub the party the "Partai Domo Indonesia."[32] Even so, the party remained divided over how fully it should support Suharto.[33]

Suharto and other senior New Order officials anticipated similar bouts of factionalism would hamstring the PPP—especially given the long history of discord within Islamic politics in Indonesia. But the PPP proved surprisingly cohesive.

Under the unifying banner of Islam, a sense of righteousness prevailed among leaders and cadres alike, and internal compromise held the party together. The PPP sustained its ties with the Indonesian masses through religious institutions, including networks of mosques and Islamic boarding schools (*pesantren*). The party held its inaugural congress in November 1975 and elected as its leaders Mohammad Syafa'at Mintaredja and Idham Chalid. The former hailed from the modernist wing of Indonesian Islam and the latter from the traditionalist wing, but the two men were united by their shared accommodationist approach to politics.[34]

It was clear that *Malari* had deeper wellsprings than a renascent civil society. A cleavage at the commanding heights of the New Order stoked the chaos during Tanaka's visit. On one side were Sumitro and the Hankam group—a coterie of principled generals determined to reduce military involvement in politics, continue the market-oriented policies pioneered by technocrats, and hew toward the United States. On the other was Murtopo and the Aspri group—a clique of pragmatic generals determined to maintain military primacy in politics, adopt nationalist economic policies akin to those pioneered by Pertamina, and lean toward Japan. In the weeks leading up to *Malari*, Sumitro became a fixture on university campuses, where he delivered speeches promising a new pattern of leadership and stoking protest against Murtopo and Sudjono.[35] On the morning of January 15, one group of demonstrators marching toward the National Monument encountered Sumitro at the southwest corner of Merdeka Square. "Long live Pak Mitro!" came shouts from the crowd.[36] But Sumitro was not alone in resorting to underhanded political maneuvering. In the weeks after *Malari*, rumors circulated that Murtopo's shadowy Opsus network had employed thugs, pedicab drivers, and Islamist activists to foment chaos during the protests and thereby discredit Sumitro.[37]

Suharto worked to close the rift within the New Order in the wake of *Malari*. He relieved Sumitro of command over Kopkamtib and offered him the ambassadorship to Washington—a manifestation of his habit of dispatching potential rivals to faraway diplomatic posts where they could pose little political threat. Sumitro refused. In March, he resigned from his other position as deputy army commander and disappeared from the political scene. Sumitro's allies General Sutopo Juwono and General Kharis Suhud accepted offers of ambassadorial posts to the Netherlands and Thailand. Suharto then assumed direct control over Kopkamtib but appointed the loyalist Sudomo as chief of staff to manage the institution's day-to-day affairs. He recalled Benny Murdani from his post as ambassador to South Korea to assume control of military intelligence and Yoga Sugama from his position as ambassador to the United Nations take the reins at Bakin. Suharto also abolished Aspri—a key target of popular protest.

Figure 8.3 General Sumitro addresses demonstrators from the top of a vehicle on January 15, 1974. *Tempo.*

Even so, key figures within Aspri maintained considerable influence. Sudjono was Suharto's spiritual advisor and won an appointment as an inspector general of development and a member of the Council on Economic Stabilization.[38] Murtopo also reached the zenith of his power. He remained deputy chief of Bakin, commander of Opsus, and a leading figure within CSIS, and he counted Murdani as a protégé. Pragmatic generals won out over their principled counterparts.

Into the institutional and ideological breach left by the delegitimization of the more principled Hankam group stepped General Sudharmono of the State Secretariat. Sudharmono recognized that the Aspri group's ties with Japanese capital and its corruption had inflamed popular discontent. He forged an alliance of convenience with the technocrats in Bappenas and various economic ministries to advocate a deeper institutionalization of policymaking in contradistinction to the more freewheeling, personalistic style embodied by Murtopo.[39] Suharto was content to allow competing factions to vie for influence as long as their rivalry did not spill into the realm of popular politics and mass mobilization. He called Sudharmono, the economic technocrats, and the Aspri group to his Bogor ranch a few months after *Malari* to foster cooperation among the mutually suspicious camps.[40] All told, the personnel changes reflected Suharto's growing confidence in the game of palace politics and delivered an unmistakable message: power and influence ultimately depended upon his favor.

II

Centralizing political power and deepening political repression would do little to address the structural conditions that gave rise to *Malari*. Some New Order officials regarded *Malari* as a malign byproduct of Indonesia's growing integration into the capitalist world economy. Adam Malik lamented that the "decadence" of the West filtered into Indonesia through a mass media that "disseminated the sensational, indecent or immodest aspects of life, depicting violence, falsehood, sadism, luxury, corruption, pornography, and the like on magazine covers, in advertisements, and in imported films."[41] Some military officials went so far as to question students detained during the *Malari* riots about the extent of their contacts with the United States.[42] Ali Murtopo blamed the disorder on adherents of the defunct Socialist Party of Indonesia and Masyumi—parties implicated in the 1958 regional rebellions and associated with a modernizing intelligentsia.[43] That was an assessment with which Suharto and other senior Indonesian military officials agreed. Suharto claimed that "the *Malari* incident was not simply a stand-alone event but was instead an integral part of a conception and plan prepared far in advance with the goal of aim of overthrowing the legitimate government."[44]

Suharto's paranoia about the roots of *Malari* was baseless. But even if such a plan existed, it succeeded only because the intelligentsia's critiques of the New Order resonated with large segments of the Indonesian population. Whatever their diagnosis of the causes behind *Malari*, most New Order figures recognized a need to redress persistent inequalities within Indonesian society and expand access to the fruits of development.

Suharto convened the Council on Economic Stabilization in the wake of *Malari* and unveiled a raft of economic initiatives designed to improve the welfare of Indonesia's *pribumi* (indigenous) population. He instructed his underlings to expand the flow of credit to small businesses—generally owned by *pribumi* Indonesians—and lower the prices of meat and vegetables in Jakarta. He also announced a tripling of salaries for civil servants, a 60 percent increase in grants to regional governments, and an expansion of subsidies for rice, fertilizer, and fuel. Other policies were more targeted. For instance, Suharto ordered a hike in wages for dockworkers at the port in Tanjung Priok, who had displayed some sympathy for the protests during *Malari* and were critical to the key artery connecting Indonesia's economy to the outside world.[45]

The Suharto regime's program of *pribumisasi* (indigenization) preceded *Malari*. It most likely drew inspiration from Malaysia's New Economic Policy— adopted to counteract racial inequalities that contributed to the eruption of deadly communal riots in 1969.[46] PT Asuransi Kredit Indonesia (Askrindo), founded in 1971, made investment credit worth up to 75 percent of the value of a project available to small and medium-sized enterprises in the agriculture, commerce, and handicraft sectors. But the need to post the remaining 25 percent collateral ensured that most credits flowed to established ethnic Chinese entrepreneurs rather than cash-poor *pribumi*. In 1973, Suharto established PT Bahana Pembinaan Usaha Indonesia to provide *pribumi* entrepreneurs with the remaining 25 percent collateral as well as 12.5 percent equity financing and managerial assistance. Toward the end of the year, the central bank established two additional initiatives—the Small Investment Credit (KIK) and Permanent Working Capital Credit (KMKP) programs—to finance fixed investment and working capital for *pribumi* entrepreneurs in the small business sector.[47]

But these programs rarely reached beyond Jakarta and other major urban centers.[48] Suhud, deputy chief of the investment agency BKPM, lamented in December 1974 that "the lion's share of investment credits flow to non-*pribumi*" in spite of the New Order's policies of credit indigenism. He presented a framework for *pribumisasi* through which 50 percent of the stock in both new and existing domestic investments would be allocated to indigenous Indonesians. He also urged the government to "act as a national guardian for the *pribumi* group" and fund a national trust that could "lighten the burden on *pribumi* investors."[49] In the year following *Malari*, the volume of KIK and KMKP credit outstanding soared from under 7 billion rupiah to almost 30 billion rupiah.[50] By the end of 1975, the chief of Askrindo boasted that his agency had facilitated the extension of 81 billion rupiah in credit to *pribumi* entrepreneurs.[51] Yet the requirements of regime maintenance constrained the New Order's *pribumisasi* project. The persistent threat of communal violence tamed ethnic Chinese capitalists and ensured they continued to remit resources to the state and parastatal "foundations." A strong indigenous capitalist class would face no such threat and could therefore grow to pose a meaningful challenge to the political authority of the Suharto regime and the Indonesian military more broadly. The government-guaranteed credit that flowed to *pribumi* Indonesians thus paled in comparison to the total volume of credit outstanding in Indonesian society.[52] The lack of internal cohesion within the *pribumi* community around the vision Suharto and the army held for Indonesia's future ensured that ethnic Chinese *cukong* remained vital to the political economy of the New Order.

More expansive than the New Order's policies of indigenization were its policies of economic nationalism. At the first meeting of the Council on Economic Stabilization following *Malari*, Suharto ordered a ban on the import of completely built-up and luxury vehicles, which would benefit the domestic automobile industry and diminish the number of ostentatious cars owned by politico-business elites on the streets of Jakarta. Suharto also instructed his underlings to direct foreign firms to train, employ, and promote a greater number of Indonesians. The following month, the New Order required all foreign investors to form joint ventures with Indonesian partners within ten years; the regime also mandated that half of the domestic interest in existing joint ventures be transferred to *pribumi* Indonesians and that ethnic Chinese participation in new joint ventures be prohibited. Tax holidays and customs privileges for foreign investors would be curbed and certain provinces and sectors closed to foreign investment entirely.[53]

Suharto's announcements served a domestic propaganda purpose. But they also marked an inflection point in the New Order's economic development strategy away from the Bappenas group's emphasis on the labor-intensive agricultural and commodity sectors and toward CSIS and Pertamina's emphasis on capital-intensive projects in the steel, fertilizer, and even aircraft industries. In a January 1974 article, Daud Jusuf of CSIS explained that it was necessary to establish "a pattern of close cooperation between the government, bureaucrats, technocrats and businessmen so as to facilitate the development of a power entity on a national scale which can serve as a countervailing power against both multinational corporations and foreign national (read Chinese) enterprises."[54] The state assumed a much larger role in promoting industrial development in Indonesia and working to alter the terms of trade that governed Indonesia's place in the global economy.

It took considerable time to translate Suharto's promises of sweeping reform into concrete policy proposals. A chaotic process emerged in which some bureaucrats worked toward Suharto and competed to prove their nationalist mettle while others sought to carve out exceptions to prevent Indonesia from being starved of investment by both foreign and ethnic Chinese entrepreneurs. The forestry sector was closed to foreign investment in April 1974. But joint ventures were permitted in certain industrial estates and land development schemes as well as in downstream lumber processing. The construction sector was closed to foreign investment in July. But joint ventures were allowed in certain large projects for which Indonesian firms lacked the necessary capital or expertise, including harbors, dams, airports, and luxury hotels. "Don't eat the soup as hot as it is served," remarked one key official about the disjuncture between Suharto's dramatic announcements and the more moderate policies that followed.[55]

Even as it imposed additional hurdles on foreign investment, the Suharto regime worked to reassure foreign capitalists. "Many foreign circles were asking questions about the future of their investments in Indonesia," recalled Yoga Sugama. "If Japan was the target this time, it was not impossible that other countries would follow."[56] Vice President Hamengkubuwono's assistant for governmental affairs, Julian Dharman, reported in February 1974 that *Malari* was "jarring for foreign entrepreneurs and investors." Even though no current international investors had pulled out of Indonesia, some foreign capitalists had postponed or reconsidered new investments and adopted a more cautious posture. Reasoning that releasing a white paper to reassure international investors would likely inflame nationalist sentiment at a fragile political juncture, he urged the government to provide reassurances through briefings in foreign capital networks.[57] Not long thereafter, Yoga and Minister of Defense Maraden Panggabean traveled across the world to meet with international investors to explain that the *Malari* riots were the result of an accumulation of grievances within Indonesia rather than a manifestation of dissatisfaction with foreign investment. This tour helped ensure continuing private capital inflows into Indonesia, which outpaced foreign aid beginning in 1974.

The Second Five-Year Development Plan (Repelita II) marked the apotheosis of the Suharto regime's efforts to address public disaffection with the New Order through indigenization and industrialization. "The aim of Repelita II," the document proclaimed, "is first to improve the standard of living and welfare of the entirety of the people" and "second to lay a strong foundation for the next stage of development." Submitted to parliament only a week before *Malari* upended Indonesian politics, Repelita II was four times the size of its predecessor in financial terms. It envisioned an expansive effort to meet the health, housing, educational, employment, and infrastructural needs of ordinary Indonesians. The plan included money for the construction of tens of thousands of new homes and schools as well as thousands of new community health centers. It also called for state investment to propel annual growth rates of 13 percent in industry—faster than any other sector—by building the domestic capacity to refine raw materials and meet the needs of the agricultural and construction sectors. The agricultural sector received the largest share of development funding, but that owed to the fact that it still produced 40 percent of national output and accounted for 65 percent of employment. Whereas Repelita I counted on international aid for 60 percent of its expenditures, Repelita II counted on international aid for only 30 percent of its expenditures.[58] The New Order had embarked upon a new era of economic nationalism.

III

The shift in economic governance reflected both crisis and opportunity: the crisis of *Malari* revealed the depth of the Indonesian population's disaffection with the New Order, while the opportunity of the oil boom provided the means to pursue state-led industrialization. Foreign exchange earnings derived from oil skyrocketed from $1.7 billion in 1973 to $5.1 billion in 1974. Meanwhile government revenues derived from oil spiked from $836 million to $2.3 billion, reaching about 50 percent of total government receipts. But even as Suharto

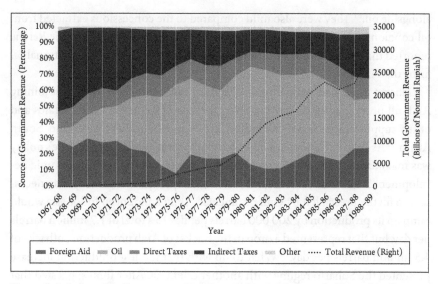

Figure 8.4 Indonesian Government Revenue, 1967–1989. Compiled by author from Government of Indonesia, *Nota Keuangan dan Rancangan Anggaran Pendapatan dan Belanja Negara* (Jakarta: Departemen Keuangan, 1969–1989).

channeled petrodollars toward his Cold War projects of political stabilization and economic development, the oil shocks themselves reflected a shift in the key axis of international relations from East-West to North-South and presented new challenges for Indonesian foreign policy.

Two immediate questions confronted the Suharto regime at the moment of the oil shock. Should Indonesia raise the price for its oil? And should Indonesia join the oil embargo against supporters of Israel?

Indonesia followed other OPEC member states in raising the price of its oil exports from $3.80 per barrel before the price revolution to $6 in November 1973 and then to $10.80 in January 1974. Although one high-placed Indonesian oil official remarked he "would prefer $4.00 per barrel oil and a stronger dollar," Ibnu told an American diplomat in early March 1974 that he believed the increased oil price was "about right" and said he "did not believe price roll-back [was] possible."[59] At the same time, New Order officials told representatives of multinational oil companies involved in production-sharing agreements with Pertamina that they would seek to increase the Indonesian share of after-cost proceeds above $5 per barrel from 65 to 85 percent—a departure from Ibnu's traditional emphasis on production-sharing toward profit-sharing.[60] These demands were the least the New Order could do in the face of domestic complaints that the government was not obtaining the maximum return for its oil resources, especially in light of Indonesia's ballooning import bill as the prices of manufactured goods and other commodities like food and fertilizer spiked alongside oil.[61] They were also mild compared to the concessions extracted from oil conglomerates by other OPEC members. The *Far Eastern Economic Review* reported that "no other major producer offered a better deal" to international oil firms than Indonesia.[62]

Suharto expressed sympathy for the Arab cause but decided against joining Arab oil-producing states in boycotting the sale of oil to the United States and other supporters of Israel, including the Netherlands, Portugal, and South Africa.[63] As Ibnu explained in a mid-October speech, the Suharto regime's policy was maximizing oil production in order to accelerate Indonesia's economic development.[64] But Indonesia did not possess the spare production capacity necessary to fill the breach left by Gulf producers.[65] Ibnu announced Indonesia would ramp up its production by 200,000 barrels per day to a total of 1.7 million barrels per day, but that represented a drop in the bucket of Arab production cutbacks of 4.5 million barrels per day.[66] What to do with that modest production increase presented the Suharto regime with another dilemma. After Ibnu suggested that Indonesia might ship some of its new production to the United States, a domestic outcry forced Malik to deny the existence of any such arrangements and proclaim support for the Arab boycott.[67] Meanwhile, facing requests for oil from other ASEAN governments as well as Cambodia and Burma, the Suharto regime protested that Indonesia lacked the capacity to expand production to a level necessary to meet the entirety of its neighbors' needs.[68] Suharto and Malik instead worked to prevent the oil shocks from undermining the stability of Southeast Asia. While Malik maneuvered within ASEAN to produce a collective statement condemning Israel for its occupation of Arab territories, Indonesian officials worked within OPEC in November to secure exemptions for its neighbors from reductions in oil shipments.[69]

The oil shock presented dilemmas beyond the questions of whether to raise prices and embargo the United States. It both reflected and reinforced a broader realignment of international relations around North-South material conflicts rather than East-West ideological conflicts. Suharto remained wedded to his Cold War outlook and his partnership with the United States and other major capitalist powers. Moreover, Indonesian economic policymakers anticipated that high oil prices would be fleeting. Suharto therefore worked to hinder the reorientation of international relations around longitudinal rather than latitudinal lines. But he also sought to derive as much benefit as possible from the oil shocks and maintain the Third Worldist credentials that served a legitimating role in Indonesian domestic politics.

Suharto did not object to American efforts to cultivate monopsony power among major oil consumers through the convening of a Washington Energy Conference in February 1974.[70] But Indonesian officials exulted when French recalcitrance led the conference to end without a unanimous communiqué.[71]

The Suharto regime then signed on to an Algerian effort to convene a special session of the United Nations General Assembly (the sixth in the organization's history) on raw materials and development in April 1974. Malik, who represented Indonesia at the session, endorsed Algerian president Houari Boumédiène's call for a New International Economic Order (NIEO).[72] But the Suharto regime's overarching focus remained on preserving high oil prices rather than remaking the global economy. On the eve of the UN session, Bakin reported that "the development of proper and proportionate terms of trade commensurate with the needs of developing countries must be continuously pursued, but within limits that don't endanger trends in oil prices." Consequently, Bakin urged an intensification of Indonesian diplomacy with Saudi Arabia and Egypt, which it reported were willing to consider reducing oil prices in light of their desire to pursue "normalization of economic relations and trade with Western countries."[73] Amid a resurgence of domestic unrest, escalating threats to the flow of international aid, and a yawning current account deficit, oil rents were becoming integral to Suharto's Cold War agenda.

Indonesia thus worked to maximize its oil revenues. Pertamina raised prices to $11.70 per barrel in April 1974 following an OPEC meeting in Vienna. At the next OPEC conference, held in Quito in June, Indonesia and ten of the eleven other member states agreed to raise prices once again. But Saudi Arabia, the swing producer, refused and threatened to ramp up production to keep prices down. The other OPEC member states bowed to Saudi influence and agreed not to raise prices until October.[74] Indonesia nevertheless chose to raise the price of Pertamina's oil to $12.60 per barrel, above the $11.65 per barrel then being charged for Persian Gulf crude, in light of its lower sulfur content and transportation costs. As preparations for the September 1974 OPEC conference commenced, most OPEC members, notably Iran, favored another price hike to keep pace with inflation in developed economies, with some endorsing renewed production cutbacks of 10 to 20 percent to support high crude prices. But Saudi Arabia continued to work to reduce prices.[75] A last-minute compromise saw OPEC agree to once again keep prices steady but to raise the royalty and income tax collected from international oil firms by 3.5 percent per barrel.[76] For the first time since the beginning of the oil price revolution in October 1973, Pertamina did not raise the price it charged for Indonesian crude. Thereafter Indonesia displayed price forbearance—a stance that reflected predictions of an oil glut due to a recession in the developed world, increasing competition from low-sulfur Chinese oil, and Japanese investments in desulfurization capacity.[77]

Ibnu Sutowo took stock of the dramatic year in global oil markets at a gathering of the Pacific Coast Gas Association in Honolulu in September 1974. Echoing the conservationist rhetoric that had become commonplace among citizens of oil-consuming countries and policymakers in oil-producing countries, Ibnu explained that "oil is a non-renewable resource. . . . No developing country can be expected to subsidize the continued industrialization and growth of advanced countries by accepting inequitable or unrealistically low prices for its own raw materials, especially those that are depletable, such as oil and minerals."[78] Indonesia's population dwarfed that of major Gulf producers and remained mired in deep poverty. Moreover, the archipelago's oil exports constituted only 2 percent of the global market and added only about $20 to per capita national income. Maximizing revenue thus remained imperative. The Suharto regime consequently displayed little enthusiasm for efforts devised by IMF chief Johannes Witteveen to recycle petrodollar earnings to oil-importing countries. The New Order also chose not to contribute to an OPEC special fund that would offer $800 million to help oil-importing developing countries address balance-of-payments challenges.[79]

The Suharto regime's approach to oil did not extend to other commodities and broader issues of North-South relations. Indonesian officials generally discouraged agricultural commodity producers from establishing cartels to mimic OPEC. As Minister of Research Sumitro Djojohadikusumo asserted, "the range of factors that have helped OPEC achieve such wonderful results do not all apply to other commodities."[80] Unlike oil, most agricultural commodities were perishable, renewable, and substitutable and thus poor candidates for cartelization strategies.[81] Moreover, pursuing widespread cartelization risked alienating the United States, Japan, and other key purveyors of aid and investment.

A similar ambivalence characterized the New Order's approach toward Boumédiène's effort to forge a New International Economic Order. Indonesian officials generally supported the NIEO project as long as it did not threaten oil revenues. In the year following the April 1974 Sixth Special Session of the UN General Assembly, Indonesian diplomats participated in a number of specialized international conferences on food, population, trade, industry, raw materials, and more. Suharto convened the Council on Economic Stabilization in June 1975 and explained that, "as a developing country, Indonesia must contribute ideas and concepts for the formation of a New International Economic Order."[82] He ordered the creation of a committee led by Sumitro Djojohadikusumo and including Minister of Mining Mohammad Sadli, Minister of Communications Emil Salim, and Minister of Finance Ali Wardhana to formulate Indonesia's official position toward the broader NIEO project.[83]

The committee delivered its recommendations two months later. Emphasizing the importance of "avoiding attitudes and approaches that are confrontational," the committee recommended that governments of the Global South align around four distinct objectives: reorienting international trade through asymmetric preferences and various commodity price arrangements, addressing global inequality through real resource transfers and an array of automatic lending facilities, promoting industrialization through technology transfers and a code of conduct for multinational firms, and reshaping international politics through a restructuring of the United Nations. Insisting on the need for a "pragmatic and realistic" approach, Sumitro's team emphasized that meetings of diplomats "cannot immediately recast or change the existing International Economic Order" and suggested that the influence of the NIEO "will be felt over the long term." He hoped that Indonesia's position as an exporter of both oil and other primary commodities, as well as its position as a partner of both the United States and the Third Worldist movement, could enable the New Order to play a meaningful role in "moderating" between the demands of developed and developing countries.[84]

The Suharto regime's determination to adopt a moderate posture reflected domestic difficulties in addition to its enduring Cold War orientation. Ibnu Sutowo's Pertamina had by the end of 1974 amassed towering debt obligations to finance its octopus-like extension into all manner of development programs, white elephant projects, and simple corruption schemes. But as soaring oil prices contributed to mounting deficits and tightening money markets in creditor countries, Ibnu found himself unable to continue rolling over Pertamina's approximately $1.5 billion in short-term loans. Pertamina fell $850 million behind on its tax obligations to the Indonesian government by March 1975. The oil giant then failed to meet its debt servicing obligations on a $40 million loan from Republic National Bank of Dallas, which called in the remainder of the loan and threatened to begin default proceedings. A cross-default clause embedded in Indonesia's sovereign debt contracts then risked throwing the country's entire debt burden into default. "The implications of default, therefore, were catastrophic," recalled Minister of Trade Radius Prawiro.[85] "A wide range of big foreign banks who had once been falling all over each other to lend him [Ibnu] money . . . were now, in some cases, lining up lawyers to make sure they got it back," reported one of the few correspondents who retained access to the Pertamina chief. Ibnu himself "was looking tired; his eyes were bloodshot."[86]

The New Order once again required massive capital inflows to surmount domestic challenges. Ibnu first sought to obtain a $1.7 billion loan from Arab oil-exporting countries in order to cover the entirety of Pertamina's short-term debts. That effort quickly came to naught.[87] As the debt crisis became public in March 1975, New Order officials worked with their American counterparts to ensure the oil company's creditors did not initiate default proceedings that would imperil the "credit rating of Indonesia itself."[88] Indonesia's central bank chief furnished Pertamina with $100 million to meet its past-due obligations and traveled around the world converting most of Pertamina's remaining short-term loans into medium-term loans that were liabilities of the Indonesian state rather than the oil giant. Suharto then contracted the American firm Arthur

Young to work through the conglomerate's unkempt books from six uncoordinated accounting departments. He also prohibited Pertamina and all other state-owned enterprises from borrowing without the central bank's permission and transferred authority over most of the conglomerate's non-oil-related assets to ministries controlled by Ibnu's technocratic rivals.[89] Bappenas chair Widjojo delivered the government's first public report on Pertamina's debt crisis in June 1975 and estimated that Ibnu had amassed some $1.6 billion in debt.[90] But over the second half of the year it became clear that Pertamina's debts totaled approximately $10.5 billion—more than the combined sovereign indebtedness of both the Sukarno and Suharto regimes and almost three times the Indonesian government budget in 1975.[91] Ibnu was finally sacked in early 1976.

Amid the escalating Pertamina scandal within Indonesia and a global recession that led to a precipitous decline in the prices of many commodities, Malik led the Indonesian delegation to the Seventh Special Session of the United Nations General Assembly in September 1975. There Daniel Patrick Moynihan, then serving as US ambassador to the UN, read a speech by Henry Kissinger blaming developing countries for the "mounting confrontations" entangling the global economy. Malik rebuked Kissinger for adopting "neither a correct nor a helpful approach to our deliberations."[92] Despite Kissinger's provocations, Malik, along with other Indonesian diplomats, worked to ensure that a conciliatory approach prevailed in discussions over the NIEO. Closed-door negotiations over an array of topics, Malik reported back to Jakarta, underwent "a very difficult and convoluted process . . . and were often delayed to wait for a 'green light' from various national capitals, especially from Washington." Patient diplomacy by Indonesia and other "moderate countries" ultimately overcame the confrontational posture of the United States and the "radical group like Iraq, Senegal, Chad, Libya, and Peru."[93] The session concluded with a resolution accepted without a vote on reshaping the structures of trade and aid and no movement on more radical proposals surrounding expropriation and reparations.

The Seventh Special Session would come to represent the high-water mark of the NIEO—a utopian project whose most strident proponents seemed almost willfully ignorant of the realities of the international economy and the fissures within the developing world. Postcolonial elites across the Global South were enmeshed in their own projects of domestic coalition-building that depended on the extraction and distribution of resources, which made it extraordinarily challenging to sustain collective action through the deprivations that any meaningful economic confrontation with the Global North would entail. Kissinger recognized as much and devised a gambit to preserve the unity of the West, split the developing world between oil producers and oil consumers, and slow the gears of international negotiations with a disorienting torrent of position papers and policy proposals.[94] "Obviously we can't accept the new economic order," he explained to senior US officials, "but I would like to pull its teeth and divide these countries up, not solidify them."[95] At the Seventh Special Session, Kissinger had rejected the idea of indexing the prices of commodities to those of manufactured goods but expressed a willingness to increase aid and pursue stabilization agreements on a case-by-case basis. The leaders of the United States, France, West Germany, and the United Kingdom also decided to convene a dialogue between developed and developing countries over energy, commodities, development, and finance. The resulting Conference for International Economic Cooperation opened in Paris in December 1975.

Indonesia assumed the role of coordinator for developing countries on commodity issues in what became known as the North-South Dialogue. At a series of conferences in far-flung world capitals, New Order diplomats worked to sustain cooperation among developing countries and to prevent proposals such as that for a "Third World Conference" (floated by Pakistan) from gaining traction. But after a year of negotiations, Indonesian officials described the results of the North-South Dialogue as "very minimal."[96] Suharto even worked to bring OPEC into the fold. At a May 1976 meeting of OPEC oil ministers in Bali, he explained that OPEC countries have "a legitimate right to obtain a fair price for the oil they produce" but must also "recognize their responsibility toward global welfare and the fate of other developing countries."[97] On Indonesia's initiative, an OPEC conference convened in Qatar in December 1976. The oil cartel issued a statement supporting "the stabilization of raw material prices at equitable and remunerative levels" while also pledging an additional $800 million to the OPEC Special Fund.[98] Even so, Indonesia and ten other members of OPEC announced they would raise oil prices by $2 per barrel over the subsequent six months. In June 1977, an Indonesian official lamented that the North-South dialogue "lasted 18 months and faced many difficulties in its negotiations."[99] Malik himself remembered that the series of conferences quickly devolved into mutual recriminations in which "the South accused the North of practicing the politics of protectionism and vice versa the North accused the South of practicing the politics of blackmail."[100]

The Suharto regime thus continued to devote its attention to maximizing oil revenues. At the president's behest, the new director of Pertamina, Piet Haryono, embarked upon an aggressive effort to wring more out of foreign oil companies in Indonesia. He negotiated with Caltex and Stanvac to secure a $1 per barrel surcharge that would raise the government's share of each barrel to more than 85 percent and would mean hundreds of millions of dollars per year in additional revenue. He also imposed a new arrangement on Pertamina's smaller production-sharing contractors for a flat 85–15 split in Indonesia's favor (replacing an existing two-tier 65–35/85–15 split) that would net the government hundreds of millions of dollars more. But after foreign firms responded by slowing the pace of exploration and investment, causing stagnation in aggregate Indonesian oil production, Haryono relented and offered a mixture of exemptions and incentives to revamp the oil industry.[101]

IV

The oil shock altered the coalitional logic of the New Order and tilted the axis of global politics. But Suharto remained wedded to his Cold War outlook. He worked to preserve Indonesian ties with the capitalist world and continued to seek Cold War capital through the IGGI. A number of obstacles cropped up to impede his effort, including political and economic crisis in the developed world and the flowering of the human rights revolution.

The IGGI convened for the first time since the price of oil stabilized above $10 per barrel in May 1974. Earlier in the year, the Nixon administration warned Indonesian officials that congressional resistance to furnishing oil-producing countries with aid would likely force the United States to abandon the formula whereby it provided at least one-third of IGGI aid to Indonesia—it could offer only $176 million of the $233 million it pledged at the December 1973 meeting of the IGGI.[102] Indonesian diplomats responded by noting that US aid cuts risked precipitating a domino effect and leading other major donors to reduce their aid commitments. These fears were not altogether misplaced. Officials in Japan's Ministry of Foreign Affairs told their American counterparts that the planned reduction in US aid would weaken their position against tight-fisted skeptics in the Ministry of Finance during internal negotiations over aid to Indonesia.[103] Only announcements of increased multilateral contributions from the World Bank and Asian Development Bank allowed the United States to maintain its one-third policy. Under considerable American pressure, Japanese officials told Indonesian diplomats that they would continue to meet their historic responsibility for one-third of IGGI aid.[104] Ultimately, the IGGI ratified the $850 million pledge endorsed at the previous meeting of the IGGI, but it also asserted that Indonesia's increasingly favorable economic outlook meant it could receive aid on harder terms than the concessional aid of years past. The body declared 1974 a "transition year" toward an Indonesia less dependent on international aid.[105]

It was not only the oil shocks and the attendant economic dislocations in advanced economies that threatened the flow of aid. The deepening Watergate scandal was eroding President Nixon's authority and empowering congressional skeptics of foreign aid. Opposition to the ongoing conflict in Indochina and competing demands for security assistance in the Middle East led some lawmakers to adopt skeptical outlooks toward military aid to all Southeast Asian states. In May 1974, the Senate passed an amendment sponsored by Senator

Ted Kennedy prohibiting funds appropriated for the Defense Department from being spent "in, for, or on behalf of any country in Southeast Asia" for the remainder of the fiscal year. Although only two months remained in the fiscal year, this served as a powerful indication of congressional hostility toward military aid and alarmed Indonesian diplomats in Washington.[106] Meanwhile in the House, Representative Otto Passman, the powerful head of the Appropriations Subcommittee on Foreign Operations, renewed his opposition to furnishing Indonesia with military aid.[107] Suharto told an American diplomat that he "was convinced that continuation of this assistance would depend on President Nixon's overcoming domestic difficulties and legal restrictions on such assistance."[108]

Nixon's resignation in August 1974 thus demanded quick action. The disgraced president was a long-standing ally of the Suharto regime and a known quantity in Jakarta, unlike his unelected successor, President Gerald Ford. The US embassy in Jakarta reported in the clipped language of diplomatic telegrams that the "Watergate challenge to President Nixon caused considerable worry in GOI [Government of Indonesia] leadership circles because of adoration for Nixon's foreign policies and belief that personal link between Suharto and Nixon was important element in US support for Indonesia."[109] Malik quickly traveled to the United States to meet the new American president. He delivered a letter from Suharto and asked Ford to "consider continuing U.S. aid to Indonesia." Ford promised to "do the best we can" but noted that "the Congressional attitude is to reduce and restrict" the nation's foreign aid budget.[110]

The burgeoning human rights revolution also imperiled the Suharto regime's ability to mobilize international capital. Ironically, the success of Suharto's Cold War in Southeast Asia imperiled the sustainability of his Cold War in Indonesia. Following President Ferdinand Marcos's Indonesian-inspired declaration of martial law in the Philippines in September 1972, a diffuse network of human rights and diasporic activists lobbied strenuously against the provision of US military aid to the Marcos regime.[111] These activists helped drive broader debates over US sponsorship of right-wing authoritarian regimes into mainstream American political discourse—and into the halls of the legislative branch. In April 1973, California senator Alan Cranston praised "the conscientious and energetic efforts" of anti–martial law activists and lamented that "foreign dictators seem to feel that all they have to do is proclaim their anticommunism and we will rush to their side with dollars and arms."[112] In March 1974, Minnesota representative Donald Fraser's House subcommittee issued a report castigating the US relationship with Indonesia, the Philippines, Greece, Chile, and other countries as emblematic of "how we have disregarded human rights for the sake of other assumed interests."[113] Fraser and his allies subsequently shepherded an amendment to the Foreign Assistance Act through Congress. Known as Section 502B, the amendment stated in non-binding "sense of Congress" language that,

"except in extraordinary circumstances, the President shall substantially reduce
or terminate security assistance to any government which engages in a consistent pattern of gross violations of internationally recognized human rights."
If the president chose to invoke extraordinary circumstances and override the
sense of Congress, he was required to submit a report outlining his rationale and
the status of human rights in the relevant countries.

Cognizant of the deluge of challenges to his ability to mobilize foreign aid,
Suharto redoubled his efforts to cultivate members of Congress. He hosted
Senator Vance Hartke, an antiwar Indiana Democrat, in early 1974 and insisted
that "military needs had been sacrificed for economic development in [the] first
five-year plan." According to an American diplomat's summary of the meeting,
Suharto "indicated he was particularly anxious for more of [the] kind of military assistance which U.S. had already provided Indonesia in [the] form of
second-hand destroyers and airplanes at bargain prices."[114] But anti–New Order
activists in the United States proved themselves equally adept at cultivating
congressional opinion. In mid-1974, Carmel Budiardjo of the advocacy group
TAPOL published a brief on political imprisonment in Indonesia in the *Bulletin
of Concerned Asian Scholars*. Recognizing that opportunities for Indonesians
themselves to protest the Suharto regime's repressive policies had narrowed
considerably, and aware that the New Order "relies heavily on foreign aid and investment" and has "shown itself to be extremely sensitive to criticism that comes
from any of those countries" that furnish large amounts of aid, she advocated a
concerted campaign of "pressure from abroad."[115]

American diplomats briefed a wide array of New Order officials on congressional efforts to curb the provision of foreign aid to dictatorial regimes
in the summer of 1974.[116] Syarif Thayeb returned from his post as ambassador to the United States and brought mounting congressional hostility
to Indonesia to Suharto's attention. The new Indonesian ambassador in
Washington, Rusmin Nuryadin, was given instructions to explain the situation
to key American lawmakers and invite several senators and representatives to
travel to Indonesia.[117] A group of staffers from Democratic Senator J. William
Fulbright's Foreign Relations Committee visited the archipelago in late 1974,
and a Republican delegation comprising Senator Strom Thurmond and Senator
William Scott followed in early 1975.[118]

The churn of the human rights revolution beyond the United States posed
similar challenges to the Suharto regime's ability to secure international aid. In
the Netherlands, the colonial lawyer turned scholar-activist W. F. Wertheim
established the Indonesia Committee in the late 1960s. He met regularly with
Indonesian refugees and exiles who kept him abreast of the latest developments
in the archipelago and found in Wertheim an impassioned advocate.[119] The
Indonesia Committee published a regular bulletin called *Indonesia: Facts and*

Views beginning in 1974, and Wertheim wrote a polemic entitled *Ten Years of Injustice in Indonesia: Military Dictatorship and International Support.* These publications argued for a cutoff in international aid to the Suharto regime.[120] The committee's perspective was at first endorsed only by radical left-wing parties in the Netherlands, but it gradually won adherents within the more mainstream Labour Party.[121] Foreign Minister Max van der Stoel raised the issue of political prisoners during a visit to Jakarta in January 1974. Four months later, Minister of Development Cooperation and IGGI chairman Jan Pronk made known his intent to apply strict "conditions" to continued Dutch aid to Indonesia—including the criteria that aid should not support "capitalist" development, should help small farmers and urban masses, and must facilitate a linkage between economic and sociopolitical development.[122] In an attempt to assuage human rights concerns, the Suharto regime hosted a delegation of Dutch parliamentarians in September 1974. Indonesian officials argued that security concerns militated against the release of tens of thousands of political prisoners of dubious loyalty and urged Dutch lawmakers not to apply alien standards to an Indonesian problem.[123]

Australian human rights activists likewise continued to lobby against the provision of aid to Indonesia. Prime Minister Gough Whitlam was intent on reorienting Australian foreign policy toward Asia, and closer relations between Canberra and Jakarta constituted a key plank of his agenda. But roughly thirty Australian lawmakers drawn mostly from Whitlam's Labor Party pressed the prime minister to demand amnesty for Indonesia's political prisoners.[124] When Whitlam traveled to Yogyakarta in September 1974, Suharto knew his Australian counterpart was caught between countervailing imperatives of domestic politics and foreign policy. He accordingly worked to forge a bond with Whitlam. During a break in the talks, he took Whitlam on a tour of the Dieng Plateau, a misty highland area dotted by millennium-old Hindu temples whose name means "abode of the gods." Suharto led Whitlam to a cave called Gua Semar, renowned as the birthplace of Semar—a ubiquitous presence in *wayang kulit* shadow theater and the guardian spirit of Java.[125] This was an unusual gesture by the traditionally aloof Suharto. His translator told an Australian diplomat that "he had not seen the President so relaxed and open with another leader."[126] Suharto's personal diplomacy appeared to win Whitlam over. The Australian prime minister admitted that "individuals in the Labor Party or in the trade unions" might criticize the New Order, but he emphasized that he "believed that such action interfered in the domestic jurisdiction of Indonesia and it would be offensive to attempt to advise another government about its own internal affairs or to demand changes in domestic policy." He also expressed his desire to continue Australian military and economic aid to Indonesia, though he noted that "from time to time developments within Indonesia would continue to have repercussions within Australia."[127]

Shortly after Whitlam's departure, Bakin urged the New Order to expand "people-to-people" ties to place Indonesian-Australian relations on a stronger foundation and counter a mounting anti-Indonesia movement within the ruling Labor Party.[128] Suharto himself told Polkam that "another term for 'political prisoner' should be found," which he hoped would diminish the controversy in countries where human rights activists excoriated the New Order and demanded aid cutoffs.[129] A few weeks later, Kopkamtib prohibited the use of the portmanteau *tapol*, asserting that "it is incorrect to call them political prisoners" because "they have all committed crimes."[130] The Jakarta daily *Kompas* reported that "the change in expression is probably intended primarily to clarify misunderstandings which arise abroad."[131] At the same time, the detention camps that held political prisoners were renamed from "special prisons" to "rehabilitation centers."[132] The rhetorical whitewashing did little to stanch international criticism. Not long after Kopkamtib's announcement, the United Nations Commission on Human Rights asked the Suharto regime to provide information on the status of Indonesia's political prisoners.[133]

As international pressure on the New Order mounted in 1974, Sudomo presided over the elaboration of *Operasi Ksatria* within Kopkamtib. Aware that the Suharto regime would have little alternative but to placate the concerns of its most important international donors, Sudomo sought to find creative ways to preserve political stability while releasing political prisoners. *Operasi Ksatria* proposed the creation of "an integrated system of surveillance and control of former G-30-S/PKI detainees and prisoners that is both efficient and effective." It also aimed to "increase the national resilience of the people in the ideological field to reject communism" and "continue the cleansing of G-30-S/PKI elements within the government, the armed forces, and the population."[134] With such precautions in mind, the framers of *Operasi Ksatria* envisioned the release of approximately 35,000 political prisoners.[135] Most sources indicated that these releases would take place in phases at the rate of roughly 2,500 per year—implying the last prisoner would not be released until 1990.[136] The plan thus struck a compromise between competing poles in the New Order: the Ali Murtopo group that favored a more rapid release of political prisoners to placate international donors and investors, and older military officials at Hankam who feared prisoner releases would undermine political stability and inspire demands for additional concessions from opposition groups.[137]

The collapse of anticommunist regimes in Indochina in the spring of 1975 both stoked the Suharto regime's anxieties about releasing political prisoners and provided a cudgel with which to beat back human rights concerns. In June 1975, Suharto told Polkam that the release of prisoners "need not be rushed" even in the face of foreign governments urging their release.[138] Meanwhile, Suharto and his lieutenants played on the Ford administration's anxieties about

American credibility to encourage the White House to override mounting congressional opposition to aiding Indonesia. In March 1975, as communist forces closed in on Saigon and Phnom Penh, Murdani told the American ambassador in Jakarta that Indonesia "gets less than $15 million from U.S. in comparison with vast sums put into Indochina. How can Indonesia face up to communist Southeast Asia if Saigon with a million and a half men and millions in aid cannot do it?" If Indonesia did not possess the "strength to oppose," Murdani warned, "it must accommodate."[139] Suharto himself reiterated these concerns during a state visit to the United States in July 1975. "Even if it takes some time to consolidate," he told Ford and Kissinger, "events will certainly encourage similar [communist] elements in Thailand, Malaysia, the Philippines, and elsewhere. . . . When they have built up the Communist movements, the Vietnamese will be able to supply the military equipment necessary for them to undertake military activities." Ford lamented that "this Congress is difficult" but reassured Suharto that "it is my intention to increase aid to Indonesia." In particular, he promised several naval vessels and transport aircraft, which Suharto had sought since *Malari*.[140]

The IGGI convened in May 1975 amid the depths of the Pertamina scandal and the turmoil in Indochina. There Indonesian diplomats secured international agreement for an astonishing $2 billion in aid. But the Suharto regime's emissaries were subjected to unusually harsh questioning on the status of Indonesia's political prisoners. In the wake of the meeting, Pronk told the press that, "if there is no improvement in the situation of the political prisoners in Indonesia, it is not unlikely that there will be a reappraisal of Dutch aid to Indonesia."[141]

Suharto recognized the pivotal role of the United States in shepherding Indonesian aid requests through the IGGI and jawboning other governments and multinational institutions to make aid commitments. He therefore redoubled his efforts to cultivate pro-Indonesia sentiment in the United States, particularly in Congress. Already in June 1975 he noted that the "balance of power between the Executive and Legislature in the United States" had shifted. He ordered Polkam to assemble teams that could present the New Order's views "both to the Executive and the Legislature, both through diplomatic channels and conveyances to other groups."[142]

Murtopo and Murdani led a CSIS delegation to the United States in October 1975. In Los Angeles, Minneapolis, Washington, New York, and Ithaca, they met with policymakers, lawmakers, scholars, and entrepreneurs. Congress was the delegation's primary focus. In a report to Suharto, Ambassador Rusmin wrote that the delegation had persuaded several influential lawmakers that Indonesia represented a "guardian of stability in Southeast Asia" deserving of American support. In Washington, the Indonesians met with the House and Senate committees on foreign affairs and armed services, with a group of the so-called Watergate Babies elected to the House in 1974, and with individual congressional leaders. In New York, they spent an hour with Representative Fraser, regarded as the foremost advocate of human rights in Congress. Murtopo and Murdani told Fraser that the continuing detention of suspected leftists was necessary for the preservation of political stability in Indonesia and for the safety of the prisoners themselves—reasoning that, if they were returned home, their communities would subject them to a fate worse than imprisonment. They also suggested that the reports of groups like Amnesty International were "used by leftists in foreign countries" to tarnish Indonesia's image. Murtopo and Murdani invited Fraser to observe the conditions of the prisoners for himself.[143] Rusmin reported to Suharto that the conversation with Fraser was "especially productive." More broadly, he claimed that the delegation successfully indulged the "psychological atmosphere" in the Capitol by "giving the impression that Congress is considered important"—an impression one rookie lawmaker confirmed when he enthused that the Indonesian delegation's visit represented "a mark of the new era of congressional dynamism."[144] The Indonesian ambassador concluded his report to Suharto by noting that "the things we want from the United States will increasingly be determined by Congress" and recommending that the embassy expand the New Order's efforts to cultivate American lawmakers, since the CSIS delegation had met only 45 of 435 representatives and 12 of 100 senators.[145]

The Suharto regime's efforts to court Congress continued. Suharto welcomed an eleven-member congressional delegation to Jakarta in August 1975 as part of what the Murtopo aide Jusuf Wanandi called a campaign "to foster the continued growth of mutual understanding between Congress and the government of Indonesia."[146] The Suharto regime also embraced more underhanded tactics. When Fraser's subcommittee went ahead with hearings on the status of human rights in Indonesia and the Philippines in December 1975, at which Carmel Budiardjo was a star witness, New Order officials worked to prevent her from testifying altogether and then to discredit her testimony. They provided two sympathetic lawmakers with information about Budiardjo's husband, still languishing in an Indonesian prison, alleging he was a communist who trafficked arms from China to Indonesia in preparation for the September Thirtieth Movement.[147] The two lawmakers so badgered Budiardjo that the powerhouse *Washington Post* columnists Rowland Evans and Robert Novak reported that senators and representatives "who have read the transcript of the Dec. 18 hearing" grew skeptical of her. The hearings thus inadvertently "fortified the President's arms aid program for Indonesia."[148] Not long after, Budiardjo was informed that her multiple-entry visa had been revoked, making it difficult for her to continue her human rights advocacy in the United States.[149] When Budiardjo applied for a visa to return for a speaking tour in 1976, Malik told Kissinger that "such a lecture tour could create difficulties for Indonesia."[150] Wanandi delivered a similar message on behalf of Murtopo to American diplomats in Jakarta, suggesting that Budiardjo's admittance to the United States would "harm rather than help those working for [a] resolution of the PKI prisoner problem."[151] At the same time, Indonesian officials in London met with Amnesty International staffers and urged them to disavow Budiardjo, characterizing her as a "partisan" who was "misusing" Amnesty.[152] The Suharto regime's intransigence proved effective: Budiardjo was denied a visa by the State Department and disavowed by Amnesty International.[153]

Despite this small victory for the New Order, the human rights revolution continued to pose challenges to the Suharto regime's ability to mobilize Cold War capital. In April 1976, Pronk visited Jakarta and noted that continuing aid to Indonesia would require "discernible" progress on the release of political prisoners.[154] The Dutch parliament debated aid to Indonesia in light of the continuing detention of tens of thousands of political prisoners later that year. With the 1977 elections looming, the Labour Party campaigned on abolishing all Dutch aid to Indonesia.[155] The British Labour Party also inserted language into its 1976 platform calling for aid to Indonesia to be "reviewed unless progress is made" on releasing political prisoners.[156] At the June 1976 meeting of the IGGI, British, Dutch, and West German diplomats reproached Indonesian officials about the political prisoner problem even as they endorsed $2.4 billion in aid for 1977.[157] Meanwhile the International Labor Organization, which for three years had requested reports on the mobilization of political prisoners for forced labor, came close to blacklisting Indonesia at its annual conference in June 1976.[158] The challenges mounted following the November 1976 elections in the United States, as incoming president Jimmy Carter had made human rights a cornerstone of his campaign and advocated ending US support for military dictatorships like Suharto's.[159]

Escalating international pressure convinced the Suharto regime to accelerate the release of political prisoners. After meeting with Sudomo in mid-1976, one member of a Dutch religious delegation wrote that the Indonesian security chief "seemed to be much more sensitive to world opinion than I had expected."[160] Shortly after the June 1976 IGGI meeting, Sudomo told a Dutch interviewer from *De Telegraaf* that "the problems of Indonesia's political prisoners will be solved before the end of 1978" and "those who have not been tried by that time will be released."[161] He also promised that all detention centers would be opened to inspectors from the International Red Cross and Amnesty International.[162] Although he backtracked on some of those commitments over the next several months, Sudomo remained determined to press ahead with a release of political prisoners. In late 1976, he unveiled *Operasi Sakti* before a crowd that included the ambassadors of the United States, United Kingdom, West Germany, Japan, and the Netherlands—revealing the drivers behind, and the intended audience for, policy changes on the political prisoner issue.[163] *Operasi Sakti* dictated that 10,000 prisoners would be released each year until the last was released in 1979.[164] But it quickly became clear that Sudomo was engaged in semantic games, since he implied that resettlement on the penal colony of Buru would be counted as release.

V

One final challenge confronted the Suharto regime in the mid-1970s: the collapse of the Portuguese empire and the emergence from Lisbon's rule of East Timor—a tiny colony nestled among the Indonesian islands of Nusa Tenggara. Many Indonesian military officials worried the territory would fall into communist hands and become a platform for subversion on the Indonesian periphery. But some civilian officials believed action to forestall a communist takeover of East Timor risked alienating Indonesia's ASEAN partners as well as key international partners like the United States and Australia. Could Suharto address his Cold War anxieties without sacrificing his Cold War alliances?

Faraway developments delivered this question to Suharto's desk. In April 1974, a group of left-leaning junior officers calling themselves the Armed Forces Movement (MFA) overthrew the *Estado Novo* dictatorship of Marcelo Caetano in Portugal. Determined to liquidate Portugal's overseas colonies, the MFA legalized the creation of indigenous political organizations in East Timor. Three major parties emerged, each with a different vision of the territory's future. Timorese elites who fared well under Lisbon's rule formed the Timorese Democratic Union (UDT), which advocated eventual self-government after an undefined period of continued Portuguese tutelage. A much smaller group of elites, located mostly near the border that divided the island between Indonesian and Portuguese sovereignty, established the Association for the Integration of Timor into Indonesia. After concluding that integration was an unpopular position, they hastily changed the name—but not the platform—of their organization to the Timorese Popular Democratic Association (Apodeti). Other Timorese drew inspiration from the burgeoning Portuguese Left and the national liberation movements challenging Portuguese imperialism in Africa and formed an organization to demand immediate independence known first as the Timorese Social Democratic Association (ASDT) and later as the Revolutionary Front for an Independent East Timor (Fretilin).

Adam Malik's Foreign Ministry favored continued Portuguese rule over East Timor. If Lisbon was determined to relinquish the colony, Malik regarded independence as preferable to integration with Indonesia. He was anxious to preserve Indonesia's nonaligned reputation and to avoid undermining the cohesion of ASEAN. Indonesian military and intelligence officials disagreed and favored annexation. They worried an independent East Timor would fall under the sway of Moscow or Beijing and become an Indonesian Cuba—or worse, a sanctuary for remnants of the PKI inspired by the communist victory in Vietnam. The thousands of ethnic Chinese who lived in East Timor came under considerable scrutiny by Indonesian military officials as possible vectors of subversion. Amid this bureaucratic jockeying, Suharto remained characteristically cautious. In May 1974, he instructed Polkam to "take the required steps to ensure that developments in Portuguese Timor will not disturb Indonesia's security."[165]

Indonesian military leaders were determined to leave nothing to chance. Bakin concluded by June 1974 that East Timorese preferred independence to integration by a large margin.[166] But the New Order moved to bolster pro-integration sentiment among the East Timorese population. The Bakin-linked governor of East Nusa Tenggara province, El Tari, invited an Apodeti delegation to Jakarta to meet with Murtopo.[167] The general responded favorably to appeals for support from the Apodeti envoys, and he dispatched a deputy on a clandestine trip to gather intelligence on the evolving political situation in East Timor. Murtopo also began offering Apodeti leaders advice on how to build an effective political organization as well as some modest financial assistance.[168] Finally, Bakin officials began canvassing Indonesia's international donors and creditors to make the case for East Timor's integration with Indonesia.[169]

Suharto took up the question of East Timor with Australian prime minister Whitlam and other Southeast Asian leaders over the last three months of 1974. In talks with Whitlam, Suharto explained that, "if Portuguese Timor were to become independent, it would give rise to problems" because the territory was "not economically viable" and "communist countries—China or the Soviet Union—might gain the opportunity to intervene." He characterized "the incorporation of Portuguese Timor as being in the best interests of the region." Whitlam agreed that "Portuguese Timor should become part of Indonesia."[170] After discussions with his Malaysian counterpart, Suharto reported back to Polkam that, "regarding the future of Portuguese Timor, Prime Minister Tun Razak basically agrees with the views of Australia and Indonesia."[171] One anticommunist Australian journalist-activist remembered that, by mid-1975, of the influential personages he interviewed across Southeast Asia, from Foreign Minister Carlos Romulo and Executive Secretary Alejandro Melchor in the Philippines to Foreign Minister Sinnathamby Rajaratnam and Security and Intelligence Division chief S. R. Nathan in Singapore, "most of these people were telling me that the Indonesians should act urgently in East Timor."[172] New Order delegations also traveled to Western Europe, Eastern Europe, North America, South America, Africa, and the Arab world to argue for the necessity of East Timor's integration into Indonesia.[173]

Portuguese officials intended to hold a referendum in East Timor and allow the population to determine the colony's future. But Suharto disagreed with Portugal's emphasis on self-determination. "The future of Portuguese Timor must be seen in the framework of the stability of Southeast Asia in general and Indonesia in particular," he told Polkam in October 1974. He concluded that an independent East Timor would inevitably threaten Indonesia's political stability and economic development.[174] Suharto's anxieties only escalated after ASDT rebranded itself as Fretilin and incorporated into its leadership several student activists recently returned from Lisbon, where they had absorbed the radical liberationist politics swirling across the Lusophone world.[175] Under the sway of these student leaders, Fretilin's rhetoric grew more confrontational and its grassroots programs more radical.[176] In late October 1974, the military newspaper *Berita Yudha* published three front-page articles on alleged links between Fretilin and China, and Yoga told American officials that Bakin had identified at least one Chinese agent in East Timor.[177]

Suharto ordered Murtopo to promote pro-integration sentiment in East Timor.[178] The result was *Operasi Komodo*, a multi-pronged covert operation designed to gather intelligence, sway popular opinion in favor of integration with Indonesia, cultivate international support for Indonesian annexation, and prepare the groundwork for an invasion should armed intervention become necessary. Indonesian radio stations in Kupang beamed broadcasts into East Timor, aired in Tetum and other Timorese dialects, that assailed Fretilin as communist and UDT as fascist. Hoping to use the East Timorese population's religiosity as an inoculant against communism and an "asset to improve Apodeti's growth," Indonesian intelligence operatives coordinated with indigenous priests and bishops to warn congregants against supporting Fretilin. Yoga also dispatched Secret Warfare Command (Kopassandha) units to each district of East Timor to "give moral support to Apodeti" and "work with Apodeti cadres to disrupt and thwart our opponents' strategy." *Operasi Komodo* also contributed to the militarization of political conflict in East Timor. Indonesian operatives furnished both Apodeti forces in East Timor and anti-Fretilin guerrillas in West Timor with weapons and training. Beyond Timor, the Indonesian army mobilized forces in East Nusa Tenggara and mounted exercises in Sumatra to practice an amphibious assault. If any of these operations were exposed in international media, Yoga wrote, Indonesia would defend itself by "employing the theme of the growth of communist influence in Portuguese Timor."[179]

Indonesian operatives fed Jakarta a steady diet of alarmist reports about increasing communist influence in East Timor. Yoga authored a top-secret January 1975 memo that announced "headway for communism in Portuguese Timor" and "the rise of a threat to national security." The report suggested that Fretilin and UDT planned to stage a coup and surrender East Timor to

Chinese control.[180] Aware of the Suharto regime's Cold War outlook, Fretilin leaders attempted to assuage Indonesian concerns about a communist beachhead opening up on Timor. Party officials promised an independent East Timor would pursue harmonious, neighborly relations with all countries, including Indonesia. Fretilin's secretary general told the Jakarta daily *Kompas* that, "if Fretilin embraces communism, Indonesia is welcome to invade." But these appeals fell on deaf ears. *Operasi Komodo* reports dismissed Fretilin's public repudiation of communism as disingenuous.[181]

Amid increasingly visible Indonesian interference in East Timor, Fretilin and UDT sealed a coalition and won a commanding victory in March 1975 elections.[182] The ascent of pro-independence sentiment in East Timor inspired renewed anxieties in Jakarta. Even Malik now advocated military action, guaranteeing that he "personally could cope with the international repercussions that would flow" from forcible annexation.[183] Jakarta dailies began airing alarmist reports predicting an impending communist takeover in East Timor and alleging Fretilin had launched a "hate Indonesia" campaign.[184] The military newspaper *Angkatan Bersenjata* published an editorial on East Timor asserting that "we need to eliminate the source of danger for the sake of the security, order, and survival of our country."[185]

Yet Suharto staved off demands for overt military intervention. After reports of Indonesian meddling in East Timor caused a public outcry in Australia, Whitlam penned a circumspect letter to Suharto urging moderation. The following week, the Australian prime minister told Surono, the deputy chief of the Indonesian armed forces, that the prospect of an Indonesian invasion of East Timor led him to wonder "whether defence aid might be affected."[186] Suharto quickly disavowed any Indonesian intent to invade during a meeting with the newly arrived Australian ambassador. He said he remained concerned about an invasion's possible effect on Indonesia's reputation, particularly among purveyors of military and economic aid.[187] Equally important in restraining Indonesian action was Suharto's inability to extract a green light from the United States, where the Ford administration had adopted what the US ambassador in Jakarta called a "policy of silence."[188] New Order leaders continued to press for an ex ante American authorization of annexation through the first half of 1975.[189] Suharto himself made the case for incorporation during his July 1975 visit to the United States. He warned Ford that the communist takeovers of Cambodia and Vietnam would inspire leftist movements across Southeast Asia, including the "Communist-influenced" Fretilin. Integration with Indonesia, Suharto insisted, was "the only way" forward for East Timor. Ford pledged to expand American assistance to Indonesia but did not endorse Suharto's plans to annex East Timor.[190] The following month, the CIA reported Suharto had again postponed military action because he "continues to fear an adverse reaction from Washington if he authorizes an invasion."[191]

With Suharto's unwillingness to imperil the flow of military and economic aid precluding outright invasion, Indonesian military and intelligence officials deepened their interference in East Timor. Murtopo's deputies worked to destabilize the coalition between Fretilin and UDT. They invited delegations from both parties to Jakarta but separated them upon their arrival. Fretilin's unofficial foreign minister José Ramos-Horta met Murtopo's deputies and proposed the Finlandization of East Timor. But the Fretilin delegation had little opportunity for substantive discussions and was instead ferried between factories and museums for photo-ops—the purpose of which Ramos-Horta surmised was to "discredit me . . . in the eyes of the [East Timorese] population.[192] The gambit succeeded. Ramos-Horta's authority within Fretilin waned as radical leaders less enamored of the coalition with UDT rose to challenge his authority. Meanwhile Murtopo met with the UDT delegation and promised that Indonesia would embrace an independent East Timor if its government excluded leftist elements, encouraging conservatives within the party to move against Fretilin.[193] Agence France-Press reported that UDT representatives departed Jakarta after "reassessing their anti-communist platform and pledging to cooperate with the colony's pro-Indonesian APODETI party."[194] Bakin also began subsidizing trips for UDT officials to Taiwan, South Korea, and the Philippines—reflecting the partnerships forged by anticommunist states across East and Southeast Asia amid Suharto's regional Cold War.[195] The resulting polarization between UDT and Fretilin led the parties to split in May 1975. Before the UDT delegation returned home in July, Murtopo encouraged them to move against Fretilin.[196]

UDT staged a coup d'état in August. Forces loyal to UDT seized control of Dili's communications centers, airport, police station, and government offices. Portuguese soldiers and officials retreated to a small island off the coast. But they left thousands of Timorese troops in the barracks. Most of these men quickly declared for Fretilin and joined the party's guerrillas in East Timor's rugged interior. Fretilin steadily chipped away at UDT positions, reclaiming control of the capital in September and achieving de facto control over the entirety of East Timor shortly thereafter.[197] As Fretilin consolidated its control, Yoga once again sought clarification of the Australian and American positions. In Canberra, the Indonesian ambassador received assurances that Whitlam would "not be in a position of seeking to exercise a veto" over Indonesian foreign policy.[198] In Jakarta, Yoga met with US ambassador David Newsom, who relayed a message from Kissinger that the "main American interest is in [the] impact of any change in Portuguese Timor on US relations with Indonesia" and Washington had "no objection to [the] merger of Portuguese Timor with Indonesia." Even so, Newsom warned Yoga that Congress would likely react harshly to an Indonesian effort at forcible annexation.[199]

Military preparations proceeded apace with efforts to lay the diplomatic groundwork for invasion. Suharto told Polkam that "over the long run Fretilin rule in Portuguese Timor could pose a threat to stability in Southeast Asia and the Southwest Pacific." He noted that, "If Indonesia is forced to intervene, efforts must be made to ensure the international community does not regard Indonesia as the aggressor."[200] The following month, Suharto adopted a more stringent line. He argued that "Indonesia cannot allow the presence of a force in Portuguese Timor that threatens and endangers the security of Indonesian territory."[201] He dispatched some 4,000 Indonesian troops to the East Timor border area in late September.[202] The following week, Indonesian forces helped their Apodeti clients retake the border town of Batugade—the first major engagement on East Timorese soil in which large numbers of Indonesian troops participated.[203] Indonesian forces pressed eastward from there, engaging in periodic skirmishes with dug-in Fretilin defenders. One highly placed Indonesian official told Australian diplomats that the military planned to retake Dili by mid-November.[204] Fretilin guerrillas proved more formidable than Indonesian leaders anticipated. But the tide of the battle was shifting. On November 28, 1975, in a desperate bid to forestall outright Indonesian intervention, Fretilin declared the independence of Timor-Leste and appealed to the international community for support.[205]

The Suharto regime remained unwilling to mount an outright invasion of East Timor without American approval. As it happened, Ford and Kissinger traveled to Jakarta in December 1975—a visit Kissinger anticipated would serve as a "dramatic reaffirmation of the significance we attach to our relations with Indonesia."[206] In conversations with Ford, Suharto alleged Fretilin was "infected" with communism and asked the American's understanding "if we deem it necessary to take rapid or drastic action." Ford's response, coming after months of evasion, was direct: "We will understand and will not press you on this issue. We understand the problem you have and the intentions you have."[207] The following day, Indonesian forces descended on East Timor, beginning an occupation that lasted nearly twenty-five years and resulted in the deaths of up to 200,000 people.[208] Indonesia's formal annexation of East Timor in July 1976 became a source of international opprobrium and a perennial challenge for Indonesian diplomacy.[209]

The mid-1970s was an era of unprecedented challenges for the Suharto regime. In Indonesia, the *Malari* incident fused elite opposition and mass discontent, imperiling the legitimacy of the New Order. In Southeast Asia, the fall of anticommunist regimes in Cambodia and South Vietnam and the collapse of

Portuguese authority in East Timor raised the specter of a destabilizing communist advance. And in the wider world, economic turbulence, the human rights revolution, and the reorientation of international politics along North-South lines combined to threaten Indonesia's ability to mobilize Cold War capital. But the mid-1970s was also an era of oil. The quadrupling of global oil prices following the October 1973 Arab-Israeli war resulted in massive petrodollar windfalls for Indonesia that reshaped the political economy of the New Order. Resource rents enabled Suharto to extend his control over civil society, chart a new course of economic nationalism, and aggressively assert Indonesia's regional ambitions.

Suharto's Cold War thus reached full bloom. But much as Suharto's earlier improvisations had generated unexpected problems, the New Order's escalating repressiveness would eventually prompt a resurgence of domestic opposition organized largely along Islamic lines. The oil boom also contributed to a sense of escalating Islamic power on the international stage that reinforced domestic unrest. This coalescence of an Islamist threat both at home and abroad would vex the Suharto regime—which originated in an anticommunist counterrevolution and remained fundamentally anticommunist in its outlook. And a precipice loomed: elections scheduled for 1977 would once again subject the New Order to a test (albeit a rigged one) of popular opinion.

Realignments

In June 1976, Kopkamtib requested that the PPP cease using as its logo an image of the Ka'bah, the holiest site in Islam toward which all Muslims pray. Party logos appeared alongside party names on electoral ballots, and in a country where illiteracy rates reached almost 40 percent and 90 percent of the population espoused Islam, the Suharto regime feared the Ka'bah logo would afford the PPP a disproportionate advantage in elections scheduled for 1977.[1] But party leaders refused Kopkamtib's request and threatened to boycott the election if the government forced the issue. Suharto backed down.[2]

The New Order grew increasingly anxious about political Islam in the 1970s. The PPP became a surprisingly powerful opposition party and mounted vigorous challenges against what it perceived as the Suharto regime's secularizing agenda. Student activism likewise assumed an Islamic hue amid intensifying prohibitions on campus political activities. And renascent jihadist organizations like Darul Islam staged a series of bold terrorist attacks and even plotted to assassinate Suharto. Changes beyond the archipelago's borders reinforced the Suharto regime's sense that political Islam rather than communism posed the most pressing threat to Indonesia. The oil shocks and the Iranian revolution heralded the resurgence of a new Islamist internationalism, one embraced by figures as diverse as Libya's Muammar Qaddafi and Iran's Ruhollah Khomeini. Transnational inspiration contributed to the emergence of a similar impulse of religious rebellion in Indonesia. Finally, the eruption of tripartite conflict between China, Vietnam, and Cambodia in the Third Indochina War fractured the myth of communist ideological solidarity and ultimately led the Suharto regime to sacrifice its anti-Chinese, anticommunist regional outlook in favor of an effort to sustain regional cohesion.

Suharto's Cold War waned as the threat of political Islam eclipsed the threat of communism. In the 1955 elections generally regarded as a barometer of the primordial loyalties of the Indonesian population, the parties that were eventually subsumed within the PPP won more than 40 percent of the vote—compared to

Suharto's Cold War. Mattias Fibiger, Oxford University Press. © Oxford University Press 2023.
DOI: 10.1093/oso/9780197667224.003.0010

only 16 percent for the PKI. Eradicating the PKI required a profound moment of rupture and a world-historic campaign of bloodletting animated by a relatively broad domestic coalition and enabled by a permissive international context. Given that Islam claimed much deeper roots and wider influence in Indonesia than communism ever did, and given the flourishing international human rights movement, Suharto could not hope for a similar opportunity to use violence to purge Indonesia of his domestic political opponents. He therefore altered his approach to governance. He worked to anchor the New Order within Indonesian life by fashioning Golkar into a genuine political party, proselytizing his regime's ideology of development, and fostering an indigenous economic elite. As he did so, he abandoned some of the policies that served as hallmarks of his Cold War, including the detention of tens of thousands of political prisoners and the containment of Chinese influence in Southeast Asia.

I

The 1977 elections confirmed religion as the key vector of opposition within the New Order. As the PPP waged a surprisingly effective campaign against the Suharto regime, Islamist movements began challenging the New Order outside the political system. At the same time, students and youth hewed toward religious identities and once again assumed the role of political vanguard. These countervailing forces grew more powerful as the national assembly prepared to convene to re-elect Suharto for a third term as president.

The emergence of religious opposition came to the fore during the so-called Sawito affair. Sawito Kartowibowo, a forty-five-year-old mystic and registered employee of the Ministry of Agriculture, began publishing tracts critical of Suharto in the second half of 1976. "Toward Salvation" excoriated the moral decay that accompanied Indonesian economic development. "Retreat in Order to Advance More Perfectly" condemned Suharto himself as having "betrayed his holy struggle, failed to provide a role model, violated the oath of office of the Head of State, including by giving opportunities to others, especially family members and friends and others close to him to enrich themselves." But the most inflammatory was "Letter of Transfer." Modeled on the *Supersemar* that brought Suharto to power a decade earlier, it proposed the transfer of power to a ruling council led by former vice president Mohammad Hatta and included a space for Suharto's signature. Among the signatories to Sawito's documents were not only Hatta but also the chiefs of the key bodies of Protestants, Catholics, Muslims, and mystics in Indonesia. The Suharto regime responded swiftly to Sawito's provocations. State Secretary Sudharmono announced that the authorities had uncovered a plot to overthrow the New Order. Sawito was arrested and eventually sentenced to eight years in prison for subversion. The signatories to his letters were pressured to recant.[3]

The Sawito affair occurred at the dawn of an efflorescence of Islamic political activism in Indonesia. By agglomerating the archipelago's Muslim parties within the PPP, the New Order provided the Islamic community with a measure of institutional unity that had eluded it since the Japanese occupation. Institutional coherence dovetailed with a broader social cohesion—itself also the result of state policy, as New Order's anticommunist and bureaucratic impulses encouraged Indonesians to hew toward religious identities.[4] As Sumitro remembered, in the aftermath of the September Thirtieth Movement, "many people . . . who never prayed began praying and studying Islam."[5] Increasingly devout Indonesian Muslims began partaking of a transnational Islamic discourse emanating from Saudi Arabia, Egypt, Iran, and elsewhere in the 1970s. The number of worshipers at Friday services surged and prayer groups cropped up in universities and government offices.[6] "Pop Islam" gained traction as devout performers earned ever-larger radio and television audiences. Among them was the *dangdut* music star Rhoma Irama. After returning from a *hajj* journey in November 1975, he imposed Islamic behavioral norms on members of his band (including prohibitions on drinking alcohol and extramarital sex), altered his image to become more pious (adopting shorter, neater hair and more recognizably Muslim dress), and injected what one journalist called a "proselytizing intent" into his music and performances.[7] The PPP capitalized on this rising sense of religious identification among Indonesian Muslims and proved itself a formidable political adversary.

Other Islamists disaffected by the challenges and compromises inherent in New Order politics adopted alternative strategies. Some turned to programs of religious proselytization at the grassroots level. Others embraced programs of violent mobilization against the state. In the period immediately following the September Thirtieth Movement, Ali Murtopo and other senior New Order officials resuscitated defunct jihadist groups like Darul Islam as anticommunist proxies.[8] These jihadist organizations began to mobilize against the New Order in the mid-1970s. The Suharto regime sensed the emerging religious opposition and established the Indonesian Ulama Council (MUI) in 1975 in an effort to coopt the Muslim community.[9] But the New Order's corporatist impulses failed to reach the deepest levels of religious society. "The people, particularly the Islamic community, are now against the Suharto regime," read one captured document from Darul Islam, and as a result "at present we do not have too difficult a task" in recruiting new members.[10] Jihadists began orchestrating terrorist attacks against symbols of what they regarded as moral decay. Emblematic was a series of grenade attacks on a Methodist church, a nightclub, and a cinema in Medan on Christmas Eve of 1976.[11]

Meanwhile Hasan de Tiro, who in 1953 proclaimed himself the foreign minister of the Darul Islam rebellion, began agitating for the independence of the famously pious province of Aceh. De Tiro returned from exile in 1976 and proclaimed Acehnese independence from "all political control of the foreign regime of Jakarta and the alien people of the island of Java."[12] He soon thereafter established the Free Aceh Movement (GAM) and began waging a guerrilla war against what he regarded as the occupying forces of the Suharto regime. The earliest GAM attacks took place in 1977 and targeted a lucrative local Mobil Oil facility—erected following the 1971 discovery of vast natural gas deposits in the province.[13] Although de Tiro articulated a conceptual architecture of opposition that was nationalist rather than religious in nature, he drew upon long-standing ideas about Acehnese Islamic piety and Aceh's advocacy for a greater role for Islam in the Indonesian national project.[14] The Suharto regime understood the motive behind de Tiro's separatist campaign as at least partly religious in nature, designed to "split Aceh from Indonesia by way of launching uprisings against the central government and proclaiming an Islamic state," as one internal government report put it.[15]

As Islamist mobilization against the New Order escalated and the 1977 electoral campaign got underway, Kopkamtib chief Sudomo announced the existence of a terrorist organization he called Komando Jihad. Although Sudomo went to great lengths to disavow any connection between Komando Jihad and the PPP, some observers assumed the group was a fabrication of the regime designed to justify the surveillance and arrest of Islamist politicians.[16] Over the course of the campaign and during the election itself, Kopkamtib arrested more than 700 Islamists it accused of belonging to Komando Jihad.[17] The government also cited the PPP for violations at five times the rate of Golkar over the same period.[18] The regime's growing concern with the threat of political Islam suggested a waning of Suharto's Cold War orientation. He went so far as to call political Islam "our common enemy" during a meeting with Catholic politicians held in advance of the campaign.[19]

Student activism resurged as Islamist political mobilization escalated. After being snuffed out by the crackdown following *Malari*, embers of opposition flickered within university student councils. They were stoked by a seemingly endless series of revelations about corruption among New Order leaders. In January 1977, for instance, Seymour Hersh of the *New York Times* reported that an official in the Department of Communications requested a $40 million bribe from General Telephone and Electronics in exchange for a contract to build a domestic satellite system; when the firm refused, the contract instead went to Hughes Aircraft, with allegations of bribery hanging over the arrangement.[20] Student delegations visited members of parliament in advance of the 1977 polls to complain about the prevalence of corruption among Suharto's cronies.[21]

Amid mounting Islamic and student activism, Indonesians embarked upon a campaign period lasting from late February to late April before heading to the polls in early May. The 1977 elections unfolded in much the same way as the 1971 polls and featured widespread intimidation and coercion of opposition parties. Sudomo began the campaign by issuing a list of "four don'ts": don't intimidate your opponents, don't offend the dignity of the government and its officials, don't disrupt national unity, and don't criticize the policies of the government. Civilian and military officials across the archipelago regularly intimidated party leaders, disqualified candidates from running, denied parties permits for rallies, scheduled collective work during party meetings, and pressured local power-brokers to deliver votes for Golkar.[22]

The PPP mounted an energetic campaign in spite of the inhospitable environment. Two prominent Islamic political figures proclaimed that "every Muslim participant in the 1977 Election, whether man or woman, especially members of the PPP, is required to vote for the PPP when the time comes in order to uphold the law and religion of Allah." Those Muslims who ignored this diktat, "out of fear of losing their position or livelihood or due to other reasons, are among those who forsake Allah's Law."[23] Golkar responded with its own appeals to the Islamic community. The party elevated the figure of Vice President and Yogyakarta Sultan Hamengkubuwono IX, whose religious bona fides were unimpeachable. Golkar also relied on a number of sympathetic *ulama* as campaign surrogates and even unveiled party banners that included calligraphy of Qur'anic verses and assurances that "It's not true that a person who joins Golkar is an infidel."[24] One group of observers lamented that the campaign was "narrow, shallow, recriminatory, filled with lies and false promises, dishonest and not objective."[25] It was also violent. The PPP complained often that its cadres were being kidnapped, shot, and murdered during the campaign. But the Suharto regime required the party to bring these accusations to a government-controlled "Contact and Communication Forum" rather than the press. Even before the government announced the final results in June, both youth and religious groups challenged the elections. A group of young people who called themselves "exponents of the Young Generation of Indonesia" wrote to the Supreme Court and asked for a review of a number of "irregularities." The PPP alleged the government rejected a large number of ballots and deliberately disenfranchised voters suspected of favoring the Islamic party; its representatives refused to sign the tallies.[26]

When the election results were finally released, Golkar earned 62.1 percent of the vote, a dip of half a percentage point from its performance in 1971. The PPP won 29.3 percent and the PDI only 8.6 percent. Among voters in Jakarta, the PPP secured a plurality and dealt Golkar a symbolic defeat. Commentators divided over whether the party's impressive performance in the capital reflected the presence of plentiful foreign observers impeding the Suharto regime's underhanded efforts at manipulation, or whether it reflected the unique characteristics of Jakarta voters—more Muslim, more cynical, more modern. Anecdotal evidence suggested that political Islam was on the ascent across the archipelago. Observers often remarked on the raucous, enthusiastic environment at PPP campaign rallies in comparison to rather staid Golkar affairs.[27] In addition to its strong national showing, the PPP won control of 40 of the archipelago's 282 regional assemblies.

The widespread discontent revealed by the 1977 election only escalated in the months following, as the national assembly prepared to convene to elect the president and establish the Broad Outlines of State Policy. A former chairman of the University of Indonesia Student Council went so far as to publicly nominate as president Ali Sadikin, a Sukarno appointee known as a critic of the New Order who had recently been sacked from the Jakarta governorship—likely because of his failure to secure a Golkar victory in the capital. Shirts emblazoned with Sadikin's portrait and the slogan "why not the best?" became a hot commodity on university campuses.[28] Army chief of staff General Panggabean allowed student activism to flare so long as it did not move beyond university walls. "From campus, students can become a moral force to drive renewal," Suharto remembered. "But if student activities spread beyond campus, or if other groups sneak onto campus, then students lose their prestige as a moral force, because they have become a political force."[29] It was not long before protest exploded beyond university campuses. Dramatist W. S. Rendra staged a new play entitled *Sekda* (Regional Secretary), which depicted a venal local official skimming from a famine relief fund and offering his immiserated constituents help through mind-numbing seminars instead. Although Bandung and Jakarta represented the epicenter of renewed student activism, student groups in Aceh, Medan, Palembang, Yogyakarta, Surabaya, and Makassar also staged protests against the New Order.[30] Particularly worrying for the regime was the fact that, as one contemporary observer put it, "most student activists appeared to be associated with . . . Islamic groups."[31]

The New Order sought to mollify public discontent in the wake of the election. Suharto launched *Operasi Tertib* (Operation Discipline) to root out crooked officials from the state apparatus and combat perceptions of corruption.[32] Sudomo explained to the newsmagazine *Tempo* that he would investigate how "an official can live a luxurious life when the wealth reported is only so-and-so much." Kopkamtib operatives showed up unannounced at government offices down to the lowest rungs of the bureaucracy to expose instances of bribery.[33] Over the next five years, *Operasi Tertib* investigations recouped 700 billion rupiah for the Indonesian government. Even so, most corruption prosecutions targeted small-time local officials rather than figures at the top of the New Order.[34] To repel perceptions of inequality, Suharto called a group of ministers to the *Bina Graha* presidential office complex and instructed them to "invite students to engage in a dialogue with the Government" about economic development.[35] Minister of Research Sumitro Djojohadikusumo led a delegation of technocrats to university campuses in August and September 1977. The first destination on Sumitro's whistle-stop tour was the University of Indonesia, where restive students castigated the government for widespread corruption. Five days later, at Gadjah Mada University in Yogyakarta, students denounced the doctrine of *dwifungsi* that afforded the military a sociopolitical role and demanded the dissolution of Kopkamtib. At Pajajaran University in Bandung, students greeted the technocrats with large posters with slogans like "Eradicate corruption entirely—change the Government." Instead of asking questions of Sumitro, they read a statement entitled "Attitude of Stupefaction" that disavowed any intent to engage in a dialogue with the Suharto regime.[36] Sumitro and his colleagues canceled the remainder of their tour.[37]

Protest only escalated after the regime's retreat from dialogue. At a summit held in October 1977, students from across Indonesia agreed to stage periodic "down to the street" protests—the first since the *Malari* incident. Six thousand students staged a "long march" in Jakarta on November 10 and carried posters with slogans like "Return ABRI to the People." The following day, Suharto called together various government ministers as well as all the governors and military commanders in Java to demand that they contain resurgent student activism lest it disturb the forthcoming session of the national assembly.[38]

Elements of the armed forces began criticizing the Suharto regime as well. Nasution toured university campuses in the autumn of 1977 and lamented the lack of religiosity in the New Order, which he suggested could serve as a source of conscience in policymaking and check against corruption.[39] Alamsjah delivered a speech in November 1977 arguing that the New Order's development efforts had failed to narrow the gap between rich and poor, between urban and rural, and between regions and the capital. He also acknowledged a long list of other failures, including food shortages, crime, scandals, smuggling, bribery, and abuses of power. The following month, Nasution and Alamsjah both appeared at a rally of 20,000 Muslims at the Istora Senayan stadium in Jakarta to celebrate the Islamic New Year. Nasution condemned the New Order in front of a boisterous crowd. Intelligence reports suggested that Nasution had told students in Surabaya that "some brigades" would rally behind him and the student cause—though the former army leader disavowed those reports when questioned about them.[40] The rise of opposition sentiment within the military reflected the diminishing salience of Cold War concerns. As one keen observer of Indonesian politics put it, "with the decline of the vividness and plausibility of the 'communist threat,' the prime cement of the 1965 coalition necessarily grew brittle."[41]

The prospect of a split within the military coinciding with a wider social cleavage reminded Bakin chief Yoga Sugama and other senior New Order security officials of the *Malari* incident.[42] But the coalescence of an Islamic-student-military axis of opposition would represent a far greater threat to the Suharto regime than *Malari*. Had Muslim groups not abstained from the 1974 protests, one scholar suggested, "disaster could have turned into holocaust, and out of the chaos a nationalist-populist-religious contender for power with partial Army backing might possibly have emerged."[43] As students, Islamists, and soldiers moved toward an inchoate alliance, Suharto immediately worked to shore up his support in the military. He called Panggabean and expressed a desire for a demonstration of loyalty from the armed forces. Panggabean organized a meeting of Indonesian generals to discuss the escalation of political discontent, especially among high-ranking military figures. After several days of negotiations, the leadership of the military issued a statement explaining that the armed forces would "take firm measures on the basis of their authority against anyone carrying out activities that would undermine the authority of the national leadership and disrupt or foil the coming MPR [national assembly] session."[44]

This warning did not curb the surge of protest. On January 10, 1978, students in Medan, Palembang, Bandung, Yogyakarta, and Surabaya demonstrated in honor of the twelfth anniversary of the *Tritura*. A Jakarta university held a panel discussion about presidential term limits at which one speaker alleged Suharto held a private fortune of 140 billion rupiah at one of his crony's banks.[45] Two erstwhile New Order radicals, General Hartono Rekso Dharsono and General Kemal Idris, spoke at universities in January 1978. Proclaiming that the New Order had abandoned its founding ideals, they demanded the military acknowledge public discontent.[46]

Student grievances crystallized in mid-January 1978 with the publication of the *White Book of the 1978 Students' Struggle* by the student council of the Bandung Institute of Technology (ITB). The book presented a laundry list of grievances against the New Order. In politics, it alleged that "the *innermost voice of the little people*, who live under the *oppression* and *repression* of the 'elite' forces, never reaches the ears of the government." In economics, it charged that development policies "do not benefit the common man." The *White Book* concluded that the Suharto regime was guilty of "deviations and abuses of power" that revealed "the failure of the national leadership in carrying out its functions." In order for "democratic life" to be realized, the students concluded, Suharto should resign from the presidency and "all social groups in society" should "participate in determining the national leadership."[47] On January 18, a delegation of five student council leaders from universities in Jakarta, Bandung, Bogor, and Surabaya sneaked into the presidential office complex and demanded a meeting with the president. They planned to urge Suharto to step down and suggested that, if he won re-election, "there will be a repetition of the overthrow of the government like that which happened in the final moments of the deceased President Sukarno."[48] The very cohort that had acted as shock troops for Suharto in 1965 and 1966 were now lined up squarely against him.

The Suharto regime quickly clamped down. Dharsono and other military officials who expressed support for the student movement were sacked or reprimanded. Kopkamtib banned seven Jakarta dailies and seven student newspapers on January 20, 1978, severing the connection between university protests and national politics. The non-student papers were allowed to resume publication within weeks, though only after their editors stood before Suharto to express support for Kopkamtib's decision and pledge to "always engage in introspection."[49] One study of the Indonesian press concluded that the newspapers were subsequently drained of their "spirit of struggle."[50] Meanwhile Sudomo ordered the arrest of student council leaders across Indonesia and froze the activities of all student councils. One intelligence official said that "the reason we arrested them was, because tensions were high, we needed to give shock therapy to the students."[51] Among the 143 student leaders arrested were ITB student council head Heri Akhmadi, who would eventually be put on trial for insulting the president.[52] Troops occupied university campuses across the archipelago, stationing tanks in front of academic buildings, ripping down political posters, and roughing up students suspected of involvement in protests. At a meeting with Suharto the following month, Sudomo explained that further student activism would be met with "decisive measures."[53]

Jakarta resembled a military garrison when the national assembly convened in March 1978 despite the fact that the outcome of the proceedings was all but foreordained. Soldiers were posted at every major intersection, with reinforcements positioned strategically across the city and helicopters hovering low scanning for trouble.[54] Sudharmono remembered that the PPP was emboldened by its performance in the 1977 elections and disheartened by the crackdown against the student movement and chose to "show its teeth." Party spokesperson Chalid Mawardi delivered a bitter speech assailing the Suharto regime for suppressing student protests and working to corporatize students through the KNPI, for meddling in the 1977 campaign and preventing an honest accounting of electoral irregularities, for remaining dependent upon the IGGI and contravening Indonesia's *bebas aktif* foreign policy heritage, and for doing too little to address the corruption and the uneven distribution of the fruits of development—an echo of the rhetoric emanating from university campuses. Most powerfully, Chalid accused the Suharto regime of being "Islamophobic" and fabricating Komando Jihad as a pretext to suppress political Islam.[55] PPP delegates from the Nahdlatul Ulama wing of the party organized a walkout to protest the inclusion of Javanese mysticism (*kepercayaan*) within the GBHN. So contentious were the proceedings that senior New Order officials had to engage in painstaking backroom negotiations to prevent the PPP from putting forth its own presidential candidate to challenge Suharto.[56]

Suharto was re-elected as president on March 22, 1978. But that was not the end of the drama at the assembly. Vice President Hamengkubuwono, whose relationship with Suharto had grown strained as a result of the corruption and authoritarianism of the New Order and the limitations of his own role in policymaking, wrote to inform the president that he would not serve in his post for a second term.[57] Suharto sought first to tap NU leader Idham Chalid as vice president, but he refused and the position instead fell to Adam Malik—the third member of the troika that held sway in the formative months of the New Order.[58] The drama in the year preceding Suharto's re-election confirmed that the New Order rested upon exceedingly narrow domestic foundations.

II

During the period following his re-election, Suharto concluded political Islam represented the most pressing threat facing the New Order. That was true domestically, as the PPP grew increasingly powerful and attracted sympathizers among retired generals and student activists, and as jihadist organizations staged a series of increasingly bold terrorist attacks. And that was true internationally, as Libya continued to engage in acts of subversion and the Iranian revolution inspired huge numbers of Muslims toward political activism.

Ensuring that university campuses did not again become sources of instability was imperative in the wake of the 1978 protests. Suharto called university rectors from across Indonesia to Jakarta in February 1978 to remind them he viewed academic freedom as "the freedom to study, to teach, and to research," and nothing more.[59] The rectors of Indonesia's forty largest universities were told that they would be held "personally responsible" for the eruption of disorder on their campuses.[60] Minister of Education and Culture Daud Jusuf soon thereafter announced a policy called the "Normalization of Campus Life" (NKK), which would be implemented through new "Campus Coordinating Bodies" (BKK). Jusuf's NKK policy held that student councils would be appointed by university rectors rather than elected by student bodies. It also introduced new curricular requirements that necessitated students spend more time on coursework. Finally, NKK inhered an absolute ban on campus political activity. As Jusuf put it, "if students are engaged in political 'action and policy,' they are engaging in activity inconsistent with their mission and students and it is therefore inappropriate for them to do so as students."[61] The security organs of the New Order worked with BKK bodies to dramatically expand their surveillance of student activities to "prevent the spread of negative student solidarity."[62] Even seemingly innocuous campus events like a panel on "Indonesian Democracy after 35 Years of Independence" were discussed at the highest levels of the New Order's coercive institutions.[63] In effect, the NKK/BKK policies amounted to an extension of the New Order's corporatist impulse over university campuses. But the Suharto regime's efforts to tighten its grip on campus activism ironically reinforced the nascent threat of political Islam. The imposition of barriers to political activism on campus led many oppositionist students to seek shelter within campus mosques and prayer groups.[64]

No less important was guaranteeing the loyalty of the military. In the wake of the criticisms leveled at the Suharto regime by retired officers like Nasution and Dharsono, Panggabean established a Forum for Study and Communication (Fosko) to serve as a conduit between active and retired military officers. But Fosko dispatched a series of reports to army headquarters arguing that the military should re-evaluate *dwifungsi*, end its entanglement with Golkar, cease imposing conformity upon social groups, and allow a greater role for democracy.[65] Fosko also helped convene a week-long commemoration for National Awakening Day at which Malik intoned that natural disasters that had recently struck the country were "a warning from God to us," invoking Javanese folklore about the role of climatic disturbances in signaling the decay of regnant political orders. "We all have sinned," Malik lamented. The army froze Fosko as a result of the ensuing brouhaha."[66] Other retired generals also began discussing the idea of presidential succession—long a taboo in New Order politics.[67]

Suharto lashed out at his military critics in a pair of speeches delivered in March and April 1980. In the first, he lamented that the New Order had not yet forged a consensus around the role of Pancasila as the sole national ideology.[68] In the second, he rebutted rumors that his wife was involved in the dispensation of government largesse and suggested that such gossip was intended to undermine the New Order and Pancasila.[69] These speeches, evincing a profound conflation of personal and national interest, inspired yet another round of criticism. Fifty luminaries signed a "Statement of Concern" that they submitted to parliament in May 1980. What became known as the "Petition of Fifty" accused the president of manipulating Pancasila and using it "as a threat against political opponents" rather than "a means to unite the Nation," of persuading the military to "take sides" rather than "standing above all societal groups," and of giving "the impression that he is the personification of Pancasila as such."[70] Its signatories were a mix of generals, politicians, and student activists—most of whom were devout Muslims—whose criticism centered on Suharto's repression of political Islam.[71] Although he was incensed, Suharto chose to address the matter quietly.[72] Signatories to the petition were denied exit visas, work permits, business licenses, and credit lines. The Petition of Fifty group survived and articulated proposals for reform including the abolition of Kopkamtib and the implementation of free and fair elections. But it gained little traction amid persistent media blackouts of its activities.[73]

As strictures on Islamic politics narrowed under the Suharto regime, some Islamists turned to violent jihadist tactics. One example of this pathway was Abdullah Sungkar, a Solo native and an admirer of Mohammad Natsir, the former Masyumi leader whom Suharto had banned from involvement in politics. After being arrested and imprisoned for broadcasting anti-government rhetoric in 1978, Sungkar used his defense plea to inveigh against the New Order for its cooptation and suppression of political Islam. He bristled against the government for blacklisting 2,500 former leaders of Masyumi, surveilling Islamic organizations, and interfering in the internal politics of the Parmusi and other Muslim parties. So too did he denounce the New Order's efforts to control civil society groups through various corporatist arrangements and the run-rampant activities of Kopkamtib and Opsus. Such activities, Sungkar said, "only occur in fascist countries like Germany in the era of Hitler and Italy in the era of Mussolini."[74] After his release from prison, Sungkar and his associate Abu Bakar Ba'asyir fled to Malaysia and helped establish a network that sent Indonesian jihadists to Afghanistan before eventually founding Jema'ah Islamiyah, one of Southeast Asia's most fearsome terrorist networks. One scholar of Indonesian jihadism has concluded that "it is questionable whether a man like Abdullah Sungkar" would have embraced violence if "New Order had allowed a party like Masyumi . . . to function freely."[75]

International developments inclined other Indonesian Muslims toward radicalism. Sungkar and Ba'asyir were devotees of the Wahhabist ideas gaining traction as a result of a Saudi proselytization campaign financed by petrodollars. Other Indonesian jihadists embraced the ideals of the Muslim Brotherhood in Egypt. But it was the Iranian Revolution that did the most to inspire Indonesian Muslims. Many members of Darul Islam considered Indonesia as ripe for revolution as Iran. Even though Indonesian Muslims were Sunni, posters of Khomeini cropped up at Islamic boarding schools across the country.[76] "He was like our Che Guevara," said one Indonesian of the Iranian revolutionary ideologue Ali Shiriati. "I read his book from cover to cover when I was in high school in Central Java." The Iranian embassy in Jakarta distributed a free magazine called *Yaum al-Quds*, which contained Khomeini's speeches encouraging Muslims to rise up against non-Islamic regimes.[77]

Revulsed by Suharto's authoritarianism and inspired by Khomeini's revolution, jihadist organizations engaged in criminal activities ranging from robberies and murders to bombings and hijackings. During the assembly session that reelected Suharto in March 1978, a bomb was discovered in the hall; suspicion quickly converged on a radical Islamist group called the March 20 Movement.

The following month, a bomb exploded in the Istiqlal Mosque in Jakarta.[78] Between 1978 and 1980, an Islamist band carried out a series of assaults and murders in Central Java that came to be known, after the name of group's leader, as *Teror Warman*.[79] In August 1980, a bomb exploded at a hospital in Jakarta only weeks after Ali Murtopo received treatment there. The escalating tempo of Islamist violence led Sudomo to launch *Operasi Sapujagat* (Operation Clean-Up) in September 1980.[80] But Kopkamtib proved unable to curb Islamist violence. The most dramatic event occurred in March 1981, when Komando Jihad operatives hijacked a Garuda Indonesia flight and forced it to divert to Bangkok. The hijackers threatened to blow up the plane unless the Suharto regime deported (nonexistent) Israeli military advisors from Indonesia, ousted Malik from the vice presidency, and released scores of jihadists held in Indonesian prisons. Generals Benny Murdani and Yoga Sugama traveled with Indonesian troops to Thailand and orchestrated a daring rescue operation.[81] In late 1982, members of Darul Islam began plotting to kill Suharto with a bomb attack and kidnap and assassinate his inner circle, including Murtopo, Murdani, and Amirmachmud—a scheme that bore a startling resemblance to the September Thirtieth Movement.[82]

The Suharto regime had long recognized political Islam as a potential international threat. The dispute between Malaysia and the Philippines over Sabah served as an early manifestation of the destabilizing potential of transnational political Islam. Although Indonesian officials prevented the dispute from undermining the institutional mechanisms of ASEAN in the late 1960s, the Sabah chief Tun Mustapha bin Harun continued to provide secessionists in the Muslim-majority Philippine south with aid, likely in an attempt to force the Philippine government to concentrate its resources on maintaining internal stability rather than pressing its claim to Sabah. Among the other sponsors of what was known as the Moro National Liberation Front (MNLF) was Libya's Qaddafi, who sought to seize the internationalist mantle of his recently deceased idol, Egyptian president Gamal Abdel Nasser.[83] Libyan diplomats began railing against the Marcos government's treatment of its Muslim subjects and sending money to the MNLF—$3.5 million in 1972 alone. The leader of the MNLF, Nur Misuari, also broadened his appeals to the wider Muslim world with Libyan and Malaysian assistance. The Organization of the Islamic Conference (OIC) passed a resolution expressing "serious concern over the plight of Muslims living in the Philippines" in February 1972. Marcos's declaration of martial law later that year prompted the MNLF to turn to militancy. The resulting conflict led to the deaths of approximately 100,000 people and the displacement of upward of a million.[84]

Misuari and the MNLF continued to seek aid from an increasingly self-conscious Islamic bloc in international politics. Indonesian diplomats worked to prevent the OIC from taking up the Moro issue at its subsequent conference in March 1973. But the conference's Libyan hosts orchestrated a dramatic interruption of the proceedings by introducing a seven-year-old Filipino Muslim boy named Hareth Salem, who was missing a hand and an ear. Hoisting Salem above his shoulders, a Libyan delegate accused the Marcos regime of brutalizing the inhabitants of Mindanao and Sulu and urged all Muslim states to sever economic ties with the Philippines.[85] The OIC once again passed a resolution expressing "deep concern over the reported repression and mass extermination of Muslims in South Philippines." In June 1973, Misuari proclaimed that "We, the five-million Bangsa Moro people, are engaged in a revolutionary struggle for national-freedom from the stranglehold of Filipino colonialism." He appealed for aid from his "Muslim Brothers of the World."[86]

The Suharto regime was determined to prevent the emergence of transnational Islamic solidarity movements. By the time Misuari delivered his appeal to the Muslim world, Kopkamtib had received reports about the emergence of ties between Indonesian Muslims and their coreligionists in the southern Philippines. General Sumitro quickly delivered an order to military commanders across Indonesia stating that "Indonesian foreign policy is to preserve the integrity of the nation and neighboring ASEAN states" and adding that "whatever happens inside a given country is the business of that country alone." He instructed his subordinates in no uncertain terms: "Do not allow the development of any type or form of Islamic solidarity activities about the events/upheavals in the Philippine south."[87] Sumitro's worries were exacerbated during a September 1973 trip to a summit of the Non-Aligned Movement in Algiers. He recalled being asked by Qaddafi about the alleged forcible conversion of Indonesian Muslims to Christianity. Sumitro batted the allegations aside and, back in Jakarta, warned the Foreign Affairs Committee about "a tendency toward a new kind of imperialism which uses religion as its medium."[88]

As the security organs of the Suharto regime tried to stymie the development of transnational ties between Muslim dissidents, New Order diplomats worked to halt the international sponsorship of Islamist movements. The Moro struggle in the Philippines was front of mind. Indonesian diplomats at the Second Islamic Summit, held in Lahore in February 1974, sought to ensure that the experience of Philippine Muslims was "not included in the official agenda of the conference."[89] They succeeded inasmuch as the final communiqué of the conference did not include any reference to the Bangsamoro struggle. But in the wake of the conference, Marcos told American officials that he was "convinced that [Malaysian prime minister Tun Abdul] Razak personally is involved" in "training, supplying, and organizing anti-government forces in in Mindanao and Sulu."[90] Suharto himself worked to patch up the relationship between Malaysia and the Philippines. In May 1974, he met with Razak in Penang, and shortly thereafter with Marcos in Manado, apparently seeking a solution whereby the

Philippines would cede its claim to Sabah in exchange for Malaysian promises to halt support for the MNLF. Suharto and Razak agreed that the Bangsamoro rebellion should receive no official mention at an OIC conference that would be held in Kuala Lumpur in June, and MNLF representatives who traveled to Kuala Lumpur were denied access to the conference site. The Libyan delegate demanded the plight of Philippine Muslims be included in the conference, exclaiming that their situation was "worse than that faced by the Arabs . . . in Palestine."[91] Ultimately, Indonesian diplomacy reoriented the position of the OIC, which passed a resolution once again expressing "deep and continuing anxiety" over the situation in the Philippine south but urging the parties to reach a solution "within the framework of the national sovereignty and territorial integrity of the Philippines."[92] In subsequent years, the OIC refrained from criticizing the Philippines and endorsed negotiations between the Marcos regime and the MNLF.

The Suharto regime effectively de-internationalized the secessionist struggle in the southern Philippines. But it remained wary of the destabilizing potential of transnational political Islam. Malik suggested in 1974 and again in 1975 that Indonesia permit the Palestinian Liberation Organization to open an office in Jakarta. But the military was anxious about the potential radicalization of Indonesian Muslims and twice vetoed the proposal.[93] Senior New Order officials also became convinced that Libya was funneling aid to the burgeoning Free Aceh Movement.[94]

The New Order's concerns about the destabilizing potential of political Islam mounted following the Iranian Revolution. The military expanded its surveillance of the Iranian embassy in Jakarta after Khomeini's ascent to power and attempted to confiscate the Islamist literature emanating from the facility.[95] The coordinating minister for security affairs expressed concern to a group of staffers about Indonesian citizens traveling to Tehran to celebrate the first anniversary of the Iranian Revolution.[96] Indonesian students were prohibited from studying in Iran without government permission, though many simply evaded these restrictions by transiting through Pakistan.[97] Later that year, security ministers decided not to allow Iranian college students marooned by the shuttering of higher education institutions in Iran to transfer to schools in Indonesia because "pro-Iranian revolution citizens of Iran tend to propagandize the Iranian revolution."[98] Even as the New Order worked to contain Iranian influence within Indonesia, however, the Suharto regime pursued cordial relations with the Islamic Republic.[99] Indonesia did not take sides when war broke out between Iran and Iraq in September 1980 and limited itself to encouraging the two parties to find a peaceful resolution to the conflict.[100]

The combination of domestic and international changes prompted a major revision of the Suharto regime's sense of threat. As the CSIS leaders Jusuf Wanandi and Hadi Susastro remarked in 1983, "communism will not be an urgent problem for at least the next ten years" because "the communists do not have the power to destabilize the country." Instead, they pointed "extremist groups employing the banner of Islam" as the most urgent threat facing the New Order.[101] To respond to that newfound threat, Suharto would call an end to his Cold War.

III

The threat of political Islam was fundamentally different from the threat of communism. Islam possessed a broader, deeper hold on the Indonesian population and could not be excised through violence and repression. A greater measure of inclusion was required. After a decade of relying mostly on the military to sustain his political authority, mobilizing and demobilizing auxiliary institutions as the situation demanded, Suharto turned toward formalization and bureaucratization. He worked to anchor the New Order in the Indonesian body politic by refashioning Golkar into a cadre party with a permanent base of popular support and implementing a large-scale program of ideological indoctrination. He also worked to coopt the most pliable elements of the Islamic community, suppress those he regarded as irredeemably hostile, and cultivate the PDI as an alternative to the PPP.

Suharto was determined to devote additional attention to what he called "political development" during his third term as president. He tasked Sudharmono with assembling a program known as the Directive for the Realization and Implementation of Pancasila (P4).[102] The program consisted of two-week-long training courses in which Indonesians studied Pancasila and the 1945 constitution but devoted disproportionate time to understanding the Broad Outlines of State Policy through "open, directed" conversations.[103] P4 courses thus amounted to an effort to indoctrinate all Indonesians in the stifling worldview of the New Order and preempt criticisms of the Suharto regime—a shift from the "floating mass" doctrine that saw the Suharto regime attempt to insulate the population from politics entirely. Ali Murtopo described P4 as nothing less than an effort to "Indonesianize Indonesians" and render it "impossible for them to be penetrated by communist ideology, or by any other ideology."[104] The New Order first required all civil servants below the level of cabinet minister to participate in the P4 program, but Sudharmono remembered the regime's ambition was to reach "all Indonesian citizens."[105] Suharto enthused in his memoirs that approximately 2 million Indonesians, mostly civil servants and soldiers, had taken the P4 courses by 1983.[106]

Institutionalization occurred alongside ideologization. Suharto assumed leadership of the Golkar Advisory Board in October 1978—the first sign that he intended to build Golkar into a genuine mass organization capable of sustaining the New Order rather than a mere vehicle of electoral legitimation activated every five years for perfunctory campaigns. He eventually ordered Golkar to "consolidate" itself and grow into something more akin to a political party.[107] Sudharmono worked to transform Golkar into a cadre party with a base of support among the Indonesian masses and an autonomous political infrastructure. As he remembered in his memoirs, he wanted Golkar to become an organization that could "determine its own policies and make its own decisions, not be determined or dictated from the outside" and thereby evolve into "a force for national development" in and of itself. Golkar subsequently recruited 10 percent of all Indonesian voters in each village as cadres who would receive training modeled on the P4 program. About 9 million cadres underwent the training before the next elections held in 1987.[108]

As the Suharto regime worked to institutionalize Golkar, so too did it sustain the PDI and PPP as legitimate if timid rivals. The PDI needed reinforcing after its dismal electoral showing in 1977. Likely at the initiative of Ali Murtopo, the New Order announced it would refurbish Sukarno's gravesite in Blitar into a veritable memorial, which would endow the PDI with a political touchstone.[109] But the party remained riven by bitter and public factional disputes and dependent on Sudomo to enforce some measure of internal cohesion.[110]

The PPP by contrast required domestication. A number of leading Islamists, including the vice secretary general of the PPP and a leading Jakarta imam, were arrested in the wake of Suharto's re-election in 1978.[111] The Suharto regime then worked to ensure leadership of the PPP fell from Mohammad Syafa'at Mintaredja to Djaelani Naro.[112] A Murtopo ally who spent most of his career in government rather than in religious organizations, Naro purged PPP lists of candidates overtly hostile toward the New Order, especially those associated with Nahdlatul Ulama.[113] The purge of politicians who considered themselves part of the "loyal opposition" radiated down the party's ranks as Naro's appointees replicated in local branches what Naro performed at the national level.[114] The steady marginalization of the opposition-inclined NU within the PPP led first to a struggle for leadership within NU and ultimately to NU's withdrawal from the PPP as the organization eschewed political activism in favor of social engagement.[115] The enfeebling of the PPP then led the party to win 7 million fewer votes (and 10 percent less of the overall vote) in 1987 than it did in 1982.

Meanwhile the Suharto regime and Golkar worked to bring moderate Muslims into the New Order fold. Alamsjah unveiled a series of sops to the Islamic community. He convinced Suharto to offer his blessing to a ruling that *kepercayaan* did not constitute a religion, ending what Islamic politicians regarded as a looming threat to the interests of their community.[116] And amid escalating anxiety about the prevalence of Christian missionary activity in

Indonesia, he issued an array of decrees that restricted proselytizing activities and curbed foreign financial contributions to missionary groups while also removing restrictions on Islamic preaching.[117] For its part, Golkar established an Islamic Missionary Council, and some members of the party's executive board expressed opposition to Minister of Education Daud Jusuf's decision to abolish the Ramadan vacation.[118]

The culmination of the Suharto regime's program of political development was a series of laws passed in 1985. The first was the election bill, which required political parties to adopt symbols that aligned with Pancasila. The bill forced the PPP to abandon the Ka'bah symbol that party leaders believed attracted many Indonesian voters. The second bill reshaped parliament and the national assembly, increasing the size of Indonesia's legislative bodies and affording the military with greater representation within them. By diluting the number of elected officials, the bill made it even more difficult for party leaders to envision legitimate pathways to political change. The third was the political parties bill, which required Golkar, PDI, and PPP to adopt Pancasila as their "sole foundation." The bill forced the PPP to abandon its Pancasila-and-Islam foundation and the PDI to abandon its Pancasila-and-nationalism foundation, which undermined the very notion of politics as a site for the elaboration of divergent visions of the nation's future. The fourth was the mass organizations bill, which stipulated the same "sole foundation" requirement for social organizations and empowered the government to advise, amalgamate, and ban nongovernmental organizations at a whim. The fifth and final was the referendum bill, which required a referendum that garnered the support of 90 percent of the citizenry to modify the constitution. Sudharmono remembered that the passage of the bills created for the first time "a strong legal foundation to implement a system of national leadership and political infrastructure for the implementation of Pancasila Democracy."[119]

The economy constituted another site for the institutionalization of the New Order. The first oil shock had accelerated an ongoing spiral of inflation in Indonesia and precipitated the Pertamina debt crisis. To stymie resurgent inflationary pressures, the Suharto regime implemented monetary austerity, but Indonesian inflation nevertheless outpaced worldwide inflation and led to a steady erosion in the archipelago's terms of trade, dulling the New Order's developmentalist impulse.[120] Exports of textiles, handicrafts, and other labor-intensive manufactured products decreased considerably in 1975 and led to predictions of an imminent devaluation of the rupiah. Adjustment finally occurred in November 1978, when the Indonesian currency was devalued by 50 percent against the dollar. In a television interview two weeks later, Widjojo explained that the purpose of devaluation was to "create as many job opportunities as possible" by incentivizing the development of the agricultural, manufacturing, and transportation sectors.[121] A memorandum to Malik reported that a key basis for the devaluation was motivated by a determination that "the likelihood of an increase in revenues from oil exports is not large" and Indonesia consequently needed to increase its non-oil exports.[122]

Indonesian economic forecasters proved entirely mistaken. Only months after the devaluation, the Shah of Iran fled his country. The resulting tumult in the Persian Gulf led the price of oil to skyrocket once again. Indonesian crude doubled in price from $15.65 in 1979 to $29.50 in 1980. Indonesia's current account surplus rose from $708 million to $2.4 billion while oil revenues surged to reach 60 percent of total government receipts.[123] Suharto's determination to anchor the New Order in the Indonesian population in the face of an escalating threat from political Islam then overcame his historic reluctance to promote the development of a *pribumi* capitalist class. He unveiled a massive program of public investment through the dispensation of petrodollar windfalls through a body called Team 10. Established in January 1980 to dispose of a surplus of about $1.4 billion deriving from the spike in oil prices, Team 10 comprised representatives of Sudharmono's State Secretariat and technocrats from Bappenas and various economic ministries. At its first meeting, the group unveiled a "crash program" for development and dispensed more than $800 million in largesse. Prioritizing domestic procurement, the team purchased equipment for transportation, electrification, and irrigation from *pribumi*-owned firms and encouraged foreign suppliers to develop production capacity in Indonesia.[124]

Team 10 was made permanent in April 1980 and granted authority to oversee government procurements valued at 500 million rupiah or more. Over the following year, the authority of Team 10 was both deepened to encompass purchases by Pertamina and other state-owned enterprises and widened to encompass purchases by provincial governments. Team 10 assumed control over military procurement in 1985 over the strident objections of Murdani and other key military leaders. Over its eight-year existence, it awarded more than $83 billion in government contracts. Sudharmono's aide Ginandjar Kartasasmita remembered that the team's purpose remained to "accelerate development" in the wake of "the oil bonanza" by using "government procurements to trigger the development of domestic industries."[125]

But Team 10 had a number of particularistic political purposes as well. Sudharmono recalled that a key objective was to "prevent the field of commerce from being centered within only one group," referring to ethnic Chinese Indonesians. Cultivating a *pribumi* capitalist class would address popular complaints about ethnic inequality that had been "muted under the pretext of smelling SARA" (*suku, agama, ras, antargolongan,* or ethnicity, religion, race, intergroup)—a taboo subject in New Order Indonesia.[126] So too would it create a network of indigenous businesses capable of supporting Sudharmono in his effort to build Golkar into a full-fledged political party. Sudharmono therefore channeled contracts to powerbrokers who delivered political support to Golkar (of which he was named chairman in 1983) in key provinces and regencies. The Golkar-Team 10 axis became a locus of institutionalization in the 1980s. It signaled the erosion of Suharto's Cold War in favor of a more inclusive approach to political and economic management whose purpose was to preserve the support of the broad masses of the Indonesian citizenry.

IV

There was perhaps no greater indication of Suharto's reorientation of the New Order away from its anticommunist roots than the release of Indonesia's political prisoners. As the human rights revolution crested with the rise of the Carter administration in the United States, and as the New Order came to regard political Islam as the overriding threat facing the archipelago, Suharto accelerated a release program and signaled a shift in the legitimacy narrative undergirding Indonesia's appeals to the outside world: from anticommunist stability to economic development.

The Carter administration posed a number of challenges to the Suharto regime. As Jusuf Wanandi put it in the flagship journal of CSIS, Carter's "emphasis on basic human rights has been greeted by Southeast Asian leaders in general and Indonesian leaders in particular with feelings of ambivalence." But it was not only the apparent shift from realism to idealism that vexed the Suharto regime. Wanandi explained that "the present government has many 'centers of power' which attempt to influence President Carter's decision-making," representing a "source of confusion which makes it difficult for both Congress and the general public to understand which is the real policy being implemented." While National Security Advisor Zbigniew Brzezinski put little weight on human rights issues, Coordinator for Human Rights and Humanitarian Affairs Patricia Derian told lawmakers the Carter administration would hold "discussions of security assistance and the possibility of cuts" with the Suharto regime.[127] The New Order's sense of bewilderment about the future of American foreign policy reflected developments in Congress as well. Wanandi noted that "a large number of new young members with more independent attitudes ... weakened both party discipline and the previously strong seniority system" and resulted in "a splintering of ideological groupings in Congress and increased difficulty in determining membership attitudes towards even a proposal coming from a president who was the acknowledged leader of their own party."[128] In particular, left-wing human rights activists had made common cause with right-wing foreign aid skeptics to threaten the continuing flow of aid to Indonesia. In the official mind of the New Order, the American political system seemed shorn of its coherence.

Seeking to counteract pressure from human rights groups, the Suharto regime lobbied the Carter administration, Congress, and the wider American public by emphasizing the New Order's developmental credentials. Adam Malik derided Amnesty International as working to undermine international confidence in Indonesian development.[129] In mid-1977, the regime contracted with the New York public relations firm Hill & Knowlton to publish *Indonesia Development News*. The publication's first issue featured a note from Ismail Saleh, chief of the National Development Information Office, who described the publication's goal as providing "a better understanding of Indonesia's commitment to progress in the field of economic growth."[130] CSIS also expanded its international outreach efforts. Jusuf Wanandi published a rejoinder to a *Far Eastern Economic Review* exposé on Indonesia's political prisoners by noting that "Indonesian cultural values as in many other developing societies tend to emphasize communalism over individualism." He argued that the Suharto regime had little alternative but to privilege economic development over human rights.[131]

But international criticism of the New Order rose to something of a fever pitch at the end of 1977. Amnesty International was awarded the Nobel Peace Prize in October.[132] The following week, the organization released a 148-page report alleging that Indonesia held roughly 100,000 political prisoners—roughly triple the prevailing estimate in Western policy circles.[133] Amnesty staffers testified about the contents of the report to Representative Donald Fraser's House subcommittee in October.[134] World Bank officials threatened to revoke an offer of a $1 billion loan for the Suharto regime's transmigration initiative if it continued to pressure former prisoners to participate in the program.[135] In November, American diplomats told Indonesian officials that the continued detention of large numbers of political prisoners "can be grounds for U.S. opposing loans to a country through international financial institutions . . . and automatically weighs heavily in consideration by Congress and administration on levels of military and economic assistance." They remarked that any delay in the release of 10,000 political prisoners anticipated by the close of 1977 would "undercut USG [US Government] support of GOI [Government of Indonesia] intentions and immeasurably strengthen GOI critics here and abroad. In such circumstances, the potential international costs to Indonesia would far outweigh any temporary domestic convenience." The incoming US ambassador delivered similar messages in his initial calls on Indonesian officials and made clear that the "next several months are a potentially critical period in US-Indonesian relations."[136]

The mounting possibility of an aid cutoff led the Suharto regime to relent. In December 1977, Sudomo announced the imminent release of 10,000 political prisoners, only 10 percent of whom had allegedly volunteered for resettlement. This marked the first time the New Order agreed to release large numbers of political prisoners to their homes rather than resettle them in what amounted to faraway prison camps.

Pressure from the United States abated in the wake of Sudomo's announcement. Derian visited Indonesia in January 1978 for discussions on human rights issues with Suharto, Sudomo, and other senior New Order officials. She also visited Salemba prison in Jakarta and spoke with former political prisoners. In a press statement issued upon her departure from Jakarta, Derian struck conciliatory notes.[137] Vice President Walter Mondale traveled to the archipelago a few months later. By the time he arrived, the Carter administration was determined to heal the rift that human rights concerns had opened in relations between the United States and Indonesia. A briefing memorandum for Mondale instructed him to use a "very light touch" in raising human rights issues given "our determination not to impose our values, our understanding of local cultural and historical factors, [and] our recognition of recent progress."[138] Even as the Carter administration moderated its attitude in light of the release of large numbers of prisoners, Amnesty International, the International Labor Organization, TAPOL, and other nongovernmental organizations continued to demand the rapid release of the approximately 20,000 prisoners who remained in confinement. The Suharto regime refused to accelerate the pace of its release program. Roughly 10,000 more prisoners were freed over the second half of 1978, and the remaining prisoners were released by the turn of the decade.

The release of tens of thousands of suspected communists whom the Suharto regime had for more than a decade insisted represented a dire security threat owed to the growing influence of the global human rights movement. But it also reflected the dramatic loss of anticommunism's cohesive power within the New Order coalition. As the regime became fixated on the threat posed by political Islam, its determination to hold the line against international pressure lapsed.

V

The waning of Suharto's Cold War became evident in Indonesian foreign policy in addition to domestic politics. Although Suharto clung to his policy of formally isolating the People's Republic of China, the complex diplomacy surrounding the recurrence of conflict in Indochina ultimately led him to embrace a tacit alliance with Beijing.

Indonesian relations with the communist superpowers underwent changes in the 1970s. Indonesian and Soviet diplomats inked agreements on economic and cultural cooperation in 1974, and two years later Moscow offered Jakarta financial and technological assistance for mining and hydroelectric projects. Suharto continued to oppose any moves toward normalizing Sino-Indonesian relations. But some Indonesian interest groups advocated a thaw following Mao's death in October 1976. Malik declared in December that "the time has come for Indonesia not to ignore a country of 800 million people any longer." The Chamber of Commerce and Industry (Kadin) concurrently made the case for a thaw in Sino-Indonesian relations based on economic considerations.[139]

The communist takeovers of Cambodia and South Vietnam in the spring of 1975 set in motion developments that would reveal the end of Suharto's Cold War in Southeast Asia. The Suharto regime had long held sanguine views about the nature of Vietnamese communism as nationalist rather than internationalist.[140] But other ASEAN states grew alarmed at the possibility of Vietnamese aggression and subversion in Southeast Asia, especially in light of Vietnamese leaders' linkage of their revolution to the "just struggle" of other Southeast Asian peoples.[141] Vietnamese policymakers attempted to assuage regional anxieties. The deputy foreign minister of the reunified Socialist Republic of Vietnam met with the Indonesian ambassador in Hanoi in December 1976 and expressed a desire to cooperate with Indonesia in promoting economic development.[142] Indonesian military officials likewise sought to foster ties with Vietnam. Wanandi recalled that Murdani and other key military leaders were "more sympathetic towards Vietnam because they saw it as a strategic issue. To them China was the big threat, and Vietnam was an important part of Southeast Asia to keep the balance with China on an even keel. For that reason, Pak Benny rationalised, we should support Vietnam as the region's bulwark against a strong China in the future."[143] Moreover, a Southeast Asia polarized between an anticommunist ASEAN and a communist Indochina, and an Indochina divided between a Soviet-aligned Vietnam and a Chinese-aligned Cambodia, would invite further destabilizing superpower interventions in the region.[144]

Both Indonesian and Vietnamese policymakers worked to integrate Vietnam into the Southeast Asian regional order. In an effort to mollify anxieties about Vietnam in other ASEAN states, General Widodo declared in March 1977 that a Vietnamese attack on Thailand would be construed as an attack on ASEAN as a whole.[145] Meanwhile Vietnamese diplomats undertook goodwill tours of Southeast Asia and sought to cultivate relationships with ASEAN states. The Vietnamese ambassador in Jakarta met with Suharto in July 1978.[146] Prime Minister Pham Van Dong traveled to ASEAN capitals a few months later.[147] When Pham visited Jakarta, Suharto hailed the journey as "opening a new page of mutual understanding, the growth of friendship, and the possibility of cooperation for the benefit of both our countries." The two leaders released a joint communiqué disavowing interference in the internal affairs of other states.[148]

The Vietnamese invasion of Cambodia in late 1978 undermined Indonesian efforts to integrate Vietnam into an anti-Chinese regional order.[149] The Vietnamese ambassador met with Suharto on December 30, five days after the invasion commenced, suggesting Hanoi hoped to win Indonesian understanding.[150] But Thailand faced what its leaders regarded as a dire threat. Vietnamese hegemony over all of Indochina would enable Hanoi to control the 1,800 miles of border that connected Thailand with Cambodia and Laos—and to exact revenge on Thai participation in the Vietnam War by sponsoring insurgencies active in the country's north and northwest. Thai leaders correspondingly engaged in secret negotiations with communist Chinese officials to provide material support for a Khmer Rouge insurgency against the Vietnamese-imposed regime of Heng Samrin. Chinese diplomats also worked to address Southeast Asian anxieties about subversion sponsored by Beijing. During a November 1978 tour through several ASEAN capitals, Chinese leader Deng Xiaoping pledged not to interfere in the internal affairs of other countries. Yet the Chinese invasion of Vietnam in March 1979, ostensibly to protect the region's ethnic Chinese community, did little to salve Indonesian anxieties about Beijing's regional ambitions—even if Ali Murtopo suggested it was in reality undertaken "to validate the U.S. expectation of the PRC to share international responsibility."[151] ASEAN was presented with a dilemma in Cambodia: whether to align with China or Vietnam.

Still suspicious of Chinese communist subversion, Indonesian military leaders preferred to align with Vietnam as a buffer against China. In early 1978, General Panggabean accused China of sending exiled PKI leaders back to Indonesia to foment unrest.[152] One Indonesian scholar who interviewed senior Indonesian military officials in the 1980s found "trust in Vietnam's role as a buffer against China . . . based on the fact that the Vietnamese were extremely nationalistic and had shown great determination and capability in resisting much greater powers," including China following its March 1979 invasion.[153] Moreover, Indonesian military officials feared that, by forging a tacit partnership with China against Vietnam, ASEAN would encourage Vietnam to invite Soviet power more deeply into Southeast Asia. That would undermine the Suharto regime's long-running efforts to construct an autonomous architecture of regional security. Murdani therefore spearheaded an effort to establish a dialogue with Vietnam. One of his deputies who traveled to Hanoi in early 1980 was overheard telling the Vietnamese foreign minister, "you take care of the field, and we'll take care of diplomacy," meaning Vietnam would continue occupying Cambodia and Indonesia would provide diplomatic cover.[154] By contrast, the Foreign Ministry under Mochtar Kusumaatmadja favored maintaining ASEAN unity against Vietnam, even if that entailed reestablishing diplomatic relations with China.

Suharto ultimately sided with the Foreign Ministry. The imperative of sustaining ASEAN unity trumped the imperative of containing China. That signaled that Indonesian foreign policy had moved beyond a Cold War mentality and had begun to focus instead on sustaining an architecture of regional stability based on ASEAN unity above all else.[155]

Even in 1984 the Indonesian military argued that "the PRC has certain political intentions towards the 17 million overseas Chinese in Southeast Asia, who generally hold dominant economic positions, whom China can use as tools for propaganda or for collecting capital for its domestic needs."[156] But the balance of power on China policy within the Suharto regime shifted toward those who favored a measure of rapprochement, including the Foreign Ministry and CSIS. It would take years of patient diplomacy, which progressed in fits and starts, but the thaw in relations between Jakarta and Beijing had begun. By 1984, the leaders of Golkar, PPP, and PDI reacted favorably to a statement by Mochtar that the New Order was considering normalizing economic relations with the People's Republic. The collapse in oil prices in the mid-1980s made the economic rationale behind normalization all the more compelling, given that growth slowed from its average of about 7 percent per annum over the preceding fifteen years. Mochtar argued in 1984 that Indonesia needed to open trade relations to take advantage of the massive Chinese market lest it be left behind by Malaysia and other regional competitors. Suharto went so far as to agree to meet with Chinese foreign minister Wu Xuqian when he visited Jakarta to celebrate the twenty-fifth anniversary of the Bandung Conference in April 1985. Scheduling conflicts ultimately scuppered the meeting, but it confirmed a fundamental shift in the foreign policy of the Suharto regime.[157]

Suharto's Cold War waned in the late 1970s. In Indonesia, Islamist parties allied with student dissidents and mounted an unprecedented challenge to the New Order, winning converts among former military leaders and delivering impressive results even in highly controlled elections. Restrictions on Islamic political activism also fueled a resurgence of jihadist organizations that staged increasingly bold terrorist attacks against the Indonesian state. Beyond the archipelago's borders in Southeast Asia, the outbreak of the Third Indochina War revealed the declining salience of communism as a geopolitical force and led Indonesia's ASEAN partners to enlist the New Order's paramount Cold War enemy, the People's Republic of China, as a counterweight against Vietnam. And in the wider world, the rivalry between Saudi Arabia and Iran for the loyalty of the Muslim *ummah* precipitated a deluge of capital and propaganda that and stoked Islamist sentiment across the globe. The Cold War no longer structured politics in Indonesia or Southeast Asia, and it lost its monopoly on the broader field of international relations. In that context, Suharto's Cold War project ceased to provide an adequate framework for understanding events or guiding policy.

Sustaining the New Order in this novel environment led Suharto to adopt a different set of strategies. Rather than rely on the military to violently repress all countervailing forces, he sought to establish a genuine base of popular support. He transformed Golkar into a genuine political party independent of military control and implemented a massive program of ideological indoctrination. So too did he inaugurate a renewed effort to foster the development of an indigenous capitalist class within Indonesia. As his regime evolved, Suharto dispensed with the hallmarks of his Cold War, releasing tens of thousands of political prisoners suspected of holding communist sympathies and abandoning his determination to contain China. Although the New Order would survive until 1998, anticommunism was no longer its overriding impulse.

Conclusion

Indonesia, Southeast Asia, and the World

Suharto's Cold War reshaped Indonesia, Southeast Asia, and the world. It began on the morning of October 1, 1965, when Suharto and the army launched an anticommunist politicide. But its roots lay in the ideological polarization of Indonesia and the geopolitical bifurcation of the world. It also endured beyond the cataclysmic violence of 1965–1966, as Suharto marshaled international capital to construct a counterrevolutionary dictatorship in Indonesia and promote authoritarian reaction across Southeast Asia.

Indonesian politics assumed the logic of Cold War in the decade before the September Thirtieth Movement. The PKI was established in 1920—the first communist party in all of Asia. But it represented only one of countless movements seeking to usher the Indonesian archipelago toward an imagined future. Islamic activists and secular nationalists elaborated their own conceptions of the Indonesian nation, while countless ethnic and regional associations contested the nationalist movement's vision of a unified territorial space.[1] This plenitude of political imaginaries re-emerged during the Indonesian national revolution that followed Japan's defeat in August 1945. The competing *aliran* (streams) of Indonesian nationalism also confronted a novel institutional force: a nascent army, forged by the fascist Japanese empire and the inheritor of its militarist and organicist values. Amid the tumult of revolutionary years, the army reinforced its illiberal outlook with a skepticism toward civilian authority and an antipathy toward communism. When Indonesia finally secured its independence in 1949, neither the army nor any single *aliran* reigned supreme.[2] The archipelago remained wracked by debates over individualism versus collectivism, federalism versus unitarism, civilianism versus militarism, and secularism versus Islamism. A proliferation of political parties catered to ever-narrower constituencies, causing ceaseless gridlock and imparting a centrifugal

Suharto's Cold War. Mattias Fibiger, Oxford University Press. © Oxford University Press 2023.
DOI: 10.1093/oso/9780197667224.003.0011

dynamic to Indonesian politics.³ Sukarno ultimately despaired of Indonesia's experiment with liberal democracy. In concert with the army, he declared martial law and erected an authoritarian system that he dubbed Guided Democracy. To counterbalance the burgeoning power of the army, the president then cultivated the PKI and embraced its radical ideas. Sukarno thus collapsed the kaleidoscope of political conflicts in postcolonial Indonesia into a single axis of contestation between anticommunist army and communist PKI.

As the Cold War emerged in Indonesia, Indonesia entered the global Cold War. The army began building ties with the United States, the world's foremost counterrevolutionary power, and the PKI leaned toward the People's Republic of China, the world's preeminent anti-imperialist power. Sukarno embarked upon a series of adventurist foreign policy crusades that served to bolster his domestic legitimacy and displace the conflict inherent to his anticommunist-communist coalition. Indonesia's bids to assert control over West Papua and oppose the creation of Malaysia rewarded the PKI with a tempestuous political climate conducive to radicalism and provided the army with a perilous security atmosphere beneficial to militarism. But Sukarno's efforts to preserve the balance between the army and the PKI could merely postpone rather than resolve the fundamental contradiction of Guided Democracy. Postponement also came at a heavy cost. It sank Indonesia into a pit of debt from which it would take decades to escape. So too did it lead factions of the army and the PKI to engage in increasingly contentious, violent forms of politics. The festering tensions within Indonesia ultimately exploded when elements of the PKI mounted a preemptive strike against the army and assassinated its most leaders.

The September Thirtieth Movement marked the beginning of Suharto's Cold War. The murder of the leadership of the Indonesian army provided Suharto with a pretext to purge the country of communism.⁴ Over the ensuing six months, the army orchestrated the mass slaughter and imprisonment of hundreds of thousands of suspected leftists.⁵ But Suharto's aspirations spanned far beyond perpetrating a politicide. He was determined to establish a political system that would guarantee national harmony and ignite processes of economic development that would diminish the appeal of revolutionary ideologies. He wanted not only to destroy the PKI but also to ensure that the Left could never again pose a threat to the regnant order in Indonesia.

A broad constellation of forces supported Suharto's campaign against the PKI. In addition to the Indonesian army, the New Order coalition included an array of political parties, religious organizations, and student and youth groups dissatisfied with the course of Guided Democracy. These disparate groups held widely divergent visions of Indonesia's future. Some favored a pluralistic political system based upon democratic principles and multiparty competition; others favored a monistic political system based upon organicist-integralist principles and technocratic management. Some advocated export-oriented development based upon primary commodities and labor-intensive industries; others advocated import-substitution development based upon high technology and capital-intensive industries. What united such divergent interests behind Suharto was little more than antipathy toward the PKI. It was therefore unsurprising that Suharto's anticommunist coalition splintered as soon as the PKI had been vanquished in 1966. Many student and youth groups mobilized in favor of a liberal-democratic order. Some political party leaders rallied in favor of a more elite-consociational system. And radicals within the Indonesian army pressed for a rapid reorganization of Indonesian life along structural-functionalist lines.[6] Much as was the case in the aftermath of the Indonesian revolution, no single vision of Indonesia's future claimed widespread legitimacy. The period following the September Thirtieth Movement was thus suffused with contingency—a critical juncture in which the existing order was overturned and myriad alternative futures became possible.[7]

The interlocking of Suharto's Cold War and the global Cold War solidified Indonesia's trajectory. Suharto invoked the specter of communist resurgence to appeal for debt relief, foreign aid, and private investment from the capitalist world. Purveyors of aid and investment furnished the nascent Suharto regime with Cold War capital—resources delivered for the purpose of geopolitical advantage rather than maximum return. International capital allowed Suharto to bankroll projects of political transformation and economic development that could not obtain the support of a critical mass of the domestic population. His ability to finance his agenda without extracting additional resources out of the Indonesian body politic enabled him to alter his approach toward the processes of bargaining and compromise that undergird all political orders. The New Order was thus an international construct.

Suharto faced a seemingly endless series of challenges in preserving the link between his Cold War and the global Cold War. At first, international creditors were unwilling to furnish Suharto with the resources necessary to implement his most expansive plans, which forced him to restrain his ambitions and permit a limited role for political parties and civil society groups within Indonesia. The late 1960s represented the apogee of the partnership between the Suharto regime and international capital, as the New Order channeled external savings to finance political consolidation, economic development, and regional stabilization. But the certainties of the global Cold War soon melted into an inchoate future as geopolitical realignment, economic turmoil, and transnational activism imperiled the Suharto regime's ability to secure Cold War capital. In the wake of the oil shocks, the New Order came to rely on petrocapital to fuel its domestic and international programs. Eventually, the Cold War ceased to provide a viable framework for the Suharto regime's approach to national and regional policy.

Political Islam became the primary vector of opposition to the New Order within Indonesia, and the Third Indochina War discredited the idea of a coherent communist threat in Southeast Asia. Suharto thus called an end to his Cold War even as the renewed rivalry between the United States and Soviet Union reached one of its most dangerous phases.

The relationship between Suharto's Cold War and Cold War projects centered in Washington, London, Tokyo, and elsewhere was a temporary alignment of autonomous yet interdependent counterrevolutionary movements rooted in idiosyncratic national struggles. Together they constituted half of the structure of international relations known as the global Cold War. Yet scholars have too often neglected the roles of peripheral actors in the anticommunist international, implying they exercised little agency unless they explicitly contravened the wishes of the United States—unless the tail wagged the proverbial dog. Power was admittedly not equally distributed between the Suharto regime and its international sponsors. But agency was nevertheless positive-sum. Both patrons and client exerted agency *through* rather than *against* one another, working in tandem toward the achievement of similar objectives.

The New Order endured beyond the end of Suharto's Cold War. Having constructed an anticommunist order in a polarized society, Suharto turned toward managing an established order in a more quiescent society. He relied less on the military, built Golkar into a cadre party with a mass base, and loosened restrictions on public expression.[8] He also embarked on a program of export-oriented industrialization and deregulated the financial system amid the oil "countershock" of the 1980s.[9] There was no greater indication of the shift in the regime's animating impulse than Suharto's crowning as the "Father of Development" by the national assembly in 1983.[10] Some facets of the regime remained the consistent. Notably, a thick web of corruption continued to extract value from economic production and provide Suharto with a reservoir of patronage resources he could tap to guarantee the support of various domestic constituencies. But the nature of the regime had unmistakably changed. It lost its ideological propulsion and much of its world-historic significance and devolved into a delicate system of coalition management.

For better and for worse, Suharto's Cold War transformed Indonesia. The New Order steered the archipelago away from a trajectory of internecine conflict that could have led the Indonesian state down a path akin to that taken by Nigeria, devoid of all capacity, or Brazil, subject to ceaseless politicization. Indonesia was endowed with a capacious, autonomous state critical to the achievement of catch-up growth. Over the course of the New Order, real GDP per capita rose at an average rate of more than 4 percent per annum. The share of manufacturing in overall economic output increased from below 10 percent to more than 25 percent. And economic change delivered salutary social results.

The share of the population living in poverty declined from more than 50 percent to only 11 percent. Life expectancy rose from fifty years to more than sixty-five years. Secondary school enrollment skyrocketed from below 20 percent to almost 55 percent.[11] It is true that Indonesia sustained this remarkable rate of economic success after the collapse of the New Order. But establishing a record of growth is far more challenging than maintaining one. Indonesia's impressive economic trajectory during the latter years of the Suharto regime and the subsequent years of democratic governance owed a great deal to institutions and conditions established as a result of Suharto's Cold War.

Suharto's Cold War also bestowed less favorable legacies on Indonesia. The New Order never surmounted its dependence on foreign aid and investment. Regimes that live by international capital often die by international capital—a lesson Suharto learned when the devaluation of the Thai baht in July 1997 precipitated massive capital flight across Asia. Indonesia was plunged into a searing economic crisis. New Order policymakers abandoned the peg that linked the rupiah to a basket of foreign currencies, whereupon the rupiah lost almost 90 percent of its value. Inflation and unemployment spiked, generating widespread popular suffering. Suharto was left with little alternative but to request assistance from the IMF. But the relationship between the Suharto regime and its Western sponsors had changed without the logic of Cold War binding them together. It was no longer possible for Suharto to balance his domestic and international constituencies, and the exercise of agency between the regime and its external sponsors became zero-sum. The IMF demanded a series of far-reaching reforms, including the dismantling of the patronage arrangements undergirding the New Order. Elites began defecting from the regime while civil society groups staged aggressive demonstrations against Suharto. The country threatened to descend into chaos as anti-Chinese pogroms erupted in cities across the archipelago and elements of the military kidnapped student activists. On May 21, 1998, after thirty-two years in power, Suharto finally announced his resignation.[12]

Indonesia became a democracy after the collapse of the New Order. But the archipelago's politics bore the imprint of Suharto's Cold War. The Indonesian Left never recovered from the devastating blow struck by the army-led politicide. Nor did the political parties and civil society organizations subjugated through corporatist arrangements evolve into institutions that articulated and aggregated diverse societal interests. Few vehicles of mass mobilization emerged in post-Suharto Indonesia. In that context the politico-business elites nurtured under the Suharto regime reconstituted their political and economic power under more pluralistic institutional arrangements. They used their financial wherewithal to capture political parties and media outlets. The result was a "cartelized" system in which major parties cooperated with one another to divvy up the

spoils of power and restrict the entry of new rivals.[13] Political contestation continued to revolve around clientelism and patronage—mechanisms of legitimation that flourished under the New Order.[14] The military ultimately disavowed
the doctrine of *dwifungsi* that asserted a sociopolitical role for the armed forces.
But retired officers eked out positions of influence in politics and business from
which they protected military prerogatives, including the territorial command
system that stationed military personnel parallel to the civilian bureaucracy
across the archipelago and served as focal points for the projection of military
influence and the collection of off-budget revenues.[15] The illiberal ideologies
entrenched during Suharto's Cold War persisted as well. The key figures within
post-authoritarian Indonesian politics were themselves products of the New
Order who had internalized the regime's skepticism about mass mobilization
and popular politics. Even the student groups that assumed a leading role in the
protests that accompanied the downfall of the New Order exhibited a reluctance
to engage in interest group politics and forge alliances with workers and peasants. And post-authoritarian elites continued to wield the national ideology of
Pancasila to enforce what one observer has aptly dubbed a "repressive pluralism"
amid an Islamic turn in Indonesian society.[16] Today Indonesia's is an inspiring but
flawed democratic system—and its flaws trace their roots to Suharto's Cold War.

Suharto's Cold War reached beyond the Indonesian archipelago. The president was convinced that Indonesia's neighbors in Southeast Asia were vulnerable
to communist aggression and subversion, which he believed emanated primarily
from the People's Republic of China. If Indonesia were surrounded by hostile
communist powers, Suharto reasoned, the New Order would be forced to divert
resources away from political stabilization and economic development and toward national security, which would impede his efforts to establish conditions
inimical to a recrudescence of communist influence. Suharto's Cold War consequently included an effort to contain Chinese influence in Southeast Asia.

The anti-Chinese component of Suharto's Cold War emerged first within
Indonesia. Suharto regarded the millions of ethnic Chinese in Indonesia as potential conduits of Chinese influence and subjected them to discrimination and
violence. But his anti-Chinese campaign quickly assumed regional dimensions.
The New Order cohered the anticommunist states of Southeast Asia within a
new regional organization whose fundamental purpose was the containment
of Chinese influence: ASEAN. Enduring anxieties about Indonesian expansionism in other Southeast Asian capitals prevented the Suharto regime from
building ASEAN into a formal military pact. Even so, Indonesian strategists
believed ASEAN could give rise to an autonomous architecture of regional security in Southeast Asia. The New Order used ASEAN to promulgate its security doctrine of *ketahanan nasional*, or national resilience, which prescribed an
array of techniques of authoritarian governance—an official state ideology that

delegitimized political contestation and a bevy of institutional structures including a dictatorial leader, a technocratic bureaucracy, and a militarized society. Remaking the region in Indonesia's developmental authoritarian image would render Southeast Asian states more secure against communism and generate a broader form of regional resilience. Suharto's regional Cold War thus provides a new answer to the age-old question of "does ASEAN matter?"[17] The multilateral organization became a transmission mechanism for authoritarianism.

Scholars have traditionally understood the rise of authoritarianism in the Global South in the 1960s and 1970s as the result of large-scale structural forces. The threat of communist subversion, the imperative of economic development, and the availability of international capital undoubtedly propelled a shift toward more exclusionary and coercive forms of governance. But structural conditions cannot alone explain Southeast Asia's convergence toward a particular form of authoritarianism. The region's leaders exercised agency. Suharto and other New Order officials traversed the region and evangelized the national resilience doctrine. When national leaders elsewhere faced political shocks—from race riots in Malaysia to youth protests in the Philippines—they consciously adapted the Indonesian model to construct newly authoritarian regimes. They pioneered institutional and ideological formations with few domestic precedents that would have been unthinkable absent international inspiration and assistance. The New Order internationalized counterrevolution across the region. Suharto's Cold War was not solely responsible for the turn toward authoritarianism in Southeast Asia, nor did it dissolve all national distinctions, but it reshaped the foundations of political order in Southeast Asia as the Vietnam War came to an end.

Many of the techniques of authoritarian rule that Suharto promulgated remain prevalent across the region today. In the Philippines, for instance, President Rodrigo Duterte mobilized the military for the preservation of internal order in the face of what he described as existential threats from communist and Islamist terrorists. In Malaysia, meanwhile, Prime Minister Najib Razak pilfered vast sums of money from public coffers and channeled state resources toward various clientelist obligations. Many of the leaders whom Suharto aided and inspired also entrenched themselves in power, establishing political dynasties that continue to menace the region and hinder the development of accountable states.[18] The process of authoritarian convergence propelled by Suharto's regional Cold War thus helps explain why Southeast Asia remained "recalcitrant" through the third wave of democratization and into the twenty-first century.[19]

The global Cold War sustained Suharto's domestic and regional Cold Wars. In recent years, scholars have emphasized the diffusion of universalist ideologies to explain how various political projects in the Third World attached themselves to the superpowers. But the distribution of capital was equally vital to the solidification of Cold War blocs. The global Cold War was an economically intensive competition between different forms of modernity, and the generation and distribution of surplus was decisive to how that competition unfolded across the world. Indeed, what made the Cold War anomalous relative to the imperialist international systems that preceded it was the direction of capital flows. Most imperial systems hinged upon the extraction of surplus value from colonies, which then flowed "uphill" toward metropoles where, in modern times, it contributed to processes of capital deepening that enabled industrial revolutions.[20] During the Cold War, by contrast, capital flowed "downhill" from metropole to (post) colony—at least until the gravity governing capital flows reversed over the course of the 1970s. Neoclassical economic theory dictated that capital would flow where it could reap the highest marginal returns, which after the devastation of the Second World War was beyond American borders. But the United States also presided over the creation of an international economic order favorable to the outward dissemination of capital, for instance by permitting nonreciprocal trade privileges and prohibiting dollar devaluation. From time to time, policymakers in Washington and other centers of capitalist power also deliberately funneled capital to accomplish their geopolitical objectives.[21] More broadly, whereas the Soviet bloc generally expanded its influence in the Third World by establishing ties with communist parties dedicated to Marxist-Leninist policies, the capitalist bloc proved highly accommodating of diverse forms of resource extraction and allocation, enabling it to enlist a wider array of counterrevolutionary movements in the Global South in its Cold War project.

This is precisely what transpired in Indonesia. The United States played a leading role in cohering the capitalist world behind a program of aid and investment for the New Order. The rhythms of aid disbursement then determined the scope, pace, and intensity of Suharto's domestic and regional Cold Wars. Capital flows could knit a Cold War bloc together because material power was more fungible than other forms of power. Suharto used material power to purchase mobilizational power, bringing untold numbers of students and youth onto the streets to protest against the faltering Sukarno regime. He also used material power to purchase coercive power, channeling materiel to the navy and air force to secure the loyalty of the divided military.[22] International capital functioned as an accelerant in Indonesia, guiding processes of political change in particular directions, notably toward the consolidation of the New Order and its partnership with the United States. By the time Suharto finally resigned, Indonesians had internalized the versatility of material power. Explaining the newly democratic state's inability to tame the oligarchs nurtured under Suharto, the finance minister lamented that "legitimacy is just one source of power. Money, weapons, and experience can also create power."[23]

But material power was not infinitely fungible. The nature of the international aid Suharto received shaped the nature of the regime he built. Indonesia received relatively little military aid as a percentage of overall aid. Less than 5 percent of all US aid to Indonesia in the four years after the birth of the Suharto regime (1966–1969) went toward military purposes. By contrast, about 45 percent of all US aid to Ethiopia in the four years following the rise of the Derg (1974–1977) went toward military purposes.[24] It is perhaps not surprising that the Derg continuously subjugated its population through terror while the New Order, after perpetrating a politicide, coopted its population through growth.[25] And given the New Order's violent origins and Indonesia's history of international aggression, it is worth remembering that the Suharto regime could have evolved into something far more terrifying had the capitalist world indulged the Indonesian army's more destructive impulses after the mass killings subsided.

Suharto's domestic and regional Cold Wars in turn reshaped the global Cold War. Consider the trajectory of the People's Republic of China. Suharto's eradication of the PKI and displacement of Sukarno meant the loss of Beijing's closest international ally.[26] Historian Taomo Zhou argues that the communist setback in Indonesia was politicized in China and "contributed to the growing sociopolitical mobilization during the early stages of the Cultural Revolution."[27] The chaos of the Cultural Revolution then undermined the planned economy, razed the remnants of the Confucian value system, and discredited Marxism as a political framework for China's modernization—sowing a profound alienation among high policymakers and ordinary people alike.[28] Meanwhile the Suharto regime helped entrench an array of anticommunist governments elsewhere in Southeast Asia. Beijing thus found itself facing a ring of hostile states—not only the anticommunist ASEAN states to the south but also India to the west; the Soviet Union to the north; Japan, South Korea, and Taiwan to the east.[29] What emerged in Beijing was a recognition that Mao Zedong's revolution had failed to achieve its utopian domestic objectives and its progressive-chauvinist international objectives. The People's Republic consequently pursued rapprochement with the United States and ceased providing aid to national liberation movements in Southeast Asia, which Chinese leaders had once called the "cradle of revolutions."[30] Soon thereafter, Deng Xiaoping embarked upon a program of reform and opening that signaled China's turn toward state capitalism.[31]

Suharto's Cold War thus contributed to a process that anthropologist Heonik Kwon calls the "decomposition of the Cold War"—the geographically and temporally uneven erosion of the Cold War as a social reality and the gradual elaboration of a post–Cold War era.[32] China's abandonment of its Cold War project of promoting socialist revolution meant that Cold War logic no longer defined Southeast Asia's regional order. The region escaped the surge of Cold War violence that tormented Africa and Latin America in the 1980s. Instead, the Third Indochina War pitted communist countries against each other and delivered another decade of strife to an already war-ravaged peninsula. In much the same way, a new generation of conflicts erupted in Southwest Asia, the epicenter of what American policymakers conceived as an "arc of crisis."[33] Historian Paul Thomas Chamberlin argues that these conflicts, too, signified a decomposition of the Cold War, as the clash of ideologies between capitalism and communism yielded to a "sectarian revolt" symbolized by the renascent power of political Islam.[34] Suharto's Cold War encouraged this shift in the engine of revolution, at least within Indonesia, as oppositionists gravitated toward Islamism to articulate grievances against the New Order. The inescapable conclusion is that Suharto's Cold War bore within itself the seeds of its own decay. The New Order's success in eradicating communism in Indonesia and containing communism in Southeast Asia ensured that novel problems would emerge for which the Cold War did not provide a compelling organizing framework.

The history of Suharto's Cold War reveals the afterlives of Cold War conflicts in the Global South. The ideological clash between capitalism and communism and the geopolitical conflict between the United States and the Soviet Union suffused the globe, fracturing societies, communities, and even families across the world. Elites across the Third World then tapped deep reservoirs of superpower resources, both material and ideational, to underwrite their domestic political struggles—often over ideology, but sometimes over race, religion, territory, and economy. Superpower aid and investment in the Global South built institutions, alleviated suffering, and promoted economic growth; but so too did it militarize societies, facilitate coercion, and undermine dissent. For Indonesia the legacy of the Cold War was ambiguous. If it is unlikely that Suharto could have established a regime as exclusionary as the New Order absent the global Cold War, it is also unlikely that the broad masses of Indonesians would be as prosperous as they are today absent the global Cold War. Like much of the Global South, Indonesia still lives in the Cold War's shadow.

NOTES

Abbreviations

AAD	Access to Archival Databases
ACDA	Arms Control and Disarmament Agency
AIPT	Department of Foreign Affairs and Trade, *Australia and the Incorporation of East Timor, 1974–1976* (Carlton Melbourne University Press, 2000)
ANM	Arkib Negara Malaysia
ANRI	Arsip Nasional Republik Indonesia
ASSUS	Asisten Sekretaris Negara Urusan Khusus (ASSUS), 1968–1976
BL	Bancroft Library, University of California at Berkeley
CUML	Columbia University Manuscript Library
CURML	Cornell University Rare and Manuscript Library.
EKUIN	Menteri Negara Bidang Ekonomi, Keuangan, dan Industri, 1966–1973
EOB	Executive Office Building
GFPL	Gerald Ford Presidential Library
H Files	NSC Institutional ("H") Files
HAK	Henry A. Kissinger Office Files
HAK Telcons	Henry A. Kissinger Telephone Conversation Transcripts (Telcons)
HB IX	Sekretariat Wakil Presiden Sri Sultan Hamengku Buwono IX, 1973–1978
HUA	Harvard University Archives
IMS	Subject Files of the Office of Indonesia, Malaysia, and Singapore Affairs, 1965–1974
Malik	Sekretariat Wakil Presiden Adam Malik, 1978–1982
NAA	National Archives of Australia
NSC	National Security Council
Polkam	Risalah Petunjuk-Petunjuk dan Putusan-Putusan Presiden pada Sidang Dewan Stabilisasi Politik dan Keamanan Nasional
PPS	Pidato Presiden Soeharto, 1966–1998
RG	Record Group
RNPL	Richard Nixon Presidential Library
Sekkab	Sekretariat Kabinet, 1966–1971
UKNA	United Kingdom National Archives
USNA	United States National Archives

Introduction

1. Abdul Gafar, *Siti Hartinah Soeharto: First Lady of Indonesia* (Jakarta: Citra Lamtoro Gung Persada, 1992), 202.
2. Soeharto, *Pikiran, Ucapan, dan Tindakan Saya: Otobiografi Seperti Dipaparkan kepada G. Dwipayana dan Ramadan K.H.* (Jakarta: Citra Lamtoro Gung Persada, 1989), 118–119.
3. "Selected Documents Relating to the 'September 30th Movement' and Its Epilogue," *Indonesia* no. 1 (April 1966): 134–135 (hereafter "Selected Documents").
4. Soeharto, *Pikiran*, 119–121.
5. "Selected Documents," 136–142.
6. Quoted in John Roosa, *Pretext for Mass Murder: The September 30th Movement and Suharto's Coup d'État in Indonesia* (Madison: University of Wisconsin Press, 2006), 51.
7. For interpretations of the September Thirtieth Movement see Angkatan Bersendjata Republik Indonesia, *40 Hari Kegagalan G-30-S* (Jakarta: Staf Pertahanan Keamanan, 1966); Nugroho Notosusanto and Ismail Saleh, *The Coup Attempt of the "September 30 Movement" in Indonesia* (Jakarta: Pembimbing Massa, 1968); Benedict Anderson and Ruth McVey, *A Preliminary Analysis of the October 1, 1965 Coup in Indonesia* (Ithaca, NY: Cornell Modern Indonesia Project, 1971); Douglas Kammen, "World Turned Upside Down: Benedict Anderson, Ruth McVey, and the 'Cornell Paper,'" *Indonesia* 104 (October 2017): 1–26; W. F. Wertheim, "Suharto and the Untung Coup—The Missing Link," *Journal of Contemporary Asia* 1, no. 1 (1970): 50–57; W. F. Wertheim, "Whose Plot?—New Light on the 1965 Events," *Journal of Contemporary Asia* 9, no. 2 (1979): 197–215; Geoffrey Robinson, *The Killing Season: A History of the Indonesian Massacres, 1965–66* (Princeton, NJ: Princeton University Press, 2018), 66–81; the most plausible interpretation remains Roosa, *Pretext*, 202–226.
8. Arnold Brackman, *The Communist Collapse in Indonesia* (New York: W. W. Norton, 1969), 98.
9. "Selected Documents," 158.
10. "Selected Documents," 151.
11. Robinson, *The Killing Season*; Jess Melvin, *The Army and the Indonesian Genocide: Mechanics of Mass Murder* (New York: Routledge, 2018); Douglas Kammen and Katherine McGregor, eds., *The Contours of Mass Violence in Indonesia, 1965–68* (Singapore: NUS Press, 2012); Vanessa Hearman, *Unmarked Graves: Death and Survival in the Anti-Communist Violence in East Java, Indonesia* (Singapore: NUS Press, 2018); Bradley Simpson, *Economists with Guns: Authoritarian Development and U.S.-Indonesian Relations, 1960–1968* (Stanford, CA: Stanford University Press, 2008); John Roosa, "The State of Knowledge about an Open Secret: Indonesia's Mass Disappearances of 1965–66," *Journal of Asian Studies* 75, no. 2 (May 2016): 281–297; Mark Winward, "Capture from Below: Civil-Military Relations during Indonesia's Anticommunist Violence, 1965–66," *Indonesia* 106 (October 2018): 111–136; Douglas Kammen and Faizah Zakaria, "Detention in Mass Violence: Policy and Practice in Indonesia, 1965–1968," *Critical Asian Studies* 44, no. 3 (2012): 441–466; Siddharth Chandra, "Glimpses of Indonesia's 1965 Massacre through the Lens of the Census: Migration and Refuge in East Java," *Indonesia* 104 (October 2017): 27–39; Siddharth Chandra, "New Findings on the Indonesian Killings of 1965–66," *Journal of Asian Studies* 76, no. 4 (November 2017): 1059–1086.
12. Quoted in Simpson, *Economists with Guns*, 146.
13. "Text of Secretary McNamara's Address on United States Policy in South Vietnam," *New York Times*, March 27, 1964.
14. Robin Hodess, "Introduction," in *Transparency International Global Corruption Report 2004* (Sterling, VA: Pluto Press, 2004), 13.
15. William Liddle, "Dua Wajah Orde Baru," *Tempo*, June 28, 2010.
16. Ruth McVey, "The Beamtenstaat in Indonesia," in *Interpreting Indonesian Politics: Thirteen Contributions to the Debate*, ed. Benedict Anderson and Audrey Kahin (Ithaca, NY: Cornell Southeast Asia Program Publications, 1982), 137–148; Benedict Anderson, "Old State, New Society: Indonesia's New Order in Comparative Historical Perspective," *Journal of Asian Studies* 42, no. 3 (May 1983): 477–496.
17. Karl Jackson, "Bureaucratic Polity: A Theoretical Framework for the Analysis of Power and Communications in Indonesia," in *Political Power and Communications in Indonesia*, ed. Karl

Jackson and Lucian Pye (Berkeley: University of California Press, 1978), 3–22; Harold Crouch, "Patrimonialism and Military Rule in Indonesia," *World Politics* 31, no. 4 (July 1979): 571–587; Dwight King, "Indonesia's New Order as a Bureaucratic Polity, a Neopatrimonial Regime or a Bureaucratic-Authoritarian Regime: What Differences Does It Make?," in *Interpreting Indonesian Politics*, 167–186; for a related debate over the extent of pluralism within the New Order see Donald Emmerson, "Understanding the New Order: Bureaucratic Pluralism in Indonesia," *Asian Survey* 23, no. 11 (November 1983): 1220–1241; William Liddle, "Soeharto's Indonesia: Personal Rule and Political Institutions," *Pacific Affairs* 58, no. 1 (Spring 1985): 68–90; William Liddle, "The Relative Autonomy of the Third World Politician: Soeharto and Indonesian Economic Development in Comparative Perspective," *International Studies Quarterly* 35, no. 4 (December 1991): 403–427; John Bresnan, *Managing Indonesia: The Modern Political Economy* (New York: Columbia University Press, 1993).

18. Benedict Anderson, "Exit Suharto: Obituary for a Mediocre Tyrant," *New Left Review* 50 (March–April 2008): 27–59; R. E. Elson, *Suharto: A Political Biography* (New York: Cambridge University Press, 2001); Margot Lyon, "Mystical Biography: Suharto and Kejawen in the Political Domain," in *Indonesian Political Biography: In Search of Cross-Cultural Understanding*, ed. Angus McIntyre (Clayton, Victoria: Monash University Centre for Southeast Asian Studies, 1993), 211–238.

19. Dan Slater, *Ordering Power: Contentious Politics and Authoritarian Leviathans in Southeast Asia* (New York: Cambridge University Press, 2010).

20. For a useful discussion of the complex statistics surrounding foreign investment see Hal Hill, *Foreign Investment and Industrialization in Indonesia* (New York: Oxford University Press, 1988), 33–40.

21. Rex Mortimer, "Indonesia: Growth or Development?," in *Showcase State: The Illusion of Indonesia's "Accelerated Modernisation,"* ed. Rex Mortimer (Sydney: Angus and Robertson, 1973).

22. Richard Robison, *Indonesia: The Rise of Capital* (Sydney: Allen & Unwin, 1986), 120, 349.

23. Jeffrey Winters, *Power in Motion: Capital Mobility and the Indonesian State* (Ithaca, NY: Cornell University Press, 1996); see also Jeffrey Winters, "Indonesia: The Rise of Capital: A Review Essay," *Indonesia* 45 (April 1988): 109–128.

24. Charles Tilly, *Coercion, Capital, and European States, AD 990–1992* (Cambridge: Blackwell, 1990), 99–103; see also Margaret Levi, *Of Rule and Revenue* (Berkeley: University of California Press, 1989).

25. Wen-Qing Ngoei, *Arc of Containment: Britain, the United States, and Anticommunism in Southeast Asia* (Ithaca, NY: Cornell University Press, 2019).

26. Charles A. Fisher, "Southeast Asia: The Balkans of the Orient?: A Study of Continuity and Change," *Geography* 47, no. 4 (November 1962): 347–367.

27. World Bank, *The East Asian Miracle: Economic Growth and Public Policy* (New York: Oxford University Press, 1993), 1–26; International Monetary Fund, *Directions of Trade: Yearbook* (Washington, DC: International Monetary Fund, 1967–1979).

28. See Ariel Armony, *Argentina, the United States, and the Anti-Communist Crusade in Central America, 1977–1984* (Columbus: Ohio University Center for International Studies, 1997); Tanya Harmer, *Allende's Chile and the Inter-American Cold War* (Chapel Hill: University of North Carolina Press, 2011); Tanya Harmer, "Brazil's Cold War in the Southern Cone, 1970–1975," *Cold War History* 12, no. 4 (November 2012): 659–681; Jamie Miller, *An African Volk: The Apartheid Regime and Its Search for Survival* (New York: Oxford University Press, 2016).

29. Lorenz Lüthi, *Cold Wars: Asia, the Middle East, Europe* (New York: Cambridge University Press, 2020); see also Lorenz Lüthi, ed., *The Regional Cold Wars in Europe, East Asia, and the Middle East: Crucial Periods and Turning Points* (Washington, DC: Woodrow Wilson Center Press, 2015).

30. Barry Buzan, Jaap de Wilde, and Ole Wæver, *Security: A New Framework for Analysis* (Boulder, CO: Lynne Rienner, 1998).

31. David Motadel, ed., *Revolutionary World: Global Upheaval in the Modern Age* (New York: Cambridge University Press, 2021); Jeremy Friedman, *Ripe for Revolution: Building Socialism in the Third World* (Cambridge, MA: Harvard University Press, 2022); Nicole

CuUnjieng Aboitiz, *Asian Place, Filipino Nation: A Global Intellectual History of the Philippine Revolution, 1887–1912* (New York: Columbia University Press, 2020); Matthew Galway, *The Emergence of Global Maoism: China's Red Evangelism and the Cambodian Communist Movement, 1959–1979* (Ithaca, NY: Cornell University Press, 2022); Tim Harper, *Underground Asia: Global Revolutionaries and the Assault on Empire* (Cambridge, MA: Harvard University Press, 2020); John Sidel, *Republicanism, Communism, Islam: Cosmopolitan Origins of Revolution in Southeast Asia* (Ithaca, NY: Cornell University Press, 2021); see also Samuel Huntington, *The Third Wave: Democratization in the Late Twentieth Century* (Norman: University of Oklahoma Press, 1991).

32. An exception is the literature on the diffusion of corporatism between Europe and Latin America. See António Costa Pinto and Federico Finchelstein, eds., *Authoritarianism and Corporatism in Europe and Latin America: Crossing Borders* (New York: Routledge, 2020); for theoretical elaborations see Thomas Ambrosio, "Constructing a Framework of Authoritarian Diffusion: Concepts, Dynamics, and Future Research," *International Studies Perspectives* 11 (2010): 375–392; Marianne Kneuer and Thomas Demmelhuber, "Gravity Centres of Authoritarian Rule: A Conceptual Approach," *Democratization* 23, no. 5 (2016): 775–796.

33. Odd Arne Westad, *The Global Cold War: Third World Interventions and the Making of Our Times* (New York: Cambridge University Press, 2004), 86–97, 152–157.

34. See David Painter and Gregory Brew, *The Struggle for Iran: Oil, Autocracy and the Cold War, 1951–1954* (Chapel Hill: University of North Carolina Press, 2023); Greg Grandin, *The Last Colonial Massacre: Latin America in the Cold War* (Chicago: University of Chicago Press, 2004); Thomas C. Field Jr., *From Development to Dictatorship: Bolivia and the Alliance for Progress in the Kennedy Era* (Ithaca, NY: Cornell University Press, 2014); Simpson, *Economists with Guns*; for vertical versus horizontal logics see Seva Gunitsky, "Democratic Waves in Historical Perspective," *Perspectives on Politics* 16, no. 3 (September 2018): 634–651.

35. Jeffrey James Byrne, *Mecca of Revolution: Algeria, Decolonization, and the Third World Order* (New York: Oxford University Press, 2016).

36. See David Bourchier, *Illiberal Democracy in Indonesia: The Ideology of the Family State* (New York: Routledge, 2015); Richard Tanter, "Intelligence Agencies and Third World Militarization: A Case Study of Indonesia, 1966–1989, with Special Reference to South Korea, 1961–1989" (PhD diss., Monash University, 1991); Sulfikar Amir, *The Technological State in Indonesia: The Co-Constitution of High Technology and Authoritarian Politics* (New York: Routledge, 2015).

37. Colleen Woods, *Freedom Incorporated: Anticommunism and Philippine Independence in the Age of Decolonization* (Ithaca, NY: Cornell University Press, 2020).

38. John Ravenhill, "East Asian Regionalism: Much Ado about Nothing?," *Review of International Studies* 35 (2009): 215–235.

39. Michael Leifer, *ASEAN and the Security of South-East Asia* (London: Routledge, 1989).

40. Amitav Acharya, *Constructing a Security Community in Southeast Asia: ASEAN and the Problem of Regional Order*, 2nd ed. (New York: Routledge, 2001).

41. John Lewis Gaddis, *Strategies of Containment: A Critical Appraisal of American National Security Policy During the Cold War*, rev. ed. (New York: Oxford University Press, 2002); Raymond B. Garthoff, *Détente and Confrontation: American-Soviet Relations from Nixon to Reagan* (Washington, DC: Brookings Institution, 1985).

42. Francis J. Gavin, *Gold, Dollars, and Power: The Politics of International Monetary Relations, 1958–1971* (Chapel Hill: University of North Carolina Press, 2004); Barry Eichengreen, *Globalizing Capital: A History of the International Monetary System*, 2nd ed. (Princeton, NJ: Princeton University Press, 2008); Judith Stein, *Pivotal Decade: How the United States Traded Factories for Finance in the Seventies* (New Haven, CT: Yale University Press, 2010); Niall Ferguson, Charles Maier, Erez Manela, and Daniel Sargent, eds., *The Shock of the Global: The 1970s in Perspective* (Cambridge, MA: Belknap Press, 2010); Greta Krippner, *Capitalizing on Crisis: The Political Origins of the Rise of Finance* (Cambridge, MA: Harvard University Press, 2011); Daniel Sargent, *A Superpower Transformed: The Remaking of American Foreign Relations in the 1970s* (New York: Oxford University Press, 2015).

43. Terry Anderson, *The Movement and the Sixties: Protest in America from Greensboro to Wounded Knee* (New York: Oxford University Press, 1996); Jeremi Suri, *Power and Protest: Global*

Revolution and the Rise of Détente (Cambridge, MA: Harvard University Press, 2003); Roderick MacFarquhar and Michael Schoenhals, *Mao's Last Revolution* (Cambridge, MA: Belknap Press, 2006); Daniel Rodgers, *Age of Fracture* (Cambridge, MA: Belknap Press, 2011); Shen Zhihua and Li Danhui, *After Leaning to One Side: China and Its Allies in the Cold War* (Washington, DC: Woodrow Wilson Center Press, 2011); Jeremy Friedman, *Shadow Cold War: The Sino-Soviet Competition for the Third World* (Chapel Hill: University of North Carolina Press, 2014).

44. John Lewis Gaddis, *The Long Peace: Inquiries into the History of the Cold War* (New York: Oxford University Press, 1987); Westad, *Global Cold War*, 398; see also Paul Thomas Chamberlin, *The Cold War's Killing Fields: Rethinking the Long Peace* (New York: Harper, 2018), 6, 175–182.

45. Heonik Kwon, *The Other Cold War* (New York: Columbia University Press, 2010).

46. David Engerman, *The Price of Aid: The Economic Cold War in India* (Cambridge, MA: Harvard University Press, 2018), 2–3.

47. James Scott, *Seeing like a State: How Certain Conditions to Improve the Human Condition Have Failed* (New Haven, CT: Yale University Press, 1998).

48. Bresnan, *Managing Indonesia*, 105; for the importance of statistics to governmentality see Adam Tooze, *Statistics and the German State, 1900–1945* (New York: Cambridge University Press, 2001); Arunabh Ghosh, *Making It Count: Statistics and Statecraft in the Early People's Republic of China* (Princeton, NJ: Princeton University Press, 2020).

49. Jennifer Alexander and Anne Booth, "The Service Sector," in *The Oil Boom and After: Indonesian Economic Policy and Performance in the Soeharto Era*, ed. Anne Booth (New York: Oxford University Press, 1992), 293–295.

50. Robert McMahon, "Introduction," in *The Cold War in the Third World*, ed. Robert McMahon (New York: Oxford University Press, 2013), 4.

51. Lorenz Lüthi, *Cold Wars: Asia, the Middle East, Europe* (New York: Cambridge University Press, 2020).

52. For a similar analysis of contradictions within "the politics of nation building" see Edward Miller, *Misalliance: Ngo Dinh Diem, the United States, and the Fate of South Vietnam* (Cambridge, MA: Harvard University Press, 2013).

53. John Lewis Gaddis, *The Landscape of History: How Historians Map the Past* (New York: Oxford University Press, 2002), xi, 92–109.

54. Melvin, *The Army and the Indonesian Genocide*, 298.

55. This is not to say that resistance was not present. For resistance within Indonesia see Robinson, *Killing Season*; for resistance beyond Indonesia see Katharine McGregor, "The World Was Silent?: Global Communities of Resistance to the 1965 Repression in the Cold War Era," in *Truth, Silence, and Violence in Emerging States: Histories of the Unspoken*, ed. Aidan Russell (London: Routledge, 2018), 147–168.

Chapter 1

1. Takashi Shiraishi, *An Age in Motion: Popular Radicalism in Java, 1912–1926* (Ithaca, NY: Cornell University Press, 1990).

2. The two preceding paragraphs draw on Soeharto, *Pikiran*, 6–25; and David Jenkins, *Young Soeharto: The Making of a Soldier, 1921–1945* (Singapore: ISEAS Yusof Ishak Institute, 2021), 1–123.

3. Benedict Anderson, "Japan: The Light of Asia," in *Southeast Asia in World War II: Four Essays*, ed. Josef Silverstein (New Haven, CT: Yale University Southeast Asia Studies, 1966), 13–50..

4. Bourchier, *Illiberal Democracy in Indonesia*, 93.

5. Rudolf Mrázek, *The United States and the Indonesian Military, 1945–1965: A Study of an Intervention*, Vol. I (Prague: Oriental Institute, 1978), 13–28.

6. Dewi Fortuna Anwar, *Indonesia's Strategic Culture: Ketahanan Nasional, Wawasan Nusantara and Hankamrata* (Queensland: Griffith University Centre for the Study of Australia–Asia Relations, 1996), 13–14.

7. Nugroho Notosusanto, *Pemberontakan Tentera Peta Blitar Melawan Djepang, 14 Pebruari 1945* (Jakarta: Departemen Pertahanan-Keamanan—Lembaga Sedjarah Hankam, 1968);

Shigeru Sato, "Gatot Mangkupraja, PETA, and the Origins of the Indonesian National Army," *Bijdragen Tot de Taal-, Land- en Volkenkunde* 166, no. 2–3 (2010): 189–217.

8. Soeharto, *Pikiran*, 25.

9. Christopher Bayly and Tim Harper, *Forgotten Wars: Freedom and Revolution in Southeast Asia* (Cambridge, MA: Belknap Press, 2007).

10. Sukarno, "Nasionalisme, Islamisme, dan Marxisme," in *Nasionalisme, Islamisme, Marxisme*, ed. Yanuar Arifin (Yogyakarta: IRCiSoD, 2021), 9–45.

11. J. D. Legge, *Sukarno: A Political Biography* (London: Allen Lane, 1972), Kindle locations 3523–3591.

12. Fredrik Logevall, *Embers of War: The Fall of an Empire and the Making of America's Vietnam* (New York: Random House, 2012), 175.

13. F. E. Crockett, "How the Troubles Began in Java," *Harper's*, March 1946, 281–282.

14. Selosoemardjan, *Social Changes in Jogjakarta* (Ithaca, NY: Cornell University Press, 1962), 59–72.

15. Soeharto, *Pikiran*, 29.

16. Abdul Haris Nasution, *Tentara Nasional Indonesia* (Bandung: Ganaco, 1963), 154–155; for Islamic *lasykar* see Kevin Fogg, *Indonesia's Islamic Revolution* (New York: Cambridge University Press, 2020), 66–78.

17. Soeharto, *Pikiran*, 31–34.

18. Sutan Sjahrir, *Perjuangan Kita* (Jakarta: Pusat Dokumentasi Politik "Guntur 49," 1995).

19. Benedict Anderson, *Java in a Time of Revolution: Occupation and Resistance, 1944–1946* (Ithaca, NY: Cornell University Press, 1972), 232–268.

20. Elson, *Suharto*, 17–20; for a broader narrative of the so-called July Third Affair see Anderson, *Java in a Time of Revolution*, 370–403.

21. Robert McMahon, *Colonialism and Cold War: The United States and the Struggle for Indonesian Independence, 1945–49* (Ithaca, NY: Cornell University Press, 1981), 130–132.

22. Elson, *Suharto*, 21–22; Robert Cribb, "Opium in the Indonesian Revolution," *Modern Asian Studies* 22, no. 4 (1988): 701–722; Richard Borsuk and Nancy Chng, *Liem Sioe Liong's Salim Group: The Business Pillar of Suharto's Indonesia* (Singapore: ISEAS-Yusof Ishak Institute, 2014), 41–46.

23. Soeharto, *Pikiran*, 41.

24. Samuel Crowl, "Indonesia's Diplomatic Revolution: Lining Up for Non-Alignment, 1945–1955," in *Connecting Histories: Decolonization and the Cold War in Southeast Asia, 1945–1962*, ed. Christopher Goscha and Christian Ostermann (Washington, DC: Woodrow Wilson Center Press, 2009), 238–257; for Indonesian advocacy in Australia and the Middle East, respectively, see Mohamad Bondan, *Genderang Proklamasi di Luar Negeri* (Jakarta: KAWAL, 1971); and Muhammad Zein Hassan, *Diplomasi Revolusi Indonesia di Luar Negeri* (Jakarta: Bulan Bintang, 1980).

25. See Chiara Formichi, Islam and the Making of the Nation: Kartosuwiryo and Political Islam in 20th Century Indonesia (Leiden: KITLV Press, 2012), 109–144.

26. George Kahin, *Nationalism and Revolution in Indonesia* (Ithaca, NY: Cornell University Press, 1952), 252.

27. See Abdul Haris Nasution, *Pokok-Pokok Gerilya dan Pertahanan Republik Indonesia dimasa jang Lalu dan jang Akan Datang* (Jakarta: Pembimbing, 1954).

28. Kahin, *Nationalism and Revolution*, 256–303; David Charles Anderson, "The Military Aspects of the Madiun Affair," *Indonesia* 21 (April 1976): 1–63; Ann Swift, *The Road to Madiun: The Indonesian Communist Uprising of 1948* (Ithaca, NY: Cornell Modern Indonesia Project, 1989); Karl Hack and Geoff Wade, "The Origins of the Southeast Asian Cold War," *Journal of Southeast Asian Studies* 40, no. 3 (October 2009): 441–448; Harry Poeze, "The Cold War in Indonesia, 1948," *Journal of Southeast Asian Studies* 40, no. 3 (October 2009): 497–517; Larisa Efimova, "Did the Soviet Union Instruct Southeast Asian Communists to Revolt? New Russian Evidence on the Calcutta Youth Conference of February 1948," *Journal of Southeast Asian Studies* 40, no. 3 (October 2009): 449–469.

29. Soeharto, *Pikiran*, 53.

30. Kahin, *Nationalism and Revolution*, 291–293.

31. Soeharto, *Pikiran*, 56–64; Elson, *Suharto*, 33–38.

32. Harold Crouch, *The Army and Politics in Indonesia*, rev. ed. (Ithaca, NY: Cornell University Press, 1988), 25.
33. Ulf Sundhaussen and C. L. M. Penders, *Abdul Haris Nasution: A Political Biography* (St. Lucia: University of Queensland Press, 1985), 75.
34. NSC-51: U.S. Policy toward Southeast Asia, July 1, 1949, *U.S. Declassified Documents Online*, Document CK2349354016 (accessed July 20, 2022).
35. McMahon, *Colonialism and Cold War*, 292–295.
36. Elson, *Suharto*, 46–49.
37. Anne Booth, *Economic Change in Modern Indonesia: Colonial and Post-colonial Comparisons* (Cambridge: Cambridge University Press, 2016), 38.
38. Herbert Feith, *The Decline of Constitutional Democracy in Indonesia* (Ithaca, NY: Cornell University Press, 1962), 199.
39. Feith, *Decline of Constitutional Democracy*, 256–257.
40. For a narrative of the October Seventeenth Affair and its aftermath see Ulf Sundhaussen, *The Road to Power: Indonesian Military Politics 1945–1967* (New York: Oxford University Press, 1982), 62–77; for a critique of "bapakism" within the regional commands see Abdul Haris Nasution, *Tjatatan-tjatatan sekitar Politik Militer Indonesia* (Djakarta: Pembimbing, 1955), 328–331.
41. Soeharto, *Pikiran*, 87.
42. Elson, *Suharto*, 55–56.
43. Joel Rocamora, "Nationalism in Search of Ideology: The Indonesian Nationalist Party, 1945–1965" (PhD diss., Cornell University, 1974), 49–53, 68–91, 99–102.
44. Friedman, *Ripe for Revolution*, 34–42.
45. Robin Bush, *Nahdlatul Ulama and the Struggle for Power within Islam and Politics in Indonesia* (Singapore: Institute of Southeast Asian Studies, 2009), 43–49.
46. Herbert Feith, *The Indonesian Elections of 1955* (Ithaca, NY: Cornell Modern Indonesia Project, 1957), 62.
47. Feith, *Decline of Constitutional Democracy*, 384–385.
48. Sukarno, "Opening Address," in *Asia-Africa Speak from Bandung* (Jakarta: Ministry of Foreign Affairs, 1955), 19–29.
49. Legge, *Sukarno*, Kindle location 4980.
50. Ganis Harsono, *Recollections of an Indonesian Diplomat in the Sukarno Era* (St. Lucia: University of Queensland Press, 1977), 145.
51. "Indonesians Sign Soviet Loan Pact," *New York Times*, September 16, 1956.
52. Sukarno with Cindy Adams, *Sukarno: An Autobiography* (New York: Bobbs-Merrill, 1965), 297–298.
53. Hong Liu, "Constructing a China Metaphor: Sukarno's Perception of the PRC and Indonesia's Political Transformation," *Journal of Southeast Asian Studies* 28, no. 1 (March 1997): 27–46.
54. Sukarno, "Let Us Bury the Parties," in *Indonesian Political Thinking, 1945–1965*, ed. Herbert Feith and Lance Castles (Ithaca, NY: Cornell University Press, 1970), 81–83.
55. Quoted in Sundhaussen, *Road to Power*, 81.
56. Feith, *Decline of Constitutional Democracy*, 397–402; Sundhaussen, *Road to Power*, 84–85.
57. Barbara Harvey, *Permesta: Half a Rebellion* (Ithaca, NY: Cornell Southeast Asia Program Publications, 1977), 164–167.
58. Feith, *Decline of Constitutional Democracy*, 443–444; Penders and Sundhaussen, *Nasution*, 91–102; Crouch, *Army and Politics*, 31; Ruth McVey, "The Post-Revolutionary Transformation of the Indonesian Military," *Indonesia* no. 11 (April 1971): 157–176; John Smail, "The Military Politics of North Sumatra, December 1956–October 1957," *Indonesia* no. 6 (October 1968): 128–187; Barbara Harvey, "Tradition, Islam, and Rebellion: South Sulawesi 1950–1965" (PhD diss., Cornell University, 1974), 272–383.
59. Sukarno, "Saving the Republic of the Proclamation," in *Indonesian Political Thinking*, 83–89.
60. Abdul Haris Nasution, "Apa Sebabnja Saja Bersedia Mendjadi Tjalon IP-KI," in *Menjongsong Kongres Nasional ke III–IP-KI di Surabaja* (Jakarta: Ikatan Pendukung Kemerdekaan Indonesia, 1961), 54.
61. See Daniel Lev, *The Transition to Guided Democracy: Indonesian Politics, 1957–1959* (Ithaca, NY: Cornell University Press, 1966).

62. Legge, *Sukarno*, Kindle location 5408.
63. Anne Booth, *The Indonesian Economy in the Nineteenth and Twentieth Centuries: A History of Missed Opportunities* (Basingstoke: Macmillan Press, 1998), 175.
64. "To Safeguard the State," in Abdul Haris Nasution, *Towards a People's Army* (Jakarta: C. V. Delegasi, 1964), 15.
65. See Charles Kraus, "'The Danger is Two-Fold': Decolonisation and Cold War in Anti-Communist Asia, 1955–7," *International History Review* 39, no. 2 (2017): 256–273; Hao Chen, "Resisting Bandung? Taiwan's Struggle for 'Representational Legitimacy' in the Rise of the Asian Peoples' Anti-Communist League," *International History Review* 43, no. 2 (2021): 244–263; S. R. Joey Long, *Safe for Decolonization: The Eisenhower Administration, Britain and Singapore* (Kent, OH: Kent State University Press, 2011); Joseph Chinyong Liow, "Tunku Abdul Rahman and Malaya's Relations with Indonesia, 1957–60," *Journal of Southeast Asian Studies* 36, no. 1 (2005): 87–109; Kenneth Conboy and James Morrison, *Feet to the Fire: CIA Covert Action in Indonesia* (Annapolis, MD: Naval Institute Press, 1999); Audrey Kahin and George McTurnan Kahin, *Subversion as Foreign Policy: The Secret Eisenhower and Dulles Debacle in Indonesia* (New York: New Press, 1995).
66. Feith, *Decline of Constitutional Democracy*, 585.
67. Ragna Boden, "Cold War Economics: Soviet Aid to Indonesia," *Journal of Cold War Studies* 10, no. 3 (Summer 2008): 116.
68. Ruth McVey, "The Post-Revolutionary Transformation of the Indonesian Army: Part II," *Indonesia* no. 13 (April 1972): 147–181; Crouch, *Army and Politics*, 33–51.
69. Quoted in Sundhaussen, *Road to Power*, 126.
70. Herbert Feith, "Dynamics of Guided Democracy," in *Indonesia*, ed. Ruth McVey (New Haven, CT: Yale University Press, 1963), 357; see also David Jenkins, "The Evolution of Indonesian Army Doctrinal Thinking: The Concept of *Dwifungsi*," *Southeast Asian Journal of Social Science* 11, no. 2 (1983): 15–30.
71. Legge, *Sukarno*, Kindle location 6411.
72. Rex Mortimer, *Indonesian Communism under Sukarno: Ideology and Politics, 1959–1965* (Ithaca, NY: Cornell University Press, 1974), 65–76.
73. Friedman, *Shadow Cold War*, Kindle location 1341–1359; Mortimer, *Indonesian Communism*, 175–202; David Webster, "Self-Determination Abandoned: The Road to the New York Agreement on West New Guinea (Papua), 1960–62," *Indonesia* no. 95 (April 2013): 9–24.
74. McVey, "Post-Revolutionary Transformation: Part II," 166.
75. Mrázek, *The United States and the Indonesian Military*, Vol. I, 124; Farabi Fakih, *Authoritarian Modernization in Indonesia's Early Independence Period: The Foundations of Guided Democracy* (Leiden: Brill, 2020), 60–66.
76. M. Panggabean, *Berjuang dan Mengabdi* (Jakarta: Pustaka Sinar Harapan, 1993), 227–228; Suparwan G. Parikesit and Krisna R. Sempurnadjaja, *H. Alamsjah Ratu Perwiranegara: Perjalanan Hidup Seorang Anak Yatim Piatu* (Jakarta: Pustaka Sinar Harapan, 1995), 139.
77. Memorandum, Joint Chiefs of Staff to Secretary of Defense, September 22, 1958, U.S. *Declassified* Documents Online, Document CK2349460409 (accessed July 20, 2022).
78. Simpson, *Economists with Guns*, 46–49, 62–86.
79. A paradigmatic articulation of the argument that stresses US influence on army plans is Peter Dale Scott, "Exporting Military-Economic Development," in *Ten Years' Military Terror in Indonesia*, ed. Malcolm Caldwell (Nottingham: Spokesman Books, 1975), 209–261.
80. Disjarahdam VI/Siliwangi, *Siliwangi dari Masa ke Masa*, 2nd ed. (Bandung: Angkasa, 1979), 349–351.
81. Bryan Evans III, "The Influence of the United States on the Development of the Indonesian Army (1954–1964)," *Indonesia* no. 47 (April 1989): 38.
82. Sundhaussen, *Road to Power*, 150–153.
83. See Herbert Feith, "President Soekarno, the Army, and the Communists: The Triangle Changes Shape," *Asian Survey* 4, no. 8 (August 1964): 969–980.
84. Soeharto, *Pikiran*, 88.
85. Quoted in Sundhaussen, *Road to Power*, 106.
86. Soeharto, *Pikiran*, 90–91.
87. Elson, *Suharto*, 70–71.

88. Soeharto, *Pikiran*, 89–90, 92.
89. Elson, *Suharto*, 60–66; Christopher M. Barr, "Bob Hasan, The Rise of Apkindo, and the Shifting Dynamics of Control in Indonesia's Timber Sector," *Indonesia* no. 65 (April 1998): 2–4.
90. Farabi, *Authoritarian Modernization*, 56–60.
91. Elson, *Suharto*, 71–74;
92. Sundhaussen, *Road to Power*, 137–143; Elson, *Suharto*, 76–79.
93. Elson, *Suharto*, 80–87; Soeharto, *Pikiran*, 109.
94. Abdul Haris Nasution, *Memenuhi Panggilan Tugas, Jilid V: Kenangan Masa Orde Lama* (Jakarta: Gunung Agung, 1985), 214; for a different interpretation that stresses a cleavage between offensively and defensively inclined army officers see Rudolf Mrázek, *The United States and the Indonesian Military, 1945–1965: A Study of an Intervention*, Vol. II (Prague: Oriental Institute, 1978), 35–50.
95. For Yani's life see Ismail B.D., ed., Seorang Peradjurit Meninggalkan Kita: Biografi Singkat Djenderal Anumerta Ahmad Yani (Jakarta: Sasmita Loks 1967).
96. J. A. C. Mackie, *Problems of the Indonesian Inflation* (Ithaca, NY: Cornell Modern Indonesia Project, 1967), 54–55.
97. Friedman, *Ripe for Revolution*, 60; Frederick P. Bunnell, "Guided Democracy Foreign Policy, 1960–1965: President Sukarno Moves from Non-Alignment to Confrontation," *Indonesia*, no. 2 (October 1966): 57–58.
98. Sukarno, "Deklarasi Ekonomi," in D. N. Aidit, *Dekon dalam Udjian* (Jakarta: Jajasan Pembaruan, 1963), 101–113.
99. Mackie, *Problems of the Indonesian Inflation*, 64–70.
100. "Selamatkan Dekon! Bersamaan dengan Itu Ringkus dan Ganjang Kontra-Revolusi!" in *Dekon dalam Udjian*, 93–100.
101. D. N. Aidit, *PKI dan Angkatan Darat (SESKOAD)* (Jakarta: Jajasan Pembaruan, 1963), 29–32.
102. D. N. Aidit, "Daring, Daring, Once Again Daring: Political Report to the First Plenary Session of the Central Committee of the Communist Party of Indonesia, 10 February 1963," in *Problems of the Indonesian Revolution* (Bandung: Demos, 1963).
103. "Indonesia Facing Red Power Test," *New York Times*, January 16, 1963.
104. Matthew Jones, *Conflict and Confrontation in South East Asia, 1961–1965: Britain, the United States, Indonesia, and the Creation of Malaysia* (New York: Cambridge University Press, 2001), 61.
105. "West Irian's Nationalism: Indonesian Minister Questions the Separatist Movement," *New York Times*, November 17, 1961.
106. Partai Komunis Indonesia, *Strengthen National Unity and Communist Unity: Documents of the Third Plenum of the Central Committee of the Communist Party of Indonesia* (Jakarta: Jajasan Pembaruan, 1962), 58–61.
107. Mrázek, *The United States and the Indonesian Military*, Vol. II, 94–113; Nasution, *Towards a People's Army*, 115–116.
108. Jones, *Conflict and Cooperation*, 195–199.
109. J. A. C. Mackie, *Konfrontasi: The Indonesia-Malaysia Dispute, 1963–1966* (Kuala Lumpur: Oxford University Press, 1974), 179.
110. Friedman, *Ripe for Revolution*, 59–61; Taomo Zhou, *Migration in the Time of Revolution: China, Indonesia, and the Cold War* (Ithaca, NY: Cornell University Press, 2019), 136–141.
111. Quoted in Mortimer, *Indonesian Communism*, 228, 230.
112. Sundhaussen, *Road to Power*, 192–193.
113. Selosoemardjan, "Land Reform in Indonesia," *Asian Survey* 1, no. 2 (February 1962): 23–30; E. Utrecht, "Land Reform in Indonesia," *Bulletin of Indonesian Economic Studies* 5, no. 3 (November 1969): 71–88.
114. Mortimer, *Indonesian Communism*, 276–328.
115. See *"Gerakan 30 September" Dihadapan Mahmillub, Perkara Dr. Subandrio*, Vol. 1 (Jakarta: Pusat Pendidikan Kehakiman A.D., 1967), 102–103; Sundhaussen, *Road to Power*, 199–200.
116. Simpson, *Economists with Guns*, 152–155.

117. Soekarno, *Tjapailah Bintang-Bintang Dilangit: Tahun Berdikari* (Jakarta: Departemen Penerangan, 1965).
118. For an elaboration of this thesis see Peter Christian Hauswedell, "Sukarno: Radical or Conservative? Indonesian Politics 1964–5," *Indonesia* no. 15 (April 1973): 109–143.
119. Central Intelligence Agency, *Indonesia—1965: The Coup That Backfired* (Washington, DC: CIA, 1968), 190–191.
120. Roosa, *Pretext*, 189–191.
121. Quoted in Roosa, *Pretext*, 189–190.
122. Quoted in Theodore Friend, *Indonesian Destinies* (Cambridge, MA: Belknap Press, 2003), 102. Italics in original.
123. Katharine McGregor, "A Reassessment of the Significance of the 1948 Madiun Uprising to the Cold War in Indonesia," *Kajian Malaysia* 27, no. 1–2 (2009): 103.
124. Robinson, *Killing Season*, 16.
125. Soeharto, *Pikiran*, 117.
126. Roosa, *Pretext*, 202–225.
127. Daniel Lev, "Indonesia 1965: The Year of the Coup," *Asian Survey* 6, no. 2 (February 1966): 105.

Chapter 2

1. See "Survey of Recent Developments," *Bulletin of Indonesian Economic Studies* 2, no. 3 (February 1966): 1–26.
2. B. Wiwoho and Bandjar Chaeruddin, *Memori Jenderal Yoga* (Jakarta: Pt. Bina Rena Pariwara, 1990), 148, 153.
3. "Selected Documents," 184.
4. Panggabean, *Berjuang dan Mengabdi*, 302–303.
5. Crouch, *Army and Politics*, 138.
6. "Mayjen Soeharto Saksikan Pengangkatan Pahlawan Revolusi," October 4, 1965, in *Jejak Langkah Pak Harto 01 Oktober 1965–27 Maret 1968*, ed. G. Dwipayana and Nazarudin Sjamsuddin (Jakarta: Citra Kharisma Bunda, 2003) (hereafter *Jejak Langkah 1965–68*), 8–9.
7. Soeharto, *Pikiran*, 134; Elson, *Suharto*, 109.
8. Pusat Penerangan Angkatan Darat, *Fakta-Fakta Persoalan Sekitar "Gerakan 30 September,"* *Penerbitan Chusus no. 1*, October 5, 1965.
9. Tarzie Vittachi, *The Fall of Sukarno* (New York: Frederick A. Praeger, 1967), 110–112.
10. The autopsy reports that surfaced twenty years later revealed no signs of torture. See Benedict Anderson, "How Did the Generals Die?" *Indonesia* no. 43 (April 1987): 110–111.
11. Benedict Anderson, "Impunity and Reenactment: Reflections on the 1965 Massacre in Indonesia and Its Legacy," *Asia-Pacific Journal* 11, no. 4 (April 2013): 6; Michael van Langenburg, "Gestapu and State Power," in *The Indonesian Mass Killings 1965–1966: Studies from Java and Bali*, ed. Robert Cribb (Clayton: Monash University Centre of Southeast Asian Studies, 1990), 46.
12. Wiwoho and Bandjar, *Memori Jenderal Yoga*, 165
13. Krisna R. Sempurnadjaja, ed., *H. Alamsjah Ratu Perwiranegara 70 Tahun: Pesan dan Kesan* (Jakarta: Pustaka Sinar Harapan, 1995), 83–84.
14. "Selected Documents," 204.
15. Telegram, Jakarta to State, October 8, 1965, POL 23-9 INDON, Central Files 1964–66, RG 59, USNA; John Hughes, *Indonesian Upheaval* (New York: D. McKay Co., 1967), 132–133.
16. Quoted in Melvin, *The Army and the Indonesian Genocide*, 126.
17. Melvin, *The Army and the Indonesian Genocide*, 110–240.
18. For a critical discussion about the temporal and spatial variation in the violence see Robinson, *The Killing Season*, 149–152.
19. Telegram, Jakarta to State, October 10, 1965, in *Foreign Relations of the United States, 1964–1968*, Vol. XXVI: *Indonesia; Malaysia-Singapore; Philippines* (hereafter FRUS with year and volume information), Document 151.
20. Telegram, Jakarta to State, October 14, 1965, in *FRUS 1964–68:26*, Document 154.

21. Bradley Simpson, "International Dimensions of the 1965–68 Violence in Indonesia," in *The Contours of Mass Violence in Indonesia, 1965–68*, ed. Douglas Kammen and Katherine McGregor (Honolulu: University of Hawai'i Press, 2012), 56–62.

22. Telegram, Jakarta to State, October 5, 1965, in *FRUS 1964–68:26*, Document 147.

23. Inward Cablegram, Jakarta to Department of External Affairs, November 9, 1965, A7133 1/2, Indonesia 2, NAA.

24. CIA Report, Jakarta to White House, October 8, 1965, quoted in Geoffrey Robinson, *The Dark Side of Paradise: Political Violence in Bali* (Ithaca, NY: Cornell University Press, 1995), 283.

25. Telegram, Jakarta to State, October 14, 1965, in *FRUS 1964–68:26*, Document 155.

26. Telegram, State to Jakarta, October 22, 1965, in *FRUS 1964–68:26*, Document 159.

27. Telegram, Jakarta to State, November 1, 1965, in *FRUS 1964–68:26*, Document 165.

28. Telegram, Jakarta to State, November 1, 1965, in *FRUS 1964–68:26*, Document 165.

29. Telegram, State to Bangkok, November 4, 1965, in *FRUS 1964–68:26*, Document 170.

30. Telegram, Bangkok to State, November 5, 1965, in *FRUS 1964–68:26*, Document 171; Telegram, Medan to State, November 16, 1965, in *FRUS 1964–68:26*, Document 174.

31. Telegram, Medan to State, November 16, 1965, in *FRUS 1964–68:26*, Document 174; Memorandum Prepared for the 303 Committee, November 17, 1965, in *FRUS 1964–68:26*, Document 175.

32. Telegram, Jakarta to State, December 2, 1965, in *FRUS 1964–68:26*, Document 179.

33. "US Officials' Lists Aided Indonesian Bloodbath in '60s," *Washington Post*, May 21, 1990.

34. Cablegram, Jakarta to Department of External Affairs, December 19, 1965, A1209 1962/817 Part 2, United States and Western Aid to Indonesia, NAA.

35. Wiwoho and Bandjar, *Memori Jenderal Yoga*, 153.

36. Soeharto, *Pikiran*, 129–132.

37. "Selected Documents," 152.

38. "Selected Documents," 153.

39. "Selected Documents," 143.

40. "Selected Documents," 159.

41. Soeharto, *Pikiran*, 138.

42. "Atas Nama Presiden Soekarno, Letjen. Soeharto Keluarkan Instruksi Pembersihan Pemerintah dari Unsur G.30.S/PKI," November 15, 1965, in *Jejak Langkah 1965–68*, 24.

43. "Bertempat di War Room, Jenderal Soeharto Hadiri Rapat Pimpinan Angkatan Dipimpin Jenderal Nasution," December 2, 1965, in *Jejak Langkah 1965–68*, 31-32.

44. "Jenderal Soeharto: Tidak Lagi di Bawah Mendagri, BPI Berada dalam Komando Pembangunan," December 15, 1965, in *Jejak Langkah 1965–68*, 33.

45. Wiwoho and Bandjar, *Memori Jenderal Yoga*, 161.

46. Quoted in Jenkins, *Young Soeharto*, 92.

47. Crouch, *Army and Politics*, 177–178; Sandhaussen, *Road to Power*, 227.

48. Wanandi, *Shades of Grey*, Kindle location 649.

49. See "Data on the Current Military Elite," *Indonesia* no. 3 (April 1967): 205–216.

50. Panggabean, *Berjuang dan Mengabdi*, 354; Aco Manafe, *Teperpu: Mengungkap Pengkhianatan PKI pada tahun 1965 dan Proses Hukum Bagi para Pelakunya* (Jakarta: Pustaka Sinar Harapan, 2007).

51. Report, The Economic Future in Indonesia, [1966?], A1838 2036/5 PART 8, Colombo Plan—Economic Aid—Indonesia—General, NAA.

52. Abdul Gafur, interview with Harold Crouch, May 23, 1970.

53. "Di Halaman FK UI, KAMI Gelar Rapat Umum Dukung Penghancuran Pelaku Gerakan Kontrev G.30.S/PKI," November 3, 1965, in *Jejak Langkah 1965–68*, 21.

54. "Bertempat di Lapangan Banteng, Ratusan Ribu Pemuda dan Pelajar Tuntut Pembersihan Kabinet Dwikora dari Unsur-Unsur PKI," November 27, 1965, in *Jejak Langkah 1965–68*, 27; for the trucking in of students see Soemitro, *Soemitro, Mantan Pangkopkamtib: Dari Pangdam Mulawarman sampai Pangkopkamtib* (Jakarta: Pustaka Sinar Harapan, 1994), 68–69.

55. Wanandi, *Shades of Grey*, Kindle location 642.

56. Soemitro, *Pangkopkamtib*, 70-71.

57. For the causes of the growth in the money supply see H. W. Arndt, "Banking in Hyperinflation and Stabilization," in *The Economy of Indonesia: Selected Readings*, ed. Bruce Glassburner (Ithaca, NY: Cornell University Press, 1971), 368; Mackie, *Problems of the Indonesian Inflation*, 71–74.

58. See the data in Nugroho, *Indonesia: Facts and Figures* (Jakarta: n.p., 1967), 517.

59. Cablegram, Jakarta to Department of External Affairs, January 10, 1966, Indonesia 2, A7133 1/2, NAA.

60. Nugroho, *Indonesia: Facts and Figures*, 4; International Bank for Reconstruction and Development, *Economic Development of Indonesia*, Vol. I: *Main Report* (Washington, DC: World Bank, 1968), 79–85.

61. For one example of Sukarno's misallocation of debt capital see Effendi Sahib, *Anak Penjamun Disarang Perawan (Skandal JMD)* (Jakarta: Varia, 1966).

62. Pierre van der Eng, "All Lies? Famines in Sukarno's Indonesia, 1950s–1960s," unpublished paper in author's possession; International Monetary Fund, Indonesia: Recent Economic Developments, September 12, 1966, S 1193 Indonesia Debt Renegotiation Meetings February–November 1966, Box 393, Economic Subject Files, Central Files Collection, IMF Archives.

63. Justus M. van der Kroef, *Indonesia after Sukarno* (Vancouver: University of British Columbia Press, 1971), 41.

64. Booth, *Economic Change in Modern Indonesia*, 63.

65. Quoted in Hal Hill, *The Indonesian Economy*, 1.

66. "Survey of Recent Developments," *Bulletin of Indonesian Economic Studies* 2, no. 3 (February 1966): 15.

67. Hamengkubuwono, Statement Politik Ekonomi dalam Negeri, April 12, 1966, in *Kumpulan Statement dan Ketetapan2 dalam Bidang Ekubang* (Jakarta: Jajasan Badan Penerbit Fakultas Ekonomi Universitas Indonesia, 1966), 6–15.

68. *Amanat PJM Presiden Sukarno di Sidang Paripurna Kabinet Dwikora dengan Dihadiri Djuga oleh Wakil-Wakil dari Mahasiswa-Mahasiswa dan Wartawan, Bogor, 15 Djanuari 1966* (Jakarta: Sekretariat Negara Kabinet Presiden Republik Indonesia, 1966), 16.

69. Wanandi, *Shades of Grey*, Kindle locations 733–767.

70. David Ransom, "The Berkeley Mafia and the Indonesian Massacre," *Ramparts* 9, no. 4 (October 1970).

71. Mohammad Sadli, "Recollections of My Career," *Bulletin of Indonesian Economic Studies* 29, no. 1 (April 1993): 39.

72. Soeharto, "Djer Basuki Mawa Beja," in *The Leader, the Man, and the Gun: Seminar Ekonomi K.A.M.I., Djakarta 10 s/d 20 Djanuari 1966* (Jakarta: P. T. Matoa, 1966), 20–24.

73. For a depiction of the Berkeley Mafia as market-oriented see Elson, *Suharto*, 149–150; Jeffrey M. Chwieroth, "How Do Crises Lead to Change? Liberalizing Capital Controls in the Early Years of New Order Indonesia," *World Politics* 62, no. 3 (2010): 496–527; see also Naomi Klein, *The Shock Doctrine: The Rise of Disaster Capitalism* (New York: Picador, 2007), 80–85.

74. Widjojo Nitisastro, "Economic Analysis and Development Planning (1963)," in *The Indonesian Development Experience: A Collection of Writings and Speeches of Widjojo Nitisastro* (Singapore: ISEAS, 2011), 6.

75. Mustopadidjaja AR, "His Role around Jan. 10, 1966: The New Order Economic Foundation," in *Testimonials of Friends about Widjojo Nitisastro*, ed. Moh. Arsjad Anwar, Aris Ananta, and Ari Kuncoro (Jakarta: Kompas Book Publishing, 2008), 54.

76. Sadli, "Recollections," 38; Emil Salim, "Recollections of My Career," *Bulletin of Indonesian Economic Studies* 33, no.1 (April 1997): 53–55.

77. Bruce Glassburner, "Political Economy and the Soeharto Regime," *Bulletin of Indonesian Economic Studies* 14, no. 3 (November 1978): 28.

78. Mohammad Sadli, "Masalah2 Ekonomi-Moneter Kita jang Strukturil," in *The Leader, the Man, and the Gun*, 88.

79. Cablegram, Washington to Department of External Affairs, December 16, 1965, A7133 1/5, Indonesia 5, NAA.

80. Telegram, Secretary of State for Commonwealth Relations to British High Commissioner, December 24, 1965, A1209, 1962/817 PART 2, United States and Western Aid to Indonesia, NAA.

81. Masashi Nishihara, *The Japanese and Sukarno's Indonesia: Tokyo-Jakarta Relations, 1951–1966* (Honolulu: University Press of Hawai'i, 1976), 197–200.
82. Justus M. van der Kroef, "The Sino-Indonesian Rupture," *China Quarterly* 33 (March 1968): 22.
83. Nishihara, *The Japanese and Sukarno's Indonesia*, 199.
84. Simpson, *Economists with Guns*, 203–204.
85. Telegram, Jakarta to State, December 11, 1965, POL 23-9 INDON, Central Files 1964–66, RG 59, USNA; for the intensity of the rice shortage among soldiers and civil servants see Saleh Afiff and C. Peter Timmer, "Rice Policy in Indonesia," *Food Research Institute Studies* 10, no. 2 (1971): 135.
86. Cablegram, Washington to Department of External Affairs, December 23, 1965, A1209 1962/817 Part 2, United States and Western Aid to Indonesia, NAA.
87. Memorandum from the President's Deputy Special Assistant for National Security Affairs (Komer) to President Johnson, February 15, 1966, in *FRUS 1964–68:26*, Document 192.
88. Hamish McDonald, *Suharto's Indonesia* (Victoria: Fontana Books, 1980), 58.
89. Jean Bush Aden, "Oil and Politics in Indonesia, 1945 to 1980" (PhD diss., Cornell University, 1988), 275–290.
90. Marshall Green, *Indonesia: Crisis and Transformation 1965–1968* (Washington, DC: Compass Press, 1990), 77–78; Savingram, Jakarta to Department of External Affairs, December 29, 1965, A1838 3034/2/1, Part 48, Indonesia—Political—General, NAA.
91. Green, *Indonesia*, 70; Cablegram, Jakarta to Department of External Affairs, January 7, 1966, A1838 3034/2/1, Part 48, Indonesia—Political—General, NAA.
92. Wanandi, *Shades of Grey*, Kindle locations 734–748.
93. "Of Rice and Men," *Far Eastern Economic Review*, January 27, 1966.
94. Crouch, *Army and Politics*, 172–175.
95. McDonald, *Suharto's Indonesia*, 56.
96. Peter Kasendra, "Perintis Orde Baru yang Tersisih," *Prisma* (1991); Soeharto, *Pikiran*, 163–164
97. Green, *Indonesia*, 82.
98. "Tidak Memperoleh Respon Memadai, Presiden Soekarno Tinggalkan Pertemuan dengan Parpol dan Ormas," March 10, 1966, in *Jejak Langkah 1965–68*, 51; "Subandrio Ancam Parpol untuk Mengutuk Gerakan Mahasiswa," March 10, 1966, in *Jejak Langkah 1965–68*, 51.
99. Soemitro, *Pangkopkamtib*, 89–90.
100. Soeharto, *Pikiran*, 170–171,
101. Amirmachmud's account comes from Amirmachmud, *H. Amirmachmud Menjawab* (Jakarta: CV Haji Masagung, 1987), 56–59.
102. Soeharto, *Pikiran*, 172.
103. Sudharmono S.H., *Pengalaman dalam Masa Pengabdian: Sebuah Otobiografi* (Jakarta: PT Gramedia Widiasarana Indonesia, 1997), 173–176.
104. Wanandi, *Shades of Grey*, Kindle location; Telegram, Jakarta to State, March 12, 1966, in *FRUS 1964–68:26*, Document 200.

Chapter 3

1. Memo, Parsons to Hasluck, April 5, 1966, A1838 3034/2/1/8 PART 12, Indonesia—Political—Coup D'Etat of 30th September 1965, NAA.
2. Graita Sutadi, "Operation Plan of the Wonogiri Reservoir: Central Java, Indonesia" (MA thesis, University of Arizona, 1982), 5.
3. Memo, Cook to Jockel, March 30, 1966, A1838 TS696/2/1 PART 2, Indonesia—Political and General, NAA.
4. Cablegram, Jakarta to Department of External Affairs, March 23, 1966, A1838 TS696/2/1 PART 2, Indonesia—Political and General, NAA.
5. Telegram, Jakarta to State, March 19, 1966, AID 1 INDON, Central Files 1964-66, RG 59, USNA.

6. Memorandum from James C. Thomson Jr., of the National Security Council Staff to the President's Special Assistant (Moyers), March 31, 1966, in *FRUS 1964–68:26*, Document 205; Telegram, State to Jakarta, March 31, 1966, AID (US) 15-11 INDON, Central Files 1964–66, RG 59, USNA.
7. Telegram, Bonn to State, March 31, 1966, AID 1 INDON, Central Files 1964–66, RG 59, USNA
8. Joint Intelligence Bureau, Indonesia: Requirements for Economic Recovery, July 1966, A1209 1962/817 Part 4, United States and Western Aid to Indonesia, NAA.
9. Adam Malik, "Statement Kebidjaksanaan Politik Luar Negeri," April 4, 1966, in *Statement-Statement Politik Waperdam Bidang Sospol/Menteri Luar Negeri dan Waperdam Bidang Ekubang* (Jakarta: Kementrian Penerangan, 1966), 3–5.
10. Hamengkubuwono, "Statement Politik Ekonomi Dalam Negeri," April 12, 1966, in *Statement-Statement Politik*, 13–29.
11. Cablegram, Tokyo to Department of External Affairs, May 20, 1966, A1838 2036/5 Part 8, Colombo Plan—Economic Aid—Indonesia—General, NAA.
12. Cablegram, Tokyo to Department of External Affairs, May 31, 1966, A1838 2036/5 Part 8, Colombo Plan—Economic Aid—Indonesia—General, NAA.
13. Telegram, Paris to State, June 28, 1966, AID 1 INDON, Central Files 1964–66, RG 59, USNA.
14. Cablegram, London to Department of External Affairs, July 21, 1966, A1209 1962/817 Part 4, United States and Western Aid to Indonesia, NAA.
15. Memo, Osborn to Hasluck, May 19, 1966, A1838 2036/5 Part 8, Colombo Plan—Economic Aid—Indonesia—General, NAA.
16. Cablegram, Tokyo to Department of External Affairs, June 6, 1966, A1838 2036/5 Part 8, Colombo Plan—Economic Aid—Indonesia—General, NAA.
17. Cablegram, Tokyo to Department of External Affairs, June 23, 1966, A1838 2036/5 Part 8, Colombo Plan—Economic Aid—Indonesia—General, NAA.
18. Telegram, Jakarta to State, May 27, 1966, POL INDON-US, Central Files 1964–66, RG 59, USNA.
19. Memorandum from Donald W. Ropa of the National Security Council Staff to the President's Special Assistant (Rostow), July 9, 1966, in *FRUS 1964–68:26*, Document 212.
20. "Confrontation and Economic Relations," *Indonesian Herald*, July 18, 1966.
21. Cablegram, Jakarta to Department of External Affairs, July 12, 1966, A1209, 1962/817 Part 4, United States and Western Aid to Indonesia, NAA.
22. Abdul Haris Nasution, *Memenuhi Panggilan Tugas, Jilid 7: Masa Konsolidasi Orde Baru* (Jakarta: CV Haji Masagung, 1988), 25.
23. Crouch, *Army and Politics*, 234–235.
24. Mohtar Mas'oed, "The Indonesian Economy and Political Structure during the Early New Order, 1966–1971" (PhD diss., Ohio State University, 1983), 172–178.
25. Airgram, Jakarta to State, March 11, 1967, DEF 6-1 INDON 1/1/67, Central Files 1967–69, RG 59, USNA.
26. Press Clipping, April 18, 1966, A1838 3034/2/1/8 PART 13, Indonesia—Political—Coup D'Etat of 30th September 1965, NAA.
27. "Pembukaan Kongres PNI, Letjen Soeharto Singgugn Tiga Penyelewang Revolusi," April 25, 1966, in *Jejak Langkah 1965–68*, 68–69; the quotation comes from Crouch, *The Army and Politics*, 255.
28. Angus McIntyre, "Divisions and Power in the Indonesian National Party, 1965–1966," *Indonesia* 13 (April 1972): 183–210.
29. Justus M. van der Kroef, "Indonesia: The Battle of the 'Old' and the 'New Order,'" *Australian Outlook* (April 1967): 26.
30. Savingram, Jakarta to Canberra, September 16, 1966, A1838, 3034/2/2/5 Part 1, Indonesia—Political Parties—NU (Nahdatul Ulama) [Islam], NAA.
31. Soekarno, *Nawa Aksara (Nawaksara): Amanat Presiden Sukarno didepan Sidang Umum Madjelis Permusjawaratan Rakjat Sementara ke-IV/1966, pada tanggal 22 Djuni 1966 di Istana Olah Raga* (Jakarta: Kementrian Penerangan, 1966), 2.
32. H. Rosihan Anwar, *Indonesia 1966–1983: Dari Koresponden Kami di Jakarta* (Jakarta: PT Pustaka Utama Grafiti, 1992), 4.

33. Soemitro, *Pangkopkamtib*, 89–90.
34. See "Data on the Current Military Elite," *Indonesia* no. 3 (April 1967): 205–216.
35. Crouch, *The Army and Politics*, 232.
36. "Rusmin Nuryadin Dilantik Sebagai Mepangau," in *Jejak Langkah 1965–68*, 65–66.
37. "Kapuspen AU: 306 Anggota AURI Ditindak," *Angkatan Bersendjata*, April 23, 1966.
38. Muradi, *Politics and Governance in Indonesia: The Police in the Era of Reformasi* (New York: Routledge, 2014), 35–52.
39. Sandhaussen, *Road to Power*, 249.
40. Parikesit and Sempurnadjaja, *Alamsjah*, 183–185.
41. Wiwoho and Bandjar, *Memori Jenderal Yoga*, 196.
42. Angkatan Darat, *Doktrin Perdjuangan TNI "Tri Ubaya Çakti": Buku Induk Hasil Seminar Angkatan Darat tgl. 2 s/d 9 April 1965 di "Grha Wiyata Yudha Seskoad" Bandung* (Jakarta: Departemen Angkatan Darat, 1965), 13, 30–36, 22.
43. Soemitro, *Pangkopkamtib*, 122.
44. Soemitro, *Pangkopkamtib*, 125.
45. Angkatan Darat, *Doktrin Perdjuangan TNI-AD "Tri Ubaya Çakti": Buku Induk, Djilid I: Hasil Seminar AD ke-II tanggal 25 s/d 31 Agustus 1966 di Grha Wiyata Yudha Seskoad Bandung* (Jakarta: Pertjetakan Negara RI, 1966), vi and lampiran, 1–2.
46. See "Ideal Foundation for the Struggle of the Indonesian National Army," in Nugroho Notususanto, *The Dual Function of the Indonesian Armed Forces, Especially since 1966* (Jakarta: Department of Defence & Security Centre for Armed Forces History, 1970), 22–28.
47. See Sukardi Rinakit, *The Indonesian Military After the New Order* (Singapore: Institute of Southeast Asian Studies, 2005), 26–27.
48. *Doktrin Hankamnas dan Doktrin Perdjuangan ABRI "Catur Dharma Eka Karma": Hasil Seminar Hankam ke-I tanggal 12 Nopember s/d 21 Nopember 1966 di Djakarta* (Jakarta, 1966).
49. "Seminar Hankamnas Melahirkan Doktrin 'Catur Dharma Eka Karma,' Jenderal Soeharto: Untuk Pertama Kalinya ABRI Memiliki Doktrin Hankamnas," November 21, 1966, in *Jejak Langkah 1965–68*, 127.
50. Wanandi, *Shades of Grey*, Kindle locations 893–952.
51. Julius Pour, *Benny: Tragedi Seorang Loyalis* (Jakarta: Kata Hasta Pustaka, 2007), 152.
52. "Red China Helps Malaysia Rebels," *New York Times*, January 14, 1966.
53. Ali Murtopo, Pembahasan Mengenai Politik Diplomasi dalam Rangka Konfrontasi terhadap "Malaysia," May 19, 1966, 1793, EKUIN, ANRI.
54. "Quick End Best: Malik," *Straits Times*, May 21, 1966.
55. Cablegram, Bangkok to Department of External Affairs, June 2, 1966, A1838 3006/4/7, South East Asia—Indonesia—Malaysia—Relations—Confrontation, NAA.
56. "After Sukarno, the Headache," *New York Times*, September 11, 1966.
57. "Terror Bomb Kills 2 Girls at Bank," *Straits Times*, March 11, 1965.
58. Cablegram, Jakarta to Department of External Affairs, August 3, 1966, A1838 3034/7/1 Part 10, Indonesia—Foreign Policy—General, NAA.
59. "Singapore: The Djakarta Deal," *Far Eastern Economic Review*, September 22, 1966.
60. Widjojo Nitisastro, "Kata Pengantar," in *Kebangkitan Semangat '66: Mendjeladjah Tracee Baru* (Jakarta: Jajasan Badan Penerbit, 1966), 2.
61. "Rantjangan Ketetapan Madjelis Purmusjawaratan Rakjat Sementara Republik Indonesia XXIII/MPRS/1966 tentang Tracee Baru dalam Kebidjaksanaan Ekonomi, Keuangan dan Pembangunan," in *Kumpulan Statement dan Ketetapan2 dalam Bidang Ekubang*, 59–65.
62. E.A. Sie Dhian Ho and Kartono Gunawan, Laporan Hasil2 Pembitjaraan Consultations Team Indonesia dengan Misi Teknis I.M.F. (27 Djuni–8 Djuli 1966), June 23, 1966, 1795, EKUIN, ANRI; Cablegram, Jakarta to Department of External Affairs, July 7, 1966, A1209 1962/817 Part 4, United States and Western Aid to Indonesia, NAA.
63. Hartono Wirjodiprodjo, "Pokok-Pokok dan Ruang-Lingkup Pembahasan Sindikat Ekonomi," in *Amanat/Pidato Pra-saran dalam Seminar AD ke-II/1966: Hasil Seminar AD ke-II tanggal 25 s/d 31 Agustus 1966 di Rgha Wiyata Yudha/Seskoad Bandung* (Jakarta, 1967), 78–82.
64. "Garis-Garis Besar Kebidjaksanaan dan Rentjana-Pelaksanaan Stablisasi Ekonomi," in *Sumbangan Fikiran TNI-AD kepada Kabinet Ampera: Hasil Seminar AD Ke-II tanggal 25 s/d*

31 Agustus 1966 di Grha Wiyata Yudha/Seskoad Bandung (Jakarta: Seksi Penerangan KOTI, 1966), 79–177.

65. Sadli, "Reflections," 40.

66. Subroto, "Recollections of My Career," *Bulletin of Indonesian Economic Studies* 34, no. 2 (August 1998): 74–75.

67. Tjatatan Rapat: Laporan Mengenai Kredit dari Amerika dalam rangka S.A.C., August 15, 1966, 2135, EKUIN, ANRI.

68. Telegram, Jakarta to Washington, October 21, 1966, S 1193 Indonesia Debt Renegotiation Meetings February–November 1966, Box 394, Economic Subject Files, Central Files Collection, IMF Archives.

69. See the collection of decisions and instructions in *Keterangan Pemerintah tentang Kebidjaksanaan Stabilisasi dan Rehabilitasi Ekonomi* (Jakarta: Departemen Penerangan R.I., 1966), 45–67.

70. Savingram, Tokyo to Department of External Affairs, March 16, 1966, A1838 3034/11/89 Part 6, Indonesia—Relations with Japan, NAA.

71. Telegram, State Circular, May 24, 1966, FN 14 INDON, Central Files 1964–66, RG 59, USNA.

72. See Amit Das Gupta, "Development by Consortia: International Donors and the Development of India, Pakistan, Indonesia and Turkey in the 1960s," *Comparativ* 19, no. 4 (2009): 96–111.

73. Memorandum, Osborn to Hasluck, May 19, 1966, A1838 2036/5 PART 8, Colombo Plan—Economic Aid—Indonesia—General, NAA.

74. Telegram, Tokyo to State, June 4, 1966, AID 9 INDON 1/1/66, Central Files 1964–66, RG 59, USNA.

75. Memorandum, Southard to Gold, Tun Thin, and Horne, August 1, 1966, S 1193 Indonesia Debt Renegotiation Meetings February–November 1966, Box 393, Economic Subject Files, Central Files Collection, IMF Archives.

76. Soeharto, Statement Made on Behalf of the Indonesian Government at the Multilateral Conference in Tokyo, September 17, 1966, 2195, EKUIN, ANRI.

77. Multilateral Conference Regarding Indonesian Problems, Tokyo, 19th and 20th September, 1966: Report of Australian Delegation, A1209 1962/817 Part 5, United States and Western Aid to Indonesia, NAA; "Indonesia's Creditors Fail to Reach Agreement," *Financial Times*, September 21, 1966; "The Burned Moneymen Appraise Indonesia," *New York Times*, September 18, 1966.

78. Hamengkubuwono IX, Laporan Perdjalanan Menteri Utama Bidang Ekonomi dan Keuangan di Eropa, Asia dan Amerika Serikat dalam Bulan September dan Oktober 1966, October 14, 1966, 2194, EKUIN, ANRI.

79. "Indonesian's Visit Canceled by Soviet," *New York Times*, September 3, 1966.

80. Tjatatan Rapat Tim Persiapan Hubungan Ekonomi Internasional, August 8, 1966, 1800, EKUIN, ANRI.

81. Hubungan Perdagangan Indonesia-Amerika, September 28, 1966, 1798, EKUIN, ANRI.

82. Perundingan Antara Menutama Ekku Sri Sultan Hamengkubuwono dengan Undersecretary of State U.S.A., September 30, 1966, 1791, EKUIN, ANRI.

83. Memorandum, Humphrey to Johnson, September 25, 1966, in *FRUS 1964–68:26*, Document 222; Memorandum of Conversation, September 27, 1966, in *FRUS 1964–68:26*, Document 223; Memorandum of Conversation, September 27, 1966, in *FRUS 1964–68:26*, Document 224.

84. "Survey of Recent Developments," *Bulletin of Indonesian Economic Studies* 2, no. 5 (October 1966): 3.

85. Telegram, Jakarta to State, October 27, 1966, in *FRUS 1964–68:26*, Document 225; Memorandum, Wheeler to McNamara, November 1, 1966, in *FRUS 1964–68:26*, Document 226.

86. Nota Dinas, Selo Soemardjan to Hamengkubuwono, October 19, 1966, 2203, EKUIN, ANRI.

87. Laporan Menteri Utama Bidang Ekonomi dan Keuangan tentang Hasil2 Pembitjaraan Penundaan Pembayaran Hutang2 dengan Negara2 Eropa Timur, April 1967, 2076, EKUIN, ANRI.

88. Soeprajogi, Laporan Missi Teknis ke Negara2 Eropah Timur (Sovjet Uni, Polandia dan Tjekoslowakia) dalam rangka Rescheduling Hutang2 Negara, Kerdjasama Ekonomi/ Perdagangan, Soal2 Project Pembangunan dan Spare-Parts ABRI, January 2, 1967, 2206, EKUIN, ANRI.

89. Cablegram, Moscow to Canberra, December 2, 1966, A1209, 1962/817 Part 5, United States and Western Aid to Indonesia, NAA.

90. Memorandum, The Secretary to Members of the Executive Board, October 6, 1966, Indonesia [1966–1969] Folder 10, Box 20, Director J. Polak Subject Files, Research Department Immediate Office, IMF Archives.

91. For US influence over the formulation of the Foreign Investment Law see Simpson, *Economists with Guns*, 229–236.

92. Undang-Undang Republik Indonesia Nomor 1 Tahun 1967 tentang Penanaman Modal Asing.

93. Memorandum, Tun Thin to Schweitzer, December 28, 1966, S1193 Indonesia Debt Renegotiation Meetings December 1966–September 1968, Box 393, Economic Subject Files, Central Files Collection, IMF Archives; International Conference on Indonesian Debt, December 1966, 2061, EKUIN, ANRI; Hamengkubuwono IX, Laporan Menutama Ekku mengenai Hasil-2 Pembitjaraan Pertemuan Paris pada tanggal 19 dan 20 Desember 1966, February 1967, 2206, EKUIN, ANRI.

94. Tun Thin, Rearrangement of Indonesian Debts, December 28, 1966, Indonesia [1966–1969] Folder 10, Box 20, Director J. Polak Subject Files, Research Department Immediate Office, IMF Archives.

95. Telegram, The Hague to State, January 5, 1967, FN 14 INDON 1967-01-01, Central Files 1967-69, RG 59, USNA.

96. "Foreign Loans Vital to Indonesia," *Financial Times*, February 7, 1967.

97. Statement atas Nama Pemerintah Republik Indonesia dalam Pertemuan "Inter-Governmental Group on Indonesia" di Amsterdam, February 20, 1967, 1832, EKUIN, ANRI.

98. Memorandum, Savkar to Schweitzer, February 28, 1967, Indonesia [1966–1969] Folder 10, Box 20, Director J. Polak Subject Files, Research Department Immediate Office, IMF Archives; Bruce Glassburner, "Pricing of Foreign Exchange in Indonesia, 1966–67," *Economic Development & Cultural Change* 18, no. 2 (January 1970): 166–187.

99. H.A. Pandelaki, Laporan Delegasi Republik Indonesia ke Konperensi Amsterdam tanggal 23–24 Februari 1967, March 2, 1967, 2223, EKUIN, ANRI.

100. "U.S. Is Ready to Reinstate Indonesia Aid," *New York Times*, February 28, 1967.

101. Tun Thin, Rearrangement of Indonesian debts, December 28, 1966, Indonesia [1966–1969] Folder 10, Box 20, Director J. Polak Subject Files, Research Department Immediate Office, IMF Archives.

102. Panggabean, *Berjuang dan Mengabdi*, 365.

103. "HUT KAMI: Jenderal Soeharto: Dalam Perjuangannya, KAMI Tak Laput Cobaan dan Fitnah," October 25, 1966, in *Jejak Langkah 1965–68*, 119.

104. Anwar, *Dari Koresponden Kami*, 20.

105. "Pernyataan Bersama Pimpinan ABRI: Tindak Tegas Penyeleng Pancasila dan UUD 1945," December 21, 1966, in *Jejak Langkah 1965–68*, 136-137.

106. Savingram, Jakarta to Canberra, January 6, 1967, A1838 TS696/2/1 Part 2, Indonesia—Political and General, NAA.

107. "Pidato Presiden Soekarno pada Pemgumuan Pelengkap Nawaksara di Istana Merdeka," January 10, 1967, in *Revolusi Belum Selesai: Kumpulan Pidato Presiden Soekarno, 30 September 1965—Pelengkap Nawaksara*, ed. Budi Setiyono and Bonnie Triyana (Jakarta: PT Serambi Ilmu Semesta, 2014), 772–791.

108. Guy Pauker, "Indonesia: The Year of Transition," *Asian Survey* 7, no. 2 (February 1967): 150; Anwar, *Dari Koresponden Kami*, 23.

109. Sumitro, *Pangkopkamtib*, 157, 165.

110. Soeharto, *Pikiran*, 187.

111. Panggabean, *Berjuang dan Mengabdi*, 370–372.

112. Sudharmono, *Otobiografi*, 190.

113. Crouch, *Army and Politics*, 214; Wanandi, *Shades of Grey*, Kindle location 975.

114. Supolo Prawotohadikusumo, *Dari Orde Lama Menudju Orde Baru* (Jakarta: Pantjuran Tudjuh, 1967), 285–317; Soeharto, *Pikiran*, 194–195.
115. For political quarantine see Panggabean, *Berjuang dan Mengabdi*, 378; Soeharto, *Pikiran*, 244.
116. Soeharto, Naskah Pidato Sambutan Pengemban Ketetapan MPRS No IX pada Penutupan Sidang Istimewa MPRS, March 12, 1967, 296, PPS, ANRI.
117. See François Raillon, *Les étudiants indonésiens et l'Ordre Nouveau: Politique et idéologie du Mahasiswa Indonesia (1966–1974)* (Paris: Association Archipel, 1984), 55–67.
118. See, e.g., Sarbini Somawinata, "Masalah Stabilisasi Politik," in *Amanat/Pidato Pra-saran dalam Seminar AD ke-II/1966: Hasil Seminar AD ke-II tanggal 25 s/d 31 Agustus 1966 di Rgha Wiyata Yudha/Seskoad Bandung* (Jakarta: n.p., 1967), 39–68; Harold Crouch, "The Army, the Parties, and Elections," *Indonesia* no. 11 (April 1971): 177–192; Sarbini Sumawinata, "Recollections of My Career," *Bulletin of Indonesian Economic Studies* 28, no. 2 (August 1992): 50–53.
119. Soenito Djojosoegito, Atrap tentang Usaha2 Terdjaminnja Kelangsungan Ketata-negaraan Rep. Indonesia, March 9, 1967, 117, Sekkab, ANRI.
120. Yahya Muhaimin, *Bisnis dan Politik: Kebijaksanaan Ekonomi Indonesia, 1950–1980* (Jakarta: LP3ES, 1991), 222.
121. "Berilah Kesempatan Bekerdja kpd. Kabinet Ampera," *Berita Yudha*, July 27, 1966.
122. Letter, Fakih Usman, Hasan Basri, and Anwar Harjono to Amirmachmud, May 9, 1966, 124, Sekkab, ANRI; letter, Prawoto Mangkusasmito to Soeharto, October 6, 1966, 124, Sekkab, ANRI.
123. See Solichin Salam, *Sedjarah Partai Muslimin* (Jakarta: Jajasan Kesedjahteraan dan Perbendaharaan Buruh Islam, 1968), 53–59; see also Nasution, *Memenuhi Panggilan Tugas, Jilid 7*, 111.
124. Airgram, Jakarta to State, April 5, 1967, DEF 6 INDON 1/1/67, Central Files 1967–69, RG 59, USNA; H. Amirmachmud, *Prajurit Pejuang: Otobiografi* (Jakarta: Panitia Penerbitan Otobiografi Bapak H. Amirmachmud, 1987), 307; Letter, Soeharto to Prawoto Mangkusasmito, January 6, 1967, 124, Sekkab, ANRI.
125. Letter, Djarnawi Hadikusuma and Nur Widjojo to Suharto, March 13, 1967, 134, Sekkab, ANRI.
126. Sambutan Pejabat Presiden Republik Indonesia pada siding Tanwir Pimpinan Muhammadiyah pada Juli 1967 di Djakarta, https://soeharto.co/1967-07-sambutan-peja bat-presiden-soeharto-pada-sidang-tanwir-muhammadiyah/ (accessed April 3, 2020); "Partai SPJ Djangan Peruntjing Ideologi," *Kompas*, August 18, 1967.
127. Ken Ward, *The Foundation of the Partai Muslimin Indonesia* (Ithaca, NY: Cornell Modern Indonesia Project, 1970), 30–39.
128. "Pejabat Presiden Jenderal Soeharto Memberi Keterangan Pers Mengenai Berbagai Persoalan," July 20, 1967, in *Jejak Langkah 1965–68*, 196–197; for meetings between Suharto and party leaders see Nugroho Notosusanto, *Tercapainya Konsensus Nasional* (Jakarta: Balai Pustaka, 1985), 49.
129. "Pimpinan DPR-GR dan Pemerintah Sepakat," *Kompas*, November 27, 1967; Abdul Haris Nasution, *Memenuhi Panggilan Tugas, Jilid 8: Masa Pemancangan Orde Pembangunan* (Jakarta: CV Haji Masagung, 1988), 14; Anwar, *Dari Koresponden Kami*, 53.
130. "Pejabat Presiden Jenderal Soeharto Memberi Keterangan Pers Mengenai Berbagai Persoalan," July 20, 1967, in *Jejak Langkah 1965–68*, 196–197.
131. "HUT Persit, Jenderal Soeharto: Orde Baru Adalah Orde Demokrasi Pancasila," April 3, 1967, in *Jejak Langkah 1965–68*, 171; Sambutan Pejabat Presiden Republik Indonesia pada Muktamar Partai Nadhatul Ulama di Bandung, July 4, 1967, 436, PPS, ANRI.
132. Bourchier, *Illiberal Democracy in Indonesia*, 2.
133. For the cabinet meeting see Annex to Letter, Kemal Siber to D.S. Savkar, May 25, 1967, C/Indonesia/810 Mission, Siber, K. and Tomasson, G. March 1967–February 1968, Box 7, Central Country Files, Central Files Collection, IMF Archives; for the Siliwangi Corps see H. W. Arndt, "Survey of Recent Developments," *Bulletin of Indonesian Economic Studies* 3, no. 7 (June 1967): 7.
134. Mohammad Sadli, Laporan: Kemadjuan mengenai, serta Masalah2 Sekitar, Pelaksanaan Projek Penanaman Modal Asing, March 9, 1967, 180, Sekkab, ANRI.

135. Hong Lan Oei, "Implications of Indonesia's New Foreign Investment Policy for Economic Development," *Indonesia* 7 (April 1969): 38.
136. Denise Leith, "Freeport and the Suharto Regime, 1965–1998," *The Contemporary Pacific* 13, no. 1 (Spring 2002): 69–74.
137. Memorandum 318/M 83/SDH/67, Bratanata to Suharto, March 27, 1967, 177, Sekkab, ANRI.
138. Memorandum, Mohammad Sadli to Suharto, March 31, 1967, 177, Sekkab, ANRI.
139. Airgram, Tokyo to State, August 13, 1968, FN-19 INDON-US 1967, Central Files 1967–69, RG59, USNA.
140. Airgram, Jakarta to State, April 29, 1967, FN-19 INDON-US 1967, Central Files 1967–69, RG59, USNA.
141. PIBA Investment Promotion Council, From Sydney to Djakarta (Report of Activities), 175, Sekkab, ANRI; Letter, Tahija to Hamengkubuwono IX, The Djakarta Meeting, July 29, 1967, 2234, EKUIN, ANRI.
142. Julius Tahija, *Horizon Beyond: Entrepreneurs of Asia* (Singapore: Times Books International, 1995), 148–150.
143. For PTPP Berdikari see Robison, *Rise of Capital*, 91–92; Suparwan and Krisna, *Alamsjah*, 196.
144. Suhardiman, Laporan Perdjalanan Dinas ke Negara2 Far East, Middle East dan Europe dari tanggal 3 April s/d 26 April 1967, 182, Sekkab, ANRI.
145. Benny G. Setiono, *Tionghoa dalam Pusaran Politik: Mengungkap Fakta Sejarah Tersembunyi Orang Tionghoa di Indonesia* (Jakarta: ELKASA, 2003), 1001.
146. Telegram, Siber to Savkar, August 5, 1967, C-Indonesia-810 Mission, Siber, K. and Tomasson, G. March 1967–February 1968, Box 7, Central Files Country Files, Central Files Collection, IMF Archives.
147. Robison, *Rise of Capital*, 229–233.
148. Aden, "Oil and Politics in Indonesia," 309–322; Robert Fabrikant, "Production Sharing Contracts in the Indonesian Oil Industry," *Harvard International Law Journal* 16, no. 2 (Spring 1975): 303–351.
149. Telegram, Jakarta to State, July 16, 1966, PET 6 INDON, Central Files 1967–69, RG 59, USNA.
150. Ramadhan KH, *Ibnu Sutuwo: Saatnya Saya Bercerita!* (Jakarta: National Press Club of Indonesia, 2008), 229.
151. Airgram, Jakarta to State, March 31, 1967, PET INDON 1/1/67, Central Files 1967–69, RG 59, USNA.
152. Memorandum of Conversation, Linen, Middleton, Berger, Green, and Underhill, January 5, 1967, FN 19 INDON-US, Central Files 1967–69, RG 59, USNA
153. Airgram, Jakarta to State, April 7, 1967, FN 9 INDON, Central Files 1967–69, RG 59, USNA.
154. Winters, *Power in Motion*, 58fn25.
155. *To Aid in the Rebuilding of a Nation: Proceedings of the Indonesian Investment Conference, Sponsored by Time Inc., Geneva, Switzerland / November 2–4, 1967* (1967), 38.
156. Hamengkubuwono, Memo EKUIN/26/Psh/68: Business International Indonesian Roundtable, January 10, 1968, 1869, EKUIN, ANRI.
157. Airgram, Tokyo to State, January 12, 1968, FN INDON-A 1/1/67, Central Files 1967–69, RG 59, USNA.
158. PIBA Investment Promotion Council, From Sydney to Djakarta (Report of Activities), 175, Sekkab, ANRI; Louis T. Wells and Rafiq Ahmed, *Making Foreign Investment Safe: Property Rights and National Sovereignty* (New York: Oxford University Press, 2007), 24–25.
159. "For Indonesians, 'No More Monuments,'" *New York Times*, January 19, 1968.
160. Telegram, Bern to Hamengkubuwono, March 16, 1967, 2220, EKUIN, ANRI.
161. Airgram, Jakarta to State, April 19, 1967, E-2 INDON 1/1/67, Central Files 1967–69, RG 59, USNA.
162. Telegram, Jakarta to State, June 10, 1967, FN 14 INDON 6/1/67, Central Files 1967–69, RG 59, USNA.
163. Memo EK/701/67, Hamengkubuwono IX to Malik, June 7, 1967, 2236, EKUIN, ANRI; Hamengkubuwono IX, Aide Memoire, June 7, 1967, 2236, EKUIN, ANRI.

164. Widjojo, *Indonesian Development Experience*, 254-255.
165. Keputusan Menteri Utama Bidang Ekonomi dan Keuangan No. Kep/70/Mekku/IX/1967, September 15, 1967, 2139, EKUIN, ANRI.
166. Telegram 3512/Sal, Washington to Suharto, July 14, 1967, 1961, EKUIN, ANRI.
167. H.A. Pandelaki, Laporan Delegasi Indonesia ke Berbagai Negara Kreditor dalam rangka Pelaksanaan Persetudjuan Paris Mengenai Rescheduling dan Follow-Up Pelaksanaan Kredit Luar Negeri Baru, August 3, 1967, 2130, EKUIN, ANRI.
168. "Indonesia Details More Friendly Policy," *Christian Science Monitor*, May 23, 1967.
169. Departemen Angkatan Darat, Laporan Chusus Nomer: 029/L.C./1967-ALa. tentang Kegiatan2 Anti Pemerintah R.I. di Eropa, July 1, 1967, 158, Sekkab, ANRI.
170. Radius Prawiro, Bank Negara Indonesia: Laporan Mingguan 82/GBNI/Biro/1967, May 27, 1967, 191, Sekkab, ANRI; International Bank for Reconstruction and Development, "Economic Development of Indonesia, Volume I: Main Report," February 12, 1968, World Bank Archives.
171. "Prof. Tinbergen Membitjarakan Prospek Ekonomi Indonesia," *Antara*, March 5, 1966; Memo, McDiarmid to Cargill, August 16, 1967, 72–178 Indonesia, Part I 1966–67, File 1, Box 35, FADAI Country Files, Fiscal Affairs Department Fonds, IMF Archives; Memo, Falcon to Papanek, April 7, 1969, DAS—Indonesia 1966–74, Box 2, UAV 462.5095.6—Development Advisory Service Administrative and Project Records, 1958–1974, HUA.
172. Green, *Crisis and Transformation*, 103.
173. Telegram, Jakarta to State, July 7, 1967, POL 15-1 INDON, Central Files 1967–69, RG 59, USNA.
174. Memorandum, Rostow to Johnson, July 22, 1967, in *FRUS 1964–68:26*, Document 238.
175. Memorandum for the Record, August 9, 1967, in *FRUS 1964–68:26*, Document 244.
176. Memo, Wright to Rostow, September 27, 1967, in *FRUS 1964–68:26*, Document 245.
177. Record of Cabinet Meeting, October 18, 1967, in *FRUS 1964–68:26*, Document 246.
178. See H. W. Arndt, "Survey of Recent Developments," *Bulletin of Indonesian Economic Studies* 3, no. 8 (October 1967): 13.
179. For an analysis of Indonesia's rice situation detailing the "strategic position" of the commodity see Badan Urusan Logistik, Politik Pemberasan Pemerintah tahun 1968, August 14, 1967, 2057, EKUIN, ANRI.
180. International Monetary Fund, Indonesia: Recent Economic Developments, October 11, 1967, S 1193 Indonesia Debt Renegotiation Meetings December 1966–September 1968, Box 393, Economic Subject Files, Central Files Collection, IMF Archives.
181. Telegram, Jakarta to State, November 18, 1967, E 8-1 INDON 1/1/67, Central Files 1967–69, RG 59, USNA.
182. "Indonesians Ask Price Cut: Students Say Regime Must Resign if Rice Stays High," *Baltimore Sun*, September 28, 1967.
183. Multilateral Conference on Indonesian Debts: Paris, October 17, 1967, S 1193 Indonesia Debt Renegotiation Meetings December 1966–September 1968, Box 393, Economic Subject Files, Central Files Collection, IMF Archives.
184. Hamengkubuwono, Laporan Pemerintah tentang Konperensi Amsterdam pada bulan Nopember 1967, 2081, EKUIN, ANRI.
185. Memorandum, Tun Thin to Schweitzer, November 28, 1967, S 1193 Indonesia Inter-Governmental Aid Meetings 1967, Box 395, Economic Subject Files, Central Files Collection, IMF Archives.
186. Tjatatan-Tjatatan Disekitar Kundjungan Wakil Presiden Amerika Serikat, 384, Sekkab, ANRI.
187. Memorandum of Conversation, February 17, 1967, in *FRUS 1964–68:26*, Document 229.
188. Telegram, Jakarta to State, November 6, 1967, in *FRUS 1964–68:26*, Document 247.
189. Editorial Note, in *FRUS 1964–68:26*, Document 248.
190. Memo, Johnson to Rostow, November 21, 1967, quoted in *FRUS 1964–68:26*, Document 249fn6.
191. Pidato Pejabat Presiden/Ketua Presidium Kabinet pada Sidang Kabinet Ampera pada tanggal 13 Juli 1967 di Jakarta, https://soeharto.co/pidato-pejabat-presiden-soeharto-pada-sidang-kabinet-ampera/ (accessed April 3, 2020).

192. Mary Sutton, "Indonesia 1966–70: Economic Management and the Role of the IMF," *Overseas Development Institute Working Paper Series*, no. 8 (April 1982): 18.

193. Pidato Pedjabat Presiden Republik Indonesia pada Sidang Kabinet Paripurna, September 18, 1967, https://soeharto.co/pidato-pejabat-presiden-soeharto-pada-sidang-paripurna-kabinet/ (accessed April 16, 2020).

194. "Pejabet Presiden Jenderal Soeharto Menerima Kebulatan Tekad Pangdam se-Jawa," July 11, 1967, in *Jejak Langkah 1965–68*, 194.

195. "Menerima Pangkostrad, Pejabat Presiden Jenderal Soeharto Paparkan Pembersihan Orde Lama," July 20, 1967, in *Jejak Langkah 1965–68*, 196-197.

196. Crouch, *Army and Politics*, 233; M. Jasin, *Saya Tidak Pernah Minta Ampun kepada Soeharto: Sebuah Memoar* (Jakarta: Pustaka Sinar Harapan, 1998), 67–69; "Jakarta Arrests as Power Struggle Continues," *The Guardian*, July 20, 1967; "Arrest of 35 Military Leaders Called Sukarno Clique Purge," *Atlanta Constitution*, July 29, 1967; "Indonesian Troops Sent to East Java," *Hartford Courant*, August 8, 1967; "Arrest 40 Indonesian Officers in Red Plot," *Chicago Tribune*, August 27, 1967.

197. "Bertempat di War Room, Jenderal Soeharto Paparkan Perubahan Organisasi Hankam," September 6, 1967, in *Jejak Langkah 1965–68*, 207–208.

198. "Jenderal Soeharto Umumkan Kabinet Ampera yang Disempurnakan," October 11, 1967, in *Jejak Langkah 1965–68*, 215.

199. Crouch, *Army and Politics*, 239.

200. Telegram, Jakarta to State, May 19, 1967, FT 25-5 INDON, Central Files 1967–69, RG 59, USNA.

201. "Diterima Jenderal Soeharto, PNI Kemukakan Kebulatan Tekad Dukung Orde Baru," December 21, 1967, in *Jejak Langkah 1965–68*, 228; "Jenderal Soeharto Instruksikan Daerah Agar Membantu PNI dalam Kristalisasinya dengan Orde Baru," December 22, 1967, in *Jejak Langkah 1965–68*, 228–229; Herbert Feith, "Suharto's Search for a Political Format," *Indonesia* no. 6 (October 1968): 96.

202. Amirmachmud, *Otobiografi*, 306–307.

203. Sudharmono, *Otobiografi*, 199.

204. Tentang Militer dan Militerisme, April 27, 1967, 111, Sekkab, ANRI.

205. Soeharto, Naskah Sambutan Ulang Tahun I Harian "KAMI" Bertempat di Gedung P.W.I. Pusat, June 17, 1967, 999-2, PPS, ANRI.

206. For hierarchical trust see Zhenhua Su, Yanyu Ye, Jingkai He, and Waibin Huang, "Constructed Hierarchical Government Trust in China: Formation Mechanism and Political Effects," *Pacific Affairs* 89, no. 4 (December 2016): 771–794.

207. "Indonesia Arrests Sukarno Followers," *New York Times*, July 17, 1967; "Indonesian Students Protest Corruption," *Washington Post*, July 23, 1967; "Students Protest in Jakarta," *New York Times*, August 20, 1967; "DPRGR Perlu Diperbaharui," *Mahasiswa Indonesia* 73, November 1967.

208. Raillon, *Les étudiants*, 59; "Jenderal Soeharto Menerima Wakil 11 Kesatuan Aksi Tingkat Pusat yang Dipimpin Adnan Buyung Nasution," January 29, 1968, in *Jejak Langkah 1965–68*, 248; "Menyambut Dua Tahun KAMI, Moga-Moga KAMI Tidak Menjadi New PPMI," *Kompas*, October 25, 1967.

209. Amanat Pejabat Presiden Republik Indonesia pada Upacara Pelantikan Haji Dokter Roeslan Abdulgani sebagai Wakil Tetap Pemerintah Republik Indonesia di PBB, dan Profesor Doktor Wijoyo Nitisastro Sebagai Ketua Bappenas pada tanggal 22 Juli 1967 di Jakarta, https://soeharto.co/1967-07-22-amanat-pejabat-presiden-soeharto-pada-pelantikan-wakil-tetap-pbb-dan-bappenas/ (accessed April 20, 2020); "Pejabat Presiden Jenderal Soeharto Harapkan Bappenas Susun Repelita yang Realistis," August 15, 1967, in *Jejak Langkah 1965–68*, 201.

210. Salim, "Recollections," 209.

211. Airgram A, Jakarta to State, September 13, 1967, E 5 INDON, Central Files 1967–69, RG 59, USNA.

212. "Jenderal Soeharto Menyampaikan Nota Keuangan 1968," October 16, 1967, in *Jejak Langkah 1965–68*, 215–216.

213. Airgram, Jakarta to State, January 12, 1968, E 2-2 INDON, Central Files 1967–69, RG 59, USNA.

214. "Hari Ketiga Demonstrasi Jakarta Menuntut Penurunan Harga Beras," January 24, 1968, in *Jejak Langkah 1965–68*, 245.
215. "Tanggapi Putusan Panglima Kodam Se-Jawa, Jenderal Soeharto: Tahun 1968 sebagai Batas Tahun Kesabaran Rakyat," January 10, 1968, in *Jejak Langkah 1965–68*, 239; "Menerima Alim Ulama, Jenderal Soeharto Meminta Ummat Islam Giat Berjuang," January 12, 1968, in *Jejak Langkah 1965–68*, 240–241; "Pimpinan Muhammadiyah Menyampaikan Saran kepada Pejabat Presiden Soeharto," January 16, 1968, in *Jejak Langkah 1965–68*, 242; "PB HMI Menyampaikan Saran-Saran kepada Pejabat Presiden Jenderal Soeharto," January 25, 1968, in *Jejak Langkah 1965–68*, 245–246; "Jenderal Soeharto Melakukan Konsultasi dengan Empat Parpol," January 26, 1968, in *Jejak Langkah 1965–68*, 246–247; "Jenderal Soeharto Menerima PB NU," January 27, 1968, in *Jejak Langkah 1965–68*, 247–248; "Jenderal Soeharto Menerima Wakil 11 Kesatuan Aksi Tingkat Pusat yang Dipimpin Adnan Buyung Nasution," January 29, 1968, in *Jejak Langkah 1965–68*, 248.
216. Soeharto, *Pikiran*, 226.
217. "Refreshing DPR-GR demi Stabilisasi Ekonomi & Politik," *Berita Yudha*, February 10, 1968.
218. Anwar, *Dari Koresponden Kami*, 66.
219. Amirmachmud, *Otobiografi*, 307.
220. Nasution, *Memenuhi Panggilan Tugas, Jilid 8*, 46.
221. "Troops Open Fire in Jakarta," *Financial Times*, March 19, 1968.
222. "Police, Students Clash in Indonesian March," *Hartford Courant*, March 19, 1968.
223. Quoted in Nasution, *Memenuhi Panggilan Tugas, Jilid 8*, 55–56.
224. Nasution, *Memenuhi Panggilan Tugas, Jilid 8*, 6.

Chapter 4

1. Adam Malik, "Promise in Indonesia," *Foreign Affairs* 46, no. 2 (January 1968): 292–303.
2. Bilveer Singh, *ABRI and the Security of Southeast Asia: The Role and Thinking of General L. Benny Moerdani* (Singapore: Singapore Institute of International Affairs, 1994), 130; L. B. Moerdani, *Menegakkan Persatuan dan Kesatuan Bangsa: Pandangan dan Ucapan Jenderal TNI (Purn) L. B. Moerdani, 1988–1991* (Jakarta: Yayasan Kejangan Panglima Besar Sudirman, 1993), 187.
3. Wen-Qing Ngoei, "The United States and the 'Chinese Problem' in Southeast Asia," *Diplomatic History* 45, no. 2 (April 2021): 240–252.
4. Presidium Kabinet Ampera, Petundjuk-Petundjuk tentang Masalah Tjina, April 1967, 111, Sekkab, ANRI.
5. Christian Chua, *Chinese Big Business in Indonesia: The State of Capital* (New York: Routledge, 2008), 31–34; "Legacy of Sukarno's Chaos," *Financial Times*, August 22, 1967.
6. Jess Melvin, "Why Not Genocide? Anti-Chinese Violence in Aceh, 1965–66," *Journal of Current Southeast Asian Affairs* 32, no. 3 (2013): 63–91.
7. Letter, Holloway to Hasluck, March 2, 1967, A1838 3034/2/5/1 PART 3, Indonesia—Chinese Minority in Indonesia, NAA.
8. J. A. C. Mackie, "Anti-Chinese Outbreaks in Indonesia, 1959–1968," in *The Chinese in Indonesia: Five Essays*, ed. J. A. C. Mackie (Honolulu: University Press of Hawai'i, 1976), 116.
9. Airgram, Indonesia to State, May 7, 1966, POL 23-9 INDON, Central Files 1964–66, RG 59, USNA
10. "Kabinet Ampera Tegaskan Tindak Tegas Tindakan Rasialis dan Tidak Sesuai Pancasila," September 15, 1966, in *Jejak Langkah 1965–68*, 112.
11. Soemitro, *Pangkopkamtib*, 118–120.
12. Letter, Chen Yu to Suharto, February 8, 1967, 111, Sekkab, ANRI.
13. Nasution, *Memenuhi Panggilan Tugas, Jilid 7*, 201; Van der Kroef, "Sino-Indonesian Rupture," 33–34.
14. Memorandum, Wells to Hasluck, April 28, 1967, A1838 3034/2/5/1 Part 4, Indonesia—Chinese Minority in Indonesia, NAA.
15. Komando Operasi Tertinggi Gabungan-I, Atrap No.Int 100/G-I/4/67 tentang Persoalan-Tjina, April 25, 1967, 111, Sekkab, ANRI.

16. Cablegram, Jakarta to Canberra, April 12, 1967, A1838 3034/2/5/1 Part 3, Indonesia—Chinese Minority in Indonesia, NAA.

17. "Capitalists, Come Back!" *The Economist*, August 19, 1967.

18. Ross McLeod, "Soeharto's Indonesia: A Better Class of Corruption," *Agenda* 7, no. 2 (2000): 99–112; "Indonesia's Burden: Army Corruption Slows Efforts to End Chaos Inherited from Sukarno," *Wall Street Journal*, May 2, 1967.

19. Presidium Kabinet Ampera, Petundjuk-Petundjuk tentang Masalah Tjina, April 1967, 111, Sekkab, ANRI.

20. Instruksi Presidium Kabinet Nomor 37/U/IN/6/1967 Tahun 1967 tentang Kebijaksanaan Pokok Penyelesaian Masalah Cina, 111, Sekkab, ANRI; Surat Edaran Presidium Kabinet Ampera Nomor SE-06/Pres.Kab/6/1967 tahun 1967 tentang Masalah Cina, 111, Sekkab, ANRI.

21. "Jenderal Soeharto Keluarkan Dua Kebijakan Masalah Cina," December 6, 1967, in *Jejak Langkah 1965–68*, 225.

22. Zhou, *Migration in the Time of Revolution*, 175–179.

23. David Mozingo, *Chinese Policy toward Indonesia, 1949–1967* (Ithaca, NY: Cornell University Press, 1976), 260–261; Barbara Barnouin and Yu Changgen, *Chinese Foreign Policy during the Cultural Revolution* (New York: Kegan Paul International, 1998), 1–27; Melvin Gurtov, "The Foreign Ministry and Foreign Affairs during the Cultural Revolution," *China Quarterly* 40 (October–November 1969): 65–102; Central Intelligence Agency, "Mao's Red Guard Diplomacy: 1967," June 21, 1968, https://www.cia.gov/library/readingroom/docs/polo-21.pdf (accessed October 25, 2022).

24. "Kuasa Usaha *Ad Interim* RRC di Jakarta *Dipersona-Non-Gratakan*," April 24, 1967, in *Jejak Langkah 1965–68*, 173; "Sidang Kabinet Ampera Putuskan Pembentukan Panitia Negara Urusan Cina, PMDN dan PMDA," April 26, 1967, in *Jejak Langkah 1965–68*, 174.

25. Tentang Kegiatan2 Tjina, April 27, 1967, 111, Sekkab, ANRI.

26. "Chinese in Jakarta Fire at Mob," *Newsday*, August 2, 1967.

27. Zhou, *Migration in the Time of Revolution*, 181.

28. "1,000 Indonesians Raid China's Embassy, Beat 9," *New York Times*, October 1, 1967; "Chinese Embassy Stormed, Ravaged by 1,000 Indonesians," *Atlanta Constitution*, October 2, 1967.

29. "Pemerintah RI Membekukan Hubungan Diplomatik dengan RRC," October 1, 1967, in *Jejak Langkah 1965–68*, 213.

30. Cablegram, Canberra to London, April 30, 1966, A2908 M120 PART 5, Malaysia/Indonesia Dispute, NAA; Cablegram, Bangkok to Canberra, June 4, 1966, A1838 3006/4/7, South-East Asia—Indonesia—Malaysia—Relations—Confrontation, NAA.

31. "A Call for Unity," *Straits Times*, May 4, 1965.

32. Pacifico Castro, *Diplomatic Agenda of Philippine Presidents, 1946–1985* (Manila: Foreign Service Institute, 1985), 144, 152–153; Carlos P. Romulo and Beth Day Romulo, *The Philippine Presidents* (Quezon City: New Day Publishers, 1988), 137.

33. Telegram, Jakarta to State, May 27, 1966, POL INDON-US, RG 59, Central Files 1964–66, RG 59, USNA.

34. "Ketua Presidium Djenderal Soeharto: Kita Harus Dapat Mentjiptakan Stabilisasi Politik jang Mantap," *Berita Yudha*, August 8, 1966.

35. "Organisasi Pertahanan," *Antara*, December 25, 1966; "Kebijakan Militer dan Kewaspadaan Militer," *Berita Yudha*, January 9, 1967; "The Question of Joint Defense," *Djakarta Times*, January 3, 1967.

36. Memorandum, Philips to Murray, January 30, 1967, A1838 3034/7/1 Part 10, Indonesia—Foreign Policy—General, NAA.

37. Dewi Fortuna Anwar, *Indonesia in ASEAN: Foreign Policy and Regionalism* (Singapore: Institute of Southeast Asia Studies, 1994), 51–52; Savingram, Jakarta to Canberra, March 3, 1967, A1838 3034/7/1 PART 10, Indonesia—Foreign Policy—General, NAA.

38. "Malik: The Bigger ASA We Are Seeking," *Straits Times*, April 12, 1967.

39. "A Larger ASA? Pointless, Says the Tengku," *Straits Times*, April 14, 1967; "Kemlu: Kami Sambut Baik 'ASA Lebeh Luas,'" *Berita Harian*, April 19, 1967.

40. Memorandum to Holyoake, February 2, 1967, A1838 3034/7/1 Part 10, Indonesia—Foreign Policy—General, NAA.

41. Quoted in Arnfinn Jorgensen-Dahl, *Regional Organization and Order in South-East Asia* (London: Macmillan, 1982), 37.

42. See *Antara*, July 21, 1967.

43. "New Defence Review Aims at Cuts East of Suez," *Financial Times*, March 17, 1967.

44. Savingram, Canberra to All Posts, March 9, 1967, A1838 3034/7/1 Part 10, Indonesia—Foreign Policy—General, NAA.

45. Soedjatmoko, "Indonesia and the World," in *Dyason Memorial Lectures 1967* (Melbourne: Australian Institute of International Affairs, 1968), 298–304.

46. See *Antara*, August 6, 1967.

47. The ASEAN Declaration (Bangkok Declaration), August 8, 1967, https://asean.org/asean2020/wp-content/uploads/2021/02/asean_declaration-1.pdf (accessed December 10, 2020).

48. Memo, Malik to Suharto, June 3, 1966, 2246, EKUIN, ANRI.

49. "Welcome ASEAN" *Far Eastern Economic Review*, August 17, 1967.

50. Adam Malik, *Mengabdi Republik, Jilid III: Angkatan Pembangunan* (Jakarta: PT Gunung Agung, 1979), 81.

51. "Our Modest Hopes Realised—Raja," *Straits Times*, August 10, 1967.

52. *National Security Institute (Lembaga Pertahanan Nasional)* (Jakarta: Lemhannas, 1965), 4; Lembaga Pertahanan Nasional, *25 Tahun Pengabdian* (Jakarta: Lembaga Pertahanan Nasional, 1990), 24–26, 38–39.

53. Lembaga Pertahanan Nasional, *Ketahanan Nasional* (Djakarta: Lembaga Pertahanan Nasional, 1968), 2.

54. Lemhannas, *Ketahanan Nasional*, 3.

55. Pidato Kenegaraan Presiden Republik Indonesia di hadapan Sidang DPR-GR pada tanggal 16 Agustus 1969 di Jakarta, 452-1, PPS, ANRI.

56. Lemhannas, *Ketahanan Nasional*, 12–13, 15.

57. "Presiden Soeharto Rapat Umum di Tanjung Karang," July 15, 1968, in *Jejak Langkah 1968–73*, 28-29.

58. Lemhannas, *Ketahanan Nasional*, 16.

59. Lemhannas, *Ketahanan Nasional*, 7.

60. For a genealogy of New Order political thought see Bourchier, *Illiberal Democracy in Indonesia*.

61. Quoted in Bourchier, *Illiberal Democracy in Indonesia*, 145.

62. See Abdul Haris Nasution, *Pokok-Pokok Gerilya dan Pertahanan Republik Indonesia dimasa jang Lalu dan jang Akan Datang* (Jakarta: Pembimbing, 1954).

63. "The Doctrine of Territorial Warfare: Translation of Document No. NS1124-01, Indonesian Army Staff and Command School, March 1962," in *The Indonesian Doctrine of Territorial Warfare and Territorial Management*, ed. Guy Pauker (Santa Monica: RAND Corporation, 1963).

64. Lemhannas, *Ketahanan Nasional*, 18.

65. "Milisi Akan Didjalankan di Indonesia," *Kompas*, April 7, 1969.

66. "Tadjuk Rentjana: Ketahanan Nasional," *Berita Yudha*, August 8, 1968.

67. A. R. Sutopo, "Masalah Komunisme di Negara-Negara ASEAN," in *Strategi dan Hubungan Internasional: Indonesia di Kawasan Asia-Pasifik*, ed. Hadi Soesastro and A. R. Sutopo (Jakarta: Centre for Strategic and International Studies, 1981), 397.

68. Memorandum, Jakarta to Wellington, April 1967, A1838 3034/7/1 Part 10, Indonesia—Foreign Policy—General, NAA.

69. Memorandum, Wells to Hasluck, May 5, 1967, A1838 3034/7/1 Part 11, Indonesia—Foreign Policy—General, NAA.

70. Wanandi, *Shades of Grey*, Kindle location 2871.

71. Arjodamar, "Konsep Gagasan tentang Pembentukan Sebuah Konfederasi Negara di Asia Tenggara," cited in Peter Polomka, "A Study of Indonesian Foreign Policy, with Special Reference to Military Involvement" (PhD diss., University of Melbourne, 1973), 133–136.

72. "Rentjana Kampanje 'Dwi Dharma': Program Pertahanan Darat Nasional sampai 1968," in *Doktrin Perdjuangan TNI-AD 'Tri Ubaya Çakti': Hasil Seminar AD ke-II tanggal 25 s/d 31 Agustus 1966 di Grha Wiyata Yudha/Seskoad, Bandung* (Bandung: Seskoad, 1966), 46–47.

73. See *Antara*, March 7, 1968.
74. "Malik Flies in with a Pledge," *Straits Times*, March 18, 1968; "Malik: We Are Prepared to Defend You," *Straits Times*, March 20, 1968.
75. Memorandum, Malik to Suharto, July 29, 1968, 71, Sekkab, ANRI.
76. Benigno Aquino, "Jabidah! Special Forces of Evil?" March 28, 1968 in *A Garrison State in the Make: And Other Speeches*, ed. Benigno Aquino (Manila: Benigno S. Aquino Jr. Foundation, 1985), 43–60.
77. "Malaysia Airs Sabah Charge," *Washington Post*, March 31, 1968.
78. "Malaysia Beritahu Dunia," *Berita Harian*, July 24, 1968; "The Break," *Philippines Free Press*, July 27, 1968; "Malaysia Suspends Links with Manila," *Washington Post*, September 20, 1968.
79. Thomas M. McKenna, *Muslim Rulers and Rebels: Everyday Politics and Armed Separatism in the Southern Philippines* (Los Angeles: University of California Press, 1998), 147–148; Sultan Rashid Lucman Statement to Islamic Conference, quoted in Tom Stern, *Nur Misuari: An Authorized Biography* (Manila: Anvil Publishing, 2012), Kindle location 757.
80. Stern, *Nur Misuari*, Kindle location 764.
81. Polomka, "A Study of Indonesian Foreign Policy," 235.
82. "Soal Sabah, Marcos Penuhi Pesan Presiden Soeharto," September 22, 1968, in *Jejak Langkah Pak Harto 28 Maret 1968–23 Maret 1973*, ed. G. Dwipayana and Nazarudin Sjamsuddin (Jakarta: Citra Kharisma Bunda, 2003) (hereafter *Jejak Langkah 1968–73*), 48.
83. Quoted in Robyn J. Abell, "Philippine Policy towards Regional Cooperation in Southeast Asia" (PhD diss., Australian National University, 1972), 372.
84. Joint Communiqué of the Third ASEAN Ministerial Meeting.
85. Adam Malik, "ASEAN," *Karya Wira Jati: Majalah Resmi Sekolah Staf dan Komando Angkatan Darat*, no. 29/30 (April 1969): 33–34.
86. Ali Moertopo, *National Resilience and Indonesia's Foreign Policy* (Jakarta, 1974), 4.
87. "Presiden Soeharto: Komunisme Dihadapi dengan Penguatan Idiologi Bangsa," August 11, 1969, in *Jejak Langkah 1968–73*, 149.
88. Telegram, Sumitro to Kissinger, September 25, 1970, Backchannel—Indonesia HAK/Sumitro 1970 [2 of 2], Box 101, HAK, RNPL.
89. Lembaga Pertahanan Nasional, Memorandum Diskusi Problema XV: Perkembangan ASEAN dalam rangka Peningkatan Ketahanan Nasional, September 24, 1970, 594, Lambertus Nicodemus Palar, ANRI.
90. *ASEAN Regional Workshop on: "The Role of Leadership in Development,"* Yogyakarta, 13–19 Dec. 1970 (Jakarta: Yayasan Tenaga Kerja Indonesia, 1971), 23.
91. "The Ismail Plan for Peace," *Straits Times*, January 24, 1968.
92. "Opening Statement by H. E. Tun (Dr.) Ismail bin Dato Abdul Rahman, Deputy Prime Minister of Malaysia," March 12, 1971, New Directions for ASEAN: Fourth Meeting of the Foreign Ministers of the Association of Southeast Asian Nations, Manila, 12–13 March, 1971, Box 3, ASEAN, Carlos P. Romulo Library, Philippines Department of Foreign Affairs.
93. "Blocks to Neutralization," *Manila Chronicle*, March 15, 1971.
94. Adam Malik, "Towards an Asian Asia," *Far Eastern Economic Review*, September 25, 1971.
95. Zone of Peace, Freedom and Neutrality Declaration, November 27, 1971, https://www.pmo.gov.my/wp-content/uploads/2019/07/ZOPFAN.pdf (accessed November 15, 2020).
96. Harry Tjan Silalahi, "CSIS Lahir dari Tantangan Jaman," in *CSIS 20 Tahun* (Jakarta: CSIS, 1991), 19–21.
97. Centre for Strategic and International Studies, Analisa Previsionil: Mengenai Asia pada Umumnja, Asia Tenggara pada Chususnja, January 1972, 2326, EKUIN, ANRI.
98. Joint Communiqué of the Fifth ASEAN Ministerial Meeting Singapore, 13–14 April 1972, http://asean.org/?static_post=joint-communique-of-the-fifth-asean-ministerial-meeting-singapore-13-14-april-1972 (accessed June 22, 2019).
99. *Nusantara*, August 11, 1972.
100. *Antara*, July 6, 1973.
101. *U.S. Overseas Loans and Grants: Obligations and Loan Authorizations, 1945–2013* (Washington, DC: US Agency for International Development, 2015).

102. Joint Press Statement of the ASEAN Foreign Ministers Meeting to Assess the Agreement on Ending the War and Restoring Peace in Vietnam and to Consider Its Implications for Southeast Asia, Kuala Lumpur, 15 February 1973, http://asean.org/?static_post=joint-press-statement-the-asean-foreign-ministers-meeting-to-assess-the-agreement-on-end ing-the-war-and-restoring-peace-in-vietnam-and-to-consider-its-implications-for-southe ast-asia-kuala-lumpur-15-f (accessed June 22, 2020).
103. "Official Week in Review, July 27–August 2, 1973," *Official Gazette*, August 6, 1973.
104. Naskah Garis-Garis Besar Haluan Negara: Ketetapan MPR RI Nomor IV/MPR/73, in *Ketetapan-Ketetapan Majelis Permusyawaratan Rakyat Republik Indonesia tahun 1973* (Jakarta: Departemen Penerangan, 1973), 92.
105. Rizal Sukma, *Indonesia and China: The Politics of a Troubled Relationship* (New York: Routledge, 1999), 81.
106. See Michael Leifer, *ASEAN and the Security of South-East Asia* (New York: Routledge, 1989), 70–73.
107. Polkam, September 10, 1974, 567, HB IX, ANRI; Polkam, November 12, 1974, 567, HB IX, ANRI.
108. Polkam, June 10, 1975, 567, HB IX, ANRI.
109. Lembaga Pertahanan Nasional, *25 Tahun*, 107.
110. "Presiden Soeharto: Untuk Ketahanan Regional Tak Berarti Hrs Ada Pakta Militer," *Sinar Harapan*, February 21, 1977; Benny Moerdani, "Negarawan Saptamarga yang Cermat dan Teguh pada Princip Perjuangan," in *Diantara para Sahabat: Pak Harto 70 Tahun*, ed. G. Dwipayana, Soeharto, Nazaruddin Sjamsuddin, and Muti'ah Lestiono (Jakarta: Citra Lamtoro Gung Persada, 1991).
111. Lembaga Pertahanan Nasional, *The Principles of Cooperation: The Association of Southeast Asian Nations* (Jakarta: Departemen Pertahanan-Keamanan, 1974), 7.
112. See Ngandani, "ASEAN and the Security of Southeast Asia: A Study of Regional Resilience" (PhD diss., University of Southern California, 1982), 17, 39-43.
113. "Political Change and Military Transformation in the Philippines, 1966–1989: From the Barracks to the Corridors of Power," *Official Gazette*, October 3, 1990.
114. Lembaga Pertahanan Nasional, *Pelita II sebagai Usaha Peningkatan Ketahanan Nasional Indonesia dan Pemantapan ASEAN dalam Rangka Kerjasama Regional* (Jakarta: Departemen Pertahanan Keamanan, 1974), 4, 27–32.
115. Fuad Hassan, "ASEAN and Its Prospect for Development," November 1974 (s.l: Lembaga Pertahanan Nasional, 1974), 1.
116. Tan Sri Ghazali bin Shafie, *ASEAN's Response to Security Issues in Southeast Asia* (Jakarta: Centre for Strategic and International Studies, 1974), 11.
117. Alejandro Melchor Jr., "Security Issues in Southeast Asia," in *Regionalism in Southeast Asia: Papers Presented at the First Conference of ASEAN Students of Regional Affairs (ASEAN I): Jakarta, October 22-25, 1974* (Jakarta: Centre for Strategic and International Studies, 1975), 39–54.
118. Polkam, September 10, 1974, 567, HB IX, ANRI.
119. Ali Moertopo, "Superpower Interests in Southeast Asia," in *Self-Reliance and National Resilience*, 52; see also T. B. Simatupang, *Ketahanan Nasional dalam Situasi Baru di Asia Tenggara: Ceramah pada tanggal 30 Juni 1975 di Gedung Kebangkitan Nasional Jakarta* (Jakarta: Yayasan Idayu, 1976), 17.
120. "Viet Communists Capture $5 Billion in U.S. Weaponry," *Washington Post*, May 1, 1975.
121. Polkam, April 8, 1975, 567, HB IX, ANRI.
122. Edward Janner Sinaga, "Developments in the ASEAN Region—A Brief Overview," in *Self-Reliance and National Resilience*, ed. K. Subrahmanyam (New Delhi: Abhinav Publications, 1975), 40.
123. Departemen Luar Negeri, Laporan Mingguan, May 14, 1975, 94, ASSUS, ANRI.
124. This was a sentiment with which most national security officials in the New Order agreed. See Polkam, April 8, 1975, 567, HB IX, ANRI.
125. Quoted in Ang Cheng Guan, *Southeast Asia and the Vietnam War* (New York: Routledge, 2010), 107.
126. Polkam, June 10, 1975, 567, HB IX, ANRI.

127. Telegram, Jakarta to State, May 27, 1975, Electronic Telegrams 1975, AAD, RG 59, USNA.

128. Risalah Petunjuk-Petunjuk dan Putusan-Putusan Presiden dalam Sidang Dewan Stablisasi Politik dan Keamanan Nasional (hereafter Polkam), September 9, 1975, 567, HB IX, ANRI; "PM Lee Bertemu Suharto Hari Ini," *Berita Harian*, September 3, 1975.

129. Polkam, November 11, 1975, 567, HB IX, ANRI.

130. See Directorate of Foreign Information Service, *The First ASEAN Summit* (Jakarta: Department of Information, 1976).

131. Anwar, *Indonesia in ASEAN*, 140–151.

132. Quoted in Leszek Buszynski, *Soviet Foreign Policy and Southeast Asia* (London: Croom Helm, 1986), 126.

Chapter 5

1. Ferdinand Marcos, *Notes on the New Society of the Philippines* (Manila: Marcos Foundation, 1973), 12, 30–31.

2. "Pakta Pertahanan Asia Tenggara," *Antara*, February 17, 1967.

3. Keputusan Presidium Kabinet No. 13/U/Kep/1/1967 tentang Pembentukan, Tugas, dan Organisasi Liaison Office Republik Indonesia di Federasi Malaysia, 69, Sekkab, ANRI.

4. For Witono's background see Harsya Bachtiar, *Siapa Dia? Perwira Tinggi Tentara Nasional Indonesia Angkatan Darat* (Jakarta: Djambatan, 1988), 468.

5. Anwar, *Indonesia in ASEAN*, 143.

6. Soemitro, *Pangkopkamtib*, 231; the best summary of the campaign is in Jamie S. Davidson, *From Rebellion to Riots: Collective Violence on Indonesian Borneo* (Madison: University of Wisconsin Press, 2008), 47–84.

7. Surat Bahagian Turus Tentara Bersama 4014/104 bth 20hb Sep 67, Logistics Assistance to Tentera Nasional Indonesia—1982/0000859—W/E/05/B/15/c/2, ANM.

8. See Edmund Terence Gomez and Jomo K.S., *Malaysia's Political Economy: Politics, Patronage, and Profits*, 2nd ed. (New York: Cambridge University Press, 1999).

9. National Operations Council, *The May 13 Tragedy* (Kuala Lumpur: Government of Malaysia, 1969), 29–35.

10. Interview with John Helble, in Frontline Diplomacy: The Foreign Affairs Oral History Collection of the Association for Diplomatic Studies and Training, https://memory.loc.gov/service/mss/mfdip/2004/2004hel01/2004hel01.pdf (accessed June 29, 2020).

11. "Some Teaparty," *Far Eastern Economic Review*, June 12, 1969; for a claim that the ethnic violence was planned by the state see Kia Soong Kua, *May 13: Declassified Documents on the Malaysian Riots of 1969* (Petaling Jaya: SUARAM, 2007).

12. "Emergency Panel Rules in Malaysia," *New York Times*, May 17, 1969.

13. Memorandum of Conversation, Tunku and Green, October 13, 1969, POL MALAYSIA-US 1/1/67, Central Files 1967–69, RG 59, USNA; Review Group Meeting, December 18, 1969, Review Group Meeting—Indonesia, Malaysia, Singapore 12/22/69, H Files, Box H-041, RNPL.

14. "The Task of Restoring National Unity," *Straits Times*, July 18, 1969.

15. "'Think Afresh' Plea to the NCC," *Straits Times*, January 28, 1970.

16. Government of Malaysia, *Rukunegara* (Kuala Lumpur: Jabatan Chetak Kerajaan, 1970).

17. Karl Von Vorys, *Democracy without Consensus: Communalism and Political Stability in Malaysia* (Princeton, NJ: Princeton University Press, 2015), 398–412; Government of Malaysia, *Rancangan Malaysia Kedua, 1971–1975* (Kuala Lumpur: Percetakan Negara Kerajaan Malaysia, 1971), 41.

18. "Perjanjian Baru Indonesia, Malaysia Di-meterai," *Berita Harian*, March 18, 1970.

19. "Kampong Pak Harto di Tanjong Nalia Malaysia (Ketahanan Nasional Merupakan Prasyarat Stabilitas Asia Tenggara)," in *Jejak Langkah 1968-73*, 210.

20. Letter, Thalib to Suharto, December 8, 1970, 394, Sekkab, ANRI.

21. Letter, Thalib to Suharto, December 8, 1970, 394, Sekkab, ANRI.

22. Letter, Kedutaan Besar Republik Indonesia to Kementrian Luar Negeri Malaysia, December 16, 1970, Indonesia—1970—1982/0005484—W/A/06/A/31/c/3, ANM.

23. Telegram, Jakarta to State, August 8, 1969, POL INDON-US, Central Files 1967–69, RG 59, USNA.

24. "Antara Indonesia dan Malaysia: Dwi Fungsi Angkatan Bersendjata Kita," *Angkatan Bersendjata,* May 3, 1969; "Antara Indonesia dan Malaysia: Perkembangan Peranan Angkatan Bersendjata," *Angkatan Bersendjata,* May 7, 1969; "Antara Indonesia dan Malaysia: ABRI Menjadi Kekuatan Stabilisasi," *Angkatan Bersendjata,* May 10, 1969.

25. "Jamu PM Malaysia, Presiden Soeharto: Stabilitas Asia Tenggara Tanggung-Jawab Negara Asia Tenggara," December 17, 1969, in *Jejak Langkah 1968–73,* 278.

26. Quoted in Hishammuddin Tun Hussein, "Managing Complex Security Challenges: Historical Perspectives, Traditional Sovereignty, Nation Building and Collective Approaches," *Journal of Defence and Security* 4, no. 2 (2013): 113.

27. Savingram, Kuala Lumpur to Department of Foreign Affairs, December 7, 1971, Malaysia—Insurgency—Internal Security, A1838 696/6/7/1 Part 1, NAA.

28. Ong Weichong, "Securing the Population from Insurgency and Subversion in the Second Emergency (1968–1981)" (PhD diss., University of Exeter, 2010), 132–150.

29. "New Bid to Curb Red Terror," *Straits Times,* April 22, 1975; "Kerahan tenaga di Malaysia," *Berita Harian,* July 25, 1975; "Malaysia Calls Up Vigilantes," *Straits Times,* July 25, 1975.

30. Suparwan and Krisna, *Alamsjah,* 191–192, 201–205.

31. "Jenderal Soeharto–Presiden Marcos Tandatangani Komunike Bersama," January 14, 1968, in *Jejak Langkah 1965–68,* 241–242; "Presiden Marcos: Dibawah Jenderal Soeharto Indonesia Menjadi Terbesar di Asia Tenggara," January 15, 1968, in *Jejak Langkah 1965–68,* 242.

32. *Foreign Affairs Bulletin* (Manila) 3, no. 4a, January 20, 1968.

33. "We Must Survive in Asia: Postulates of Philippine Foreign Policy—Speech at the Manila Overseas Press Club, February 24, 1968," in Ferdinand Marcos, *Presidential Speeches,* Vol. I (Manila: Ferdinand Marcos, 1978).

34. Memorandum, Soemitro Djojohadikusumo to Suharto, May 13, 1969, 1997, EKUIN, ANRI.

35. See the foreign minister's speech in Carlos Romulo, *An Innovative Approach to Our Foreign Relations* (Manila: Department of Foreign Affairs, 1969).

36. Jose F. Lacaba, *Days of Disquiet, Nights of Rage: The First Quarter Storm and Related Events* (Quezon City: Asphodel Book, 1982), 68–70.

37. "If You Can't Beat Them . . ." *Far Eastern Economic Review,* February 20, 1969.

38. "But the Cupboard Is Bare," *Far Eastern Economic Review,* February 5, 1970.

39. Benigno Aquino, "When Law and Order Went Amok," January 27, 1970, in Aquino, ed., *A Garrison State,* 231–242.

40. Lacaba, *Days of Disquiet,* 81.

41. Juan Ponce Enrile, *A Memoir,* ed. Nelson A Navarro (Quezon City: ABS-CBN, 2012), Kindle location 6288.

42. For the rivalry between the two communist parties see Joseph Scalice, *The Drama of Dictatorship: Martial Law and the Communist Parties of the Philippines* (Ithaca, NY: Cornell University Press, 2023).

43. Communist Party of the Philippines, *Rectify Errors and Rebuild the Party* (London, Filipino Support group, n.d.); "Statement of the New People's Army," *Ang Bayan: Pahayagan ng Partido Komunista ng Pilipinas Pinapatnubayan ng Marxismo-Leninismo-Kaisipan Mao Tsetung,* July 1, 1969.

44. Amado Guerrero, *Lipunan at Rebolusyong Pilipino* (Manila: Lathalaang Pulang Tala, 1971), 65.

45. "Marcos at Bay," *Far Eastern Economic Review,* February 12, 1970.

46. Enrile, *A Memoir,* 276.

47. Quoted in William Rempel, *Delusions of a Dictator: The Mind of Marcos as Revealed in His Secret Diaries* (Boston: Little, Brown & Company, 1993), 35.

48. Ferdinand Marcos, "To Fight Alone, If Necessary," August 27, 1971, in Ferdinand Marcos, *Presidential Speeches,* Vol. III (Manila: Marcos Foundation, 1978), 429.

49. Primitivo Mijares, *The Conjugal Dictatorship of Ferdinand and Imelda Marcos* (San Francisco: Union Square, 1976), 137–138; Alfred W. McCoy, *Policing America's Empire: The United States, the Philippines, and the Rise of the Surveillance State* (Madison: University of Wisconsin Press, 2009), 395–396.

50. "Enrile—Ambush Fake," *Philippine Daily Inquirer*, February 23, 1986. Enrile later recanted, claiming not to have faked the ambush after all. See Enrile, *A Memoir*, Kindle location 8529.

51. Ferdinand Marcos, Diary Entry, September 22, 1972, http://philippinediaryproject.com/1972/09/22/sept-21-1972-thursday-sept-22nd-at-145-am/ (accessed July 5, 2020).

52. First Address to the Nation under Martial Law," in Ferdinand E. Marcos, *Presidential Speeches*, Vol. IV (Manila: Marcos Foundation, 1978), 136, 139.

53. Enrile, *A Memoir*, Kindle location 13424.

54. Pidato Balasan pada Djamuan Makan Malam Kenegaraan jang Diselenggarakan oleh Paduka jang Mulia Presiden Marcos, February 13, 1972, 107, PPS, ANRI.

55. "Suharto: Ang Kasuklam-suklam na Larawan ng Isang Pasistang Halimaw," *Ang Bayan: Pahayagan ng Partido Komunista ng Pilipinas Pinapatnubayan ng Kaisipan Mao Tsetung* 4, no. 2 (March 1972): 8.

56. Raymond Bonner, *Waltzing with a Dictator: The Marcoses and the Making of American Policy* (New York: Times Books, 1987), 95–96.

57. "Week in Review, September 1–7, 1972," *Official Gazette*, September 11, 1972.

58. "Official Week in Review, December 7–13, 1973," *Official Gazette*, December 17, 1973.

59. Marcos, *Notes on the New Society*, 70–71.

60. Ferdinand Marcos, "The True Filipino Ideology," *Official Gazette*, May 12, 1982.

61. See *An Ecosystem Approach to Southeast Asian Economic Integration Regional Meeting of Economic Planners on Southeast Asian Economy in the 1970s* (Bangkok: Ministerial Conference for Economic Development of Southeast Asia, 1972).

62. Presidential Decree No. 107: Creating the National Economic and Development Authority, January 24, 1973; Republic of the Philippines, *The National Economic and Development Authority* (Manila: NEDA, 1975).

63. Gerardo Sicat, *Cesar Virata: Life and Times through Four Decades of Philippine Economic History* (Quezon City: University of the Philippines Press, 2014), 260.

64. For a standard treatment see Gary Hawes, *The Philippine State and the Marcos Regime: The Politics of Export* (Ithaca, NY: Cornell University Press, 1987); see also Albert Celoza, *Ferdinand Marcos and the Philippines: The Political Economy of Authoritarianism* (Westport, CT: Praeger, 1997).

65. Marcos, *Notes on the New Society*, 99.

66. "The Need for Vigilance," in Ferdinand Marcos, *Presidential Speeches*, Vol. IV (Manila: Ferdinand E. Marcos, 1978), 218.

67. See Carolina Galicia Hernandez, "The Extent of Civilian Control of the Military in the Philippines: 1946–1976" (PhD diss., State University of New York, 1979), 160–161.

68. For the military's role in education, agriculture, and industry during Marcos's first term in office see Government of the Philippines, *Four-Year Economic Program for the Philippines: Fiscal Years 1967–1970* (Manila: Office of the President, 1966).

69. Alfred McCoy, *Closer than Brothers: Manhood at the Philippine Military Academy* (New Haven, CT: Yale University Press, 1999).

70. ACDA, *World Military Expenditures and Arms Transfers, 1972–1982*.

71. Jose P. Magno Jr. and A. James Gregor, "Insurgency and Counterinsurgency in the Philippines," *Asian Survey* 26, no. 5 (May 1986): 507–508.

72. Enrile, *Autobiography*, Kindle location 6631.

73. "The Final Report of the Fact-Finding Commission: II: Political Change and Military Transmission in the Philippines, 1966–1989: From the Barracks to the Corridors of Power," *Official Gazette*, October 3, 1990.

74. Memorandum, Thomson to Rostow, April 2, 1966, *U.S. Declassified Documents Online*, Document CK2349491744 (accessed July 20, 2022).

75. Howard Loewen, "Foreign Relations between the Philippines and the United States," in *Routledge Handbook of the Contemporary Philippines*, ed. Mark R. Thompson and Eric Vincent C. Batalla (New York: Routledge, 2018), 165; for Marcos's invocation of East Asian developmental states as models see "Land Reform and Democracy," July 12, 1969, in Ferdinand Marcos, *Presidential Speeches*, Vol. II (Manila: Ferdinand Marcos, 1978), 314–320.

76. Jusuf Wanandi, "Sociopolitical Development and Institution Building in Indonesia," in *Asian Political Institutionalization*, ed. Robert A. Scalapino, Seizaburo Sato, and Jusuf Wanandi (Berkeley: Institute of East Asian Studies, 1986), 183.

77. Memorandum, Jakarta to Wellington, April 1967, A1838, 3034/7/1 Part 10, Indonesia—Foreign Policy—General, NAA.

78. Memorandum, Cook to Hasluck, August 25, 1967, A1838 3034/7/1 Part 11, Indonesia—Foreign Policy—General, NAA.

79. "Broadcast Excerpts from an Address Given by the Prime Minister, Mr. Lee Kuan Yew, on 'Changing Values in a Shrinking World' at the Political Study Centre," July 13, 1966, https://www.nas.gov.sg/archivesonline/data/pdfdoc/lky19660713.pdf (accessed July 10, 2020).

80. "Transcript of a Speech Made by the Prime Minister, Mr. Lee Kuan Yew, at a Seminar on 'International Relations,' Held at the University of Singapore," October 9, 1966, https://www.nas.gov.sg/archivesonline/data/pdfdoc/lky19661009a.pdf (accessed July 10, 2020).

81. Visit of the Prime Minister of Singapore to London, January 1968, Cabinet Papers 133/374, UKNA.

82. Ibrahim Adjie, Memorandum Pol 2/68: P.M. Lee Kuan Yew di London, January 22, 1968, 150, Sekkab, ANRI.

83. Boni Ray Siagian, ed., *Eighth Year Cycle of ASEAN: With Forewords/Messages of ASEAN Foreign Ministers* (Jakarta: Department of Information, 1976), 117.

84. Muchtaruddin Ibrahim, *Usman bin Haji Muhammad Ali Alias Janatin* (Jakarta: Departemen Pendidikan dan Kebudayaan, 1993), 42–44; "Singapura Tolak Permintaan Presiden Soeharto," *Kompas*, October 16, 1968.

85. Soemitro, *Pangkopkamtib*, 200.

86. "Presiden Soeharto Bahas Kemungkinan Tindakan Balasan kepada Singapura," October 30, 1968, in *Jejak Langkah 1968–73*, 57.

87. Lee Khoon Choy, *An Ambassador's Journey* (Singapore: Times Books International, 1983), 192, 196–197.

88. Lee Kuan Yew, *From Third World to First: The Singapore Story, 1965–2000* (New York: HarperCollins, 2000), 264–265.

89. For descriptions of the meeting see Soemitro, *Pangkopkamtib*, 211–215; Lee, *An Ambassador's Story*, 202–207; Lee, *Third World to First*, 265.

90. Lee, *Third World to First*, 266.

91. "Raja: A Change in Attitude to the Third World," *Straits Times*, April 14, 1972.

92. Lee, *An Ambassador's Journey*, 209–210.

93. Lee, *Third World to First*, 267.

94. Joint Communiqué Issued on the Occasion of the Official Visit of the Prime Minister of the Republic of Singapore to the Republic of Indonesia, May 27, 1973, https://www.nas.gov.sg/archivesonline/data/pdfdoc/lky19730527.pdf (accessed July 10, 2020).

95. Graham Allison and Robert D. Blackwill, eds., *Lee Kuan Yew: The Grand Master's Insights on China, the United States, and the World* (Cambridge, MA: MIT Press, 2012), 131.

96. See Chan Heng Chee, *Singapore: The Politics of Survival, 1965–1967* (Singapore: Oxford University Press, 1971).

97. Mattia Tomba, *Beating the Odds Together* (Singapore: World Scientific, 2019).

98. See Tim Huxley, *Defending the Lion City: The Armed Forces of Singapore* (St. Leonards: Allen & Unwin, 2000), Kindle locations 516–614.

99. "Hot Cross Lines," *Far Eastern Economic Review*, June 12, 1969.

100. "Southeast Asia's Concern: A New Balance of Power," *Singapore Bulletin* 1, no. 9 (1973): 41.

101. Norodom Sihanouk and Bernard Krisher, *Sihanouk Reminisces: World Leaders I Have Known* (Bangkok: Editions Duang Kamol, 1990), 66.

102. Nazaruddin Nasution, Diddy Hermawan, and Lily Meiliani, eds., *Indonesia-Cambodia: Forging Ties through Thick and Thin* (Jakarta: PT Metro Pos, 2002), 32–35; Soedjono Hoemardani, "Yang Benar adalah Keseimbangan Rasio dan Intuisi," in *CSIS 20 Tahun*, 3.

103. Quoted in George McTurnan Kahin, *Southeast Asia: A Testament* (New York: Routledge Curzon, 2003), 282.

104. Norodom Sihanouk, *My War with the CIA: The Memoirs of Prince Norodom Sihanouk* (New York: Pantheon Books, 1973), 216.

105. "Periscope," *Newsweek*, May 25, 1970.
106. Kahin, *Testament*, 282.
107. Nasution, *Memenuhi Panggilan Tugas, Jilid 8*, 230.
108. Telegram, State to Jakarta, April 10, 1970, POL 7 INDON 1/1/70, Subject Files 1970–73, RG 59, USNA; Minutes of WSAG Meeting, April 14, 1970, Originals, 1969 and 1970, WSAG Minutes, H-114, H Files, RNPL.
109. Richard Hunt, *Melvin Laird and the Foundation of the Post-Vietnam Military, 1969–1973* (Washington, DC: Office of the Secretary of Defense Historical Office, 2015), 158.
110. Telegram, Jakarta to State, April 2, 1970, in *FRUS 1969–76:20*, Document 285; Telegram, Jakarta to State, April 26, 1970, POL 7 INDON, Subject Files 1970–73, RG 59, USNA.
111. Biro Analisa dan Perundang-undangan, Memorandum tentang Bantuan Militer kepada Kambodja dan Politik Bebas Aktif R.I., June 18, 1970, 122, Sekkab, ANRI.
112. See *FRUS, 1969–76:20*, 624 fn 2.
113. "Adam's Prayer," *Far Eastern Economic Review*, May 7, 1970; Telegram, Jakarta to State, April 20, 1970, POL 7 INDON, Subject Files 1970–73, RG 59, USNA.
114. Telegram, State to Jakarta, March 31, 1970, POL CAMB-INDON, Subject Files 1970–73, RG 59, USNA.
115. Telegram, Jakarta to State, April 23, 1970, POL 7 INDON, Subject Files 1970–73, RG 59, USNA.
116. Telegram, Jakarta to State, April 24, 1970, POL 7 INDON, Subject Files 1970–73, RG 59, USNA.
117. Cablegram, Jakarta to Canberra, May 12, 1970, A1838 696/9/6 PART 2, Cambodia—Regional Conference on Cambodia 1970, NAA
118. Richard Nixon, "Address to the Nation on the Situation in Southeast Asia," April 30, 1970, https://www.presidency.ucsb.edu/documents/address-the-nation-the-situation-southe ast-asia-1 (accessed July 20, 2020).
119. Amanat pada Upatjara Pembukaan Konperensi para Menteri Luar Negeri Asia di Djakarta, May 16, 1970, 337, PPS, ANRI.
120. "Whispers from the Sideline," *Far Eastern Economic Review*, June 4, 1970.
121. Telegram, Jakarta to State, May 17, 1970, POL 7 INDON, Subject Files 1970–73, RG 59, USNA.
122. Memorandum of Conversation, Nixon, Kissinger, and Suharto, May 26, 1970, MemCon—The President/Pres. Suharto/Kissinger May 26, 1970, Box 1024, NSC Files, RNPL "Suharto Says Red Troop Intervention in Asia Must Be Prevented," *New York Times*, May 28, 1970.
123. Telcon, Kissinger and Moorer, May 27, 1970, May 21–31, 1970, Box 5, HAK Telcons, RNPL.
124. Telcon, Kissinger and Nixon, May 26, 1970, May 21–31, 1970, Box 5, HAK Telcons, RNPL.
125. Memorandum of Conversation, Kissinger and Sumitro, July 8, 1970, Backchannel—Indonesia HAK/Sumitro 1970 [2 of 2], Box 101, Backchannel—Indonesia HAK/Sumitro 1970 [2 of 2], RNPL.
126. "Minta Bantuan Indonesia, Menlu Kamboja Temui Presiden Soeharto," January 13, 1971, in *Jejak Langkah 1968–73*, 229.
127. Ken Conboy, *Kopassus: Inside Indonesia's Special Forces* (Singapore: Equinox, 2003), Kindle locations 3149–3208; "Jakarta Drilling Cambodian Group," *New York Times*, March 29, 1972.
128. Adam Malik, Laporan Khusus tentang Pembicaraan dengan Brigjen. Lon Non, Utusan Khusus Presiden Republik Khmer, October 30, 1972, in *Naskah Sumber Arsip Adam Malik Menembus Empat Zaman: Memperingati 100 Tahun Adam Malik* (Jakarta: Arsip Nasional Republik Indonesia, 2017), 103.
129. Government Proclaims National Mobilization, June 25, 1970, A1838 3016/1/1 Part 4, Cambodia—Internal—General, NAA.
130. Telegram, Jakarta to State, December 2, 1970, POL 7 INDON, Subject Files 1970–73, RG 59, USNA.
131. "Marshal Lon Nol Addresses the National Assembly on the Inaugural Day," *Khmer Republic* 1, no. 5 (December 1972): 43–44.
132. "Le maréchal Lon Nol renforce ses pouvoirs pour faire face à l'opposition cambodgienne une république déchantée I.—'Les campagnes nous échappent," *Le Monde*, March 13, 1972.

133. Robert Sam Anson, *War News: A Young Reporter in Indochina* (New York: Simon & Schuster, 1989), 130–131.

134. David Chandler, *A History of Cambodia*, 4th ed. (Boulder, CO: Westview Press, 2008), 249–252.

135. Lon Nol, *Le Néo-Khmérisme* (Phnom Penh: Republique Khmere, 1972), 34; Margaret Slocomb, "The Nature and Role of Ideology in the Modern Cambodian State," *Journal of Southeast Asian Studies* 37, no. 3 (October 2006): 381–384.

136. Telegram, Jakarta to State, February 26, 1975, Indonesia—State Department Telegrams to SECSTATE—NODIS (3), Box 6, National Security Adviser—Presidential Country Files for East Asia and the Pacific, GFPL.

137. Nazaruddin et al., *Indonesia-Cambodia*, 49–50; "Ambassador Richard C. Howland Interviewed by Charles Stuart Kennedy," January 26, 1999, The Association for Diplomatic Studies and Training Foreign Affairs Oral History Project, https://adst.org/wp-content/uploads/2012/09/Howland-Richard-C.1.pdf (accessed July 20, 2020), 262–267.

138. Quoted in Weinstein, *Indonesian Foreign Policy*, 198.

139. Pidato Pelantikan Duta Besar Luar Biasa dan Berkuasa Penuh Republik Indonesia Masing-Masing untuk Singapura dan Muang Thai, July 19, 1969, 719, PPS, ANRI.

140. "Presiden Soeharto Kunjungan Kenegaraan ke Malaysia dan Muangthai," March 16, 1970, in *Jejak Langkah 1968–73*, 138–139.

141. Leszek Buszynski, "Thailand: The Erosion of a Balanced Foreign Policy," *Asian Survey* 22, no. 11 (November 1982): 1039–1043.

142. Ali Moertopo, "Convergence and Divergence of Japan's and Indonesia's Interest and Responsibility in Southeast Asia," in *Japanese-Indonesian Relations in the Seventies: Papers Presented at the First Japanese-Indonesian Conference, December 6–8, 1973* (Jakarta: Centre for Strategic and International Studies, 1974), 40.

143. Benedict Anderson, "Withdrawal Symptoms: Social and Cultural Aspects of the October 6 Coup," *Bulletin of Concerned Asian Scholars* 9, no. 3 (1977): 13–30.

144. Telegram, State to Jakarta, July 18, 1975, Indonesia—State Department Telegrams from SECSTATE—EXDIS, Box 6, National Security Adviser—Presidential Country Files for East Asia and the Pacific, GFPL.

145. Kamol Somvichian, "'The Oyster and the Shell': Thai Bureaucrats in Politics," *Asian Survey* 18, no. 8 (August 1978): 829–837.

146. "Menerima PM Muangthai, Presiden Soeharto Ajak Tumbuhkan Semangat ASEAN," December 10, 1976, in *Jejak Langkah Pak Harto 27 Maret 1973–23 Maret 1978* (Jakarta: Citra Kharisma Bunda, 2003) (hereafter *Jejak Langkah 1973–78*), 418.

147. "Pidato pada Jamuan Santap Malam Kenegaraan untuk Menghormat yang Mulia Perdana Menteri Muangthai Tanin Kraivixien," December 10, 1976, 180-2, PPS, ANRI.

148. "Menerima Kunjungan PM Thailand, Presiden Soeharto Ajak Tingkatkan Ketahanan Nasional untuk Ketahanan Regional," February 17, 1978, in *Jejak Langkah 1973–78*, 598–599.

149. Daniel Fineman, *A Special Relationship: The United States and Military Government in Thailand, 1947–1958* (Honolulu: University of Hawai'i Press, 1997).

150. Michael Kelly Connors, *Democracy and National Identity in Thailand* (New York: RoutledgeCurzon, 2003), 130–142; Paul Handley, *The King Never Smiles: A Biography of Thailand's Bhumibol Adulyadej* (New Haven, CT: Yale University Press, 2006); for a skeptical analysis of the term ideology in Thai discourse see Michelle Tan, "Passing Over in Silence: Ideology, Ideals, and Ideas in Thai Translation," *Journal of Southeast Asian Studies* 43, no. 1 (February 2012): 32–54; for secular demystification see Benedict Anderson, "Withdrawal Symptoms: Social and Cultural Aspects of the October 6 Coup," *Bulletin of Concerned Asian Scholars* 9, no. 3 (1977): 13–30

151. "Thailand's 'Village Scouts' Prove to Be Too Zealous for Leaders," *New York Times*, November 29, 1976; Marjorie A. Muecke, "The Village Scouts of Thailand," *Asian Survey* 20, no. 4 (April 1980): 407–427.

152. Surachart Bamrungsuk, "From Dominance to Power Sharing: The Military and Politics in Thailand, 1973–1992" (PhD diss., Columbia University, 1999), 129.

153. Lie Tek Tjeng, "Vietnamese Nationalism: An Indonesian Perspective," *National Resilience* 1 (March 1982): 72–75.

154. For a broader narrative of Indonesian policy toward Vietnam see See Ngoc-Diep thi Trinh, "Indonesia's Foreign Policy toward Vietnam" (PhD diss., University of Hawai'i, 1995).
155. Adam Malik, *Politik Luar Negeri Indonesia Dipimpin oleh Falsafah Pantja-Sila: Pidato Waperdam/Menlu Adam Malik Dimuka Sidang DPR-GR pada tanggal 5 Mei 1966* (Jakarta: Kementrian Penerangan, 1966), 27–28.
156. "Bekas Dubes ke Hanoi Tidak Melihat Akhir yang Terlihat Perang Vietnam," *Kompas*, January 13, 1971.
157. Foreign Minister's Press Conference—ASEAN, Vietnam, China and Taiwan, September 1, 1967, A1838 3006/4/6 Part 1, Indonesian Relations with South Vietnam, NAA.
158. "Diperlukan Evaluasi Ulang Kebijakan Kita terhadap Perang Vietnam?" *Angkatan Bersendjata*, October 23, 1967.
159. Cablegram, Saigon to Canberra, March 30, 1967, A1838 3034/7/1 Part 10, Indonesia—Foreign Policy—General, NAA.
160. Wanandi, *Shades of Grey*, Kindle location 1970; Pour, *Benny*, 164; Memorandum, McLennan to Hasluck, March 6, 1967, A1838 3006/4/6 Part 1, Indonesian Relations with South Vietnam, NAA.
161. Indonesian Relations with North Vietnam and South Vietnam, August 25, 1967, A1838 3006/4/6 Part 1, Indonesian Relations with South Vietnam, NAA.
162. Inward Savingram, Jakarta to Canberra, January 3, 1968, A1838 3006/4/6 Part 2, Indonesian Relations with South Vietnam, NAA.
163. Memorandum, McLennan to Hasluck, December 3, 1968, A1838 3006/4/6 Part 2, Indonesian Relations with South Vietnam, NAA.
164. Soemitro, *Pangkopkamtib*, 161–162.
165. Lien-Hang Nguyen, *Hanoi's War: An International History of the War for Peace in Vietnam* (Chapel Hill: University of North Carolina Press, 2012), 141–160.
166. "Presiden Soeharto: Islam Agama Kemajuan, Jangan Perlebar Perbedaan (Melanjutkan Pertemuan dengan Para Menteri Luar Negeri," May 18, 1970, in *Jejak Langkah 1968–73*, 226; "Pertemuan Tutup 9 Parpol di Slipi," *Harian Kami*, March 3, 1971; Republic of Vietnam Representation in Indonesia, October 27, 1970, A1838 3006/4/6 Part 3, Indonesian Relations with South Vietnam, NAA.
167. "Presiden Soeharto: Penyelesaian Indocina Berpengaruh pada Pembangunan Asia Tenggara," July 3, 1972, in *Jejak Langkah 1968–73*, 451; Nguyen Phu Duc, *The Viet-Nam Peace Negotiations: Saigon's Side of the Story* (Christianburg: Dalley Book Service, 2005), 336.
168. Memorandum of Conversation, Kissinger and Indonesian Leaders, July 28, 1969, MemCons—The President's Asian and European Trip July–August 1969, Box 1023, NSC Files, RNPL.
169. Suli Suleiman, *Garis-Garis Besar Politik Luar Negeri Republik Indonesia* (Jakarta: Direktorat Research, 1973), 13–15.
170. Gareth Porter, *A Peace Denied: The United States, Vietnam, and the Paris Agreement* (Bloomington: Indiana University Press, 1975), 224.
171. M. Kharis Suhud, Delegasi Republik Indonesia pada I.C.C.S. di Vietnam, March 24, 1975, 430, HB IX, ANRI.
172. M. Kharis Suhud, "Intuisinya Sangat Tajam," in *Diantara Para Sahabat Pak Harto 70 Tahun*, ed. G. Dwipayana and Nazaruddin Sjamsuddin (Jakarta: Citra Lamtoro Gung Persada, 1991), 734–736.
173. Simon Toner, "Imagining Taiwan: The Nixon Administration, the Developmental States, and South Vietnam's Search for Economic Viability, 1969–1975," *Diplomatic History* 41, no. 4 (September 2017): 772–798; Sean Fear, "Saigon Goes Global: South Vietnam's Quest for International Legitimacy in the Age of Détente," *Diplomatic History* 42, no. 3 (June 2018): 428–455.

Chapter 6

1. Sofjan Wanandi and J. Soedjati Djiwandono, "Soedjono Hoemardani dan Hubungan Indonesia-Jepang," in *Soedjono Hoemardani: Pendiri CSIS, 1918–1986* (Jakarta: Centre for Strategic and International Studies, 1987), 81–83; see also Soedjono Hoemardani, "Aspek

Strategi dari Hubungan antara Indonesia dan Jepang," in *Strategi dan Hubungan Internasional,* 565–566.

2. "Djepang Berusaha Keras Memenuhi Permintaan Indonesia," *Kompas,* January 24, 1968.

3. Franklin Weinstein, "The Uses of Foreign Policy in Indonesia" (PhD diss., Cornell University, 1972), 635n115.

4. Memorandum: Indonesia—Request for Stand-By Arrangement, Schweitzer to Members of the Executive Board, February 7, 1968, IMF Archives.

5. H. W. Arndt, "Survey of Recent Developments," *Bulletin of Indonesian Economic Studies* 4, no. 10 (June 1968): 2.

6. Statement by U Tun Thin, Chief of IMF Staff Team at the Meeting of the Inter-Governmental Group on Aid to Indonesia, at Rotterdam, April 22–24, 1968, S 1193 Inter-Governmental Aid Meeting Indonesia—Rotterdam April 1968, Box 395, Economic Subject Files, Central Files Collection, IMF Archives.

7. Statement of the Indonesian Delegation at the Meeting of the Inter-Governmental Group on Indonesia at Rotterdam, 22–24 April 1968, S 1193 Inter-Governmental Aid Meeting Indonesia—Rotterdam April 1968, Box 395, Economic Subject Files, Central Files Collection, IMF Archives.

8. Laporan Delegasi Republik Indonesia ke Konperensi Inter-Governmental Group on Indonesia ke-4 di Rotterdam tanggal 22, 23 dan 24 April 1968, 2215, EKUIN, ANRI; Laporan Tambahan Mengenai Konperensi I.G.G.I. di Rotterdam pada tanggal 22–24 April 1968, 2215, EKUIN, ANRI.

9. Final Statement by the Head of the Indonesian Delegation to the Inter-Governmental Group on Indonesia Meeting of April 22–24, 1968, Rotterdam, S 1193 Inter-Governmental Aid Meeting Indonesia—Rotterdam April 1968, Box 395, Economic Subject Files, Central Files Collection, IMF Archives.

10. "Presiden Soeharto Naikkan Harga BBM," April 24, 1968, in *Jejak Langkah 1968–73,* 11.

11. Statement by U Tun Thin, Chief of IMF Staff Team at the Meeting of the Inter-Governmental Group on Aid to Indonesia, at Rotterdam, April 22–24, 1968, S 1193 Inter-Governmental Aid Meeting Indonesia—Rotterdam April 1968, Box 395, Economic Subject Files, Central Files Collection, IMF Archives.

12. Soeharto, *Pikiran,* 441.

13. Telegram, Jakarta to State, April 22, 1968, E 8-1 INDON, Central Files 1967–69, RG 59, USNA.

14. Van der Kroef, *Indonesia since Sukarno* (Singapore: D. Moore for Asia Pacific Press, 1971), 67.

15. Telegram, Jakarta to State, April 27, 1968, E 1-1 INDON, Central Files 1967–69, RG 59, USNA.

16. Telegram, Jakarta to State, April 25, 1968, E 8-1 INDON, Central Files 1967–69, RG 59, USNA; Airgram, Jakarta to State, May 21, 1968, FN 10 INDON, Central Files 1967–69, RG 59, USNA.

17. Memorandum of Conversation, Widjojo, Salim, Humphrey et al, May 3, 1968, E 8-1 INDON 1/1/1967, Central Files 1967–69, RG 59, USNA.

18. Airgram, Jakarta to State, February 21, 1968, POL 1 INDON, Central Files 1967–69, RG 59, USNA.

19. Memorandum, Rostow to Johnson, June 18, 1968, in *FRUS 1964–68:26,* Document 258.

20. Airgram, Jakarta to State, May 24, 1968, FN 6-1 INDON, Central Files 1967–69, RG 59, USNA; Telegram, State to Jakarta, June 6, 1968, AID (GERM) 8 INDON, Central Files 1967–69, RG 59, USNA; Telegram, Jakarta to State, June 14, 1968, FN 14 INDON, Central Files 1967–69, RG 59, USNA.

21. Sambutan Presiden Republik Indonesia Djenderal Soeharto pada Pembukaan Diskusi Besar Dewan-Dewan Mahasiswa Universitas/Institut Negeri se-Indonesia, May 19, 1968, 1010, PPS, ANRI.

22. "Cabinet of Experts," *Far Eastern Economic Review,* June 20, 1968.

23. Letter, Siber to Tun Thin, June 18, 1968, File 4 INDONESIA—Relations with IBRD, Box 49, ASDAI Country Files, Asian Department Immediate Office, IMF Archives.

24. Soeharto, *Pikiran,* 238.

25. Quoted in Winters, *Power in Motion*, 78.
26. Widjojo Nitisastro, "Basic Aims of Economic Planning," *Financial Times*, October 24, 1968.
27. "Text of Secretary McNamara's Address on United States Policy in South Vietnam," *New York Times*, March 27, 1964.
28. Letter, Tazi to Soeharto, May 16, 1968, 76, Sekkab, ANRI.
29. World Bank History Project, Transcript of Interview with Robert McNamara, April 1, May 10, and October 3, 1991, http://documents.worldbank.org/curated/en/981971468149966185/pdf/790840TRN0McNa001000October03001991.pdf (accessed January 8, 2019).
30. Memorandum, William Clark to Robert McNamara, June 27, 1968, Contacts with Member Countries: Indonesia—Correspondence 01, Contacts—Member Countries Files, Records of President Robert S. McNamara, Records of the Office of the President, World Bank Archives.
31. World Bank History Project, Transcript of Interview with Robert McNamara, April 1, May 10, and October 3, 1991, http://documents.worldbank.org/curated/en/981971468149966185/pdf/790840TRN0McNa001000October03001991.pdf (accessed January 8, 2019).
32. IBRD President McNamara's Principal Conclusions on Indonesian Economic Problems as Prepared by the Indonesians, June 1968, Contacts with Member Countries: Indonesia—Correspondence 01, Contacts—Member Countries Files, Records of President Robert S. McNamara, Records of the Office of the President, World Bank Archives.
33. Letter, Siber to Tun Thin, June 16, 1968, File 4 INDONESIA—Relations with IBRD, Box 49, ASDAI Country Files, Asian Department Immediate Office, IMF Archives.
34. Letter, Savkar to Southard, May 20, 1968, File 4 INDONESIA—Relations with IBRD, Box 49, ASDAI Country Files, Asian Department Immediate Office, IMF Archives.
35. Letter, Siber to Tun Thin, June 15, 1968, File 4 INDONESIA—Relations with IBRD, Box 49, ASDAI Country Files, Asian Department Immediate Office, IMF Archives.
36. William Hollinger, Harvard University Development Advisory Service: Advisory Project—Indonesia, July 1, 1968–September 1, 1969, September 1, 1969, Indonesia—Folder 1 of 3, UAV 462.5010.5—Institute for International Development Project Records, 1957–1982, HUA.
37. "The Basic Framework of the Five-Year Development Plan (Repelita) (1968)," in *Indonesian Development Experience*, 105–106.
38. Government of Indonesia, *Rentjana Pembangunan Lima Tahun 1969/70–1973/74* (Jakarta: Departemen Penerangan, 1969), 36, 20, 46.
39. "Repelita," in *Menuju Masyarakat Adil Makmur: 70 Tahun Prof Sarbini Sumawinata*, ed. Sjahrir (Jakarta: Gramedia, 1989).
40. Airgram, Jakarta to State, February 7, 1969, E 5 INDON/FIVE YEAR PLAN, Central Files 1967–69, RG 59, USNA.
41. Memorandum, Savkar and Finch to Schweitzer and Southard, July 11, 1968, S 1193 Indonesia Debt Renegotiation Meetings December 1966–September 1968, Box 393, Economic Subject Files, Central Files Collection, IMF Archives; for a detailed analysis of Indonesia's debt service costs see IMF Technical Assistance Mission to Indonesia, Indonesia: Debt Profile and Export Projections, 1968–81, September 30, 1968, S 1193 Indonesia Debt Renegotiation Meetings December 1966–September 1968, Box 393, Economic Subject Files, Central Files Collection, IMF Archives.
42. Radius Prawiro, *Indonesia's Struggle for Economic Development: Pragmatism in Action* (New York: Oxford University Press, 1998), 67; Memorandum, Mohammed to Sture, December 31, 1968, File 5 INDONESIA—Abs Debt Study (1968–70), Box 45, ASDAI Country Files, Asian Department Immediate Office, IMF Archives.
43. "Creditors Defer Payment," *Financial Times*, October 18, 1968.
44. Letter to Hermann Abs, 1968, File 5 INDONESIA—Abs Debt Study (1968–70), Box 45, ASDAI Country Files, Asian Department Immediate Office, IMF Archives.
45. Telegram, The Hague to State, October 28, 1968, FN 1-1 INDON, Central Files 1967–69, RG 59, USNA.
46. Inter-Governmental Group on Indonesia, Meeting at Scheveningen on 21, 22, and 23 October, 1968: Summary of Proceedings, FN 1-1 INDON, Central Files 1967–69, RG 59, USNA; G. A. Posthumus, *The Inter Governmental Group on Indonesia (I.G.G.I.)* (Rotterdam: Rotterdam University Press, 1971), 36–37.

47. Memorandum, Mohammed to Schweitzer, April 29, 1969, File 5 INDONESIA—Abs Debt Study (1968–70), Box 45, ASDAI Country Files, Asian Department Immediate Office, IMF Archives.

48. Mohammed, Memorandum for the Files: Indonesia, May 12, 1969, File 5 INDONESIA—Abs Debt Study (1968–70), Box 45, ASDAI Country Files, Asian Department Immediate Office, IMF Archives.

49. Telegram 103/bon/vii/69, Bonn to Suharto, July 14, 1968, 78A, Sekkab, ANRI.

50. Hermann J. Abs, The Problem of Indonesia's External Debt and Reflexions on Its Solution, July 30, 1969, 186, Sekkab, ANRI.

51. Telegram, Bali to State, August 5, 1969, Tony Lake Chron File [6 of 6] [June 1969–May 1970], Box 1048, NSC Files, RNPL.

52. Telegram, Paris to State, October 28, 1969, FN 14 INDON, FN 14 INDON, Central Files 1967–69, RG 59, USNA; Telegram, Widjojo to Suharto, November 1, 1969, 78A, Sekkab, ANRI.

53. MemCon, Nakajima, Kikuchi, Barnett, et. al, October 20, 1969, FN 14 INDON, Central Files 1967–69, RG 59, USNA.

54. MemCon, Widjojo, Saleh, Barnett, et al., October 26, 1969, FN 14 INDON, Central Files 1967–69, RG 59, USNA.

55. Meeting of the Indonesian Paris Club, December 12, 1969, FN 14 INDON, Central Files 1967–69, RG 59, USNA; Telegram, Widjojo to Suharto, December 14, 1969, 78A, Sekkab, ANRI.

56. Agreed Minute of Meeting, December 12, 1969, FN 14 INDON, Central Files 1967–69, RG 59, USNA.

57. Telegram, Paris to Jakarta, March 7, 1970, 78A, Sekkab, ANRI.

58. Telegram, Paris to Jakarta, April 25, 1970, 78A, Sekkab, ANRI.

59. Telegram, Jakarta to State, March 13, 1970, FN 14 INDON, Subject Files 1970–73, RG 59, USNA; "Soviet Agrees to Extend Term of Indonesian Debt," New York Times, August 28, 1970; Widjojo, Indonesian Development Experience, 398–416.

60. MemCon, Nixon and Malik, November 17, 1969, in FRUS 1969–76:20, 597.

61. Telegram, The Hague to State, December 10, 1969, FN 14 INDON, Central Files 1967–69, RG 59, USNA.

62. International Monetary Fund, Report on Meeting of Inter-Governmental Group on Indonesia and Indonesian Debt Meeting, December 29, 1969, IMF Archives.

63. Letter, Soedjatmoko to Suharto, December 22, 1969, in Surat-Surat Pribadi Soedjatmoko kepada Presiden (Jenderal) Soeharto (16 Juni 1968–26 April 1971), ed. M. Nursam (Jakarta: PT Gramedia Pustaka Utama, 2002), 148–149.

64. "Build the PKI along the Marxist-Leninist Line to Lead the People's Democratic Revolution of Indonesia (Self-Criticism of the Political Bureau of the CC PKI), September 1966," in Build the PKI along the Marxist-Leninist Line to Lead the People's Democratic Revolution in Indonesia: Five Important Documents of the Political Bureau of the CC PKI (Delegation of the CC PKI, 1971), 85–208.

65. Soemitro, Pangkopkamtib, 100–101.

66. Nurinwa Ki S. Hendrowinoto, ed., M. Jasin: "Saya Tidak Pernah Minta Ampun kepada Soeharto" (Jakarta: Pustaka Sinar Harapan, 1998), 68.

67. Crouch, Army and Politics, 232–234; Surat Keputusan No. Kep-001/ORBA/9/1967 Panglima Daerah Militer VIII Brawidjaja selaku Pembina Orde Baru Tingkat 1/Propinsi Djawa Timur, 316-B, Arsip Komando Daerah Militer V/Brawijaya, Museum Brawijaya.

68. Justus M. van der Kroef, "Indonesian Communism since the 1965 Coup," Pacific Affairs 43, no. 1 (Spring 1970): 38–43; Hearman, Unmarked Graves, 112–137.

69. Semdam VIII Brawidjaja, Operasi Trisula Kodam VIII Brawidjaja (Surabaya: Jajasan Taman Tjandrawilwatika, 1969); "Reds Renew Campaign in Indonesia," New York Times, August 11, 1968.

70. "Tadjuk Rentjana: Hari Ini," Berita Yudha, September 7, 1968.

71. "Presiden Soeharto: Pembangunan Irian Barat Menjadi Prioritas Nasional," May 4, 1968, in Jejak Langkah 1968–73, 15.

72. Quoted in van der Kroef, Indonesia after Sukarno, 128.

73. See Pietr Drooglever, *An Act of Free Choice: Decolonization and the Right to Self-Determination in West Papua*, trans. Theresa Stanton, Maria van Yperen, and Marjolijn de Jager (New York: Oneworld, 2009), 651–658.
74. Soeharto, *Pikiran*, 109–110.
75. Van Der Kroef, *Indonesia after Sukarno*, 137.
76. Airgram, Jakarta to State, January 24, 1968, E 2-2 INDON, Central Files 1967–69, RG 59, USNA.
77. See Daniel Lev, "Judicial Authority and the Quest for an Indonesian Rechtsstaat," in *Legal Evolution and Political Authority in Indonesia: Selected Essays* (The Hauge: Kluwer Law International, 2000), 215–244.
78. MemCon, Lim Bian Kie and Barber III, March 24, 1969, DEF INDON, Central Files 1967–69, RG 59, USNA.
79. Telegram, Jakarta to State, February 29, 1968, POL 19 WEST IRIAN, Central Files 1967–69, RG 59, USNA.
80. Airgram, Jakarta to State, June 18, 1968, DEF 6 INDON, Central Files 1967–69, RG 59, USNA.
81. Telegram, Jakarta to State, July 23, 1968, DEF 9 INDON, Central Files 1967–69, RG 59, USNA.
82. Airgram, Jakarta to State, July 9, 1969, POL 19 WEST IRIAN, Central Files 1967–69, RG 59, USNA.
83. See Peter King, *West Papua and Indonesia since Suharto: Independence, Autonomy or Chaos?* (Sydney: UNSW Press, 2004), 28.
84. Telegram, Jakarta to State, June 20, 1969, E 5 INDON, Central Files 1967–69, RG 59, USNA.
85. Airgram, Jakarta to State, November 19, 1969, PET 2 INDON, Central Files 1967–69, RG 59, USNA.
86. Pidato di depan Anggota DPR-GR dan Gubernur Irian Barat pada tanggal 1 September 1969 di Jayapura, Irian Barat, https://soeharto.co/1969-09-16-pidato-presiden-soeharto-di-depan-anggota-dpr-gr-dan-gubernur-irian-barat/ (accessed September 22, 2020).
87. Lee Hong Oey, *Indonesian Government and Press during Guided Democracy* (Zug: Inter Documentation Company, 1971).
88. Quoted in Mary E. McCoy, *Scandal and Democracy: Media Politics in Indonesia* (Ithaca, NY: Southeast Asia Program Publications, 2019), 19.
89. David Hill, *The Press in New Order Indonesia* (Jakarta: Equinox Publishing, 2007), 34.
90. Adam Schwarz, *A Nation in Waiting: Indonesia's Search for Stability*, 2nd ed. (St. Leonards: Allen & Unwin, 1999), 32.
91. See *Indonesia Raya*, November 22, 24, and 25, 1969; "Pertamina Menjawab," *Angkatan Bersendjata*, November 25, 1969; "Manajemen, Hambatan Pembangunan," *Indonesia Raya*, April 9, 1970; for Ibnu's rebuttal see *Ekspres*, November 7, 1970.
92. *Sinar Harapan*, January 19, 1970
93. Anwar, *Dari Koresponden Kami*, 65–66.
94. "Konferensi di Amsterdam," *Indonesia Raya*, December 5, 1969.
95. Telegram, Jakarta to State, November 26, 1969, PET 6 INDON, Central Files 1967–69, RG 59, USNA; Telegram, State to Jakarta, November 27, 1968, PET 6 INDON, Central Files 1967–69, RG 59, USNA.
96. See *Sinar Harapan*, July 18–24, 1970.
97. "Gerakan Pemuda/Mahasiswa sebagai *Pressure Group*" and "Polarisasi dan Konsolidasi Mahasiswa," in Arief Budiman, *Kebebasan, Negara, Pembangunan: Kumpulan Tulisan 1065–2005* (Jakarta: Freedom Institute, 2006), 267–274; Ramadhan, *Ibnu Sutowo*, 249–263.
98. "Pemerintah Bubarkan Komite Anti Korupsi," August 15, 1970, in *Jejak Langkah 1968–73*, 248; Rosihan Anwar, *Menulis dalam Air: Di Sini Sekarang Esok Hilang: Sebuah Otobiografi* (Jakarta: Sinar Harapan, 1983), 243–44, 250; Sambutan pada Pembukaan Kongres Nasional ke-XIV Persatuan Wartawan Indonesia, pada tanggal 14 Oktober 1970, di Palembang, https://soeharto.co/1970-10-sambutan-presiden-soeharto-pada-pembukaan-kongres-nasional-ke-xiv-pwi/ (accessed September 28, 2020).
99. Janet Steele, *Wars Within: The Story of "Tempo," an Independent Magazine in Soeharto's Indonesia* (Jakarta: Equinox Publishing, 2005), 61–62.

100. Memorandum 320/KD/70, Soekanto to Malik, September 25, 1970, 1894, EKUIN, ANRI.
101. "Foreign Aid Program Slowly Loses Support," *Los Angeles Times*, January 15, 1970; "Military Aid Limits Fought by Pentagon," *Hartford Courant*, February 9, 1970; Robert David Johnson, *Congress and the Cold War* (New York: Cambridge University Press, 2005), 179.
102. Amnesty International, "Monthly Newsletter from Amnesty International Postcards for Prisoners Campaign," October 1969, 1.
103. Memorandum, Ennals to All Sections, January 30, 1970, Folder 4, Box II.5 7, Amnesty International U.S.A. National Office Records, CUML.
104. Anwar, *Dari Koresponden Kami*, 58.
105. "Tadjuk Rentjana," *El Bahar*, July 19, 1968.
106. Airgram, Jakarta to State, July 30, 1968, DEF 6 INDON, Central Files 1967–69, RG 59, USNA.
107. Crouch, *Army and Politics*, 240.
108. Airgram, Jakarta to State, February 21, 1968, POL 1 INDON, Central Files 1967–69, RG 59, USNA.
109. Letter, Soedjatmoko to Suharto, June 16, 1968, in *Surat-Surat Pribadi*, 4–5.
110. Richard Nixon, Handwritten Notes: Indonesia, [April 1967], Far East and Middle East Trips 1967 (RN's Handwritten Notes), Series 347, Pre-Presidential Papers, RNPL.
111. Badan Koordinasi Intelidjen Negara, Laporan Intelidgen Berkala—Minggu ke-III & IV bulan "Mei—1967"—R-072/Lap/Kin/1967, 122, Sekkab, ANRI.
112. Richard Nixon, "Asia after Viet-Nam," *Foreign Affairs* 46, no. 1 (October 1967): 111, 123.
113. Telegram, Jakarta to State, March 23, 1969, POL INDON-US, Central Files 1967–69, RG 59, USNA.
114. Memorandum, Kissinger to Nixon, March 26, 1969, in *FRUS 1969–76:20*, Document 266.
115. Telegram, Jakarta to State, March 25, 1969, POL INDON-US, Central Files 1967–69, RG 59, USNA.
116. Richard Nixon, "Informal Remarks in Guam with Newsmen," July 25, 1969, https://www.presidency.ucsb.edu/documents/informal-remarks-guam-with-newsmen (accessed March 13, 2023); for the background to the Nixon Doctrine see Mattias Fibiger, "The Nixon Doctrine and the Making of Authoritarianism in Island Southeast Asia," *Diplomatic History* 45, no. 5 (November 2021): 958–961.
117. Apa dan Siapa Richard Milhous Nixon, 389, Sekkab, ANRI; Amerika Serikat dan Masalah-2 Utama jang Dihadapinja, 389, Sekkab, ANRI; Tjatatan Singkat: Hubungan Ekonomi Indonesia—A.S., 389, Sekkab, ANRI.
118. Telegram, Bali to State, August 5, 1969, Tony Lake Chron File [6 of 6] [June 1969–May 1970], Box 1048, NSC Files, RNPL.
119. Memorandum for the Record, Meeting with Indonesian Generals, July 27, 1969, Tony Lake Chron File [6 of 6] [June 1969–May 1970], Box 1048, NSC Files, RNPL.
120. Memorandum, Nixon to Kissinger, August 7, 1969, President/Kissinger Memos, Box 341, NSC Files, RNPL.
121. NSSM-61 Indonesia, Review Group Meeting—Indonesia, Malaysia, Singapore 12/22/69, H Files, Box H-041, RNPL.
122. Memorandum, Haig to Lake, August 11, 1969, Indonesian Generals, Box 101, HAK, RNPL.
123. "Reorganisasi ABRI," *Indonesia Raya*, October 11, 1969.
124. "Susunan Personalia Baru Dilingkungan Hankam," *Kompas*, November 11, 1969; "Kilasan Hidup para Kepala Staf Angkatan," *Kompas*, October 12, 1969; see also Julius Pour, *Laksamana Sudomo: Mengatasi Gelombang Kehidupan* (Jakarta, 1997), 217–221.
125. "Kesedjahteraan Pradjurit akan Langsung Ditangani," *Kompas*, February 2, 1970; "Perintah Harian Kepala Staf Angkatan Laut Berkenaan Dengan Serah Terima Djabatan Kepala Staf Angkatan Laut," December 16, 1969, in *Himpunan Amanat Kepala Staf Angkatan Laut (Periode 16 Desember 1969–31 Desember 1970)* (Jakarta, 1971), 3.
126. James Goldrick and Jack McCaffrie, eds., *Navies of South-East Asia: A Comparative Study* (New York: Routledge, 2013), 74.
127. "Lantik KSAU, Presiden Soeharto: Pembersihan Sisa-Sisa G.30.S/PKI bukan Karena Ketakutan, tapi Kewaspadaan," January 6, 1970, in *Jejak Langkah 1968–73*.

128. Memorandum, Holdridge to Kissinger, October 30, 1969, in *FRUS 1969–76:20*, Document 275.
129. Memorandum, Kissinger to Laird and Rogers, March 11, 1970, Backchannel—Indonesia HAK/Sumitro 1970 [2 of 2], Box 101, HAK, RNPL.
130. Memo, Ruslan Abdulgani to Suharto, January 6, 1970, 397, Sekkab, ANRI.
131. Departemen Pertahanan-Keamanan G-I/Intel, Laporan Chusus Nomor R/G-I/LC/008/ IV/1970 tentang: Amerika Serikat, April 29, 1970, 161, Sekkab, ANRI.
132. Memorandum of Conversation, Nixon, Suharto, and Kissinger, May 26, 1970, MemCon— The President/Pres. Suharto/Kissinger May 26, 1970, Box 1024, NSC Files, RNPL.
133. MemCon, Kissinger, Alamsjah, and Holdridge, May 27, 1970, MemCon—The President/ Pres. Suharto/Kissinger May 26, 1970, Box 1024, NSC Files, RNPL.
134. Letter, Masters to Purnell, May 28, 1970, POL 7 SUHARTO Talking Points, Memos 1970, Box 6, IMS, RG 59, USNA.
135. Memorandum of Conversation, Kissinger and Sumitro, July 1, 1970, Backchannel— Indonesia HAK/Sumitro 1970 [2 of 2], Box 101, HAK, RNPL; Memorandum, Lynn to Kissinger, July 7, 1970, Backchannel—Indonesia HAK/Sumitro 1970 [2 of 2], Box 101, HAK, RNPL.
136. Memorandum of Conversation, Sumitro and Kissinger, July 7, 1970, Backchannel— Indonesia HAK/Sumitro 1970 [2 of 2], Box 101, HAK, RNPL.
137. Memorandum, Panggabean to Galbraith, August 19, 1970, DEF 19-1 Combat Equipment, Box 5, IMS, RG 59, USNA.
138. Telegram, Fulton to CINCPAC, August 1970, DEF 19-1 Combat Equipment, Box 5, IMS, RG 59, USNA.
139. Ikrar Kebulatan Tekad Rakjat Djawa Barat ke-II untuk Meningkatkan Perdjuangan Orde Baru, January 18, 1968, 110, Sekkab, ANRI; H.R. Dharsono, Pedoman Pelaksanaan Ikrar Kebulatan Tekad Rakjat Djawa Barat ke-II, March 7, 1968, 110, Sekkab, ANRI
140. Amirmachmud, Djawaban Pemerintah atas Pertanjaan Anggota-Anggota DPR-GR Sdr. M. Jusuf Hasjim dkk. tentang "Perombakan Struktur Politik dengan Dibentuknja Dwi Grup Sistem" di-Daerah Djawa Barat, May 1969, 110, Sekkab, ANRI.
141. "Pemilu Pemalu," *Far Eastern Economic Review*, November 6, 1969.
142. Sekretarat Bersama Golongan Karya, Pokok-2 Pikiran tentang Pemilu jang Perlu Diungkapkan dalam Briefing dengan Presiden tanggal 17 Oktober 1969, October 17, 1969, 107, Sekkab, ANRI.
143. Pemilu dalam Strategi Nasional, October 1969, 114, Sekkab, ANRI.
144. See "Tadjuk Rentjana," *Suluh Marhaen*, October 7, 1969; "Partai Politik Terima Penundaan Pemilu?" *Indonesia Raya*, October 11, 1969; "Tegaknja Kedaulatan Rakjat Melalui Pemilu," *Sinar Harapan*, September 4, 1969.
145. Wanandi, *Shades of Grey*, Kindle location 1539.
146. Sekretariat Bersama Golongan Karya Pusat, Surat Keputusan No. Kep/507/Sekber Golkar/1969 tentang Ketentuan-Ketentuan Pokok Konsolidasi dan Regrouping Sekretariat Bersama Golongan Karya, November 22, 1969, 107, Sekkab, ANRI; for membership see Leo Suryadinata, *Military Ascendancy and Political Culture: A Study of Indonesia's Golkar* (Athens: Ohio University Center for International Studies, 1989), 27–28.
147. Golongan Karya, *Beberapa Tanja Djawab tentang Pemilu* (Jakarta: Golongan Karya, 1971), 1.
148. Sekretariat Bersama Golongan Karya, "Progress Report," 1970, 107, Sekkab, ANRI.
149. Wanandi, *Shades of Grey*, Kindle location 1545; Hill, *Press in New Order Indonesia*, 36.
150. Airgram, Jakarta to State, July 23, 1971, POL 14 INDON, Subject Files 1970–73, RG 59, USNA.
151. Amirmachmud, *Prajurit Pejuang*, 341–343, 372–374; Masashi Nishihara, *Golkar and the Indonesian Elections of 1971* (Ithaca, NY: Cornell Modern Indonesia Project, 1972), 24.
152. Quoted in Crouch, *Army and Politics*, 258.
153. For details of the Parmusi split see Allan A. Samson, "Army and Islam in Indonesia," *Pacific Affairs* 44, no. 4 (Winter 1971–1972): 557–560.
154. Nishihara, *Golkar*, 25–27; Amirmachmud, *Prajurit Pejuang*, 364–365.

155. Arief Mudatsir Mandan, *Subchan Z.E., sang Maestro Politisi-Intelektual dari Kalangan N.U. Modern* (Jakarta: Pustaka Indonesia Satu, 2001), 127–140.
156. Ken Ward, *The 1971 Elections in Indonesia: An East Java Case Study* (Melbourne: Monash University Centre of Southeast Asian Studies, 1974), 106.
157. "Presiden Soeharto Bahas Golput," June 12, 1971, in *Jejak Langkah 1968–73*, 336.
158. Wanandi, *Shades of Grey*, Kindle location 1563.
159. Airgram, Jakarta to State, February 24, 1971, POL 14 INDON, Subject Files 1970–73, RG 59, USNA.
160. Telegram, Jakarta to State, May 11, 1971, POL 14 INDON, Subject Files 1970–73, RG 59, USNA.
161. Bureau of Intelligence and Research, Indonesia: On the Eve of the Election, July 2, 1971, POL 14 INDON, Subject Files 1970-73, RG 59, USNA.

Chapter 7

1. "The Technocrat Cometh," *Far Eastern Economic Review*, September 18, 1971.
2. H. W. Arndt, "Survey of Recent Developments," *Bulletin of Indonesian Economic Studies* 5, no. 2 (July 1969): 1.
3. *Buku Saku Statistik Indonesia, 1964–1967* (Jakarta: Biro Pusat Statistik, 1968), 97.
4. Quoted in Graeme Thompson and Richard C. Manning, "The World Bank in Indonesia," *Bulletin of Indonesian Economic Studies* 10, no. 2 (July 1974): 61–62.
5. World Bank, "Project Performance Audit Report: Indonesia (First) Irrigation Rehabilitation Project (Credit 127-IND), May 4, 1978, http://documents.worldbank.org/curated/en/820801468913922453/pdf/multi0page.pdf (accessed May 20, 2021).
6. Gary Hawes, "Rice in Indonesia," AID US-INDON, Subject Files 1970–73, RG 59, USNA; Gary Hansen, "Indonesia's Green Revolution: The Abandonment of a Non-Market Strategy toward Change," *Asian Survey* 12, no. 11 (November 1972): 932–946; C. Peter Timmer, "The Political Economy of Rice in Asia: Indonesia," *Food Research Institute Studies* 14, no. 3 (1975): 197–231.
7. Pantar Simatupang and C. Peter Timmer, "Indonesian Rice Production: Policies and Realities," *Bulletin of Indonesian Economic Studies* 44, no. 1 (March 2008): 66–67; H. W. Arndt, "Survey of Recent Developments," *Bulletin of Indonesian Economic Studies* 10, no. 2 (July 1974): 23.
8. *Statistik Indonesia: 1968 & 1969* (Jakarta: Biro Pusat Statistik, 1971), 230; Peter McCawley, "Rural Electrification in Indonesia—Is It Time?" *Bulletin of Indonesian Economic Studies* 14, no. 2 (July 1978): 36.
9. Peter McCawley, "Infrastructure Policy in Indonesia, 1965–2015: A Survey," *Bulletin of Indonesian Economic Studies* 51, no. 2 (2015): 268, 270, 272, 275.
10. Ali Sadikin, *Bang Ali Demi Jakarta (1966–1977): Memoar Dituliskan oleh Ramadhan K.H.* (Jakarta: Pustaka Sinar Harapan, 1992), 230–233.
11. Pidato Presiden Mengenai Kebijaksanaan Ekonomi Disampaikan Melalui Radio dan Televisi, April 17, 1970, 715, PPS, ANRI; for the IMF's role in the elaboration of these policies see Memo, Abadjis to Saleh and Salim, February 8, 1970, File 4 INDONESIA—Relations with IBRD, Box 49, ASDAI Country Files, Asian Department Immediate Office, IMF Archives.
12. International Monetary Fund, *Balance of Payments Yearbook Volume 22: 1965–1969* (Washington, DC: International Monetary Fund, 1971); International Monetary Fund, *Balance of Payments Yearbook Volume 28: 1969–1976* (Washington, DC: International Monetary Fund, 1977).
13. Bernard Gruss and Suhaib Kebhaj, "Commodity Terms of Trade: A New Database," IMF Working Paper WP/19/21, https://www.imf.org/en/Publications/WP/Issues/2019/01/24/Commodity-Terms-of-Trade-A-New-Database-46522 (accessed October 20, 2020).
14. Memorandum, Tun Thin to Ali Wardhana, August 6, 1968, File 1 INDONESIA—Correspondence—Memos July '68, Box 7, ETRAI Country Correspondence Files, Exchange and Trade Relations Department Immediate Office, IMF Archives.
15. John R. Hansen, "The Motor Vehicle Industry," *Bulletin of Indonesian Economic Studies* 7, no. 2 (July 1971): 47–51, 53–56.

16. Ian M. Chalmers, "Economic Nationalism and the Third World State: The Political Economy of the Indonesian Automotive Industry, 1950–1984" (PhD diss., Australian National University, 1988), 145.

17. Hal Hill, *Indonesia's Textile and Garment Industries: Developments in an Asian Perspective* (Singapore: Institute of Southeast Asian Studies, 1992), 6–12.

18. Robison, *Rise of Capital*, 271–320.

19. Memo, Ansberry to Hamengkubuwono, January 6, 1970, 2020, EKUIN, ANRI; "Indonesian Investment Mission to U.S.A.," Folder 8, Carton 15, Personal Files, 1923–96, Edmund G. Brown Papers, BL; "Indonesia Asks 'New Approach' to 'Burden of Debt Repayment,'" *New York Times*, September 25, 1969.

20. Telegram, Sadli to Deplu, March 23, 1970, 2024, EKUIN, ANRI.

21. Robison, *Rise of Capital*, 142.

22. A. R. Soehoed, *Asahan: Impian yang Menjadi Kenyataan* (Jakarta: s.n., 1983), 31.

23. Bisuk Siahaan, *Sejarah Pembangunan Proyek Asahan: Membangunkan Raksasa Sedang Tidur* (Jakarta: s.n., 1984), 242.

24. Quoted in Michael Sean Malley, "A Political Biography of Major General Soedjono Hoemardani, 1918–1986" (MA thesis, Cornell University, 1990), 83.

25. "Indonesia Delays Sumatra Project," *Christian Science Monitor*, September 6, 1972.

26. A. R. Soehoed, "Never Far from the People," in *Among Friends: Pak Harto at 70*, ed. G. Dwipayana and Nazaruddin Sjamsuddin, trans. Muti'ah Lestiono (Jakarta: PT Citra Lamtoro Gung Persada, 1993), 589–599; Memorandum, Sadli to Hamengkubuwono, October 1, 1973, 317, HB IX, ANRI.

27. Anne Booth, "Poverty and Inequality in the Soeharto Era: An Assessment," *Bulletin of Indonesian Economic Studies* 36, no.1 (April 2000): 75–77.

28. "The Taxman Cometh," *Far Eastern Economic Review*, January 2, 1969.

29. "Growing Demand in Japan, U.S. for Low-Sulphur Product," *Wall Street Journal*, March 30, 1972.

30. Airgram, Jakarta to State, May 3, 1968, PET 1 INDON, Central Files 1967–79, RG 59, USNA.

31. "Beberapa Pertanyaan tentang Minyak," *Indonesia Raya*, August 2, 1972.

32. Ramadhan, *Ibnu Sutowo*, 236.

33. See the issues of Government of Indonesia, *Anggaran dan Rancangan Anggaran Pendapatan dan Belanja Negara* (Jakarta: Departemen Keuangan, 1969–1974).

34. For a list of the subsidiaries see H. W. Arndt, "Survey of Recent Developments," *Bulletin of Indonesian Economic Studies* 10, no. 2 (July 1974): 26–28; for Ibnu's Japanese inspiration see "Sutowo: Down but Not Out," *Far Eastern Economic Review*, May 30, 1975.

35. Robison, *Rise of Capital*, 233–242.

36. For the full text of the report see the July 18–24, 1970, issues of *Sinar Harapan*.

37. Ibnu Sutowo, *Pertamina for a Closer Indonesian Relationship with the Developed Countries in Its Second Five-Year Development Plan* (Jakarta: Pertamina, 1973), 2.

38. Ramadhan, *Ibnu Sutowo*, 344.

39. "Oil and Nationalism Mix Beautifully in Indonesia," *Fortune*, July 1973.

40. "The Brown Link to Indonesian Firm," *Lodi News-Sentinel*, October 17, 1990.

41. Letter, Seligson to Brown, April 10, 1973, Folder 11, Carton 15, Personal Files, 1923–96, Edmund G. Brown Papers, BL; Memorandum, Goodman to Records, Visit of General Sutowo, December 2, 1968, Contacts with Member Countries: Indonesia—Correspondence 01, Contacts—Member Countries Files, Records of President Robert S. McNamara, World Bank Archives; "Pertamina Sets $200 Million in Loans via Citibank Group," *Wall Street Journal*, November 6, 1973.

42. "Indonesia to Borrow $68 Million from U.S., Japan, 2 Organizations," *Wall Street Journal*, June 5, 1970; "Japan's Banks Engage in Major Dollar Loans," *Globe and Mail*, August 5, 1972; "Indonesia Prime Test for Japan," *Washington Post*, March 2, 1973; see also Takashi Shiraishi, "Japan and Southeast Asia," in *Network Power: Japan and Asia*, ed. Peter Katzenstein and Takashi Shiraishi (Ithaca, NY: Cornell University Press, 1997), 180–185.

43. Wing Thye Woo and Anwar Nasution, "External Debt Management," in *Developing Country Debt and Economic Performance, Volume 3: Country Studies—Indonesia, Korea, Philippines, Turkey*, ed. Jeffrey Sachs and Susan Collins (Chicago: University of Chicago Press, 1989), 122.

44. "The Pertamina Affair," *Euromoney*, June 1975, 3.
45. "Pertamina: Lesson for World Banking," *New York Times*, November 17, 1977.
46. Sturc and Mohammed, Indonesian Debts, June 20, 1969, S 1193 Indonesia Debt Renegotiation Meetings October 1968–October 1969, Box 394, Economic Subject Files, Central Files Collection, IMF Archives; Selo Soemardjan, Catatan tentang Pembicaraan antara para Menteri R.I. Dibidang Ekonomi dengan Perdana Menteri Australia pada tanggal 21 Pebruari 1973 di Bina Graha, February 23, 1973, 1897, EKUIN, ANRI.
47. Telegram, Jakarta to State, March 15, 1973, Electronic Telegrams 1973, AAD, RG 59, USNA.
48. Keputusan Presiden Republik Indonesia Nomor 59 tahun 1972 tentang Penerimaan Kredit Luar Negeri, October 12, 1972, Pasal 4.
49. Telegram, State to Jakarta, February 16, 1973, POL INDON-US, Subject Files 1970–73, RG 59, USNA.
50. *The Witteveen Facility and the OPEC Financial Surpluses: Hearings before the Subcommittee on Foreign Economic Policy of the Committee on Foreign Relations, United States Senate* (Washington, DC: Government Printing Office, 1978), 93.
51. P. A. Wellons, *Borrowing by Developing Countries on the Euro-Currency Market* (Paris: OECD, 1977), 214–215.
52. "The High Price of Pertamina's Big Dreams," *Far Eastern Economic Review*, May 30, 1975.
53. See the various issues of Government of Indonesia, *Nota Keuangan dan Rancangan Anggaran Pendapatan dan Belanja Negara* (Jakarta: Departemen Keuangan, 1969–1973). The figure is calculated by comparing expenditures devoted to the Ministry of Defense and Security to total routine expenditures.
54. "Tadjuk Rentjana," *Angkatan Bersendjata*, March 4, 1970.
55. ACDA, *Worldwide Military Expenditures and Arms Transfers, 1970–1979* (Washington, DC: US Arms Control and Disarmament Agency, 1982).
56. Soemitro, *Pangkopkamtib*, 233, 242–244.
57. "Harga Indonesia Mini," *Tempo*, June 15, 1971; "Projek Miniatur Indonesia Indah: Sikap jang Tepat Perlu Segera Dinjatakan," *Kompas*, December 30, 1971; "Projek Mini: Adakah Jalan Keluar?" *Kompas*, January 3, 1972; see also Yulia Nurliani Lukito, *Exhibiting Modernity and Indonesian Vernacular Architecture: Hybrid Architecture at Pasar Gambir of Batavia, the 1931 Paris International Colonial Exhibition and Taman Mini Indonesia Indah* (Wiesbaden: Springer VS, 2016).
58. Benedict Anderson, "Last Days of Indonesia's Suharto?" *Southeast Asia Chronicle* 63 (July–August 1978): 2–17.
59. Loren Ryter, "Pemuda Pancasila," in *Violence and the State in Suharto's Indonesia*, ed. Benedict Anderson (Ithaca, NY: Cornell University Press, 2001), 137–141.
60. Quoted in Steele, *Wars Within*, 58.
61. "Resmikan RSP Pertamina, Presiden Soeharto: Saya Akan Hantam Pelanggar Konstitusi," January 6, 1972, in *Jejak Langkah 1968–73*, 401; "Presiden Beri Tanggapan Keras," *Kompas*, January 7, 1972.
62. Quoted in Ryter, "Pemuda Pancasila," 140; Telegram, Jakarta to State, January 18, 1972, POL 23-8 INDON, Subject Files 1970–73, RG 59, USNA; Airgram, Jakarta to State, May 1, 1972, POLITICAL AFF. & REL. INDON, Subject Files 1970–73, RG 59, USNA; for long-haired *pemuda* see Nasution, *Tentara Nasional Indonesia*, 105.
63. "Bukan Hanya Isu-Isu," *Indonesia Raya*, December 8, 1972.
64. Food and Agriculture Organization, *The State of Food and Agriculture in 1973* (Rome: FAO, 1973), 14.
65. Stephen Grenville, "Survey of Recent Developments," *Bulletin of Indonesian Economic Studies* 9, no. 1 (March 1973): 1–9; C. Peter Timmer, "The Political Economy of Rice in Asia: Indonesia," *Food Research Institute Studies* 14, no. 3 (1975): 216–218; "Asia Threatened by Rice Shortage," *New York Times*, December 6, 1972.
66. Ali Moertopo, *Politik Nasional: Strategi, Taktik dan Tehnik Implementasinja* (Jakarta: Departemen Pertahanan Keamanan, 1970), 17–18.
67. MemCon, Lim Bian Kie, Purnell, and Swift, February 15, 1971, POL 14 INDON, Subject Files 1970–73, RG 59, USNA.
68. Soeharto, *Pikiran*, 266.

69. For the PPP leader's views see H. M. S. Mintaredja, *Renungan Pembaharuan Pemikiran Masjarakat Islam dan Politik di Indonesia* (Jakarta: Permata, 1971).
70. Quoted in Radi Umaidi, *Strategi PPP, 1973–1982: Suatu Studi tentang Kekuatan Politik Islam Tingkat Nasional* (Jakarta: Integrita Press, 1984), 81.
71. Ali Moertopo, *Dasar-Dasar Pemikiran tentang Akselerasi Modernisasi Pembangunan 25 Tahun* (Jakarta: Yayasan Proklamasi, 1973).
72. "Seperti Parpol Golkar Djuga Dilarang Didesa-desa," *Harian Kami*, October 12, 1971.
73. Telegram, Jakarta to State, March 23, 1973, POL 15-1 INDON, Subject Files 1970–73, RG 59 USNA.
74. MemCon, Sutopo, Suhud, Galbraith, September 7, 1973, POL 23-8 INDON, Subject Files 1970–73, RG 59, USNA.
75. See Donald Emmerson, *Indonesia's Elite: Political Culture and Cultural Politics* (Ithaca, NY: Cornell University Press, 1976), 229–236.
76. Yong Mun Cheong, "Indonesia in Focus," *Southeast Asian Affairs* 1 (1974): 101–105.
77. See Heru Cahyono, *Peranan Ulama dalam Golkar, 1971–1980: Dari Pemilu sampai Malari* (Jakarta: Pustaka Sinar Harapan, 1992); Soemitro, *Pangkopkamtib*, 284–285.
78. Raillon, *Les étudiants*, 88–92; Amir Hasin Daulay and Hasibuan Imran, eds., *Hariman dan Malari: Gelombang Aksi Mahasiswa Menentang Modal Asing* (Jakarta: Q-Communication, 2011).
79. Government of Indonesia, *14 Tahun Komite Nasional Pemuda Indonesia, 23 Juli 1973–1987* (Jakarta: Departemen Penerangan, 1987), 39–63.
80. Hans Thoolen, ed., *Indonesia and the Rule of Law: Twenty Years of "New Order" Government* (London: Frances Pinter, 1987), 138–140; MemCon, Napitupulu, Monjo, and Pringle, June 1, 1973, POL 13-2 INDON, Subject Files 1970–73, RG 59, USNA.
81. "Demonstrasi: Impala Udin Versus VW," *Tempo*, August 11, 1973; Helius Sjamsuddin, "Rusuh di Bandung: Peristiwa 5 Agustus 1973 dalam Liputan Media Massa," *HISTORIA: Jurnal Pendidikan Sejarah* 3, no. 6 (December 2002): 113–136; for a higher estimate of deaths see MemCon, Tjan and Pringle, September 12, 1973, POL 13-3 INDON, Subject Files 1970–73, RG 59, USNA.
82. *Mahasiswa Indonesia* no. 371, 32.
83. Risalah Putusan-Putusan dan Petunjuk-Petunjuk Presiden pada Sidang Dewan Stabilisasi Ekonomi Nasional, August 7, 1973, 225, HB IX, ANRI; "Presiden Soeharto: Hindari Hal-Hal yang Merugikan Integrasi (Pemerintah Tidak Ubah Kurs Rupiah)," August 7, 1973, in *Jejak Langkah 1973–78*, 41.
84. Bresnan, *Managing Indonesia*, 145.
85. "Tri Tura Baru," *Tempo*, January 19, 1974.
86. Ignatius Haryanto, *Indonesia Raya Dibredel!* (Yogyakarta: LKiS, 2006), 89.
87. Heru Cahyono, *Pangkopkamtib Jenderal Soemitro dan Peristiwa 15 Januari '74* (Jakarta: Pustaka Sinar Harapan, 1998), 137.
88. W. S. Rendra, *Mastodon dan Burung Kondor* (Jakarta: Burung Merak Press, 2011).
89. Ashadi Siregar, *Kugapai Cintamu* (Jakarta: PT Gramedia, 1974); Ashadi Siregar, *Cintaku di Kampus Biru* (Jakarta: PT Gramedia, 1974); for a more thorough analysis of Ashadi's works and their readership see David Hill, "Alienation and Opposition to Authoritarianism in the Novels of Ashadi Siregar," *Review of Indonesian and Malayan Affairs* 13, no. 1 (June 1979): 25–43.
90. Soemitro, *Pangkopkamtib*, 304–305.
91. Telegram, Jakarta to State, November 15, 1973, Electronic Telegrams 1973, AAD, RG 59, USNA.
92. Soemitro, *Pangkopkamtib*, 261; MemCon, Toussaint, Siddique, Sindjelic, August 14, 1973, FN 14 INDON, Subject Files 1970–73, RG 59, USNA.
93. Surat Kopkamtib R-026/Kopkam/II/1973, Usaha Pengamanan dan Pensuksesan Program Pemerintah Melalui HUMAS dan Mass Media, February 22, 1973, 1287, EKUIN, ANRI.
94. Risalah Putusan-Putusan dan Petunjuk-Petunjuk Presiden dalam Sidang Kabinet Paripurna, November 27, 1973, 225, HB IX, ANRI.
95. Team Pelaksana Inpres No. 6/1971, Naskah Induk tentang Subversi dan Penanggulangannya, December 1973, 551, HB IX, ANRI.

96. MemCon, Soedjatmoko, Surjo, Webbert, and Harary, December 9, 1970, POL INDON-US, Subject Files 1970–73, RG 59, USNA.

97. Soemitro, *Pangkopkamtib*, 197.

98. Amnesty International, *Annual Report, 1969–70* (London: Amnesty International, 1970), 8.

99. "Indonesia," *Amnesty International Review: A Quarterly Review of News and Comment on International Human Rights*, no. 29 (November 1969): 4–5.

100. "Presiden Soeharto Menuju Jerman Barat," September 4, 1970, in *Jejak Langkah 1968–73*, 254–255.

101. Telegram, The Hague to State, September 4, 1970, POL 7 INDON, Subject Files 1970–73, RG 59, USNA; Telegram, Bonn to State, September 9, 1970, Subject Files 1970–73, RG 59, USNA.

102. Memorandum, Sudharmono to Sumitro et al., October 13, 1970, 392, Sekkab, ANRI.

103. Extracts from Memorandum to President Suharto and the Government of Indonesia Submitted by the Chairman of Amnesty International, February 1971, in Amnesty International, *Indonesia: An Amnesty International Report* (London: Amnesty International Publications, 1977), 141–143.

104. Press Statement, "Political Imprisonment in Indonesia," August 11, 1971, Folder 4, Box II.5 7, Amnesty International U.S.A. National Office Records, CUML.

105. Telegram, State to Jakarta, December 28, 1971, POL 29 INDON, Subject Files 1970–73, RG 59, USNA.

106. "Tadjuk Rentjana," *Angkatan Bersendjata*, May 29, 1972.

107. Amnesty International, *Indonesia Special*, 31.

108. "Statement of David Hinkley, Coordinator for Indonesia, Amnesty International, U.S.A., and Member of Board of Directors, U.S. Section," in *Human Rights in Indonesia: A Review of the Situation with Respect to Long-Term Political Detainees: Hearing before the Subcommittee on International Organizations of the Committee on International Relations: House of Representatives, Ninety-Fifth Congress, First Session, October 18, 1977* (Washington, DC: Government Printing Office, 1977), 9.

109. Djamal Marsudi, Masalah Tahanan Politik G.30.S/PKI dan Laporan dari Pulau Buru, 76, Djamal Marsudi, 1947–79, ANRI.

110. Centre for Strategic and International Studies, Analisa Previsionil Mengenai Asia pada Umumnja, Asia-Tenggara pada Chususnja, January 1972, 2326, EKUIN, ANRI.

111. "Mansfield's Life with Foreign Aid," *The Sun*, November 14, 1971.

112. Robert David Johnson, *Congress and the Cold War* (New York: Cambridge University Press, 2005), 179.

113. Frank Church, "Farewell to Foreign Aid: A Liberal Takes Leave," *Congressional Record*, October 29, 1971.

114. "Senate Kills Foreign Aid Bill: Program Defeated 41 to 27," *Washington Post*, October 30, 1971; "Interim Foreign Aid Bills Approved by Senate Panel," *New York Times*, November 5, 1971; "Senate, 65 to 24, Votes $1.5-Billion for Military Aid," *New York Times*, November 12, 1971.

115. Telegram, State to Jakarta, November 5, 1971, AID (US) INDON, Subject Files 1970–73, RG 59, USNA.

116. Telegram, Tokyo to State, November 12, 1971, POL 7 US/CONNALLY, Subject Files 1970–73, RG 59, USNA.

117. EOB 296-16, November 14, 1971, White House Tapes, RNPL.

118. See Telegram, State to USUN, October 1, 1971, POL 7 INDON, Subject Files 1970–73, RG 59, USNA

119. Memorandum, Rogers to Nixon, December 1, 1971, INDONESIA Suharto corres. [1970–1974] [1 of 1], Box 755, NSC Files, RNPL.

120. Letter, Suharto to Nixon, December 3, 1971, INDONESIA Suharto corres. [1970–1974] [1 of 1], Box 755, NSC Files, RNPL.

121. Letter, Sumitro to Kissinger, December 5, 1971, Backchannel—Indonesia HAK/Sumitro 1970 [1 of 2], Box 101, HAK, RNPL.

122. Memo, Holdridge and Hormats to Kissinger, December 8, 1971, INDONESIA Suharto corres. [1970–1974] [1 of 1], Box 755, NSC Files, RNPL; Message, Kissinger to Sumitro, December 11, 1971, Backchannel—Indonesia HAK/Sumitro 1970 [1 of 2], Box 101, HAK, RNPL.

123. Quoted in Peter Polomka, "Indonesia's Future and South-East Asia," *Adelphi Papers* no. 104 (Spring 1974): 19.

124. Telegram, Jakarta to State, July 29, 1969, in *FRUS 1969–76:20*, Document 272.

125. Sukma, *Indonesia and China*, 81–82.

126. Anwar, *Dari Koresponden Kami*, 120–121; MemCon, Galbraith and Pauker, March 22, 1972, POL 15 INDON, Subject Files 1970–73, RG 59, USNA.

127. See the editorial by Juwono Sudarsono in *Harian Kami*, November 10, 1971.

128. Centre for Strategic and International Studies, Analisa Previsionil Mengenai Asia pada Umumnja, Asia-Tenggara pada Chususnja, January 1972, 2326, EKUIN, ANRI.

129. For these conversations see Telegram, Jakarta to State, January 11, 1972, POL 7 US/ NIXON, Subject Files 1970–73, RG 59, USNA; Telegram, Jakarta to State, January 12, 1972, POL 15-1 INDON, Subject Files 1970–73, Subject Files 1970–73, RG 59, USNA.

130. Letter, Nixon to Suharto, January 21, 1971, INDONESIA Suharto corres. [1970–1974] [1 of 1], Box 755, NSC Files, RNPL; Presidential Directive 72-3, September 7, 1971, 71-1–72/ 09/71, Presidential Determinations, Box 370, Subject Files, RNPL.

131. Dewan Pertahanan Keamanan Nasional, Lembaran Kerdja No. 006/1972: Apresiasi tentang Pola Hubungan Super Power dan Usaha Indonesia Mengamankan Kepentingan Nasionalnya, 1284, EKUIN, ANRI.

132. Dewan Pertahanan Keamanan Nasional, Lembaran Kerdja No. 006/1972: Apresiasi tentang Pola Hubungan Super Power dan Usaha Indonesia Mengamankan Kepentingan Nasionalnya, 1284, EKUIN, ANRI.

133. "Asian Defence—Communist Style," *Far Eastern Economic Review*, July 3, 1969; Alexander Ghebhardt, "The Soviet System of Collective Security in Asia," *Asian Survey* 13, no. 12 (December 1973): 1075–1091; Arnold Horelick, "The Soviet Union's Asian Collective Security System: A Club in Search of Members," *Pacific Affairs* 47, no. 3 (Fall 1974): 269–285.

134. Memorandum, Sumitro to Cabinet, May 12, 1972, 1904, EKUIN, ANRI.

135. Risalah Petunjuk-Petunjuk dan Putusan-Putusan Presiden pada Sidang Dewan Stabilisasi Ekonomi Nasional, November 27, 1973, 225, HB IX, ANRI.

136. Bureau of Intelligence and Research, "Indonesia: Suharto Emphasizes Regional Cooperation During Visits to Three Neighbors," March 3, 1972, POL 7 INDON, Subject Files 1970–73, RG 59, USNA.

137. See John Piccini, *Human Rights in Twentieth-Century Australia* (New York: Cambridge University Press, 2019).

138. "Kunjungi Wellington, Presiden Soeharto Jelaskan Tapol Pulau Buru," February 11, 1972, in *Jejak Langkah 1968–73*, 415.

139. "Kunjungi Selandia Baru, Presiden Soeharto: Amankan Pancasila Harus Tegas ke Komunis," February 10, 1972, in *Jejak Langkah 1968–73*, 414.

140. MemCon, Donald and Hatano, May 1, 1972, POL 7 INDON, Subject Files 1970–73, RG 59, USNA.

141. Telegram, Tokyo to State, May 18, 1972, POL-INDON-JAPAN, Subject Files 1970–73, RG 59, USNA.

142. Ichtisar Bahan-Bahan Bagi KTT. Non-Aligned ke-III, July 31, 1970, 87, Sekkab, ANRI.

143. Elson, *Suharto*, 182; Savingram, Jakarta to Canberra, September 25, 1970, A1838 3034/ 7/1 PART 13, Indonesia—Foreign Policy—General, NAA; Landjutan Laporan Chusus Pembitjaraan Radio Telefoni (SSB) antara Dubes Otto Abdurrachman dengan Kol Satari a/ n Ka Bakin, September 1970, 1892, EKUIN, ANRI.

144. "Viet Cong Seated at Guyana Meeting; 3 Nations Leave," *Globe and Mail*, August 11, 1972.

145. Soemitro, *Pangkopkamtib*, 267.

146. Basarudin Nasution and R. Juniarta, S.H., Bantuan dari Industri Minyak dan Gas Bumi untuk Mengadakan Stabilisasi Keuangan Negara R.I., January 5, 1973, 157, HB IX, ANRI.

147. Memorandum, Rus'an to Malik, April 18, 1973, 402, HB IX, ANRI.

148. Memo, Basarudin and Juniarta to Hamengkubuwono, April 9, 1973, 157, HB IX, ANRI; "Indonesian Gas Could Be Imported to West Coast to Ease Shortage," *Offshore*, November 1972.

149. Memo, Dharman to Hamengkubuwono, June 4, 1973, 315, HB IX, ANRI.

150. Barbara Keys, *Reclaiming American Virtue: The Human Rights Revolution of the 1970s* (Cambridge, MA: Harvard University Press, 2014), 140–148.

151. Memo, Kissinger to Nixon, March 18, 1972, Foreign Aid, Vol II 1972 [3 of 3], Box 324, NSC Files, RNPL.

152. MemCon, Thajeb and Green, April 4, 1972, POL INDON-US, Subject Files 1970–73, RG 59, USNA.

153. 1972 Democratic Party Platform, July 10, 1972, American Presidency Project, http://www.presidency.ucsb.edu/ws/index.php?pid=29605 (accessed November 5, 2020).

154. Memorandum, Lehman to Kissinger, December 10, 1972, Congressional Vol #7 Sep 72–Dec 72 [1 of 1], Box 317, NSC Files, RNPL.

155. Telegram, Jakarta to State, November 14, 1972, POL 15-1 INDON, Subject Files 1970–73, RG 59, USNA.

156. Airgram, Jakarta to State, December 11, 1972, POL 7 INDON, Subject Files 1970–73, RG 59, USNA.

157. International Monetary Fund, Report of the Thirteenth Meeting of the Intergovernmental Group on Indonesia, December 29, 1972, IMF Archives; Widjojo, *Indonesian Development Experience*, 170–171.

158. "Boycott of Suharto Functions," *Irish Times*, November 15, 1972; "Letters to the Editor: How Suharto Stays in Power," *The Guardian*, November 17, 1972; "France Assures More Aid to Indonesia," *Times of India*, November 18, 1972.

159. Telegram, The Hague to State, December 21, 1972, AID 9 INDON, Subject Files 1970–73, RG 59, USNA.

160. See Adam Hughes Henry, "Gough Whitlam and the Politics of Universal Human Rights," *The International Journal of Human Rights* 24, no. 6 (2020): 796–803.

161. Soemitro, *Pangkopkamtib*, 257.

162. Telegram, Jakarta to State, February 10, 1973, Vice President's SEA Visit Jan 28–10 Feb 73 [1 of 3], Box 952, NSC Files, RNPL.

163. Memorandum, Agnew to Nixon, February 9, 1973, Vice President's SEA Visit Jan 28–10 Feb 73 [2 of 3], Box 952, NSC Files, RNPL.

164. Laporan Mingguan, December 25, 1973 424-B, HB IX, ANRI.

165. Bahan-Bahan Briefing Hubungan Indonesia-Australia Bidang Ekonomi, February 1973, 1897, EKUIN, ANRI.

166. Komunike-Bersama Australia-Indonesia, February 1973, 1897, EKUIN, ANRI.

167. "Soal Asia Pasifik, Presiden Soeharto-PM Selandia Baru Keluarkan Pernyataan," December 17, 1973, in *Jejak Langkah 1973–78*, 73.

168. Bank Indonesia, *Report for the Financial Year* (Jakarta: Bank Indonesia, 1973), 47–48; H. W. Arndt, "Survey of Recent Developments," *Bulletin of Indonesian Economic Studies* 9, no. 2 (July 1973): 9–17; Tarmiden Sitorus, "The Role of Financial and Exchange Rate Policies in Indonesia's Macroeconomic Adjustment" (PhD diss., University of Illinois at Urbana-Champaign, 1989), 83–88.

169. "Investment: Indonesian Perils," *Newsweek*, April 9, 1973.

170. Risalah Petunjuk-Petunjuk dan Putusan-Putusan Presiden pada Sidang Dewan Stabilisasi Ekonomi Nasional, May 18, 1973, 225, HB IX, ANRI.

171. Risalah Petunjuk-Petunjuk dan Putusan-Putusan Presiden pada Sidang Dewan Stabilisasi Ekonomi Nasional, September 25, 1973, 225, HB IX, ANRI.

172. Memo, Dharman to Hamengkubuwono, September 25, 1973, 175, HB IX, ANRI.

173. Telegram, Jakarta to State, October 3, 1973, Electronic Telegrams 1973, AAD, RG 59, USNA.

174. Amnesty International Dutch Section, *Indonesia Special* (Amsterdam: Wordt Vervolgd, 1973).

175. Telegram, State to Jakarta, June 12, 1973, POL 29 INDON, Subject Files 1970–73, RG 59, USNA.

176. Memorandum, Secretary General to National Sections, November 20, 1973, Folder 5, Box II.5 7, Amnesty International U.S.A. National Office Records, CUML; Letter, Ennals to Moller, March 6, 1973, Folder 5, Box II.5 7, Amnesty International U.S.A. National Office Records, CUML; "The Prisoners of Buru," *Asia Magazine*, March 5, 1972, 3–17.

177. Carmel Budiardjo, *Surviving Indonesia's Gulag: A Western Woman Tells Her Story* (London: Cassell, 1996), 208–209.

178. "General Sumitro: 'Juridically We're Weak, from a Humanitarian Point of View, We're Even Weaker,'" *TAPOL Bulletin* 1, no. 1 (August 1973): 1.

179. "M.P.s Visit Indonesian Embassy in London," *TAPOL Bulletin* 1, no. 2 (November 1973): 3.

180. MemCon, Galbraith, Said, and Wilcox, July 5, 1973, POL 29 INDON, Subject Files 1970–73, RG 59, USNA.

181. MemCon, Combs, Furlonger, Jalink, Galbraith, Toussaint, August 21, 1973, POL 29 INDON, Subject Files 1970–73, RG 59, USNA.

182. Letter, Seda to Widjojo, November 2, 1973, 423, HB IX, ANRI. Emphasis in original.

183. "Revolusi di Negeri Pagoda," *Indonesia Raya*, November 1–5, 1973; "Indonesia, Mindful of Thai Overthrow, Heeds New Student Stirrings," *New York Times*, January 2, 1974; Soemitro, *Pangkopkamtib*, 337; "Kisah dari Muangthai," *Mahasiswa Indonesia* no. 392, October 1973.

184. Memorandum of Conversation, Wilcox and Suleiman, November 13, 1973, POL INDON-US, Subject Files 1970–73, RG 59, USNA.

185. "Bappenas Terbuka?" *Indonesia Raya*, December 22, 1973.

186. For an analysis of the student movement's efforts to consolidate itself see Wiwoho and Bandjar, *Memori Jenderal Yoga*, 232–236.

187. Telegram, Jakarta to State, December 4, 1973, Electronic Telegrams 1973, AAD, RG 59, USNA.

188. David Hill, *Journalism and Politics in Indonesia: A Critical Biography of Mocthar Lubis (1922–2004) as Editor and Author* (New York: Routledge, 2010), 106.

189. Soedjono Hoemardani, "To Promote Good Relations between the Republic of Indonesia and Japan," in *Japanese-Indonesian Relations in the Seventies* (Jakarta: Centre for Strategic and International Studies, 1974), 5, 9–10.

190. Wanandi and Djiwandono, "Soedjono Hoemardani," 89.

191. Anonymous, "The Bangkok-Jakarta Connection," *Journal of Contemporary Asia* 4, no. 2 (1974): 239; "Api Bagi Penjual Bangsa," *Mahasiswa Indonesia* 393, January 1974.

192. Soemitro, *Pangkopkamtib*, 312.

193. Memo, Dharman to Hamengkubuwono, September 12, 1973, 315, HB IX, ANRI.

194. Giuliano Garavini, *The Rise and Fall of OPEC in the Twentieth Century* (New York: Oxford University Press, 2019), 216–228.

Chapter 8

1. Soemitro, *Pangkopkamtib*, 274.

2. Telegram, Jakarta to State, January 15, 1974, Electronic Telegrams 1974, AAD, RG 59, USNA.

3. Panggabean, *Berjuang dan Mengabdi*, 410.

4. "Usai Lepas PM Tanaka, Presiden Soeharto Bahas Keamanan," January 17, 1974, in *Jejak Langkah 1973–78*, 94.

5. Wanandi, *Shades of Grey*, Kindle location 1782.

6. Pidato di Depan Para Tamtama, Bintara, dan Perwira ABRI pada tanggal 17 Januari 1974 di Jakarta, https://soeharto.co/1974-01-17-pidato-presiden-soeharto-di-depan-para-tamt ama-bintara-dan-perwira-abri/ (accessed December 29, 2020).

7. Hill, *The Press in New Order Indonesia*, 37–39.

8. "Dewan Stabilisasi Politik dan Keamanan Nasional Dibentuk," *Kompas*, February 5, 1974.

9. "Presiden Soeharto Bahas Laporan Penanganan Malari," February 12, 1974, in *Jejak Langkah 1973–78*, 101.

10. Polkam, October 8, 1974, 567, HB IX, ANRI.

11. Polkam, May 14, 1974, 567, HB IX, ANRI.

12. Polkam, March 12, 1974, 567, HB IX, ANRI

13. Polkam, October 8, 1974, 567, HB IX, ANRI.
14. "Presiden Soeharto: KNPI Wadah Pengembangan Orientasi Baru Pemuda," October 28, 1974, in *Jejak Langkah 1973–78*, 167.
15. Telegram, Jakarta to State, November 11, 1974, Electronic Telegrams 1974, AAD, RG 59, USNA.
16. Polkam, November 12, 1974, 567, HB IX, ANRI.
17. "Presiden Kepada DPP KNPI: Petani2 Didesa Nantikan Uluran Tangan," *Berita Yudha*, November 29, 1974.
18. Polkam, November 12, 1974, 567, HB IX, ANRI.
19. Polkam, May 11, 1976, 567, HB IX, ANRI.
20. "Presiden Soeharto Sambut Gembira Terbentunknya FBSI," *Antara*, April 25, 1973.
21. See Vedi Hadiz, *Workers and the State in New Order Indonesia* (New York: Routledge, 1997), 59–90.
22. Ali Moertopo, *Buruh dan Tani dalam Pembangunan* (Jakarta: Centre for Strategic and International Studies, 1975), 19–20; Richard Robison, "The Politics of 'Asian Values,'" *Pacific Review* 9, no. 3 (1996): 309–327.
23. Peter McCawley, "Survey of Recent Developments," *Bulletin of Indonesian Economic Studies* 12, no. 1 (March 1976): 38.
24. Sapardjo, "Kindling the Peaceful Revolution," in *Among Friends*, 615.
25. Polkam, March 12, 1974, 567, HB IX, ANRI
26. Polkam, May 14, 1974, 567, HB IX, ANRI.
27. "Presiden Soeharto Menerima Pimpinan-Pimpinan Parpol," June 25, 1975, in *Jejak Langkah 1973–78*, 258.
28. "Kata-Akhir Fraksi-Fraksi terhadap RUU Parpol-Golkar," *Kompas*, August 15, 1975; Direktorat Jenderal Hukum: *Sekitar Pembentukan Undang-Undang No. 3 tentang Parpol dan Golkar Beserta Peraturan Pelaksanaannya* (Jakarta: Departemen Kehakiman, 1975); Memo, Hartanto and Warsito to Hamengkubuwono, December 17, 1974, 468, HB IX, ANRI.
29. Polkam, May 14, 1974, 567, HB IX, ANRI.
30. C. van Dijk, "Survey of Major Political Developments in Indonesia in the Second Half of 1978: (1) The Partai Demokrasi Indonesia (2) Golkar's Second National Congress," *Review of Indonesian and Malayan Affairs* 13, no. 1 (June 1979): 117–119.
31. Polkam, April 13, 1976, 567, HB IX, ANRI.
32. Pour, *Sudomo*, 255.
33. Anwar, *Dari Koresponden Kami*, 177–178.
34. Umaidi Radi, *Strategi PPP 1973–1982: Suatu Studi tentang Kekuatan Politik Islam Tingkat Nasional* (Jakarta: Integrita Press, 1984), 101–136; Syamsuddin Haris, *PPP dan Politik Orde Baru* (Jakarta: PT Gramedia Widiasarana Indonesia, 1991), 8–13.
35. "Pangkopkamtib Akui Semakin Banyak Kontradiksi Sosial," *Mahasiswa Indonesia* no. 384, November 1974.
36. Soemitro, *Pangkopkamtib*, 319–320.
37. See Cahyono, *Pangkopkamtib Jenderal Soemitro*; Daoed Joesoef, *Dia dan Aku: Memoar Pencari Kebenaran* (Jakarta: Buku Kompas, 2006), 445–449.
38. "Presiden Soeharto Bentuk Irjenbang (Menerima Menteri Keuangan AS dan Imelda Marcos)," April 22, 1974, in *Jejak Langkah 1973–78*, 118.
39. See Robinson Pangaribuan, *The Indonesian State Secretariat, 1945–1993*, trans. Vedi Hadiz (Perth: Murdoch University Asia Research Centre on Social, Political, and Economic Change, 1995), 37–38.
40. Sudharmono, *Otobiografi*, 246–249.
41. Malik, *Mengabdi Republik, Jilid III*, 63.
42. Bresnan, *Managing Indonesia*, 146.
43. Marzuki Arifin SE, *Peristiwa 15 Januari 1974* (Jakarta: Publishing House Indonesia, 1974), 75.
44. "Presiden Soeharto Terbitkan Keppres Kopkamtib," February 21, 1974, in *Jejak Langkah 1973–78*, 102.
45. Risalah Petunjuk-Petunjuk dan Putusan-Putusan Presiden pada Sidang Dewan Stabilisasi Ekonomi Nasional, January 29, 1974, 225, HB IX, ANRI; Risalah Petunjuk-Petunjuk dan Putusan-Putusan Presiden pada sidang Dewan Stabilisasi Ekonomi Nasional, February 19,

1974, 225, HB IX, ANRI; Risalah Petunjuk-Petunjuk dan Putusan-Putusan Presiden pada sidang Dewan Stabilisasi Ekonomi Nasional, March 19, 1974, 225, HB IX, ANRI.

46. M. J. Kasiyanto, *Mengapa Orde Baru Gagal?* (Jakarta: Yayasan Tri Mawar, 1999), 88.

47. Soeharsono Sagir, *Analisa Kebijaksanaan Ekonomi Indonesia, 1971–1975: Kumpulan Tulisan Populer-Ilmiah mengenai Masalah-Masalah Ekonomi Terpenting di Indonesia* (Jakarta: Maha Anoegerah, 1975), 147–149.

48. Dorodjatun Kuntjoro-Jakti, "The Political-Economy of Development: The Case of Indonesia under the New Order Government, 1966–1978" (PhD diss., University of California, Berkeley, 1981), 225–230.

49. Memo, Dharman to Hamengkubuwono, December 7, 1974, 410, HB IX, ANRI.

50. Bank Indonesia, *Report for the Financial Year 1974/1975* (Jakarta: Bank Indonesia, 1975), 29.

51. "PT Askrindo Mendorong Usaha Kecil dengan Kredit," *Angkatan Bersenjata*, April 19, 1976.

52. Yoon Hwan Shin, "Demystifying the Capitalist State: Political Patronage, Bureaucratic Interests, and Capitalists-in-Formation in Soeharto's Indonesia" (PhD diss., Yale University, 1989), 317–318; David Cole and Betty Slade, *Building a Modern Financial System: The Indonesian Experience* (New York: Cambridge University Press, 1996), 84–88.

53. "Pemerintah Tetapkan Kebijakan PMA, Pola Hidup Sederhana dan Pelangaran Impor Kendaraan Bermotor *Built Up*," January 22, 1974, in *Jejak Langkah 1973–78*, 95; Telegram, Jakarta to State, January 23, 1974, Electronic Telegrams 1974, RG 59, USNA; Risalah Petunjuk-Petunjuk dan Putusan-Putusan Presiden pada Sidang Dewan Stabilisasi Ekonomi Nasional, January 29, 1974, 225, HB IX, ANRI; Risalah Petunjuk-Petunjuk dan Putusan-Putusan Presiden pada sidang Dewan Stabilisasi Ekonomi Nasional, February 19, 1974, 225, HB IX, ANRI.

54. Daoed Joesoef, "Knowledge Economy and World Economy," *Indonesian Quarterly* 2, no. 2 (January 1974): 41–43.

55. U.S. Embassy (Indonesia) Economic-Commercial Section, *Changes in Indonesian Investment Climate, 1974–75* (Jakarta: s.n., 1975), 2, 21–24.

56. Wiwoho and Bandjar, *Memori Jenderal Yoga*, 223.

57. Memo, Dharman to Hamengkubuwono, February 18, 1974, 563, HB IX, ANRI.

58. Republik Indonesia, *Rencana Pembangunan Lima Tahun Kedua 1974/75–1978/79* (Jakarta: Departemen Penerangan, 1974), 1–2; Republik Indonesia, *Statistik Indonesia 1974/1975* (Jakarta: Biro Pusat Statistik, 1975), 62–63.

59. Telegram, Jakarta to State, January 7, 1974, Electronic Telegrams 1974, AAD, RG 59, USNA; Telegram, Manila to State, March 8, 1974, Electronic Telegrams 1974, AAD, RG 59, USNA.

60. Telegram, State to Jakarta, January 21, 1974, Electronic Telegrams 1974, AAD, RG 59, USNA.

61. Telegram, Jakarta to State, January 23, 1974, Electronic Telegrams 1974, AAD, RG 59, USNA.

62. "Roll Me Over in the Clover," *Far Eastern Economic Review*, November 15, 1974.

63. "Presiden Soeharto Serukan DK PBB Hentikan Perang Arab-Israel," October 13, 1973, in *Jejak Langkah 1973–78*, 58.

64. Telegram, Jakarta to State, October 20, 1973, Electronic Telegrams 1973, AAD, RG 59, USNA.

65. Memo, Dharman to Hamengkubuwono, January 22, 1974, 318, HB IX, ANRI.

66. "Indonesia to Raise Output," *Financial Times*, November 7, 1973.

67. "Tajuk Rencana," *Abadi*, November 12, 1973; Telegram, Jakarta to State, November 23, 1973, Electronic Telegrams 1973, AAD RG 59, USNA; Risalah Petunjuk-Petunjuk dan Putusan-Putusan Presiden pada Sidang Dewan Stabilisasi Ekonomi Nasional, November 20, 1973, 225, HB IX, ANRI.

68. Memo, Dharman to Hamengkubuwono, November 30, 1973, 315, HB IX, ANRI.

69. Telegram, Singapore to State, November 28, 1973, Electronic Telegrams 1973, AAD, RG 59, USNA; Risalah Petunjuk-Petunjuk dan Putusan-Putusan Presiden pada Sidang Dewan Stabilisasi Ekonomi Nasional, November 20, 1973, 225, HB IX, ANRI.

70. Telegram, Jakarta to State, January 24, 1974, Electronic Telegrams 1974, AAD, RG 59, USNA.

71. Memo, Dharman to Hamengkubuwono, February 16, 1974, 319, HB IX, ANRI.

72. United Nations, *Proceedings of the Sixth Special Session of the General Assembly, April 9–May 2, 1974* (New York: United Nations, 1974), 2214th Plenary, 7–11.

73. Memo, Dharman to Hamengkubuwono, April 9, 1974, 321, HB IX, ANRI.

74. Memo, Dharman to Hamengkubuwono, June 26, 1974, 326, HB IX, ANRI.

75. Memo, Dharman to Hamengkubuwono, September 3, 1974, 326, HB IX, ANRI; "Saudis Drop Call for Oil Price Roll Back," *Financial Times*, September 2, 1974.

76. Memo, Dharman to Hamengkubuwono, September 25, 1974, 326, HB IX, ANRI.

77. Memo, Dharman to Hamengkubuwono, September 3, 1974, 326, HB IX, ANRI; Sevinc Carlson, *Indonesia's Oil* (Boulder, CO: Westview Press, 1977), 81; Anonymous, "Survey of Recent Developments," *Bulletin of Indonesian Economic Studies* 11, no. 3 (November 1975): 3–4.

78. Ibnu Sutowo, New Energy Realities Confronting Producing and Consuming Nations: Address Made at the Pacific Coast Gas Association Convention, Honolulu, September 12, 1974, 2005/0010321W, ANM.

79. Memo, Dharman to Hamengkubuwono, October 8, 1974, 190, HB IX, ANRI; Departemen Luar Negeri, Pembentukan Dana Pembangunan OPEC, January 1976, 200, HB IX, ANRI.

80. Sumitro Djojohadikusumo, *Indonesia dalam Perkembangan Dunia: Kini dan Masa Datang* (Jakarta: Lembaga Penelitian, Pendidikan dan Penerangan Ekonomi dan Sosial, Jakarta, 1976), 47.

81. Sumitro Djojohadikusumo, *The Political Economy of ASEAN Resources* (Jakarta: Sekreteriat Menteri Negara Riset, 1974), 35–41.

82. Departemen Luar Negeri, *Orde Ekonomi Internasional Baru dan Posisi Indonesia* (Jakarta: Departemen Luar Negeri, 1975), 1, 3, 5–6, 11–15.

83. "Sidang Kabinet Bentuk Panitia Penyusunan Orde Ekonomi Internasional Baru," June 3, 1975, in *Jejak Langkah 1973–78*, 253–254.

84. Departemen Luar Negeri, *Orde Ekonomi Internasional Baru*, 3.

85. Prawiro, *Indonesia's Struggle for Economic Development*, 107–108.

86. "Sutowo: Down but Not Out," *Far Eastern Economic Review*, May 30, 1975.

87. Telegram, Singapore to Jakarta, February 22, 1975, Electronic Telegrams 1975, AAD, RG 59, USNA; Ramadhan, *Ibnu Sutowo*, 344–347.

88. Telegram, Jakarta to State, March 18, 1975, Electronic Telegrams 1975, AAD, RG 59, USNA; Telegram, Jakarta to State, April 24, 1975, Electronic Telegrams 1975, AAD, RG 59, USNA; see also *The Witteveen Facility and the OPEC Financial Surpluses: Hearings Before the Subcommittee on Foreign Economic Policy of the Committee on Foreign Relations* (Washington, DC: Government Printing Office, 1978), 95–97.

89. Keputusan Presiden Republik Indonesia Nomor 15 Tahun 1975, April 17, 1975.

90. Widjojo Nitisastro, *Indonesian Development Experience*, 183.

91. "Bank Indonesia Seeks Funds from Banks in U.S. and Europe for Pertamina Debts," *Wall Street Journal*, April 15, 1975; Seth Lipsky, "The Billion Dollar Bubble," in *The Billion Dollar Bubble and Other Stories from the Asian Wall Street Journal*, ed. Seth Lipsky (Hong Kong: Dow Jones Publishing Company, 1978), 16–17.

92. Statement by His Excellency Mr. Adam Malik, Foreign Minister of the Republic of Indonesia, Head of the Indonesian Delegation to the 7th Special Session of the General Assembly of the United Nations, September 2, 1975, 202, HB IX, ANRI.

93. Adam Malik, Laporan Delegasi R.I. ke Sidang Khusus ke-VII Majelis Umum PBB Mengenai Pembangunan dan Kerjasama Ekonomi Internasional di New York, tgl. 1–16 September 1975, September 19, 1975, 202, HB IX, ANRI.

94. Daniel Sargent, "North/South: The United States Responds to the New International Economic Order," *Humanity* 6, no. 1 (Spring 2015): 201–216.

95. MemCon, Ford, Kissinger, et al., May 26, 1975, in *FRUS 1969–76:31*, Document 294.

96. Departemen Luar Negeri, Konperensi Kelompok-77 Mengenai Kerjasama Ekonomi Antara Negara-Negara Berkembang di Mexico City, September 1976, 200, HB IX, ANRI; Departemen Luar Negeri, Masalah Kerjasama Ekonomi Internasional dalam Rangka Menciptakan Orde Ekonomi Internasional Baru, December 1976, 200, HB IX, ANRI.

97. "Buka Sidang OPEC, Presiden Soeharto: Negara-Negara OPEC Berhak Harga Minyak yang Adil," May 27, 1976, in *Jejak Langkah 1973–78*, 364.

98. "Text of Oil Ministers' Statement," *New York Times*, December 18, 1976.

99. Julian Dharman, Konperensi Kerjasama Ekonomi Internasional (Konperensi Paris Mengenai Utara-Selatan), June 7, 1977, 206, HB IX, ANRI.

100. Malik, *Mengabdi Republik*, 106–107.

101. Aden, "Oil and Politics in Indonesia," 445

102. Telegram, Jakarta to State, February 20, 1974, Electronic Telegrams 1974, AAD, RG 59, USNA; Telegram, State to Jakarta, March 9, 1974, Electronic Telegrams 1974, AAD, RG 59, USNA.

103. Telegram, Tokyo to State, April 12, 1974, Electronic Telegrams 1974, AAD, RG 59, USNA.

104. Telegram, The Hague to State, May 10, 1974, Electronic Telegrams 1974, AAD, RG 59, USNA.

105. Report, Sidang IGGI ke XVI, May 9, 1974, 171, HB IX, ANRI.

106. Rusmin Nuryadin, Laporan Fakta Mingguan, May 12, 1974, 424-B, HB IX, ANRI.

107. Memorandum, Smyser to Kissinger, July 9, 1974, Indonesia (1), Box 3, National Security Adviser—NSC East Asian and Pacific Affairs Staff Files, GFPL.

108. Telegram, Jakarta to State, January 24, 1974, Electronic Telegrams 1974, AAD, RG 59, USNA.

109. Telegram, Jakarta to State, August 22, 1974, Electronic Telegrams 1974, AAD, RG 59, USNA.

110. MemCon, Ford, Kissinger, and Malik, September 25, 1974, September 25, 1974 - Ford, Kissinger, Indonesian Foreign Minister Adam Malik, Box 6, National Security Adviser—Memoranda of Conversations, GFPL.

111. "Oppose the U.S.-Marcos Fascist Dictatorship!" *Kalayaan International*, October–November 1972; National Committee for the Restoration of Civil Liberties in the Philippines, "Is the Philippines the Next Vietnam," October 1972, Box 12, Philippine Radical Papers, Aklatan ng Unibersidad ng Pilipinas, Diliman; "Petition to the U.S. Congress to Cut Off American Aid to the Philippines," *Pahayag*, April 1973; Raul Manglapus, *A Pen for Democracy: A Decade of Articles, Speeches, Letters, Interviews, and Committee Testimony Published in the International Press and the U.S. Congressional Record in the Tradition of the Filipino Democrats a Century Ago* (Washington, DC: Movement for a Free Philippines, 1983).

112. Alan Cranston, "Repression in the Philippines," *Congressional Record*, April 12, 1973, 12135–12137.

113. "Human Rights Emphasis Urged for US Diplomacy," *Boston Globe*, March 27, 1974.

114. Telegram, Jakarta to State, January 30, 1974, Electronic Telegrams 1974, AAD, RG 59, USNA.

115. Carmel Budiardjo, "Political Imprisonment in Indonesia," *Bulletin of Concerned Asian Scholars* 6, no. 2 (April–August 1974): 23.

116. Telegram, Jakarta to State, July 3, 1974, Electronic Telegrams 1974, AAD, RG 59, USNA.

117. Telegram, Jakarta to State, July 12, 1974, Electronic Telegrams 1974, AAD, RG 59, USNA.

118. Telegram, Jakarta to State, October 24, 1974, Electronic Telegrams 1974, AAD, RG 59, USNA; Telegram, Jakarta to State, January 9, 1975, Electronic Telegrams 1975, AAD, RG 59, USNA.

119. Jan Breman, "W. F. Wertheim: A Sociological Chronicler of Revolutionary Change," *Development and Change* (August 2017): 1130–1153.

120. *Indonesië: Feiten an Meningen* 1, no. 1 (March 1974); W. F. Wertheim, *Tien Jaar Onrecht in Indonesië: Militaire Dictatuur en Internationale Steun* (Amsterdam: Van Gennen, 1976).

121. Peter Baehr, "Problems of Aid Conditionality: The Netherlands and Indonesia," *Third World Quarterly* 18, no. 2 (June 1997): 363–376.

122. Telegram, The Hague to State, January 28, 1974, Electronic Telegrams 1974, AAD, RG 59, USNA; Telegram, Jakarta to State, June 4, 1974, Electronic Telegrams 1974, AAD, RG 59, USNA.

123. Telegram, Jakarta to State, September 26, 1974, Electronic Telegrams 1974, AAD, RG 59, USNA.

124. Telegram, Canberra to State, August 2, 1974, Electronic Telegrams 1974, AAD, RG 59, USNA.

125. McDonald, *Suharto's Indonesia*, 1–2.

126. Report of Visit to Indonesia 5–13 September: G. Forrester, September 25, 1974, A1838 3034/10/11/24 Part 3, Visit to Indonesia by Prime Minister—Mr [Edward Gough] Whitlam 1974, NAA.

127. Record of Second Meeting between Whitlam and Soeharto, September 6, 1974, A10463 801/13/11/1 Part 3, Jakarta—Portuguese Timor, NAA; for Sudharmono's evaluation of the visit see "Pentingnya Pembicaraan Informal," *Antara*, September 7, 1974.
128. Memo, Dharman to Hamengkubuwono, September 26, 1974, 428, HB IX, ANRI.
129. Polkam, September 10, 1974, 567, HB IX, ANRI.
130. See *Suara Karya*, October 1, 1974; *Kompas*, December 9, 1974.
131. *Kompas*, January 8, 1975.
132. "Sudomo on Releases," *Tapol Bulletin* no. 25 (December 1977): 2.
133. Polkam, November 12, 1974, 567, HB IX, ANRI.
134. Angkatan Bersenjata Republik Indonesia, Langkah Mendasar untuk Penanggulangan dan Pencegahan Bahaya Latent Subversi Kiri (Ops Ksatria 1974), n.d., unpublished document in author's possession (courtesy of Geoffrey Robinson).
135. Julius Pour, *Laskamana Sudomo: Mengatasi Gelombang Kehidupan* (Jakarta: PT Gramedia, 1997), 225.
136. "14½ Year Release Plan for Tapols?" *Tapol Bulletin* no. 13 (December 1975): 20; "Ramai-Ramai Debebaskan," *Tempo*, December 13, 1975.
137. Greg Fealy, "The Release of Indonesia's Political Prisoners: Domestic Versus Foreign Policy, 1975–1979," *Monash University Centre of Southeast Asian Studies Working Papers* no. 94 (1995): 19–21.
138. Polkam, June 10, 1975, 567, HB IX, ANRI.
139. Telegram, Jakarta to State, March 31, 1975, Indonesia—State Department Telegrams to SECSTATE—EXDIS, Box 6, National Security Adviser—National Security Council East Asian and Pacific Affairs Staff Files, GFPL.
140. MemCon, Ford, Kissinger, and Suharto, July 5, 1975, July 5, 1975—Ford, Kissinger, Indonesian President Suharto, Box 13, National Security Adviser—Memoranda of Conversations, GFPL.
141. "Dutch Warn: Free Tapols or Face Aid Cut," *Tapol Bulletin* no. 10 (June 1975): 1.
142. Polkam, June 10, 1975, 567, HB IX, ANRI.
143. Telegram, New York to State, October 24, 1975, Electronic Telegrams 1975, AAD, RG 59, USNA.
144. "Future Indonesian-American Relations," *Congressional Record*, October 20, 1975, 10096–10097.
145. Memorandum, Roesmin Nurjadin to Soeharto, October 30, 1975, 203, HB IX, ANRI; Telegram, State to Jakarta, October 31, 1975, Electronic Telegrams 1975, AAD, RG 59, USNA.
146. Jusuf Wanandi, "President Carter's Foreign Policy and the Role of the American Congress," *Indonesian Quarterly* 6, no. 2 (April 1978): 73.
147. Letter, Ali Murtopo to Donald Fraser, November 14, 1976, G9, Subject Committee Files 1976, Donald Fraser Papers, Minnesota State Historical Society.
148. "Aid vs. Human Rights," *Washington Post*, January 15, 1976.
149. "Congressional Hearing on Indonesia," *Tapol Bulletin* 14 (February 1976): 3.
150. Telegram, State to Jakarta, October 7, 1976, Electronic Telegrams 1976, AAD, RG 59, USNA.
151. Telegram, Jakarta to State, November 2, 1976, Electronic Telegrams 1976, AAD, RG 59, USNA.
152. Letter, Jones to Huang, January 31, 1977, Folder 7 Box II.5 7, Amnesty International U.S.A. National Office Records, CUML.
153. Fealy, "The Release of Indonesia's Political Prisoners," 42; Letter, Hinkley to Zeltmana, December 7, 1976, Folder 7 Box II.5 7, Amnesty International U.S.A. National Office Records, CUML.
154. Telegram, Jakarta to State, April 28, 1976, Electronic Telegrams 1976, AAD, RG 59, USNA.
155. Maarten Kuitenbrouwer, *Dutch Scholarship in the Age of Empire and Beyond: The Royal Netherlands Institute of Southeast Asian and Caribbean Studies, 1815–2011*, trans. Lorri Granger (Boston: Brill, 2014), 179–181.
156. "Labour Party on Tapols," *Tapol Bulletin* no. 17 (August 1976): 6.
157. Fealy, "The Release of Indonesia's Political Prisoners," 27.

158. "Indonesia at the I.L.O.," *Tapol Bulletin* no. 17 (August 1976): 2–3; "ILO Given Indonesia Pledge on Prisoners," *Guardian*, June 17, 1976.
159. "Presidential Challengers Diverge on Foreign Policy," *New York Times*, April 6, 1976.
160. Quoted in Robinson, *Killing Season*, 374n14.
161. "Release Pledges Reneged," *Tapol Bulletin* no. 18 (October 1976): 2; Memorandum, Research Department to All National Sections, July 30, 1976, Folder 8 Box II.5 7, Amnesty International U.S.A. National Office Records, CUML.
162. "Sudomo's New Pledges," *Tapol Bulletin* no. 17 (August 1976): 6.
163. Fealy, "The Release of Indonesia's Political Prisoners," 29; "Inside Suharto's Prisons," *Far Eastern Economic Review*, October 28, 1977.
164. Memorandum, Sudomo to Umar Seno Aji, Permohonan Prioritas Penyidangan Perkara G-30-S/PKI, Subversi dan Pengerahan Bantuan Tenaga Jaksa sebagai Payek/Calon Penuntut Umum, August 18, 1977, in H. M. Fauzan, *Peranan PERMA dan SEMA sebagai Pengisi Kekosongan Hukum Indonesia Menuju Terwujudnya Peradilan yang Agung* (Jakarta: Kencana, 2015), 445–447.
165. Polkam, May 14, 1974, 567, HB IX, ANRI.
166. Memorandum to Canberra, June 28, 1974, in *AIPT*, 60.
167. Soekanto, ed., *Integrasi: Kebulatan Tekad Rakyat Timor Timur* (Jakarta: Yayasan Parisekit, 1976), 103–109.
168. Conboy, *Kopassus*, Kindle locations 3305 and 3403.
169. Cablegram to Canberra, May 22, 1974, in *AIPT*, 56.
170. Record of Second Meeting between Whitlam and Soeharto, September 6, 1974, A10463 801/13/11/1 Part 3, Jakarta—Portuguese Timor, NAA
171. Polkam, September 10, 1974, 567, HB IX, ANRI.
172. Frank Mount, *Wrestling with Asia: A Memoir* (Ballan: Connor Court, 2012), 273.
173. Joint Intelligence Organisation, Brief for Visit of Minister of Defence to Indonesia: Indonesian Attitudes to Military Intervention in Portuguese Timor, December 5, 1974, A1838 3038/10/1/2 PART 1, Submissions to Ministers and Briefs on Portuguese Timor, NAA; Soekanto, *Integrasi*, 155–157.
174. Polkam, October 8, 1974, 567, HB IX, ANRI.
175. José Ramos-Horta, *Funu: The Unfinished Saga of East Timor* (Lawrenceville: Red Sea Press, 1987), 36–37.
176. Michael Leach, *Nation-Building and National Identity in Timor-Leste* (New York: Routledge, 2017), 56–69.
177. Telegram, Jakarta to State, October 25, 1974, Electronic Telegrams 1974, AAD, RG 59, USNA.
178. Polkam, October 8, 1974, 567, HB IX, ANRI.
179. Yoga Sugama, Progress Report: Bulan January 1975, January 29, 1975, 589, HB IX, ANRI.
180. Yoga Sugama, Progress Report: Bulan Januari 1975, January 29, 1975, 589, HB IX, ANRI.
181. Yoga Sugama, Progress Report: Bulan Januari 1975 ke-II, February 4, 1975, 589, HB IX, ANRI; Cablegram to Canberra, October 26, 1974, in *AIPT*, 113; Cablegram to Canberra, March 18, 1975, in *AIPT*, 228.
182. Soekanto, *Integrasi*, 134–146.
183. Cablegram to Canberra, February 13, 1975, in *AIPT*, 183.
184. See the February 23, 24, and 27, 1975 issues of *Antara* as well as the February 26 issue of *Berita Yudha*.
185. "Tajuk Rencana: Indonesia-Australia dan Timport," *Angkatan Bersenjata*, March 8, 1975.
186. Letter from Whitlam to Soeharto, February 28, 1975, in *AIPT*, 200–202; Record of Conversation between Whitlam, Surono, and Her Tasning, March 4, 1975, in *AIPT*, 208–209.
187. Telegram, Canberra to State, March 10, 1975, Australia—State Department Telegrams yo SECSTATE—EXDIS, Box 2, National Security Adviser—Presidential Country Files for East Asia and the Pacific, GFPL; see also Pidato Jawaban pada Upacara Peneyrahan Surat-Surat Kepercayaan Yang Mulia Richard Arthur Woolcott Duta Besar Luar Biasa dan Berkuasa Penuh Australia, March 8, 1975, 26-3, PPS, ANRI.
188. Memorandum, Smyser to Kissinger, March 4, 1975, Indonesia (2), Box 6, National Security Adviser—Presidential Country Files for East Asia and the Pacific, GFPL.

189. Telegram, Jakarta to State, March 31, 1975, Indonesia—State Department Telegrams to SECSTATE—EXDIS, Box 6, National Security Adviser—Presidential Country Files for East Asia and the Pacific, GFPL.
190. Memorandum of Conversation, Ford, Suharto, Kissinger, and Scowcroft, July 5, 1975, July 5, 1975—Ford, Kissinger, Indonesian President Suharto, Box 13, National Security Adviser—Memoranda of Conversations, GFPL.
191. The President's Daily Brief, August 18, 1975, Central Intelligence Agency Electronic Reading Room, https://www.cia.gov/library/readingroom/docs/DOC_0006014878.pdf (accessed March 31, 2021).
192. Ramos-Horta, *Funu*, 66.
193. Helen Hill, *The Timor Story* (Melbourne: Timor Information Service, 1976), 10.
194. Foreign Broadcast Information Service, *Daily Report*, April 24, 1975, N3.
195. James Dunn, "The Timor Affair in International Perspective," in *East Timor at the Crossroads: The Forging of a Nation*, ed. Peter Carey and G. Carter Bentley (London: Cassell, 1995), 63.
196. Soekanto, *Integrasi*, 198; Helen Hill, *Stirrings of Nationalism in East Timor: Fretilin 1974–1978: The Origins, Ideologies and Strategies of a Nationalist Movement* (Sydney: Otford Press, 2002), 139; McDonald, *Suharto's Indonesia*, 205.
197. Press Statement, September 13, 1975, in *Facts about Fretilin: A Collection of Statements Made by Fretilin Itself* (Sydney: Campaign for an Independent East Timor, 1975).
198. Cablegram to Canberra, August 14, 1975, in *AIPT*, 307; Cablegram to Canberra, August 26, 1975, in *AIPT*, 346.
199. Telegram, Jakarta to State, August 21, 1975, Indonesia—State Department Telegrams to SECSTATE—EXDIS, Box 6, National Security Adviser—Presidential Country Files for East Asia and the Pacific, GFPL.
200. Polkam, September 9, 1975, 567, HB IX, ANRI.
201. Polkam, October 21, 1975, 567, HB IX, ANRI.
202. Cablegram to Canberra, September 29, 1975, in *AIPT*, 437; Cablegram to Canberra, September 30, 1975, *AIPT*, 439.
203. "Big Indonesian Attack in Timor Reported," *New York Times*, October 8, 1975.
204. Submission to Willesee, October 14, 1975, in *AIPT*, 463; Cablegram to Canberra, October 16, 1975, *AIPT*, 473.
205. For the international politics of the invasion see Mattias Fibiger, "A Diplomatic Counter-Revolution: Indonesian Diplomacy and the Invasion of East Timor," *Modern Asian Studies* 55, no. 2 (2021): 618–624.
206. Memorandum, Kissinger to Ford, n.d., President Ford's Trip to the Philippines and Indonesia, December 1975 (1), Box 18, National Security Adviser—Presidential Country Files for East Asia and the Pacific, GFPL.
207. Telegram, Jakarta to State, December 6, 1975, Indonesia—State Department Telegrams to SECSTATE—NODIS (3), National Security Adviser—Presidential Country Files for East Asia and the Pacific, GFPL.
208. See *Chega! Laporan Komisi Penerimaan, Kebenaran, dan Rekonsiliasi (CAVR) di Timor-Leste* (Jakarta: KPG, 2010).
209. Polkam, November 16, 1976, 567, HB IX, ANRI.

Chapter 9

1. Polkam, June 22, 1976, 567, HB IX, ANRI; for illiteracy see Government of Indonesia, *Ringkasan Penduduk Indonesia Menurut Propinsi dan Pulau 1976* (Jakarta: Biro Pusat Statistik, 1976), 34.
2. Amirmachmud, *Prajurit Pejuang*, 384.
3. Anwar, *Dari Koresponden Kami*, 143–146; Sudharmono, *Otobiografi*, 252-256; for a narrative of the Sawito affair see David Bourchier, *Dynamics of Dissent in Indonesia: Sawito and the Phantom Coup* (Ithaca, NY: Cornell Modern Indonesia Project, 1984).
4. See John Sidel, *Riots, Pogroms, Jihad: Religious Violence in Indonesia* (Ithaca, NY: Cornell University Press, 2006), 50–60.
5. Soemitro, *Pangkopkamtib*, 147.

6. "Masa Baru dalam Dakwah, Mudah-Mudahan," *Tempo*, August 12, 1978.
7. "Hak Asasi Dilarang," *Tempo*, December 17, 1977; for the broader context of "pop Islam" see François Raillon, "L'Ordre Nouveau et l'Islam ou l'imbroglio de la foi et de la politique," *Archipel* 30 (1985): 229–261; for Rhoma Irama see Andrew Weintraub, *Dangdut Stories: A Social and Musical History of Indonesia's Most Popular Music* (New York: Oxford University Press, 2010), 86–93.
8. Cahyono, *Pangkopkamtib Jenderal Soemitro*, 92–93, 195.
9. "MUI, Kisah Sebuah Jembatan," *Tempo*, May 30, 1981.
10. Solahudin, *The Roots of Terrorism in Indonesia: From Darul Islam to Jema'ah Islamiyah*, trans. Dave McRae (Ithaca, NY: Cornell University Press, 2013), 80–81.
11. June Chandra Santosa, "Modernization, Utopia, and the Rise of Islamic Radicalism in Indonesia" (PhD diss., Boston University, 1996), 304 fn101.
12. Hasan de Tiro, *The Price of Freedom: The Unfinished Diary of Tengku Hasan de Tiro* (Banda Aceh: National Liberation Front of Acheh Sumatra, 1984), 15.
13. Michael Ross, "Resources and Rebellion in Aceh, Indonesia," in *Understanding Civil War: Evidence and Analysis*, Vol. 2: *Europe, Central Asia, and Other Regions*, ed. Paul Collier and Nicholas Sambanis (Washington, DC: World Bank, 2005), 41.
14. Edward Aspinall, *Islam and Nation: Separatist Rebellion in Aceh, Indonesia* (Stanford, CA: Stanford University Press, 2009), 49–83.
15. Memo, Staf Kesra to Selo Sumarjan, November 28, 1974, 585, HB IX, ANRI; Memo, Soenandar Prijosoedarmo to Selo Sumarjan, November 18, 1975, 597, HB IX, ANRI.
16. "Presiden: Pangdam se Kowilhan II Supaya Selalu Siap Sedia," *Antara*, February 26, 1977; "Kalau Perlu Ambil Tindakan Pengamanan," *Berita Yudha*, February 28, 1977; for a claim that the organization was a creation of the Suharto regime see Bourchier, *Illiberal Democracy in Indonesia*, 180–181; see also David Jenkins, *Suharto and His Generals: Indonesian Military Politics, 1975–1983* (Ithaca, NY: Cornell Modern Indonesia Project, 1984), 56–59.
17. Tapol, Human Rights Violations in Indonesia: A Chronology, May 1978, A10463 801/11/1 PART 8, Jakarta—Indonesia—Political Prisoners, NAA.
18. "Peringatan Keras Presiden," *Kompas*, May 31, 1977.
19. Quoted in Jenkins, *Suharto and His Generals*, 29.
20. "Hughes Aircraft Faces Allegation That It Used Bribery in Indonesia," *New York Times*, January 25, 1977.
21. Suryadinata, *Military Ascendancy and Political Culture*, 88.
22. Soeharto, *Pikiran*, 330; William Liddle, "Indonesia 1977: The New Order's Second Parliamentary Election," *Asian Survey* 18, no. 2 (February 1978): 181.
23. Quoted in Haris, *PPP dan Politik Orde Baru*, 1.
24. Haris, *PPP dan Politik Orde Baru*, 12-13.
25. "Bicaralah, Pak Kimin!" *Tempo*, May 7, 1977.
26. William Liddle, "The 1977 Indonesian Election and New Order Legitimacy," *Southeast Asian Affairs* (1978): 128–129.
27. Bourchier, *Illiberal Democracy in Indonesia*, 181; "Suatu Analisa tentang Pemilu 1977," *Kompas*, May 30, 1977.
28. "Sadikin: Going Out with a Bang," *Far Eastern Economic Review*, July 15, 1977.
29. Soeharto, *Pikiran*, 332.
30. Edy Budiyarso, *Menentang Tirani: Aksi Mahasiswa '77/'78* (Jakarta: PT Gramedia Widiasarana Indonesia, 2000), 112–160.
31. Leo Suryadinata, "Indonesia: A Year of Continuing Challenge," *Southeast Asian Affairs* (1979): 108.
32. Instruksi Presiden Republik Indonesia Nomor 9 Tahun 1977 tentang Operasi Tertib, September 5, 1977.
33. "Kita Sendiri Harus Bersih Dahulu," *Tempo*, October 1, 1977.
34. Richard Tanter, "Intelligence Agencies and Third World Militarization: A Case Study of Indonesia, 1966–1989, with Special Reference to South Korea, 1961–1989" (PhD diss., Monash University), 227–228.
35. "Presiden Soeharto Beri Arahan Dialog dengan Dunia Kampus," July 23, 1977, in *Jejak Langkah 1973-78*, 516–517.

36. "Campus 'Gibberish' Halts Dialogue," *Far Eastern Economic Review*, September 2, 1977.
37. Bresnan, *Managing Indonesia*, 197.
38. "Mencoba 'Jalan yang Baik,'" *Tempo*, November 19, 1977.
39. "Pembangunan Kita Masih Bertitikberat pada Stabilitas Keamanan dan Ekonomi," *Kompas*, September 28, 1977.
40. Jenkins, *Suharto and His Generals*, 77–82.
41. Anderson, "Last Days of Indonesia's Suharto," 7.
42. Wiwoho and Bandjar, *Memori Jenderal Yoga*, 283.
43. See Donald Emmerson, *Indonesia's Elite: Political Culture and Cultural Politics* (Ithaca, NY: Cornell University Press 1976), 247.
44. "Pernyataan Pimpinan ABRI Soal Kewibawaan Pimpinan Nasional dan Pengganggu SU MPR," December 15, 1977, in *Jejak Langkah 1973–78*, 580.
45. Edy, *Menentang Tirani*, 174–176, 181.
46. "The Second Time Around," *Far Eastern Economic Review*, February 3, 1978.
47. "White Book of the 1978 Students' Struggle," *Indonesia* no. 25 (April 1978): 151–182. Emphasis in original.
48. Hariyadhie, *Perskpektif Gerakan Mahasiswa 1978 dalam Percaturan Politik Nasional* (Jakarta: Citra Mandala Pratama, 1994), 92.
49. Atmakusumah, *Kebebasan Pers dan Arus Informasi di Indonesia: Beberapa Cermin Perkembangan 12 Tahun* (Jakarta: Lembaga Studi Pembangunan, 1981).
50. Hill, *The Press in New* Order Indonesia, 39.
51. Quoted in Edy, *Menentang Tirani*, 204.
52. Heri Akhmadi, *Breaking the Chains of Oppression of the Indonesian People: Defense Statement at His Trial on Charges of Insulting the Head of State* (Ithaca, NY: Cornell Modern Indonesia Project, 1981).
53. "Laporkan Hasil Opstib, Sudomo: Mogok Kuliah Ditindak Tegas," March 7, 1978 in *Jejak Langkah 1973–78*, 608.
54. "Mirror, Mirror on the Wall . . ." *Far Eastern Economic Review*, March 31, 1978.
55. McDonald, *Suharto's Indonesia*, 247–249.
56. Sudharmono, *Otobiografi*, 276–279.
57. John Monfries, *A Prince in a Republic: The Life of Sultan Hamengku Buwono IX of Yogyakarta* (Singapore: Institute of Southeast Asian Studies, 2015), 289-293; "The Sultan Upstages Suharto," *Far Eastern Economic Review*, March 24, 1978.
58. Wiwoho and Bandjar, *Memori Jenderal Yoga*, 281.
59. "Mencari Rumusan Kebebasan 1978," *Tempo*, February 25, 1978.
60. Telegram, Jakarta to State, April 13, 1978, Electronic Telegrams 1978, AAD, RG 59, USNA.
61. Didik Supriyanto, *Perlawanan Pers Mahasiswa: Protes Sepanjang NKK/BKK* (Jakarta: Pustaka Sinar Harapan, 1998), 39.
62. See Risalah Putusan-Putusan Rapat Koordinasi Bidang Polkam Tingkat Menteri, December 13, 1979, 179, Malik, ANRI.
63. Bahan Rapat Koordinasi Bidang Polkam Tingkat Menteri, October 20, 1980, 180, Malik, ANRI.
64. Ed Aspinall, *Opposing Suharto: Compromise, Resistance, and Regime Change in Indonesia* (Stanford: Stanford University Press, 2005), 132.
65. Jenkins, *Suharto and His Generals*, 90–98.
66. "Kita Semua Telah Berdosa," *Tempo*, June 9, 1979.
67. See the editorial by Sumitro in *Kompas*, May 11, 1979.
68. "Presiden Soeharto Meninggalkan Kuantan Menuju Pekanbaru," March 27, 1980, in *Jejak Langkah 1978–83*, 279.
69. "Hadapi Pemilu, Presiden Soeharto Jelaskan Berbagai Tudingan," April 16, 1980, in *Jejak Langkah 1978–83*, 286.
70. P. Bambang Siswoyo, *Sekitar Petisi 50, 61, 360* (Solo: Mayasari, 1983), 27–28.
71. Jenkins, *Suharto and His Generals*, 162–170.
72. Soeharto, *Pikiran*, 346–348.
73. Aspinall, *Opposing Suharto*, 61.

74. Berita Acara Persidangan Abu Bakar Ba'asyir dan Abdullah Sungkar, No.1/Pid.Subv/1982/ P.N. Smh, CD 1: Ba'asyir-1 – From Trial 1982 – 1ˢᵗ of Bap 2003, Indonesian Terrorism Documents, Rare and Manuscript Collections, CURML.

75. Sidney Jones, "New Order Repression and the Birth of Jemaah Islamiyah," in *Soeharto's New Order and Its Legacy: Essays in Honour of Harold Crouch*, ed. Edward Aspinall and Greg Fealy (Canberra: ANU Press, 2010), 40.

76. Solahudin, *Roots of Terrorism*, 85–86, 91–92, 99–103.

77. Krithika Varagur, *The Call: Inside the Global Saudi Religious Project* (New York: Columbia Global Reports, 2020), 62.

78. "Bom di Istiqlal," *Tempo*, April 22, 1978; Letter, Kafrawi to Umar, June 12, 1978, 282, Malik, ANRI.

79. Noorhaidi Hasan, *Laskar Jihad: Islam, Militancy, and the Quest for Identity in Post-New Order Indonesia* (Ithaca, NY: Southeast Asia Program Publications, 2006), 41.

80. Pour, *Sudomo*, 248–249.

81. Conboy, *Kopassus*, Kindle locations 4745–4760; see also Pour, *Benny*, 209–229; Wiwoho and Bandjar, *Memori Jenderal Yoga*, 305–314.

82. Solahudin, *Roots of Terrorism*, 111–112.

83. For an early depiction see "Colonel Qadhafi—Libya's Mystical Revolutionary," *New York Times*, February 6, 1972.

84. Marites Dañuilan Vitug and Glenda M. Gloria, *Under the Crescent Moon: Rebellion in Mindanao* (Manila: Ateneo Center for Social Policy & Public Affairs, 2000).

85. "Uproar at Islamic Conference," *Times of India*, March 27, 1973.

86. Nur Misuari, "Statement of the Chairman of the Central Committee of the MNLF to the Muslim Brothers of the World," June 25, 1973, in International Studies Institute of the Philippines, *Conference on the "Tripoli Agreement: Problems and Prospects, September 12–13, 1985"* (Quezon City: University of the Philippines, 1985), 1.

87. Formulir-Berita, Sumitro to Hamengkubuwono et al., 1973, 532, HB IX, ANRI.

88. Soemitro, *Pangkopkamtib*, 269-270.

89. Laporan Delegasi Indonesia ke Konperensi Tingkat Tinggi Islam kedua di Lahore, Pakistan, 18–24 Pebruari 1974, 178, HB IX, ANRI.

90. Telegram, Manila to State, March 5, 1974, Electronic Telegrams 1974, AAD, RG 59, USNA.

91. Airgram, Manila to State, August 30, 1974, President Ford's Trip to the Philippines and Indonesia, December 1975 (7), Box 19, National Security Adviser - NSC East Asian and Pacific Affairs Staff Files, GFPL; "Presiden Soeharto-PM Tun Abdul Razak Adakan Pembicaraan Tidak Resmi," May 4, 1974, in *Jejak Langkah 1973–78*, 121; "Presiden Soeharto-Presiden Marcos Sepakati Pentingnya ASEAN," May 30, 1974, in *Jejak Langkah 1973–78*, 125–126; "Razak: The Peacemaker," *Far Eastern Economic Review*, July 1, 1974; James Piscatori, "Asian Islam: International Linkages and Their Impact on International Relations," in *Islam in Asia: Religion, Politics, and Society*, ed. John Esposito (New York: Oxford University Press, 1987), 237.

92. Organization of the Islamic Conference, *Declarations and Resolutions of Heads of State and Ministers of Foreign Affairs Conferences, 1969–1981* (Jeddah: Organization of the Islamic Conference, 1981), 100.

93. Gordon Hein, "Soeharto's Foreign Policy: Second-Generation Nationalism in Indonesia" (PhD diss., University of California at Berkeley, 1986), 243.

94. Leo Suryadinata, "Islam and Suharto's Foreign Policy: Indonesia, the Middle East, and Bosnia," *Asian Survey* 35, no. 3 (March 1995): 296.

95. Suryadinata, "Islam and Suharto's Foreign Policy," 295.

96. Catatan Terhadap Rapat Koordinasi Polkam Tingkat Staf, March 6, 1980, 179, Malik, ANRI.

97. "Terjun Bebas di Qum," *Tempo*, September 7, 1991.

98. Laporan Rapat Koordinasi Bidang Polkam Tingkat Menteri, November 17, 1980, Malik, ANRI.

99. Letter, Rajaie to Soeharto, February 13, 1981, 348, Malik, ANRI.

100. Laporan Khusus Mengenai Krisis Iran-Irak, September 26, 1980, 406, Malik, ANRI.

101. Jusuf Wanandi and M. Hadisoesastro, "Indonesia's Security and Threat Perceptions," in *Threats to Security in East-Asia Pacific: National and Regional Perspectives*, ed. Charles Morrison (Lexington: LexingtonBooks, 1983), 85.
102. See Sudharmono, *Otobiografi*, 269–275; Moerdiono, "Father, Leader, and Statesman" in *Among Friends*, 307–326.
103. Government of Indonesia, *Pedoman Penghayatan dan Pengamalan Pancasila (Ekaprasetia Pancakarsa) & Garis Besar Haluan Negara (GHBN)* (Jakarta: Departemen Penerangan, 1978).
104. Government of Indonesia, *Peningkatan Penerangan yang Berwibawa: Himpunan Pidato Menteri Penerangan RI, 1978–1982* (Jakarta: Departemen Penerangan, 1983), 209–210.
105. Sudharmono, *Otobiografi*, 273.
106. Soeharto, *Pikiran*, 337.
107. "Buka Munas Golkar, Presiden Soeharto: Pembangunan Politik Merupakan Bagian Pembangunan Nasional yang Sulit," October 20, 1983, in *Jejak Langkah Pak Harto 16 Maret 1983–11 Maret 1988* (Jakarta: Citra Kharisma Bunda), 209–210.
108. Sudharmono, *Otobiografi*, 330, 337–340.
109. "Di Sini Proklamator Dimakamkan," *Tempo*, June 30, 1979.
110. See C. van Dijk, "Survey of Major Political Developments in Indonesia in the Second Half of 1980: Crime Prevention, Anti-Chinese Riots and the PDI Party Congress," *Review of Indonesian and Malayan Affairs* 15, no. 1 (1981): 101–124.
111. "Orang-Orang yang Ditahan," *Tempo*, April 22, 1978.
112. Martin van Bruinessen, *NU, Tradisi, Relasi-Relasi Kuasa, Pencarian Wacana Baru* (Yogyakarta: LKiS and Pustaka Pelajar, 1994), 104–112.
113. "NU Akan Bilang Selamat Tinggal?" *Tempo*, November 7, 1981.
114. Radi, *Strategi PPP*, 153.
115. Robin Bush, *Nahdlatul Ulama and the Struggle for Power within Islam and Politics in Indonesia* (Singapore: Institute of Southeast Asian Studies, 2009), 66–78.
116. "Kepercayaan Setelah Ketegangan," *Tempo*, January 21, 1978.
117. Alamsjah, *Perjalanan Hidup*, 243–246.
118. Suryadinata, *Military Ascendancy and Political Culture*, 91.
119. Sudharmono, *Otobiografi*, 285.
120. See H.W. Arndt, "Survey of Recent Developments," *Bulletin of Indonesian Economic Studies* 10, no. 2 (July 1974): 1–34.
121. Widjojo, *Indonesian Development Experience*, 196–197.
122. Memo, Dharman to Malik, December 21, 1978, 468, Malik, ANRI.
123. "Why Indonesia Is Asking for More Money," *Financial Times*, May 7, 1980.
124. Sudharmono, *Otobiografi*, 295–299.
125. Ginandjar, *Managing Indonesia's Transformation*, 49–50.
126. Sudharmono, *Otobiografi*, 300.
127. *Foreign Assistance and Related Agencies Appropriations for 1978: Hearings Before a Subcommittee of the Committee on Appropriations, House of Representatives, Ninety-Fifth Congress*, Part III (Washington, DC: Government Printing Office, 1977), 348; for Brzezinski see Bradley Simpson, "Denying the 'First Right': The United States, Indonesia, and the Ranking of Human Rights by the Carter Administration, 1976–1980," *International History Review* 31, no. 4 (December 2009): 805–806.
128. Jusuf Wanandi, "President Carter's Foreign Policy and the Role of the American Congress," *Indonesian Quarterly* 6, no. 2 (April 1978): 52, 58, 55.
129. "Indonesian Assails Human Rights Groups," *Washington Post*, August 19, 1977.
130. *Indonesia Development News* 1, no. 1 (September/October 1977): 1.
131. Jusuf Wanandi, "Human Rights: An Indonesian View," *Far Eastern Economic Review*, December 2, 1977; for the broader context see Roland Burke, *Decolonization and the Evolution of International Human Rights* (Philadelphia: University of Pennsylvania Press, 2010), 129–141.
132. "Amnesty Unit, 16 Years Old, Gains Ends by Pressure and Publicity," *New York Times*, October 11, 1977.

133. Amnesty International, *Indonesia: An Amnesty International Report* (London: Amnesty International Publications, 1977).
134. *Human Rights in Indonesia: A Review of the Situation with Respect to the Long-Term Political Detainees: Hearing Before the Subcommittee on International Organizations of the Committee on International Relations, House of Representatives, Ninety-Fifth Congress* (Washington, DC: Government Printing Office, 1977).
135. "Prison Algebra," *The Economist*, December 24, 1977.
136. Telegram, State to Jakarta, November 4, 1977, Electronic Telegrams 1977, AAD, RG 59, USNA.
137. Telegram, Jakarta to State, January 14, 1978, Electronic Telegrams 1978, AAD, RG 59, USNA.
138. Quoted in Simpson, "Denying the 'First Right,' " 821.
139. Sukma, *Indonesia and China*, 108.
140. Hardi, *Api Nasionalisme: Cuplikan Pengalaman* (Jakarta: Gunung Agung, 1983), 203–206.
141. Leifer, *ASEAN and the Security of South-East Asia*, 73–74.
142. Departemen Luar Negeri, Keinginan RSV untuk Kerjasama Dibidang Ekonomi dengan Indonesia, December 1976, 200, HB IX, ANRI.
143. Wanandi, *Shades of Grey*, Kindle location 2107.
144. See Wanandi and Hadisoesastro, "Indonesia's Security and Threat Perceptions," 91–92.
145. "Suspicion Lingers On," *Far Eastern Economic Review*, June 24, 1977.
146. "Menghadap Presiden Soeharto, Dubes Vietnam Jelaskan Konflik Negaranya dengan Kamboja dan RRC," July 8, 1978, in *Jejak Langkah 1978–83*, 41.
147. "Viet Chief on Fence-Mending Mission," *Boston Globe*, September 6, 1978.
148. "Presiden Soeharto Menerima PM Vietnam Pham Van Dong," September 21, 1978, in *Jejak Langkah 1978–83*, 64–65; "Komentar di DPR Atas Hasil Kunjungan PM Phan Van Dong ke Indonesia," *Antara*, September 25, 1978.
149. See Christopher Goscha, "Vietnam, the Third Indochina War, and the Meltdown of Asian Internationalism," in *The Third Indochina War: Conflict between China, Vietnam and Cambodia, 1972–79*, ed. Odd Arne Westad and Sophie Quinn-Judge (New York: Routledge, 2006), 152–186.
150. "Presiden Soeharto Menerima Pesan Lisan PM Vietnam," December 30, 1978, in *Jejak Langkah 1978–83*, 99.
151. Ali Murtopo, "Great Powers Configuration in the Asia-Pacific Region: An Indonesian View," *Asian Perspective* 4, no. 1 (Spring-Summer 1980): 15.
152. "Panggabean Accuses Peking," *Straits Times*, February 24, 1978.
153. Anwar, *Indonesia in ASEAN*, 187.
154. Wanandi, *Shades of Grey*, Kindle location 2107.
155. For a more detailed narrative of the Suharto regime's about-face on China see Mattias Fibiger, "Indonesia and the Third Indochina War: The End of Containment," *Journal of American-East Asian Relations* 29, no. 3 (2022): 240–270.
156. Kelompok Bidang Internasional (KRA XVII), *Upaya Mewujudkan ZOPFAN di Asia Tenggara* (Jakarta: Angkatan Bersenjata, 1984), quoted in Anwar, *Indonesia in ASEAN*, 237fn60.
157. Wanandi, *Shades of Grey*, Kindle locations 2335.

Conclusion

1. See R. E. Elson, *The Idea of Indonesia: A History* (New York: Cambridge University Press, 2008).
2. For an analogous argument in comparative context see Tuong Vu, *Paths to Development in Asia: South Korea, Vietnam, China, and Indonesia* (New York: Cambridge University Press, 2010), 50–70.
3. Marcus Mietzner, "Comparing Indonesia's Party Systems of the 1950s and the Post-Suharto Era: From Centrifugal to Centripetal Inter-Party Competition," *Journal of Southeast Asian Studies* 39, no. 3 (October 2008): 433–438.
4. Roosa, *Pretext*, 176–201.
5. Robinson, *Killing Season*, 118–176.

6. For an insightful analysis of the divisions within Sukarno's Indonesian Nationalist Party (PNI) between radicals, moderates, and conservatives at the dawn of the New Order see Rocamora, "Nationalism in Search of Ideology," 498–554.

7. For a useful meditation on critical junctures see David Collier and Gerardo Munck, eds., *Critical Junctures and Historical Legacies: Insights and Methods for Comparative Social Science* (Lanham, MD: Rowman & Littlefield, 2022).

8. See Edward Aspinall, "The Broadening Base of Political Opposition in Indonesia," in *Political Oppositions in Industrializing Asia*, ed. Garry Rodan (London: Routledge, 1996), 215–240.

9. Duccio Basosi, Giuliano Garavini, and Massimiliano Trentin, eds., *Counter-Shock: The Oil Counter-Revolution of the 1980s* (London: I. B. Tauris, 2018).

10. *Presiden Soeharto, Bapak Pembangunan Indonesia: Ditetapkan dalam Sidang Umum I–II Maret 1983 oleh Majelis Permusyawaratan Rakyat R.I.* (Jakarta: Yayasan Dana Bantuan Kesejahteraan Masyarakat Indonesia, 1983).

11. For poverty data see Booth, "Poverty and Inequality," 78; all other data courtesy of the World Bank.

12. Thomas Pepinsky, *Economic Crises and the Breakdown of Authoritarian Regimes: Indonesia and Malaysia in Comparative Perspective* (New York: Cambridge University Press, 2009); Edward Aspinall, *Opposing Suharto: Compromise, Resistance, and Regime Change in Indonesia* (Stanford, CA: Stanford University Press, 2005); Donald Emmerson, "Exit and Aftermath: The Crisis of 1997–98," in *Indonesia beyond Suharto: Polity, Economy, Society, Transition*, ed. Donald Emmerson (Armonk: M. E. Sharpe, 1999); Robert Hefner, *Civil Islam: Muslims and Democratization in Indonesia* (Princeton, NJ: Princeton University Press, 2000); William Liddle, "Indonesia's Unexpected Failure of Leadership," in *Politics of Post-Suharto Indonesia*, ed. Adam Schwarz and Jonathan Paris (New York: Council on Foreign Relations, 1999); Andrew MacIntyre, "Institutions and Investors: The Politics of the Economic Crisis in Southeast Asia," *International Organization* 55, no. 1 (2001): 81–122; Benjamin Smith, "'If I Do These Things, They Will Throw Me Out': Economic Reform and the Collapse of Indonesia's New Order," *Journal of International Affairs* 57, no. 1 (2003): 113–128.

13. See Richard Robison and Vedi Hadiz, *Reorganizing Power in Indonesia: The Politics of Oligarchy in an Age of Markets* (New York: Routledge, 2004); Dan Slater, "Indonesia's Accountability Trap: Party Cartels and Presidential Power after Democratic Transition," *Indonesia* no. 78 (2004): 61–92; for contrary views that question the cartelization thesis and emphasize the persistence of *aliran*-based political participation see Marcus Mietzner, *Money, Power, and Ideology: Political Power in Post-Authoritarian Indonesia* (Singapore: NUS Press, 2013); Dwight King, *Half-Hearted Reform: Electoral Institutions and the Struggle for Democracy in Indonesia* (Westport, CT: Praeger, 2003).

14. Edward Aspinall and Ward Berenschot, *Democracy for Sale: Elections, Clientelism, and the State in Indonesia* (Ithaca, NY: Cornell University Press, 2019); Edward Aspinall, Meredith Weiss, Allen Hicken, and Paul Hutchcroft, *Mobilizing for Elections: Patronage and Political Machines in Southeast Asia* (New York: Cambridge University Press, 2022).

15. Marcus Mietzner, *Military Politics, Islam, and the State in Indonesia: From Turbulent Transition to Democratic Consolidation* (Singapore: Institute of Southeast Asian Studies, 2009); Jun Honna, *Military Politics and Democratization in Indonesia* (New York: Routledge, 2013).

16. Greg Fealy, "Jokowi in the Covid-19 Era: Repressive Pluralism, Dynasticism and the Overbearing State," *Bulletin of Indonesian Economic Studies* 56, no. 3 (2020): 301–323; David Bourchier, "Two Decades of Ideological Contestation in Indonesia: From Democratic Cosmopolitanism to Religious Nationalism," *Journal of Contemporary Asia* 49, no. 5 (2019): 713–733; Thomas Power, "Jokowi's Authoritarian Turn and Indonesia's Democratic Decline," *Bulletin of Indonesian Economic Studies* 54, no. 3 (2018): 307–338; Vedi Hadiz, "Retrieving the Past for the Future? Indonesia and the New Order Legacy," *Southeast Asian Journal of Social Science* 28, no. 2 (2000): 10–33.

17. Marty Natalegawa, *Does ASEAN Matter? A View from Within* (Singapore: ISEAS Yusof Ishak Institute, 2018).

18. See the essays in Nicole Curato, ed., *The Duterte Reader: Critical Essays on Rodrigo Duterte's Early Presidency* (Ithaca, NY: Southeast Asia Program Publications, 2018); Thomas

Pepinsky, "Southeast Asia: Voting Against Disorder," *Journal of Democracy* 28, no. 2 (April 2017): 120-131.

19. Donald Emmerson, "Region and Recalcitrance: Rethinking Democracy through Southeast Asia," *World Politics* 8, no. 2 (1995): 223–248.

20. The literature on colonial drain/colonial surplus is too voluminous to cite in its entirety. For one example see Elise Brezis, "Foreign Capital Flows in the Century of Britain's Industrial Revolution: New Estimates, Controlled Conjectures," *Economic History Review* 48, no. 1 (1995): 46–67; for a comparative articulation see Charles Maier, *Among Empires: American Ascendancy and Its Predecessors* (Cambridge, MA: Harvard University Press, 2006), 273–275; for the paradox of "uphill" capital flows see Robert Lucas, "Why Doesn't Capital Flow from Rich to Poor Countries?" *American Economic Review* 80, no. 2 (May 1990): 92–96.

21. Fritz Bartel, *The Triumph of Broken Promises: The End of the Cold War and the Rise of Neoliberalism* (Cambridge, MA: Harvard University Press, 2022); Daniel Sargent, "Pax Americana: Sketches for an Undiplomatic History," *Diplomatic History* 42, no. 3 (2017): 357–376.

22. For the fungibility of material power see Jeffrey Winters, *Oligarchy* (New York: Cambridge University Press, 2011), 6–20.

23. Quoted in Borsuk and Chng, *Liem Sioe Liong's Salim Group*, 431.

24. Data available through USAID, *U.S. Overseas Loans and Grants*.

25. For the Derg see Andargachew Tiruneh, The Ethiopian Revolution 1974–1987: A Transformation from an Aristocratic to a Totalitarian Autocracy (Cambridge: Cambridge University Press, 1993); Tefarra Haile-Selassie, The Ethiopian Revolution 1974–1991: From a Monarchical Autocracy to a Military Oligarchy (London: Kegan Paul, 1997); Fred Halliday and Maxine Molyneux, The Ethiopian Revolution (New York: New Left Books, 1981); Westad, Global Cold War, 250–273.

26. Friedman, *Shadow Cold War*, Kindle location 3060.

27. Zhou, *Migration in the Time of Revolution*, 174.

28. Odd Arne Westad, "The Great Transformation: China in the Long 1970s," in *The Shock of the Global*, 65–79; Ci Jiwei, *Dialectic of the Chinese Revolution: From Utopianism to Hedonism* (Stanford, CA: Stanford University Press, 1995).

29. Niu Jun, "The Background to the Shift in Chinese Policy Toward the United States in the Late 1960s," in *Behind the Bamboo Curtain: China, Vietnam, and the World beyond Asia*, ed. Priscilla Roberts (Washington, DC: Woodrow Wilson Center Press, 2006), 319–320, 341; Li Danhui, "The Sino-Soviet Dispute over Assistance for Vietnam's Anti-American War, 1965–1972," in *Behind the Bamboo Curtain*, 289; Wen-Qing Ngoei, "'A Wide Anticommunist Arc': Britain, ASEAN, and Nixon's Triangular Diplomacy," *Diplomatic History* 41, no. 5 (November 2017): 903–932.

30. Chen Jian, "China's Changing Policies toward the Third World and the End of the Global Cold War," in *The End of the Cold War and the Third World: New Perspectives on Regional Conflict*, ed. Artemy M. Kalinovsky and Sergey Radchenko (New York: Routledge, 2011), 110.

31. Ezra Vogel, *Deng Xiaoping and the Transformation of China* (Cambridge, MA: Belknap Press, 2011).

32. Heonik Kwon, *The Other Cold War* (New York: Columbia University Press, 2010), 8.

33. Memorandum from the President's Assistant for National Security Affairs (Brzezinski) to President Carter, December 2, 1978, in *FRUS, 1977–1980:1*, Document 100.

34. Chamberlin, *The Cold War's Killing Fields*, 361–365.

INDEX

For the benefit of digital users, indexed terms that span two pages (e.g., 52–53) may, on occasion, appear on only one of those pages.

Note: Tables and figures are indicated by *t* and *f* following the page number.

350   INDEX

Association of Southeast Asian Nations
    (ASEAN) (cont.)
  institutionalization through, 9–10
  Islamic threat and, 263, 273–75
  oil industry and, 230
authoritarianism
  counterrevolution and, 129–30, 132, 133, 138–
    39, 142–43, 146, 147, 154, 158
  developmental authoritarian, 4–10,
    103, 282–83
  economic development and, 199, 203, 209,
    213, 214–15
  Guided Democracy, 12–13, 30, 32, 34, 37,
    38–40, 44–45, 48–49, 52–53, 70–71, 158,
    173, 277–79
  international capital and, 6–7, 10–11, 13–14,
    170, 171, 174, 175
  Islamic threat and, 260, 262–63
  Malari Incident and, 216, 237–38
  national resilience and, 114, 120

balance-of-payments challenges, 68, 80, 82, 96,
    160, 231–32
Bandung Conference (1955), 37, 155, 275
Bandung Institute of Technology (ITB), 258–59
Barli Halim, 212
Beamtenstaat, 5–6
Beautiful Indonesia-in-Miniature Park (Taman
    Mini), 195–96
bebas aktif (free and active), 27, 106, 110, 148–50,
    208, 259–60
Bell, Bernard, 165
berdikari (berdiri diatas kaki sendiri, standing on
    one's feet), 56–57
Berita Yudha, 246
Berkeley Mafia, 59–60, 61, 77–79, 88–89,
    91, 164–65
Bretton Woods, 14, 202–3, 214–15
Broad Outlines of State Policy (GBHN), 197–98
Brown, Edmund "Pat," 192–93
Brzezinski, Zbigniew, 270
Budiardjo, Carmel, 212–13, 238
Buscayno, Bernabe, 138

Cabinet Secretariat, 14–15
Caetano, Marcelo, 244
Cambodia, 147–52, 273–74
Campus Coordinating Bodies (BKK), 260–61
Carter, Jimmy, 243, 270–72
Çatur Dharma Eka Karma (Four Missions, One
    Deed), 75
Center for Strategic and International Studies
    (CSIS), 121–22, 124–25, 203, 205–6, 214,
    223–24, 227
Central Intelligence Agency, 1–2
Central Intelligence Board (BPI), 53, 73
Chaerul Saleh, 63–64, 72

Chalid Mawardi, 259–60
Charter of Unity, 30
Charter of Universal Struggle, 30–31
Chicago Boys, 59–60
Chinese Communist Party, 25–26, 274
Church, Frank, 203
civil service, 11, 69, 185, 196–97
civil society groups, 49, 54–55, 75, 104, 161, 214–
    15, 262, 279–80, 281
coercive institutions, 10–11, 97, 195–96, 219–
    20, 260–61
Cold War capital, 10–11, 104, 236, 243, 249–
    50, 279–80
collapse of Portuguese empire, 244–50
Communist Party of Indonesia (PKI). See also
    anticommunism; September Thirtieth
    Movement
  campaign of eradication against, 15–16, 44,
    66, 278–79
  domestic politics of, 24, 277–78
  economic development and, 200
  international capital and, 170–71
  introduction to, 1–2, 4, 8
  Islamic threat and, 251–52
  parliamentary democracy and, 27
  political offensive by, 40
  Republic's suppression of, 25–26
  rivalry with Indonesian army, 18, 34–37
  September Thirtieth Movement and, 47–51
  unilateral action (aksi sepihak) campaign, 42
Communist Party of the Philippines (CPP), 138
Consultative Body for Indonesian
    Citizenship, 106–7
Coordinating Ministry of Economy, Finance, and
    Industry, 14–15
Council of Generals, 1–2, 42–44
Council on Economic Stabilization, 198–99, 223–
    24, 225, 226–27, 232
Council on Political Stabilization and National
    Security (Polkam), 125–27, 219–21
counterrevolution
  authoritarianism and, 129–30, 132, 133, 138–
    39, 142–43, 146, 147, 154, 158
  Cambodia and, 147–52
  introduction to, 13
  Marcos, Ferdinand and, 129–30, 136–43
  national resilience and, 129–30, 131, 133–47,
    152–53, 157–58
  New Order and, 130, 131, 134, 135, 136–37,
    139, 143–44, 145, 147–59
  scholarship on, 9
  South Vietnam and, 152, 153, 155–58
  Thailand and, 152–55
coup d'état, 22, 24, 51–52, 101–2, 248
Cranston, Alan, 237–38
Crush Malaysia Command (Kogam), 62
cukong (ethnic Chinese capitalists), 107–8, 189, 199